4th edition

W9-CAX-402

criminal

investigation

a method for reconstructing the past

James W. Osterburg
University of Illinois

Richard H. Ward
Sam Houston State University

LexisNexis™

anderson publishing
A member of the LexisNexis Group

Criminal Investigation: A Method for Reconstructing the Past, Fourth Edition

Copyright © 1992, 1997, 2000, 2004
Matthew Bender & Company, Inc., a member of the LexisNexis Group

Phone 877-374-2919
Web Site www.lexisnexis.com/anderson/criminaljustice

LexisNexis and the Knowledge Burst logo are trademarks of Reed Elsevier Properties, Inc.
Anderson Publishing is a registered trademark of Anderson Publishing, a member of the LexisNexis Group

Osterburg, James W.
    Criminal investigation: a method for reconstructing the past / James W. Osterburg,
  Richard H. Ward—4th ed.
      Includes index.
      ISBN 1-59345-960-2 (paperback)

Cover design by Tin Box Studio, Inc./Cincinnati, Ohio

Editor   Ellen S. Boyne
Acquisitions Editor   Michael C. Braswell

There is no accepted test of civilization. It is not wealth, or the degree of comfort, or the average duration of life, or the increase of knowledge. All such tests would be disputed. In default of any other measure, may it not be suggested that as good a measure as any is the degree to which justice is carried out, the degree to which men are sensitive to wrongdoing and desirous to right it?

Sir John Macdonell. *Historical Trials.* London: Oxford University Press, 1927, 148.

To Julia, wife and life-long companion since high school days, mother of our children, and early copy editor of this book. She made it readable by refusing to type any paragraph she could not understand. She is missed, having battled and was felled by ovarian cancer. In loving memory of a remarkable woman—Julia Mary Osterburg.

—Jim Osterburg

For Michelle, Jeanne, Jon, Juli, and Sophia.

—Dick Ward

Dedication

In the history of a field of study, landmark events chronicle the stages of its progress toward a discipline. We have chosen to commemorate three such events in the evolution of criminal justice: the establishing of university programs in the early 1940s, New York's Police Department joining with the City University in the 1950s, and the endowing of the first research chair in 1980.

Well before the designation of our field as criminal justice a few universities were prodded by a progressive police chief to set up departments centered largely on the study of the police. Leading the way were the Departments of Police Administration at Indiana University, Michigan State University, Washington State University, and the (now defunct) School of Criminology at the University of California, Berkeley. The latter school's demise reflects an academic unwillingness to accept new departments, and the uneasy alliance between some in academia and criminal justice.

The affiliation of the New York City Police Department with the City University of New York (The Baruch School and John Jay College) was the first collaborative effort to make a college education possible for *on-duty* police officers. Joining ranks in the belief that higher education for sworn officers would humanize law enforcement, their conviction sowed the seeds for the development of a profession. The implementation of the plan fell on the shoulders of Donald H. Riddle; under his leadership, it was brought to fruition a decade later.

Dr. Donald H. Riddle (1921-1999) was a distinguished leader and innovator in the field of criminal justice education. When President of John Jay University, he was once asked "How do you educate the police?" His answer: "Like everyone else," became legendary and helped set the direction for curriculum and research in the field. His vision and understanding of the special mission of an urban university was realized during his tenure as Chancellor of the University of Illinois at Chicago. His wisdom and dedication to higher education and the field of criminal justice were an inspiration to faculty and students. The authors were privileged to know Don Riddle as a friend and mentor and are honored to dedicate this book to his memory.

We also honor (former) Dean Victor Strecher and the faculty of the School of Criminal Justice at Sam Houston State University for securing the funding for the first endowed chair in criminal justice—the George J. Beto Chair. Sam Houston remains an important institution of higher learning that emphasizes and supports research in criminal justice.

James W. Osterburg
Richard H. Ward

Acknowledgments

An early version of this book was read in its entirety by Professors Robert F. Borkenstein of Indiana University and Ralph F. Turner of Michigan State University. They had a major input on what was covered and how it was treated. We are deeply grateful to them both. Thereafter, several people in academia and law enforcement were kind enough to read our material, check for accuracy, and improve its character with their thoughtful criticism.

James Adkins	Chief, Brooksville Fire Department (Brooksville, FL)
Mike Ahearn	Special Agent in Charge, U.S. Postal Inspector (Boston)
Paul Beachem	Lieutenant Colonel (retired), U.S. Army
Jeff Builta	Research Analyst, Department of Defense
J. David Coldren	Vice President and Director, Advanced Information Systems, Office of International Criminal Justice
Matt Casey	Deputy Superintendent, Chicago Police Department
John Conley	Special Agent (retired), FBI Academy (Quantico, VA)
Thomas Constantine	Director (retired), Drug Enforcement Administration
John DeHaan	Program Manager, Bureau of Forensic Services, Department of Justice, State of California; author of *Kirk's Fire Investigation,* 3rd ed.
Rolando del Carmen	Professor, College of Criminal Justice, Sam Houston State University
Duayne J. Dillon	Assistant Sheriff and Chief Executive Officer (retired), Sheriff's Department, Contra Costa County, CA; founder and former Director, Criminalistics Laboratory, Contra Costa County, CA
Dave Donnersberger	Judge, Circuit Court, Cook County, IL
William Dyson	Supervisory Special Agent and Head of Joint FBI Terrorist Task Force in Chicago (retired)
Ahmed Galal Ezeldin	General (retired), Egyptian Police Academy (Cairo)
Thomas Fitzgerald	Chief of Police, Cook County, IL, Sheriff's Police
Robert Gaensslen	Professor of Forensic Science, University of Illinois at Chicago
Terry Gainer	Deputy Chief, Washington, DC Police Department
Tony Grubisic	Chicago Police Department
Marshall J. Hartman	Public Defender, Lake County, IL

Sean Hill	Research Associate, College of Criminal Justice, Sam Houston State University
Terry Hillard	Superintendent, Chicago Police Department
David Kalish	Assistant Chief, Los Angeles Police Department
James L. Kennedy	Director, Office of Administration and Assistant to the Vice President, Indiana University; former Director, Indiana University Police
Wayne A. Kerstetter	Professor of Criminal Justice, University of Illinois at Chicago
Kathleen Kiernan	Division Head (Chicago), Bureau of Alcohol, Tobacco, and Firearms.
Keith Killacky	Associate Professor of Criminal Justice, St. Louis University; Federal Bureau of Investigation (retired)
Joseph King	U.S. Customs Service
John C. Klotter	Professor Emeritus and former Dean, School of Justice Administration, University of Louisville
Henry C. Lee	Director, Connecticut State Police Department
John J. Lentini	Fire Investigation Chemist, Applied Technical Services (Marietta, GA)
Thomas Linkowski	Deputy Chief, Evanston Fire Department (Evanston, IL)
Mickey Lombardo	Deputy Chief, Cook County Sheriff's Police
Herbert L. MacDonell	Director, Laboratory of Forensic Science, Corning, NY; Adjunct Professor, Corning Community College, Corning, NY
James Malinowski	First Deputy, Cook County, IL, Sheriff's Police
Sean Malinowski	Los Angeles Police Department
Michael D. Maltz	Professor of Criminal Justice and Professor of Information and Decision Sciences, University of Illinois at Chicago
Patrick McCarthy	Chicago Police Department, FBI Asian Crime Task Force
Robert McCormack	Professor, Trenton State College
Gordon E. Misner	Professor of Criminal Justice, University of Illinois at Chicago
Cindy Moors	Research Associate, College of Criminal Justice, Sam Houston State University
John Murray	Sergeant (retired), Chicago Police Department
Richard A. Myren	Professor Emeritus, School of Justice, American University, (Washington, DC); founding Dean, School of Criminal Justice, SUNY at Albany
John O'Neill	Federal Bureau of Investigation
Joseph L. Peterson	Professor of Criminal Justice, University of Illinois at Chicago
Frank Pierczynski	Sergeant, Chicago Police Department
John E. Pless	Culbertson Professor of Pathology and Professor of Pathology, School of Medicine, Indiana University
Michael A. Prieto	Director, American Institute of Applied Sciences (Syracuse, NY)

Charles Ramsey	Chief of Police, Washington, DC Police Department
Fred Rice	Superintendent (retired), Chicago Police Department; Professor, University of Illinois at Chicago
Jack Ridges	Sergeant, Central Homicide Evaluation and Support Squad, Chicago Police Department
Matt Rodriguez	Superintendent (retired), Chicago Police Department
Sheldon Rosenberg	Professor of Psychology, University of Illinois at Chicago
Dennis Rowe	Chief Superintendent (deceased), Metropolitan Police, London
Joe Ryan	Professor, Pace University; New York City University Police Department (retired)
Gene Scaramella	Associate Professor, Western Illinois University
Joseph Serio	Consultant, Organized Crime
Robert "Jerry" Simandl	Detective, Gang Unit, Chicago Police Department
Darrel Stephens	Chief of Police, Charlotte, NC
Mark J. Stolorow	Manager, Forensic Sciences, Cellmark Diagnostics (Germantown, MD); former Director, Research and Development, Illinois State Police, Bureau of Forensic Science
Tim Stone	Federal Bureau of Investigation
William Tafoya	Special Agent, FBI Academy (Quantico, VA) (retired)
Ian Watt	Dean, Police Staff College, Bramshill, England (retired)
Jeffrey D. Wells	Professor of Justice Sciences, University of Alabama at Birmingham
Ed Worthington	Federal Bureau of Investigation
Joe Zhou	Office of International Criminal Justice

A special note of thanks to Sam Houston State University, where much of the early planning and organization of the text was undertaken, and to Harold Smith, a friend and colleague who passed away during the preparation of the text.

Many others offered their advice or otherwise helped to improve the quality of the work; they are:

Mary Bartucci	Administrative Secretary, Office of the Vice Chancellor for Special Programs, University of Illinois at Chicago
Frank Bolz	Commander, Hostage Negotiation Team, New York Police Department (retired)
André Bossard	Former Executive Director, INTERPOL (Paris)
Tony Bouza	Chief (retired), Minneapolis Police Department
Harriet Brewster	Director, Graphic Arts, Criminal Justice Center, Sam Houston State University

Jane Buckwalter	Illinois Criminal Justice Information Authority (Board Member)
Bill Burnham	United Nations Crime Prevention and Criminal Justice Branch (retired)
T.J. Chung	Research Associate, Sam Houston State University
Stan Delaney	Vice Chancellor for Administration, University of Illinois at Chicago
Jerry L. Dowling	Professor, College of Criminal Justice, Sam Houston State University
Susan Flood	U.S. Customs Service
Randy Garner	Director, Law Enforcement Management Institute of Texas (LEMIT), Huntsville, TX
Aldo Grassi	Judge of the Supreme Court, Italy
Wu Han	Professor, East China Institute of Politics and Law (Shanghai)
Ron Hauri	Director of Security, Merchandise Mart, Chicago, IL
Mary Hoag	Federal Bureau of Investigation
Wayne Johnson	Chief Investigator, Chicago Crime Commission
John Kennedy	Research Associate, Sam Houston State University
Bruce Lewis	Chief of Police, University of Illinois at Chicago
Ray Liu	Professor of Forensic Sciences, University of Alabama at Birmingham
Tonya Matz	Director of Women's Athletics, University of Illinois at Chicago
Debra McCall	Executive Assistant to the Dean, Criminal Justice Center, Sam Houston State University
Michelle Moran	Secretary to the Dean, College of Criminal Justice, Sam Houston State University
Bette Naysmith	Chair, Committee on Ritual Abuse, Cult Awareness Network
Harry O'Reilly	Detective Sergeant (retired), New York Police Department
Dave Peters	Deputy Chief of Police, University of Illinois at Chicago
Larry St. Regis	Sunnyvale California Department of Public Safety
Victor Strecher	Professor and former Dean, School of Criminal Justice, Sam Houston State University (retired)
John Truitt	Criminal Justice Consultant
Marie Tyse	Chief of Police (retired), University of Illinois at Chicago
Hubert Williams	President, Police Foundation
David Zemke	Graphic Artist, University of Illinois at Chicago

Several firms that market equipment used in law enforcement generously provided illustrative material. Our thanks to John Carrington of Sirchie Finger Print Laboratories (Raleigh, NC); Elliot L. Parker of Instant Image Systems (Plainfield, NJ); Doug Peavey of Lynn Peavey Company (Lenexa, KS); Michael A. Prieto of the American Institute of Applied Sciences (Syracuse, NY); Robert Smith of UNISYS Corporation; and James D. Werner of Cellmark Diagnostics (Germantown, MD).

Permission was granted to use material that first appeared in the publications of Clark Boardman Co., Ltd. (New York, NY); the *Journal of Police Science and Administration* (International Association of Chiefs of Police, Inc., Gaithersburg, MD); and the National Center for Missing and Exploited Children (Arlington, VA). We thank Judge William S. Sessions, former Director of the Federal Bureau of Investigation, for permission to reprint "FBI Suggestions for Packaging Physical Evidence."

The collection of several libraries were available. We thank the staffs of University of Illinois at Chicago; Sam Houston State University; Northwestern University; University of Alabama, Birmingham; University of South Florida; Pasco-Hernando Community College; Lykes Memorial (Hernando) County Library; and Evanston Public Library.

Cheerful editorial assistance and encouragement were provided by Anderson Publishing Co. in the persons of William L. Simon, Vice President (retired); Ellen S. Boyne, Editor; and Kelly Grondin, Editor in Chief. They have been most patient with our many delays in preparing the manuscript. We also wish to acknowledge the suggestions made by Professors Larry Miller and Larry Myers of East Tennessee State University and David L. Carter of Michigan State University. Although we received numerous suggestions and acted upon most of them, we rejected some; in the final analysis, therefore, the text is our responsibility and not that of any of the readers listed above who, no doubt, offered good advice we could not use.

J.W.O.
R.H.W.

Preface

The aim of this text is to present the fundamentals of criminal investigation, and throw light on their application to some of the more important felonies. Issues presently plaguing law enforcement world-wide, such as terrorism and enterprise crime, also pass under review. It immediately becomes obvious that the scope of the material is so wide it cannot all be covered in one college course. Accordingly, the instructor may choose to emphasize certain areas because they are timely, or are more difficult to comprehend and can profit from classroom discussion. One teacher might emphasize the fundamentals of the investigative process treated in Section I; another, the solution of specific crimes, the subject of Sections II and III. Selected specialized topics covered in Section IV may appeal to one instructor more so than another.

Another goal is to help the general reader understand how detective work should be performed, and, most important, to demystify the investigative process. To the extent that criminal investigation is perceived as part and parcel of a more universal kind of inquiry, we will have succeeded. Human beings, it must be agreed, have always acknowledged their need to understand the past. In the study of ancient history, this understanding relies largely on what records survive from that era; in criminal investigation, on the other hand, reconstructing a past event (i.e., a crime) is based on evidence developed by the forensic laboratory, from questioning people, and from examining records.

There are numerous reminders throughout the text that criminal investigation must be conducted within the framework of our democratic system. Hence, those U.S. Supreme Court decisions that affect the investigative function are quoted extensively. They reveal the inherent tension created by the state's obligation to enforce the law while protecting a citizen's rights under the Constitution. In addition, the Court's carefully crafted opinions expose the student to legal reasoning at its best. Although courses in criminal procedure are covered in the criminal justice curricula, we believe that issues which have been or will be brought before the court are better comprehended when there is an awareness of law enforcement's perspective as well as that of the civil libertarian's.

Whatever may be the need for information, it is fairly obvious that the ability to conduct any type of inquiry can be honed by studying the investigative process. For example, one of the most important decisions a person ever has to make involves the purchase of a house. If the buyer acts in the knowledge that all three sources of information—physical evidence, people, and records—must be examined before making an evaluation, the decision is more likely to be wise and prudent. By physical evidence we mean the quality of materials and construction; the environment (water supply, air quality); and the existence of alternative modes of transportation. As for people, information can be gleaned from potential neighbors, school officials, real estate agents, and friends; whereas records comprise such things as deed of ownership, taxes, and mortgages. The point of this example is that the study of the investigative process is educational in the best sense, and not merely vocational training.

We believe this text will have a wide appeal. Its heuristic approach to the investigative function—which stresses the significance of the three basic sources of information—will not only enlighten the average reader and serve the needs of the police detective, but those of many other kinds of investigator. A partial list might include: those employed by public prosecutors, criminal defense attorneys, public defenders, medical examiners and coroners; the army, navy, air force, coast guard, and inspectors general of governmental departments; insurance companies; and crime commissions; as well as arson investigators, fish and game wardens, investigative reporters, and private detectives.

The authors have continued with the reorganization adopted for the second edition, better to accommodate the text for a quarter or semester course of study. It is now divided into four sections. The first discusses the basics of criminal investigation. The second illustrates their application to many of the major felonies. Instructors and students are given several kinds of specialized investigations and topics to choose from in the remaining two sections. We believe that dividing the material in this fashion has not only preserved the text's comprehensiveness, but it has also rendered the material eminently more teachable. The first two sections constitute the heart of the investigative process; the last two offer enrichment—to be savored as time and desire permit. A new chapter on automobile theft and its use in crime has been added in response to user request. The chapters on terrorism and computer crime have been substantially rewritten; and text throughout the book has been updated where appropriate.

The authors thank the many users who have commented on the readability of our text, and trust that the new material is of similar quality. Suggestions from instructors and students alike are most welcome.

Table of Contents

SECTION IV
SPECIALIZED TOPICS

SECTION I

THE FOUNDATION AND PRINCIPLES OF CRIMINAL INVESTIGATION

This section on criminal investigation comprises three parts: the first emphasizes the uses that can be made of the basic sources of information; the second is concerned with the problems associated with obtaining information; and the third focuses on the kinds of follow-through activities necessary for capitalizing on the efforts described in the first two parts. Considered together, these three parts are the foundation and principles of criminal investigation.

PART A

Part A begins with a discussion of the detective's responsibilities and the personal attributes that are required for success. A brief history of criminal investigation follows (touching on a sometimes less-than-honorable past). Part A concludes with a look at the trends and future developments that are likely to occur.

The three principal sources of information in criminal investigation (physical evidence, people, and records) are studied first from the standpoint of *what* information may be obtained and *why* it can be of help. Then, because understanding physical evidence—its development, interpretation, and investigative use—is fundamental, some familiarity with criminalistics is recommended. The O.J. Simpson trial graphically demonstrated that the means by which evidence is collected, preserved, and transmitted must preclude any possibility of contamination. Such considerations, coupled with a treatment of the crime scene—its limits, the purpose for a search, legal constraints on the discovery of physical evidence—are presented next. Finally, the other appropriate sources of information are considered: people (criminals, victims, witnesses, friends) and records (public and private).

CHAPTER 1

The Investigator

Responsibilities and Attributes; Origins and Trends

This chapter integrates and summarizes the criminal investigation function, including its history, current obligations, and future prospects. It defines criminal investigation and the responsibilities of the investigator, together with the attributes and skills required to discharge them. The reader will find a brief review of the origins of criminal investigation and the developments that brought it to its present stage or that may result from ongoing research.

CRIMINAL INVESTIGATION DEFINED

A group of scholars looking into police work defined criminal investigation as "the collection of information and evidence for identifying, apprehending, and convicting suspected offenders."[1] Professor Ralph F. Turner of Michigan State University prefers: "A criminal investigation is the reconstruction of a past event."[2] Either definition may be clarified further by examining the specific responsibilities of the investigator.

RESPONSIBILITIES OF THE INVESTIGATOR

1. Determine whether a crime has been committed.

2. Decide if the crime was committed within the investigator's jurisdiction.

3. Discover all facts pertaining to the complaint.
    a. Gather and preserve physical evidence.
    b. Develop and follow up all clues.

4. Recover stolen property.

5. Identify the perpetrator or eliminate a suspect as the perpetrator.

6. Locate and apprehend the perpetrator.

7. Aid in the prosecution of the offender by providing evidence of guilt that is admissible in court.

8. Testify effectively as a witness in court.

The date and time when each responsibility was carried out should be recorded. Being unable to answer confidently "when" a task was carried out affords defense counsel the opportunity to cast doubt on the investigator's capability. If a witness repeatedly responds to the question "At what time did you do_____?" with "I don't remember" or "as best as I can recall," defense counsel will use this technique to impugn a witness's competence.

Determine if a Crime Has Been Committed

In general, the responsibility for determining whether a crime has been committed is easily discharged. An investigator familiar with the elements of at least the more common crimes will be able to handle most situations. (Arson is an exception: when committed by professionals for profit, it is often easy to suspect but hard to prove.) First, the investigator should have available a copy of both the penal law and case law of the state; this ought to suffice for many of the more difficult cases. Second, the prosecuting attorney can be consulted. Third, if it is determined that no crime is involved or the issue is one for the civil courts, with rare exceptions criminal law enforcement personnel have no responsibility.

Verify Jurisdiction

If a crime is not within the investigator's jurisdiction, there is no responsibility for its investigation, but the complainant may need to be referred to the proper authority. Occasionally a crime is committed on the border line of two jurisdictions. Depending on whether it has the potential for publicity (especially a high-profile case), it affords the chance to make a "good arrest," or it is inherently interesting or important, an investigator will seek to retain authority over the case, remain involved in it; otherwise, talk the other jurisdiction into accepting it.

When two investigators have concurrent jurisdiction, the issue of who will handle the case becomes complicated. The following set of circumstances will illustrate. When the leader of a 19-member United States weather observation team was shot to death on a drifting ice mass in the Arctic Ocean, the immediate problem was not what happened or finding the perpetrator—it was where it happened and who had jurisdiction. "Where" was a 28-square-mile, 50-foot-thick slab of ice drifting back and forth within a limited area close to the North Pole. Since World War II and perhaps for much longer, it had been moving approximately two miles a day; at the time of the shooting, it lay west of Greenland, about 325 miles from the Pole.

Who had jurisdiction? The United States government contended that the moving ice should be likened to a ship on the high seas, hence subject to maritime law—as would be any vessel flying the American flag. Indeed, the flag had flown continuously in the midnight sun over the huts of the Eskimos and weather scientists from the States. Another contention asserted the drifting ice to be in Canadian jurisdiction, having once been contiguous to

Canada. Still another maintained (after he was caught) that the defendant's first step on any national territory was at Thule Air Force Base in Greenland; it being Danish, Denmark held jurisdiction.

Although the ultimate disposition of this case was not reported in the press from which this account was taken, and jurisdictional questions are only occasionally of concern for the investigator (certainly not of paramount significance), its unique circumstances suggest possibilities that might otherwise be difficult to imagine.

Discover All Facts and Collect Physical Evidence

The facts available to the first officer to arrive at a crime scene are provided by the victim or complainant and any eyewitness(es). Except in departments with programs in place for managing criminal investigations (see Chapter 24), they will be communicated to the detective dispatched to investigate the crime. He or she may decide to verify and pursue all of them, or to home in on specific details. This verification and follow-up process usually furnishes the answers to: what, when, where, and possibly, how and why the crime was committed. In addition, the detective will collect any physical evidence, or arrange for its collection (preferably by an evidence technician) and examination in the criminalistics laboratory. Depending on the kind of information provided, immediate follow-up might be required or the investigator may have to await laboratory results. In either event, it is essential at this point to follow through on any clue that holds promise for the identification of the perpetrator, and promptly exploit it.

The investigator must be mindful that the information developed may be tested in court, and should prepare for this ultimate possibility. At the first opportunity, a careful, comprehensive record of the crime scene should be made by means of notes, photographs, and sketches. This task should not be put off until later when memory must be trusted or objects may have been moved. The process of sifting facts and collecting evidence can result in the prompt apprehension of the perpetrator; more likely, however, additional time will be required to develop what is necessary for an identification and eventually an apprehension.

In longer investigations the use of records is more likely to contribute to the solution. If the victim furnishes the suspect's name to the detective, the case may be solved promptly. Then the chief problem is proving that the particular individual did in fact commit the crime. If the identity of the perpetrator must be developed, the effort required is much greater and, for certain crimes, often not successful. When it is, there comes a point not unlike that reached in solving a jigsaw puzzle: when the crucial piece is found, those remaining quickly fall into place.

Recover Stolen Property

The recovery of stolen property has a significance on a parallel with the identification of the perpetrator. The reports required of secondhand dealers and pawn shops are of great help to criminal investigators. They facilitate the identification of items brought in for pawn, since many thieves use this means to convert their loot into cash. But the dual description supplied by victim and pawn shop of the purloined and the pawned item must be accurate if it is to be matched in the stolen property file. Accuracy is assured if the forms the pawnbroker and the investigating officer must complete are designed so that each collects and provides identical details. When utilized properly, the information they elicit will be quite similar, and both forms should fall into the same slot in the stolen property file.

Identify the Perpetrator

In addition to the role secondhand dealers and pawnbrokers play in the recovery of stolen property, there is a chance that other merchants engaged in buying and selling may be able to describe who brought in a particular item. Usually the seller is required to fill out a form giving name, address, telephone number, and place of employment, thereby unwittingly making a sample of handwriting or printing available. Surprisingly, the individual pawning stolen goods will, more than the inexperienced might guess, provide factually correct information. When this occurs, the case solution is quite simple.

Motive as a Means of Identification

In addition to the identification of the perpetrator from records, physical evidence, and eyewitnesses, the value of motive must be examined. Certain crimes, such as burglary, robbery, and rape, seem to have a universal motive; others, such as homicide, arson, and assault, have what might be called "particularized motives," because they often relate victim to criminal. Once established, it would be practical to develop a short list of persons who might have a particularized motive; then, if the investigator considers who had the opportunity and the temperament to carry out the crime, one or perhaps a few suspects may remain on the list. When physical evidence is available, as it often is in these crimes, this extends the possibility of a solution beyond what can be accomplished by interrogation alone.

Locate and Apprehend the Perpetrator

When people who know the perpetrator are unwilling or unable to provide an address or a clue to his or her whereabouts (should the suspect be elusive or have escaped), records may provide the information. (See Chapters 5 and 7, which discuss the value and utilization of records.) When the suspect is located, apprehension seldom presents difficulties; if it does, a raid may be called for. Planning and staging a raid require coordination, but this is essentially a police function rather than an investigative one. Owing, however, to several raids that received world-wide attention and, to some extent, had a deleterious impact on *all* law enforcement agencies, it is important to consider these events. Therefore, a commentary on the Waco Branch Davidians, Philadelphia's MOVE, and the Chicago Black Panther raids is provided as one of the specialized topics in Chapter 30 in Section IV.

Aid the Prosecution by Providing Evidence of Guilt Admissible in Court

Largely as a result of plea bargaining, only a few cases that are investigated and solved eventually go to trial, but the detective must operate on the assumption that each will be tried. This necessitates that proper notes, photographs, and sketches are made in a timely fashion from the very beginning and that the physical evidence present is properly handled and examined. A case in which this was not done involved a burglary that was interrupted by the return of the owner. Heading for the fire escape from a freshly painted, still tacky step stool at the kitchen window, the intruder left a distinct imprint of his shoe on its adhesive surface. In a search of the neighborhood, the suspect was found hiding under a blanket on the floor of a parked automobile, wearing shoes with crepe soles that seemed to match the pattern left on the stool (see Figure 1.1).

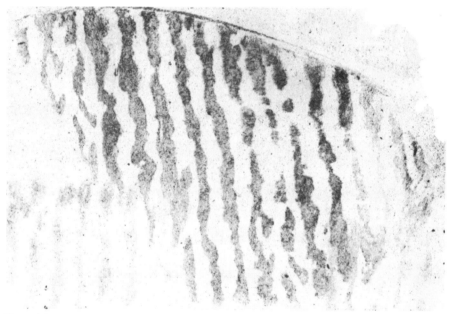

Figure 1.1
Crepe-sole impression left by a burglar on a freshly painted step stool. *(From* The Crime Laboratory, *2nd ed. Courtesy, Clark Boardman Co., Ltd. and the New York City Police Department.)*

At this point in the investigation, unfortunately, the physical evidence was improperly handled. Rather than transport both shoes and step stool to the crime laboratory, the detective made his own test impression. As can be seen from Figure 1.2, this impression was rather poor. This is a reversal of the norm: typically, the crime scene impression is poor and the known (comparison) impression is good. However poor its quality, the test impression sufficed to establish an identity. A bit of luck for the investigator.

Though this detective had handled 75 burglary cases, none had gone to trial (each defendant having pleaded guilty to a reduced charge). Based on this experience, and because the suspect had confessed verbally, the detective believed that it was but a needless exercise to submit the shoes and stool to the laboratory. Instead, the prisoner was allowed to be placed in a police station cell wearing the incriminating evidence; once there, he ripped the crepe soles into pieces and flushed them down the toilet. At a preliminary hearing he then repudiated the confession and demanded a trial. A four-time offender, he faced a life sentence if convicted.

Problems concerning physical evidence can arise needlessly when it is presumed that a case will involve plea bargaining. Here, the detective was caught off guard; even though the blunder was offset, an investigator ought not bank on such luck.

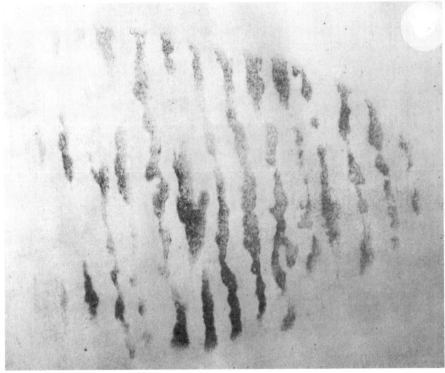

Figure 1.2
Impression made by a detective using suspect's shoe. *(From* The Crime Laboratory, *2nd ed. Courtesy, Clark Boardman Co., Ltd., and the New York City Police Department.)*

Testify Effectively as a Witness in Court

Although few people are comfortable when called to the witness stand, the experienced investigator who has testified often can appear jaded. Yet testimony is effective only when it is credible. When sincerity, knowledge of the facts, and impartiality are projected, credibility is established. In all events, it is helpful that the investigator be familiar with the rules of evidence and the pitfalls of cross-examination (see Chapter 26).

ATTRIBUTES DESIRABLE IN AN INVESTIGATOR _____

Abilities and Skills

The attributes that enable a person to be an accomplished investigator are twofold:

1. the ability, both physical and mental, to conduct an inquiry; together with

2. those skills necessary to reach the intended objectives.

ABILITIES	RELATED SKILLS
Conduct a proper crime scene search for physical evidence.	Know how to recognize, collect, and preserve physical evidence.
	Know the varieties of *modus operandi*.
Question complainants, witnesses, and suspects.	Know how to use interviewing techniques.
	Know interrogation methods.
	Have a knowledge of local street jargon, and if pertinent, any foreign language spoken in the community.
	Be sensitive to the constitutional and civil rights of *all*: rich or poor, witness or suspect.
	Have a developed sense of *mind-set*.
Develop and follow up clues.	Know sources of records and how to check them.
	Know how to cultivate and use informants.
	Know how to conduct surveillances.
	Know how to check pawn shops, secondhand dealers, and the like.
Prepare written reports of case activity as it develops.	Have knowledge and skill in English.
Obtain legal search warrants based on evidence of probable cause.	Know how to use departmental and court forms to secure a search warrant.
Conduct raids, possibly under adverse conditions.	Know the techniques of cover and concealment.
Act with initiative, as the fluidity of the (raid) situation demands.	Acquire skill in silent communication. Use teamwork— within and between agencies.
Apprehend violators in a lawful manner.	Acquire a working knowledge of applicable laws, departmental rules and regulations.
	Know about the use of "come-along," handcuffs, and service revolver.

<u>**ABILITIES**</u>	<u>**RELATED SKILLS**</u>
	Know search and seizure techniques for prisoners, houses, and automobiles.
Assist prosecuting attorney in presentation to the grand jury or trial court.	Know how to prepare clear, comprehensive reports.
	Know how to serve subpoenas, when necessary.
	Know how to have witnesses available or willing to appear on notice.
Appear as a witness in court.	Testify effectively in court.

Qualifications of Mind, Personality, Attitude, and Knowledge

The following list of traits, which are desirable and help to qualify an individual for investigative work, was developed through classroom discussions (including many detectives who were students) and by conferring with police administrators interested in the topic of qualifications.

1. Intelligence and reasoning ability.

   A score of 110 or better on a General Classification Test (GCT).

   Ability to analyze and interrelate a large number of facts.

2. Curiosity and imagination.

   Taking nothing for granted.

   Skeptical of the obvious.

   A sense of the unusual: anything out of place or not in keeping with the norm.

   An inquisitive mind.

   A suspicious nature with respect to the behavior of people.

   A sense of awareness.

   Insight.

   A flair for detective work.

3. Observation and memory.

   All five senses are intact and functioning.

   The investigator is alert and attentive.

4. Knowledge of life and people.

   Includes all strata of society; especially necessary to deal with the heterogeneous population of large cities. Also helpful: common sense, an outgoing personality, a spirit of cooperativeness, emotional stability, and some acting ability for role playing.

5. Possession of technical "know-how."

> Implies training and knowledge of statutory and case law, as well as in the recognition, collection, preservation, and investigative value of physical evidence.

6. Perseverance, "stick-to-itiveness," and energy.

> Many who wish to become detectives believe the job involves a glamorous life style, but the ability to be indefatigable, survive boredom, and keep energy in reserve to carry on, is more suggestive and realistic.

7. Ability to recognize and control bias and prejudice in one's self and on the job.

> Owing to bias and prejudice, for example, there may be a preconceived idea as to the perpetrator. Other truths may be ignored, such as: a chronic complainant can have a legitimate grievance; a prostitute can be raped; etc.

8. Sensitivity to people's feelings; acts with discretion and tact; respects a confidence.

9. The honesty and courage to withstand temptation and corruption.

10. When testifying, is not overzealous and does not commit perjury.

11. Miscellaneous characteristics:

> Physically fit appearance, report writing skills, awareness of good public relations as a future source of cooperation and information.

Some police administrators believe that the traditional means of selecting detectives—written and oral examinations—have proved to be unsatisfactory:

> Prepared written examinations have not proved predictive in the selection of outstanding candidates for the position of investigator. . . . No theoretical foundation exists for the oral board portion of the current testing process, other than a belief in its content validity.[3]

It is suggested that future performance can be gauged by an individual's "past work product." Further, good prospects must be recruited—not merely a fallout of the hiring process. Selection should include such considerations as: computer literacy, superior analytical capability, and good communication and reading skills.[4] Another prerequisite is education.

> . . . [The] most important requirement is education. Study after study produces the same conclusions: that college educated people make better law enforcement officers.[5]

The National Institute of Justice published the results of a more comprehensive study of the detective selection process. In the Foreword, James K. Stewart wrote:

. . . managers and line personnel alike could identify some officers who were much better investigators than others. Studies bear out their observation: a small proportion of officers in any department is responsible for the majority of cases that successfully result in convictions.[6]

The concept of "past work product" is again endorsed as a predictor of success, yet criminal justice researchers have paid scant attention to the problem of detective selection, despite the impact of crime on the quality of life in communities across the nation.

ORIGINS OF CRIMINAL INVESTIGATION

The Industrial Revolution in Europe drew the peasant class from the countryside into the towns, and the crime wave that swept through the burgeoning cities forced governments to make hasty, *ad hoc* responses to the crisis. As one writer describes it:

> . . . The rapid expansion of London since the Great Fire had taken place in a haphazard, undisciplined way, and the increased population . . . was protected merely by a system of purely local constables and watches which had been inadequate to the needs of a far smaller community, and was now hopelessly overwhelmed.[7]

Thus "thief-catchers" were not ordinarily sought from among those already part of the underworld, yet it was the criminal element in their midst to which authorities eventually turned for help. The rank and file of those recruits constituted a distinct breed, but two clear-cut differences in motivation set some apart from others. One kind were hirelings; with mercenary motives, they would play both sides of the street. The other kind were social climbers who, in order to move into respectable society, would incriminate their confederates.

Figure 1.3
Jonathan Wild
(Courtesy, Metropolitan Police, New Scotland Yard, London.)

An example of the former may be found in eighteenth-century England where one Jonathan Wild personified the old saying, "Set a thief to catch a thief" (see Figure 1.3). Wild was well-acquainted with London's riffraff, having operated a brothel that served as headquarters for the gang of thieves and cut-throats under his tight control. Simultaneously, he was the public servant doing undercover work for the authorities. A rogue on the grand scale, Wild was both law enforcer and law breaker. He soon realized, however, that there was more profit to be made arranging for the return of stolen goods than for its disposal at the stiff discounts taken by the fence. Therefore, throughout the period he worked for the authorities, he was actually a receiver of stolen goods posing as the recoverer of lost property—the middle man exacting his cut while protecting the criminals in his employ. Even today, there are resemblances between his fictitious "Lost Property Office" and the "no questions asked" practices of individuals (even of some insurance companies) when stolen property, such as valuable jewelry and priceless paintings, is ransomed.

The earliest police in England worked only at night. First known as the "Watch of London," and later as the "Old Charleys," they were paid by the inhabitants in the vicinity of the watchman's box from which they regularly made the rounds of their beat. These parish constables had been appointed in 1253; they lasted until 1829 in London. About 20 years after Jonathan Wild was hanged, novelist Henry Fielding (who wrote about Wild's exploits in a genial, tolerant vein, believing humankind to be a mix of good and bad) accepted an appointment as a London Magistrate. Taking his call to the bar seriously, Fielding was promptly embroiled in the sorry state of England's penal codes and its administration of justice (see Figure 1.4). The new magistrate tried to deal with the rising crime rate by enlarging the scope of the government's crime fighting methods and assigning to his court a few parish constables accustomed to night watchman duties. These pursuers were soon performing some criminal investigative functions, and they were successful "thief-takers," owing to the use of informants and their close ties with the underworld. First called "Mr. Fielding's People," they later came to be known as the "Bow Street Runners" (see Figure 1.5). Unofficial and unpaid, the constables wore no uniforms and were ranked directly under the magistrate, who had to fight for their fair share of the reward moneys for apprehending criminals.

HENRY FIELDING (1707-1754)

Figure 1.4
Henry Fielding
(Courtesy, Metropolitan Police, New Scotland Yard, London.)

When the public finally became aware of their goings-on, the Bow Street Runners were perceived as thief-takers of the Jonathan Wild mold. Inevitably, abuses followed hard upon their close ties with the underworld, resulting in widespread criticism and loss of public trust. Then, around 1790, a staff of trained detectives was established, known as the "Runners." Officially recognized and paid, they were plainclothesmen who wore no uniforms and coexisted with the constables until the passage of the Metropolitan Police Act in 1829. The constables were replaced by a professional police force of 1,000 men, the "Runners" lasting another 10 years until the passage of the Metropolitan Police Act and Metropolitan Police Courts Act of 1839.[8] The members of this first professional force, organized by Sir Robert Peel (Britain's Home Secretary), were called the "Peelers" (see Figure 1.6); later and up until the present, they became known as the "Bobbies."

About a decade later, a small number of full-time plainclothes officers had become an integral part of the new force. Because it was quartered in the Scotland Yard, an ancient structure that once protected Scottish kings and royal visitors, the police force in general and the detective force in particular were dubbed with that name.

Figure 1.5
One of "Mr. Fielding's People," who came after the "Old Charleys," and were later known as the "Bow Street Runners." They covered all of London, yet were never greater than 10 in number. *(Courtesy, Metropolitan Police, New Scotland Yard, London.)*

In the early nineteenth century, French authorities also sought out convicted criminals to do undercover work. A notorious example of the thief-turned-informer, Francois Eugene Vidocq quickly set an enviable arrest and conviction record for the Paris police (see Figure 1.7). Taking advantage of expertise acquired during his long association with thieves, Vidocq enabled the police to wipe cases from their books that they had hitherto been unable to clear. Yet throughout 1812 the high crime rate in Paris continued and Vidocq's suggestion to establish a plainclothes bureau was finally adopted. The Brigade de la Sûreté, created by the Ministry of Police, would function in all of the city's districts and report directly to the Prefect (the head of the Paris police force). Then Vidocq, the thief-turned-informer-turned-detective, became chief of this cohort of ex-convicts.

The role of thief-taker evolved gradually, despite rapid social change in Europe. In the nineteenth century, the function of criminal investigator or detective became a specific, identifiable one. It no longer required criminal apprenticeship; the detective was merely expected to mingle with and watch criminals. Meanwhile, in the United States, Thomas Byrnes was appointed detective bureau chief for the New York Police Department. His stewardship in 1880 exemplifies this gradual shift in direction—from one who consorted with criminals to one who was first and foremost a policeman. But just as the Bow Street Runners' close ties with the underworld were unethical, so were Byrnes's. With his coterie of informers, and his system of singling out which criminals to prosecute and which to tolerate—a system almost as corrupt as that of Jonathan Wild (who actually set up, or framed, his own confederates)—this chief of detectives, like Wild, gave the impression that crime was under control. If valuables were stolen from anyone of importance, it lay within Byrnes's power not only to guarantee their return, but to specify the day and time that their owners could expect it. All he need do was put out a verbal signal; if it was ignored, harsh retribution was exacted of (and by) the underworld.

Crime that victimized the average citizen was not treated with similar tact. There can be

Figure 1.6
A member of the professional police force organized by Sir Robert Peel. Initially referred to as "Peelers," they later came to be known as "Bobbies." *(Courtesy, Metropolitan Police, New Scotland Yard, London.)*

little doubt that police morale was low, yet the mighty—those who commanded the attention of the press and who were a political force in the city—were complacent about Byrnes. Whether all of them understood how his selective system operated is not certain;

that some did becomes evident from one of Theodore
Roosevelt's first acts upon assuming the post of President
of the Board of Police Commissioners in 1895. Byrnes
was forced out. Some time later in another larger city, it
was rumored that a chief of detectives was picked
allegedly because of his ability to have the bodies of
gangland slayings dumped outside the borders of his
jurisdiction. Apocryphal perhaps, but such a practice is
not totally beyond belief considering the rough-and-
tumble turn-of-the-century politics in some large cities
and the heritage of criminal investigation.

The foregoing has briefly touched on the history of
investigation at the local level in the United States.
Because federal laws also need to be enforced, it is
informative to do the same at the national level. When the
Department of Justice was created by Congress in 1870,
the investigative forces of the federal government consisted largely of the Treasury Department's Secret Service
and Bureau of Customs, together with the U.S. Postal

Figure 1.7
Francoise Eugene Vidocq.
*(Courtesy, Metropolitan Police, New Scotland
Yard, London.)*

Inspection Service. All were essentially *ad hoc* agencies with restricted jurisdictions. The
next year, limited funds were appropriated for the newly formed Department of Justice;
its mandate, the detection and prosecution of federal crimes. As investigators it employed
part-time outsiders, some Pinkerton detectives, paid informers, political patronage
workers, and occasionally agents borrowed from the Secret Service and other units. This
practice continued for 30 years, until the administration of Theodore Roosevelt in
1901. Among the many concerns of this conservationist, activist, reformer president were
the "public be damned" attitude of big business and its flouting of the Sherman Antitrust
Act. The effort to make it subservient to law and government was evident from the
angry force of Roosevelt's speeches about the large-scale thefts of public lands in the western states; he was advancing the new idea that natural resources should be held in trust.
Subsequently, two politicians (a senator and a congressman, both from Oregon) were
convicted for "conspiracy to defraud the United States out of public lands." A historic
investigation, it was accomplished with borrowed Secret Service agents.

> Roosevelt's administration called "The attention of Congress . . . to the
> anomaly that the Department of Justice has . . . no permanent detective
> force under its immediate control . . . it seems obvious that the Department
> . . . ought to have a means of . . . enforcement subject to its own call; a Depart-
> ment of Justice with no force of permanent police in any form under its con-
> trol is assuredly not fully equipped for its work."[9]

Not only did Congress ignore the request, it retaliated by initiating an inquiry into the
Justice Department's habit of employing the investigative forces of other federal agencies.
Indeed, just before adjournment, Congress amended an appropriation bill to expressly
forbid the department's use of Secret Service or other agents. Roosevelt's response to the
challenge was characteristically quick. Rather than accede to a continual hamstringing

of the new department, his attorney general established an investigative unit within the Department of Justice soon after Congress adjourned. Named "The Bureau of Investigation" a short time later, the unit was to report only to the attorney general.

Two of the men who directed this unit formerly had been in command of the Secret Service. President Harding's appointee, the director since 1921, was replaced by another former Secret Service head, William J. Burns. Burns, however, was responsible for bringing Gaston B. Means, a man of unsavory reputation, into the Bureau. It was not long before the new agent was suspended for such unethical deals as selling departmental reports to underworld figures and offering to fix federal cases. The attorney general suspended Means; quietly, Burns brought him back, ostensibly because of Means's underworld contacts. Under such stewardship, needless to say, the prestige of the Bureau declined; it sank even further when Harding's attorney general used the agency to frame a senator. This scandal, among the many others in Harding's administration, brought about the appointment of a new attorney general when, upon the sudden death of the president in 1923, Calvin Coolidge was catapulted into office.

President Coolidge did not equivocate about replacing Harding's corrupt cabinet members. The first decision of Harlan Fiske Stone, the new Attorney General (later Chief Justice of the Supreme Court,) was to demand Burns's resignation and offer the directorship to a 29-year-old attorney in the Justice Department. J. Edgar Hoover accepted the post, but only under certain conditions. The first applied to the Bureau's personnel practice: it must be divorced from politics, cease to be a catch-all for political hacks, and base appointments on merit. The director's authority was the subject of his second condition: he must have full control over hiring and firing (with promotion solely on proven ability), and be responsible only to the attorney general. Appointed to clean up the scandals, Stone not only agreed, he asserted that J. Edgar Hoover would not be allowed to take the job under any other conditions.

The sweeping powers given the new director brought a radical improvement in personnel quality. Although such sweeping authority was certainly necessary to effect change, the seeds of disaster accompanied it nonetheless. As Lord Acton's aphorism aptly warns, "Power tends to corrupt, and absolute power corrupts absolutely." It should not be unexpected, therefore, that absolute power corrupted once more. Toward the close of Hoover's distinguished 48-year regime, some investigative practices were viewed critically, first by a senate committee, and then by the press. What should be surprising is that the far greater excesses proposed were not countenanced. Indeed, they were rejected by the director.[10]

Of all the executive departments of government, those having the power to investigate crime represent a potential threat to freedom. In a democracy, therefore, civilian supervision of the exercise of such power is crucial. Those entering the field of law enforcement must always be mindful that they are citizens first, investigators second.

Shift in Investigative Methods

When formally organized police departments came into being in response to crime conditions, the use of informers as the main staple in the investigative cupboard was supplemented by the use of interrogation, though the methods permitted to secure confessions varied widely from country to country. In the United States in 1931, the Wickersham Commission (appointed by President Herbert Hoover) employed the term "third degree" to characterize the extraction of confessions accompanied by brute force. It was, said the report, a widespread, almost universal police practice. Then the Supreme Court began to apply the provisions of the Bill of Rights to the states. Its judicial decisions, together with the potential offered by the application of science to the examination of physical evidence, brought an end to brutal methods of interrogation.

Europe was well ahead of the States in recognizing that potential. In 1893, Hans Gross, an Austrian who might be called the father of forensic investigation, wrote a monumental treatise so advanced for its time that it was unmatched for decades. *Handbuch fur Untersuchungsrichter* when translated became *Criminal Investigation*. At about the same time in England, Sir Francis Galton's landmark book, *Fingerprints*, was published (in 1892). It led to the identification of criminals based on fingerprint evidence found at the crime scene. The marks or visible evidence left on an object by a person's fingers had long been observed, but such observations lacked any understanding of the intrinsic value of a human fingerprint. A somewhat similar situation prevailed with respect to bloodstain evidence. For a long time it could not be proved that a suspected stain was in fact blood; when it could, its presence would be explained by alleging the source to be that of a chicken or other animal. Prior to 1901, such allegations could neither be proved nor disproved; then, a German, Paul Uhlenhuth, discovered the precipitin test for distinguishing human blood from animal blood. In the field of firearms identification, it was not until 1923 that Calvin Goddard, an American, developed (with others) the comparison microscope; it helped to determine whether a particular gun fired a bullet or cartridge found at a crime scene.

These scientific developments, when applied to the examination of physical evidence, pointed to the need for properly equipped crime laboratories. In 1910 the first police laboratory was established by Edmond Locard in Lyon, France. In the United States it ultimately led, in the mid-1920s to early 1930s, to the installation of crime laboratories in a few of the larger cities. In Washington, DC, one was established in the Bureau of Investigation (renamed the Federal Bureau of Investigation in 1935). The expansion of crime laboratories proceeded slowly: by 1968, there still were none within the borders of 17 (mostly western) states. The availability of Law Enforcement Assistance Administration (LEAA) funds, however, soon permitted each state to install a criminalistics laboratory. Incidentally, the term *criminalistics*, first used by Hans Gross, was not to reappear in the title of a book until 1948 when it was used for the publication, *An Introduction to Criminalistics*. This text provided in-depth coverage of the scientific principles and instruments employed at that time for the examination of physical evidence in a forensic laboratory. In California, a university program in criminalistics, coupled with strong support from the law enforcement community, led to the greatest proliferation of county laboratories in this country. With his research contributions and headship of the program at the University of California, Professor Paul L. Kirk must be viewed as one of the few major figures in the field of criminalistics. In the midwest, another major figure, Professor Ralph F. Turner, integrated criminalistics with the teaching of criminal investigation at Michigan State University's strong police/law enforcement program, turning out criminalists to serve that area of the country.

Forensic medicine, the other main branch of forensic science, developed outside the control of police agencies. For this reason and because it otherwise contributes to the general well-being, forensic medicine evolved sooner and grew more quickly, remaining well ahead of criminalistics. This was the state of affairs until the 1960s when both branches benefitted from the infusion of LEAA funds. Just the same, forensic medicine and its subdivisions are largely, but not exclusively, concerned with homicide; their use within the totality of criminal investigation is more limited than is that of criminalistics. Owing to the importance attached to homicide, however, forensic medicine is of vital significance to the criminal investigator.

TRENDS IN INVESTIGATION

To conclude, several developments attributable to the social unrest of the 1960s in the United States must be mentioned because they will affect the investigative function in the future. With "crime-in-the-streets" a priority campaign issue in the 1964 presidential election, it became clear that something was going to be "done." But what? A typical solution: establishing and funding yet another federal program. Moneys finally became available to study crime from the Office of Law Enforcement Assistance (OLEA). A beneficial result affecting criminal investigation was supposed to be an improvement in the techniques for analyzing crime-related data, with the following objectives in mind:

- To increase the number of cases cleared by arrest by correlating the MOs of arrested suspects to other current offenses.

- To provide investigative leads for detectives by furnishing lists of suspects whose MOs match those of current offenses.

- To provide a greater number of crime pattern bulletins for the patrol function, and thereby increase the awareness of field officers and the potential for earlier arrests.

- To provide a means for influencing citizen groups to observe criminal activity as it directly pertains to them, and thereby aid in enlisting their support for crime-specific prevention programs.

- To provide information relating to security considerations for external design of new residential communities and commercial developments.

- To provide early identification of crime patterns through MO correlations.

- To increase the number of discovered crime patterns capable of being identified.

- To provide a means of measuring the results of crime-specific prevention or suppression programs.

- To provide staff recommendations on possible program solutions to crime problems.

- To aid in the coordination of special crime suppression task forces.

- To provide information on projected levels of offender activity and to identify future problem areas.[11]

These obviously worthwhile, ambitious objectives must be balanced in the short run by practical considerations. For example, Block and Weidman state:

> Of course, a team commander (or analyst in a team) is more likely to spot the patterns of offenders who are working intensively in a small neighborhood. As the area increases, the more distinctive the pattern of activity will need to be before it will stand out. The more common the crime pattern, the more likely that analysis will be a waste of time. Indeed, statistical programs [that] will attempt to find geographical or MO patterns by operating on a large data base are doomed to failure unless methods of seeking unusual patterns have been built in. The machine is no more capable of finding patterns among masses of mundane events than is a person.
>
> The involvement of investigative personnel in crime analysis and crime-analysis planning may be very helpful. These officers will have a sense, from their everyday experience, of the kinds of patterns which are distinctive. In general, they can help provide the hunches which may pay off either in a manual analysis system or in a machine-assisted system.[12]

As sophisticated information systems become prevalent, the long-term implications are indicated by the proposed (but disputed) reforms of the investigative process suggested by Greenwood and Petersilia: "Increase the use of information processing systems in lieu of investigators."[13]

Although computers are now commonly used in police work, their ultimate contribution is yet to be realized. As electronic information becomes more sophisticated, it will have a major effect on case investigations: helping the detective cull a quantity of data efficiently and effectively; providing clues and identifying potential suspects; making it possible to prepare reports quickly and assemble evidence for presentation in court. Present technology allows for the transfer of photographs, fingerprints, and other forms of visual information through networks. Technology makes it possible for an investigator to carry a small "notebook," e.g., a laptop computer, containing as many as 20,000 pages of information that can be called up by means of code and search systems or through a modem hooked to a computer. It would be perfectly feasible, for example, to conduct on-site "mug shot" presentations.

On the international level, the need for enhanced computer systems increases as the world seems to become smaller owing to rapid global travel. Computerized databases will be critical in combating terrorism and fraud. INTERPOL, the International Police Organization, acknowledged this by significantly upgrading its computer systems when moving to new headquarters in Lyon, France. The United Nations Crime Prevention and Criminal Justice Branch also views the goal of worldwide computerization as crucial. Indeed, large criminal syndicates and those involved in "enterprise crime" are in many respects much further ahead in their use of computer technology than are many law enforcement agencies.

In the early 1980s, a great amount of work was going on with regard to the use of artificial intelligence, but progress in this field was slow and results have not yet lived up to expectations.[14] Nevertheless, there are those who believe the computer will revolutionize criminal investigation. When such claims were made 20 years ago by several major police departments, they soon found the determinant to be the quality of information fed into the system. In computer language: "garbage in, garbage out." Ultimately, benefits will come from computer programs designed to facilitate and enhance, rather than replace, good detective work.

Another development to be considered is the emergence of the female detective. In the United States, the passage of the Equal Employment Opportunity Act has accelerated this trend, yet the overall progress of assimilation has not been as rapid as some had anticipated. Prior to 1968, for example, the investigation of rape was male-dominated; today, many departments assign female detectives to rape cases. They work with and support the victim through the entire investigation. Thus far, however, there are but a handful of female undercover narcotics agents in the United States—even though their effectiveness could be attested to by the experience of the New York City Police Department, which employed women for this purpose well before drugs became a nationwide problem. The same department used women for surveillance work; the female officers also proved to be more than capable at these tasks. A trend is discernible, but the number of women assigned as criminal investigators is unlikely to swell unless the stereotyped concept of detective work as a male occupation changes.[15]

The scrutiny of the criminal investigation process by police administrators, researchers, and scholars is another important development. Patrick V. Murphy, first in his role as a police administrator and Commissioner of the New York City Police Department, and then as the President of the Police Foundation, was a prime mover in the genesis and germination of this idea.[16] A serious dialogue between practitioners and researchers was a potentially valuable result of such scrutiny.[17] With the loss of federal funding, it unfortunately has lapsed; there is virtually no ongoing dialogue. Nevertheless, research across the spectrum of the behavioral and information sciences holds great promise for improvement in the investigative function—if criminal justice is able to digest and adopt it for practical use. Such research might involve: psychology as it applies to interviewing and interrogation; artificial intelligence as it may apply to criminal investigation (as a means of plotting investigative strategy, for example); or the use of laptop computers to improve the quality of the information gathered initially, while transferring and storing it and all subsequent information in the memory of a large computer for the purpose of case management.[18]

Finally, there is the recognition of the need for improving police performance when making arrests; it is an example of how the criminal investigation process can be scrutinized through academic research. Interest in doing so arose from the fact that fewer than half of all felony arrests in the United States result in conviction.

> This failure . . . to come to trial, referred to as *case attrition*, has become a matter of serious public and policy concern. Many arrestees whose cases are dropped quickly return to crime and are rearrested, only to slip through the system again. This pattern creates an impression of "revolving door" justice that not only undermines public confidence, but also may make criminals cynical about their chances of being punished, thus undercutting the deterrent effect of "swift and certain punishment."

The gravity of the situation has made case attrition a major target for reform efforts, most of them focused on the police. Although attrition may occur anywhere in the process of arrest, filing, and prosecution, most of the onus has fallen on police handling of cases. Statistics play a part in this placing of blame. On average, 80 percent of the cases accepted for prosecution nationwide result in conviction. However, only about 50 percent of arrests are accepted for prosecution. Thus, it is clear that most case attrition occurs between arrest and filing.[19]

This situation would be alleviated if investigators routinely conducted competent investigations—if, as they search for the information needed to sustain a conviction, they kept uppermost in mind the principles and practices that govern evidence gathering. Then the number of arrests accepted for prosecution and the number of convictions will surely rise. With "swift and certain" punishment closer to reality, any resulting deterrent effects that result will be to the benefit of all.

REFERENCES

[1]   E. Ostrum, R.B. Parks, and G. Whitaker, *Patterns of Metropolitan Policing* (Cambridge, MA: Ballinger, 1978), 131.

[2]   Ralph F. Turner, personal communication, 1987.

[3]   Frank Adams, "Selecting Successful Investigative Candidates," *The Police Chief, 61*(7), 12-14 (July 1994), 12.

[4]   Ibid., 12, 14.

[5]   Ibid., 14.

[6]   Bernard Cohen and Jan Chaiken, *Investigators Who Perform Well*. Washington, DC: U.S. Department of Justice (National Institute of Justice), September 1987, iii.

[7]   Henry Fielding, *Jonathan Wild*, ed. David Nokes (New York: Penguin Books, 1982), 8.

[8]   R.L. Jones, "Back to the Bow Street Runners," *Police Journal* 63:3 (1990), 246-248.

[9]   D. Whitehead, *The FBI Story* (New York: Random House, 1956), 19.

[10] W.C. Sullivan with Bill Brown, *The Bureau: My Thirty Years in Hoover's FBI* (New York: Norton, 1979), 205-217, 251-257.

[11] G.A. Buck, *Police Crime Analysis Unit Handbook* (Washington, DC: U.S. Government Printing Office, 1974), 7.

[12] P.B. Block and D.R. Weidman, *Managing Criminal Investigations* (Washington DC: U.S. Government Printing Office, 1976), 28-29.

[13] P.W. Greenwood and J. Petersilia, *The Criminal Investigative Process*, Vol. I: Summary and Policy Implications (Santa Monica, CA: RAND, 1975), 30.

[14] J. Brian Morgan, *The Police Function and the Investigation of Crime* (Aldershot, England: Avebury/Gower, 1990).

[15] R.L O'Block and V.L. Abele, "The Emergence of the Female Detective," *The Police Chief* 47:5 (May 1980), 54.

16   Patrick V. Murphy and Thomas Plate, *Commissioner: A View from the Top of American Law Enforcement* (New York: Simon and Schuster, 1977), 183-216.

17   National Institute of Law Enforcement and Criminal Justice, *The Criminal Investigation Process: A Dialogue on Research Findings* (Washington, DC: U.S. Government Printing Office, 1977).

18   J. Brian Morgan, *loc. cit.*

19   J. Petersilia, A. Abrahamse, and J.Q. Wilson, "A Summary of RAND's Research on Police Performance," *Journal of Police Science and Administration* 17:3 (1990), 219-227.

SUPPLEMENTAL READINGS

Amidon, H.T. "Law Enforcement: From The Beginning to the English Bobby," *Journal of Police Science and Administration* 5:3 (1977), 355-367.

Anon. *Investigators Who Perform Well.* Washington, DC: U.S. Department of Justice, National Institute of Justice, 1987.

Berman, Jay S. *Police Administration and Progressive Reform: Theodore Roosevelt as Police Commissioner of New York.* Westport, CT: Greenwood Press, 1987.

Brown, Jerrold G. and Clarice R. Cox. *Report Writing for Criminal Justice Professionals.* 2nd ed. Cincinnati: Anderson, 1998.

Defoe, Daniel. Introduction and notes to "The True and Genuine Account of the Life and Actions of the Late Jonathan Wild." Pages 225-227 in *Jonathan Wild*, by Henry Fielding, edited by David Nokes. New York: Penguin Books, 1982.

Edwards, Samuel. *The Vidocq Dossier: The Story of the World's First Detective.* Boston: Houghton-Mifflin, 1977.

Ericson, R.V. *Making Crime: A Study of Detective Work.* Toronto: Butterworth, 1984.

Hopkins, Ernest Jerome. *Our Lawless Police.* New York: Viking Press, 1931; New York: Da Capo Press, 1971.

Horne, Peter. *Women in Law Enforcement.* 2nd ed. Springfield, IL: Charles C Thomas, 1980.

Lockley, Thomas. "The Heart and Art of a Detective Officer: I through VII." *Police Journal of Britain* 43: 2, 3, 4, 5, 6, 7 (February 1970-August 1970), 73-80, 141-149, 177-181, 223-229, 269-277, 327-330, 385-394.

Mones, Paul. *Stalking Justice: The Dramatic True Story of the Detective Who First Used DNA Testing to Catch a Serial Killer.* New York: Pocket Books, 1995.

Morgan, J. Brian. *The Police Function and the Investigation of Crime.* Aldershot, England: Avebury/Gower, 1990.

National Commission on Law Observance and Enforcement. *Report on Lawlessness in Law Enforcement.* Washington, DC: U.S. Government Printing Office, 1931. [Report No. 11 of the Wickersham Commission appointed by President Herbert Hoover in 1929.]

Sanders, W.B. *Detective Work: A Study of Criminal Investigations.* Riverside, NJ: The Free Press, 1977.

Stead, Philip J., ed. *Pioneers in Policing.* Montclair, NJ: Patterson Smith, 1978.

Thornwald, Jurgen. *The Century of the Detective.* New York: Harcourt, Brace & World, 1965.

Thornwald, Jurgen. *Crime and Science.* New York: Harcourt, Brace & World, 1967.

U.S. Department of the Treasury. *Report to the Bureau of Alcohol, Tobacco and Firearms Investigation of Vernon Wayne Howell, also known as David Koresh.* Washington, DC: Department of the Treasury, September 30, 1993.

CHAPTER 2

Physical Evidence

Development, Interpretation, Investigative Value

FORENSIC SCIENCE

The word *forensic* is derived from the Latin *forensis*, meaning "forum." A town square or marketplace in ancient cities, the forum was the arena of discussion and disputation in judicial and other public matters. As society became more complex, disputes were argued and settled in formally organized courts. Today, the term *forensic* still applies to and is used in courts of law or public discussion and debate. *Forensics*, a fairly new, all-encompassing term, characterizes the scientific examination of evidence. Owing largely to television shows and motion pictures, the term *forensics* is now generic and part of the vocabulary of the average person—and, therefore, jurors. At least two major branches of forensic science are recognized, the most obvious being criminalistics and forensic medicine. Each has several subdivisions. The less obvious branches of forensic medicine will be discussed later in this chapter.

Criminalistics	**Forensic Medicine**
Wet Chemistry	Pathology
Instrumental Chemistry	Serology
Firearms and Toolmarks	Toxicology
Questioned Documents	Odontology
Fingerprints	Psychiatry
Photography	
Lie Detection	
Voice Spectroscopy	

The purpose of this chapter is to further the reader's understanding of the principles involved in converting physical clues into evidence that has investigative or probative value—or both. The help given to law enforcement by the work of forensic laboratories is treated later in the chapter. Discussed later are the most common kinds of clue materials to be found at crime scenes (in terms of the information provided the investigator if they are examined by a forensic scientist). DNA analysis, having just become visible on the horizon of criminal justice and holding great promise for serving the needs of law enforcement, is treated at some length.

Criminalistics: The Development and Interpretation of Physical Evidence

Criminalistics, the branch of forensic science concerned with the recording, scientific examination, and interpretation of the *minute details* to be found in physical evidence, is directed toward the following ends:

1. To identify a substance, object, or instrument.

2. To establish a connection between crime scene evidence and a known comparison specimen obtained from a suspect, thus linking the suspect to the crime scene or victim.

3. To reconstruct how a crime was committed.

4. To protect the innocent by developing evidence that may exonerate a suspect.

5. To provide expert testimony in court.

Occasionally, those *minute details* are visible to the naked eye; more often, scientific instrumentation must be used to make them so. In either circumstance, they must be evaluated and interpreted by the criminalist as to their investigative significance for the detective and their probative significance for the jury (or judge in a nonjury trial).

Basic Concepts—Details in Physical Evidence

What Are They?

The *details* that may be found in physical evidence are best illustrated by examples— some from actual cases and some by line drawings (see Figures 2.1–2.7). With evidence such as fingerprints, these details are given specific names (e.g., ridge ending, bifurcation, short ridge; with bullets, cartridge casings or tool marks), a more general descriptive term is used—*striations*. Essentially a series of roughly parallel lines of varying width, depth, and separation, striations are scratch marks caused by irregularities or a lack of microfine smoothness on the barrel of a gun, head of a firing pin, or working face or edge of a tool. In DNA fingerprinting and emission spectrography, striations are like a bar pattern similar to the line codes a supermarket register scans to record sales. With evidence like paint, hair, grease, and glass, the chemical composition (qualitative and quantitative) provides the significant details. Particularly important are those chemical elements present in trace amounts resulting from accidental impurities or environmental conditions.

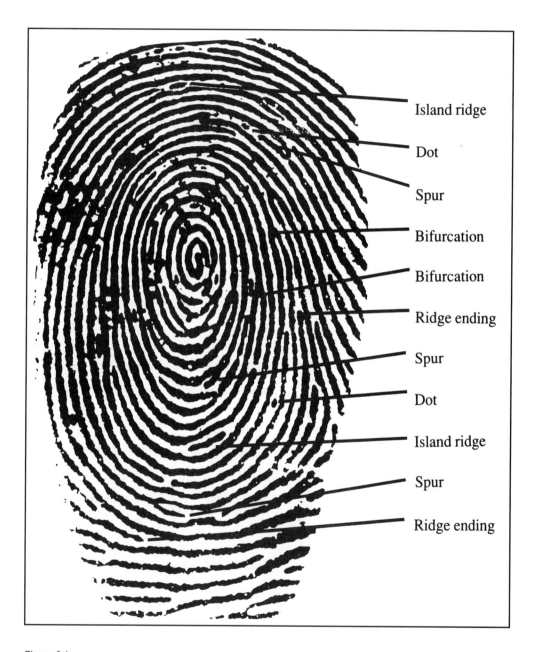

Figure 2.1
An inked fingerprint with some ridge line details marked. *(Courtesy, American Institute of Applied Science, Syracuse, NY.)*

Types of individual characteristics	Illustration of individual characteristics
Ending ridge	
Fork (bifurcation)	
Island ridge or short ridge	
Dot	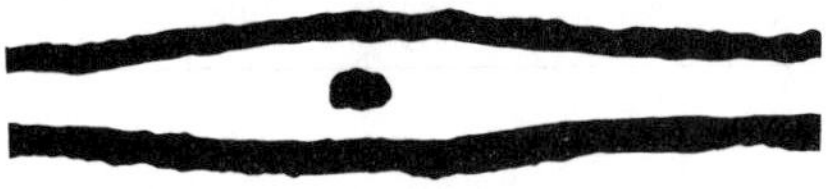
Bridge	
Spur	
Eye (island)	
Double bifurcation	
Trifurcation	

Figure 2.2
Examples of individual characteristics (Galton minutiae or ridge line details) used to individualize a fingerprint—latent or inked. (*Courtesy, American Institute of Applied Science, Syracuse, NY.*)

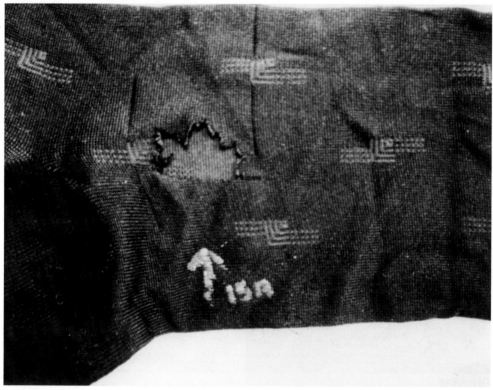

Color Figure A

The <u>outside</u> of <u>left</u> (ankle) panel of one of the woven socks found in O.J. Simpson's bedroom. A portion was cut out for DNA testing. The part visible through the cut-out area is the <u>inside</u> of the <u>right</u> ankle panel (side 3 in Color Figure B). *Courtesy, Professor Herbert L. MacDonell and Dr. Henry C. Lee.*

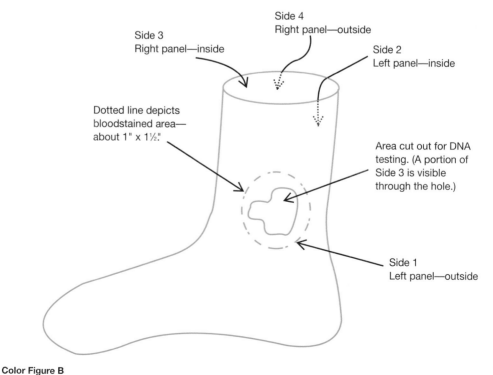

Color Figure B

Schematic drawing of Color Figure A. The four sides of a sock are numbered to assist in understanding the significance of trial testimony. Dotted arrows point to invisible surfaces (sides 2 and 4). *Courtesy, David Zemke.*

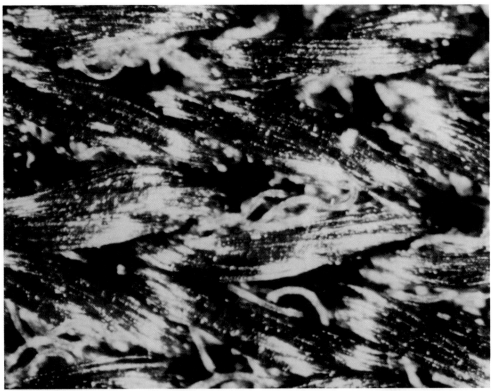

Color Figure C
Photomicrograph (about 70x) taken of the fibers (around the cut-out hole) on the <u>outside</u> surface of the <u>left</u> (ankle) panel (see Color Figure A and side 1 in Color Figure B). Blood is visible, but only on the surface of some fibers. *Courtesy, Professor Herbert L. MacDonell and Dr. Henry C. Lee.*

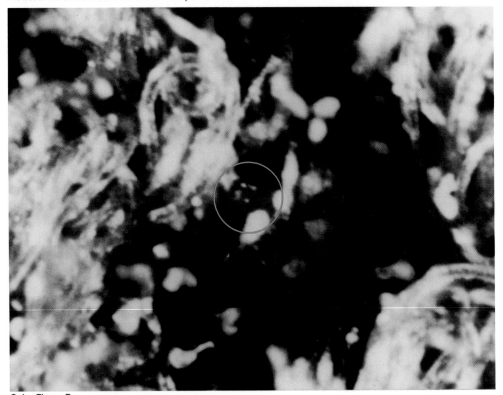

Color Figure D
Photomicrograph (about 150x) taken of the <u>inside</u> of the <u>right</u> (ankle) panel (side 3 of Color Figure B and visible through the cut-out hole in Color Figure A). The circled shiny red ball-like object (one of several) must originally have been in the liquid state, thus permitting it to flow around the fiber and solidify. *Courtesy, Professor Herbert L. MacDonell and Dr. Henry C. Lee.*

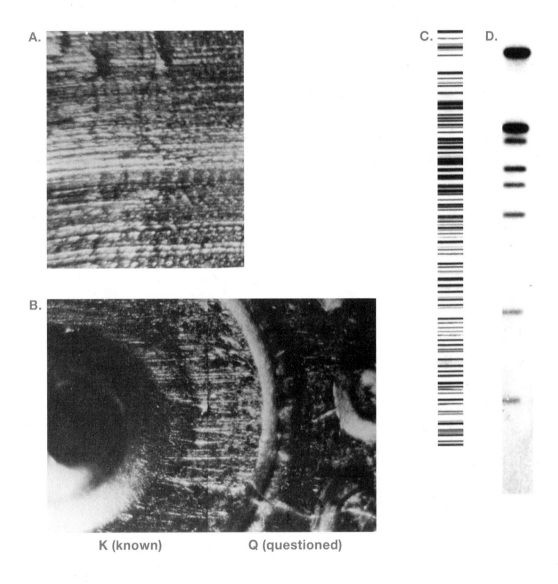

Figure 2.3
Striations and bar code patterns. Such details are used to analyze, compare, and identify some kinds of physical evidence from a crime scene (Q) with physical evidence from a suspect (K). **A.** Striations left by a tool used as a jimmy on a safe. **B.** Striations on the breech face of a revolver left on the head of a cartridge fired in a suspect's weapon (K). The vertical dividing line in the middle separates images K and Q as seen in the comparison microscope. **C.** Line bar code pattern or spectrogram of the chemical element iron. Each metal trace impurity in a clue material provides a different spectrogram when analyzed by the spectrograph. **D.** A DNA bar code pattern revealed through analysis of biological specimens. *(Figure 2.2D, courtesy, Mark D. Stolorow, Cellmark Diagnostics, Germantown, MD.)*

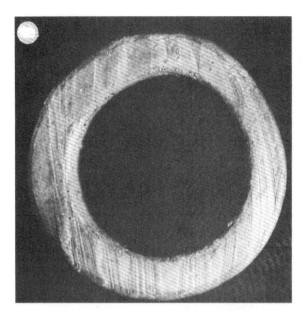

Figure 2.4
Tool mark striations left by a knife on the
end(s) of a hose that was connected to an
illicit still. *(From The Crime Laboratory,
2nd ed. Courtesy, Clark Boardman Co., Ltd.
and the Columbus Police Department,
Columbus, OH.)*

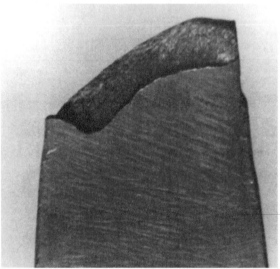

Figure 2.5
The irregularity in shape of the broken tip of
a screwdriver is a morphological detail
used to link a jimmy impression left on a
doorjamb at the scene of a burglary to a
suspect's screwdriver. *(From The Crime
Laboratory, 2nd ed. Courtesy, Clark Boardman Co., Ltd. and the Santa Ana Police
Department,
Santa Ana, CA.)*

Morphology

With some types of evidence, the general term *morphology* describes the structure and shape (or form)—hence, the details. Figure 2.5 illustrates the morphology of a screwdriver, the tip of which was broken during the commission of a burglary. In the examination of an undergarment for a suspected seminal stain, the presence of at least one intact spermatozoon, identifiable under the microscope by its structure and form, helps to corroborate a charge of rape. In addition, the jigsaw-puzzle fit of several pieces of evidence—for example, the glass fragments of a broken automobile headlight (or radiator grill) in a hit-and-run homicide—illustrates morphological details effectively put to work in criminalistics (see Figure 2.6). Figure 2.7 is another illustration of the morphological linking of crime scene evidence to a suspected source.

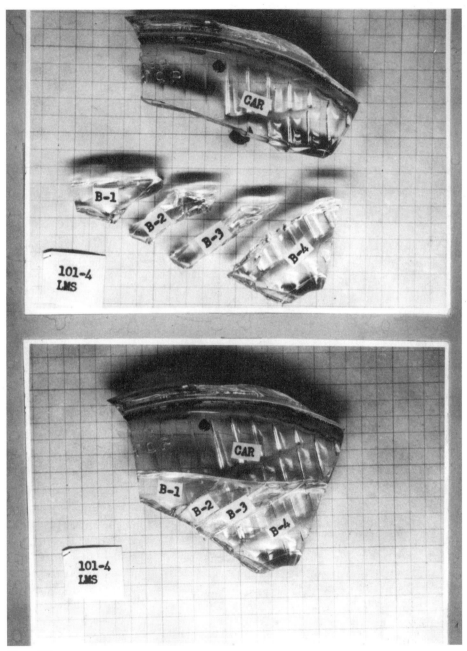

Figure 2.6
The morphological or jigsaw puzzle fit of the crime scene glass lens fragments (B-1 through B-4) with a piece of headlight lens removed from a car suspected in a hit-and-run case. *(From* The Crime Laboratory, *2nd ed. Courtesy, Clark Boardman Co., Ltd. and the Columbus Police Department, Columbus, OH.)*

Figure 2.7
A photomacrograph depicting the morphological detail and consequently a physical match between a piece of automobile grill (bottom) with a piece of metal found at the scene of a hit-and-run accident. *(From* The Crime Laboratory, *2nd ed. Courtesy, Clark Boardman Co., Ltd. and the New York City Police Department.)*

How Are They Developed?

The means now at the disposal of the criminalist to make visible the forensic details in physical evidence include the altering of contrast and the use of optical and analytical instruments.

Contrast

The most familiar way to bring out details is by altering contrast. One method uses black or white powder to process a crime scene for fingerprints. With the possible exception of small children, people seldom leave visible fingerprints after touching an object; therefore, the indistinct image or latent print must be converted to one that can be seen. This is achieved by "dusting" it with black or white fingerprint powder, the color of the object dictating the choice of powder: on a white kitchen appliance, black powder; on a green bottle, white powder. The latent fingerprint developed by dusting will contrast with the object on which it is located.

Photography is another well-known means of altering contrast. The type of film (emulsion) and developer, illumination (oblique lighting and filters), enlarger, and photographic paper can all affect contrast. The criminalist is generally concerned with increasing contrast, but occasionally it must be reduced. If so, the process is reversed and many of the same means that enhance contrast are then employed to decrease it.

Optical Instruments

Invaluable optical devices, the microscope and camera make details visible that are difficult, or even impossible, to see with the unaided eye. Mere enlargement, however, is not enough: there must be enlargement with *resolution*. This term describes the ability of a microscope or camera lens to separate what, to the unaided eye, appears to be one object (or point) into two or more objects (or points), and thus yield details not perceptible in any other way. It might be easier to understand this concept if the reader imagines he or she is looking down a railroad track. At some distant spot the rails will appear to converge. With binoculars, however, this spot can be separated into two objects (the rails), the lenses having given an enlarged image with resolution.

It is possible to have enlargement or magnification without resolution. For example, in the enlargement of a fingerprint negative made with a fingerprint camera, no details other than those present in the negative can be reproduced. The term 1 to 1 (1:1) describes the size of the image produced on a negative by the fingerprint camera lens. If larger than life-size—2 to 1 or greater—it is termed a *photomacrograph* (not to be confused with a *photomicrograph*, i.e., a photograph of an object as seen in the eyepiece of a microscope). Both photomacrographs and photomicrographs furnish resolution of details, and though the practical limit of photomacrography is about 25 to 1, it is still a powerful tool in the hands of the criminalist. Much physical evidence, fortunately, yields the necessary details at magnifications between 2x and 10x.

Analytical Instruments

The need for quality control in World War II weapons production brought unique scientific analytical instruments (heretofore found only in isolated university laboratories) to the commercial arena. Coupled with the vast financial support given to science after the war, this development greatly enhanced the capabilities of forensic laboratories to examine clue materials. Samples considerably smaller than those required by traditional wet chemistry—with its emphasis on test tubes, beakers, and flasks—could now be analyzed. Available clue material at a crime scene being limited, such instrumentation was particularly suited to the needs of the criminal investigator. Today, the problem of the small-sized specimen is mitigated owing to the development and availability of:

> Spectrophotometers
>> Ultraviolet
>> Visible
>> Infrared
>> Atomic Absorption (AA)
>
> Emission Spectrograph
>> Arc Excitation Method
>> Laser Excitation Method
>
> Mass Spectrograph (MS)
>
> X-ray Diffraction Camera (XRD)
>
> Neutron Activation Analysis (NAA)
>
> Scanning Electron Microscope/Energy
>> Dispersive X-Ray (SEM/EDX)
>
> Chromotography
>> Gas-liquid (GLC)
>> Thin layer (TLC)
>> Electrophoresis

The mere mention of such instruments makes them seem formidable and intimidating, but the criminal investigator need not understand how they work; after all, tuning a radio hardly requires a grasp of physics and electronics. It is sufficient to know their capabilities: that analytical instruments can furnish essential qualitative and/or quantitative details about a substance. Interpreting the investigative and probative value of this information is another role the criminalist ultimately fills for the detective, jury, and judge.

There are two major classes of instruments—destructive and nondestructive. The destructive class consumes the sample during analysis; the nondestructive does not alter the sample, leaving it available for further instrumental analysis or for presentation as evidence in court. If applicable, nondestructive methods should be tried first. For each instrument, Table 2.1 summarizes the type of clue material that can be analyzed, whether or not it is destroyed by the method, and what kind of information can result.

Table 2.1
Instrumental Methods: Type of Sample—How Effected and Information Acquired

INSTRUMENT	TYPE OF SUBSTANCE	EFFECT ON SAMPLE	INFORMATION	
			Qualitative	Quantitative
SPECTROPHOTOMETERS				
Infrared (IR)	Organic compounds	Nondestructive	Yes	Difficult
Visible	Organic compounds, inorganic elements	Nondestructive	No	Yes
Ultraviolet (UV)	Organic compounds, inorganic elements	Nondestructive	No	Yes
Atomic Absorption (AA)	Inorganic elements	Destructive	No	Yes
SPECTROGRAPH				
Arc excitation	Inorganic elements	Destructive	Yes	Yes
Laser excitation	Inorganic elements	Destructive	Yes	Semi-quantitative
Mass	Organic compounds	Destructive	Yes	Difficult
X-RAY DIFFRACTION	Cyrstalline substances (organic and inorganic)	Nondestructive	Yes	No
NEUTRON ACTIVATION (NAA)	Inorganic elements	Nondestructive	Yes	Yes
SCANNING ELECTRON MICROSCOPE (SEM)	Organic compounds, inorganic elements	Nondestructive	NA	NA
SEM coupled to an X-ray dispersive analyzer (EDX)	Inorganic elements	Nondestructive	Yes	Difficult
CHROMATOGRAPHY				
Gas-liquid (GLC)	Organic compounds	Nondestructive	Yes	Yes
Thin Layer (TLC)	Organic compounds	Nondestructive	Yes	Difficult
Electrophoresis	Organic (large biomolecules)	Nondestructive	Yes	Difficult

Perhaps the terms *organic* and *inorganic* in Table 2.1 need review. An organic substance is one that contains carbon; all other substances are inorganic. Table 2.2 lists clue materials in accordance with this chemical dichotomy. Because there are more than 90 chemical elements besides carbon, it may surprise the reader to learn that organic substances are far more common than inorganic. Materials comprising a mixture rather than a single chemical substance are listed in both categories.

Table 2.2
Some Examples of Clue Materials Characterized as Organic or Inorganic Substances

---

ORGANIC

Petroleum products (arson accelerants)
Gunpowder and gunshot residue
Controlled substances and other drugs:

    Heroin, morphine, cocaine, and so on
    Marijuana
    LSD and other hallucinogens
    Phenobarbital and other barbiturates
    Benzedrine and other amphetamines
    Valium and other tranquilizers

Ethyl alcohol
Explosives
Hair and polymer fibers (e.g., nylon, Dacron)
Paint (some constituents)
Dyes in gasoline, cosmetics, and some inks
Poisons (e.g., digitalis, strychnine)
Biological fluids (e.g., proteins and enzymes)
Plastics (e.g., automobile tail lights)

INORGANIC

Dirt
Gunpowder and gunshot residue (e.g., lead, antimony,
    and barium)
Hair (trace elements)
Poisons (e.g., arsenic, mercury)
Paint (some constituents)
Glass (e.g., windows, automobile headlights)
Safe-lining material

The instruments of most significant value would seem to be the gas chromatograph in combination with the mass spectrometer (GC/MS), and the scanning electron microscope (SEM). Many listed in Table 2.1 are costly; only large forensic laboratories are likely to have them. Once acquired, their operation may have some handicaps, for clue material must be in an acceptable form. In arson cases for example, the spectrometer (IR) can identify the organic liquid employed to accelerate the spread of the fire, but the sample must be free of water (which fogs the salt optics of the instrument). Firefighters battling a blaze cannot concern themselves with the criminalist's needs; consequently, additional painstaking work is created for the analyst because of the copious applications of water necessary to douse the flames.

Nevertheless, there are great advantages attached to these advanced analytical methods:

1. The sample may often be preserved for future use as evidence, many of these instruments being nondestructive.

2. A permanent record is obtained for presentation in court, in the form of a photograph, chart on graph paper, or computer printout.

3. Personal error is minimized; one analyst's results can be checked by another.

4. A smaller amount of clue material is required than for wet chemistry.

5. More definitive results are obtained than from classical methods of analysis.

6. The information (or details) provided by one instrument supplements rather than duplicates what is provided by another instrument.

7. The instrument and techniques apply to the evidence. It is not the nature of the crime that counts; it is the nature of the evidence.

Basic Concepts—Identification and Identity

Identification, a significant term in criminalistics, describes the classification process by which an entity is placed in a predefined, limited, or restricted class. For example, if the entity is a packet of white powder, the crime laboratory report on such evidence seized in a narcotics arrest might read: "The powdered substance submitted in Case 123 contains heroin." Two other examples: If the physical evidence is a typed ransom note, the laboratory might inform the investigator that of all typewriters, the one used was in the IBM Selectric class; if a bullet (perhaps in a homicide case before a weapon is recovered), the finding might be that it was fired from a .25 caliber automatic pistol with a left twist and six lands.

In a rape case, the crime laboratory report might state that the fiber found beneath the victim's fingernail is a naturally occurring filament (distinct from a synthetic) in the class of human hair. However unequivocal this identification, it has not linked the physical evidence to the crime scene or victim. When it does, an *identity* has been established. Therefore, if the criminalist is able to state that the strand is the pubic hair of the suspect—and *only* the suspect's—an identity has been established. At present, DNA (deoxyribonucleic acid) technology is opening up new possibilities in this important aspect of the criminalist's work. An identity, therefore, extends the classification process to the point at which the entity is in a class by itself—a class of one. It has been *individualized*—effected by comparing physical evidence discovered at the crime scene with apparently similar evidence obtained from a suspect (or defendant). The following will illustrate:

• The partial fingerprint found at the crime scene matches the inked impression of the right ring finger of the suspect (or defendant).

- The .25 caliber bullet retrieved by the medical examiner from the deceased's body was fired from a Beretta .25 caliber automatic pistol (Serial #01234C) found in the possession of the suspect (or defendant).

- The kidnapper's typed ransom note was typed on an IBM Selectric Model II (Serial #2379406).

A criminalist's finding that a unique connection existed between the victim or crime scene and the suspect prompted Paul L. Kirk, a major figure in the field, to define criminalistics as "the science of individualization."[1] Taken together, the details that uniquely characterize the entity—that is, put it in a class of one (by itself) and thereby establish an identity—are called *individual characteristics*. When a sufficient number of individual characteristics in the crime scene evidence and a specimen of known origin (the exemplar obtained from a suspect) can be matched, the criminalist is said to have developed associative evidence and established an identity.

Figures 2.1 and 2.2 indicate the points of identity (Galton details) that an expert uses to establish and demonstrate that a latent crime scene fingerprint and an inked record print were made by the same finger—and no other finger in the world. The general patterns of fingerprints (whorls, loops, arches) are shown in Figure 2.8; all fingerprints are divided into the three major groups. Called *class characteristics*, each can be subdivided further: loops into ulnar and radial; arches into plain and tented; whorls into six subgroups. Because a fingerprint falls into one or the other, these subcategories are also class characteristics.

Another illustration: the class characteristics of rubber shoe heels include the name of the manufacturer (e.g., Cat's Paw, O'Sullivan, Florsheim), the decorative pattern, and the heel size. When comparing a Cat's Paw heel impression with an O'Sullivan impression, their dissimilar class characteristics make an identity impossible. The individual characteristics found in or on a heel (or tool) are those cuts, nicks, and gouges acquired through wear (Figures 2.9 and 2.10). Table 2.3 summarizes class and individual characteristics in various types of evidence. If the individual characteristics are the same, and are found in sufficient number each at the same location, then two specimens under comparison may be judged an identity. What constitutes a sufficient number is a judgment call, an integral part of the criminalist's work.

There are rare occasions when an imprint (sole, heel) is so unusual that its class characteristic renders it of probative value in and of itself. To illustrate, a bloody heel print (see Figure 2.11) was found on the walkway of murder victim Nicole Simpson's condominium. Its distinctive pattern, an S-like waffle design, was not in the FBI's computerized shoe print library or in any other country's file (Japan excepted). In due course, FBI agent William Bodziak determined that it was designed for Bruno Magli shoes. Being an expensive Italian brand and a model marketed for only two years in but 40 locations in the United States and Puerto Rico, the number sold was limited. Likewise, the number of potential suspects was limited to a crime scene print estimated to be size 12: at most, 9 percent of the United States population wears size 12 shoes.

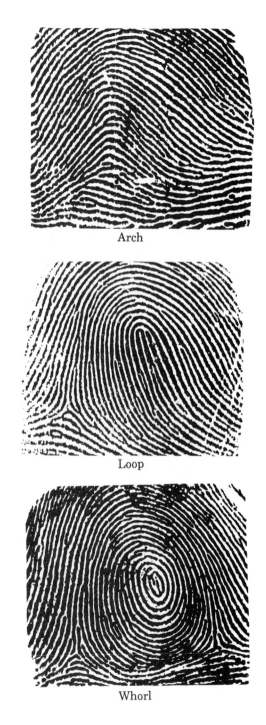

Arch

Loop

Whorl

Figure 2.8
Basic fingerprint patterns: arches, loops, and whorls. *(Courtesy, American Institute of Applied Science, Syracuse, NY.)*

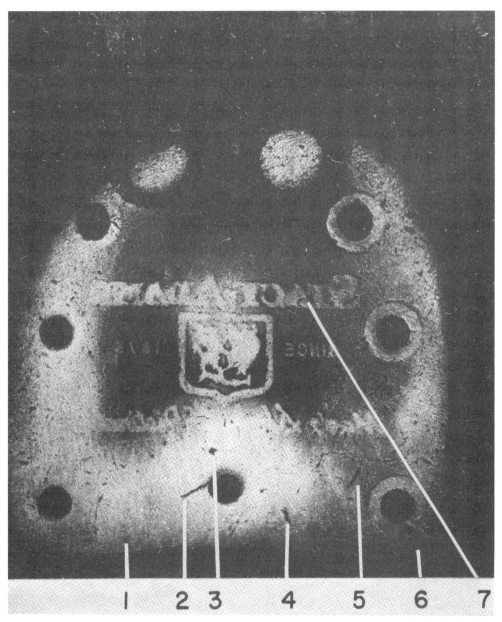

Figure 2.9
Impression found at a crime scene. The nicks, cuts, and gouges—the details that individualize this heel—are marked. *(From* The Crime Laboratory, *2nd ed. Courtesy, Clark Boardman Co., Ltd. and the Los Angeles Police Department.)*

Figure 2.10
Face of hammer head damaged by misuse. Nicks and gouges present, as well as the shape (morphology) of the upper edge, provide a basis for establishing an identity. *(Courtesy, New York City Police Department.)*

Table 2.3
Class and Individual Characteristics in Various Types of Evidence

Type of Evidence	Characteristics		
	CLASS	INDIVIDUAL	
	Example	*Example*	*Visual Appearance*
Fingerprints	arches loops whorls	ridge ending, bifurcation, short ridge, enclosure, dot, bridge, spur, trifurcation	see Figs. 2.1 and 2.2 for class characteristics
Bullets and Cartridges	caliber; number of lands and grooves; direction of twist or rifling	scratch marks or striations in the lands and grooves; casing head, firing pin	see Fig. 2.3B
Handwriting	school of handwriting; hand printing; cursive printing	any deviation from the model letters of the system used to teach handwriting, i.e., peculiarities of letter formation	*R* for R *y* for g
Shoe impressions	heel design; sole design; manufacturer's name	gouges, cuts and other marks acquired accidentally through wear	see Fig. 2.9
Tool impressions	hammer screwdriver jimmy cutting devices	nicks, dents, broken edges, and other damage from misuse or abuse; striations are left by some tools when drawn across a suitable surface	see Figs. 2.3A, 2.4, 2.5, and 2.10

The point is that a class characteristic can have probative value and be utilized as evidence even though it is not conclusive proof of a suspect's involvement in the crime. (It *is* conclusive when class characteristics are not the same.)

So long as a Bruno Magli shoe was never recovered, there is no way of knowing whether the apparent individual characteristics in Figure 2.11 are "real." If they are real (that is, not altered because of the concrete surface on which it was found or by other factors), then a criminalist could have compared a suspect shoe (had there been one) with the crime scene imprint.

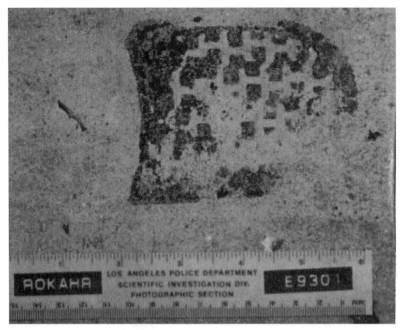

Figure 2.11
Bloody heel print found on the walkway outside of Nicole Brown Simpson's
condominium (*Courtesy, Federal Bureau of Investigation*).

Unfortunately, the science of criminalistics has not yet evolved to the point at which
it is always possible to establish an identity. Consider the following statements in regard
to bloodstain and pubic hair evidence. Each illustrates a comparison that has greater probative value than a mere identification, but less than a conclusion of an identity.

> This reddish brown stain on the suspect's underwear contains group AB blood
> of human origin.

Approximately 5 percent or less of humanity has AB blood (groups A, O, B, and AB being
class characteristics). If a stain is AB, approximately 95 percent is thereby eliminated
as suspect.

> The strand lodged beneath the rape victim's fingernail matches in all observ-
> able details the pubic hair specimen obtained from the suspect.

This statement is open to misinterpretation. Does it mean that the strand is from the defendant (suspect)? It might seem so to some. However, the informed defense attorney, prepared to cross-examine rigorously, should not allow a jury to make this mistake. Until
recently, this was an accurate statement and if asked by defense counsel a criminalist would
explain and interpret what it meant—that it could be, but is not necessarily, the defendant's hair. The development of DNA short-tandem repeat (STR) technology now permits
hair to be individualized.

This illustration reinforces the importance of the *interpretive* role of the criminalist, not only for the investigator and prosecutor but for the defense attorney, judge, and jury as well. The following dialogue will emphasize this point. It is taken from the direct testimony of the firearms examiner in a *cause célèbre*, the trial of Sacco and Vanzetti.

District Attorney:	"Have you an opinion as to whether bullet Number 3 [the fatal bullet] was fired from the Colt automatic [Sacco's gun] which is in evidence?"
Firearms Examiner:	"I have."
District Attorney:	"And what is your opinion?"
Firearms Examiner:	"My opinion is that it is consistent with being fired from that pistol."[2]

What does the last statement mean? For some it will mean that Sacco's pistol fired bullet Number 3. Indeed, when charging the jury, the judge indicated just that—the fatal bullet was fired through the barrel of Sacco's gun.[3] The judge, however, was wrong (along with any present-day reader who might have agreed with him). The firearms examiner's testimony means only that bullet Number 3 had the class characteristics of a bullet fired through a Colt automatic of the kind found on Sacco. This is certainly not the conclusion of an identity—a fact that should be brought out and made clear by a defense counsel's cross-examination.

The Role of the Crime Laboratory

The definition of criminalistics (given earlier) can be expanded by illustrating what the laboratory does to assist the detective: namely, establish an element of the crime, link the crime scene or victim to the criminal, and reconstruct the crime.

Establish an Element of the Crime

Heroin is proscribed by law, and alcohol is regulated. If the pertinent law is to apply, their presence in seized evidence must be established. The concept of identification is involved and chemistry is needed to effect the determination. The presence of heroin or alcohol is an element of the crime.

Link the Crime Scene or Victim to the Criminal

Associative evidence, a nonlegal term, describes the aspect of laboratory work involving the concept of identity (i.e., linking a subject to the crime scene or victim— such as by a fingerprint). The most effective means of developing associative evidence are instrumental chemistry, photomacrography, microscopy, other optical methods, and morphology.

Crime Scene Reconstruction[4, 5]

The reconstruction of a crime has long been of interest to detectives. Until fairly recently, however, the ability to do so was limited, and grounded, for the most part, on experience in the field. For example, Arthur Carey, the first head of homicide in the New York Police Department, described how he began to recognize "a crime picture"—to formulate the image from certain aspects common to homicides he had investigated successfully. With the aid of inductive reasoning (i.e., utilizing particulars of the crime he was attempting to solve and any similarities to past crimes), Carey speculated about the kind of person who might be guilty of such an act. Coupling this with additional information gathered in the investigative process enabled him to get a mental "fix" on the crime—how it was committed and who may have committed it.

By the 1980s, the FBI Behavioral Science Unit had turned to the principles of psychology, raising recreative crime assessment to a far more mature level than any conceived of by Carey. *Pychological profiling* (see Chapter 4) provides investigative leads by evaluating intangible evidence such as emotions apparently underlying a criminal act, a rapist's remarks to the victim, or interviews of witnesses.

Are the Facts Consistent with the Story?

A crime is reconstructed for other equally important reasons; for example, to check details provided by a suspect or witness against those disclosed by the crime scene examination. The laws of physics are helpful here: a bullet travels in a straight line (unless it ricochets off a solid object); therefore, by sighting from the point of impact (on a wall) through the bullet hole (in a window shade or sofa), it is possible to decide whether the shot indeed came from the location claimed by a witness (or suspect).

Just as the laws of physics (and chemistry) apply when determining the distance between victim and gun muzzle at time of firing, or whether the weapon had a hair trigger, so too must spattered blood from a gunshot (or bludgeoned) victim obey the laws of momentum, gravity, and surface tension. Accordingly, the inductive method (i.e., moving from the specific to the general) can determine where the criminal stood to fire the shot (or deliver the blows). Reconstruction also can find out: Was the window of a burglarized warehouse broken from the outside to gain entrance or from the inside to conceal employee theft? Was the driver killed when his motorcycle smashed into the telephone pole or was he the victim of a hate crime—beaten to death, and the cycle subsequently damaged (by running over it with an automobile) to simulate the effects of striking the pole? Scientific reconstruction can provide answers to these and similar questions on how a crime or event occurred. (See Chapter 13 for a more detailed discussion of reconstructing the past.)

Any significant discrepancy between an individual's statement and the physical evidence will raise suspicion if not explained satisfactorily. Is a suspect trying to cover up? Is a witness trying to mislead? Whatever the logical follow-up steps entail, the outcome can either be more incriminating or it may diminish initial suspicions; therefore, the development of inculpatory evidence or exculpatory evidence that protects the innocent is another reason for undertaking crime reconstruction. The cause of justice is served by permitting the statements of complainants and witnesses to be proved or challenged, corroborated or refuted.

Time: The question of whether a suspect had sufficient time to commit the crime is occasionally of investigative and prosecutorial interest. When the window of opportunity is quite narrow, a defendant's lawyer is likely to argue that there was insufficient time. If there apparently would not have been enough time to carry out the crime, the police must exercise caution and weigh all the circumstances. For example, if a victim has been seriously assaulted (skull crushed, large bones broken, body mutilated), the interval between the time when the report came in and when the suspect was last seen can be crucial. If that interval is too short, it should create doubt in the minds of the police. It also may very well create doubt in the minds of the jury. Physical evidence, the testimony of witnesses, and the opinion of a forensic pathologist can provide answers to the "time" issue.

The time required for blood to dry can also be a crucial factor in a case. Because blood can seep through a metal watchband or the weave of a garment's fabric, the question is: how much time would elapse before an impression (of watchband or fabric) is left dried on the skin of the deceased? In one homicide case, the watch worn by the (suspect's) murdered wife had been removed, presumably by the intruder the husband claimed to be the killer; on the dead woman's wrist the dried-blood impression of the metal watchband was clearly visible. Investigators did not think it feasible for an intruder-turned-killer to wait around for the blood to dry before removing the watch. On the other hand, they reasoned, the killer's attempt to divert suspicion required time to concoct a story and set the scene by removing the watch to suggest a motive of burglary.

The question of time was the focus of a well-known double-homicide trial. A few hours of the accused's time were unaccounted for, during which the accused supposedly had the opportunity to commit the crime. The delayed arrival of the pathologist to the crime scene added to the uncertainty of his opinion regarding when the deaths occurred. Such a delay can result through failure to notify the pathologist promptly, or through the pathologist's failure to respond forthwith. Both situations demonstrate unprofessional behavior; absent other exigent circumstances, this can be considered dereliction of duty. This illustrates the importance of a forensic pathologist's expeditious arrival at the scene of a homicide. As delay in response time increases, so does the imprecision of expert opinion as to time of death. However, if the time of death can be based on information aside from forensic evidence—when victim or suspect was last seen walking the dog, receiving a telephone call, purchasing cigarettes, etc.—and, thereby, can be asserted with relatively greater precision, the window of opportunity provided by a pathologist may be narrowed.

Future Prospects

The blossoming of interest in crime scene reconstruction is marked by the founding in 1992 of an association of police investigators with the purpose of exchanging information on reconstruction learned through case experience. The Association of Crime Scene Reconstruction has a rapidly expanding membership. At the end of this section, two cases illustrate how crime reconstruction offers assistance to the cause of justice.

Induce an Admission or Confession

A necessary condition for obtaining a confession is for the person to believe incriminating evidence exists. This condition having been met, the guilty may either be sufficiently troubled to make an admission against interest ("I own the gun but I did not use it") or confess ("Yes, I did it"). In rape cases, on learning that "a group A bloodstain was found on your underwear" and "the victim is also group A, but you are not," or "a pubic hair specimen taken from the victim's fingernail matches yours," the guilty may confess. Evidence clearly indicating involvement induces an inner turmoil that seeks relief. An innocent person, however, would not feel pressure arising from self-generated guilt, there being no guilt to build up, even when there appears to be incriminating physical evidence. With no need for relief, confession by the innocent is unlikely.

Protect the Innocent

Though the crime laboratory is more often involved in developing evidence to establish guilt, an equally consequential aspect of its work is the protection of the innocent. Physical evidence that discloses unbiased facts that are not subject to the distortions of perception or memory can weaken an apparently strong case. Should those facts be in conflict (e.g., if the white powder does not contain heroin; if the suspected weapon did not fire the fatal shot; if the stain was not human blood; or if the available light or vantage point made it impossible for the witness to have observed what was claimed), then the innocent person may be protected—provided the crime scene search for physical evidence is diligent and knowledgeable.

In this regard, lack of diligence is the most troubling aspect. As research indicates, physical evidence is invariably undercollected and underutilized at crime scenes, despite its availability.[6] Because a democratic society prizes individual freedom, the price is continual vigilance—a citizenry watchful for any abuses of power by the state. Accordingly, if a fair chance to limit that power is lost when physical evidence that might have exculpated a suspect went uncollected or unused, not only is the suspect harmed, but the government is as well. A double blow is dealt: the first tarnishes democracy; the second adversely affects a department's reputation. The latter result may be intangible, but the former can, over time, be calamitous.

The absence of forensic evidence can occasionally be of assistance in protecting the innocent. As a *Chicago Tribune* editorial serves to illustrate, ignoring forensic evidence can be detrimental to the suspect:

> . . . the case of [E.H.] who was 15 when he was charged with murder last year, had an amazing twist. He allegedly confessed to stabbing a woman . . . but an autopsy conducted a few hours after his arrest didn't show any stab wounds on the victim.
>
> Unfazed by this whopping contradiction—the lack of any physical evidence implicating [E.H.]—prosecutors kept him locked up for 16 months at the county's juvenile detention center.
>
> [E.H.'s] sad saga . . . came to an end when . . . a criminal court judge formally acquitted [him] and set him free.[7]

Provide Expert Testimony in Court

For cases that go to trial, a criminalist's ultimate task is the presentation of laboratory findings to the jury. To do this, the criminalist must first be *qualified* as an expert. At each and every trial, either the judge qualifies proposed experts, or their qualifications are stipulated to by defense counsel and accepted by the judge. It is necessary to demonstrate to the court that the "expert" possesses specialized, relevant knowledge ordinarily not expected of the average layperson. Such knowledge can be acquired through any combination of education and practical experience, and augmented through a study of books and journals in the field. Writing, research, and active membership in pertinent professional organizations are expected of most experts if they are to be considered current in the field.

The effective expert is able to describe his or her work and its significance to the jury in plain, everyday language. A faculty for putting scientific concepts into lay terms cannot be overrated; neither can the ability to remain cool under cross-examination. These attributes, inherent for some people, must be acquired by others through experience and hard work. Yet, diligence in recognizing and collecting physical evidence, and competence in the laboratory, are of no avail if the results are not readily perceived by the jury— if credibility is damaged by defense counsel's success in rattling the expert, causing testimony to be modified or weakened.

Examples of Crime Reconstruction

The Bombing of Pan Am Flight 103[8,9]

On December 21, 1988, on the last leg of its return to New York, Pan Am Flight l03, a jumbo jet flying six miles high and filled with 270 holiday travelers and crew, fell out of the sky over Lockerbie, Scotland. The cause—whether engine failure, collision, structural failure, bomb, etc.—was not immediately known. In a short time FAA investigators had ruled out structural failure; after several more days of intensive inquiry and forensic tests on recovered baggage, they concluded that a bomb was responsible for the disaster. The next steps in the inquiry were focused on: Whose luggage contained the bomb? When was it loaded on the aircraft? Where was it placed in the plane?

Thousands of interviews were conducted over the next eight months. In addition, more than 800 square miles of Scottish countryside were combed for the debris that was not only scattered by the explosion and crash, but also by the prevailing 130 m.p.h. winds at 30,000 feet (see Figure 3.1 in Chapter 3). Ultimately, 4 million pieces of crash litter were collected and catalogued, permitting a rebuilding of 80 percent of the Boeing 747. The blast damage identified which luggage container had stored the bomb bag, and established that the bomb had exploded near the bottom of that container. This indicated that the fatal suitcase was among the first loaded. Analysis of baggage handling records divulged that it had been placed aboard in Frankfurt, Germany.

Twenty-seven fragments (recovered in an area about 25 miles from Lockerbie) appeared to be from a Samsonite suitcase. Independent forensic examination concluded that it had contained the bomb. Eight Samsonite bags were loaded at Frankfort;

only one had an owner who did not come aboard. Subsequently, a computer printout from Frankfort's baggage sorting system revealed that an unaccompanied suitcase was transferred to Flight 103 from an Air Malta aircraft.

Some clothing labeled "Malta Trading Company" and exhibiting scorch marks had been recovered in the extensive, scattered-scene search. Upon further examination and comparison, fibers from that clothing matched fibers found fused to the lining of the suspected Samsonite suitcase. Once again Malta was the focus of investigative interest. With old-fashioned detective work and a bit of luck, the trail led to a Maltese merchant who recognized some of the clothing that apparently had been packed in the bomb suitcase. Because of the buyer's random, mismatched selection and the sale of a heavy wool men's jacket the shop had long been trying to be rid of, the shopkeeper remembered—and ultimately identified—the customer.

As they were recovered, all items scattered over the crime scene had been bagged for further study. When one torn shirt was shaken out, a green piece of debris about the size of a small fingernail dropped onto the examiner's paper-lined table. Ultimately, the green fragment was traced to a Swiss manufacturer of digital electronic timers, only 20 of which had been made to fill a special order from the Libyan Government. Earlier, another small piece, found in a corner of the luggage container that had stored the bomb, was subsequently identified as a part of the circuit board of a Toshiba radio-cassette player. Linking the fragment to that device was significant because terrorists had previously used it to hide Semtex—a plastic explosive that defies detection by airport X-rays—in an unsuccessful attempt to bomb another plane.

This, perhaps the largest crime scene search in history, meant the combing of an 800-square-mile area for physical evidence. Astonishingly successful, it permitted investigators to rebuild the jet and prove thereby that an exploding bomb caused it to fall. They reconstructed the luggage container, the suitcase, and the bomb (through its fragments), and determined the origin of some of the clothing carried in the suitcase. These activities led to the identification of the perpetrators. If an inquiry is to benefit from forensic expertise, develop investigative leads, and ultimately establish what happened and who were the perpetrators, the prerequisites are thoroughness and patience, plus a willingness to devote the resources required for the discovery and collection of physical evidence left at the crime scene.

Criminal Negligence or Accident?[10]

If essential clues or objects are moved, altered, or destroyed, reconstruction of the crime is rendered impossible. The same outcome can result when potential physical evidence goes unrecovered because it is not recognized or is disregarded because its importance is not comprehended. The following homicide case involving the shooting of one hunter by another is illustratative of the latter scenario. It demonstrates the value of having a criminalist review and examine physical evidence obtained from the crime scene or the body of a victim to attempt to reconstruct what happened.

Convinced that a death resulted from criminal negligence, the county sheriff secured a signed confession in short order. Apparently, neither he nor any other investigator regarded the shotgun slug recovered from the deceased's body as peculiar, even though its wadding had not become detached. (Upon exiting a weapon, the metal slug and wadding normally separate within 18 to 36 inches of the gun barrel.) Called by the defense, Herbert L. MacDonell, a well-known criminalist (but research chemist at the time), examined the slug. Noting a bit of lead hooked around the wadding and bonding it to the slug, MacDonell inquired if the sheriff (a hunter himself) had ever found wadding in the body of a deer. When he indicated that he had not, the expert remarked on this interesting phenomenon. The sheriff, annoyed, insisted that "It didn't mean a damned thing" and that MacDonell was wasting his time. MacDonell had also noticed a tiny particle that looked like wood embedded in the slug. Weighing the slug, he found it to be 45 grains lighter than slugs from the same lot of ammunition used by the defendant. Microscopic examination confirmed that the embedded particle was indeed wood.

MacDonell's observations (aided by inductive reasoning) led him to conclude that the shotgun slug had first struck a tree; then (through deductive reasoning) that it had ricocheted and mortally wounded the defendant's hunting companion. The death of his friend left him so distraught that he refused to reenact the incident. (Some homicide investigators would regard this refusal as a sign of guilt.) The trial (at which MacDonell took the stand) resulted in an acquittal. It was several years before the defendant could be persuaded to return to the scene to demonstrate how and where he had pointed the gun. This enabled MacDonell to recover a section of tree bark, which still contained some of the lead missing from the slug.

In how many other cases, one might ask, is such crucial physical evidence ignored or simply overlooked? And why? Reasons may include investigative inexperience or lack of training, a mind closed to anything unfavorable to the belief that the offender has been caught, or even indolence. A defendant's disinclination to cooperate in a reconstruction of the event might contribute to a guilty verdict. Such unwillingness, however, might instead be the result of pain or regret.

The O.J. Simpson Case: The Sock Evidence Reconstructed

The pair of socks allegedly found in the O.J. Simpson bedroom was an important piece of evidence in this case. When defense lawyers studied the two sets of images (video and photographic) made by the Los Angeles Police Department, they noted that in the video set (taken to protect the LAPD against damaged property claims), there were no socks to be seen at the foot of the defendant's bed. Yet, in the photographic set (taken to record the crime scene), a pair of socks appears.

The defense made further inquiry, studying the documentary evidence specifically with regard to time; that is, when did the criminalist examine the socks in the bedroom, and when was the video made? Their conclusion was that the video was taken before the criminalist examined the socks. The fact that they were not to be seen in the video was significant: it allowed the defense to assert that they were planted, and supported the theory that their defendant was being framed. Thus, for crime scene reconstruction purposes, pinpointing the exact time of certain actions or events can be crucial.

In the Simpson case the criminalist's chronological notes indicated that the stains in the downstairs foyer were tested for blood at 4:30 P.M., the second-floor bedroom's socks were tested at a time not specified, and the second-floor bathroom was tested at 4:50 P.M. The criminalists testified that they did not go upstairs until after testing the stains in the foyer; the socks, therefore, were examined in those intervening 20 minutes. The video camera's clock timer indicated that the bedroom pictures were made at 3:15 P.M.; the prosecution, however, introduced evidence that the actual time was 4:15 P.M., the clock not having been adjusted for Daylight Saving Time. If the jury accepted this explanation, it still means that for at least 15 minutes before the criminalist got to the bedroom, no socks were present at the foot of the bed. One can only wonder how much this weighed in the verdict.

Upon being examined for blood a month or so later, one of the socks was found by prosecution experts to contain blood from the victim, Nicole Brown Simpson. Subsequently, it was examined by defense bloodstain expert Professor Herbert L. MacDonell. Color Figures A–D (see color photos) and the paragraphs following will explicate some of the details in his testimony. If we think of the human foot as two-sided (its ankle bone having a left and a right side), we can refer to one side of a sock on its wearer's foot as the left (ankle) panel and the other side, the right (ankle) panel. Each panel can have an inside and an outside surface (see Color Figure B).

When MacDonell and Dr. Henry C. Lee examined the sock from which a piece of the stained area was missing (Color Figure A), using a stereo microscope, they noted the presence of blood on the surface of some fibers surrounding the hole (side 1 in Color Figure B). By no means were all of these fibers covered with blood (Color Figure C). On the inside of the right panel (opposite the site of the cut-out portion in Color Figure A, and represented as side 3 in Color Figure B) they observed about 12 microscopically small "balls" or solidified drops of a reddish-colored substance, each having hardened around a strand of fiber (see Color Figure D, a photograph of one of the red "balls" magnified about 150X). This indicates that the substance had to have been in a liquid state when it came in contact with the fiber, thus allowing it to flow around the fiber and then solidify. Clearly, this could not happen while the sock was on the suspect's foot.

Blood dries quickly, especially the small quantity present here. Accordingly, the transfer to side 3 could not have occurred after the sock was worn for more than a few minutes, since travel time from the homicide scene to Simpson's home was sufficient for the crime scene blood to dry.* The shiny red balls (Color Figure D), coupled with the partial transfer of blood (limited to the top surface of the woven fibers—see Color Figure C), allowed MacDonell to testify that the sock was lying on a flat surface when the reddish liquid was applied by means of a swiping, lateral motion. Some liquid penetrated the outside of the left panel (side 1 of Color Figure B) to the inside surface of the left panel (side 2 of Color Figure B), with some liquid passing through to the inside of the right panel (side 3 of Color Figure B). A portion of the left panel was cut out subsequently for DNA testing: no blood was present on the outside of the right panel (side 4 of Color Figure B).

---

*This statement is based on empirical evidence generated by MacDonell in his Blood Spatter Laboratory Courses, as well as by experimentation undertaken for the Simpson trial.

FORENSIC MEDICINE: INVESTIGATIVE VALUE _____

Forensic medicine is also referred to as *legal medicine* or *medical jurisprudence*. The branch of medicine offering training in the study of diseases and trauma (their causes and consequences) is pathology. Forensic pathology goes beyond the normal concern with disease, to the study of the causes of death—whether from natural, accidental, or criminal agency. Forensic medicine—including forensic pathology, forensic serology, toxicology, forensic odontology, and forensic psychiatry—contributes not only to homicide investigation, but to other kinds of criminal investigation, in the following ways.

Forensic Pathology

1. Establish the cause and manner of death—natural, suicide, accident, homicide.

2. Establish the time of death.

3. Indicate the type of instrument used to commit the homicide.

4. Indicate whether injuries to the body were postmortem or antemortem.

5. Establish the identity of the victim.

6. Determine the age of the victim.

7. Determine the sex, height, weight, and age of mutilated or decomposed bodies and skeletons.

8. Determine virginity, defloration, pregnancy and delivery, sodomy.

Forensic Serology

Forensic serology (or the study of blood) historically was viewed as a branch of forensic medicine. Now, crime laboratories are proliferating, and blood has become a major concern to the criminalist. A fairly common clue material, blood is given detailed treatment in this chapter.

Toxicology

Toxicology is the study of poisons: their origins and properties, their identification by chemical analysis, their action upon humans and animals, and the treatment of the conditions they produce. Most crucial to the criminal investigator is the toxicologist's work of identifying a poison; then, there is the significant issue of quantity: was there or was there not a lethal amount present? The detection of poison may also allow the pathologist to exclude all other causes of death.

Forensic Odontology

Forensic odontology is the study of teeth, dentures, and bite marks for the following purposes:

1. To connect a bite mark to a particular person.

2. To identify an individual through an examination of fillings, missing teeth, and root canal work. If a silver amalgam or other type of metal restoration is present, X-rays can be compared.

3. To estimate a person's age.

Forensic Psychiatry

Forensic psychiatry, the study of a criminal's mental state and probable intent, is applicable to three areas of criminal justice: law enforcement, the courts, and the correctional system. Unfortunately for our purposes, it offers less assistance to the criminal investigator than to other actors in the criminal justice field.

Law Enforcement

With a skyjacker, terrorist, or barricaded malefactor who perhaps has taken hostages, a psychiatrist's evaluation of the criminal's mental state and probable intent can be useful in formulating plans to deal with the situation. In other cases, where the manner of death is in doubt, the likelihood of accident or suicide must be considered. To provide answers to the latter possibility, a technique called *psychological autopsy* was developed in Los Angeles in the 1950s. Working in concert, a team of specialists and nonspecialists might include: the pathologist who performed the medical autopsy, a psychiatrist, a social worker, the deceased's family, friends and acquaintances, as well as the criminal investigator. Each member of the team discusses, from his or her own perspective, what is known about the deceased. Then the team arrives at a consensus (a psychological autopsy) as to whether or not death was by suicide.

A police department is occasionally confronted with a series of heinous crimes committed against prostitutes or the homeless, or such well-defined targets as utility companies subjected to sporadic bombings. An unusual investigative technique that has had some success is an "open letter" appeal printed on the front page of a newspaper, or read over television and radio. The intention is to frame an irresistible plea for the offender to seek help by surrendering to a well-known newspaper columnist or TV reporter; in return, the interests of the offender will be protected. Profiting from insights provided by psychiatrists, psychologists, and other behavioral scientists, the Mad Bomber Case in New York City and the Skid Row Slasher Case in Los Angeles were solved in this fashion.

The Courts

Forensic psychiatry is more often employed in the courtroom than anywhere else in the criminal justice system. It offers expert testimony on the following issues:

1. Did the accused's state of mind at the time of the offense comport with the definition of insanity used in the jurisdiction in which the crime was committed? Legal insanity is established by applying one of the following tests:

    The M'Naghten Rule [11]
    This rule is the common law test for criminal responsibility. It provides for an acquittal by reason of insanity if the accused did not know the difference between right and wrong at the time of the act or did not understand the nature of the act because of impaired reasoning and/or mental disease.

    The Concept of Irresistible Impulse [12]
    An irresistible impulse is one in which the individual knew the act to be wrong but was unable to resist the psychological forces driving him to commit the forbidden act.

    The Concept of Diminished Responsibility [13]
    Diminished responsibility or diminished capacity involves mental impairment to the extent that it prevented the individual from acting with premeditation and deliberation.

    The American Law Institute Test [14]
    A person is not responsible for criminal conduct, if at the time of such conduct, as a result of a mental disease or defect, he or she lacks substantial capacity to appreciate the wrongfulness of his or her conduct or to conform his or her conduct to the requirements of the law.

2. Does the accused understand the nature and purpose of the proceedings against him or her, and assist in his or her own defense?

3. Did the accused have the capacity to pursue deliberately the criminal course of action? What was his or her state of mind? Was there intent to commit the act?

4. Was the defendant capable of intelligently waiving constitutional rights?

5. Was the defendant's confession made voluntarily?

6. Is a witness competent to testify?

The Correctional System

Although the potential contribution of psychiatry to correctional administration is fairly obvious, it has never received commensurate funding. As long as society talks about prisoner rehabilitation but practices warehousing, this should not be surprising. The parolee returned to the community with prospects no better than before incarceration will almost certainly resume a delinquent lifestyle, and again become a police problem. Once criminal justice operates like a system whose components function compatibly, perhaps society will begin to act more sensibly toward preventing crime. Preparing prisoners to cope with a return to society will require a heavy monetary outlay for social workers, psychiatrists, and educators. In calculating the cost-benefit of such a policy, the actual dollar cost may be seen in a different light if the loss of life, property, and peace of mind for the population in general are taken into account.

CLUE MATERIALS AS INFORMATION SOURCES

Physical evidence may be removed from or brought to and left at the crime scene. In either event, such an occurrence is seldom deliberate, but rather a natural consequence of committing the crime. A shoe impression left by a burglar on breaking into a house through the back yard unavoidably remains in receptive soil. In an assault with a knife, the victim's blood can drop on the shoes or spurt on the criminal's clothing. Other possibilities include handwriting; teeth marks; finger, palm, foot, and even ear prints; wearing apparel (glove, shoe, heel) impressions; or traces of a distinctive weave in cloth or stitching pattern made by a sewing machine. Impressions of a victim's clothing fabric have been found on the hood or fender of an automobile suspected of being involved in a hit-and-run case.

Other sources of physical evidence are the instruments used to commit the crime: for example, jimmies, metal cutters, axes, and hammers to gain access; firearms and knives to threaten a victim; shovels to bury a body; a kidnapper's note; metal punches to open a safe. All are examples of what to look for at the crime scene.

Familiarity with actual crime scene evidence is a prerequisite for the recognition of clues. For example, Figure 2.12 is a partial heel mark found on the back of one of the office file papers scattered by a safe burglar. Is it worth preserving? Can such a poor impression link the criminal to the crime scene? Can it be developed into associative evidence? The criminalist can answer each question with an emphatic "Yes!"

To learn how such a decision is made, and to acquire a familiarity with other crime scene evidence, the serious student might attempt to "solve" the case exercises in *The Crime Laboratory: Case Studies of Scientific Criminal Investigation.*[15] That book's photographs of actual police crime scene evidence show both typical and unusual types of evidence that can be (and were) found by a police officer or criminal investigator. Each exercise provides an opportunity to compare the crime scene evidence with that obtained from a suspect. The actual comparison points or individual characteristics, which are usually marked by the criminalist who worked on the case, are illustrated in a separate section. That section should be consulted only after the student has tried to make the comparison unassisted.

When the details permitting the formation of an identity become familiar, the steps necessary to preserve crime scene evidence are fairly obvious. Unless details are kept intact and undisturbed, the criminalist is unable to establish an identity (if one indeed exists). Should they be damaged or destroyed by improper handling, the possibility of establishing an identity is lost forever.

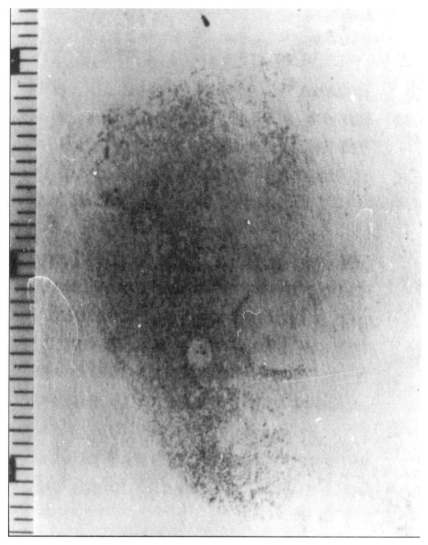

Figure 2.12
An indistinct, partial heel print left at the scene of a burglary. It was compared and identified as made by the shoe of a suspect. *(From* The Crime Laboratory, *2nd ed. Courtesy, Clark Boardman Co., Ltd. and the Michigan State Police.)*

Information of investigative or probative value may often be developed by the laboratory when any of the following common clue materials are encountered:

- Fingerprints
- Firearms
- Blood
- Semen, other biological materials

- Documents
- Glass
- Trace evidence

Fingerprints

A person reporting a crime—especially a burglary—expects the police to find fingerprints of the offender(s). Few detectives share this unrealistic expectation; most recognize that even if fingerprints are not always left by a criminal, the crime scene should still be examined for them.

Fingerprints will be considered in this section. What are they? How are they developed and preserved? When was the fingerprint made? Are there different kinds of fingerprint experts? What is the probative value of a single, partial fingerprint?

What are fingerprints? The friction ridges on the hands (fingers and palms) and feet (toes, soles, and heels), which facilitate gripping an object and the sense of touch, form on the fetus before birth. They do not change during life. The prints of either the hands or feet can be a means of identifying an individual, but only the fingers are used routinely. Extensive files are maintained for this purpose.

A fingerprint is an impression of the friction ridges on the skin of the fingers. In leaving an impression, an outline of the ridges is transferred and duplicated by the deposit of perspiration and other substances on the object handled. If the impression is not visible, which is most often the case, it must be made visible. To do so, certain conditions must prevail as to the fingers themselves and the surface with which they come in contact (see Latent Fingerprints later in the chapter). The friction ridges must contain either a substance already present on the fingers or one purposefully rolled on (for example, the printer's ink used by the police). Printer's ink can register each finger in the proper order on a fingerprint card, producing a set of *record fingerprints* (see Figure 2.13). Later, these prints become the exemplars needed by the fingerprint expert to identify (individualize) prints found at the scene of a crime. When touching an object or surface and thereby depositing some natural or environmentally acquired material, the impression is usually an invisible or *latent print* ("latent" from the Latin for "hidden"). This necessitates that something be done to make it visible; called "developing the print," it is the result of processing the crime scene for fingerprints. It is quite possible to handle an object (for example, a gun) and leave no latent fingerprint on it; it also is possible to leave a partial impression (often the case) or a smudged and blurred print in which no useful ridge line details remain (see Figure 2.14).

Latent Fingerprints—Constituents and their Sources

The two kinds of sources for the material on the fingers that produces latent fingerprints are natural and environmental.

Natural Sources

The natural materials are perspiration and the residue left by the evaporation of its water content, and sebum—a semifluid, fatty substance secreted by sebaceous glands at the base of the hair follicles. Although perspiration is about 99 percent water, it also contains some dissolved solids that are the by-products of food metabolism: organic compounds (amino acids, urea, and lipids—fats, oils, waxes) and an inorganic compound (table salt). The presence of some vitamins in perspiration makes development by lasers feasible.

| Name_____ | Classification_____ |

(Please type or print plainly)

Alias_____

No_____ Color_____ Sex_____   Reference_____

RIGHT HAND

1. Thumb	2. Index finger	3. Middle finger	4. Ring finger	5. Little finger

LEFT HAND

6. Thumb	7. Index finger	8. Middle finger	9. Ring finger	10. Little finger

Impressions taken by: Note amputations   Subject's signature:

(Signature of official taking prints)

Date impressions taken_____

Four fingers taken simultaneously	Thumb plain impressions		Four fingers taken simultaneously
Left Hand	Left thumb	Right thumb	**Right Hand**

Figure 2.13
Set of record fingerprints. *(Courtesy, American Institute of Applied Science, Syracuse, NY.)*

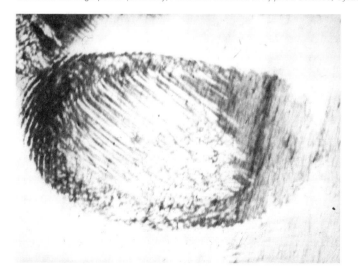

Figure 2.14
A smudged (blurred) fingerprint impression. Note lack of ridge line detail—making identification impossible. *(From* The Crime Laboratory, *2nd ed. Courtesy, Clark Boardman, Co., Ltd. and the New York City Police Department.)*

Environmental Sources

In the course of daily living, the hands touch and thereby pick up foreign matter from the environment such as: dust, soot, cooking oils, kitchen grease, and hair preparations, as well as pollen and other plant particulate matter.

Latent Fingerprints—Controlling Factors

Whether a latent impression is left depends on physiology (does the person perspire?) and what substances are present on the fingers, the nature of the surface, and the manner in which it was touched; and such environmental factors as temperature and humidity.

Surface

A latent print requires a suitable surface for it to be registered. Whereas porous surfaces such as unpainted wood and some paper products are unlikely to yield a useful impression, smooth surfaces like glass, enamel, and glossy paper are ideal. Rough surfaces are unsuitable because the friction ridge lines will be recorded only partially on their flat, high spots, and completely lost in their troughs or valleys (although attempts to develop latents on leather have been successful). When called to the scene of a burglary, evidence technicians are not surprised to find that the safe they are expected to process for fingerprints has a crinkled surface that will not take a fingerprint. (Perhaps a case of form preceding rather than following function?)

Finger Pressure

A fingerprint requires firm but not heavy pressure; otherwise, ridges will be flattened and the details distorted or not registered at all. Moreover, if a good print rather than a smudged one is to be left behind, the fingers must not be pulled or slipped across the surface, but lifted in a perpendicular motion. Needless to say, criminals seldom satisfy these conditions. Latent prints of the perpetrator are not found as often as most crime victims believe; one or more of the necessary conditions—a deposit on the fingers, suitable surface, or correct pressure—is usually missing.

Other Kinds of Fingerprints

A few fingerprints found at the crime scene are visible owing to the (largely environmental) substances present on the fingers. They also can be on partially dried, tacky paint, or even on a bar of butter, cream cheese, or chocolate that a burglar may take from the refrigerator. In burglary cases in which access was through a window, they may be found in soft window putty. In assault cases, they may be found on adhesive tape that had been left on a finger for several days (for example, a Band-Aid dislodged in a struggle), or on tape removed from a bound victim or an explosive device. If the impression is three-dimensional, it is called a *plastic* print. Plastic prints are encountered far less than other visible prints, but all visible prints combined are far less common than latent prints.

How Are Latent Fingerprints Made Visible?

The means available for developing latent fingerprints run the gamut from powders to chemical methods to different kinds of radiation.

Powders

The most common practice is to "dust" an object or crime scene with fingerprint powder. The color of the powder is selected to provide contrast between the developed print and its background: black powder on light-colored backgrounds, white powder on dark. Other colors are available and sometimes used, but white and black are customary. Fingerprint powders are designed to cling to natural and/or environmental source material; this makes the development of fingerprints possible. The powders must not cling to the background; the friction ridge lines should remain clearly delineated. In processing an object, powders are applied with an ostrich feather, a camel hair or nylon brush, or an atomizer. Herbert L. MacDonell invented the Magna-Brush and a magnetic powder. His method develops and preserves ridge line details better than any other mechanical means. In all dusting attempts, however, great care must be taken not to distort or destroy those details by using too much powder or by brushing too vigorously.

Investigators can learn to process a crime scene with fingerprint powder. More technically difficult methods require an evidence technician or criminalist; they rely on specific kinds of radiation—ultraviolet light or illumination by laser light—or involve a chemical reaction with a component of the residue left after an object has been touched. Brief descriptions of a few of these methods follow.

Chemical Methods

Several methods employ specific chemicals to process an object. The most common are: iodine, ninhydrin, silver nitrate, or cyanoacrylate esters. The process involves fuming, spraying, brushing, or dipping the object in a solution of the chemical.

Iodine: At room temperature (or slightly above), iodine, a crystalline solid, has the capability of changing directly to a vapor. This is called *sublimation*. The iodine vapor, interacting with the fatty material present in fingerprint residue, yields a temporary brownish-colored print that fades within a few hours. In addition to photography, there are several chemical means of "fixing" the print to preserve it. Iodine fuming is especially useful in kitchens and restaurants where airborne oily material has been deposited on appliances, windows, sills, walls, and exhaust fan blades. If these surfaces are subsequently touched, a plastic print can be the result, or a secondary (oily) print may be left on another surface. Because iodine fumes fade so quickly, this method is ideal for secret or internal investigations in which documents must be returned to an unsuspecting person under investigation.

Ninhydrin: Ninhydrin, an organic chemical, reacts with amino acids and other products of protein metabolism to yield purple-colored fingerprints. It takes from one to three days for a print to be developed fully, but this can be hastened with controlled heat and humidity. The relatively stable prints will last many months, possibly years; like iodine prints, they can be "fixed" chemically and, of course, photographed. Ninhydrin is particularly useful in developing prints on paper, including cardboard. It is not useful on paper money; because it is handled so often, the entire bill turns purple. Ninhydrin is very sensitive and can bring up old prints; however, others of recent origin may be partially superimposed on them, producing a dual impression of no value.

Silver Nitrate: Silver nitrate is an inorganic chemical, the silver part of which reacts with the chloride excreted in perspiration (resulting from sodium chloride ingested as common table salt). The silver chloride print is developed by exposure to intense ultraviolet light or sunlight. Developed prints are reddish-brown in color. Because they will lose contrast over time, they should be photographed quickly. When silver nitrate is used to bring up prints on brass cartridges, the prints are longer lasting, but they too should be photographed. An early attempt to use silver nitrate to develop fingerprints on wood was made by Dr. Erastus M. Hudson. He examined the wooden ladder left at the scene of the kidnapping of the Lindbergh baby in 1932, but was unsuccessful in raising any prints.

Cyanoacrylate Fuming: The cyanoacrylate fuming method came about in the 1950s by chance, when cyanoacrylate esters (resins) were first discovered as a means for bonding plastics and metals. To the surprise of observers, fingerprints were often seen on the bonded objects. In 1978 Japan's National Police were first to employ the method in criminal investigations and, through contacts with the U.S. Army crime laboratory in the far east, brought their observations to the attention of law enforcement in the United States. The first source of cyanoacrylate esters was an adhesive called "Super Glue," and the method is still referred to as the *superglue procedure*. Marketed directly to law enforcement as a volatile liquid, it is now used (in an enclosed space) to fume an object for latent fingerprints, detecting them on such nonporous surfaces as glass, gun metal, plastic steering wheels, and other plastic objects—such as the packages in which street narcotics are sold. The resulting impression is white in color; it should be photographed or dusted with powder and lifted. Although employed largely in the laboratory, fuming an automobile or a room is safe if special circumstances dictate and precautions are taken. It should also be noted that cyanoacrylate fumes interfere with the examination of the following biological materials: blood, semen, and hair. Such evidence, therefore, should be collected or examined beforehand.

Radiation

Two distinct kinds of radiation—ultraviolet and laser—are used to render latent fingerprints visible.

Ultraviolet Rays: Sunlight consists of the many colors in a rainbow; collectively, these colors constitute the visible spectrum. Just beyond the visible spectrum lies the ultraviolet (UV) region. Though imperceptible to the human eye, UV light can be produced by commercially available lamps. It is of interest here because certain substances respond to UV, including some materials found in the residue left on an object after it was handled. Substances that absorb ultraviolet radiation, and instantaneously re-emit it in the visible region of the spectrum, are said to *fluoresce*—they can be seen by the naked eye. Not all fingerprints fluoresce naturally; dusting with fluorescent powder can enhance ridge line details (when viewed in UV light in a darkened room). The use of these powders is most appropriate when a multicolored background must be examined, black or white powder alone producing insufficient contrast to make the ridge lines clear. The investigator will not often run across fingerprints that necessitate development by fluorescent powders.

Laser Radiation: Laser detection of fingerprints was first accomplished in the mid-1970s. Riboflavin and a few other vitamins are the organic solids in perspiration that can be detected by lasers. The vitamin molecules absorb the laser illumination, re-emitting it almost immediately at a wave length different from the incident laser light. Called *luminescence*, this phenomenon is akin to fluorescence. The inherent luminescence of fingerprints can be enhanced by dusting them with luminescent material or by using chemicals that react with fingerprint residue to form compounds that luminesce.

Surfaces normally regarded as unsuitable for registering a fingerprint, such as live human skin and paper toweling, may sometimes display the ridge lines of a print when illuminated by a laser. Not durable on skin, they must be looked for without delay. When a laser is employed, it should be utilized before regular dusting or any chemical method is tried.

Preserving Fingerprint Evidence

Basically, there are two means of preserving fingerprint evidence if the object bearing the print cannot be moved or protected: photographing and "lifting." Photography, the most common method, is preferred, especially from a legal viewpoint. Whether visible naturally or made so by dusting or other means, the print should be photographed life-size (1 to 1). For this purpose, an easily mastered, specially designed fingerprint camera is available. Anyone who is steady of hand and able to push a button and count to 10 can, with a minimum of training, produce consistently reliable photographs of latent prints (see Figure 2.15). A one-inch scale and the date and initials of the investigator or evidence technician should be included, particularly if a fingerprint camera is not used.

Sometimes a fingerprint is hard to photograph because of its location—for example, on the side of a filing cabinet that is close to a wall and too heavy to

Figure 2.15
Fingerprint camera.
(Courtesy, Sirchie Finger Print Laboratories, Inc., Raleigh, NC.)

move. In these situations, it can be "lifted" using a special cellophane transparent tape or other commercially available lifter. This lift may be accomplished with ease on a flat surface, but a print on a curved surface presents some difficulty. The use of clear, stretchable bookbinding tape, which conforms to the shape of the object and does not distort the print, will minimize or eliminate the problem.

It is important to keep careful notes describing the object and the location of the print. A photograph has the advantage of recording an object's background, serving to establish the source (which seldom can be done from a lift). A photograph would preclude a defense attorney's challenging the source of the print or claiming it was lifted while the defendant was in custody. The prudent investigator will attempt to preserve all objects bearing a fingerprint and, if possible, photograph the print *in situ* (in its original location) before lifting.

The defense of Count Alfred de Marigny, indicted for the murder of Sir Harry Oaks in a famous homicide case in the Bahamas, rested largely on the source of a latent fingerprint. Although the print was identified as that of de Marigny, defense counsel brought out the fact that it (allegedly lifted from a moveable Chinese screen at the crime scene, the victim's bedroom) was not photographed *in situ* because a fingerprint camera was not available. On examining the background of the lifted print, an investigator for the defense noted the presence of circular marks that could not be duplicated on lifts taken from any part of the Chinese screen. The defense made another telling point: there was no need to lift the developed print; the lightweight screen could have been carried to a place to be photographed. Largely because of the suspicious circumstances under which the latent print was allegedly obtained, the case was lost.[15] The lesson for the evidence technician and the investigator is that developed latent prints should be photographed first, then lifted. Many departments ignore this admonition, perhaps for reasons of economy. Should they have jurisdiction over an important case and the identity of a lifted fingerprint becomes an issue at trial, the price paid for a damaged reputation as a competent law enforcement agency may be far greater than the money saved by not providing film for the evidence technician to record the latent print properly.

How is a Fingerprint Classified and Identified?

Fingerprint bureaus were established about three decades before crime laboratories; hence, the identification of a latent print is often not considered the responsibility of the crime laboratory. Another reason for keeping the process in the fingerprint bureau is that the latent print examiner has ready access to the exemplars needed for comparison with latent impressions. Because fingerprint personnel generally are not trained in science, such identification work traditionally has not been thought of as a criminalist's work. Fortunately, James F. Cowger corrected this in 1983 with his book, *Friction Ridge Skin*. The present text emphasizes the basis on which a fingerprint identity is established. It avoids the complicated, arbitrary rules for building fingerprint classification schemes, with the exception of those rules necessary to understand why some inked record prints are rejected by the FBI.

How fingerprints are classified and filed is not given an extended explanation in this text because:

1. The field investigator generally does not possess the know-how to classify a set of fingerprints, and only a general understanding is required to answer a complainant's questions.

2. Unless utilized on a regular basis, classification rules beyond the few described are arbitrary and soon forgotten. In addition, because fingerprint files grow in size, so does the need to define more subtypes. As this need is met, variations will be found between agencies, there being no single authority for the introduction of new rules. Classification schemes thus require a text of their own.

Ridge Line Details

Different features of the friction ridge lines are significant in the classification and the individualization of fingerprints. Classification details are largely concerned with line patterns, whereas individualization (comparison) details focus on deviations from a straight or curved continuous ridge line. To the criminalist, ridge line patterns represent *class characteristics*; ridge line deviation details, *individual characteristics*.

Classification by Ridge Line Patterns: Listed in increasing order of complexity, there are three basic patterns: arches, loops, and whorls. About 5 to 10 percent of all patterns are arches, 60 to 65 percent are loops, and 25 to 30 percent are whorls (see Figure 2.8 on page 38). Fingerprint patterns are used to classify, not to individualize, a print. When a complete (as opposed to a partial) latent print is developed, and the pattern on each finger of a suspect differs from that of the latent, that suspect is definitively eliminated as the source.

In building the classification scheme, arches are further divided into *plain* and *tented* arches; loops into *radial* patterns (the open end leads out to the thumb) and *ulnar* patterns (the open end leads out to the little finger). An ulnar loop on one hand becomes a radial loop on the other. Ulnar loops are far more common than radial loops. Whorls, the most complex pattern, have four subdivisions: plain, central pocket loop, double loop, and accidental. Too complicated for the purposes of this text, they need not be explained in detail.

—Ridge Counting: Loops

Loops are further divided by counting ridges between the delta and the core, the count running from 1 to 30 (but rarely higher) (see Figure 2.16).

—Ridge Tracing: Whorls

Starting at the left delta and tracing the ridge line toward the right delta, if the traced ridge comes within three ridges (at its closest point) to the right delta, the pattern is called a *meet*. If there are three or more ridge lines between the traced ridge and the right delta, and if the trace ridge runs between that delta and the core, the pattern is called an *inner tracing*. If the right delta lies three lines or more above the traced ridge—between the core and the traced ridge, it is an *outer tracing*. (see Figure 2.17).

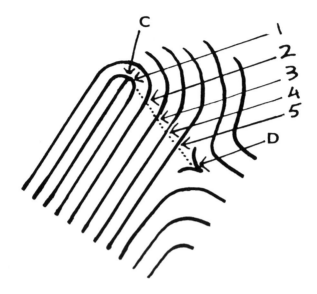

Figure 2.16
Loop pattern with a ridge count—from core (C) to delta (D)—of five. *(Courtesy, American Institute of Applied Science, Syracuse, NY.)*

A - Inner Whorl   B - Meeting Whorl   C - Outer Whorl

Figure 2.17
Three kinds of whorls as determined by ridge tracing from the left delta to the right delta. "D" points to the two deltas. The dotted line is adjacent to the traced ridge. *(Courtesy, American Institute of Applied Science, Syracuse, NY.)*

A fingerprint cannot be classified if the ridge lines are blocked out by too much ink having been rolled onto the finger. If the lines between the delta and core are not clear in a loop pattern, a ridge count cannot be made; therefore, the print is unclassifiable. Similarly, if ridge tracing between deltas is not possible, the whorls cannot be classified. Any blockage of details in these critical areas requires that the person's prints be taken over again.

Individualization by Ridge Line Deviations

A ridge line, whether straight or curved, can deviate from its course in the ways depicted in Figure 2.1. To the criminalist such divergences are *individual characteristics*; to the latent print examiner they are *points of identification* (also called minutiae, Galton details, or ridge characteristics). By means of these characteristics or points, a latent fingerprint is shown to be that of a particular individual. No standard terminology has been established. Most terms being sufficiently descriptive, the average juror encounters little difficulty in following expert testimony on the identification of a fingerprint.

Identifying a Latent Fingerprint: A latent fingerprint cannot be identified unless one of known origin is available for comparison. For this, fingerprint exemplars must be acquired. The sources through which known fingerprints are secured and the way the comparison is made are discussed below.

—Fingerprint Exemplars: Sources

The three sources providing the exemplars needed for comparison with a latent print are: police fingerprint files, a set of prints taken from a suspect who has no arrest or fingerprint record, and a set of prints taken from each person who frequents the area in which the latent print was found. The last set, called *elimination prints*, is used to determine whether the latent print is that of a stranger or someone who is customarily present. An unidentified latent print found on an object or in places that a stranger would be unable to justify is potentially valuable evidence.

—Comparison of a Latent with a Known Fingerprint

The first step toward identifying a latent fingerprint is to scrutinize it for any discernible class characteristics in order to eliminate comparison prints that are not of the same pattern type. The next task is to find a cluster of individual characteristics—two or three points bunched together. This grouping is chosen as a landmark to be searched for in the known comparison print. If a corresponding cluster is not noted, the known print is eliminated. If one is noted, the third step is to examine the latent for the next point of identification closest to the landmark cluster; then compare it to the known print to see if that characteristic is present in the same location, based on ridge counting. If it is, the latent is further examined for yet another individual characteristic, and the known is checked to see if there is a match. When all points of identification in each print are of the same type (bifurcation, dot, etc.) in the same unit relationship (same location), and no inexplicable differences are noted in either print, a conclusion that both impressions were made by the same person may be warranted.

—Number of Points Necessary for an Identification

The question of how many individual characteristics are needed for "a conclusion of an identity" (in the language of criminalistics) or "an identification" (in the language of latent print examiners) has not been definitively settled. Among European countries, the minimum number of points is set in France at 17, in England at 16, and in Spain at 10 to 12. In the United States at one time, 12 was common. Nevertheless, in 1973 following a three-year study, the International Association for Identification (IAI) pronounced: ". . . no valid basis exists at this time for requiring that a pre-determined number of friction ridge characteristics must be present in two impressions in order to establish a positive identification."[17]

The qualitative value of each kind of individual characteristic is a matter largely ignored in establishing a minimum quantitative standard as proof of an identity. For example, about half of all characteristics present in a fingerprint are ridge endings; fewer than one in 100 are trifurcations. Obviously, one trifurcation is worth several ridge endings. This is an area worthy of further research that, if fruitful, will make latent print identification less subjective. When the requisite statistical means are developed and applied to the evaluation of individual characteristics in other areas of criminalistics—firearms and tool marks, for instance—it will render decision-making more precise and scientific.

Automated Fingerprint Identification Systems (AFISs)

Not until the mid-1980s (and then only in a few law enforcement agencies) did it become possible by means of scanners and computers to inspect file (record) prints for specified ridge line details. By 1990, more than 100 agencies had databases in the United States, and there were close to 400 remote-site AFIS (automated fingerprint identification system) agencies. It will take time and money for all police fingerprint files to be stored in computers. Until this is possible, the investigator must submit a record card number for the individual whose prints are on file, to have them used for comparison with a latent impression.

Automated fingerprint identification systems (AFISs) scan the file record prints in the computer for possible matches with those of a latent print. A computer printout lists them in order—from the most probable down to the least probable. This allows files to be pulled for submission to a latent print examiner, who makes the final determination as to whether there is or is not a match.

A crucial problem remains to be solved if maximum results are to be achieved from the AFIS. Having been developed independently, the existing systems lack compatibility with each other. The three major AFIS vendors—computer software vendors with large potential profits at stake—are unlikely to share the technical information that would allow systems to interconnect. Such compatibility issues, fortunately, are being addressed by law enforcement agencies.

Progress, however, has not been rapid:

> . . . AFIS is quite costly—a significant obstacle for small departments with even smaller resources. More than 75 percent of the agencies in this country are only beginning to automate. . . . communication between AFIS computers can

be complicated, even among agencies located in the same state. Differences in current technology, operational approaches, equipment, interfaces and network compatability make it difficult to "ship" fingerprints to other agencies for access to other fingerprint data bases.[18]

In an attempt to deal with this situation, the FBI created an Integrated Automated Fingerprint Identification System (IAFIS). The system went online in 1999. Since then, its use has grown to the point where more than 60 percent of submissions are now received electronically.[19]

Evidentiary Value

When the friction ridge lines of a fingerprint are properly examined, and an identity between the latent print and a known print can be shown, there is irrefutable evidence that the identified individual made the latent print. This is true whatever the source—finger, palm, or foot. Its value lies in the connection established between the crime scene (or victim) and the identified individual. A defense attorney confronted with such convincing evidence has little chance of disputing it as long as investigators have seen to it that the evidence was legally collected and preserved.

Occasionally, however, defendants will either assert that they were at the crime scene at some earlier time or that they had previously handled the object in question. Two cases come to mind: the first involved a burglary in which one latent print was developed on a broken piece of window glass found on a bedroom floor; the other was a homicide in which the latent was developed on a soft drink can found on a table next to the victim. In the first case, the alleged burglar (the victim's former live-in companion) claimed that his latent print on the window was left six months earlier; the claim gained credence when the evidence was shown to be on the inside rather than the outside of the window glass. This raised the question of how long a latent print lasts. In the second case, the defendant asserted that—a few days before the crime—he had, while trying to make up his mind, handled several cans of the soft drink in the only store in which it was sold in the small town. Again, the issue was the age of the print.

How Long Do Fingerprints Last?

Determining the age of a latent fingerprint, especially one developed with powders, receives meager, conflicting treatment in the literature of the field. Moreover, except for a study by Barnett, it has rarely been the subject of systematic research.[20] Many evidence technicians incorrectly believe that the ease with which a latent print "grabs" the powder is indicative of its age. Cowger, one of the few to refute this commonly held view, wrote:

> [T]hat a latent print develops strongly and quickly does not provide much of a clue as to its age, since many substances that could cause the print may have sufficient viscosity to remain in one place for long periods of time and do not necessarily dry out even in harsh environments. . . . For an examiner to conclude that a particular print is "old" because little powder adheres or because the print has diffused through the substrate would be to ignore the fact that many latent prints that are quite new have those characteristics.[21]

Additional Factors to be Considered

There is no reason to believe that a latent print will improve over time; sooner or later it will deteriorate, depending on its environment. In a protected environment it is likely to last longer than when exposed to rain, sun, dust, and wind. If the object bearing the print—e.g., counter top, kitchen appliance, or window—receives frequent cleaning, the last time it was cleaned fixes the maximum possible age of the latent print. To evaluate the feasibility of its having lasted for the period claimed, the conditions prevailing during the interval the print was supposedly present must be ascertained. If time permits, a criminalist can be asked to place a print on a surface similar to the one bearing the incriminating print to determine empirically whether a useful latent of a particular age can last and ultimately be developed.

In checking out the explanation of the presence of such a print, the investigator need not rely entirely on forensic considerations. For example, does a code mark on a soda can indicate when and if that can was distributed in the area? If brought in from elsewhere, from where? In general, the investigator must check all the circumstances that either support or contradict any and all such explanations, keeping in mind the equally important task of protecting the innocent.

Levels of Expertise

To make fingerprints serviceable in the criminal justice system, several kinds of expertise are required. First are the inked record prints made of arrestees for police files or, when no file record print exists, taken expressly for comparison with a latent impression. Making a set of acceptable record prints is easily learned and relatively simple; even so, it entails a modicum of expertise. Otherwise, the prints may be rejected as "unclassifiable" by the FBI.

Special training is required to classify a set of inked fingerprints. After several years of experience, a "classifier" may be selected for training as a "latent print examiner." The two tasks are quite different, and experience alone is not sufficient. Yet apprenticeship, long abandoned by the learned professions, is still the mode for creating a "fingerprint identification expert." As pointed out earlier in this chapter, establishing a fingerprint identity is a criminalistics problem, and some criminalists are now performing this work.

Processing a crime scene for fingerprints calls for some training. The necessary skills for the use of powders can be mastered quickly. Chemical methods and laser radiation, however, require more formal education in science—especially in chemistry and physics.

Expert testimony in court is required of the following people:

1. The evidence technician (or investigator) who developed the latent impression.

2. The file supervisor or detective who can vouch for the authenticity of the known fingerprint record used to identify the defendant.

3. The expert (a latent print examiner) who can prove the source of the latent print (i.e., to whom it belongs).

Probative Value

A single, partial, latent fingerprint identified as that of a defendant—absent any other evidence—is sufficient proof to convict the accused. It must be shown, however, that the defendant's print was present under circumstances that exclude any reasonable possibility consistent with innocence. Accordingly, the prosecution may have to prove that any object bearing the latent print was inaccessible to the accused. If the defendant had legitimate access to the location before (and reasonably close to when) the crime was committed, the value of the fingerprint evidence is largely negated.

Firearms

Whenever a firearm is discharged in the commission of a crime, physical evidence is likely to be available. The investigator will have several questions to ask concerning its investigative worth:

1. Can the crime scene bullet or cartridge casing be linked to a suspected weapon (if one is located)?

2. Relative to the gun and its mechanical condition:
   a) What is a correct description of the weapon?
   b) Is it capable of firing a cartridge?
   c) Is there evidence of the bullet's trajectory that will permit a determination of the line of fire?
   d) Can the weapon be discharged accidentally?
   e) What is the trigger pull?
   f) Can the serial number (if removed) be restored?

3. What was the muzzle-to-victim (or shooting) distance at the time the weapon was discharged?

4. Is there gunpowder evidence on the firing hand, revealing that it had recently discharged a firearm?

5. Was the weapon recently fired? How many shots?

6. Can the type of gun be determined from an examination of the class characteristics of a bullet or cartridge recovered at the crime scene?

Crime Scene Bullet or Cartridge and Suspected Weapon

Linking a suspected weapon, when one is recovered, to a crime scene bullet or cartridge has both investigative and probative value. The owner or person in possession of the weapon has some explaining to do—certainly to a jury—if put on trial. The owner might have loaned it to another person; if so, that person's name must be disclosed and the alibi checked.

Establishing that a particular weapon fired a bullet is determined by using an instrument designed for this purpose. Figure 2.18 depicts an early (1938) comparison microscope originally developed in the 1920s by Calvin Goddard and others. A comparison microscope is used to compare tool marks as well as bullets and cartridges.

Figure 2.18
An early comparison microscope used in the Kansas City Police Laboratory by Ralph F. Turner. *(Courtesy, Professor Ralph F. Turner, Michigan State University.)*

Make and Mechanical Condition of Gun

Several matters concerning the make and mechanical condition of a firearm arise when a detective prepares a report or needs information to reconstruct the crime:

1. What is the proper description of the weapon?

2. Is it in working order?

3. Can the trajectory of the bullet be established?

4. Can the weapon be accidentally discharged?

5. Does it have a hair trigger?

Description of a Weapon

It is widely assumed that because police officers carry guns, they are familiar with weapons in general. For many officers nothing is further from the truth. As President Kennedy's assassination illustrates, the correct description of a gun is best left to the firearms examiner because an incorrect description creates difficulties. Initially, a deputy sheriff reported that the rifle discovered on the sixth floor of the book depository building in Dallas was a 7.65 mm. German Mauser; later, it was accurately described as a

Mannlicher-Carcano 6.5 mm. Italian carbine. In this case, a result of the confusion ensuing from the incorrect identification of the weapon was the credence it gave to a conspiracy theory.

Operating Condition of a Weapon

Is a particular gun capable of firing a cartridge? This determination is made simply by loading the weapon with proper cartridge and attempting to fire it in an appropriate place such as a range or other facility in which thorough safety precautions have been taken. Then, by firing into cotton, oiled waste, or a water recovery tank, the test bullet can be retrieved for examination under the comparison microscope. If a bullet is found at a crime scene, it can be compared with bullets and cartridges from these test firings, and with evidence on file from other apparently unrelated crimes.

Bullet Trajectory

If there are two or more holes made by one bullet, it may be feasible to determine the line of fire and the firing position of the shooter. Such determinations are made by sighting through the holes (or at night, by directing the beam of a flashlight through them) to trace the line of flight back to the source. The line of fire cannot be established with accuracy, however, when a bullet is diverted from a straight line by an object that causes it to ricochet, or because of a mechanical defect in the weapon.

Accidental Discharge

Whether a gun is defective or was accidentally discharged because it was tampered with should be determined solely by someone thoroughly familiar with guns and their mechanisms. Reputable manufacturers are quite reliable, and their products rarely go off by chance. However, the "Saturday-Night Special" and the zip gun are dangerous; if dropped, they can be set off. Official concern over the question of accidental discharge is yet another illustration of the need to reconstruct the event under investigation.

Trigger Pull

A gun is said to have a hair trigger when the force required to pull it is less than that normally set by the factory. For a .38 caliber revolver, a hair trigger pull would be 2.5 pounds to 3.5 pounds with the hammer uncocked, i.e., double action. Trigger pull can be determined by using a spring scale (tension method), or by adding weights to a pan scale hooked over the trigger until the hammer falls (inertia method).

Restoration of Serial Numbers

The serial numbers on a weapon are useful in proving ownership or in tracing a gun from the time of its manufacture. By filing, grinding, punching, or drilling, serial numbers in metal can be obliterated. It should be noted that there are other stolen items such as typewriters, automobile engines, and cameras that also may have their serial numbers altered or obliterated.

An etching process can often restore the original numbers or marks. After the area has been cleaned and polished, a suitable reagent is chosen (depending on the metal: steel, copper, aluminum, or brass) and applied with a cotton swab. Because the original stamping process sets up a strain in the metal by compressing the area beneath the stamp, the etching rate for the metal under pressure and that not so compressed is not the same. This differential causes the original numbers to be restored.

The etching process requires great care and patience; it can take from a few minutes to several hours—even days. During this time the numbers may not appear simultaneously, and the criminalist's attention to reconstituting them must be continuous. Because they may suddenly appear then disappear (usually forever), it is imperative that the details be photographed quickly.

Shooting Distance

The question of the distance between the muzzle of the gun and the victim at the time of the shooting can be significant. The following situations will illustrate:

1. When suicide or foul play is a possibility.

2. In a claim of self-defense or other allegation.

3. Where poor lighting conditions make the victim's recognition of the perpetrator questionable.

With regard to suicide, it is clearly impossible to shoot oneself if the trigger is out of reach. When the firing distance is very small (as in a contact wound) or when it is measured in inches, probative support is given a claim of self-defense. Firing distance is also important when victim recognition is the issue. In New York City—where not many harbor waterfront homicides are brought to trial—one such case was influenced by the criminalist's testimony that the shooting distance was less than six inches. This apparently convinced the jury that the victim's *dying declaration* identifying an old friend as the killer was believable although the illumination was very poor at the time.

The basis for the determination of shooting distance is found in the smoke halo and powder pattern of the burned, partially burned, and unburned powder particles blown from the muzzle of a gun when fired (see Figure 2.19). Should the victim have been wearing dark clothing, however, a powder pattern may not be discernible. Several technical procedures can be used to make such details visible:

- Contrast photography

- Infrared photography

- Soft X-rays (produced by a low-voltage X-ray tube)

- The Walker nitrite test

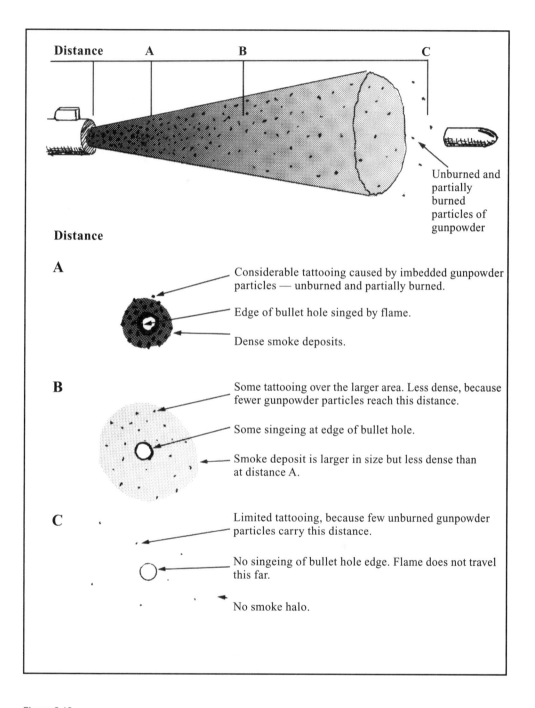

Figure 2.19
Patterns of the smoke halo and gunpowder particles blown out of muzzle upon discharge of a firearm. *(Prepared by Jerzy J. Hoga, graphic designer.)*

Powder Traces on Gun Hand

In addition to powder residue from the muzzle, powder is blown out laterally in the area of the revolver's cylinder or, when an automatic pistol is fired, during the ejection of the cartridge casing. One of the first tests proposed to detect such traces on the hand that fired the gun, the *dermal nitrate* or *paraffin test*, has since proved unreliable and lost credibility. A person can fire a gun yet have no detectable traces on the hand, or not fire a gun and have traces of a nitrate present from a source other than gunpowder.

In place of the dermal nitrate test, neutron activation analysis (NAA) detects the metal residue (barium and antimony) that comes from the primer of the cartridge. Although residue levels are substantially reduced by wiping or washing the hands with soap, the sensitivity of NAA is so great that even minute traces are readily detected. The sample must be taken within a few hours of the shooting. The hand is coated with melted paraffin (as it was in the now little-used dermal nitrate method); upon cooling, the hardened paraffin cast transfers any primer (metal) residue from the skin. This is then tested. An alternative method utilizes a cotton swab saturated with dilute nitric acid to obtain the sample. Atomic absorption (AA) and scanning electron microscopy/energy dispersive X-ray (SEM/EDX) analysis are also employed to detect primer residue elements.

Weapon Recently Fired? — How Many Shots?

The question of whether a gun was recently fired cannot be decisively answered. The best that can be said is that the gun was fired since it was last cleaned. This determination is easily made by running a cleaning patch through the barrel of the weapon. The information provided, however, does not reveal whether the gun has been fired recently.

If cartridge casings are recovered at the crime scene or bullet holes are found, the minimum number of shots fired may be ascertained. This can sometimes be useful in checking out descriptions of the event.

Type and Model of Weapon Used

Following the commission of a crime in which a gun was discharged, notifying area police forces about the type of weapon sought could be productive. Many police officers believe that the crime laboratory can pinpoint the weapon by examining the spent bullet or cartridge casing. It may be feasible to determine caliber this way, but it is seldom possible to identify a specific manufacturer or model. Elimination is a more viable procedure. If a bullet has a left twist to the rifling, then any gun with a right twist would be eliminated automatically based on class characteristics.

Cartridge casings are more useful for identifying the weapon: their shape and size reveal type (revolver or automatic pistol) and caliber. The absence of cartridge casings at the crime scene indicates that a revolver was probably used, since an automatic ejects its casing with each shot fired. The offender, however, may have had the presence of mind to retrieve the ejected cartridge cases, not necessarily to have it appear that a revolver was used, but to eliminate the prospects of the weapon being linked to the crime scene.

Blood

Blood is a common clue material in many of the more serious crimes against the person: homicide, felonious assault, robbery, and rape. Occasionally, it is available in crimes against property. When breaking and entering, a burglar may cut himself or herself—the odds increasing in proportion to the haste or carelessness typical in a crime like automobile larceny. Although fresh blood is easy to discern, its appearance can be altered even after a short time by sunlight, heat, airborne bacteria, age, and other factors; then it is difficult to recognize. Blood that was removed by washing or covered with paint might go unnoticed unless suspicion of such a circumstance is aroused. Fortunately, very sensitive, simple field tests using a chemical reagent permit detection of the slightest residues. Called *presumptive tests*, they are not specific for blood, are only preliminary, and are of little value for court purposes. Still, they have great investigative potential and can be performed at the crime scene. The following are several field color tests presumptive for blood:

- Leuco-Malachite Green Test
- Reduced Phenolphthalein Test
- Luminol Test
- Tetramethyl Benzidine Test

Other tests performed on suspected stains can yield additional information. For example, the hemin crystal test proves the actual presence of blood in a stain; the precipitin test establishes its origin (human, animal, or a mixture of both); and, if a stain has been satisfactorily preserved and is of sufficient quantity, its blood group(s) may be determined as well. In addition, DNA tests became a reality in 1989. Most of these tests are usually not possible in the field; they call for laboratory equipment and carefully controlled conditions. When the amount of clue material is limited, it is best not to expend it by field testing. Although sensitive and requiring small samples of blood, field tests can in some cases make the precipitin test impossible.

The degree of investigative value for each of the examinations on a suspected bloodstain varies.

Investigative Uses

From the viewpoint of the investigator, the concern is not with how blood tests are performed but with the investigative prospects they hold. The following practical results have been achieved through the examination of suspected bloodstains:

- The crime scene has been located.
- The crime weapon has been identified.
- A link has been established between criminal and victim—or, one or both of them has been connected to the crime scene.
- A reconstruction of the crime (how it was committed) has been accomplished.

- An alibi has been corroborated or disproved.

- A suspect has made an admission or a confession during an interrogation after having been informed of blood test results.

Locate the Crime Scene

In homicide cases, a body is sometimes discovered at a location other than where the assault occurred. In the meantime, of course, if the original crime scene can be found, the investigation has taken a step forward. Moving the body suggests a deliberate attempt by the criminal to dissociate himself or herself from the killing. It is often apparent from the nature of the injuries that a significant quantity of blood is likely to be present at the crime scene, making it equally likely that the criminal will take countermeasures to forestall discovery of that site. This, however, is not easy to do, because the guilty person is hindered by internal pressures to avoid exposure.

Here are a few circumstances that have alerted investigators and aroused their suspicion that blood might have been present:

- In an otherwise grubby home, the kitchen floor had been immaculately cleaned.

- Only one wall of a living room had been freshly painted.

- A rug was missing from a floor that obviously had been previously covered (judging by a color difference in the varnish at the room's borders and the lack of scratch marks in the middle).

- A bedspread could not be located, nor its whereabouts satisfactorily explained.

- The seat covers of an automobile had been removed, though reported to have been in good condition the day before the crime.

- A few tons of coal had been moved within a coal bin (shoveled to another side and away from where it would normally be), making it inconvenient to use.

- Ketchup had been smeared over the kitchen floor and rubbed into the carpet.

In such circumstances, when a positive preliminary blood test is obtained despite an effort to cover it up, the clue must be followed up. Although not admissible as evidence in court, preliminary blood tests have significant investigative value. Additional information can become available when the original crime scene is located.

Identify the Weapon or Instrument

Although the law does not require that a weapon be produced as evidence in court, an intensive search is generally made to recover it. The impact on the jury is considerable if an unusually terrifying instrument was wielded to wound or injure. On observing the injuries on the victim's body, the pathologist—and in many cases the detective—may be able to arrive at some conclusion with respect to the type of weapon; obviously, the search is more likely to be successful when one knows what to look for.

The presence of blood on a hammer or other bludgeon, knife, ice pick, heavy boot, or spike heel can expose it as the likely assault weapon. When the blood group can be determined, evidentiary value is enhanced. Most weapons seem to present difficulties regarding removal of all residual traces. This is often true despite precautions taken by the perpetrator soon after committing the crime. Careful washing of cutting or stabbing instruments, on the other hand, is quite effective; if done thoroughly, even the most sensitive reagent fails to detect blood. Fortunately, most criminals are satisfied if their weapon appears free of visible traces of blood; hence, there is always the chance that invisible traces remain. For example, a boot thought to be implicated in a stomping homicide may retain traces of blood on its welt or on the side or inside of the shoelace. Therefore, even when no signs of blood are apparent, it will profit the conscientious investigator to submit a suspected weapon to the crime laboratory.

Develop Associative Evidence

Relating the criminal to the victim—or either of them to the crime scene—through the discovery and grouping of a bloodstain or through DNA content are examples of associative evidence. It is not unusual to find the victim's blood on the perpetrator's clothing or body, or alternatively, the criminal's blood at the crime scene. There are a few cases on record in which a trail of the perpetrator's blood was tracked from the crime scene back to the perpetrator's house. Usually, however, the identity of the suspect is gradually disclosed through normal investigative techniques. Then the crime laboratory's ability is called on to process the physical evidence. Two extreme investigative possibilities for blood are represented in the following examples:

1. No test other than normal visual observation—tracking a trail of blood—is required.

2. Significant investigative results are provided when the bloodstain can be grouped or analyzed for DNA.

Identifying the source, especially of animal blood, can be significant in some circumstances. For example, illegal cattle slaughtering in uninspected barns was somewhat common during World War II while there was a meat shortage. Just as meat prices rise, so does the incidence of cattle rustling and illegal slaughtering. In addition, wild game shot out of season must be transported covertly. Because the detection of animal blood in unusual places can expose the owner (of the barn or vehicle) to further investigation, state conservation officers can probably make profitable use of this investigative tool.

Reconstruct How the Crime was Committed

Reconstructing the crime, an increasingly important laboratory function, can be accomplished through the study of blood groups and bloodstain patterns. One of the authors is familiar with a case of a double homicide by a third person. Despite the perpetrator's attempt to have it appear that a duel with carving knives had taken place, the homicide was reconstructed in the crime laboratory by the blood grouping of stains found throughout the apartment. The apparent duelists obviously dead, this strategy might have been successful and the case closed had the unusual distribution of blood in widely separated areas not aroused the suspicion of the investigator. Blood was found on the back of the entrance door to the apartment, on the inside of the bathroom door, on the telephone ripped from the wall, and on a window shade (normally open, but closed when the crime was discovered).

The samples were sufficient in quantity for grouping purposes, and two different blood groups were present. The laboratory ascertained the specific objects each victim had touched and, through a reconstruction of how the crime was committed, was able to explain the wide distribution of blood. It became clear that the criminal had been unable to deal lethally with two victims at the same time. When switching from one to the other, he would find the first attempting to escape or call for help. The bloody doors, the ripped telephone wire, and the closed window shade testified to the killer's resolve to prevent such attempts. Although the perpetrator was ultimately apprehended by conventional techniques, his confession was corroborated by the crime laboratory's blood grouping, which reconstructed how the crime was committed. In many jurisdictions, corroboration of a confession is a requisite in more serious crimes. Corroboration through independent evidence is desirable in all crimes. Sometimes blood examinations have this potential.

In a monograph on the interpretation of bloodstain patterns, MacDonell describes how knowledge of the flight characteristics and the stain patterns of spattered blood can be employed to determine several things:

1. The distance between the surface bearing the stain and the origin of the blood at the time it was shed;

2. The point(s) of origin of the blood (see Figure 2.20);

3. The type of impacting object (bludgeon or gunshot) that produced the bloodstains, and the direction of its force;

4. The movement and direction of the person(s) and/or object(s) during the shedding of blood;

5. The number of blows or shots; with arterial gushing, the number of heart-beats;

6. The position(s) of the victim and/or object(s) during the shedding of blood;

7. The movement of the victim and/or object(s) following the shedding of blood.[22]

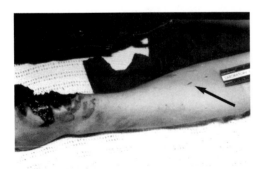

Figure 2.20
Blood spatter on arm (to the left of ruler) shows directionality to be from right to left. These small stains establish that the arm was outstretched when the slug struck the victim's chin. The origin of spatter was not from the thumb but from the other area of damage (or impact), i.e., the chin. *(Courtesy, Herbert L. MacDonell, Laboratory of Forensic Science, Corning, NY.)*

In one case, MacDonell's expertise was called on to examine blood spatter stains on the clothing of an individual who claimed he found the victim in a pool of blood and dragged the body to get help, thereby causing the stains. MacDonell, however, testified that the blood pattern on the defendant's clothing could not have resulted as described—from mere contact with the victim. It could only have been produced by blood spattering with great velocity, as from a beating or stabbing.[23]

Corroborate or Disprove an Alibi

Suspects finding it somewhat disconcerting when a bloodstain is discovered in their home or automobile, or on their clothing, often proffer an explanation for its presence. Typical alibis include: a recent visit to the butcher shop, a cookout, a hunting trip, or a nosebleed. They may be proved or disproved in the laboratory by determining the origin of a stain (animal, human, or both), its blood group, or DNA content. Simplistic excuses that wine, ketchup, or iron are the cause can be readily checked in the field by one of the preliminary catalytic color tests (such as the Leuco-Malachite Green Test).

Interrogate a Suspect

The average suspect does not know the difference between a blood examination that is no more than an investigative technique and one with genuine evidentiary value. One of the prerequisites of effective interrogation is met when suspects understand that evidence exists that can be used against them; at least they must *believe* it is available. To invoke this belief, a color test (such as the Leuco-Malachite Green Test) performed in the presence of the suspect on a stain that seems to be implicative can be effective. If the other conditions necessary for a confession are satisfied (see Chapter 11), a formal declaration of guilt can result.

Evidentiary Value

A laboratory finding that a suspicious stain contains blood of human origin may work against a defendant on trial, and laboratory testimony on its blood group will carry greater weight. A determination, therefore, that incriminating stains on the suspect's clothing are of the same group as the victim's (and different from the suspect's) represents a contribution to the evidence that few juries would ignore. This also applies to a determination resulting from DNA analysis. Any explanation of why the same DNA or blood group as the victim's should have been found on the defendant must satisfy the jury. Should it fail to, the consequences are apt to be grave when the jury deliberates on the evidence.

Semen, Other Biological Material, and DNA Profiling

DNA (deoxyribonucleic acid) technology is a relative newcomer to serving the needs of law enforcement. Developed in the 1970s as a tool for the molecular biologist, and coming as a surprise spin-off from gene splicing, it was first applied to forensic matters in 1985. Not since Neutron Activation Analysis (NAA) was viewed as a godsend in the late 1940s has a promising new method for the examination of physical evidence caused such a stir in the world of forensic scientists, prosecutors, and defense attorneys. Particularly in rape cases, prosecutors see the possibility of presenting positive DNA (semen) results as associative evidence or proof that the defendant's ejaculate was present at the crime scene or on the victim's clothing or body. The linkage of suspect to crime scene has strong probative value and is likely to be persuasive to a jury. Defense attorneys are also tantalized by the prospect that DNA findings may (and can) eliminate their client as a rape suspect, or free him should he have been convicted and the test not done. Similarly, interest is aroused because other kinds of biological evidence are suitable for DNA analysis: blood (if white cells are present), hair (if the root is present), saliva, skin (if nucleated epithelial cells are present), bone, and urine.

DNA analysis (profiling) is regarded by some in law enforcement as the greatest breakthrough since the advent of fingerprinting and the police radio. By 1989, the courts in 25 states had allowed DNA test results to be admitted as evidence; this has withstood its first appeal in a Florida criminal case. Of the first 54 cases handled by the FBI Laboratory, 29 suspects were linked to the crime through a comparison of DNA profiles obtained from the suspect's specimen and the biological crime scene specimen. Fourteen suspects were cleared when DNA results did not match.

DNA profiling would, therefore, appear to be a powerful forensic tool for protecting the innocent. And yet it could be used maliciously to do just the opposite; namely, frame a victim. Specimens of hair, blood, and semen could be procured (though not without some difficulty), then placed at a crime scene to incriminate the "patsy" selected to take the "fall." Great care must therefore be taken to gather evidence independent of DNA results to corroborate that the suspect did, in fact, commit the crime or at least had the opportunity and compelling motive to do so.

DNA—What Is It?

A naturally occurring substance, and the principal component of cellular chromosomes, DNA is responsible for the hereditary (genetic) characteristics in all life forms. It is a large, heavy macromolecule consisting of two strands coiled about each other—like a spiral staircase—forming DNA into the structure of a double helix. The steps in the staircase are composed of four nitrogenous bases known as adenine, guanine, cytosine, and thymine—each represented respectively by A, G, C, and T. Only when A is paired with T, or G with C, can a step be built in the staircase. In nature, when a sugar (deoxyribose) is linked to a phosphate group and to one of the four nitrogenous bases (A, G, C, T), the resultant molecule is called a nucleotide.

The number of arrangements for nucleotides is almost infinite, the human genetic code comprising three billion combinations. For example, base pairings in a nucleotide and its two-strand structure can be depicted for one possible fragment of the DNA code as follows:

```
-A-G-T-T-C-A-G-G-G-T-C-C-A-
 | | | | | | | | | | | | |
-T-C-A-A-G-T-C-C-C-A-G-G-T-
```

Within a human cell, each of the 46 chromosomes (23 from each parent) has a DNA structure built from the randomly alternating base pairings:

The vast majority of the 3 billion nucleotides are shared in common by all human beings. Only a small portion is sufficiently variable in base pairing sequence to permit discriminating one individual from another through the variations of genetic material at the molecular level.

DNA—How Is It Analyzed?

Certain nucleotide combinations, however, repeat themselves at random intervals throughout the length of the DNA chain. The sequence is called a *restriction site*, the term coming from the naturally occurring restriction enzymes obtained from certain bacteria. Restriction enzymes can be purified for use in fragmenting DNA after it is extracted from the specimen (Step 1 in Figure 2.21); they act like chemical scissors, cutting or breaking the DNA chain at its restriction sites (Step 2 in Figure 2.21). The resultant fragments, varying in length and weight, are separated by *gel electrophoresis* (Step 3 in Figure 2.21). The double stranded DNA fragments are further broken apart (*denatured* by heat or chemical means), resulting in single-stranded fragments. These single strands can be joined together again under certain conditions to reform the original double stranded DNA. The process of recombining single DNA strands to form a double strand is called *hybridization* (Step 4 in Figure 2.21). It is possible to hybridize (combine) the denatured single strands of DNA obtained from the questioned biological evidence with other single (complementary) strands obtained through laboratory recombinant techniques. If the complementary strands (or probes) are tagged (by incorporating radioactive phosphorous into the DNA molecule), the resulting hybrid is detected by using X-ray film (Step 5 in Figure 2.21). The process is repeated with a known sample obtained from the suspect or victim. Laboratory-tagged single-stranded DNA molecules are again used to detect any complementary single strands of DNA obtained by denaturing the known sample. The labeled (or tagged) molecules used for this purpose are called *probes*.

There are several methods available for DNA profiling. They differ from each other in the amount of sample required for analysis. The accuracy of the results is dependent on the quantity and quality of the sample. The laboratory-made probes used to identify the DNA denatured fragments obtained from the crime scene evidence also differ significantly. *Restriction Fragment Length Polymorphism* (RFLP) analysis, the earliest known technique (Steps 3 through 7 in Figure 2.21), involves either of two kinds of probes. Originally called Jeffreys probes and White probes (named after the scientists who developed them), they are now better characterized as *multilocus* and *single-locus*

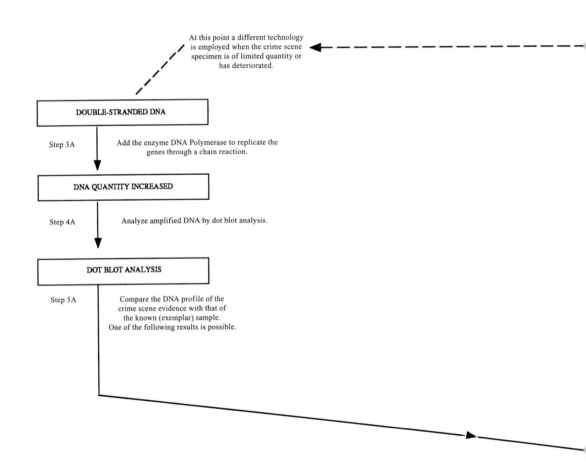

At this point a different technology
is employed when the crime scene
specimen is of limited quantity or
has deteriorated.

DOUBLE-STRANDED DNA

Step 3A   Add the enzyme DNA Polymerase to replicate the
                 genes through a chain reaction.

DNA QUANTITY INCREASED

Step 4A   Analyze amplified DNA by dot blot analysis.

DOT BLOT ANALYSIS

Step 5A   Compare the DNA profile of the
                 crime scene evidence with that of
                 the known (exemplar) sample.
                 One of the following results is possible.

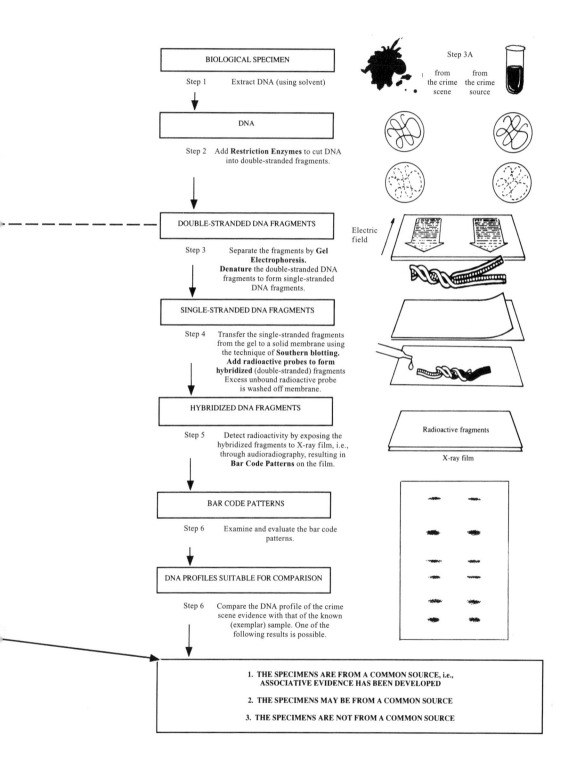

Figure 2.21

Schematic outline for the analysis of DNA. *(Prepared with the assistance of Mark D. Stolorow, Cellmark Diagnostics, Germantown, MD; drawing by Jerzy J. Hoga, graphic designer.)*

probes. A multilocus probe (MLP) can, in one test, simultaneously bind many DNA fragments from many different chromosomes; this process is a *multilocus probe* test. A *single-locus probe* (SLP) test, on the other hand, identifies a fragment whose sequence appears only once in a chromosome. (However, several single locus tests can be performed using different probes.) At the beginning of DNA testing for forensic purposes, only the SLP method was used in North America; both were used in Europe. Of the two, the MLP is less costly and does not require as much time because only one test need be made. A drawback of both methods is the requirement that the DNA sample be of high molecular weight, i.e., a sample that has not begun to deteriorate or decompose in stages—resulting in lower molecular weights. Because heat, bacteria, and moisture can cause it to decompose, the preservation of DNA evidence is critical.

Fortunately, another procedure is useful when a crime scene specimen has undergone some deterioration, is of insufficient molecular weight, or was limited in quantity to begin with. This procedure involves a chain reaction that amplifies certain (target) DNA sequences in the specimen. To accomplish this, the enzyme *DNA polymerase* is used, and the procedure is known as the *polymerase chain reaction* (PCR), or alternatively, the *gene amplification technique* (Steps 3A through 5A in Figure 2.21). Although the time needed to complete a PCR procedure is measured in hours, it takes additional time to complete any of the several identification methods that must then be used.

Newer DNA Technology

A new approach to DNA analysis involves *short tandem repeats* (STRs). Individually, STRs are less discriminating, but when multiple ones are examined, the combined probability can equal that of RFLP results. Similarly, Y-chromosome DNA typing is on the horizon as yet another form of STR analysis. This technology could help identify males involved in sexual assault cases. At the cutting edge of DNA technology is the study of *single nucleotide polymorphism* (SNP) sites, with the future prospect of their use as an additional kind of DNA evidence.

Another development enhancing the value of DNA as evidence is the utilization of a different DNA that is also found in body cells: *mitochondrial DNA* (mtDNA). The more familiar DNA, found only in the nucleus of the cell, is properly designated as nDNA.

Short Tandem Repeats (STRs)

The DNA molecule is chemically stable, long-living, and quite resistant to environmental factors. Although preserved by dessication or cold storage, it can be degraded by enzyme action (cellular or bacterial) when damp; then, it separates into fragments with far fewer base pairs than are present in intact DNA, which has 3 billion base pairs.

The greater the DNA degradation, the more likely the survival of only the shortest fragments. Such small DNA fragments are still useful for analyzing old specimens and crime scene evidence. Short Tandem Repeat (STR) defines a small region (locus) in which different numbers of tandemly repeated core DNA sequences, two to eight base pairs in length, are found. The DNA database now being compiled uses 13 core STR loci in the DNA molecule (see CODIS, below). "Core" STR loci refers to the fact that the forensic science laboratories in the United States, which are cooperating with the FBI in CODIS, will type the same DNA regions. This way, they can exchange and compare case work and database typing information. By selecting 13 loci, the power of discrimination rivals that of RFLP analysis, which is expensive and requires considerably more time and DNA to complete.

Mitochondrial DNA

The cell is the basic building block of all living things. Although it contains many components, two are of interest from a DNA standpoint: the *nucleus* and the *mitochondrion*. The nucleus is the source of the DNA (more properly nDNA) that is commonly tested for. The mitochondrion is a specialized part of the cell, the function of which is to produce energy for the body by using the food digested. It too has a DNA molecule, mitochondrial DNA (mtDNA), which is relatively small, compared to the 3 billion base pairs in nDNA. Although mtDNA offers much less discriminatory information than nDNA, the hundreds or thousands of mitochondria per cell (compared to one nucleus per cell) make it much easier to extract mtDNA from biological specimens. Thus, a very small sample or one that is badly degraded may not be suitable for nDNA analysis, yet could be fit for mtDNA analysis. Moreover, mtDNA can often be recovered from samples that will not yield much nDNA, such as hair shafts, saliva, and skeletal remains.

Unlike nDNA (which is inherited from both parents), mtDNA is passed only through the mother. This fact, coupled with the fact that mtDNA is recoverable from ancient bones, has led to the solution of some interesting historical questions. For instance, were the bodies buried in an unmarked grave those of the Romanov family, the Russian royal family believed to be shot more than 70 years ago at the start of the Russian Revolution? Typing revealed that the mtDNA sequences obtained from the Romanov descendants matched that extracted from the bones believed to be those of the royal family.

DNA—Investigative Use

DNA tests for forensic evidence were first performed in the United States by commercial laboratories. In 1989 the FBI Laboratory began to offer them for law enforcement purposes.[24] Since then the agency has received thousands of submissions of evidence from federal, state, and local law enforcement agencies.

> DNA results are obtained in about seventy-five percent of cases studied. DNA testing eliminates the suspect in about one-third of these cases. . . . The FBI has testified in over 360 cases in 47 states . . . and there . . . are numerous criminal cases in which the defendant pleads guilty in the face of compelling DNA evidence.[25]

To push the potential of DNA even further and use it to generate investigative leads, the FBI Laboratory's Combined DNA Index System (CODIS) blends forensic science and computer technology to create an effective tool for solving violent crimes. CODIS enables federal, state, and local crime labs to exchange and compare DNA profiles electronically, thereby linking crimes to each other and to convicted offenders. All DNA profiles originate at the local level, then flow to state and national levels.[26]

Ever since the first United States case solved by searching convicted offender DNA records—a 1991 Minnesota rape-homicide, CODIS has solved "otherwise unsolvable violent crimes" with increasing frequency.[27]

In 1993, crime laboratories in the United States had collected 142,000 samples and analyzed more than 7,000. By 2003, however, almost 1.5 million profiles were stored in the national CODIS database. Moreover, all 50 states passed legislation requiring convicted offenders to provide samples for DNA databases.[28] In the United States thus far, DNA samples are for the most part analyzed in cases involving sexual assault and homicide, whereas in the UK, evidence obtained in burglary cases is also analyzed. Even in the 1990s, the British were getting between 300 and 500 "hits" weekly, largely for burglary. These include crime-scene-to-crime-scene hits (in CODIS, the Forensic Index), but also convicted-offender-to-crime-scene matches (in CODIS, the Convicted Offender Index).[29]

DNA Results—Evidence and Proof

The probe patterns obtained from crime scene biological evidence and those from the suspect's known biological sample must match if an identity is to be established (Steps 5A and 7 in Figure 2.21). When there are no matching patterns, the suspect clearly is not the source of the crime scene evidence.

Proponents of the Jeffreys method use the term *DNA fingerprinting* to describe the results obtained through MLP testing. To approach the same certainty, the SLP procedure must employ several single-locus probes. Just the same, there are those in the forensic science community who share the belief that, as yet, DNA profiling offers a promise rather than a realization of the individualization of some biological evidence.

In 1988 the FBI undertook an ambitious research program to perfect the method used in its laboratory, and to establish its scientific validity and reliability.[30] It is important to recognize that DNA test patterns depend on the restriction enzyme(s) and probe(s) employed. Different enzyme/probe combinations will produce different DNA patterns. Standardization of DNA technology, therefore, is important when the results are to be used as evidence in a court of law. The ultimate goal of the FBI is to ensure that DNA-based evidence withstands the inevitable legal challenges.

Another aspect of the need and importance of standardization for DNA testing methods relates to the desirability of creating a DNA file (or database) comparable to that of a fingerprint file. DNA technology was in its infancy in the late 1980s, and it is probably premature to start compiling such a database on a wide scale. But, as a means of tying together apparently unrelated rapes or homicides—establishing that they are the work of one person (a serial murderer, for example)—DNA has an important immediate contribution to make.

Those who use the term "fingerprinting" to imply certitude regarding DNA profiling inevitably invite comparison. Identical twins yield identical DNA profiles that cannot be distinguished from one another; however, with their real fingerprints, there is no problem. In addition to theoretical (*a priori*) reasons for believing fingerprints are unique, there is considerable empirical (*a posteriori*) evidence to confirm the absolute nature of fingerprint identification. Except for identical twins, there is good theoretical reason to support individualization by DNA testing. However, until the necessary database and file are fully constructed and tested, it is premature to rank DNA profiling with the certainty of an identity established by matching a latent print with a known print.

New forensic examination methods have given rise to a similar set of concerns among those interested in evidence and proof. Yale H. Caplan, co-editor of *Academic News*, in a column on professional issues in forensic science, wrote:

> With the use of a new technology, the interpretation of the results becomes critical. Serious consequences may result if the expert overinterprets or overextends the technology. This occurred in the application of neutron activation analysis (NAA) to hair examinations; result, NAA is no longer utilized for this purpose. . . . It is incredibly powerful to be able to state in a courtroom that a bloodstain came from a particular person to the exclusion of everyone else in the world. It is hoped that such statements can be backed up by a valid statistical base and that such studies have been verified by peer review.[31]

Caplan further stated:

> In this early stage in the application of DNA probe technology to forensic cases, it is vital that the laboratories conducting such tests employ stringent quality control in their procedures. The experts testifying should be conservative in their use of statistics. The greater concern is the manner in which this technology will be transferred from the few highly specialized laboratories performing this test today to crime laboratories throughout the country. This will require extensive training and must include stringent quality control, certification and proficiency testing.[32]

Early in 1989, the FBI's capabilities had developed to the point at which it was ready to accept evidence for analysis of its DNA content:

> The FBI Laboratory is now prepared to accept physical evidence for deoxyribonucleic acid (DNA) testing. Because the FBI Laboratory is presently the only police crime laboratory in the United States with this capability, a significant increase in case submission is anticipated. . . . [Therefore] a selective case acceptance policy has been established to handle these requests effectively. In general, this policy states that the FBI Laboratory will accept evidence for DNA analysis from current, violent personal crimes where appropriate standards for comparison are available. Specifically, DNA analysis on state and

local cases will be limited to homicide, sexual assault, and serious aggravated assault cases in which a suspect has been identified. In certain cases, evidence will be accepted . . . even though a suspect has not been identified. These exceptions include serial homicide/rape cases and sexual assaults on young children. A known blood sample from the victim and suspect is required for comparison purposes.[33]

Documents

The examination of the handwriting, printing, or typewriting on a document (in addition to the paper itself) affords opportunities to develop useful information.

Handwriting and Hand-Printing Examinations

Questions that should be asked include:

1. Did the suspect write, print, or sign the document? This question arises with kidnap ransom notes, anonymous letters, and signatures that are questioned.

2. Is the document genuine? This question arises with receipts and bills, suicide notes, letters, diaries, and wills suspected of being forgeries.

3. Are there any additions or deletions? If so, were they made at the time of original preparation or at a different time? These questions arise in forgery cases.

4. Was the document written or printed by one or more than one person? This is usually a civil rather than a criminal matter.

Typewriting Examinations

The availability of typewriters makes their use very likely when a document is employed in the commission of a crime. Kidnap and ransom notes, threatening letters, forged documents, and bank robber notes give rise to the following questions:

1. Can the make and perhaps the model of the typewriter be identified? This information limits the inquiry to those who have such an instrument available.

2. Can it be shown that a specific machine typed the questioned document? If so, associative evidence has been developed.

3. Were any additions or changes made by a typewriter other than the one used to type the original document? This question is more often raised in civil matters.

4. Was the typewriter manufactured after the ascribed date of the document? Again, this usually (but not exclusively) involves a civil rather than a criminal matter.

Paper and Other Examinations

Investigators are often familiar with the potential value of handwriting and typewriting evidence, yet they frequently fail to ask if other information could be developed by further examination of the document—in particular, the paper itself. They should ask:

1. Can a sheet of paper, which was directly beneath another at the time of the writing, be used to restore the original writing, if the top sheet was not recovered? In one case, a patrol officer stopped a vehicle, but before approaching the driver, wrote the license number on his paper pad. The driver shot and killed the officer as he approached, then went to the patrol car and tore off the incriminating top page. The pad was brought to the laboratory, where the indented writing was made visible and photographed by means of sidewise (oblique) illumination, which provided the needed contrast. With the license number known, the killer's apprehension resulted.

2. Can writing that has been obliterated by covering it with scratch marks be restored? In a conspiracy case, the obliterated name of a hotel, the telephone and room numbers, and alias of its occupant were revealed by means of infrared photography. A red ink pen had been used to scratch out the writing.

3. Can a mechanical or chemical erasure be restored? These and other alterations are found on affidavits, ballots, checks, and receipts.

4. Was one piece of paper torn from another? A jigsaw-puzzle-like reassembly of the evidence answers this question.

5. What company manufactured the paper? When was it manufactured? Such information is often involved with civil matters, but sometimes it bears on the crime of forgery.

Glass

Window glass broken during the commission of a crime retains details in its cracks that permit the event to be reconstructed. For example, it might be important to determine whether the glass was broken from the outside or inside. Determining whether a bullet (or other breaking force) came from the outside or the inside of a dwelling can be crucial; sometimes it can reverse the direction of an investigation. For example, a visiting child was shot dead while seated at a table having lunch. An aunt, an uncle, and two nephews were in the apartment at the time; all said a sniper's bullet had been the cause of death. Examination of the window, however, disclosed that the breaking force had come from the inside (see Figure 2.22). Then, by separating and reinterrogating the witnesses, the actual events were revealed: toying with an unfamiliar gun, the aunt had accidentally killed the child; to account for the tragedy to the mother, the uncle broke the window from the inside with a ball-peen hammer and concocted the sniper story.

A.

C.

B.

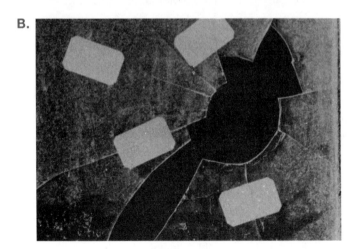

Figure 2.22
A. Sash of broken window removed from its frame. B. Same window, but the piece in the 7 o'clock position has been removed for an examination of its radial and spiral cracks. C. A photomacrograph of a radial edge of B, depicting its rib marks. See Figures 2.26 and 2.27 to determine direction of force. *(From* The Crime Laboratory, *2nd ed. Courtesy, Clark Boardman Co., Ltd. and the New York City Police Department.)*

Direction of Break

The details needed by a detective (or criminalist) to determine where the breaking force was applied to a pane of glass are developed as follows:

1. To obtain the required details, a piece of the broken window is used.

2. The inside and outside surfaces of the piece must be identified. If a piece of the broken pane can be removed from the window, the respective sides should be carefully marked with gummed labels. The outside surface of a window is generally dirtier and streaked by rain, and often has paint or putty serving as a tell-tale sign indicating that it was on the outside.

3. One edge of a crack in the broken piece of glass must be examined for its rib marks (see Figure 2.22C). It is customary to examine the edge of a radial crack, but the edge of a spiral crack will serve equally well, as long as the examiner is certain which edge—radial or spiral—is being studied. This visual examination involves scrutinizing the edge for the rib mark pattern. There are two types: in one pattern, the rib marks run perpendicular to the right side of the glass; in the other, they run to the left side (see Figure 2.23).

Should the rib mark pattern be difficult to see, the illumination may need to be subdued. This can be done simply by turning one's back to the light, or by viewing the edge beneath a table and gently turning or rocking the glass until the light reveals the rib mark pattern. Figure 2.24 is a worksheet that facilitates the recording of the observation and provides other details necessary to arrive at a conclusion. The interpretation of the recorded details is illustrated in Figure 2.25.

Which Bullet Hole Was Made First?

When two bullets are fired through opposite sides of a window, the crucial question can be: which bullet hole was made first? A reconstruction can resolve which person fired first so a claim of self-defense can be checked.

The determination is very simply made. In Figure 2.26, it is possible to determine that the bullet on the right was fired last because its cracks were stopped by the cracks made by the bullet on the left. Crack lines represent the transmission and dissipation of energy. Energy can be transmitted through a solid, but upon reaching a break, cannot go beyond it. Thus, the bullet hole cracks on the left were not stopped by those of the right, because the right cracks were not there when the left cracks were made.

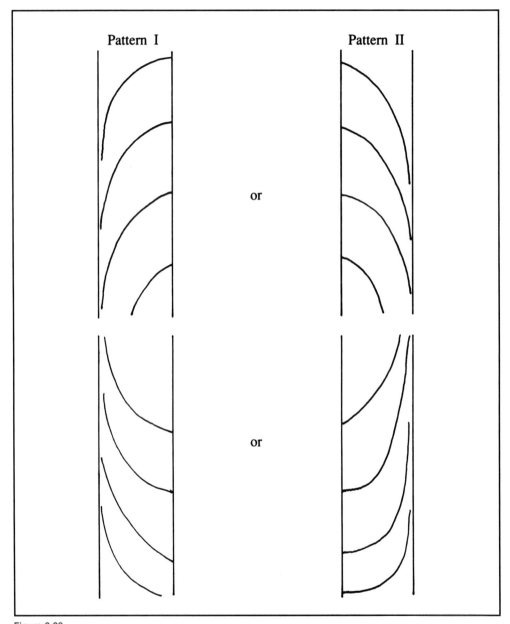

Figure 2.23
Types of rib mark patterns that may be seen on the edge of a glass crack. *(Drawing by Jerzy J. Hoga, graphic designer.)*

**STEPWISE
DIRECTIONS**

1. Indicate type of edge: Radial ☐   or Spiral ☐

2. Indicate outside and inside surfaces by labeling each side:

   Outside surface is labeled: ....
   Inside surface is labeled: ....

3. Draw in the space below the type of pattern observed when the edge of the glass crack is examined in subdued light:

   SIDE A   **SIDE B**

3. See Figure 2.25 for interpretation of these data.

Figure 2.24
Worksheet for the examination of a glass crack: gathering the data necessary to determine the direction of the breaking force. *(Drawing by Jerzy J. Hoga, graphic designer.)*

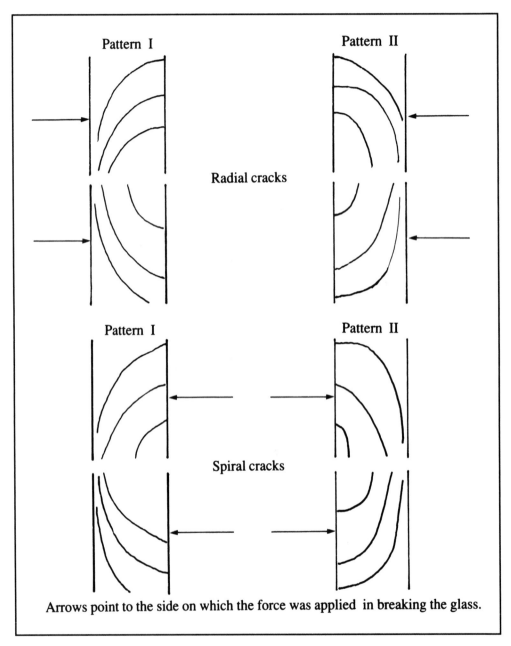

Arrows point to the side on which the force was applied in breaking the glass.

Figure 2.25
Interpretation of rib mark patterns. *(Drawing by Jerzy J. Hoga, graphic designer.)*

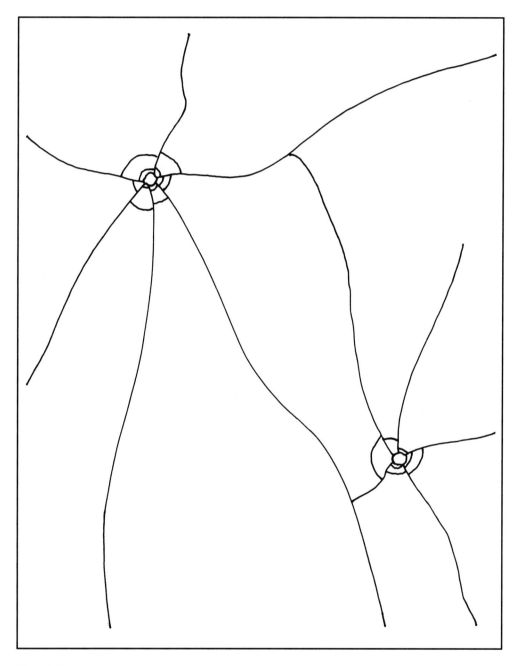

Figure 2.26
Two bullet holes in a window made at different times. Hole in lower right was made after that of upper left. *(Drawing by Jerzy J. Hoga, graphic designer.)*

The Jon Benet Ramsey Case

Jon Benet Ramsey was a six-year-old beauty pageant queen who was first reported kidnapped by her parents but, several hours later, was found dead by her father in a remote basement room of their house. The Jon Benet Ramsey case was extensively covered by the media (especially television), using film footage of the pageants Jon Benet had entered and usually won. "During 1997, seventy-four worldwide news agencies came to Denver to cover the Oklahoma City bombing trials of Timothy McVeigh and Terry Nichols. One hundred sixty such organizations have requested credentials to travel to Boulder should the Jon Benet case ever reach the courtroom.[34]

The police and much of the public believed Jon Benet's parents, John Ramsey and Patsy Ramsey, were involved in the death of their child. The Ramseys never appeared before the grand jury, which was desired by the police, because the district attorney thought they did not have probable cause. The Ramseys' claim in their book *The Death of Innocence* that they "offered to testify before the Grand Jury, but they were never subpoenaed."[35] The following discussion suggests how probable cause could (or perhaps not) be established through an examination of the basement broken window by disproving Ramsey's volunteered statement.

John Ramsey and his friend Fleet White were sent by the police officer left in charge to search again throughout the house for Jon Benet. Ramsey recounted: "We head down stairs, and I take Fleet over to the broken window pane and explain my breaking in their last summer. We look for glass splinters and find some small ones." Does it not appear strange that this wealthy man would not have the broken pane replaced? Remember this is now December and cold air is seeping into his basement. Why was it important for Ramsey to point out to Fleet that the window was broken in the summer from the outside? Perhaps because it was recently broken from the inside? Why Ramsey would break the window from the inside is of legitimate interest to investigators. Elsewhere in this text is a discussion of the difficulty an inexperienced person has in staging a crime (see Chapter 4). If the Ramseys are guilty, this is a possibility. Alternatively, they may have changed their minds about how to misdirect the investigation by suggesting with the ransom note that the child was kidnapped. If the broken pane of glass or window was removed and retained by the police, it still may be possible to determine if it was broken from the outside. The authors have not been able to become informed whether the window was ever so examined. If broken from the outside, the Ramseys are less suspect; however, if broken from the inside, they are more so and could be subjected to a grand jury inquiry.

As noted in the section on "Cover-Up Attempts" in Chapter 14, sometimes a killer makes an effort to disguise a crime. Several means can be employed to make a death appear accidental or explainable, to misdirect the efforts of investigators, or to conceal the perpetrator's own involvement. This possibility is further supported by the anomalous kidnap note in the Ramsey case. Among other unusual things was its length (about 400 words), compared to an average length of about 40 words (as in the first Lindbergh ransom note). Investigators might have considered this an example of overstaging.

Trace Evidence

It is a common belief that an offender's whereabouts can be tracked through trace evidence. Although this is usually not the case, such evidence can be of help to the investigator in other ways (see the Coors homicide case at the end of this chapter). *Trace evidence* is a criminalistics term; it describes physical evidence so small (in size or forensic details) that an examination usually requires either a stereomicroscope, a polarized light microscope, or both. It is not practical to list every conceivable trace material to be found at a crime scene. Based on routine case work experience, however, Nicholas Petraco has categorized the most commonly encountered types as either fibrous substances or particulate matter.[36] Fibrous substances include: hair (human or animal); plant fibers (sisal in cordage or rope, linen, and cotton); mineral fibers (asbestos, glass wool); and synthetic fibers (nylon, rayon, and Dacron in fabrics and carpeting). Particulate matter includes: building material, safe insulation, paint chips, metal filings or shavings, soil, seeds, pollen, wood chips (or splinters or sawdust), and cosmetics—to name some of the more obvious kinds. Because trace evidence can be minuscule, it is located and collected by means of: (1) a vacuum cleaner, (2) adhesive tape, or (3) by shaking it loose over a large, clean, white sheet of paper (see Chapter 3).

Petraco notes that human hair and other fiber evidence are frequently encountered at the scenes of violent crimes such as homicide and robbery; particulate matter is often available in burglary cases; and human hair is discovered in just under 75 percent of those cases in which trace evidence was present.[37] More significant is the "regularity with which the various forms of trace evidence occur, rather than the fact that one form occurs more or less frequently than another."[38] The most common source of trace evidence is the crime scene, then the victim's home or business, followed by the victim's body and the clothing of the suspect and victim. The least productive source is "things"—vehicles, hats, furniture, and bludgeons (such as baseball bats or pipes).[39] Petraco finds disturbing

> . . . the low percent occurrence of fibers and particulate matter for the category of rape and sex crimes. One possible explanation for this unexpected finding might be the prevalent use of commercially available rape kits for collecting evidence in these cases. The prepared kits usually concentrate on the collection of physiological fluids and hair specimens, while giving little attention to the collection of fibers and particulate matter."[40]

In a later paper, Petraco states that trace evidence can be used to:

1. Reconstruct the event.

2. Associate people, places, and things involved with the event.

3. Surmise (with some accuracy) the occupations of the principals in the case.

4. Describe the environment or location involved in the event. Then, armed with such information, use it to establish *probable cause* for a warrant to search a home, vehicle, garage or other area specified on the basis of the trace evidence found.[41]

Petraco makes a shrewd observation: "All this is achieved without the aid of an eyewitness. It is a powerful source of information indeed, and one that is barely utilized in our criminal justice system."[42]

THE ADOLPH COORS HOMICIDE

The utility of trace evidence for the criminal investigator is illustrated by the Adolph Coors homicide, a case of murder and attempted kidnapping.[43] The perpetrator had come to Denver with the fixed purpose of making himself rich quick. To accomplish this he gave careful thought and much time to devising a plan. After studying the (illegal) money-making potential of the Denver area, he decided that what he had in mind could be obtained by abducting the wealthy head of the Coors Brewing Company.

The victim now under his scrutiny had moved with his family from a well-populated suburb to a ranch in the foothills of the front range, just west of Denver. The site made the kidnapper's strategy clear: he would pose as a hunter, carry a rifle, and park where he could check on the movements of Coors and his family. This plan succeeded so well that after a time the family became accustomed to seeing the yellow car; indeed, they took the stranger for a poacher, scouting out deer. The perpetrator then calculated that his best opportunity would come when the victim made his customary morning run across the one-lane bridge over the creek. On the day of the crime, Coors arrived punctually at 8:00 A.M. to find a yellow car directly in his path.

Absent any eyewitness, the encounter can only be partially reconstructed from what physical evidence was to be found at the scene: the hats of both men on the edge of the creek, and Coors's eyeglasses (with one lens broken) in the stream. Blood was present on the bridge's railing and on its road surface, and there were tire marks dug into the dirt just off the bridge. Seven months later, at and around a dump site, the murder victim's clothing and other belongings were found, including his windbreaker with bullet holes in its back.

When neighbors were questioned, those living several hundred yards away reported having heard shouting, then gunfire. A more distant neighbor also heard gunfire. A miner prospecting the area had observed on several occasions a yellow Mercury with license plates that began with "AT" and included a "62." Registration records did not require a car's color to be listed; therefore, every Mercury in the Denver area had to be located. The tedious search finally accounted for all of them but one. The missing vehicle was traced to place of purchase, its owner's name, address, and driver's license number were obtained, and its yellow color confirmed.

The follow-up investigation traced the car owner's place of employment, but having anticipated this, the owner had destroyed all files on himself. Coworkers, however, had useful information: he had once worked for an ice company in Los Angeles. There he joined a union that required the name of a beneficiary. The name of Joseph Corbett Sr. had been provided along with a Seattle address. Meanwhile, the FBI had identified a fingerprint found on his Colorado driver's license application as that of a fugitive: Joseph Corbett Jr.

About eight days after the crime in an Atlantic City (NJ) dump, a yellow Mercury had been torched. Shortly thereafter, an FBI agent in New Jersey learned that a yellow Mercury was being sought in connection with the Coors case. Remembering the description of the car burned in the dump, he checked it out. Its motor number matched that of the Colorado Mercury. In order to trace the car's movements from Colorado to New Jersey, the forensic geology section of the FBI Laboratory examined the road debris collected underneath its fenders. During its travels, four distinct types of soil were deposited on the car. To determine if these soils had come from Colorado or New Jersey, numerous soil samples had to be gathered. The outer or topmost layer came from the Atlantic City area; the innermost layer was compatible with the mineral content of the Rocky Mountain Front Face. The second layer was from the Coors ranch (thereby placing the vehicle close to the crime scene); the third layer was consistent with soil where Coors's body was found. Because the Mercury had been driven over unpaved dirt roads and their soils were rich in minerals, these conclusions were possible. They permitted a reconstruction of the criminal's itinerary and helped establish the localities associated with the crime and its perpetrator.

Back in Colorado, meanwhile, investigators checking for traffic violations, found that a traffic ticket was issued to the driver of the Mercury for crossing a yellow line and passing a truck near the crest of a hill just a few miles away from the crime scene. The offender had paid the fine with a National Check Cashing Company money order. A search of more than 400,000 money orders led to the discovery that he had purchased several sets of handcuffs, as well as one set of leg irons. In addition, one of the hats found at the scene led investigators to a department store clerk who (when shown five different photographs) identified Corbett as the purchaser. After trial, and without any confession, Corbett was found guilty and sentenced to life imprisonment.

Although forensic geology helped in the solution of the Coors case, dirt splashed on a vehicle while it is being driven about, or is stuck in mud, is not always useful. This fact is made plain by the vexing situation that confronted detectives in the John Wayne Gacy case:

> We were stalled. The surveillance team still hadn't connected with Gacy, and in these crucial hours he was unobserved, free to do whatever he needed to do to cover up his tracks. . . .
>
> Two questions about Gacy still nagged at us. Why were Gacy and his car covered with mud? Why was he more than four hours late in reporting to the police station early Wednesday morning? We now suspected that if he had killed Rob Priest, he had disposed of the body before coming to the station—that would account for the mud. *But where was it from?*
>
> Knautz (one of the detectives) called the soil chemistry testing laboratory at the University of Illinois. They could test samples from Gacy's car, they told him, but only for such things as farmers want to know—soil structure, acidity, and nutrient content. There was no way they could tell where the mud came from.[45]

Unfortunately, the clay soil of the Chicago area of Illinois is not as rich and diverse in mineral content as is that of the Rocky Mountain region.

CONCLUSION

Of the common clue materials, fingerprints, firearms evidence, and blood are encountered far more often than documents, glass, or biological material (including semen). Trace evidence is present at many crime scenes, but is frequently overlooked despite its considerable potential. In varying degrees, therefore, each clue material can serve to link an offender to the crime scene or victim. If an investigator is to recognize, collect, and preserve such evidence, there must be an appreciation of the needs of—and the means used by—the forensic laboratory to make that linkage.

REFERENCES

1   P.E. Kirk, "The Ontogeny of Criminalistics," *Journal of Criminal Law, Criminology, and Police Science* 54 (1963), 236.

2   *The Sacco-Vanzetti Case: Transcript of the Record of the Trial of Nicola Sacco and Bartolomeo Vanzetti in the Courts of Massachusetts and Subsequent Proceedings*, 1920-1927, vol. I (New York: Henry Holt & Co., 1929), 896.

3   Ibid., vol. III, 4322.

4   Joseph M. Rynearson and Wm. J. Chisum, *Evidence and Crime Scene Reconstruction*. 3rd ed. (Redding, CA: National Crime Investigation and Training, 1993).

5   Henry C. Lee, *Crime Scene Investigation* (Taoyuan, Taiwan (Republic of China): Central Police Agency, 1994), Chapter 10.

6   B. Parker and J.L. Peterson, "Physical Evidence Utilization in the Administration of Criminal Justice," (Washington, DC: U.S. Department of Justice, 1972).

7   *Chicago Tribune*, 1 May 1999, 26.

8   Steven Emerson and Brian Duffy, *The Fall of Pan Am 103: Inside the Lockerbie Investigation* (New York: G.P. Putnam's Sons, 1990).

9   Matthew Cox and Tom Foster, *Their Darkest Day: The Tragedy of Pan Am 103 and Its Legacy of Hope* (New York: Grove Weidenfeld, 1992).

10   Alfred A. Lewis with Herbert L. MacDonell, *The Evidence Never Lies* (New York: Holt, Rinehart and Winston, 1984), Chapter 1.

11   *The Queen v. M'Naghten*, 8 Eng. Rep. 718, 10 Cl. & Fin. 200 (1843).

12   *Commonwealth v. Rogers*, 7 Metc. 500 (1844).

13   Homicide Act, 5 & 6 Eliz. II C. II. Sec.2 (1957).

14   American Law Institute. Model Penal Code. Section 401(1) 1962.

15   James W. Osterburg, *The Crime Laboratory: Case Studies of Scientific Criminal Investigation*, 2nd ed. (New York: Clark Boardman, 1982).

16   Frank Smyth and Myles Ludwig, *The Detectives: Crime and Detection in Fact and Fiction* (Philadelphia: J.B. Lippincott, 1978), 25-6.

17   Paul D. McCann, "Report of the Standardization Committee of the International Association for Identification," *Identification News* 23:8 (August 1973), 13-14.

18   Lois Pilant, "Exploiting Fingerprint Technology," *The Police Chief, 61*(2), 29-35 (Feb. 1994), 31.

19 *Guidelines for the Developed Automated Fingerprint Identification (AFIS).* *<http://www.interpol. int/Public/Forensic/fingerprints/WorkingParties/IAEG/afis.asp>*

20 P.D. Barnett and R.A. Berger, "The Effects of Temperature and Humidity on the Permanency of Latent Fingerprints," *Journal of Forensic Science Society,* 16 (1977), 249.

21 James F. Cowger, *Friction Ridge Skin: Comparison and Identification of Fingerprints* (New York: Elsevier, 1983).

22 H.L. MacDonell, *Bloodstain Pattern Interpretation* (Corning, NY: Laboratory of Foresnic Science, 1982).

23 *State v. Hall,* 28 Cr. Lo. 2106 (Iowa 1980).

24 John R. Brown, "DNA Analysis: A Significant Tool for Law Enforcement," *The Police Chief, 61*(3), 51-52 (Mar. 1994), 51.

25 Ibid.

26 *<http://www.fbi.gov/hq/lab/codis/program.htm>*

27 John W. Hicks, "DNA Profiling: A Tool for Law Enforcement," *FBI Law Enforcement Bulletin* 57:8 (Aug. 1988), 3.

28 4th Annual CODIS User Group Meeting, Nov. 1998, Arlington, VA; *<http://www.fbi.gov/hq/lab/codis/ clickmap.htm>*

29 Barry Scheck, "Getting Smart About DNA," *Newsweek*, Nov. 16, 1998, 69.

30 Hicks, *loc. cit.*, 3.

31 Yale H. Caplan, "Current Issues in Forensic Science: DNA Probe Technology in Foresnic Serology: Statistics, Quality Control and Interpretation," [American Academy of Forensic Science] *Academy News* 18:6 (Nov. 1988), 1.

32 Ibid., 11.

33 Anon., "Focus on Forensics: FBI Announces New DNA Policy," *FBI Law Enforcement Bulletin,* 59:3 (Mar. 1989), 23.

34 Stephen Singular, *Presumed Guilty* (Beverly Hills, CA: New Millenium Press, 1999), 170.

35 John and Patsy Ramsey, *The Death of Innocence* (Nashville, TN: Thomas Nelson, 2000), 394.

36 N. Petraco, "The Occurrence of Trace Evidence in One Examiner's Casework," *Journal of Forensic Sciences,* 30:2 (1985), 486.

37 Ibid., 487-490.

38 Ibid., 487-488.

39 Ibid., 492 (Table 7).

40 Ibid., 487.

41 N. Petraco, "Trace Evidence—The Invisible Witness," *Journal of Forensic Sciences,* 31:1 (1986), 321, 327.

42 N. Petraco, *loc. cit.* (1985), 493.

43 John McPhee, "The Gravel Page," *The New Yorker*, XLXXI (46), 44-52 (Jan. 29, 1996).

44 Terry Sullivan with Peter T. Maiken, *Killer Clown: The John Wayne Gacy Murders* (New York: Gossett & Dunlop, 1983), 4.

Supplemental Readings _____

Criminal Evidence

Klotter, John C. *Criminal Evidence*, 7th ed. Cincinnati: Anderson, 2000.

Criminalistics

Bodziak, W.J. *Footwear Impression Evidence*. Boca Raton, FL: CRC Press, 1992.

Cowger, James F. *Friction Ridge Skin: Comparison and Identification of Fingerprints*. Boca Raton, FL: CRC Press, 1992.

DeForest, Peter R., R.E. Gaensslen, and Henry C. Lee. *Forensic Science: An Introduction to Criminalistics*. 2nd ed. New York: McGraw-Hill, 1995.

Eckert, William G., and James H. Stuart. *Interpretation of Blood Stain Evidence at Crime Scenes*. Boca Raton, FL: CRC Press, 1992.

Fisher, Barry A.J. *Techniques of Crime Scene Investigation*. 6th ed. Boca Raton, FL: CRC Press, 1999.

Kirk, Paul L., and John I. Thornton. *Crime Investigation*. 2nd ed. Reprint. New York: Wiley & Sons, 1974; Melbourne, FL: Krieger, 1985.

Lambourne, Gerald. "Glove Print Identification," *J. For. Ident., 38*(1), 7-24 (1988).

Lee, Henry C. *Crime Scene Investigation*. Taoyuan, Taiwan (Republic of China): Central Police University Press, 1994. Chapter 10.

Lee, Henry C., and Robert F. Gaensslen, eds. *Advances in Fingerprint Technology*. Boca Raton, FL: CRC Press, 1994.

McDonald, P. *Tire Print Identification: Practical Aspects of Criminal Forensic Investigation*. Boca Raton, FL: CRC Press, 1992.

Miller, L.S., and A.M. Brown. *Criminal Evidence Laboratory Manual: An Introduction to the Crime Laboratory*. 2nd ed. Cincinnati: Anderson, 1990.

Osterburg, James W. *The Crime Laboratory: Case Studies of Scientific Investigation*. 2nd ed. New York: Clark Boardman, 1982.

Palenik, S. "Microscopic Trace Evidence: The Overlooked Clue," *The Microscope* 30, Part I (1982), 93-100; Part II (1982), 163-169; Part III (1982), 163-169; 31 Part IV (1983), 1-14.

Rynearson, Joseph M., and W.J. Chisum. *Evidence and Crime Scene Reconstruction*, 3rd ed. Reading, CA: National Crime Investigation and Training (P.O. Box 492005), 1993.

Safferstein, Richard. *Criminalistics: An Introduction to Forensic Science*. 5th ed. Englewood Cliffs, NJ: Prentice Hall, 1995.

Forensic Psychiatry

Brussel, James A. *Casebook of a Crime Psychiatrist*. New York: Bernard Geis Associates, 1968; distributed by Grove Press.

Forensic Medicine

Adelson, Lester. *The Pathology of Homicide*. Springfield, IL: Charles C Thomas, 1974.

DiMaio, D.J., and V.J.M. DiMaio. *Forensic Pathology*. Boca Raton, FL: CRC Press, 1992.

Spitz, Werner. *Spitz and Fischer's Medicolegal Investigation of Death: Guidelines for the Application of Pathology to Crime Investigation*. 3rd ed. Springfield, IL: Charles C Thomas, 1993.

Forensic Dentistry (Odontology)

Cottone, James A., and S. Miles Standish, eds. *Outline of Forensic Dentistry*. Chicago: Year Book Med., 1982.

Rogers, Spencer, L. *The Testimony of Teeth: Forensic Aspects of Human Dentition*. Springfield, IL: Charles C Thomas, 1988.

Sopher, Irvin M. *Forensic Dentistry*. Springfield, IL: Charles C Thomas, 1976.

Stimson, Paul G., and Curtis A. Mertz. *Forensic Dentistry*. Boca Raton, FL: CRC Press, 1997.

Forensic Science

Eckert, William G. *Introduction to Forensic Sciences*. 2nd ed. Boca Raton, FL: CRC Press, 1995.

DNA Profiling

Dabbs, D., and P.D. Cornwell. "The Use of DNA Profiling in Linking Serial Murders," *Medico-Legal Bulletin* 37:6 (Nov.-Dec. 1988), 2-10.

Esteal, Simon, Neal McLeod, and Ken Reed. *DNA Profiling: Principles, Pitfalls, and Potential*. New York: Harwood Academic Publishers, 1992.

Farkas, Daniel H. *DNA Simplified II: The Illustrated Hitchhiker's Guide to DNA*. Washington, DC: AACC Press, 1999.

Farley, Mark A., and James J. Harrington. *Forensic DNA Technology*. Boca Raton, FL: CRC Press, 1991.

Ford, S., and W.C. Thompson. "A Question of Identity: Some Reasonable Doubts About DNA Fingerprints," *The Sciences* 30:1 (1990), 37-43.

Gill, P., A.J. Jeffreys, and D.J. Werrett. "Forensic Applications of DNA Fingerprints," *Nature* 318 (1985), 577-579.

Inman, Paul G., and Curtis A. Mertz. *Forensic Dentistry*. Boca Raton, FL: CRC Press, 1997.

Jeffreys, A.J., V. Wilson, and S.L. Thein. "Individual-Specific 'Fingerprints' of Human DNA," *Nature* 316 (1985), 76-79.

Kelly, K.F., J.J. Rankin, and R.C. Wink. "Method and Applications of DNA Fingerprinting: A Guide for the Non-Scientist," *Criminal Law Review* (Feb. 1987), 105-110.

Kirby, L.T. *DNA Fingerprinting: An Introduction*. New York: Stockton Press, 1990.

Levy, Harlpin. *And the Blood Cried Out*. New York: Basic Books, 1996.

Lomax, I.S. "DNA Fingerprints—A Revolution In Forensic Science," *Law Society's Gazette* (April 23, 1986), 1213-1214.

Maidment, S. "DNA Fingerprinting," *New Law Journal* 326 (April 11, 1986).

Mones, Paul. *Stalking Justice: The Dramatic Story of the Detective Who First Used Testing to Catch a Serial Killer.* New York: Pocket Books, 1995.

Neufeld, P.J., and N. Colman. "When Science Takes the Witness Stand," *Scientific American* 262:5 (May 1990), 46-53.

Sylvester, John T., and John H. Stafford. "Judicial Acceptance of DNA Profiling," *FBI Law Enforcement Bulletin* 60:7 (July 1991), 26-32.

Werrett, D.J. "DNA Fingerprinting," *International Criminal Policy Review* (Sept.-Oct. 21-25, 1987).

Document Examinations

Ellen, David. *The Scientific Examination of Documents: Methods and Techniques.* New York: Wiley & Sons, 1989.

Harrison, Wilson R. *Suspect Documents: Their Scientific Examination.* Chicago: Nelson-Hall, 1981.

Hilton, Ordway. *Scientific Examination of Questioned Documents.* Rev. ed. Boca Raton, FL: CRC Press, 1992.

Huber, Roy A., and Alfred M. Headrick. *Handwriting Identification: Facts and Fundamentals.* Boca Raton, FL: CRC Press, 1999.

Soil Evidence Examinations

Murray, Raymond C., and John C.F. Tedrow. *Forensic Geology: Earth Sciences and Criminal Investigation.* New Brunswick, NJ: Rutgers University Press, 1975.

Police Photography

Miller, Larry S. *Police Photography.* 4th ed. Cincinnati: Anderson, 1998.

Redsicker, David R. *The Practical Methodology of Forensic Photography.* Boca Raton, FL: CRC Press, 1992.

Ethical Issues in Forensic Science

Lucas, D.M. "The Ethical Responsibilities of the Forensic Scientist: Exploring the Limits," *Journal of Forensic Science* 34:3 (1989), 719-729.

Peterson, J.L. "Ethical Issues in the Collection, Examination and Use of Physical Evidence," in *Forensic Science*, 2nd ed., G. Davies, ed. Washington, DC: American Chemical Society, 1986.

Schroeder, O.C. "Ethical and Moral Dilemmas Confronting Forensic Scientists, *Journal of Forensic Science* 29:4 (1984), 966-986.

CHAPTER 3

Physical Evidence

Discovery, Preservation, Collection, Transmission

DEFINING THE LIMITS OF THE CRIME SCENE

The crime scene encompasses all areas over which the actors—victim, criminal, and eyewitness—move during the commission of a crime. Usually it is one, readily defined area of limited size, but sometimes it comprises several sites. A case example of the latter is to be found in the abduction of a bank manager as he left for work one morning. The car that conveyed him to the bank, the vault and other areas in the bank, the vicinity of the place in the woods where he was found tied to a tree—each site is a part of the crime scene. Another example is a homicide in which the murder is committed in one place and the body is dumped or buried in another.

Although the precise boundary lines of a crime scene are most often well-defined, sometimes they can be in dispute. In the case of an attempted murder of a prominent black civil rights leader as he returned to his motel, the question was whether the shots came from one spot or from three different areas. Had a lone shooter lay hidden in the patch of weeds across the street from the motel? If so, it would support the local police view that the ambush was sexually motivated, a response to the victim's visit with a white woman, a local civil rights activist. On the other hand, the three separate matted areas found in the weeds the next day supported federal investigators' belief in a conspiracy—and the presence of three shooters would put the crime under federal as well as local jurisdiction. Disputing a conspiracy theory, the police asserted that the weeds were trampled by reporters converging on the scene and not by one restive shooter.

It is clear from the preceding cases that the crime scene must be conceptualized. Once its position and boundaries are defined, the scene must then be made secure, the physical evidence discovered and collected, and the crime reconstructed (if needed). Had the correct procedure been followed in the ambush investigation—boundaries defined and protected, and the area within them recorded—there would not have been a question of whether there were one or three sites or perpetrators. In this case, ensuring that the boundaries were "properly protected" would have meant cordoning it off until daylight, when the cursory search in the dark turned up little evidence. In all cases it means excluding reporters, government officials, even superior police officers who are not directly involved in the investigation; not to mention local residents and curiosity seekers. In any ambush investigation it is important to establish where the perpetrator was concealed and to record details of activity within that area. Afterward, it can be searched for other physical evidence, such as spent cartridges, food containers, or discarded cigarettes and matches. In this ambush, a thorough search conducted the next morning led to the discovery of a spent shell casing (from a 30.06 rifle) that had been overlooked.

Figure 3.1
Scene of the crash of Pan Am Flight 103 in Lockerbie, Scotland. Crucial fragmentary evidence was recognized and collected in an area about 25 miles away from Lockerbie. The Pan Am Flight 103 evidence scene is the largest crime scene ever (more than 800 square miles) that needed to be searched.

The in-flight bombing of Pan Am Flight 103 over Lockerbie, Scotland, gave new meaning to the concept of the limits of a crime scene. Fragments of physical evidence—plane parts, bomb bits, personal belongings, body parts—were scattered over 800 square miles of countryside (see Figure 3.1). The painstaking recovery of four million pieces of physical evidence attests to the diligence and thoroughness of the effort to solve the case.

THE CRIME SCENE AS AN EVIDENCE SOURCE

An offender brings physical evidence to the crime scene: in burglary cases, tools needed to break into the premises or a safe; in robbery or homicide cases, a weapon used to threaten, assault, or kill; in arson cases, a container of flammable fluid. During the commission of a crime, an offender may inadvertently leave evidence behind (*in situ*): fingerprints, tool marks, shoe prints, blood-spatter patterns, spent bullets, fired cartridge casings. Other physical evidence can by its very nature be unavoidably left behind: in kidnapping cases, the ransom note; in bank robbery cases, the note handed to the teller. For instance, it may be left on a record tape. In one homicide case, the suspect's name first emerged in a message left on the deceased's answering machine.[1] The caller asked that a meeting be set up at a specific time in the owner's home, and when the latter was found dead there and time of death was determined to be an hour or two after the proposed meeting, this crucial piece of information had to be followed up. In this instance, it was—with success.

When searching the crime scene (and afterward), an investigator's observations and interviews might develop intangible evidence. For example, the emotional factors involved in motivating and carrying out a homicide become manifest as intangible evidence through an assessment of such observations as: grossly excessive stab wounds, bones unnecessarily broken, parts of the body cut out or cut off, or the choice and kind of lethal weapon employed. A shrewd appraisal of intangible evidence (as in psychological profiling) can provide leads to possible perpetrators. Interviewing also can be used to develop intangible evidence. Witnesses or victims may report on the language used during the commission of the crime. How exactly did the robber convey intentions and demands? What did the rapist say, before, during, and after the assault? Because such commands and comments are elements of the perpetrator's *modus operandi*, they have investigative and probative value.

OPPORTUNITY FOR DISCOVERY

The crime scene provides the major opportunity to locate physical evidence. The initial response should be regarded as the only chance to recognize, record, and collect physical evidence. The investigator must make the most of it. This search, however, must be conducted properly and lawfully, or the evidence will be suppressed in the course of a trial. Police should not relinquish control over the scene and its environs until all evidence has been discovered and collected. If it must be gone over again later, legal difficulties may be created because pertinent evidence was not recognized or collected initially.

In 1984, the U.S. Supreme Court in *Michigan v. Clifford* reversed a decision based on evidence obtained by investigators who entered the scene of a suspected arson five hours after the blaze had been extinguished.[2] Another case, *Michigan v. Tyler*, also illustrates the need to collect evidence without unnecessary delay, otherwise a warrant must be obtained.[3] In the *Tyler* arson case there were three searches. The first was within one and a half hours after the fire; the second, four hours later (dense smoke having caused the delay); but the third was made three weeks later. Evidence from the first two was held admissible, but the evidence seized in the third attempt was not, because no emergency validated the warrantless search. Delayed or late attempts are legal if the permission of the owner or occupant of the premises is obtained, preferably in writing. Figure 3.2 is a consent form for this purpose.

In *Mincey v. Arizona*, involving the homicide of a narcotics officer, the identity of the offender (Mincey) was known from the outset.[4] Investigators took four days to search his apartment, and the evidence they discovered led to a conviction. On appeal, the Court noted that no occupant of the premises had summoned police and that the search continued for four days. It held, therefore, that no justification for the warrantless search existed under the Fourth Amendment. A few years later in *Thompson v. Louisiana* the Court invalidated a general exploratory search of the premises by homicide investigators 35 minutes after the police were called by a daughter to the scene of a homicide in which her father had been killed by her mother. The wife was convicted as the killer. She appealed to the U.S. Supreme Court on the grounds that a pistol and suicide note discovered by the investigators were obtained in violation of the Fourth Amendment and therefore must be suppressed. The Court held:

> . . . Although we agree that the scope of the intrusion was certainly greater in *Mincey* than here, nothing in *Mincey* turned on the length of time taken in the search or the date on which it was conducted. A 2-hour general search remains a significant intrusion of petitioner's privacy and therefore may only be conducted subject to the constraints—including the warrant requirement—of the Fourth Amendment.[5]

State of _____

County of _____

I, _____, hereby permit

(name of searcher) _____ of the

(name of agency or dept.) _____

to search my * _____

located at _____

described as ** _____

I authorize them to process, collect and take *any* relevant object including, *but not limited to,* latent fingerprints, hairs, fiber, blood, tracks, impressions, clothing, criminal instruments, contraband, and fruits of a crime.

I further authorize the making of photographs, videotapes, and sketches of the area being searched.

I understand that I have the right to refuse such consent.

I freely and voluntarily give this consent this _____ day of

_____, 19_____.

Witnessed

_____

         (name)   (date)

* Entire home; basement only, if one or more rooms, specify which; garage; locker; automobile or truck; and so on.

** Single family house; condominium, apartment number; a four-door sedan (make and model); mobile home; and so on.

Figure 3.2
Consent-to-search form.

An extended discussion of the need to comply with the search requirements of the Fourth Amendment can be found in an *FBI Law Enforcement Bulletin* article.[6] Its author, Special Agent Kimberly Crawford, points out that the Supreme Court, in *Katz v. United States*, created the presumption that all searches conducted without warrants are unreasonable. Accordingly, a valid search warrant must be secured before any crime scene search is undertaken; that is, unless it falls under the exceptions allowed by the Court (consent-to-search or emergency situations).

A *consent to search* must be given voluntarily by a person reasonably believed to have control over and legal access to the premises.[7]

There are two kinds of emergency situations:

1. Those involving an attempt or opportunity to carry off or destroy evidence. To support this contention, belief must meet the standard of probable cause.

2. Those involving threats to safety or life. In these cases, a lower level of proof—reasonable suspicion—is acceptable (see Table 13.2).

In an emergency situation, a warrantless search is lawful, but it must not go beyond the limits of the emergency; thus, a general exploratory search of the premises cannot be conducted lawfully. This limitation also applies in a consent search.

Crawford offers an example of a crime scene search for evidence that exceeded the scope of the emergency.[8] In this case, a 14-year-old kidnap victim, upon being liberated by police officers, told them where the kidnapper kept his guns and ammunition. Beyond retrieving the weapons from a closet, no further search of the apartment was made. On appeal, it was held that the emergency situation ("exigent circumstances," in the Court's language) justified entry into the apartment, but the emergency ended when it was determined that neither the defendant nor anyone else was in the apartment. Entering the closet to locate the weapons exceeded the scope of the emergency search. The evidence, therefore, was not admissible. Because the 14-year-old victim did not have control over the apartment, the consent exception was not applicable.

PURPOSE OF SEARCH

To understand the numerous precepts imposed on police behavior at a crime scene, one must be aware of the reasons for conducting a search. The most common reason is to develop *associative evidence;* that is, to find evidence that could link a suspect to the crime or the victim. Should some linkage be developed, its probative strength can range from an intimation of who may have been involved up to actual proof of something (as when a fingerprint is developed at the scene). Accordingly, nothing at the crime scene should be touched or stepped on.

Another purpose for the crime scene search is to seek answers to: *What* happened? *How, When,* and *Where* did it happen? In a homicide the forensic pathologist is usually able to provide answers after the autopsy, and sometimes (in other kinds of cases) answers are obvious even to the detective. When they are not, however, it is essential that nothing be moved or altered. Then, at least some of the questions may be satisfied when a reconstruction of the crime is attempted. In all events, before the criminalist can collect associative evidence or undertake a reconstruction, the scene must first be carefully recorded and photographed.

The police sometimes have other reasons for making a crime scene search: (1) to recognize evidence from which a psychological profile may be developed, and from which, conceivably, a motive may be determined (i.e., *why* the crime was committed); (2) to identify an object the use or purpose of which is not readily apparent or is foreign to the scene, thereby calling for efforts to trace ownership—through a serial number (as with Oswald's rifle in the Kennedy assassination) or by locating its source, through point of sale (as in an item of clothing bought in the Pan Am Flight 103 bombing case) or manufacturer; or (3) to recognize a perpetrator's *modus operandi* (MO). In a burglary, for example, the use of a push drill to make a hole in the top sash of the bottom half of a window (to insert a wire and open the catch) is sufficiently unusual to be viewed as the MO of that criminal. Pooling clues from several burglaries with the same tell-tale marks increases the chances of a suspect's apprehension.

ARRIVAL OF THE FIRST POLICE OFFICER

When the criminal has not been caught red-handed and has fled the scene before the first officer arrives (which is what generally happens), several responsibilities devolve upon this officer:

1. To ascertain any facts pertinent to the criminal(s) that should be immediately transmitted to the patrol force—personal description, make and model of vehicle used, direction fled from scene.

2. To isolate the crime scene (and if necessary, its environs). To limit access to those with responsibility for its examination and processing.

3. To detain and separate any eyewitnesses so they cannot discuss their individual observations with each other.

4. To call for medical aid for the injured. In those cases where a person is seriously injured, the first three steps (above) may be deferred until this is attended to. Stretcher bearers, nurses, and doctors should be admonished not to step on footprints or other clues, and not to move anything beyond what is required to assist the injured. They should be instructed to carry a victim out on a stretcher. This is preferred because a wheeler or cart makes it difficult to avoid disturbing blood spatters, foot or shoe impressions, or other evidence on the floor or pathways to and from the scene.

5. To continue to protect the scene until the officer who is to be responsible for the continuing investigation arrives. This authority is determined by departmental policy.

The time of any significant subsequent action (as well as its nature, the reasons for taking it, and people involved) should be carefully noted and recorded. Not doing so permits defense counsel to create the impression that an investigator is lazy, not thorough, or incompetent. Being well-informed on the rules of evidence, attorney's often attack the collection and handling of physical evidence at the crime scene. Their aim is often to have it ruled inadmissible should there have been any procedural lapse. In the Nicole Brown Simpson/Ronald Goldman double-murder case, for example, investigators left the original scene early on, only to run into what they believed to be a second crime scene. As a consequence, the protection of the original scene, the reasons for leaving it, and the processing of both scenes for physical evidence became matters of intense interest to the defense. In such cases it is crucial that the investigator takes good notes in a timely fashion, recording the investigative actions taken and the reasons why.

ARRIVAL OF THE INVESTIGATOR

On arrival at the crime scene, the investigator must note the following details to write a report and, possibly much later, to answer questions by defense counsel at trial:

1. Who made the notification; the time of arrival; and how long it took to respond.

2. The weather conditions and visibility.

3. The names of persons at the scene; in particular, the names of those who already went through the scene or any part of it.

4. The facts of the case as ascertained by the first officer(s) at the scene.

5. Subsequent actions on taking responsibility for the crime scene from the uniformed officer who was in charge up to that point.

OTHER SOURCES OF PHYSICAL EVIDENCE

In addition to the crime scene, there are two other possible sources of physical evidence:

1. The clothing and body of the victim (if not at the crime scene).

2. The suspect: the body, clothing, weapon, automobile, house, garage, or other area or article under his or her control.

Whatever the source—crime scene, victim, or suspect—the basic precepts governing the discovery, preservation, and collection of physical evidence apply equally.

DISCOVERY OF PHYSICAL EVIDENCE

James K. Stewart, Director of the National Institute of Justice wrote:

> Because of the increased value given to physical evidence in the judicial process and the advanced ability of criminalistics laboratories to analyze that evidence, the responsibility has fallen increasingly upon the investigating officer for conducting a thorough, careful investigation of the crime scene and for the proper collection and transport of physical evidence."[9]

It should be noted, however, that before any physical evidence can be collected and transported, it must first be recognized as such. Recognition is a routine matter when clue materials are familiar, like bullets, cartridge casings, tool marks, and blood. When materials are unfamiliar, recognition depends on the investigator's education, training, and imagination. Large police departments today have technicians and scientific equipment available for collecting and preserving physical evidence. In small departments the investigator shoulders this responsibility, responding to the extent possible with skills acquired through training, self-study, and experience on the job.

For readers who are looking for vicarious hands-on experience, a book such as *The Crime Laboratory* is a good starting point. *The Crime Laboratory* includes some of the common and, more important, some of the *uncommon* types of physical evidence encountered at crime scenes.[10] It is illustrated with police photographs (one-to-one or photomacrograph) of evidence discovered at the crime scene, together with those of a known comparison specimen (exemplar) obtained from the suspect (see Figures 3.3 and 3.4). By comparing the two pieces of evidence, the reader determines whether an identity exists. For many of

Figure 3.3
Impression in wood. *(Courtesy, Clark Boardman Co., Ltd. and Herbert MacDonell, Laboratory of Forensic Sciences, Corning, NY.)*

the case examples, solutions arrived at by the criminalist who worked on the investigation are provided. When the exercises are mastered, the details upon which an identity depends will be recognized. The trainee will appreciate what specific aspects of physical evidence covered in the exercises need protection when being collected and transmitted to the laboratory. In addition, he or she will better understand the principles underlying the FBI's recommendations for the handling of physical evidence (see Appendix 1). For those already in law enforcement, a local laboratory may be able to provide photographs of crime scene evidence and known comparison samples.

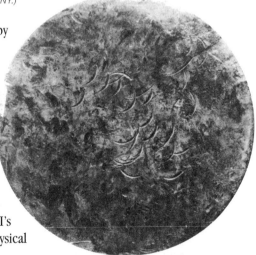

Figure 3.4
Hammer face is reproduced to permit a direct comparison with Figure 3.3. These pieces of potential evidence can be compared to determine whether a common origin exists. *(Courtesy, Clark Boardman Co., Ltd. and Herbert MacDonell, Laboratory of Forensic Sciences, Corning, NY.)*

Overview, Walk-Through, and Search

The process of discovery begins after the complainant (and often before an eyewitness, if any) has been questioned. When information is not otherwise available, the investigator's experience with that type of crime is put to use in forming a general impression of what happened and where to look for physical evidence. The search should include:

1. The most probable access and escape routes. When fleeing the scene, some criminals deliberately discard a weapon or burglar's tools, or on occasion, the proceeds of the crime.

2. Any area where the perpetrator waited before committing the crime. Burglars often gain entrance to a building just before closing time, then wait until it has been vacated. Killers or robbers also wait in ambush for their victims. In these areas, such clues as used matches, burned cigarettes, spent cartridge casings, food containers, etc., may be found.

3. The point of entry to the premises.

4. The route used within the premises where signs of the perpetrator's activity—such as objects that have been moved or places broken into—are apparent.

5. Any objects that seem to have received the attention of the criminal, such as a safe.

6. Some unusual places where evidence might be looked for:

    A. refrigerator
        a) half-eaten food (this actually happens)
        b) latent fingerprints on handle

    B. bathroom
        a) toilet seat—fingerprints—hairs
        b) trash can

A walk-through of the crime scene is first undertaken to observe the actual physical evidence and to ascertain which locations and articles require processing; namely, dusting for fingerprints or photographing blood-spatter details. If an outdoor search must be made during the hours of darkness, the scene should be protected and searched again in daylight. Under these circumstances, the first search should be confined to the fairly obvious and to what could be of immediate value in identifying or apprehending the perpetrator. Priority must be given to evidence that has a short life and is easily destroyed unless prompt action is taken to preserve and protect it. Whether indoors or out, sufficient illumination is crucial: it will prevent the mistake of walking on or missing evidence that cannot be seen.

The preliminary walk-through process helps to define the boundaries of the areas to be examined. Regardless of the search pattern employed, it must be systematic and thorough. When the area is large, a piecemeal probing of small sections (or strips) is effective. However, this task can be shortened. In a homicide committed in a sand pit, in which the victim's skull was fractured, the search for the missing weapon could start where the body was found. A better idea, however, would be to divide the area surrounding the sand pit area into a large grid. Those cells in the grid along the possible escape route (which, owing to foliage, offered a place to discard and conceal the weapon) might be searched after the sand pit area. If unsuccessful, the search could be directed to other cells in the grid and, upon completion, the entire process reviewed to make certain none were overlooked.

RECORDING CONDITIONS AND EVIDENCE FOUND AT THE CRIME SCENE

For a number of reasons, it is essential upon arrival to record the investigative evidence or clue materials that were noted during the search of the crime scene:

1. Writing an official report of the day's activities provides a record of information that will be useful later for jogging the memory and assuring accuracy.

2. Details that the criminalist can use for reconstructing the crime or developing associative evidence will be available.

3. As an investigation progresses and the suspect or witness makes statements, some aspects of the crime scene that did not initially appear significant can become important. A record made before anything was disturbed will permit such a reevaluation.

4. Records are useful in preparing for the interrogation of a suspect.

5. Defense attorneys, legitimately, will be curious about where and when the evidence was found and by whom. The investigator's preparation for cross-examination should begin at this early stage, not delayed until the trial date is set.

6. The effectiveness of courtroom testimony is enhanced when more than mere memory is available to recall events.

Methods of recording the situation, conditions, and physical evidence found at the crime scene include: notes, photographs, and sketches. Another method now used by some agencies requires video equipment, i.e., a camcorder equipped with at least an 8:1 power zoom lens with macro capability that functions even when lighting conditions are poor. This means the camera is rated to function at a minimum of 1 lux (a measure of illumination). Each method has a distinct value in that it supplements the others; in general, however, all three should be used to document the crime scene.

Notes

Recording the activities upon the arrival of the first officer and investigator at the scene is best accomplished with notes kept on a chronological basis. Many believe that a loose-leaf notebook is preferable to a bound one for logging the arrivals, departures, and assignments of assisting personnel, as well as the directions given to evidence technicians for processing the scene. It facilitates having material pertinent to the case at hand. If the notes are needed to refresh the investigator's memory when testifying, or should the court grant defense permission to examine them, then only the applicable jottings are open to inspection. If in a bound notebook, all information—confidential and otherwise, or pertaining to other cases—could be revealed.

Some people believe a bound notebook is best because it makes it difficult to change facts as first recorded should there be an attempt later to corrupt the officer. For the same reason, ink is preferable for crime scene notes. Should a correction be necessary, it is admissible to draw a line through the original notes and initial the alteration. Regardless of what form they take, the notes may become part of the *res gestae*, a record of what was said or done by the complainant, witness, or suspect in the first moments of the investigation. *Res gestae* (statements or acts), being an exception to the hearsay rule, may be admitted as evidence for consideration by a jury.

Photographs

Two kinds of photographs are taken at the crime scene. The first is intended to record the overall scene: the approach to the premises used by the criminal, the point of entrance, the pathway through the premises, the various rooms the criminal entered, and the location of any physical evidence. The second kind records details needed by the criminalist to reconstruct the crime or establish an identity. They are preserved by life-size or one-to-one photographs (of fingerprints, blood spatter patterns, tool marks) or occasionally by a photomacrograph of the evidence. A specially designed camera for one-to-one recording of fingerprints and other objects is commercially available and simple to operate (see Chapter 2). A photomacrograph, which requires a camera with a bellows extension, sturdy tripod, suitable focal length lenses, and illumination, should be left to a trained evidence technician. The introduction of the video camcorder with a power zoom lens and macro capability has simplified both the taking of record pictures and the preservation of evidence details by photograph or photomacrograph.

A more detailed treatment of the photography of a crime scene can be found in Fox and Cunningham's classic handbook on crime scene search[11] (see Appendix 2).

Sketches

The advantage of a sketch is that it includes only essential details; also, it best indicates distances or spatial relationships between items of evidence, indoors or out. There are two kinds: rough and finished. The *rough sketch*, a relatively crude, free-hand representation of all essential information, including measurements, is made at the crime scene (see Figure 3.5). Because there is great variation in individual sketching ability, changes are often needed in tracing outlines. It is best to use pencil for this task. The *finished sketch* is more precise: its lines are clean and straight and its lettering is either typeset or typewritten. Usually prepared later when time is available, it uses information from the rough sketch, notes, and photographs taken at the crime scene.

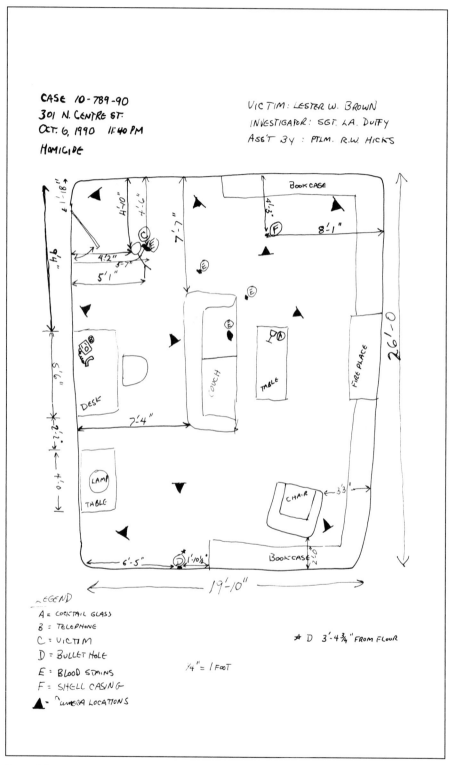

Figure 3.5
Rough sketch of a homicide crime scene. *(Courtesy, Sirchie Finger Print Laboratories, Inc., Raleigh, NC.)*

When the distances in the finished sketch are precise and proportional, with lines drawn by a skilled drafter, it is termed a *scale drawing* (see Figure 3.6). Scale drawings can be helpful in court to demonstrate exact distances. For example, in a case involving an unsuccessful attempt to choke the victim, the issue of manslaughter versus murder came up at trial. The jury had to decide whether the time it took for the killer to run down a hallway to the kitchen for a knife and return to the bedroom to finish the job was sufficient to constitute premeditation. A scale drawing would help in making this determination.

Commercially available crime scene sketch kits provide several templates: some for house furnishings, others for store and office layouts, and so on (see Figure 3.7). Computerized systems (such as Compu-Scene, by Digital Descriptor Systems, Inc.) are also available. In addition to routine drawing materials, a 100-foot steel tape and two people are needed to make the measurement. Each person must verify the distance between the item (the physical evidence) and a fixed object (a wall, boulder, house, telephone pole, or tree). Indoor measurements (from item of evidence to wall) are made along the shortest perpendicular lines, with two such right-angle measurements required to locate it. Each measurement is best made to the nearest walls not parallel to each other. This is known as the coordinate method for locating an object (see Figure 3.8). Another method (the triangulation method) is employed outdoors, the measurements being made from two fixed objects such as the corner of a house, a telephone pole, fence post, or tree (see Figure 3.9). If the direction and angle (obtained from a compass) are known for each measurement, the location of the object or item of evidence can be established (see Figure 3.10). Even when the angles are unknown, if each distance is considered the radius of a circle, the two circles can intersect at two points only, and the evidence will be located at but one of these two points. If the measurer records the general direction of the evidence from each fixed object, it is possible to select the correct intersecting point of the two circles.

Exact measurements are important for two reasons: one, to reconstruct the crime—namely, to check the account given by a suspect or witness; and two, to give clear-cut, precise answers to defense counsel's questions, and ensure that counsel is provided no opportunity to impugn the investigator's competence or confidence.

COLLECTION AND PRESERVATION

When each item of physical evidence has been properly recorded, it must then be collected separately and preserved for examination in the laboratory and eventually in court. The requirements of both scientist and lawyer therefore must be kept in mind. Because improperly collected or preserved evidence will fail to meet the tests defense counsel can apply in court, legal requirements will be considered first.

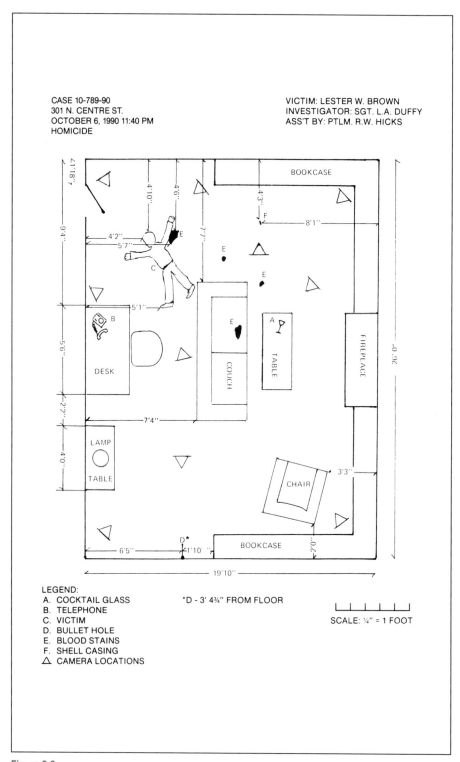

Figure 3.6
Finished sketch and scale drawing of same scene as Figure 3.5. *(Courtesy, Sirchie Finger Print Laboratories, Inc., Raleigh, NC.)*

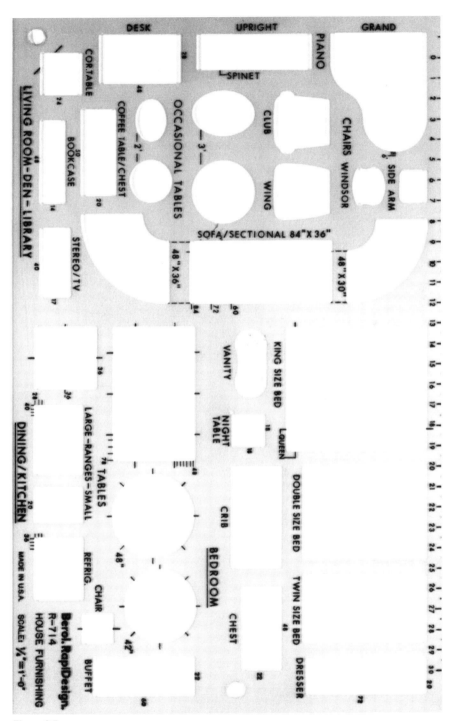

Figure 3.7
Template for house furnishings—Berol Rapid Design. *(Courtesy, Sirchie Finger Print Laboratories, Inc., Raleigh, NC.)*

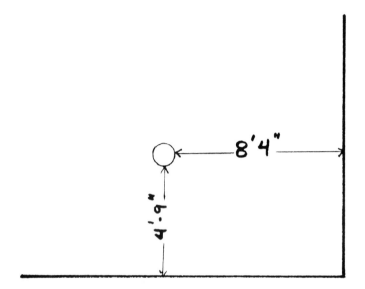

Figure 3.8
Coordinate method for locating an object. *(Courtesy, Sirchie Finger Print Laboratories, Inc., Raleigh, NC.)*

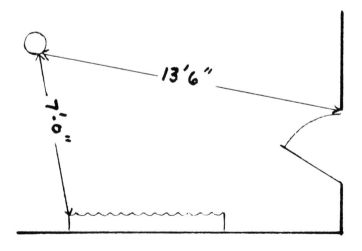

Figure 3.9
Triangulation method for locating an object. *(Courtesy, Sirchie Finger Print Laboratories, Inc., Raleigh, NC.)*

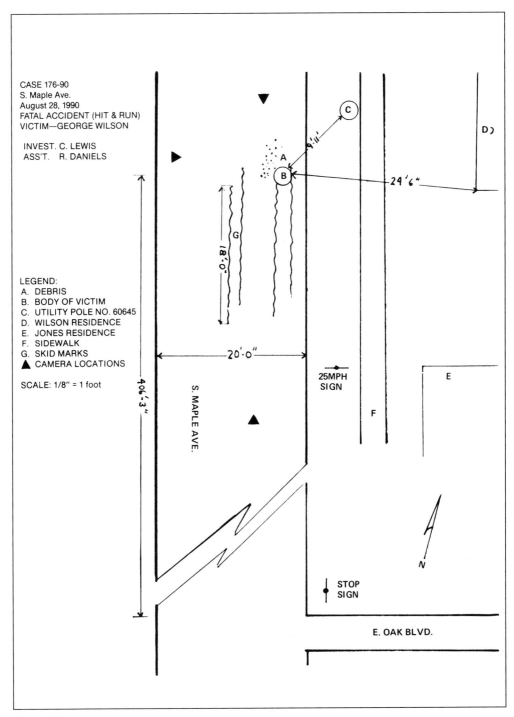

Figure 3.10
Finished sketch and scale drawing of a homicide that took place outdoors. *(Courtesy, Sirchie Finger Print Laboratories, Inc., Raleigh, NC.)*

Preservation—Legal Requirements

The same information used by the criminalist to reconstruct the crime serves to answer defense counsel's questions at trial. For example, the distribution pattern of spent cartridges ejected from an automatic pistol may allow the criminalist to determine where the shooter stood when firing the weapon, and defense counsel will certainly ask how he or she knows the exact position of each cartridge. An admissible set of photographs and a sketch can defuse this challenge. Other tests lawyers can apply in attempting to exclude evidence involve the certainty of the identification (of the cartridges in this example) and the issue of continuity of possession—the chain of custody of each item of evidence.

Identification

To be admissible in court, an item of evidence must be shown to be identical with that discovered at the crime scene or secured at the time of arrest. Thus, any alleged marijuana cigarettes found in the defendant's possession on arrest or bullets removed from the bedroom mattress after a homicide must be shown to be *the* cigarettes or *the* bullets acquired originally. To make identifications with certainty and thereby preclude a successful challenge, some method of marking each item of evidence must be devised, the marks serving to connect each bit of evidence to both investigator and defendant or scene. If possible, they should include the date and location of the acquisition of the evidence. Attempting to squeeze this information onto a small item would be impractical, but an envelope, bottle, or other container provides an enlarged labeling surface. Plastic containers are preferred because this material is less likely to break or contaminate the evidence. Any receptacle must be sealed and initialed on the seal.

Figure 3.11
An all-in-one evidence tag/label. It is supplied with tamper-proof ties for tagging and peel-off backing with a permanent adhesive to make it into a label. *(Courtesy, Lynn Peavey Co., Lenexa, KS.)*

An all-in-one evidence tag/label is available that can be used for the identification of many kinds of evidence. Printed on heavy-duty stock, it can be either threaded using tamper-proof ties through a pre-punched hole to form an evidence tag or made into an adhesive backed evidence label by peeling off the protective backing (see Figure 3.11).

In large police departments the storage and retrieval of evidence from the property clerk or evidence custodian is somewhat complicated. For simplification, a voucher number system may be utilized to account for the evidence. Some large departments use a computer to inventory and track evidence as it is examined within the laboratory. This has little to do with the identification of the original evidence by the detective; rather, it is related to the other legal requirement: chain of custody.

Continuity of Possession/Chain of Custody

Evidence must be continuously accounted for from the time of its discovery until it is presented in court. Anyone who had it in their possession, even momentarily, may be called upon to testify as to when, where, and from whom it was received; what (if anything) was done to it; to whom it was surrendered, and at what time and date. The greater the number of people handling the evidence, the greater the potential for conflict in, or contradiction of, their testimony. Any disruption in the chain of custody may cause evidence to be inadmissible. Even if it is admitted, a disruption can weaken or destroy its probative value. Accordingly, the rule is to have the least possible number of persons handle evidence. If at all practical, the investigator should personally deliver evidence to the laboratory. If the facility is far away, the use of the U.S. Post Office (Registered) or United Parcel Service (Acknowledgment of Delivery) is permissible. Their signed receipts usually suffice to satisfy the court. The court appearance of a postal or delivery clerk is not usually required.

Police departments normally specify how physical evidence should be marked, transported, and stored. These procedures are not specified here, as they vary from department to department, but the general considerations can be met in a number of ways. Any practice that ignores them can create major problems regarding the admissibility of evidence in court.

Vulnerability

If investigators do not comprehend the legal aspects intrinsic to the preservation of physical evidence, they become vulnerable to attack by defense counsel. The lessons of the Nicole Brown Simpson/Ronald Goldman murder case underscore how effective such challenges can be. In this double homicide, numerous bloodstains were discovered at the original crime scene and, subsequently, at O.J. Simpson's home.

A (known) sample of O.J. Simpson's blood was drawn for comparison purposes. The investigator had the option of logging it into one of two forensic evidence facilities nearby. Instead, he opted to deliver it (almost three hours later) to the criminalist, who was still collecting evidence at the crime scene. He took this step because he did not have the case number needed to log it in. Keeping the chain of custody as short as possible may also have motivated his decision to hand-deliver the blood sample to the criminalist. Although the bureaucratic mindset may well account for believing that a case number is required before evidence can be logged in, this is an administrative rather than legal requirement. Moreover, chain of custody was in no way shortened by delivering the tube to the criminalist who had to in turn deliver it to the evidence custodian. Rather it was lengthened, because a serologist (or DNA expert) would most likely be the next person to handle the tube had the crime scene criminalist not been involved.

The main lesson to be learned is that bringing exemplars (or a suspect) back to the crime scene provides defense counsel with an opportunity to raise a doubt as to whether the questioned evidence was there originally or was there because it was taken to the scene. This is exactly the opportunity the defense grasped in the Simpson case, as one of the jurors remarked after the trial:

Juror Brenda Moran told the press that the jury found Vanatter's decision to carry Simpson's blood sample around with him for several hours "suspicious because it gave him the opportunity to plant evidence": he's walking around with blood in his pocket for a couple of hours. How come he didn't book it at Parker Center or Piper Tech? He had a perfect opportunity. Why walk around with it? He was my biggest doubt . . . There was an opportunity to sprinkle it here or there.[12]

Preservation—Scientific Requirements and Means

Scientific Requirements

The criminalist also has scientific requirements for the preservation of evidence, the primary one being that there be no alteration in its inherent quality or composition. Sometimes, deterioration may occur in such biological materials as blood, semen, and vomit before the investigator arrives at the scene. Any change after that must be minimized by taking proper precautions promptly. Physical evidence may undergo change in the following ways:

1. Loss by leakage (of a powder) from an opening in the seam of an envelope; or by evaporation (of a volatile liquid) from an improperly stoppered container.

2. Decomposition through exposure to light, heat, or bacteria; for example, direct exposure to summer sun can alter a bloodstain in a very short time. It may not be recognized; most likely, it cannot be grouped or have its DNA content analyzed.

3. Intermingling of evidence from various sources and locations in a common container. In a sex crime, the suspect's and victim's underwear should not be placed in the same bag. Such commingling, surprisingly, is not uncommon.

4. Alteration by the unwitting addition of a fresh fold or crease in a document; or a tear or cut in a garment. For example, hospital personnel in haste to remove clothing, have cut right through the powder mark on the victim's shirt (see Figure 3.12). They also have disposed of such clothing. If it has any potential as evidence, immediate measures must be taken to retrieve it.

5. Contamination, bacterial or chemical, resulting from the use of unclean containers.

A few precautions can minimize or eliminate these problems:

1. Use only fresh, clean containers.

2. Use leak-proof, sealable containers.

3. Uphold the integrity of each item of evidence by using separate containers.

4. Keep evidence away from direct sunlight and heat. Refrigerate biological evidence (such as whole blood, urine, and rape kits) when not being transported.

5. Deliver evidence as quickly as possible to the laboratory.

6. Handle evidence as little as possible.

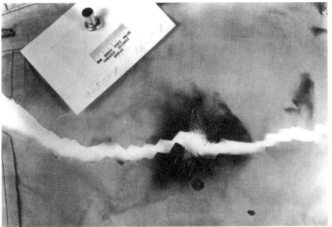

Biological specimens, particularly blood and semen stains, are best preserved by permitting them to dry at room temperature, away from direct sunlight. No air currents (e.g., from a fan) or heat (e.g., from a blow dryer) should be directed at them. Appendix 1 contains FBI recommendations for collecting and preserving various types of physical evidence.

Figure 3.12
Powder mark on victim's shirt cut through by hospital personnel unmindful of its potential evidentiary value. *(Courtesy, New Jersey State Police.)*

Collection—Scientific Requirements and Means

Scientific Requirements

It was pointed out earlier that the comparison and interpretation of details in physical evidence—especially the development of associative evidence—is a major activity for the criminalist. As part of this process, the criminalist requires that a specimen from the suspect be checked against the evidence from the crime scene. Therefore, an inked set of the suspect's fingerprints must be at hand for comparison with a latent print found at the scene, or a bullet fired from the suspected weapon must be available to link the crime scene bullet to a certain weapon. Generally, comparison specimens of known origin (*exemplars*) must be collected and made available to criminalists. Three considerations should govern the collection:

1. Whenever possible, variables must be controlled.

2. Background material must be collected.

3. The quantity of the sample must be sufficient.

Control of Variables

It is fundamental to scientific experimentation that, where feasible, all variables except one be controlled during the test. Because controlling the variables is not always possible in criminalistics, all variables that can possibly be eliminated should be. Thus, when collecting handwriting specimens for comparison with a forged check, variables to be eliminated include: the size, color, and printing on the check; and the type of writing instrument (by employing the same type—ball point pen, pencil, pen nib with nutgall ink, etc.—used in the original forgery). Similarly, when examining a firearm, the same ammunition used in the commission of the crime, if available, should be employed in the test firing. The aim in controlling variables is to have the evidence specimen duplicated to the fullest extent possible in the exemplar.

Background Material

A material that has been bloodstained or has had paint transferred to it (in a hit-and-run accident, for instance) contains valuable physical evidence. Something, however, may have been present on the material prior to the crime that could interfere with the tests that the criminalist performs. For this reason, an unstained sample that is quite close to the stained area should be collected. A bloodstained mattress for instance can yield misleading results if perspiration or saliva was already on the ticking when the crime was committed. By testing an unstained sample of the ticking, blood type antigens can be discovered and dealt with by a serologist. Another example: When a bicycle is struck by an automobile, each vehicle's paint can be transferred to the other. To evaluate the spectrograms of each paint, a specimen of the original paint on each vehicle must be taken from a spot near the collision-transfer point. These specimens, like the unstained ticking, constitute the background samples.

Figure 3.13
Kraft bags. *(Courtesy, Lynn Peavey Co., Lenexa, KS.)*

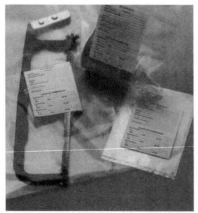

Figure 3.14
Heat sealable, clear polyethylene bags. *(Courtesy, Lynn Peavey Co., Lenexa, KS.)*

Sample Sufficiency

It is accurate to say that most investigators do not collect comparison samples of adequate size or quantity. This may partly be a result of misunderstanding, for the sensitivity of modern instrumental methods of analysis has certainly been exaggerated. Still, it is better that samples be too large rather than too small. The investigator or evidence technician, naturally, is limited to what is available at the crime scene. In general, this factor does not pertain to the known specimen (exemplar), which usually is large. As a result, the criminalist is able to establish the conditions and method of examination before comparing the crime scene evidence with it.

Means

Various tools are required to separate and remove material from its setting when collecting physical evidence at the crime scene. Special means are employed to gather trace evidence. Similarly, an assortment of containers is needed to isolate and protect each material.

Tools

In general, tools that cut, grip, or force are needed for the collection of physical evidence. They can be classified as follows:

1. Cutting Implements

    Scissors—compound-action metal snips or shears
    Saws for wood and metal
    Scalpels and razors
    Chisels for wood and metal
    Knives
    Drills with assorted bits
    Axes
    Files

2. Gripping Devices

    Assorted wrenches
    Assorted pliers
    Tweezers—straight and angled

3. Forcing or Prying Tools

    Screwdrivers—various sizes of regular and Phillips-head types
    Hammers—claw, ball-peen, chipping, mallet
    Crowbars

Containers

All items listed below are available in most communities. They are best collected in advance, in anticipation of future need:

1.	Bags	paper, plastic
2.	Boxes	pill (drug store type), shoe, large cartons
3.	Envelopes	assorted sizes and types; mail, brown manila with metal clasp, plastic.
4.	Other containers	
	Plastic	used by druggists to dispense tablets and capsules; or used to store or freeze foods.
	Glass	bottles with stoppers, Mason jars with lids
	Cans	with tight covers

Expansion envelopes; heat-sealable, extra-strength polyethylene bags; and other items for the collection of crime scene evidence are available from police equipment specialists such as Sirchie Finger Print Laboratories, Lynn Peavey Company, Ames Safety Envelope Company, and Kinderprint Company (see Figures 3.13–3.16).

Collection—Special Considerations

In addition to the routine collection of physical evidence, today's investigator should not overlook the possibility of trace evidence, and also must keep in mind the hazard imposed by AIDS-infected blood.

Figure 3.15
Evidence bags for rifles or other long items. *(Courtesy, Lynn Peavey Co., Lenexa, KS.)*

Figure 3.16
Clear evidence jars with tight-fitting screw-on caps. *(Courtesy, Lynn Peavey Co., Lenexa, KS.)*

Trace Evidence

Trace evidence, differing from ordinary physical evidence mainly because of its small size, calls for special methods. Three techniques for discovering and gathering trace evidence are: vacuuming, shaking, or sweeping, and adhesion to tape. An ordinary vacuum cleaner with good suction, equipped with a special attachment to hold filter paper in place, can be used to trap the debris as a deposit on the paper. Each item of evidence processed requires a fresh filter. Particulate matter and fibers (on clothing, automobile rug, bed sheet, blanket, etc.) are dislodged by vigorous shaking over a clean white sheet of paper laid on a large table. The adhesion technique involves pressing a three- or four-inch piece of transparent tape on the evidence to be examined; with the tape placed sticky side down on a glass slide, the debris adhering to it can be studied directly under the microscope. A stereomicroscope is employed to sort out the fibers or particles obtained from vacuuming or shaking; a polarized light microscope is used for comparison and identification.

Detective Nicholas Petraco (New York Police Department), who specializes in trace evidence examination, believes that even in this day of highly advanced laboratory instrumentation "the microscope, especially the polarized microscope, is the most important and versatile instrument available to the criminalist for the study of trace evidential materials."[13] He cites several cases that were solved because of the "vital role that the microscope and trace evidence played."[14]

AIDS as a Concern for Crime Scene Investigators

The potential of Acquired Immune Deficiency Syndrome (AIDS) as a serious hazard to the health of those charged with collecting physical evidence at scenes of violent crimes has been acknowledged.[15] A research paper by Kennedy and others points to the special vulnerability of crime scene investigators:

> [For] . . . unlike the doctor, nurse, or health worker who most often works in a controlled environment, the criminal investigator may be confronted with less manageable conditions.[16]

> . . . using conventional methods such as latex gloves for protection against the potential risk of AIDS or other infectious diseases may not be adequate at every crime scene . . . While the human skin and protective garments are barriers to exposure to the AIDS virus, there are objects and conditions present at a crime scene which may, through abrasion, puncturing, or cutting action, provide an avenue for transmission and infection.[17]

The authors raise the following problem:

> . . . If investigators believe they are not properly protected from the AIDS virus, they may limit their evidentiary searches, consciously or unconsciously, to only those scenarios they believe to be "safe." Physical evidence may only be cursorily dealt with, hunches may not be followed up, and officers may avoid specialized forensic assignments. If evidence of poor quality must be relied upon by the courts, the truly guilty may not be convicted. Worse yet, the innocent may fail to be exonerated.[18]

They conclude with some recommendations, to wit:

> . . . Notwithstanding these clear concerns for the AIDS problem in general and their own safety in particular, the vast majority of crime scene investigators and evidence technicians report that the quality of their work is not adversely affected. While policy makers at all levels of the criminal justice system may be pleased by the perseverance of forensic line officers, it is clear that their efforts must be supported by stronger departmental measures if they are to continue effectively in their work. At the very least, clear guidelines that incorporate the latest information on AIDS prevention should be developed and publicized. The feasibility of issuing various support equipment, such as specialized clothing, also needs to be explored.[19]

TRANSMISSION OF EVIDENCE TO THE LABORATORY

Delivering physical evidence to the laboratory is best done in person for legal and scientific reasons. In the case that this is not possible, the U.S. Postal Service or United Parcel Service (UPS) can be used to deliver the packaged evidence. Proper packing, wrapping, and sealing is extremely important when evidence is to be shipped. With this in mind, the FBI has prepared a helpful set of explicit recommendations and instructions, which are reprinted in Appendix 1.

This text thus far has treated investigations as though the detective and his or her partner are conducting the crime scene search by themselves. However, when a high-profile case, a large crime scene, or multiple scenes are involved, a more elaborate evidence collection process is desirable. To this end, the FBI has published a booklet with the aim of ensuring that search efforts are conducted in an organized and methodical fashion.[20] It describes the duties and responsibilities of the response team, which includes: a team leader, a photographer and photographic log recorder, an evidence recorder/custodian, and specialists (e.g., bomb expert, geologist, etc.). Other issues treated include: organization and basic stages in a search operation, documentation procedures, and equipment recommendations.

While largely concerned with how to conduct a search, the booklet also warns the user of the pitfalls involved in blindly following their recommendations. Considering the gravity of high-profile crimes, the booklet's suggestions help investigators recall things to do that can be overlooked in the heat of the moment.

FINDING PHYSICAL EVIDENCE BY CANVASSING

Canvassing is employed most often to search out witnesses who do not know they have useful information about a crime under investigation. It is also used to track down the source of crime scene evidence. For example, in the Sam Sheppard murder case, a nationwide canvass was undertaken to find a surgical instrument matching the contours of a bloodstained impression found on the pillow of the victim, Marilyn Sheppard—the defendant's wife. Despite intense efforts, it was not successful.

In kidnapping cases, a modified form of canvass for physical evidence has proved successful. A document examiner selects handwriting (or printing) characteristics in the kidnapper's ransom note that are outstanding and easily recognized. A photograph illustrating these unusual characteristics is prepared and distributed to each investigator after the document examiner has explained their significance. Then investigators are sent out systematically to examine numerous public documents for handwriting or printing characteristics resembling those in the photograph. They examine applications for state license plates, automobile operator's licenses, and marriage licenses. They scan the signatures on election voting records, financial transactions, and probation and parole records. The Lindbergh/Hauptmann kidnapping case would have been solved earlier had this procedure (which was suggested at the time) been followed. With numerous clues indicating that the kidnapper came from the Bronx, it would have been feasible to initiate and confine the search to that borough; and, had driver's license or automobile registration files been examined, the kidnapper's distinctive brand of handwriting could have been recognized.

The lessons of the Lindbergh case were not forgotten, however. They were applied successfully in the LaMarca/Weinberger kidnapping case, in which the writer of a ransom note (left in the victim's carriage) was found by assigning investigators to comb through various public documents until one was located that apparently bore the same handwriting. The discovery involved 150 detectives and FBI agents who, in a brief training session, were taught to recognize the unusual characteristics in the handwriting of the ransom note. After examining 2 million public documents, an FBI agent discovered one that appeared to contain characteristics similar to those in the note; when examined by an expert, the agent's preliminary judgment was proved correct.

REFERENCES

[1]   Shannon Tangonan, "Accused Levin Killers Due to be Arraigned." *USA Today*, 9 June 1997, 9A.

[2]   *Michigan v. Clifford*, 464 U.S. 1 (1983).

[3]   *Michigan v. Tyler*, 436 U.S. 499 (1978).

[4]   *Mincey v. Arizona*, 437 U.S. 385 (1978).

[5]   *Thompson v. Louisiana*, 469 U.S. 17 (1984).

[6]   Kimberly A. Crawford, "Crime Scene Searches: The Need for Fourth Amendment Compliance." *FBI Law Enforcement Bulletin* 68:1 (1999), 26-31.

[7]   *Illinois v. Rodriquez*, 110 S. Ct. 2793 (1990).

[8]   Crawford, *op. cit.*, 29.

[9]   Richard F. Fox and Carl L. Cunningham, *Crime Scene Search and Physical Evidence Handbook*, reprint (Washington, DC: U.S. Government Printing Office, 1973), iii.

[10]   James W. Osterburg, *The Crime Laboratory: Case Studies of Scientific Criminal Investigation*, 2nd ed. (New York: Clark Boardman, 1982), 161-381.

[11]   Fox and Cunningham, *op. cit.*, 41-46.

[12]   Alan M. Dershowitz, *Reasonable Doubts,* (New York: Simon & Schuster, 1996), 74.

[13]   Nicholas Petraco, "Trace Evidence—The Invisible Witness," *Journal of Forensic Sciences,* 31:1 (1986), 321.

[14]   Ibid., 321-327.

[15]   D.B. Kennedy, R.J. Homant, and G.L. Emery, "AIDS Concerns Among Crime Scene Investigators," *Journal of Police Science and Administration* 17:1 (1990), 12-18.

[16]   Ibid., 13.

[17]   Ibid., 14.

[18]   Ibid.

[19]   Ibid., 18.

[20]   Federal Bureau of Investigation. *Suggested Guidelines for Establishing Evidence Response Teams.* (Washington, DC: Department of Justice, no date).

SUPPLEMENTAL READINGS

Bevel, Tom, and Ross M. Gardiner. *Blood Stain Pattern Analysis*. Boca Raton, FL: CRC Press, 1997.

Bodziak, William J. *Footwear Impression Evidence*. 2nd ed. Boca Raton, FL: CRC Press, 1993.

Brown, Jerrold G., and Clarice R. Cox. *Report Writing for Criminal Justice Professionals*. 2nd ed. Cincinnati: Anderson, 1998.

Cowger, James F. *Friction Ridge Skin: Comparison and Identification of Fingerprints*. Boca Raton, FL: CRC Press, 1992.

DeForest, Peter R., R.E. Gaensslen, and Henry C. Lee. *Forensic Science: An Introduction to Criminalistics*. 2nd ed. New York: McGraw-Hill, 1995.

Eckert, William G., and James H. Stuart. *Interpretation of Blood Stain Evidence at Crime Scenes*. New York: Elsevier, 1989.

Fisher, Barry A.J. *Techniques of Crime Scene Investigation*. 6th ed. Boca Raton, FL: CRC Press, 1999.

Fox, Richard H., and Carl L. Cunningham. *Crime Scene Search and Physical Evidence Handbook*. Boulder, CO: Paladin Press, 1987.

Hawthorne, Mark R. *First Unit Responder*. Boca Raton, FL: CRC Press, 1998.

Kirk, Paul L. *Crime Investigation*. 2nd ed. Edited by John I. Thornton. Reprint. New York: Wiley & Sons, 1974; Melbourne, FL: Krieger, 1985.

Lee, Henry C. *Crime Scene Investigation*. Taoyuan, Taiwan (Republic of China): Central Police University Press, 1994.

Lee, Henry C., and Robert F. Gaensslen, eds. *Advances in Fingerprint Technology*. Boca Raton, FL: CRC Press, 1994.

McDonald, Peter. *Tire Print Identification: Practical Aspects of Criminal Forensic Investigation*. Boca Raton, FL: CRC Press, 1992.

Osterburg, James W. *The Crime Laboratory: Case Studies of Scientific Investigation*. 2nd ed. Eagan, MN: West Group, 1982.

Redsicker, David R. *The Practical Methodology of Forensic Photography*. Boca Raton, FL: CRC Press, 1992.

Rynearson, Joseph M., and Wm. J. Chisum. *Evidence and Crime Scene Reconstruction*. 3rd ed. Redding, CA: National Crime Investigation and Training, 1993.

Safferstein, Richard. *Criminalistics: An Introduction to Forensic Science*. 5th ed. Englewood Cliffs, NJ: Prentice Hall, 1995.

CHAPTER 4

People as a Source of Information

Individually and collectively, people possess a wide spectrum of information about other people. Of potential value to the criminal investigator, this information can range from what a victim plainly knows to what an eyewitness chances to see or hear prior to or during the commission of a crime. This is firsthand knowledge. People also accumulate a quantity of secondhand knowledge during the course of daily life—from intimate and casual relationships, remarks overheard, or quarrels witnessed. It may involve physical evidence such as a threatening note, or something that comes into the hands of a victim or witness by coincidence—a bullet, or an instrument used in the crime (e.g., a baseball bat or piece of pipe). Whatever the form, it is the detective's task either to find those who have such knowledge or evidence, or to persuade people to come forward and volunteer what they know. Victims and eyewitnesses are the most obvious sources of information. Others of potential value are relatives and acquaintances of the suspect, informants, and the perpetrator (when apprehended).

This chapter will discuss the kinds of information that can be obtained from people by means of interviewing, psychological profiling, surveillance, lineups, neighborhood canvasses, interrogation, hypnosis, and nonverbal clues.

THE CRIMINAL

Mind, body, words, actions—all can serve to betray the identity of the offender through a consideration of motive, the physical evidence brought to or taken from the crime scene, or the method of committing the crime. In one sense, this restates Hans Gross's thesis that:

> . . . criminal investigation consist[s] of two parts; one, the utilization by police officers of all available knowledge and information concerning the psychology, motivation, and character of the criminal before, during, and after the commission of a crime; and two, the application of all useful technological and scientific information to solve a crime and support the allegations in the courtroom.[1]

Motive

From the standpoint of motive, crime may be divided into two classes. In the first class, crimes such as robbery, rape, and burglary may have a universal motive which is—in and of itself—of little value in furthering the investigation. Those in the second class, such as homicide, arson, and assault, are more likely to have a particularized motive; when one is discovered, the connection between victim and criminal may be deduced. (The high clearance rate for homicide is based in part on this logic.)

Investigative experience is helpful in ferreting out the motive for a crime. In some cases, motive may be learned through adroit interviewing. In others, however, it is implied—when it can be determined who might benefit from committing the crime. Occasionally, a victim is able to suggest the names of suspects and their motives. When several individuals have motive, their number can be pared down by ascertaining who had the opportunity of time and place, and who among them had the enterprise. This sifting process allows investigators to channel their efforts into those aspects of the inquiry most likely to produce evidence of the offender's involvement.

There is another important reason for establishing motive—even when it is not helpful in suggesting possible suspects. Though not an element of any crime, a jury is more likely to be convinced of a defendant's guilt if a motive for committing the crime can be shown.

Modus Operandi (MO)

An offender's pattern of operation (method of preparing for and committing a crime) is called the *modus operandi* or MO (see Chapter 7). When collected, stored, and classified, MO information can assist in the identification and apprehension of a perpetrator. It also can be useful in devising strategies for deterring crime.

Identification

Ideally, MO characteristics can identify an offender. When an individual has an arrest record and a unique MO is on file, an identification may occur if the MO is used again and recognized. In general, however, MO characteristics are not sufficiently unique for this purpose. Just the same, MO can lead to the identification of an offender when a string of crimes is recognized as having a common perpetrator and the respective clues are pooled and used inductively. The pooled information also can send the investigator to search records, set up a surveillance, or seek out an informant.

Apprehension

An analysis of the pattern of operation (MO) may provide the basis for a plan to apprehend an offender. The general aim is to discover possible targets and place them under a fixed surveillance. Though this constitutes a considerable commitment of staff and resources, under the right circumstances the prospects are good. For example, because retail stores are susceptible to robbery during the Christmas season, certain establishments are targeted. Stationing a police officer hidden from view at the rear of a store that is likely to be "hit" often produces results. This could also lead to clearing other cases through an interrogation of the perpetrator. Pointing out that his MO is recognized may cause the suspect to believe incriminating evidence exists and induce him or her to confess. Suspects are not apt to volunteer a confession for crimes not specifically asked about; therefore, were it not for MO data, some otherwise apparently unrelated cases would probably remain unsolved.

MO data make another highly useful contribution to the cause of justice when a run of crimes appears to have been solved, yet the convicted person still claims innocence. Should those crimes continue after the individual has been imprisoned, and if they are characterized by the same MO (especially a somewhat unusual one), it is an indication that an innocent person may have been wronged. The case should then be thoroughly reviewed to settle the matter.

When MO analysis indicates that a previously crime-free area is beset by a series of crimes, implementation of more intensive visible patrol during the relevant period may bring about an abatement of the activity. An apprehension may also be a consequence of preventive patrol strategy. In one case involving a prowler (who typically operated between midnight and 3:00 A.M.), setting up a tactical patrol in the neighborhood was responsible for solving the double murder of a brother and sister.

The burglar, who invaded the home just after 2:00 A.M., entered through a rear bedroom window on the first floor, awakening two teenagers. A struggle ensued in which both children were killed and the burglary aborted. In the previous month, reports had been made of a backyard prowler operating in the limited time period of midnight to 3:00 A.M. Following the double homicide, all prowler calls taken between midnight and 4:00 A.M. were covered. Four detective cars were assigned, and rather than responding directly to the location calling for help, they took up positions in each direction two blocks from the complainant's address. This tactic allowed the detectives to observe anyone emerging from alleyways between the rows of houses. When a prowler call came in about 10 months later, a male was observed (from one of the parked detective cars) to cross the street midblock, continue on, and then, after cutting between the houses, reappear one block away and cross the next street. Persisting in this behavior for two more blocks, the suspect was stopped for questioning.

Detectives learned that he lived about four miles away and could not account for his presence in the neighborhood other than to claim that he "liked to walk at night." They observed he wore all dark clothing and, although the weather was bitterly cold, canvas shoes. The 15 pawn tickets in his wallet raised their suspicions that a burglar had been caught, and a search warrant was obtained. The surmise proved correct: the suspect's apartment was a storehouse. Television sets, other small appliances, and jewelry—watches, rings, necklaces—were everywhere.

The burglar was more than willing to talk about the stolen goods, perhaps to keep official attention on this activity and away from the homicide. When the investigator handling the case casually produced a flashlight with colored paper over its bulb (to reduce illumination), the suspect inquired about where it had been found in the apartment, saying that he thought it had been lost. The suspect was correct but forgetful—

the flashlight had been recovered at the scene of the double homicide. A confession was soon forthcoming; ultimately, he agreed to reenact the crime.

Taken to the crime scene, the suspect remarked on the placement of a small chest of drawers in one room, saying it had been against another wall on the night of the murder. He also indicated a cherry tree from which he had broken a branch to use as a prod on the window shade pulled down over the open window. A small twig had been found by an investigator who had unrolled the shade to examine a bump he noted in it. Though its presence made no sense at the time, it was collected and preserved for possible future use as potential evidence. Subsequently, it was learned that the prod had snapped the shade shut, breaking and trapping the twig. As physical evidence, it corroborated the defendant's confession (often a legal requirement in a first-degree murder case). A xylotomist (wood expert) could testify that it came from a particular species of cherry tree, and that its age matched that of a torn branch on the tree the defendant identified as the source of his window shade prod.

Psychological Profiling

Occasionally, a psychiatrist or psychologist is invited to make an assessment of a crime that is presenting difficulties. When the specialists are asked: "Who would do a thing like this?," their answers may provide direction to the investigation or limit the number of suspects. This procedure, confined to crimes of brutality or those in which strong emotions were manifest, has been employed to a limited extent. Psychological assessment of a crime is called *profiling*; its purpose is to recognize and interpret visible evidence at the scene as indicative of the personality type of the perpetrator. According to the FBI, it is based on the notion that:

> Clues left at the crime scene may be of inestimable value in leading to the solution of the crime; however, they are not necessarily items of physical evidence. . . .

> These aspects [the clues] may be present at the crime scene but the untrained officer will miss them . . . .

> Nonetheless, the results [of behavioral science research] may be applied to teach police officers to recognize [the visible evidence of] the existence of the emotions [of rage, hatred, fear, love] and other personality traits in a crime scene. Once recognized, police may then construct a profile of the type of person who might possess these emotions and/or personality traits . . . .

> The officer must bear in mind that the profile is not an exact science and a suspect who fits the description is not automatically guilty. The use of profiling does not replace sound investigative procedures . . . .

> The entire basis for a good profile is a good crime scene examination and adequate interviews of victims and witnesses . . . .

> The victim is one of the most important aspects of the psychological profile. In cases involving a surviving victim, particularly a rape victim, the perpetrator's exact conversation with the victim is of utmost importance and can play a very large role in the construction of an accurate profile.

The profile is not all inclusive and does not always provide the same information from one profile to another. It is based on what was or was not left at the crime scene. Since the amount of psychological evidence varies, as does physical evidence, the profile may also vary. The profile information may include:

1. The perpetrator's race
2. Sex
3. Age range
4. Marital status
5. General employment
6. Reaction to questioning by police
7. Degree of sexual maturity
8. Whether the individual might strike again
9. The possibility that he or she has committed a similar offense in the past
10. Possible police record. . . .

The primary psychological evidence which the profiler is looking for is motive. . . . [But also] the intangible evidence that the observer gathers from the crime scene [may] tell . . . whether the crime appears to be planned or whether it is the result of an irrational process . . . .

It is most important that this investigative technique be confined chiefly to crimes against the person where the motive is lacking and where there is sufficient data to recognize the presence of psychopathology at the crime scene . . . . It should be understood that analysis is for lead value only.[2]

If a potential suspect emerges as a result of profiling or routine investigation, the information may be of help during interrogation. One of the necessary conditions for confession is a feeling of guilt, and the insight gained from profiling may provide an understanding of what will and will not provoke such a feeling. This permits the avoidance of some areas of a suspect's behavior in an interrogative session and the more vigorous pursuit of other areas.

Origin

Based on experience, a few investigators have (at least since 1900) successfully utilized the equivalent of profiling.[3] Almost a century later an examination of modern psychological profiling suggests that ". . . such profiles are not as exact as we'd like and no better than a street-smart detective could dream up."[4]

This reaffirms that:

Good profiles, it seems, are generally the work of detectives; and when a psychologist produces a good profile it usually means he has been thinking like a detective.[5]

Utilizing personnel with graduate degrees in psychology and with investigative experience, the FBI Academy has established a Behavioral Science Unit to undertake applied research and publish its findings regarding offender profiles.[6]

Case Illustration: Psychological Profiling

. . . a woman on the east coast reported to the police that she had been raped. After learning the facts of this case, the investigating officer realized that this was the seventh rape in the past two years wherein the same *modus operandi* was used. There were no investigative leads remaining in any of these incidents. The investigation conducted thus far had yielded no suspect.

The incident reports, together with transcripts of interviews with the victims, were forwarded to the FBI . . . with a request . . . that a psychological profile of the suspect or suspects be provided. After careful examination of the submitted materials by the FBI Academy's Behavioral Science Unit a psychological profile was constructed . . . [in which it was] advised that these rapes were probably committed by the same person and described him as a white male, 25 to 35 years of age (most likely 20s or early 30s), divorced or separated, working at marginal employment (laborer, etc.), high school education, poor self-image, living in the immediate area of the rapes, and being involved in crimes of voyeurism (Peeping Tom). It was likely that the police had talked to the rapist in the past due to his being on the streets in the neighborhood in the early morning hours.

Three days after receiving the profile provided to them the requesting agency developed approximately 40 suspects in the neighborhood who met the age criterion. Using additional information in the profile, they narrowed their investigation to one individual and focused their investigation on him. He was arrested within a week.[7]

Clues from Evidence Brought to Crime Scene

Physical evidence brought to the crime scene by a criminal may yield a clue to his or her identity. Determining the intended use of a particular object wielded as a murder weapon has investigative value (see discussion in Chapter 5). The potential value of other foreign objects (a wallet, letter, or receipt) accidentally dropped or left at the scene hardly needs discussing. Suffice it to say such clues are not always apparent. Uncovering them calls for thoroughness; for example, an evidence technician discovered a dry cleaner's tag in a waste basket after homicide detectives had "searched" the room. This clue led to the identification of the offender.

Trampled vegetation, tracks in mud or snow, or any other visible evidence of the route taken to or from the scene, may be important—especially if the route is not one most people would choose. When no plausible reason can be inferred for not taking the most likely route (too many possible witnesses who might be encountered, for example), consideration must then be given to why the less likely one was chosen. Is it in the direction (especially in remote areas) of the offender's house? Would it lead to where a vehicle might be parked and not be noticed? Is there an attraction nearby (for example, an amusement park set up temporarily in some vacant space) that could provide a cover and explain the suspect's presence in the area? When any reason for the choice becomes apparent, investigative efforts can then be focused on this insight to see if additional leads can be developed.

Confession

A suspect is often interrogated in the latter stages of an investigation, primarily to ascertain what happened, and why, from the suspect's own mouth. The ultimate result may be a written, signed confession. A less conclusive result, a statement that stops short of a confession yet admits to facts from which guilt might be inferred, is called an *admission*. Such a statement has probative value; coupled with independent, corroborative physical evidence or testimony, an admission against interest may be sufficient to meet the reasonable doubt criterion the law imposes on a jury. (The reasons why a person may confess to a crime are discussed in Chapter 11.)

THE VICTIM

A victim is at the same time a witness and—like any other witness—is able to provide information. By virtue of being a victim, an additional contribution can be made, sometimes by suggesting the name of a suspect and sometimes by speculating about why he or she was the target. Underlying this input is motive. Even though a victim is not always aware of those who were motivated to commit the crime, such suggestions and speculations may give direction to the investigator's efforts. If blood or hair is found at the crime scene or on the victim's clothing, its potential as associative evidence should be exploited. (The discussion on "Witnesses" in the following section is equally applicable to the victim as a source of information).

WITNESSES

The Five Senses

A visual observation is the most frequent source of information contributed by a witness. The next is auditory in nature: the witness hears something said or someone speaking. Sources that are less frequent, but important at times, include: smell (e.g., the use of dogs to sniff out the presence of narcotics), touch (e.g., by a blindfolded rape victim), and taste (e.g., an odd or "off" flavor in food as in poisonings). In a series of rapes, several victims recognized the odor of home furnace heating oil in the rapist's automobile and on his clothing. Several victims described his car, and this led to a survey of parking areas adjacent to heating oil delivery companies. The victims also recalled a particular decal on the car's windshield. These visual and olfactory clues, together with an intensified, thorough investigative effort, pointed to a suspect who was later identified by each of the victims in separate lineups.

A visual observation contributed important information to the solution of a bombing case. A woman glancing out her window at the street noted six men and five women, dressed as joggers, grouped around a Volkswagen van. What caught her attention and aroused her suspicions was the strange sight of cigarettes in the mouths of joggers. Her call to the police led to the capture of Puerto Rican nationalists wanted for bombings on the island and in the United States. The recognition "that something is not right" is an ingredient of investigative mind-set; fortunately, it is not limited to detectives.

It is through eyewitnesses that the investigator may secure answers to the five questions of *who, what, when, where,* and *how*. They can make major contributions to the investigation of an event when the perpetrator, vehicle, or both are accurately described, and everything that happened is recalled in exact detail. More often than not, though, eyewitnesses are unable to meet these high standards.

Describing the Perpetrator

To some degree, an eyewitness or victim may be able to describe the perpetrator to police. This description can then be transmitted in three ways to other law enforcement personnel (or the public at large) for assistance in apprehending the offender:

1. A verbal description (*portrait parlé*) of the perpetrator's physical characteristics and clothing is taken, then printed;

2. A likeness of the perceived image is captured by a police artist (the variety of feature nuances is almost infinite);

3. A likeness of the perceived image is captured by mechanical means such as Identi-Kit or Penry Photo-Fit (a choice of features is offered: forehead, hairline, eyebrows, chin, ears, eyes, nose, and mouth). Or, a computer can be used to compose a likeness of an offender; the variety of feature nuances is comparable to that which the police artist is able to capture.

Whether hand-drawn or obtained by mechanical means, these images can be electronically transmitted to other law enforcement agencies.

Describing Vehicles or Weapons

Unfortunately, witnesses are often unable to provide a serviceable description of a vehicle or weapon used in the commission of a crime. Accurate information would permit police to alert officers on patrol about what to look for. Once such property is located, it should be placed in protective custody until examined for fingerprints or other trace evidence.

Vehicles

The following information may be provided by witnesses:

- Kind of vehicle   automobile, pickup truck, motorcycle, bicycle, etc.

- Color of vehicle   white, red, two-tone—gray on top, blue on bottom, etc.

- Body style   2-door, 4-door, station wagon, etc.

- Make or manufacturer   General Motors, Ford, Chrysler, foreign
                             (sometimes by name), etc.

- Model   Regal, Camaro, Mustang, Blazer, etc.

- License plate   the state; the number (or a part of the number)

- Distinguishing features   bumper stickers, vanity plates, wheel covers,
                             customizing

Weapons

The information obtained from witnesses is generally sketchy with respect to a weapon used in a crime, but some people may be able to provide the following details:

- Kind   Gun, knife, hatchet, club, etc.

- Color   Shiny, black, olive green, dull grey, etc.

- Type   Gun (revolver, automatic, rifle);
                    Knife (hunting, carving, pocket,
                    kitchen), etc.

- Length   Gun (short or long barrel);
                    Knife (long or short blade), etc.

- Caliber (of gun) .22, .38, .45, .357 Magnum, large bore,
                    small bore, etc.

PERSONS ACQUAINTED WITH THE SUSPECT

Relatives, friends, and business associates usually know a great deal about an individual. Not only are they familiar with the person's lifestyle and activities, but also with his or her thoughts and opinions. Some of this knowledge can be useful to the detective; even what seems to be worthless can turn out to be helpful. What a person eats on a given day can even be important. In a burglary case, a suspect under surveillance was reported to have just had a big steak for dinner. From another source it had already been learned that the burglar made a habit of eating a hearty steak dinner before going to "work." Surveillance was difficult because he was wary, and considerable resources in vehicles and personnel had to be assigned. Armed with the knowledge of the suspect's habit, the wherewithal could be assembled quickly and utilized efficiently.

Informants

Witnesses are informants in the strictest sense. Others provide information about criminal activity in the area for venal reasons. For instance, before a case has been fully made against him or her, a fence, suspect, or felon engaging in plea bargaining may offer to provide information about a major crime or a series of lesser crimes. For such proposals to be acceptable, explicit information must be supplied. Hence, even though "who," what," "where," "when" and "how" are handed up on a platter, as it were, the investigator should obtain other, independent evidence if the assertions are to be proved and have credibility in court. (The motivation and usefulness of informants are treated at greater length in Chapter 8.)

FOLLOW-UP ACTIVITIES

Regardless of the source of information, in order to bring about an arrest and prove guilt, it is the detective who must do the follow-up. The investigative potential of some follow-up activities is treated below.

Surveillance

Surveillance may be described as the unobtrusive observation of a person, place, or thing. A "person" is usually a suspect or the relative or friend of a suspect. Anyone, however, is a potential subject of surveillance—provided it is reasonable to expect that their activities would furnish significant information in a criminal investigation. A "place" might be a drug store or liquor store, supermarket, bank, or any other locus in which transactions are largely in cash, or where contraband such as narcotics is available. For the investigator, any place may become sufficiently interesting to be put under surveillance. A "thing" worthy of surveillance might include the ransom dropped at a designated spot, an automobile, or the fruits or instruments of a crime that were hidden for later recovery. In the last named circumstance, other investigative measures would have to be employed first if the perpetrator is to be caught in the act of recovering what was hidden.

Surveillance has a dual function in police work: one is investigative; the other, preventive. The specific objectives are:

1. To locate a suspect.

2. To obtain detailed information about the nature and scope of an individual's activities as they relate to suspected criminality.

3. To prevent the commission of crimes such as arson, which may put lives in jeopardy.

4. To apprehend immediately those who commit a crime while under surveillance (in a burglary for instance, the arrest is made as the perpetrators emerge from the building they broke into).

There is a temptation to discuss surveillance as though it were an independent investigative technique, but this is seldom true. On the contrary, facts acquired through interviewing, interrogation, informants, and legitimate wiretapping often supplement and confirm those developed through surveillance. And vice-versa. They are complementary, and a successful detective learns to season the investigative effort with the proper quantity of each technique.

Locating Suspect

Suspects who have absented themselves from their normal haunts present a problem for the detective. Given the gregarious nature of the human being, surveilling a relative or close friend may quickly lead to the subject's whereabouts—except in cases where extreme measures are taken (e.g., flight from the jurisdiction). Sometimes a hobby can help to locate a suspect who, for example, follows the horses from track to track, loves deep sea fishing, or has an exotic interest such as falconry.

Determining Activities of Suspect

An investigator needs details on the nature and scope of a suspect's activities for the following reasons:

1. To identify a suspect's associates; and to infer from their observed behavior (individual or group) any criminal intentions or plans.

2. To obtain evidence necessary to establish probable cause for a search warrant or an arrest.

3. To obtain information useful for interrogating a suspect.

Concluding Existence of Probable Cause for Search Warrant—Based on Behavior of Suspect

There may come a point in an investigation when it no longer seems likely that sufficient evidence will be produced to establish guilt beyond a reasonable doubt. By utilizing professional judgment and other sources (such as informants), the investigator may have grounds for believing the individual is engaging in criminal acts. Under such circumstances, suspect and associates should be put under surveillance. If a professional criminal is involved, considerable staff and equipment will be required. With some luck there will be a speedy, satisfactory outcome, but probably days, weeks, or even months will go by before results are achieved.

If contraband (such as alcohol or narcotics) is suspected, or stolen cars are involved, surveillance may permit observations to support an application for a search warrant. When the observations are correctly interpreted by the investigator, the search should uncover the necessary evidence in most situations.

Obtaining Information for Interrogation

Horowitz has analyzed the requisite conditions for obtaining a confession (see Chapter 11). Two of them may be assisted by information obtained through surveillance. They require the suspect to believe that:

1. Evidence is available against them;

2. Forces hostile to their interests are being employed with maximum effort; meanwhile, friendly forces are being kept to a minimum.

A thorough surveillance or interview of the suspect's family and friends puts detailed, personal facts at the disposal of the investigator. This, if skillfully utilized, can prove devastating. By disclosing an inconsequential detail at the proper moment during an interrogation, a suspect's life appears to be an open book. After a few repetitions of this methodology and, having met the conditions outlined by Horowitz (i.e., accusation, available evidence, friendly and hostile forces, guilt feelings), an admission or confession may result. To corroborate the confession, a diligent check on the admitted details must follow. For an innocent person, of course, guilty knowledge is not coupled with the other conditions described by Horowitz; therefore, a confession is not likely.

Judging when to invest significant surveillance resources, and at what stage in the investigative process, depends on other priority needs, the personnel available, and additional developments in the case. The economist's notion of a "trade-off" can be of help in arriving at a decision to continue or discontinue a surveillance.

Lineup (Identification Parade)

After a suspect has been apprehended, a lineup is assembled for the purpose of having the perpetrator correctly identified by those who witnessed the crime. At the same time, it is employed to protect the innocent, a correct identification eliminating an individual otherwise thought to be a suspect. A properly conducted lineup also serves to support an eyewitness concerned about making a mistake or the ability to make an identification. And, just as a perpetrator who is given a fair lineup is less likely to harbor a grudge, so will an eyewitness testify more effectively when confidence in the identification was based on and tested by the proper procedure (see Chapter 10).

Neighborhood Canvass

When all clues have been followed up without avail and a case holds little hope of solution, a canvass of the area might be productive. The British use the term *intensive inquiry* for seeking information by canvass. Law enforcement procedures in Great Britain and the United States justify neighborhood canvasses for two reasons: one, there is the possibility that someone saw or heard something that was not reported— perhaps because its importance is not realized until an inquiring officer knocks at the door; and two, there is the likelihood of a shock to the security of a criminal. Believing that he or she managed to leave the crime scene undetected, a guilty person could be unnerved by a sudden confrontation with an investigator. Because neighborhood surveillance is conducted without publicity, the customary mode in cities, the culpable may jump to the wrong conclusions and either confess or betray their involvement by their responses to questions.

Questioning People: Proposed Refinements

In seeking information from people, an investigator should be aware of two difficulties that may not immediately be recognized or comprehended. One is presented by those who are willing to talk, but cannot recall (in whole or in part) what was observed, or those who do not remember anything beyond the information already provided. The second difficulty is presented by those who refuse to talk, or do talk yet withhold what might be of use, or attempt to misdirect the investigator by providing time-consuming and ultimately unproductive leads.

Among the old and new methods proposed to remedy these difficulties and elicit useful information are: lie detection (by traditional polygraph and the voice stress analyzer), hypnosis, nonverbal communication signals, and the behavioral analysis interview (see Chapter 6). To be effective, the results obtained from any of these methods should be followed up and buttressed by independent evidence.

Lie Detection by Polygraph

The polygraph or lie detector is a mechanical device designed to ascertain whether a subject is telling the truth. It records any changes in blood pressure and pulse, breathing rate, and the electrical conductance of the skin, known as GSR (galvanic skin response). For control purposes, neutral questions like "What is your name?" are interspersed with critical questions such as "Did you kill Mary Smith?" The instrument is based on the idea that ordinarily a person is under stress when telling a lie; therefore physiological responses to psychological stimuli (the questions) are produced that can be detected and measured. They may be interpreted to mean that the subject is telling the truth, that he or she is lying, or the result may be inconclusive.

The polygraph's principal contribution to criminal investigation is that it frequently leads to a confession. It is not uncommon for confessions to be obtained from suspects when it is suggested that they take a lie detector test. At other times, people will steadfastly deny involvement until just before the test is to be administered. Confessions also occur during testing, but more often take place afterward when the visible results (a series of graphs) are shown and discussed with the suspect. Most important, the test may protect the innocent person who asserts having no knowledge of the crime under investigation.

Thirty states allow polygraph results into evidence if both parties agree (i.e., by stipulation) and 13 states do so even when opposing counsel objects. There are more than 60 appellate decisions upholding the admissibility of confessions obtained during a polygraph test.[8] Rafky and Sussman, in the introduction to their article, "Polygraph Reliability and Validity," enumerate the previous studies already published on this issue.[9] Scientists in general understand reliability to mean that the results of polygraph tests are consistent and reproducible, and validity to mean that they accurately measure truthfulness. Their research demonstrates:

the intimate relationship between validity and reliability. The finding that three components produce more valid determinations than any single component shows that additional measures stabilize the test by reducing the standard error of measurement.[10]

A secondary, though far less frequent, contribution of a polygraph test is the emergence of follow-up leads; the whereabouts of stolen property, a weapon, or a person may be determined from the reactions to direct questions about them. In addition, any inconsistencies in prior statements and explanations given to police by the suspect can be verified or challenged. Statements likely to be untruthful must be followed up by checking them against the facts as determined from the physical evidence.

When there are numerous suspects in a case, the polygraph is occasionally employed to separate the unlikely ones; however, some polygraphers regard this as a misuse. Most often, the polygraph is employed in an investigation that is already developed to a point where its test results may resolve an issue or produce further leads. In either situation, the investigator must furnish the polygraph examiner with investigative information to permit the construction of fruitful questions. Despite the claims for lie detection, it should be noted that its acceptance as an investigative tool is not universal. About 10 countries accept it; Britain's Scotland Yard does not.

Lie Detection by Voice Stress Analysis

Several names have been given to instruments designed in the early 1970s to detect voice changes in people who are upset or under stress. Among the so-called voice polygraphs are the Psychological Stress Evaluator (PSE), the Mark II Voice Analyzer, the Hagoth voice stress analyzer, and the Computerized Voice Stress Analyzer (CVSA). In certain circumstances, it is possible to use voice stress analysis even when an individual is unwilling to take the voice polygraph test, since attachments to the body need not be made as with the traditional polygraph. The value of voice stress analysis for the investigator is claimed by proponents to equal that of the traditional polygraph. Although relatively new, criticism of its scientific basis has developed; this is reviewed by Lykken, who concluded:

> There is no scientifically credible evidence that the PSE . . . can reliably measure differences in "stress" as reflected in the human voice. There is considerable evidence that the PSE, used in connection with standard lie detection test interrogations, discriminates the deceptive from the truthful at about chance levels of accuracy: that is, the PSE lie test has roughly zero validity.[11]

A later study by Timm in 1983 on the effectiveness of PSE states:

> . . . the Psychological Stress Evaluator failed to perform at a level better than chance expectancy in this study.

> . . . therefore, the poor showing of the PSE in this study appears to be a reflection of the instrument itself, as opposed to defects in the procedures used to evaluate it.[12]

Nachshon, et al., examined the PSE under field conditions, suggesting that

> . . . more research is needed before a final conclusion concerning PSE validity, its scope of applicability, and the differential contributions of the factors affecting final decisions (PSE charts, examiner's expertise) can be reached.[13]

Before widespread support and acceptance can be achieved, additional objective testing and investigative usage would appear to be necessary.

A comparison of the latest development in PSE technology—the Computer Voice Stress Analyzer (CVSA)—with traditional polygraphy, reveals several interesting facts:

1. Both the polygraph and CVSA are in use today.

2. Either machine may be effective in measuring exactly what it was designed to measure.

3. The operation of either device is an "art": it depends on skill, technique, and experience.

4. For legal and ethical reasons, permission (granted by the subject) is required before any test is run on either instrument.[14]

Many traditional polygraphers are critical of CVSA. There is a dearth of "scientifically valid, objective research," and a reliance on only one input (i.e., "microtremors" in the human voice). The polygraph, they point out, can measure several physiological inputs: blood pressure and pulse, breathing rate, and GSR. All the same, CVSA is "popular in everyday use with a growing number of law enforcement agencies." Apparently it has flourished because it seems to work "especially in child molester and rape cases . . . (with) a high confession rate."[15]

Unlike the polygraph, which must be physically connected to the subject, CVSA merely tape-records the questioning session. This can be done at the subject's home, detention facility, or hospital room. The advantages of portability and flexibility are important considerations in an investigation. The submission of CVSA data to computer analysis would appear to be the next step on the horizon.[16]

Hypnosis

Hypnosis is a method of eliciting information from victims and witnesses (and sometimes suspects) who are willing to be put into a sleep-like state in which they respond to questions about an event they have observed. Under hypnosis, such details as license plate numbers, the make or color of a car, the race of an offender, parts of conversations (including places and names incidentally referred to therein), and other details of the crime may be recalled. Facial characteristics for the police artist also may be provided under hypnosis, even though not recalled when the victim or witness is questioned under normal conditions. In traumatic, emotionally charged events like murder, rape, or kidnapping, repression of the conscious memory may be undone in the hypnotic state, and information obtained that was not forthcoming during a normal interview.

The Los Angeles Police and the Israeli National Police, pioneers in the use of hypnosis, are convinced of its value. A bizarre case in California will illustrate the basis for their faith and demonstrate how a valuable lead was elicited.[17] Twenty-six children on a school bus were kidnapped by three masked, armed men. They, together with the driver, were taken to an abandoned trailer truck that was buried in a pit and provided with a small air vent. Some 16 hours later the captives dug themselves out and escaped. When questioning failed to produce leads, the driver agreed to be hypnotized. In that sleep-like state, he recalled all but one of the eight digits of the license plate on the kidnappers' vehicle, providing the clue that led to their apprehension. Though yielding remarkable results in this case, hypnosis should not be expected to prove equally efficacious each time it is used.

There are, of course, fundamental legal questions concerning the use of hypnosis. For example, are the results of having a witness's memory refreshed by hypnosis admissible as evidence in court? This was addressed by a Michigan appellate court and the Arizona Supreme Court.[18, 19] A basic point at issue was whether the witness's testimony was a true recollection of the event, or one implanted unwittingly or deliberately by the hypnotist. Stated another way: could such testimony be "tainted" as the court declared, and therefore, constitute inadmissible evidence?

Until 1980, courts held that hypnosis did not render the testimony tainted or the witness incompetent. The shift in judicial attitude, first manifested in 1980, is best illustrated by quoting from two decisions:

> Although we perceive that hypnosis is a useful tool in the investigative stage, we do not feel the state of the science (or art) has been shown to be such as to admit testimony which may have been developed as a result of hypnosis. A witness who has been under hypnosis, as in the case here, should not be allowed to testify when there is a question that the testimony may have been produced by that hypnosis.[20]

The second decision states:

> The determination of the guilt or innocence of an accused should not depend on the unknown consequences of a procedure concededly used for the purpose of changing in some way a witness' memory. Therefore, until hypnosis gains general acceptance in the fields of medicine and psychiatry as a method by which memories are accurately improved without undue danger of distortion, delusion, or fantasy, we feel that testimony of witnesses which has been tainted by hypnosis should be excluded in criminal cases.[21]

Another legal question raised is whether hypnosis can be used to determine the state of mind of a defendant before or during the commission of a crime.[22] Although such a determination is important to prosecutors when trying a case, using hypnosis for this purpose provokes yet another issue: Is the defendant denied a basic right to confront and cross-examine a hostile witness who was previously hypnotized? Effective cross-examination is prevented when there is no recollection of questions asked, answers given, or even the subject matter. Thus, the details elicited under hypnosis cannot be probed under cross-examination because the witness is technically unaware of them.[23]

In 1987 the Supreme Court examined the right of a defendant to take the stand in her own behalf and give testimony based on her having been hypnotized.[24] The original trial judge had limited testimony to what she knew about the crime prior to hypnosis. The Supreme Court, however, refused to accept an automatic (*per se*) rule of exclusion; it ruled that a hearing by the trial judge was needed to determine the reliability of the proposed hypnosis-based testimony, and the existence of any corroboration for it. The Court also suggested that the states develop guidelines regarding such testimony, and some have done so. Its admissibility may differ, depending on whether the state or the defense seeks to offer the evidence. For a comprehensive treatment of state cases and the literature on this subject, see *People v. Zayas* (159 Ill. App. 3d 554 (1987)).[25]

Nonverbal Communication

Communication between people is not limited to the spoken or written word. Thoughts and feelings not stated openly may be expressed unconsciously through nonverbal behavior. Nonverbal methods may also be employed to change another person's unfavorable opinion to a favorable one. Generally, people use both verbal and nonverbal methods simultaneously.

> Nonverbal communication tends to be nonrational in that the response is direct and immediate, circumventing the conscious deliberative process. Nonverbal messages tend to follow a stimulus-response pattern without any intervening conscious decision-making process we call thinking. For these reasons nonverbal communication is less conscious than verbal, but it may be the more powerful force in face-to-face interaction . . . .[26]

There are many modes of nonverbal communication, including kinesics, paralinguistics, and proxemics. *Kinesics*, the study of the use of body movement and posture to convey meaning, is most important for the investigator. Serving to a lesser extent is *paralinguistics*, the study of the variations in the quality of the voice (its pitch or intonation, its loudness or softness) and the effect of these variations on the meaning conveyed. *Proxemics* pertains to the physical distance individuals put between themselves and others, as well as to the space a person occupies (in particular, the placement and use of the limbs). Nonverbal signals are referred to as "leakage" by psychologists who study the phenomenon.

Kinesics

Eye, hand, leg, and foot movement; facial expression; and body posture provide valuable cues to the investigator. In the practical application of kinesics, most people focus on the eyes and face for indications that a verbal statement is or is not in accord with the speaker's innermost thoughts and feelings. It also may be evidenced by constant crossing and recrossing of the legs, foot tapping, or finger drumming—all of which belie verbal denials of culpability or involvement.

Paralinguistics

It is possible to give a resounding "no" that, by its loudness, means "no" emphatically; or, through varying the pitch in the voice, to intone a "no" that means "maybe." Through intonation, "no" can also either ask a question or express disbelief. Similar paralinguistic clues may be communicated during an interview or interrogation by replies spoken in a low voice when the previous volume was normal, or (toward the end of the session) by those spoken in a dispirited tone. These cues may signal that the person is about to "break" and make a confession.

Proxemics

An individual at ease may sit with legs spread wide and arms at the sides. However, if questioning becomes unnerving, the subject may shift to a protective posture by crossing the legs and folding the arms across the chest. Another proxemic clue is made manifest by any movement or action taken by the subject to increase the distance between him or her and the questioner.

The Value of Nonverbal Signals

In order to obtain the most benefit from nonverbal leakage, a base line needs to be established for the nonverbal clues normally employed by the subject. This is best done by first engaging in nonthreatening conversation and looking for signs (or lack thereof) of the nonverbal clues basic to the individual's makeup. Later, when the stress of official questioning (especially that of interrogation) is felt by the subject, any new nonverbal clue or sign of increase in frequency or intensity is meaningful. The subject should be in plain view, not seated in front of a desk or allowed to have a throw pillow or other object on the lap that masks the hands.

During an interview (and particularly during an interrogation), the detective must be alert to the nonverbal clues suspects may emit. Indeed, when offenders are interrogated, they will subtly try (initially at least) to induce a belief in their innocence. Through eye contact they may attempt to demonstrate sincerity; through other body and facial expressions they may show concern for the victim or surprise and shock at a question that implies involvement. By means of such role playing, they hope to convince the investigator that the police are on the wrong track. In so doing, the guilty person must resort to lying. When contradictions are exposed by other evidence and pointed out, the symptoms of lying conveyed through body language can sometimes be observed.

At the appropriate point, the detective is at liberty to employ nonverbal behavior consciously to communicate with the suspect. Facial expressions (raised eyebrow, beady stare, smirk) or other body movements (hand gestures, head shaking, rolling of the eyes) will convey disbelief in the explanation that a suspect is providing.

In addition to serving as a kind of lie detector, nonverbal signals can provide follow-up clues. In the homicide of a young female business executive, for instance, a male neighbor in the next-door apartment was asked whether another male was or had been her lover. He gave a negative response but, before answering, a barely perceptible smile crossed his face. Making a mental note of this observation, and checking it out later, the detective learned that the two men once had a sexual affair. Although it did not help to solve the homicide, it shows how fleeting nonverbal clues can be. In this case, eliminating a possible suspect freed up the investigator's efforts, allowing them to be directed into more productive channels. In summary, nonverbal signals may serve to expose a deception, eliminate fruitless effort, or suggest possible leads for further investigation.

REFERENCES

1   R.F. Turner, "Hans Gross: The Model of the Detective," in *Pioneers in Policing*, P.J. Stead, ed., (Montclair, NJ: Patterson Smith, 1977), 148-158.

2   R.L. Ault and J.T. Reese, "Profiling: A Psychological Assessment of Crime," *FBI Law Enforcement Bulletin*, 49:3 (March 1980), 22-25.

3   Arthur A. Carey, *Memoirs of a Murder Man* (New York: Doubleday, 1930).

4   Colin Campbell, "Detectives of the Mind: Portrait of a Mass Killer," *Psychology Today* 9:12 (1976), 110-119.

5   Ibid., 115.

6   R.K. Ressler, et al., "Offender Profiles: A Multidisciplinary Approach," *FBI Law Enforcement Bulletin* 49:9 (September 1980), 16-20.

7   R. Ault and J.T. Reese, *op. cit.*

8   D.M. Rafky and R.C. Sussman, "Polygraphic Reliability and Validity: Individual Components and Stress of Issue in Criminal Tests," *Journal of Police Science and Administration* 13:4 (1985), 283.

9   Ibid., 283-284.

10 Ibid., 293.

11 David T. Lykken, *A Tremor in the Blood: Uses and Abuses of the Lie Detector* (New York: McGraw-Hill, 1981), 159-160.

12 H.W. Timm, "The Efficacy of the Psychological Stress Evaluator in Detecting Deception," *Journal of Police Science and Administration* 11:1 (1983), 65-66.

13 I. Nachshon, E. Elaad, and T. Amsel, "Validity of the Psychological Stress Evaluator: A Field Study," *Journal of Police Science and Administration* 13:4 (1985), 281.

14 Whitworth, A.W., "Polygraph or CVSA: What's the Truth About Deception Analysis?" *Law and Order*, 41(11), 29-31 (Nov. 1993), 30.

15 Ibid., 31.

16 Ibid.

17 "The Svengali Squad," *Time*, 13 September 1976, 56-57.

18 *People v. Tait*, 297 N.W.2d 853 (Mich. App. 1980).

19 *State v. Mena*, 624 P.2d 1274 (Arizona 1980).

20 *State v. La Mountain*, 611 P.2d 551 (Arizona 1980).

21 *State v. Mena, supra* note 19.

22 M. Reiser, "Hypnosis and Its Uses in Law Enforcement," *Police Journal (Brit.)* 51 (1978), 24-33.

23 B.L. Diamond, "Inherent Problems in the Use of Pretrial Hypnosis on a Prospective Witness," 68 *California Law Review*, 313 (1980).

24   *Rock v. Arkansas*, 483 U.S. 44 (1987).

25   *People v. Zayas*, 159 Ill. App. 3d 554 (1987).

26   Raymond L. Gorden, *Interviewing: Strategy, Techniques and Tactics*, 4th ed. (Florence, KY: Wadsworth, 1987).

SUPPLEMENTAL READINGS

Psychological Profiling

Anon., "Offender Profiles: A Multidisciplinary Approach," *FBI Law Enforcement Bulletin* 49:9 (September 1980), 16-20.

Ault, R.L., and J.T. Reese. "A Psychological Assessment of Crime: Profiling," *FBI Law Enforcement Bulletin* 49:3 (March 1980), 22-25.

Neighborhood Canvassing

Andrew, Allen. *Intensive Inquiries*. London: Harrap & Co., 1973.

Interrogation

Aubry, Arthur S., Jr., and Rudolph R. Caputo. *Criminal Interrogation*. 3rd ed. Springfield, IL: Charles C Thomas, 1980.

Gudjonsson, Gisli H. *The Psychology of Interrogations, Confessions and Testimony*. Text Ed., New York: Wiley, 1992.

Hess, John E. *Interviewing and Interrogation for Law Enforcement*. Cincinnati: Anderson, 1997.

Hilgendorff, Irving B., and L. Hilgendorff. *Police Interrogation: The Psychological Approach*. Research Study No. 1. Royal Commission on Criminal Procedure. London: Her Majesty's Stationery Office, 1980.

Inbau, F.E. *Criminal Investigation and Confessions*. 3rd ed. Baltimore: Williams & Wilkins, 1985.

Macdonald, John M., and David L. Michaud. *Criminal Interrogation,* Rev. & Enl. ed. Denver: Apache Press, 1992.

McDonald, Hugh C. *The Practical Psychology of Police Interrogation*. Santa Ana, CA: Townsend, 1963.

Morris, P. *Police Interrogation: Review of the Literature*. Research Study No. 1. Royal Commission of Criminal Procedure. London: Her Majesty's Stationery Office, 1981.

Rabon, Don. *Interviewing and Interrogation*. Durham, NC: Carolina Academic Press, 1992.

Zulawski, David E., and Douglas E. Wicklander, eds. *Practical Aspects of Interview and Interrogation*. Boca Raton, FL: CRC Press, 1993.

Nonverbal Communication

Archer, Dane. *How To Expand Your Social Intelligence Quotient*. New York: M. Evans and Company, 1980.

Kuhlman, Merlin S. "Nonverbal Communications in Interrogation," *FBI Law Enforcement Bulletin* 49:11 (November 1980), 6-9.

Link, Frederick C., and Glen D. Foster. *The Kinesic Interview Technique.* Anniston, AL: Interrotec Press, 1982.

Morris, Desmond. *Body Talk: The Meaning of Human Gestures.* New York: Crown Publishers, 1994.

Walters, Stan B. *Principles of Kinesic Interview and Interrogation.* Boca Raton, FL: CRC Press, 1996.

Waltman, John L. "Nonverbal Communication in Interrogation: Some Applications," *Journal of Police Science and Administration* 11:2 (1983), 166-169.

Detection of Deception

Ekman, P., and M.V. Friesen, "Leakage and Clues to Deception," *Psychiatry* 32 (1969), 88-106.

Ferguson, Robert J. *The Scientific Informer.* Springfield, IL: Charles C Thomas, 1971.

Horvath, F.S. "Detecting Deception: The Promise and Reality of Voice Stress Analysis," *Journal of Forensic Sciences* 27:1 (1982), 340-349.

Horvath, F.S. "Verbal and Nonverbal Clues to Truth and Deception During Polygraph Examinations," *Journal of Police Science and Administration* 1 (1973), 138-152.

Lykken, David T. *A Tremor in the Blood: Uses and Abuses of the Lie Detector.* New York: McGraw-Hill, 1981.

Matte, J.A. *Art and Science of the Polygraph Technique.* Springfield, IL: Charles C Thomas, 1980.

Murphy, James K. "Polygraphy Technique: Past and Present," *FBI Law Enforcement Bulletin* 49:6 (June 1980), 1.

Nizer, Louis. "How to Tell a Liar," in *Reflections Without Mirrors.* New York: Berkley, 1979.

Reid, John E., and Inbau, F.E. *Truth and Deception: The Polygraph Technique.* 2nd ed. Woburn, MA: Butterworth, 1977.

CHAPTER 5

Records and Files

Investigative Uses and Sources—Public and Private

RECORDS AS INVESTIGATIVE AIDS

It is hardly possible for people to move in modern society and not leave a trail of past activities. Recorded in one way or another, the trail is chronological, marked from earliest school days by intelligence and psychological test scores, teacher evaluations, and grades. It can be followed into adult life where business and personal dealings leave their own distinctive traces. Hence, just as school records can be used to locate a family, so can credit card purchases of goods and services account for the buyer's whereabouts. And, because the stages of life from birth to death are for the most part duly noted by government and business, the patterns of human activity can be reconstructed through diligent, informed effort. The investigator, however, must have a reason to devote time and effort on the search for information. Generally, a criminal investigation is driven by the seriousness of a crime and its impact on the community, but it may be influenced by media or other pressures on the police to find a solution.

Hence, a mass of assorted material is on record for any one individual, and the investigator must have some appreciation of the existence and possible origins of what is sought. The wide variety of sources includes the records of ownership of personal property (automobile, handgun, house); of required licenses (driver, marriage, professional); of business transactions (purchase or sale of property); of utility services received (gas, electric, telephone); and of transportation (airline, car rental). A classification scheme for record sources for investigative purposes is presented in this chapter. The following possibilities represent an overview of the kind of information that can be sought and uncovered through the study of records.

- Link a person to an object (such as a gun) through purchase or ownership;

- Link one person to another (relatives through a marriage license, friends through telephone calls, or membership in an organization);

- Link a person to a place or a time period;

- Discover something about an individual's lifestyle, personal behavior or movements.

Realizing the potential of records for the investigative process is most likely when they are perceived as stored information awaiting retrieval by the imaginative investigator. Whether maintained expressly for criminal justice purposes, or as a concomitant of good government and sound business practice, records can be used to:

- Follow up or provide additional leads;

- Identify the perpetrator;

- Trace and locate a suspect, criminal, or witness;

- Recover stolen or lost property;

- Ascertain facts about physical evidence—its source or ownership, for example.

Follow Up or Provide New Leads

The laundry and dry cleaner mark file and the fraudulent check file are sources of stored information that can serve the follow-up purposes of law enforcement. License plate registration files for motor vehicles could be made more conducive to investigative purposes if application forms were to ask for vehicle color. Feasibly, the records of one agency of government (for example, the motor vehicle bureau) could at no additional cost be designed with another's needs (the police) in mind. Even such a modest innovation would require bureaucratic imagination and cooperation.

The pawnbroker file is a good example of how new leads may be supplied. In addition to the handwriting specimen provided by the required signature on the pawn slip, a personal description of the individual who pledged the stolen goods is sometimes obtained. Occasionally, the alert pawnbroker makes a judgment call about the behavior of a customer or, recognizing that the articles were probably stolen, detains the customer on some pretext in order to telephone the local police.

The many directories compiled by telephone companies for public and intracompany use are especially helpful for follow-up purposes. The city directory (though a private publication and not available for every city) is a source of additional information on the residential and business community. It can be used to corroborate and augment incomplete information obtained verbally from people contacted during an investigation.

Identify the Perpetrator

The fingerprint record file, the criminal photograph file (sometimes called the "Rogues Gallery" or "mug shot" file), and the *modus operandi* (MO) file are quite useful for identification purposes. Often housed in the same place, they supplement each other. On the other hand, the latent fingerprint file enjoys limited success in the identification of criminals on the basis of fingerprints alone. Although the application of computer technology to the problem of fingerprint identity is a major breakthrough, it initially requires that a complete set of the subject's fingerprints be in storage. An expensive task requiring some time for completion, the problem remains formidable.

Trace and Locate a Suspect, Criminal, or Witness

When the identity of a suspect, criminal, or witness is known but he or she is absent from the usual places of abode, work, and recreation, the investigator is faced with the problem of tracing and locating that person. The investigative effort should be based on the knowledge that most people are to some extent gregarious and will tend to seek out familiar people and places. It is possible, for instance, to locate a particular individual through his or her child by arranging to be alerted to the transfer of any school records in the areas most frequented by that person. Placing relatives and friends of the fugitive under surveillance is another means to the same end. Because people generally require some continuity in their everyday business pursuits, the records of banks and public utilities are also quite useful. In important cases, "wanted" circulars can be distributed.

Figure 5.1

A woman's fingerprints are scanned into a computer at the driver's license bureau in Atlanta, Georgia. Georgia is among four states that require license applicants to provide their fingerprints for identification. *(AP Photo/Alan Mothner.)*

Recover Stolen or Lost Property

The major problem in recovering stolen or lost property is making certain that the complainant's description of the property corresponds closely with the description recorded when it is located by police, either directly or through a pawn shop. This problem is readily solved by using carefully structured forms for pawnbrokers and secondhand dealers. Computers are also useful because their large memory banks facilitate the operation of a system over a much wider geographical area than was heretofore possible. If law enforcement computer systems were linked, a criminal crossing a state line or traveling hundreds of miles to pawn stolen articles would no longer be able to avoid detection.

Ascertain Information Concerning Physical Evidence

Two distinctly different kinds of information are sought when physical evidence is discovered at a crime scene. The first has to do with tracing ownership of evidence like guns, poisons, and explosives. Ownership can often be ascertained, as many states require records of such transactions. The rifle used to assassinate President Kennedy was traced to Lee Harvey Oswald through government records on the distribution and sale of guns.

The second kind of information concerns the recognition and identification of physical evidence: what it is, what it is used for, and where it is manufactured and distributed. The Sheppard murder investigation is an example of an attempt to identify the source of a bloody imprint (found on the pillowcase beneath the victim's head). It appeared to have been made by the jaws of a surgical instrument; also, trauma was consistent with that of a heavy instrument of some kind. Because Sam Sheppard, the suspect, was a surgeon, if such an instrument could be found to exist and to have once been in the doctor's possession (or available to him), testimony on these points could have a profound impact on a jury. At the request of Ohio authorities, therefore, a search was conducted throughout the country by local police departments. Despite this painstaking effort, no instrument that might leave a mark to match the blood pattern on the pillowcase could be found. The examination of hospital and medical supply house catalogues had similar results; the existence of such an instrument was not on record. Hence, it was impossible to determine what caused the bloody impression on the pillow; and, if it were an instrument, what it was and where it might be obtained. Had an instrument been found to match the bloody imprint, but which by its nature and purpose was for nonmedical use, authorities would probably have given Sheppard's story greater credence.

TYPES AND SOURCES OF RECORDED INFORMATION _____

Because the extent and scope of stored information is extraordinarily large, it is useful to generate a classification scheme. This will help the detective to reach a record source quickly, follow up on a clue that came from an unexpected source, or develop a new clue. The following taxonomy ranks recorded information in proportion to its potential usefulness and availability:

- Files of law enforcement agencies
- Files of other governmental agencies
- Records of business organizations
- Miscellaneous sources

Law Enforcement Agencies

The files that yield the greatest amount of information and offer immediate access to the investigator are clearly those maintained for law enforcement. Hence, the value of many of the following files is self-evident from their names:

Police Files

- Fingerprint
- Arrest and conviction (rap sheet)
- *Modus operandi*
- Rogues gallery (mug shot)
- "Stop and wanted" fugitives
- Lost and stolen property
- Pawnbrokers and secondhand dealers
- Known habitual criminals
    Sex offenders
    Arsonists
    Burglars (safes; homes; factories; offices)
    Robbers (gas stations, banks, drug stores; cab drivers, doctors)
    Truck thieves
    Bookmakers
    Prostitutes
- Receivers of stolen goods
- Nicknames or aliases
- Laundry and dry cleaner marks
- Fraudulent checks
- Field contact reports

Penal Records

- Regarding an inmate:
    Names of visitors
    Names of cellmates
    Names of other friends
    Places and periods of incarceration

Probation and Parole Records

- Regarding the released offender:
    Names of friends
    Names of references for employment
    Names of employers
    Place(s) of residence
    Name(s) of person(s) supervising release

Other Governmental Agencies

The name of an agency or its subdivision is usually self-explanatory, and the information to be gleaned is obvious. The kind of information to be obtained from some other agencies needs a brief explanation:

Federal Government

Treasury Department

- Bureau of Alcohol, Tobacco, Firearms, and Explosives (formerly Bureau of Alcohol, Tobacco, and Firearms) (ATF)

    The administration of the tax levied on these items requires detailed information on the persons and firms that handle them. AFT, in the National Firearms Tracing Center, maintains records on the manufacture, distribution, purchase, and transfer of firearms. Even weapons manufactured in a foreign country, if imported legally, can be traced by the center.

- Customs Service

    Information on importers, exporters, and the licensing and registry of vessels engaged in this trade; also names of custom house brokers and truckers.

- Internal Revenue Service (IRS)

    Sources of income can reveal names and places of employment. (Much illicit income has been reported to this agency ever since Al Capone's conviction by the Intelligence Unit for tax evasion.)

- U.S. Secret Service

    Threatening letter file. (It is amazing that individuals who write threatening anonymous letters to a president or another official they dislike will subsequently send and sign letters to one they admire.)

Department of Justice

- Federal Bureau of Investigation

    FBI Laboratory

    Forensic science services are provided to all law enforcement agencies that need them and are otherwise unable to obtain such assistance. New, often expensive technology found useful in law enforcement (such as DNA "fingerprinting") is made available through the FBI laboratory.

- Fingerprint File

    This is a national resource. "Stop and Wanted" cards received from state and municipal departments result in the identification of about 1,500 fugitives a month.

- National Crime Information Center (NCIC)

    The development of electronic data processing has made the rapid storage and retrieval of criminal information a reality. The NCIC computer stores data on: guns (missing, stolen, or recovered), securities (stolen, embezzled, counterfeited, or missing), and vehicles and/or license plates (stolen). The file also contains information on missing persons of any age who are: (1) proved to be physically or mentally disabled (possibly subjecting them or others to danger); (2) in the company of other persons under circumstances suggesting they are in danger; (3) possibly abducted or kidnapped, or (4) possible catastrophe victims. The computer accepts the names of wanted persons only if a warrant has been issued and the jurisdiction involved will extradite; it responds within a few minutes to requests for information. The agency entering data is primarily responsible for keeping its input accurate and up-to-date, including removal of that which is no longer pertinent. NCIC's files are referred to as "hot" files; the center also maintains the Unidentified Person's File, and the Computerized Criminal History File (CCH).

Immigration and Naturalization Service

An immigrant's date of entry into the country. Information provided by naturalization papers, names and addresses of registered aliens, lists of the passengers and crews of foreign vessels docking at United States ports.

Drug Enforcement Administration (DEA)

This agency, together with the Food and Drug Administration (FDA), is responsible for enforcing the Controlled Substances Act, which governs the manufacturing, obtaining, and selling of—as well as the illicit trafficking in—a controlled substance. Records and files are maintained on individuals and companies that are in violation of the law. (Many crimes— e.g., theft, assault, arson, homicide—are committed to seek or maintain control over the illicit drug trade; facts gathered in the investigation of drug-related crimes should be viewed in this light.)

Federal Prison System

The names of visitors, cellmates, and friends. For those granted probation, the names of employers, employment references, places of residence, and the names of friends.

Postal Service

- Postal Inspectors

    Information on persons receiving mail at a given address. Any forwarding address left by a person. The names of those from whom mail is being received—e.g., *mail covers*. (A mail cover is a copy of the printing and writing on the outside of a piece of mail. Examples are the sender's name and address, where and when it was mailed, and all outside markings. The mail is not opened by the post office. The information furnished to the investigator is on the outside of the envelope being mailed to the person or address being covered.)

State Department

- Passport Agency
  Date and place of birth of any person who has applied for a United States passport. Information about aliens who have been admitted to or departed from the United States.

Department of Transportation

- U.S. Coast Guard
  Names of persons and vessels seized in connection with smuggling contraband into the United States. The names and birthplaces of the owners of registered vessels.

- Federal Aviation Administration
  Names of pilots, their flight plans and briefings.

State and Local Agencies

Under the federal system of government, the powers not delegated in the Constitution to the national government were retained by the states. Accordingly, most licensing and regulatory powers are exercised at the state and local levels. The process of granting or denying licenses and regulating business requires that information be provided; these documents are a resource the investigator might tap at the appropriate time. Some particularly useful sources are listed below for each level of government: state, county and municipal.

State Agencies

Motor Vehicle Bureau
The information available from a driver's license application includes name, address, date of birth, sex, height, weight, color of eyes, sometimes the social security number, and a photograph; also, a handwriting specimen (the individual's signature). The bureau also maintains a Vehicle Identification Number (VIN) file.

Department of Labor
Names and addresses of persons who have sought employment as a day laborer, domestic, or hotel/restaurant employee.

Department of Public Aid or Welfare
Names and addresses of applicants for and recipients of public aid.

Ad Hoc Agencies
An *ad hoc* or one-purpose agency is established to deal with a particularly vexatious problem, in connection, for instance, with a sport like horse-racing or boxing, or with crime on the waterfront. (To wit, a bis-

tate compact between New York and New Jersey creating the New York Harbor Waterfront Commission dealt in a coordinated fashion with the numerous issues involved.) Because activities under the surveillance of an *ad hoc* agency usually entail the licensing of personnel, considerable information is available from licensee application forms. They are designed to elicit usable investigative information in anticipation of this need.

County and Municipal Departments

Owing to the great variation in administrative practices across the United States, it is impractical to specify the name of the bureau or office housing the following records at the county or municipal level:

- Birth certificates

- Marriage licenses

- Election (voting) records

- School records

- Library cards

A birth certificate or marriage license provides such valuable information as names, addresses, and ages of the licensees and their relatives. Voting records can provide an authenticated signature that may serve as an exemplar for the questioned document examiner. School records can locate a family, because schools will transmit a child's record only by mail. The records of public libraries include the names of registered borrowers, their home addresses and telephone numbers, and sometimes names, addresses, and telephone numbers of employers.

Business Organizations

It is not possible to exist in modern society without taking part in a certain amount of business dealings. People must find shelter, buy food, meet job-related demands, and take some recreation—all of which puts them on record. Indeed, given a list of checks written and credit card purchases made each month, an accurate socioeconomic picture can be reconstructed on an individual. The following is a roster of business organizations whose records are likely to provide investigative leads:

- Public utility companies

- Credit reporting agencies

- Insurance companies

- Labor unions

- Fraternal organizations

Public Utility Companies

As long as people must supply facts to obtain or transfer any utility service, there is a reservoir of useful information in utility company files. The files of the telephone company are particularly useful. For example, information can be obtained on the telephone numbers called frequently by an individual; the unlisted numbers called; the long distance numbers called (as well as the time and length of each call); the name of the subscriber for a particular number; and the telephone numbers listed for a particular address.

The value of such information to the detective may not be readily apparent. To clear away any doubts, consider the shooting of a well-known mobster in New York City. In this case, a search of the murdered man's overcoat pockets produced a slip of paper bearing a single telephone number. This evidence, obviously, was of interest to investigators; and yet, it would certainly have been unwise at that stage of the investigation to call the number directly. However, by knowing how to obtain the name of the subscriber discreetly and quickly, a potential source of information can be identified for follow-up. What such follow-up activity would entail depends on the needs of the particular situation. The circumstances may call merely for questioning the subscriber or a household member; it might mean placing one or several of them under surveillance; or, in order to clarify a partially developed detail, it might become necessary to use an informant or (where legal) a telephone surveillance or wiretap.

Credit Reporting Agencies

The extension of credit to a business or an individual requires assurances of the borrower's ability to repay the debt. This kind of information is compiled on a historical basis; it reveals the borrower's general reputation in the community. *File-based credit reporting bureaus* collect information from creditors on how bills were paid; *investigative credit reporting bureaus* gather information on an individual's lifestyle and reputation.

Although there are many local, file-based credit reporting companies, most of which belong to the Associated Credit Bureaus of America, only a few are investigative credit reporting agencies that operate nationally. They include Dun and Bradstreet, Inc., The Retail Credit Company, Hooper Holmes Inc., and Experian. Dun and Bradstreet gathers information on a business's corporate character, capital, and capacity to repay a loan. Retail Credit and Hooper Holmes gather information on individuals; in addition to income information, they furnish facts on: marital status, number of dependents, home address, employment history, lifestyle, consumption habits, moral character, and any indications of past or present illegal practices. Experian reports on both businesses and consumers. Sometimes a local file-based credit agency will have a photograph of the individual. MasterCard, Visa, Diner's Club, Carte Blanche, American Express, and other credit card applications offer additional avenues to be pursued in the quest for recorded facts. The whereabouts of a suspected serial murderer can be checked if a credit card was used. The downfall of Ted Bundy, the notorious, multi-state serial killer, can be attributed in part to credit card records. For example, though he denied having been in Colorado, receipts for gasoline purchased by credit card led to Bundy's extradition to stand trial for murder in that state.

Insurance Companies

Most people are covered by one or more forms of insurance: life, health, accident, casualty, or fire. Regardless of the kind of insurance they sell, insurance companies share information quite freely in order to eliminate poor risks. They also exchange data with other sources such as motor vehicle and credit bureaus, social welfare agencies, and health services. As a consequence, insurance companies may possess more information than is contained in a client's initial application (considerable in itself). Pursuing this line of inquiry can serve a criminal investigator well.

Labor Unions

Well over 20 million persons belong to labor unions in the United States. Not only must a member's dues be paid on time in order for them to remain in good standing with the union, but in the case of closed shops it is necessary for continued employment. If the union is cooperative, and some are not, this dues-paying transaction can provide a means of locating an individual. Labor union publications often contain photographs and news items covering members' activities. The *Directory of National and International Unions in the United States* provides the most comprehensive list of unions. This government publication will serve as a good starting point for an investigator seeking information about a union member.

Fraternal Organizations

Some organizations exist for fellowship (e.g., Elks, Moose, Odd Fellows); others have a religious base (e.g., Knights of Columbus, Masons, B'nai Brith) or were founded on pride of national origin (e.g., Ancient Order of Hibernians, Polish National Alliance, Dante Alighieri Society). Their people usually know each other better than do the members of professionally based organizations; hence, they may provide background material on an individual's vocational and avocational interests, hobbies, community activities, and close friends.

Miscellaneous Sources

The taxonomy (classification scheme) employed to outline record sources thus far has not included the more obscure repositories of information. Public and college libraries are available of course, but the investigator also ought to be aware of sources that normally do not disclose information to the public. Examples include quasi-official *ad hoc* agencies such as the National Board of Fire Underwriters and the National Auto Theft Bureau. Other sources often overlooked are: Chambers of Commerce, Better Business Bureaus, and the morgue files of local newspapers.

The value of information stored in a reference library can be illustrated by the case of one college student found murdered on campus. The murder weapon was a fabricated piece of iron; there appeared to be a short handle at one end. No one was familiar with it, and the purpose for its manufacture could only be guessed. A visit to the university reference room, however, produced a list of trade associations that possibly could provide further insight. After several days of checking and telephoning, investigators located a company in a distant state that identified the piece of evidence as a furnace handle. It was not a familiar object because the company had foreseen a limited market and manufactured only a few such furnaces. A check of the university registry disclosed that a mere handful of students came from that distant state. After questioning them individually, the list was narrowed down to one suspect. When his car was found to have bloodstains on the door and the blood group matched that of the victim and differed from his own, the suspect confessed.

Most quasi-official *ad hoc* agencies maintain files on persons who have been suspects or have otherwise been involved in matters of specific interest to the agencies. They assist law enforcement officials in other ways as well. For example, the National Auto Theft Bureau's staff of experts can restore an obliterated or altered vehicle identification number (VIN); the Jewelers' Security Alliance in New York City maintains a file of almost microscopic scratch marks whereby jewelers identify valuable pieces they have sold. In burglary cases, such marks serve to prove possession of a stolen article, or to identify recovered valuables so they can be restored to their rightful owners.

Case Illustrations: Using Records and Files

The contribution that a record or file makes to an investigation in attaining the objectives mentioned earlier can be affected in three ways: first, by the time and order in which the information is received and evaluated; second, by how well it dovetails with or supplements other facts developed through physical evidence or obtained from people; and third, by the diligence of the investigator in following through on the insight(s) it provides. A few of the case examples described below involve the use of police files; others suggest the value of records not specifically maintained for law enforcement purposes. The investigator must be ready to exploit both kinds of sources.

Murder of a Taxicab Driver

Early one Sunday morning a man walking his dog was attracted by the animal's barking at a taxicab parked near the curb. Although the motor was running, its driver was nowhere in sight. Drawing nearer, he observed the driver slumped across the seat. When he received no response to his offer of assistance, the man called police. An autopsy determined that the taxi driver had been strangled (probably with a belt). He also had been robbed of his wallet. Investigators found his trip-destination card, with the name "Shorty" scribbled on the back. This, together with a partial palm print developed on the roof of the cab just above the front door on the passenger side constituted all the physical evidence at the crime scene.

A search of the alias (or nickname) file disclosed several "Shortys." Their palm prints were taken, but none matched the latent print. The Rogues Gallery file on some of them contained group photographs picturing others who previously had been arrested with them. Each confederate was palm printed; one print was found to match the latent. When the "Shorty" and his confederate were brought to the station house for further questioning, the pair was separated. Each suspect readily admitted to having been in the cab that night, but denied strangling the driver. Each shifted the guilt onto the other until the statute on felony murder was spelled out: in the commission of a felony in which there is a death, all participants are guilty. Then both related how they came to kill the cab driver.

Two Rape Cases

Walking home from a movie with two female companions, a woman was forced at gunpoint into an automobile that had pulled alongside, taken to the basement of a building, and gang-raped. Later, while the men quarreled about whether to kill or free their victim, she maneuvered close enough to a bank of utility company meters on the basement wall to memorize one serial number. Much later, deciding to spare her life, they drove to a deserted street and abandoned her. The investigators located the basement from the utility company's meter records, but further inquiries in the neighborhood were hampered by residents' fear of retaliation. The rapists' reputation ensured their control of the area and the basement hideout. Nonetheless, a persuasive, sympathetic interviewing of area residents eventually elicited the information needed for their apprehension.

The importance of memory is illustrated by the fact that the victim was resolved to remain calm enough to focus all her attention on one detail—the number on the gas meter. Such close attention to a circumstance or circumstances is not as unusual as it might seem. It characterized another rape case in which the victim was blindfolded and driven around for hours, then assaulted in the car. At first, she was only able to make out the word "Cadillac" on the dashboard; when the blindfold worked itself loose, she could read the city sticker on the windshield. She memorized the two-letter, four-digit number. A determination to bring her attacker to justice helped the victim keep her wits about her, thus permitting police to trace the vehicle's owner.

Each case also illustrates how a record file maintained for one purpose was put to investigative use.

Assault on a Baby

In this case, the mother of an infant daughter awakened one morning, surprised that the baby had not demanded her 6:00 A.M. feeding. Going to the crib, she found the child bleeding profusely from the vagina. Medical examination disclosed extensive damage to the genital orifice, such as might be caused by the insertion of an object too large for the opening. The mother had last seen her child at the 2:00 A.M. feeding; she heard nothing after the baby went back to sleep. There were no obvious signs of entry into the one-family house. A few hours later, the next door neighbor reported to detectives that the electricity had been turned off in the basement during the night, the turn-off occurring at 3:20 A.M., as indicated by an electric clock. A partially consumed bottle of beer was noted on a workbench close to the fuse box in the basement. The brand was unfamiliar to the investigator and the occupants of both houses. Although no usable fingerprints were to be found on the bottle, the criminalist at the scene discovered a number inside the label. Observing the number required that the bottle be held up to strong light directed at the front of the label. It was ascertained from the brewery that this number indicated a distribution area, and the name of the local distributor was furnished.

Checking with the distributor, the investigators learned that the brand in question was handled by that distributor alone and was sold only by case lots for home delivery. A search of the records on case deliveries for that month produced two names. One family lived five miles from the crime scene; the other, within half a mile. The latter had a teenaged son who claimed to know nothing of the incident; however, after a brief interrogation, his preoccupation with sex became apparent, and he revealed that he had "examined" the baby. He then confirmed the method of entry into the house (through the pantry window), which had been suggested by the criminalist but scoffed at by the investigating officer. The clue for the criminalist had been the slight disturbance of dust, revealed by means of oblique illumination on a small ledge under the pantry window.

Disappearance of a Witness

In another case, a witness suddenly decided to disappear with his wife and young son to escape retribution for agreeing to give testimony against a defendant. Although his great anxiety had certainly been manifest, he never conveyed to relatives or friends any inclination toward such drastic action. The family disappeared without a trace. About five months later, the investigator was notified by the local school district clerk (who had been alerted to such an eventuality) that a request for the transfer of school records on the son had been received from a small community in a distant state. Locating the witness was then quite simple. When offered protection, the witness agreed to return and testify.

The Amtorg Bombing Incident

In his book, *Chief*, retired Chief of Detectives Albert A. Seedman of the New York City Police Department describes the investigation of a bombing incident at the offices of Amtorg, the USSR's official trade mission in the United States.[1] Two bombs were planted in the Manhattan skyscraper housing Amtorg's offices: one exploded on the nineteenth floor, the other was disarmed seconds before it was set to explode on the twentieth floor. In tracing the physical evidence made available, investigators discovered that one part of the dismantled, unexploded bomb was a white enameled kitchen timer retailed exclusively by RadioShack and bearing the name "Micronata." The sales policy of this nationwide chain of electronic equipment stores requires the recording of the name and address of each customer on all sales slips; this practice facilitates updating its mailing lists. Somewhere in the files of a RadioShack store was the crucial document.

Painstaking, store-by-store sorting of sales slips in all Brooklyn stores ultimately led to a receipt for two Micronata timers and a package of copper wire. The purchaser was checked out, but he was unknown at the address given. However, an anonymous telephone call to news media had come in shortly before the bombs were set to explode; and because of earlier harassment of Amtorg personnel, members of the Jewish Defense League (JDL) were suspect. When shown photographs of known JDL activists, the RadioShack salesman tentatively identified two young men. Follow-up on this identification involved extensive surveillance work and, before the case was solved, the assiduous cultivation of an informant within the JDL.

The Assassination of Dr. Martin Luther King, Jr.

The last case example is drawn from the assassination of Dr. Martin Luther King, Jr. in Memphis on April 4, 1968. Immediately after Dr. King was shot, a lieutenant in charge of the Memphis Police TAC (Tactical) Squad correctly surmised that the assassin's escape route would be South Main Street. He reached South Main within minutes in the hope of seeing someone flee with a weapon, but there was nothing in motion—neither suspect nor vehicle. Racing to the nearest corner about 50 yards away, he passed the Canipe Amusement Company; lying in the doorway he noted a green bedspread partially covering a blue zippered overnight bag, and a long pasteboard box from which the barrel of a rifle protruded. Moments before the officer stopped at sight of the bundle, Guy W. Canipe (the store owner) and two customers saw a man drop it in the doorway; then, they noted a white car—a compact, possibly a Ford Mustang—take off at high speed and proceed north on South Main.

A wealth of physical evidence was found in the discarded bundle after photographs of its position in the doorway were taken:

Contents of the Overnight Bag:

- Assorted toiletry articles
- Two unopened 12-ounce cans of Schlitz beer bearing Mississippi tax stamps
- A six-transistor portable radio with "00416" scratched on its side
- A pair of flatnose, duckbill pliers with *Romage Hardware* stamped on the handle
- A tack hammer
- One section of the *Commercial-Appeal*, a Memphis newspaper, dated April 4, 1968.
- A brown paper bag on which *Homestead* was printed
- Men's underwear (T-shirt and shorts) with a laundry mark (02B-6) printed in black letters on each item

Contents of the Cardboard Box:

- A pair of binoculars 7×35 (Bushnell "Banner")

- A paper bag on which *York Arms Co.* was printed, and a sales receipt from the same company (dated April 4, 1968)

- A 30.06 caliber Remington Rifle (Gamemaster), Model 760 on which a Redfield 2×7 telescopic sight was mounted

- A cartridge case and some ammunition for the rifle

Because the manufacture, distribution, and sale of guns are regulated, the rifle and scope were easily traced to the manufacturer, then to a distributor in Birmingham, and soon after, to the Aero Marine Supply Company (also in Birmingham). Aero sold the weapon to a "Harvey Lowmyer" on March 30, 1968, and the salesman could describe Lowmyer; meanwhile in Memphis, the salesman of the York Arms Company was able to describe the purchaser of the binoculars. The descriptions matched. Although the duckbill pliers were traced (by a telephone call to a trade association, The National Retail Hardware Association in Indianapolis) to Romage Hardware on Hollywood Boulevard in Los Angeles, no description of the purchaser could be obtained from this source. Yet, a connection, however tenuous, had been established between the suspect and the Los Angeles area; it suggested that if further evidence pointing to that city was developed, intense investigative efforts should also be channeled in that direction.

This was made clear when the laundry marks (02B-6) on the underwear were found to be those used by Home Service Laundry and Dry Cleaning, just two blocks away from Romage Hardware in Los Angeles. Laundry records indicated that the number 02B-6 had been assigned to an "Eric S. Galt." In addition, a week after Dr. King's slaying, an abandoned white Mustang was located (in Atlanta) and searched. From a service station sticker it was learned that the car had been lubricated twice in Los Angeles.

Investigative efforts were also being channeled to the Alabama-Mississippi area. The beer cans had been traced through their markings and company records to a store in Mississippi where they had been purchased, but no further information of value could be obtained from that source. The rifle and scope, however, had been purchased in Birmingham, and a motel registration in Memphis in the name of Eric Starvo Galt on the day before Dr. King's death also connected Galt to Birmingham. It was learned through canvassing that when living in Birmingham in 1967, Galt had expressed an interest in dancing and had attended a dancing school there. Following up on this clue, a canvass of all dance schools in Los Angeles led to the National Dance Studio. There, Galt's name was recognized. In addition, the owner recalled that Galt had mentioned attending bartending school. A fruitful clue, it brought investigators to the International School of Bartending in Los Angeles, which provided the first photograph of Galt—in the form of a graduation picture.

In addition to systematically reconstructing the wavering, sometimes dim trail of the suspect, an effort was undertaken to determine if he had been arrested under another name. Two latent fingerprints—one on the rifle, the other on the binoculars—had been developed; and later, a third print was developed on a map found in Galt's room in Atlanta. It was not possible at that time to locate a record in the fingerprint file, when the search was based only on a latent crime scene print. Because it was an important case, however, President Johnson ensured that extraordinary measures and resources were allocated. Initially, it was decided to limit the search of the fingerprint file to those of white male ("wanted") fugitives whose physical descriptions were close to Galt's. There were 53,000 sets of prints of white "wanted" males in the files. Only a day or so after the search was undertaken (15 days after Dr. King's death) 700 fingerprint cards had been scrutinized. One card stood out—its record print matched that of the latent print. Bearing the name James Earl Ray, the record indicated among other things that Ray had escaped from the Missouri State Penitentiary in 1967.

This development remains a monument to a painstaking, tenacious investigation. And yet, from the moment the assailant discarded that bundle in Canipe's doorway, one clue was available that might quickly have led to the identification of James Earl Ray. If the reader will refer to the list of the bundle's contents, he or she will note that a portable transistor radio with the number 00416 scratched on its side was included. This was the prison number assigned to inmate James Earl Ray in the Missouri State Penitentiary.

Although hindsight is usually superior to foresight, the latter attribute is one the investigator must strive to cultivate. It is certainly true that the accumulation of recorded information is such that no one person can be expected to be familiar with it. What is interesting to speculate about is whether a "brainstorming" session of people from across the board in criminal justice might have provided the insight that 00416 was possibly a prisoner's number. A group of creative, knowledgeable criminal justice people might be such a resource. It could be assembled quickly and inexpensively; that is, if advance plans are made as to its composition, meeting place, and method of calling it into session. Depending on the issue to be examined, the composition of the group could vary. There are no certainties of course, but such an attempt might enhance the possibility of a solution.

In any event, the King case illustrates how extensively record sources were employed: banks, telephone companies, credit agencies, police departments, car rental agencies, motor vehicle departments, dance schools, hotels and motels, laundries, utility companies, selective service bureaus, and labor unions.[2]

REFERENCES

1   Albert A. Seedman and Peter Hellman, *Chief* (New York: Arthur Fields Books, 1974), 270-317.

2   U.S. Congress, House Select Committee of Assassinations, *Report of Findings and Recommendations*, 95th Cong., 2d sess., 1979, 445-446.

SUPPLEMENTAL READINGS

Carroll, John M. *Confidential Information Sources: Public and Private*. Los Angeles: Security World, 1975.

Gale Research. *Directories in Print*. 23rd ed. Detroit: Thompson Gale, 2003.

Gale Research. *Encyclopedia of Associations: National Organizations of the U.S.* 40th ed. Detroit: Thompson Gale, 2003:

Murphy, Harry J. *Where's What: Sources of Information for Federal Investigators*. New York: Quadrangle/New York Times, 1976.

PART B

SEEKING AND OBTAINING INFORMATION: PEOPLE AND RECORDS

The acquisition of facts requires specialized procedures. Doctors, mechanics, detectives—all have methods for obtaining the information necessary to deal with the particular issue confronting them. Although doctors and mechanics have innumerable technical and scientific instruments at their disposal, few diagnostic tools address the needs of criminal investigators. Hence, investigators must be resourceful, and call on diverse, special capabilities—wider in range and more difficult to apply. In short, though detective work is not easy, the task is greatly assisted by the ability to interview people, cultivate and deal with informants, and retrieve data from record sources (including the recognition of crime patterns).

Part B covers some of the methods detectives employ to elicit facts from people, and gather information from records.

CHAPTER 6

Interviews

Obtaining Information from Witnesses

QUESTIONING PEOPLE

The investigator spends a great deal of professional time talking with people after a crime is committed. The victim and eyewitness(es) are first; next are those whose identities develop in the course of the investigation. Some people furnish complete and candid information, but some are less cooperative or will deliberately mislead authorities; others must be coaxed to come forward.

The terms used to describe the questioning process are *interrogation* and *interviewing*. *Interrogation* applies to a suspect and a suspect's family, friends, or associates—people who are likely to withhold information or be deceptive. *Interviewing* applies to victims or eyewitnesses who can reasonably be expected to disclose what they know. Hence, the guiding principles and techniques of interrogation (discussed in Chapters 11 and 12) differ considerably from those of interviewing.

INTERVIEWING

There are few people who have neither been interviewed nor conducted an interview themselves. Whether formal or informal, it is the same process that is involved in job hunting, shopping, or talking over a child's progress with a teacher. Its purpose is the exchange of information. Investigators also are engaged in this exchange, and as practiced professionals they generally take in far more information than they give out. Seeking facts not divulged because there is little comprehension of their significance, the investigator needs to be intuitive, alert, and skillful—much more than a passive information-recorder. If interviewing at the crime scene is unavoidable and there is any chance that the suspect or accomplices are within hearing distance, absolute discretion is a must. The following questions—"five Ws and one H": Who?, What?, When?, Where?, Why?, and How?—should be regarded as the minimum to be covered in an interview.

Who: The question of who involves the name, address, sex, age, and occupation of the interviewee. Interviewees can be victims, witnesses, or others suggested by witnesses or friends of the victim. Who is the perpetrator? Who gains some advantage from committing the crime? The investigator taking information from a witness must make a point of verifying the name and address given. A driver's license or other identification can prevent a subpoena's being returned, marked: "Addressee Unknown." It is not uncommon to lose a case because a witness could not be contacted; numerous cases have been lost for precisely that reason.

What: What was observed by the eyewitness? What was heard or learned through any of the other senses (smell, touch, taste)? What relationship exists or existed between victim and perpetrator? Between the complainant and witness? Between complainant and other witnesses? Between participants in the crime? What objects were moved, taken, or damaged?

When: When was the crime committed? When did the interviewee acquire this information? When did a suspect last see or talk to the victim?

Where: Where did the crime take place? Where did the interviewee observe, hear, or otherwise learn what he or she is reporting? Where did the interview take place?

Why: Why was the interviewee in a position to observe the incident? Why did the crime occur (possible motive)? Why was the victim, target, or object selected? Why was a particular object moved, taken, or damaged?

How: How was the crime consummated? How was it originally conceived?

Modus Operandi: The manner in which a crime was committed can serve as the trademark or *modus operandi* (MO) of that criminal. For example, the language used to convey to the victim that a robbery is to take place differs among holdup perpetrators. In a sexual assault, a rapist's threats, demands, and remarks characterize him just as the means of breaking and entering—cutting a hole in the roof, breaking through a wall with a jack hammer, hiding in the stairwell until the building is closed, picking a lock—distinguish a burglar. Some aspects of MO must be sought at the crime scene; others are furnished by the complainant (and perhaps by witnesses) at the initial interview. The well-maintained MO file can tie several crimes together through crime analysis. Individual clues collected in each crime may not suffice, but a pool of clues from crimes sharing a common MO could suggest a strategy for identifying and apprehending the perpetrator.

ACQUIRING THE FACTS

One method of acquiring the facts is to utilize a standardized form dealing with the significant details a complainant or witness may possess. Termed "complaint report" or "investigation report," such forms are designed with questions framed to ensure that vital information is not overlooked. At the same time the forms are intended to ferret out facts that witnesses fail to volunteer because their potential value is unrealized. A note of caution:

> . . . it is not true that more information necessarily is more productive. In some circumstances the use of precoded incident forms may be counterproductive.
>
> . . . [Although] information is essential to apprehension and prosecution, [there are those who] are pessimistic about the way in which this notion has been implemented in some departments where investigating officers must wade through long, general lists of questions and precoded investigation forms. . . . [It can be argued] that the key to enhanced productivity lies in collecting only that information likely to be useful in identifying and apprehending an offender.[1]

Thus, specialized forms need to be developed and tested. Their primary function is to minimize the amount of information collected and maximize its usefulness. If investigative efficiency is to be improved, applied research in this vein is essential. A simplified identification chart designed to focus a victim's or witness's immediate attention on a particular aspect of the crime or its perpetrator is needed. Also helpful would be a greater use by business establishments of a height line marker; placed on the exit doorjamb, it allows the height of the perpetrator passing through the door to be estimated.

Describing the Offender

The victim or eyewitness can make a major contribution by providing a good description of the perpetrator. Several procedures have been developed to accomplish this. The earliest, the *portrait parlé* (loosely translated, "verbal picture"), was suggested by Bertillon of the Sûreté. It was a supplement to his identification scheme, anthropometry (the recording of certain body measurements—especially bone length), which, despite his own fanatical opposition, was eventually dropped in favor of fingerprints. But portrait parlé, utilizing facial and bodily features to describe an individual, continues to this day.

Three other methods have emerged. In one, an artist draws a likeness of the person observed. People capable of this can be found in most communities; they may be on the staff in large police departments. Another method employs a series of pre-drawn facial features—hairlines, mustaches, eyebrows, eyes, ears, noses, lips, chins, and so on. Choosing the one feature from each series most closely resembling the perpetrator's feature (see Figure 6.1), the eyewitness makes selections that form a composite picture of the perpetrator. Composite kits are commercially available. Identi-Kit is well known; other makes, such as the Penry Photo-Fit, are equally satisfactory (see Figure 6.2).

The third (and latest) method exploits the graphics capability of the computer. At least two software programs have been designed to produce images of suspects or wanted persons: Compu-Sketch and ComPHOTOfit.

Figure 6.1
A few of the 193 forehead/hair styles available in the Photo-Fit female Caucasian front face kit. *(Courtesy, Sirchie Finger Print Laboratories, Raleigh, NC.)*

Photo-Fit Female Composite   **Actual Photograph**

Figure 6.2
A comparison of a Photo-Fit composite with a photograph of the same person. *(Courtesy, Sirchie Finger Print Laboratories, Raleigh, NC.)*

Compu-Sketch, offered by Digital Descriptor Systems, Inc. in Langhorne Pennsylvania, evolved in conjunction with a California police officer, Tom Macris, who served for 12 years as sketch artist for the San Jose Police Department.[2] It has been described:

> [Compu-Sketch] combines and creates over 100,000 facial features by simply pressing a button; one feature quickly falls over another until the composite is complete. The positioning of features in their relation to each other is unlimited, while refinement of resultant images is by electronic "paint box" techniques. The product is printed out as a highly credible composite sketch for leaflets or wanted posters.

> At the system's heart is a comprehensive interview program. It provides maximum help to the witness to recall critical suspect features, while assuring completely unbiased answers with non-leading and non-suggestive queries. Incorporated into the computer program is the key interview process enabling the operator to assist the witness step-by-step with memory enhancement questions triggering other memory processes, with consistency from case to case and agency to agency.[3]

The number of facial features available in the Compu-Sketch library is shown in Figure 6.3.

ComPHOTOfit works with five features to draft the composite sketch, e.g., forehead, eyes, nose, mouth, and chin; a mustache, beard, eyeglasses, and headgear can be added if needed. The software program was described in *Law and Order*:

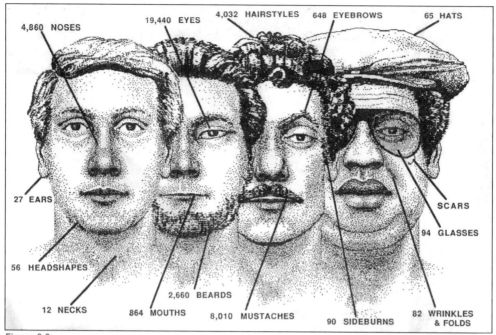

Figure 6.3
Compu-Sketch feature library. *(Courtesy, Digital Descriptor Systems, Inc., Langhorne, PA.)*

There is an image index function that displays the group of components that most closely match a description. If your technique is to let the witnesses pick the component parts, you can show him a group to pick from. Or you can use it yourself to build an interim composite for the witness to correct. With rapid scan, you can run through a variety of any particular component to see if another is closer to the subject. . . .

With the five major components making up a composite, suppose the subject's nose is a bit off-center? The forehead, nose, and chin sections can be set in any of seven vertical levels, but you can also capture a portion of the face by outlining it with the mouse, moving it wherever you want it. If the hairline isn't quite right, just use a built-in "paint brush" to erase part of the hair or add to another area.

Put glasses on the image. "But he wore them down on his nose." Just move them.

The screen is split into two image areas. The one on the right is the working image where you create the composite. When it gets close to a good likeness—but the witness wants to try something else—you can save it to the facsimile image screen, where the image enhancing is done.

If the witness frustrates your efforts by saying, "We were closer before," rather than reshuffling films, just touch a key and retrieve the earlier version.

The system includes a search routine that you can use to find all other images in the database using the same component numbers. This might tie your suspect into a previous case in which he was identified.[4]

ComPHOTOfit's developers claim that "the image generated is virtually photo quality after the image section lines of the component parts are blended out with a mouse, or moles and scars are 'painted' in."[5]

People normally see the features on a face in totality, unless one feature stands out. The totality (or gestalt) can be caught by the police artist, who offers the choice of an infinite number of facial features. Sirchie Laboratories claims that more than 12 billion faces can be composed using the Photo-Fit system. If an artist's sketch or a composite picture is distributed, the likelihood of its utilization by the patrol force, community merchants, and the general public is greater than if a verbal description alone were circulated. When the general public must be looked to for help, prospects for its involvement increase if resentment is felt about the crime, or if the request is a novelty. Of course, the ultimate result is an identification; short of that, productive results could include leads that send detectives in search of additional facts from a record file or another person.

Describing Stolen or Lost Property

The task of identifying stolen property arises when the stores of loot of a burglar or fence are located. Because theft is largely a means of acquiring cash by pawning or selling stolen goods, police monitoring of property sold to secondhand dealers or pledged as security in pawn shops can bring about its identification. For this to result, it must be described twice:

First: by the owner to the investigator handling the case;

Second: by the pawnbroker or secondhand dealer to the stolen property
                bureau of a police department

Because it would take a miracle to bring owner/victim and pawnbroker reports together (filing dates can be 30 or more days apart), the information generated by each report must be similar. To achieve this, the Stolen/Lost Property Report Form is a requisite. In some jurisdictions the law stipulates that pawnshop owners file such forms; in others, their voluntary cooperation must be sought. Owing to the nature of this business, however, it is not uncommon for pawnbrokers to contact police when merchandise brought to them arouses suspicion. Whether filing is required by law or voluntary, both reports (owner/victim and pawnbroker) should ultimately come together in the stolen property bureau records, thereby helping to clear the case as well as facilitating a return of the stolen goods to their rightful owners.

A Stolen/Lost Property Report Form can be developed in accordance with the following (or similar) taxonomy:

KIND OF OBJECT   Camera, TV, stereo set, credit card, watch, binoculars,
                                                jewelry

NAME OF MANUFACTURER
(OR OTHER SOURCE)

MODEL NUMBER*

IDENTIFYING FEATURES*   Serial number, initials, or other personal inscription

MATERIAL USED   Shiny chrome or dull black body of a camera;
IN ITS CONSTRUCTION   wood or plastic in a TV set; gold or silver in jewelry

PHYSICAL APPEARANCE   Size, shape (as of a diamond), condition (like new,
scratched)

DEALING WITH THE RELUCTANT, FEARFUL OR UNAWARE WITNESS

Securing Cooperation

It is a fact that many crimes occur in which no witnesses come forward. Several reasons account for this disinclination: a person may be concerned over loss of pay through court continuances, harbor a fear of the police, or dread the offender's retaliation. In addition, some people have information, but are unaware of its usefulness to the police. An effective way to secure cooperation is to set up a special, 24-hour "hot line"; this allows witnesses to telephone police while remaining anonymous. Offering a reward is another time-honored formula. When the investigator learns the name of a potential witness who has not come forward, the rationale for this behavior must be ascertained. The means of dealing with this phenomenon vary with the reasons that foster it.

The Reluctant Witness

It does not require great imaginative ability to reassure the reluctant witness. Recognizing and realistically dealing with a legitimate complaint will usually suffice. For instance, many people are concerned about loss of pay when repeatedly called to court only to have the case continued (set for a later date). Should this be the basis for hesitancy, the investigator can arrange to have the witness placed on a telephone alert, to be called only when the case is actually on trial and the testimony wanted within an hour or so. In the course of duty, detectives continuously work out such arrangements.

The Fearful Witness

Witnesses who dread reprisal should their identity become known can be difficult to handle. For a key witness in an important case, protective custody (agreed to or imposed) may be required—a harsh measure that is seldom taken because it is hard on the individual and expensive for the state. A sympathetic attitude and a reliable appraisal of the danger (for example, by citing a witness's safety in the jurisdiction) may remove any remaining hesitancy. Just the same, there will be those who, for cultural or other reasons, cannot be persuaded to divulge what they know.

---

*Unfortunately, many people do not keep records of this information.

The witness who is reticent owing to fear of the police presents both short-term and long-term challenges. The short-term challenge is for the detective on the case to induce a person to divulge what he or she knows; the long-term challenge is for the department to surmount the misgivings that cause people to dread contact with the police. It may surprise many police officers to learn that law-abiding citizens fear them. In small communities with relatively homogenous populations, the degree of fear is not as great and usually is not manifest, but a latent fear may well exist.

This should not be surprising to those in large communities like New York, especially in the aftermath of the notorious Kitty Genovese case. It was in March of 1964 that Genovese was stalked by an assailant from a parking lot to a point near her apartment house door, where she was stabbed repeatedly. The time was 3:20 A.M. and her screams for help awakened the neighborhood, producing a hue and cry. Seeing lights go on and hearing people's shouts, the attacker was frightened off; however, 10 minutes later, when no police cars had responded to the scene, he came back for the kill. Knowing the extent of the injuries he had inflicted, and surmising that his victim had crawled to the refuge of an apartment doorway, he searched and found her there. Again she screamed for help, but this time he cut her throat and stopped the cries.

Some 38 neighbors heard Kitty Genovese that night. Yet it was not until 3:55 A.M.— about 30 minutes after the first scream, by which time the killer had long departed— that one of them called the police. Not an unfamiliar experience for many large city departments, this phenomenon is usually written off as citizen indifference or unwillingness to get involved. Is this the answer? Thirty-eight people were right at the scene, safe in their homes, with telephones available. Why the hesitation? Why was not one in this larger-than-average number of witnesses motivated by enlightened self-interest or plain civic duty to call the police?

To clarify the issue, one of the authors made informal queries among civilians in several sections of the United States. One fairly common retort stood out: a defensive "Have *you* ever called the police?" Even an inexpert poll-taker is alerted when rhetoric is employed to dodge an awkward question. Respondents, therefore, were asked to explain further. Upon doing so, they confronted, perhaps for the first time, the fundamental cause of their hesitancy: the fact that police emergency operators invariably put callers on the defensive and require them to justify the call.

Although this claim is generally shrugged off by those in law enforcement, many respondents cited as intimidating factors the operator's indifferent tone of voice and the demand that callers identify themselves. Asked if it was not reasonable that police be enabled to verify information called in, they acquiesced; still, they persisted, the purpose of such calls is to ask for help, or to identify and expose a wrongdoer. To them, the process seemed to push this purpose to a back burner, while focusing uncomfortably long on the caller's possible motivations and identity.

This widespread civilian perspective lent credibility to an early reform implemented by O.W. Wilson on assuming the post of Chicago's Police Superintendent. His administrative assistant, Herman Goldstein, acknowledged that the critical contact between the public and the police depended on the quality of emergency personnel; hence, it was impractical to expect operators to work the usual duty chart at this post and maintain a high level of interest and concern. By shortening the work week and lengthening relief time, he proposed that it was feasible to remove the communications barrier set up by fatigue.

Whatever its cause, this barrier is real; this became apparent from some respondents' replies. When an operator's voice is an irritated monotone, it communicates "This is nothing new; what are you excited about?" To the caller, of course, the event is indeed new and unusual enough to cause great concern. By turning off the civic-minded with a seemingly indifferent response, law enforcement agencies probably forfeit future cooperation. And, since any contact with police is a rare event for most people, the experience is likely to be recounted to family and friends, producing more reticent witnesses who are unwilling to come forward.

Generating Long-Term Cooperation

In addition to the Goldstein proposal, a few progressive police departments have begun to take seriously the recommendation of President Johnson's Commission on Law Enforcement and the Administration of Justice that

> . . . the officials of the criminal justice system itself must stop operating, as all too many do, by tradition or by rote. They must re-examine what they do. They must be honest about the system's shortcomings with the public and with themselves. They must be willing to take risks in order to make advances. They must be bold.[6]

In keeping with the Commission's spirit, some departments have instituted a Victim-Witness Assistance Unit. In rape cases, for example, a female officer (who may be a trained social worker) responds to a reported rape scene. She supports the victim in a personal way throughout the questioning, then accompanies her to the hospital for medical examination, where physical evidence (semen, pubic hairs, blood) is acquired. Later, she provides follow-up counseling and sees the victim (now the witness) through the criminal justice process, explaining each step along the way—why it is necessary and what is next. A humanely treated victim is likely to be a willing witness, more so certainly than one who must—because official concern is focused only on the investigation—go over details of the ordeal while being inadvertently embarrassed by various male officers.

Some assistance programs concentrate on what is expected of the victim/witness when called to the stand. They supply transportation to court, child care, and a lounge or service center separated from the defendant. Some agencies even see to the repair of broken windows or damaged door locks in the home of a witness who has been threatened. For the witness or victim who feels intimidated, "hot line" telephones have been set up for advice, reassurance, and action.

In a study of the assistance concept, researchers concluded that:

> The question of victim/witness assistance is one for system balance. Right now, it appears that most elements of the criminal justice system are directed to conviction of the offender and the maintenance of regularized system operation. As long as the victim and witness is [*sic*] treated as an intervening actor and not a person in need within the system, he or she will respond negatively. Only when these individuals perceive their concerns are given equal atten-

tion as those related to the offender will they recognize that the system cares about them and values their participation. Until this happens the system of justice will not be completely whole.[7]

In the foreword to this study, Gerald Caplan addressed the pressing issue of generating long-term cooperation from victims and witnesses. He wrote:

How can the criminal justice system gain the cooperation of these citizens who are alienated by its often cumbersome procedures? One possible approach recommended by this research is ombudsman programs for victims and witnesses. The programs would address such problems as intimidation by defendants, loss of wages and other expenses while appearing at court and other proceedings, transportation to and from the court-house or police station, and frustration with the criminal justice system.[8]

The Unaware Witness

There are times when someone in the neighborhood sees the criminal on the way to or retreating from the crime scene. The observer could be sitting in a car, looking out a window, walking a dog, or driving a cab. Yet such observers are generally unaware of having seen anything that could be of value to the police. By revisiting the scene the following day or two, and exactly one week after the crime, the investigator may find a person who was passing when the crime was about to be (or was being) committed. In a well-publicized crime, the observer may realize he or she has something to contribute and come forward. In a major case, broadcasting an appeal is sometimes effective, as are leaflets distributed in shopping and transportation centers.

Canvass

If the case warrants it after all other measures have failed, a neighborhood canvass may be undertaken to discover the offender or unaware witness. Expensive and time-consuming, a canvass requires careful administrative control to ensure that every person in the area is contacted and interviewed. Large cities pose the greatest number of problems in conducting a store-to-store, building-to-building, house-to-house canvass. But if the area can be reasonably well-defined, its size and number of inhabitants limited, and the search is marked by patience and thoroughness, the chances of success are enhanced.

The use of the canvass is widespread in Great Britain, where it is termed "intensive inquiry." Therefore, Allen Andrews's account of some painstaking efforts and what they achieve is illuminating.[9] A large allocation of personnel is permitted for murder investigations, partly as a result of the low homicide rate in Britain. In the United States, intensive inquiry is employed less frequently; the scale of the undertaking would have to be vast to allow for its greater size and much higher homicide rate. But from time to time, on appropriate occasions, canvass has proved effective, as illustrated below.

Case Illustrations: Canvass

In the United States, a canvass is often considered in cases of homicide. The tactic works for other crimes as well. It can be productive when based on the possibility that someone saw or heard something that he or she did not bother to report until confronted by the inquiries of a police officer knocking on the door. Then, there is always the chance that the officer will knock on the very door of the perpetrator, who will be exposed by the combined effect of surprise and guilty knowledge. This, clearly, was the expectation of a New York Chief of Detectives in the homicide case below.

Homicide

This case concerns the mysterious slaying of a young woman driving alone on the Shore Parkway in Brooklyn. A motorist saw the woman's car drift slowly off the road into the bushes alongside. Others stopped to render assistance, but for no reason apparent to them, she was already dead. Indeed, the hospital staff took quite a bit of time to discover a bloodless wound on the left side of her head—a single, small bullet hole hidden by her long hair. Occurring on an isolated stretch of parkway, the crime had few eyewitnesses, and when the sparse facts they provided were checked out, there were no leads. The single piece of physical evidence was the steel-jacketed, .318 caliber copper-coated bullet that had killed her. Its unusual class characteristics (two lands and grooves with a left twist) were potentially valuable. When it was determined that an Enfield .303 rifle had these characteristics, investigators knew that if the rifle (a rarity in that area) could be found, the case would be solved.

At this point Chief Seedman decided to conduct a canvass. Meeting with his detectives, he said:

> Starting tomorrow morning, we're going to knock on every door in Brooklyn until we find the guy who has that Enfield. He isn't talking now, but when that detective comes calling, he's going to figure we've traced that gun to him somehow and he'll come clean. He can always say he didn't know we were looking for it.[10]

Although confident, even the chief expressed surprise at the very short time it took to apprehend the offender as a result of the canvass.

Another homicide case involved a baseball fan struck by a bullet while sitting in a ballpark watching a major league game. No motive could be established for the killing; no one had heard the shot. Overlooking the stadium about a quarter of a mile away was a low bluff, fronted by a public park. Apartment buildings were set further back on the bluff. The victim's seat was not visible from the apartments, but investigators determined that a gun fired with a low trajectory could have traveled to the ballpark from the apartment roof. After checking out the public park area, police found no witnesses who either saw or heard anything.

As part of a neighborhood canvass, some detectives went to the rooftops of the apartment buildings overlooking the stadium. On one was a pock-marked brick wall; it appeared to have been hit by many bullets. Concentrating on the occupants of this building, investigators learned that a youth who lived there was in the habit of target shooting at the roof's wall. As the investigation later revealed, he had discharged the bullet that accidentally killed the spectator at the game.

Larceny

This case involved the theft of a large sum of money from a private home; the crime appeared to have been an "inside job." Wanting the investigation kept secret, the complainant demanded there be no newspaper coverage of the crime. After several days, when servants, tradespersons, and others with access to the house were cleared of suspicion, a decision was made to canvass the neighborhood. One detective, working the outer limit of the half-mile circle drawn with the house at its center, was about to pass up a Western Union office when a sense of thoroughness put him on guard. It seemed a most unlikely source, yet the clue that would ultimately solve the case by pointing to the complainant's wife was furnished by the telegraph office manager. Being blackmailed for an indiscretion, and having exhausted her considerable allowance, the wife was unwilling to ask her husband for more. She had stolen and then sent via telegraph what was to be the "last" payoff to the blackmailer. Because the transaction involved such a large amount, the manager immediately recalled it; when shown the woman's picture, he readily identified her.

Robbery/Homicide

This case demonstrates that the canvass technique need not be limited to urban centers; it can be effective in open country, even over a comparatively large area. The facts are: a postal employee was killed and $25,000 in cash taken in a hold-up. The crime took place in a small community where almost everyone knew one another, but because inquiries among its residents produced no suspects or motive, investigators concluded that it had been committed by strangers who made a clean getaway. The case might have reached an impasse had investigators not hypothesized that the perpetrators cased the area thoroughly. By deduction, this premise led to the question of where they might have stayed while doing so. With a 100-mile area to canvass, the services of postmasters and rural carriers were enlisted. One response came from a farmer who said he had boarded some strangers. On being interviewed, he recalled the names they had used and snatches of conversation he overheard. This information, together with what investigators learned about the perpetrators' casing activities, furnished clues that led to the killers some months later, and to the ultimate solution of the homicide.

Indifferent Complainants

At times a complainant may display indifference or claim that he or she is too busy to be questioned. Since most victims are anxious to be helpful, such resistance raises the question: "Why?" Sometimes the answer can be found through a crime scene examination focused on how the crime was committed, e.g., through a reconstruction of the event. Re-examining the alleged facts and the physical evidence may reveal that the crime was simulated, and account for a complainant's reluctance to be interviewed and possibly exposed as the perpetrator. An interrogation then may have greater success. In addition, when evidence of a crime (a burglary, for instance) is recognized as having been simulated, Horowitz's condition that evidence be available against the individual is met. This factor can be effective when interrogating the complainant who is falsely claiming to have been the victim of a burglary. (See Chapter 11.)

BEHAVIORAL ANALYSIS INTERVIEWS

The Behavioral Analysis Interview (BAI) is an investigative technique that seeks to capitalize on the fact that a person being questioned unwittingly emits nonverbal signals. Called an interview, yet nearer to an interrogation in purpose, BAI can be likened to a bridge between the two. It also is described as an effective substitute when the polygraph is not available or acceptable for use.[11] So far, it has been of greatest help in private security work and for screening numbers of suspects when polygraph tests would be too time-consuming.

> [BAI] . . . involves a short face-to-face non-accusatory interview during which the interviewer asks a series of structured behavior-provoking questions. The interview is designed to have suspects reveal their innocence or guilt by what they say and how they look when they say it.[12]

Based on an empirical study, the following symptoms are to be noted during the interview, because:

> . . . it was clear that the innocent suspects revealed their truthfulness by their behavior, and the guilty revealed their deception by their behavior.

> . . . truthful suspects were more at ease during the interview. They were able to sit comfortably without shifting while being questioned. These suspects were straightforward in their answers and looked at the interviewer with sincere eyes.

> The guilty suspects appeared to be more nervous and uneasy during the interview. Some acted resentful or aggressive. The guilty suspects were often evasive, would not look at the examiner, and moved around frequently during the interview.

> . . . It is important to note that the interviewer does not look for just one behavior symptom from the suspect. Rather, he is evaluating a cluster of behavior symptoms.[13]

To provoke a response the person under suspicion is told that a specially trained interviewer will do the questioning and take fingerprints. If any other physical evidence has been found, this fact is also utilized; if for instance the evidence was a hair, the individual can be asked to provide a sample. The interviewer then begins with a review of some details of the crime, and watches for behavioral responses. Next, the person is turned over to another interviewer who has several prepared questions relevant to the crime; again, any behavioral reaction is noted. Finally, a third interviewer asks formulated questions based on previous responses, then terminates the session with the taking of fingerprints, watching the while for any behavioral symptoms of guilt or innocence.

Sometimes a *bait* question is employed to draw the individual into modifying or even repudiating the original assertion of noninvolvement. An example: "Why would anyone say they saw you come out of the bar and go to the parking lot just before Joe was shot there?" A truthful response would be a direct denial such as "That can't be; I wasn't there" or "Whoever told you that is full of shit." A guilty response, based on the possibility that he or she was indeed seen in the lot, would either produce a denial—usually after some hesitation—or an admission that he or she was in the lot (but on another day), and a claim that the witness made a mistake as to when this occurred.

A response suggestive of guilt requires follow-up: by surveillance; perhaps seeking an informant; tracing the weapon used—if it was recovered; questioning associates; and so on. When and if further evidence is developed, a full-scale interrogation may be in order. It is claimed that

> . . . a professional interviewer . . . can confidently eliminate over 80% of the innocent and can identify the guilty without the use of the polygraph technique.[14]

HYPNOSIS

The use of hypnosis by law enforcement as a means of interviewing has met with some criticism. Two concerns are expressed: (1) in some crimes the victim suffers severe psychological trauma, and reliving the experience through hypnosis could make it worse; (2) "facts" may be implanted to cue or lead the witness under hypnosis, he or she being suggestible in this condition. To avoid criticism while retaining the benefits of hypnosis, the FBI has established elaborate guidelines for its use as an investigative tool:

> The FBI's policy basically states that the FBI is to use hypnosis only in selected cases. This would include bank robbery, where force is used or a large amount of money is involved, kidnapping, extortion, and crimes of violence which occur where the FBI has jurisdiction. Hypnosis is confined to use with key witnesses or victims of crimes only. No one who has the potential of becoming a suspect or subject in a case is to be hypnotized for any reason. For the sake of brevity, the term "witness" will be used in this article as a substitute for "witness/victim." The FBI uses only highly qualified hypnotists to do the actual induction. The use of hypnosis must be discussed with the U.S. attorney and his permission obtained. The U.S. attorney must then obtain written permission from the Assistant Attorney General of the Criminal Division, U.S. Department of Justice. The current policy also states that no Agent may participate in a hypnotic interview without written permission from the Attorney General. Further, the hypnotic interview must be recorded in its entirety, either by audio or videotape, with video the preferred method.
>
> The guidelines specify the use of a psychiatrist, psychologist, physician, or dentist who is qualified as a hypnotist. The use of a qualified health professional provides additional protection for the witness, the cost of which is minimal. Agents have used the services of professionals who have given generously

of their time, or who have charged only a modest fee for the sessions, because of their desire to help in what is for some a new area of hypnosis. Furthermore, the FBI has found that this added protection has not restricted Agents in their use of hypnosis.

Training of Coordinator

As with many new programs, the FBI had some early problems in its use of hypnosis. The results obtained were not consistent from field office to field office. Some Agents contacted doctors who did not want anyone present, except the witness and the doctor, during the hypnosis interview. Other doctors did not want videotapes made of the session. These and other problems were not in keeping with the legal needs of either the FBI or the prosecuting attorneys. With this in mind, the Training Division of the FBI instituted a program for 60 of its Agents from field offices throughout the United States. Its purpose was "not" to train Agents as hypnotists, but to teach them the theory, techniques, and hazards of the use of hypnosis. These Agents are the FBI's "hypnosis coordinators" and are trained to bridge that gap which exists between the professional, who does not always understand our legal needs, and the FBI, which does not always understand medical needs. The coordinator is responsible for setting up every hypnosis session. This assures more centralized control of the use of hypnosis in each FBI field office.

Members of the social science community assisted in this training by participating in this seminar which was designed to provide instruction to the 60 Agents.

On completion of the first 4-day seminar, the Agents were charged with the responsibility of returning to their offices and seeking a qualified professional to assist in future hypnosis sessions. Arrangements with this professional would include such items as the doctor's willingness to allow at least the Agent coordinator to be present at the hypnosis session, possible locations for interviews, an understanding that the entire interview must be recorded and recorded in a specific way (which will be discussed), arrangements for payment, and amount charged for the service.

Specific Techniques

The area of greatest concern was the potential for "leading" witnesses. While "cueing" does exist with or without hypnosis, the suggestibility of a witness in a state of hypnosis may be even greater than when not hypnotized. To offset this tendency, and to provide a record should the witness' information be used in court, recording the hypnosis session should be conducted in three parts.

In the first segment, the psychiatrist, psychologist, or physician explains to the witness what hypnosis is, what some misconceptions are, and what should happen during the course of the session. The professional will also determine that the witness has no particular problems which preclude hypnosis. The coordinating Agent is present and may also ask questions to assure that the witness knows why he/she is participating in the hypnosis session.

In the second phase, either the professional or the coordinator asks the witness to relax and attempt to remember as much as possible concerning the incident. This is done with no prompting. Neither the Agent nor the professional should ask questions until the witness has had a chance to "run down." Then, any questions asked would be based only on what the witness has remembered during this phase.

The last phase is the actual induction. After appropriate hypnotic induction, and then regression, the witness is again asked to tell what he can remember. Once more, questions should be based only on that information produced during the hypnotic session. It is better for the hypnotist, as well as the coordinator, to know as little as possible about the case, so that cueing is minimal. With the above method, there appears less chance for the questioner to "slip," even if he does have knowledge of the case outside the witness' memory of the event.

The time involved for all three phases is usually about 1-3 hours, depending on the details recalled by the witness and the length of the professional's explanation.

Checklist

To prepare the coordinator for the task of setting up a session, each Agent was provided with an informal checklist which he could use in his operations. The checklist is set out as follows:

Preliminary

1) Only witnesses and victims should be hypnotized and only after other methods of investigation have been exhausted. (It should be noted here that the FBI does not intend hypnosis to replace normal investigative procedures. It is not meant as a "hurry up" substitute for proper investigation.)

2) Refer to and follow existing FBI policy.

3) Videotape requirements will be planned in advance of the first interview and should include:
   — Location (a quiet spot free from excess noise and large enough that those present will not crowd the individual being hypnotized; a comfortable chair; adequate heating or cooling; proper lighting).
   — Equipment (video equipment; proper number of microphones; a time-date generator, if available).
   — Properly cleared personnel to operate equipment.
   — A proper briefing for camera crew (if any).

4) Choice of professional—only a psychiatrist, psychologist, physician, or dentist. (It should be noted that the use of the terms "psychologist" and "psychiatrist" is regulated by most states and the District of Columbia. The FBI currently uses only those properly trained individuals who are licensed or certified as psychologists, psychiatrists, or physicians. Further, while our policy does include the use of dentists who are qualified as hypnotists, no dentists have

been used as of this date. The qualifications of a hypnotist are some-what vague. There is no standard for a "qualified" hypnotist per se. However, several societies, such as the American Society of Clinical Hypnosis and the Society of Clinical and Experimental Hypnosis, do set standards for the use of hypnosis and the training of hypnotists. It is to these standards the FBI refers when we speak of "qualified.")

5) Items to be discussed with professionals:
    — FBI requirements (for recording sessions; for keeping tapes; and various legal requirements.)
    — Dangers of cueing.
    — Desire for coordinator to do the interviewing. (This is not an inflexible rule. At this time, many psychiatrists and psychologists have done enough work with FBI Agents that the professional himself can and does conduct much of the interview.)
    — Agreement on payment. (Charges may be by the hour, by the session, by number of persons, or a flat rate.)
    — Long-term arrangements, such as the possibility of obtaining security clearance for the doctor and the doctor's future participation in FBI cases.
    — Comfort of witness.

The Hypnosis Session

1) The preinduction interview, that portion conducted on tape prior to the hypnosis session, should include:
    — Discussion of hypnotist's background.
    — Voluntary participation of witness. Signing consent form.
    — Brief description of procedures.
    — Removal of misconceptions.
    — Discussion of basic health of witness (back trouble; contact lenses; color blindness; heart problems, mental disorders, blood pressure, if possible; diabetes). Any health problems must be resolved prior to interview.

2) Prior to taped interview, coordinating Agent will confer with others who may be present to advise them of the need for keeping quiet and unobtrusive.

3) Prior to hypnotic induction, the witness will be allowed to relax and recount all the details he/she can recall of the incident in question. Do not lead or question. Merely allow the witness to recount details in any order he desires.

4) The induction will be done by the professional. The coordinator should note for his records the doctor's opinion of the depth of trance and by what method the doctor estimates that depth.

5) The doctor may then transfer rapport to the coordinator for questioning about the incident. The coordinator will again simply let the witness recall the incident without prompting. After the witness has recalled the incident the coordinator may go back and "zero in" on specific details.

6) Rapport will be transferred back to the doctor who will dehypnotize the witness. The doctor is in charge of the session. (If the Agent coordinator finds that the doctor's requirements do not meet the FBI's minimum legal standards, the Agent may find another doctor. In fact, he is required to do so. But once the session is started, the doctor is in charge.)

7) The original videotapes of the interview are evidence and are treated accordingly: the chain of custody is maintained and the tapes are stored in a secure location. Copies are provided the Behavioral Science Unit of the Training Division of the FBI Academy for assessment and research.[15]

The FBI has utilized hypnosis in numerous cases; for approximately 60 percent of these investigations, additional intelligence was obtained. Some was relevant and produced immediate results (e.g., an accurate sketch drawn from the witness's recall). But some is still open to question because the imprecise nature of hypnosis-based information makes corroboration difficult.

Often overlooked as a member of the investigation "team," sketch artists have sometimes proved invaluable in hypnosis sessions. Several cases in which the FBI was involved were resolved dramatically because they provided satisfactory composite sketches of suspects. An FBI artist will travel to various field offices to work with the witness, coordinator, and doctor to produce composite drawings of suspects. Outside artists should be familiarized with the use of hypnosis in aiding recall and the FBI guidelines.

The Future of Hypnosis

Hypnosis continues to be a minor tool in the investigator's repertory. Nevertheless, it can be an effective one. Not only will it save many work hours, the potential also exists for its use by investigators themselves to enhance their own recall of events or details.

The team approach has proved valuable to the FBI. Introducing a "doctor-patient" relationship into an investigation, it ensures additional protection for witness and victim, while minimizing the hazards (potential and real) of hypnosis. Most important, the team approach helps to offset doubts about professionalism. There may well be a few individuals in law enforcement whose techniques are unscrupulous, but the same might be said of the health professions, both mental and physical. The FBI does not tout its approach as the only method, but law enforcement agencies may wish to consider some of the Bureau's guidelines for improving an existing program or establishing the place of hypnosis in their departments.[16] A few municipal police departments have staff members trained in hypnosis, and the Forensic Hypnosis Society, a professional organization of police hypnotists, provides for the exchange of information and encourages research.

Finally, it must be emphasized, the credibility of information obtained through hypnosis is enhanced when the fact(s) disclosed are supported by independent evidence. It is important that such disclosures be followed up with additional investigative efforts involving other individuals, objects (physical evidence), and records to secure corroborative evidence.

EYEWITNESS EVIDENCE: THE ROLE OF PERCEPTION AND MEMORY _____

Most people have strong convictions about what they see with their own eyes, thus jurors tend to believe eyewitness testimony. However, experienced detectives have learned that eyewitnesses can be mistaken; indeed, it is not uncommon to find various eyewitness reports on an identical event to be incompatible. It is the task of the investigator to resolve such contradictions. One way is to reconstruct how the crime was committed (the use of physical evidence and the crime laboratory for this purpose are treated in Chapter 2). Another way to evaluate eyewitness reports is by understanding the psychological process involved: it begins with the original observation and proceeds to its retelling to the detective later and ultimate presentation to the court if the case goes to trial. A rather complicated process of observing and recalling, it can be divided into the following stages:

1. *Sensory input*: Information is encountered through visual observation or other senses, then encoded for storage in memory;

2. *Memory:* The storage and retention of what was observed and encoded;

3. *Retrieval:* The recovery of information through search of memory and its communication to others. The availability of cues to assist the search process is important at this stage.

Sensory Input

To understand how information is acquired, it is important to know the difference between perception and attention. Borrowing from Huxley's plain-talking style (which serves well for explaining the scientific method in Chapter 13) should be helpful. In one example, a person absorbed in reading hears a loud noise that seems to come from just outside the window. The reader, his or her attention diverted from the book, then interprets the meaning of the noise. Perception based on previous experience permits the likely cause to be determined. The sound could be of automobiles colliding, thunder, a scream, or a gunshot.

Now, consider a new baby asleep in its crib who is awakened by an identical noise. Though its attention would also be directed at the sound, having acquired no experience or knowledge in its brief life span, the baby is unable to interpret what the noise means. Like the reader, the baby's attention might be directed toward the sound; unlike the reader, however, the baby lacks any perception of its cause.

Perception is an important concept in comprehending the process of sensory input. *Memory* (essentially stored perceptions) and perception are intertwined, but for didactic reasons they are usually considered separate processes. To possess memory a person must have experiences. Something—a thought, emotion, object—must be comprehended through the mind or the senses. The person then perceives a new event in terms of experiences already stored up in memory and builds expectations and attitudes on them. So long as biases and stereotypes that can color expectations and attitudes are operative, perception may be faulty.

Perception can be considered the interpretation, classification, and conversion of sensory stimuli into a more durable configuration for memory. In other words, sensory input is assimilated to established knowledge stored in long-term memory. The discrete elements of an event are organized by the mind into meaningful categories, and stored. The aim is to assimilate the event, then reconcile it with prior experience and knowledge so as to avoid any discrepancy between them—bringing both the perceived event and prior experience into harmony and making them compatible. The mind's need to affect such a reconciliation is, however, a possible source of error. Perception also can be affected by stress or arousal felt at the time cognizance was taken of the event. Thus, the perception of how long it took for a crime to be committed (or for the police to respond) is often much greater than the actual elapsed time. Other factors affecting perception include age, health, and gender.

Memory

What the witness to a crime sees is etched on the brain; and later, on request, it can be recollected precisely. This belief is pervasive—witnesses (particularly victims) often asserting: "I'll never forget that face!" Common sense would seem to concur, yet clinical and laboratory experimentation demonstrate that memory is a complex phenomenon that cannot be explained with assumptions or beliefs. For example, common sense rejects the idea that sensory input received after an event can affect the memory of that event. Nonetheless, there is considerable empirical evidence that post-event information is indeed integrated with what already exists in memory. As a result, modifications may include: a change in the person's memory, enhancement of existing memory, or nonexistent details becoming embodied in the previous existing memory. Post-event information may arise from reading a newspaper article about it, from questions asked by an investigator or attorney, or from overhearing or talking about the event (particularly with other witnesses). The mind, therefore, is not like a videotape recorder that captures and retains what was seen (or heard) and remains unaffected by subsequent input.

Psychologists use the term *unconscious transference* to describe a witness's mistaken recollection about a crime—a recollection implicating an individual who was not involved. In one case, for instance, a young adult identified in a lineup (composed of several bank tellers) as the person who had robbed a bank was, in fact, an innocent depositor who had been in the bank the previous day. He was otherwise not connected with the institution, and certainly not with the robbery. This case illustrates the critical need to check out an accused person's explanation or alibi. Here, a review of the bank's deposit records would have challenged (and precluded) the lineup misidentification.

Information Retrieval

Two kinds of remembering are of interest to the detective: recall and recognition. In *recall* a previous event (e.g., a crime) is described verbally—in narrative form, in a portrait parlé, or to a police artist. In *recognition* there is an awareness that something was seen previously; some aspect of an event is remembered and selected from a group of similar items, persons, or photographs. This occurs when a mug shot is picked from the Rogues Gallery file or an individual is selected from a lineup. Generally, a person's ability with regard to recognition is better than it is for recall.

For retrieving information from a witness through an interview, a new technique, the result of psychological research into memory retrieval, is a major step forward. (See the section on The Cognitive Interview later in this chapter.)

WITNESS ERRORS

In addition to the possible errors associated with perception and memory, other sources of error include environmental conditions and personal factors.

Environmental Conditions

A person's ability to observe an event is limited by such factors as: the illumination of the scene, the distance of the observer from the scene, the noise level (if hearing is involved), and the weather (if the event occurred outdoors). If the evidence in a case depends largely on eyewitness testimony, it is desirable to verify whether environmental conditions existing at the time permitted such observations. Basic to the protection of the innocent, a verification can also deflect criticism by defense counsel and strengthen the confidence of the witness by establishing that there were no impediments to making the reported observations.

Personal Factors

Although sight and hearing most often provide the basis of witness testimony, any of the five senses can be involved. Again it is desirable to verify that the relevant sensory organs are or were not impaired. Taking this precaution enhances the credibility of the witness.

THE COGNITIVE INTERVIEW

In 1908 Harvard's Hugo Munsterberg (the first experimental psychologist in America) proved that although eyewitness testimony was remarkably faulty, it could be improved upon.[17] His effort was ignored by lawyers, judges, and law enforcement, and not until the 1970s would psychologists reexamine ways to improve eyewitness testimony. This kind of empirical research may have been further prompted by the RAND Corporation report noting that the single most important factor as to whether a case would be solved is the information provided by a witness or victim.[18]

This observation led R. Edward Geiselman and others to research the effectiveness of memory retrieval techniques; their program was labeled the "cognitive interview."[19] Reminiscent of Munsterberg's earlier experiment, an incident was staged and 16 undergraduates became "eyewitnesses." Divided into two groups, only one group (the cognitive interview group) was given instruction in memory-retrieval techniques. It included four recommendations for completing the test booklet, which had an open-ended question and some pointed (short-answer) questions. The recommendations were:

> First, try to reinstate in your mind the context surrounding the incident. Think about what the room looked like and where you were sitting in the room. Think about how you were feeling at the time and think about your reactions to the incident.

> Second, some people hold back information because they are not quite sure about what they remember. Please do not edit anything out. Please write down everything, even things you think may not be important. Just be sure to indicate at the right how sure you are about each item.

> Third, it is natural to go through the incident from beginning to end, and that is probably what you should do at first. However, many people can come up with more information if they also go through events in reverse order. Or, you might start with the thing that impressed you the most and then go from there, proceeding both forward and backward in time.

> Fourth, try to adopt the perspective of others who were present during the incident. For example, try to place yourself in the experimenter's role and think about what she must have seen.[20]

The researchers concluded:

> The results of this study illustrate that the cognitive interview has substantial promise as a technique for the enhancement of eyewitness memory retrieval. The cognitive interview produced significantly more correct information without an accompanying increase in the amount of incorrect information. This advantage for subjects using the cognitive interview held for both an open-ended question and for pointed questions. Overall, 84 percent of the information generated with the cognitive interview was found to be accurate. Further, the confidence of the witnesses in their correct responses was enhanced with the cognitive interview, while confidence in their incorrect responses was not reliably affected. All but one of the subjects who received the cognitive interview reported that they found the methods to be useful.[21]

The next step for the Geiselman team was to compare the cognitive interview against hypnosis, another memory enhancement technique. Then both were matched against results obtained from a standard police interview.[22] This research revealed that both the cognitive and hypnosis procedures elicited a significantly greater number of correct items of information from the subjects than did the standard interview. This result, which held even for the most critical facts from the films, was most pronounced for crime scenarios in which the density of events was high. The number of incorrect items of information generated did not differ across the three interview conditions. The observed memory enhancement was interpreted in terms of the memory-guidance techniques common to both the cognitive and hypnosis interviews. Neither differential questioning time nor heightened subject or interviewer motivation could explain the results.[23]

Three years later, Geiselman and Fischer reported on the effort to refine and revise the cognitive interview technique which, they stated, was based on four core principles: memory-event similarity, focused retrieval, extensive retrieval, and witness-compatible questioning.[24]

Memory-Event Similarity

Memory-event similarity involves an attempt to have the witness mentally recreate the environment surrounding the incident. A psychological environment similar to that which existed at the time of the crime is reproduced at the interview.

> The interviewer, therefore, should try to reinstate in the witness's mind the external (e.g., weather), emotional (e.g., feelings of fear), and cognitive (e.g., relevant thoughts) features that were experienced at the time the crime occurred.[25]

The witness is requested to think about the crime—the scene and what it looked like, where he or she was standing (or sitting), and the reaction to the crime at that time. This is a mental exercise; the witness is not physically placed at the scene. "In fact, if the crime scene has changed considerably, going back to the scene could conceivably interfere with the witness's recollection."[26]

Focused Retrieval

Because memory retrieval requires concentration, the interviewer helps witnesses to focus by refraining from asking too many short-answer, undirected, or irrelevant questions that tend to break concentration. Just as asking a series of questions can create a barrier that obstructs memory, so can interrupting the eyewitness who is responding to an open-ended question or providing a narrative description of the event. Another means of focusing memory retrieval is to have witnesses write everything down, even details they consider unimportant or about which they are unsure.

Extensive Retrieval

Memory retrieval is hard work, and witnesses are apt to terminate the effort after the first attempt. It is especially likely that the elderly will do so; they need to be encouraged to make other attempts. The usual mode is to begin at the beginning and continue chronologically to the end, but there are other ways. For example, witnesses can be asked to start with whatever detail is most indelibly inscribed in their memory, and from there, encouraged to go backward and forward. Another way is to reverse the order, urging witnesses to describe how the incident ended, and then proceed backward to the beginning.

Witness-Compatible Questioning

Just as the eyewitness is better able to retrieve memory when the environment surrounding the event is recreated, so are interviewers better able to ask questions if they can place themselves in the witness's frame of mind. The aim is to ask questions compatible with the situation in which the witness found himself or herself. To accomplish this, interviewers should try to place themselves in the witness's situation, and then frame questions on the basis of what was likely to have been observed at the time. This means adjusting to the witness's perspective rather than having the witness adjust to the investigator's. Geiselman and Fischer conclude by remarking:

> . . . cognitive interviewing reliably enhances the completeness of a witness's recollection, and without increasing the number of incorrect or confabulated (replacing facts with fantasy) bits of information generated. . . .The procedures are easy to learn and can be readily adopted in routine police interview procedures. In fact, the cognitive interview is in use as standard training at several police departments and other law enforcement agencies.[27]

REFERENCES

1   W.G. Skogan and G.E. Antunes, "Information, Apprehension, and Deterrence: Exploring the Limits of Police Productivity," *Journal of Criminal Justice* 7 (1979), 234-235.

2   R. Bocklet, "Suspect Sketches Computerized for Faster Identification," *Law and Order*, 35:8 (August 1987), 61-63.

3   Ibid., 62.

4   B. Clede, "Computerized ID Systems," *Law and Order*, 36:1 (January 1988), 201-202.

5   Ibid., 201.

6   U.S. President, 1966-1972 (Johnson), The President's Commission on Law Enforcement and Administration of Justice, *The Challenge of Crime in a Free Society* (Washington, DC: U.S. Government Printing Office, 1967), 15.

7   Richard D. Knudten, et al., *Victims and Witnesses: Their Experiences with Crime and the Criminal Justice System*, Executive Summary (Washington, DC: National Institute of Law Enforcement and Criminal Justice, 1977), 12.

8   Ibid., iv.

9   Allen Andrews, *Intensive Inquiry* (New York: St. Martin's Press, 1973).

10   Albert A. Seedman and Peter Hellman, *Chief* (New York: Avon Books, 1975), 18-19.

11   D.E. Wicklander, "Behavioral Analysis," *Security World* 17:3 (March 1980), 41.

12   Ibid., 40.

13   Ibid.

14   Ibid., 61.

15   R.L. Ault, "Hypnosis: The FBI's Team Approach," *FBI Law Enforcement Bulletin* 49:1 (Jan. 1980), 5-8.

16   Ibid., 8.

17   Hugo Munsterberg, *On The Witness Stand* (Littleton, CO: Fred B. Rothman, 1981). [A reproduction of the original 1908 edition.]

18   Peter Greenwood and Joan Petersilia, *The Criminal Investigation Process*. Vol. III: Observations and Analysis (Santa Monica, CA: RAND, 1975).

19   R. Edward Geiselman, et al., Enhancement of Eyewitness Memory: An Empirical Evaluation of the Cognitive Interview," *Journal of Police Science and Administration* 12:1 (1984), 74.

20   Ibid., 76.

21   Ibid., 79.

22   R. Edward Geiselman, et al., "Eyewitness Memory Enhancement in the Police Interview: Cognitive Retrieval Mnemonics Versus Hypnosis," *Journal of Applied Psychology* 70:2 (1985), 401-412.

23   Ibid., 401.

24   R.E. Geiselman and R.P. Fischer, "The Cognitive Interview: An Innovative Technique for Questioning Witnesses of Crime," *Journal of Police and Criminal Psychology* 4:2 (October 1988), 3.

25   Ibid.

26   Ibid.

27   Ibid., 4-5.

SUPPLEMENTAL READINGS

Interviewing

Bennett, Margo, and John E. Hess. "Cognitive Interviewing," *FBI Law Enforcement Bulletin* 60:3 (Mar. 1991), 8-12.

Fisher, Ronald P. *An R.E. Geiselman Memory-Enhancing Technique for Investigative Interviewing; the Cognitive Interview.* Text. Ed. Springfield, IL: Charles C Thomas, 1992.

Gorden, Raymond L. *Basic Interviewing Skills.* Englewood, CO: Peacock Publications, 1992.

Gorden, Raymond L. *Interviewing: Strategy, Techniques, and Tactics.* 4th ed. Florence, KY: Wadsworth, 1987.

Hess, John. *Interviewing and Interrogation for Law Enforcement.* Cincinnati: Anderson, 1997.

Kahn, R.L. *The Dynamics of Interviewing: Theory, Techniques and Cases.* Melbourne, FL: Krieger, 1983.

Rabon, Don. *Interviewing and Interrogation.* Durham, NC: Carolina Academic Press, 1992.

Royal, Robert F., and Steven R. Schutt. *The Gentle Art of Interviewing and Interrogation.* Englewood Cliffs, NJ: Prentice Hall, 1976.

Spaulding, William. *Interviewing Child Victims of Sexual Exploitation.* Arlington, VA: National Center for Missing and Exploited Children, 1987.

Zulawski, David E., and Douglas E. Wicklander, eds. *Practical Aspects of Interview and Interrogation.* Boca Raton, FL: CRC Press, 1993.

Dealing with Witnesses

Cain, Anthony, A., and Marjorie Kravitz. *Victim/Witness Assistance: A Selected Bibliography*. Rockville, MD: National Criminal Justice Reference Service, 1978.

Cannavale, Frank J., Jr., and William D. Falcon. *Witness Cooperation*. Lexington, MA: Lexington Books, 1976.

Nonverbal Communication

Ekman, Paul, and Wallace V. Friesen. *Unmasking the Face*. 2nd ed. Palo Alto, CA: Consulting Psychologist Press, 1984.

Fast, Julius. *Body Language*. New York: M. Evans and Company, 1972.

Speigel, J.P., and P. Machotka. *Messages of the Body*. New York: The Free Press, 1974.

Weaver, Richard L. *Understanding Interpersonal Communications*. 7th ed. Glenview, IL: Harper College Division, 1996.

Hypnosis

Arons, Harry. *Hypnosis in Criminal Investigation*. Springfield, IL: Charles C Thomas, 1967.

Niehaus, Joe. *Investigative Forensic Hypnosis*. Boca Raton, FL: CRC Press, 1992.

Reiser, Martin. *Handbook of Investigative Hypnosis*. Los Angeles: Lehi Publishing, 1980.

Perception, Memory, and Witness Error

Ellison, Katherine W., and Robert Buckout. Chapter 5 of *Psychology and Criminal Justice*. New York: Harper & Row, 1981.

Loftus, Elizabeth F. *Eyewitness Testimony*. Cambridge, MA: Harvard University Press, 1980.

Marshall, James. *Law and Psychology in Conflict*. Indianapolis: Bobbs-Merrill, 1966.

Wall, Patrick M. *Eyewitness Identification in Criminal Cases*. Springfield, IL: Charles C Thomas, 1971.

Yarmey, A. Daniel. *The Psychology of Eyewitness Testimony*. New York: The Free Press, 1979.

CHAPTER 7

Records and Files

Nurtured Resource or Arid Archive?

The major sources of recorded information are the files maintained by government and business organizations. Within government, the agencies contacted most are those concerned with criminal justice. They, as well as some others not part of the criminal justice system, willingly provide information to the investigator. The remaining bureaucratic agencies, however, may not be very cooperative. The investigator will find them similar to business firms that do not necessarily make it an easy matter to extract information from their files. As a rule, problems arise when a detective does not, as a matter of right, have direct access to what is sought. That being so, the file keeper's cooperation must be secured. This chapter will describe methods that facilitate the acquisition of recorded information and make its investigative value more timely.

LAW ENFORCEMENT RECORDS

Police files are often set up according to:

1. Type of offense
2. Name(s) of offender(s)
3. Name(s) of victim(s)
4. Location—where crime was committed
5. Date and time of occurrence
6. Relevant facts pertaining to the case

This system may be adequate for many departments, but once set up, lethargy and lean budgets often prevent periodic updating. To be relevant, files must be culled regularly, and after some time, purged. Outdated records clearly do not meet the investigator's needs, as community crime patterns shift to reflect social and economic change. Two developments, though, hold promise of enhancing the investigative value of law enforcement records:

1. The application of information science concepts to the storage and retrieval of information;

2. A more sophisticated use of records in crime pattern analysis.

INFORMATION SCIENCE

Today, almost all large and medium-sized departments have some form of automated data processing; only a few small departments do not utilize at least some kind of computer. Reider recognized the value of putting information science technology to work for law enforcement when he wrote that it "represents a breakthrough comparable to the adoption of radio broadcasting as a means of communication between station and field personnel."[1]

With a computerized system on line, the magnitude of information collected and filed by police every day is accessible; their daily field contact reports can receive instantaneous cross-checks for correlations with crimes already in the computer. The following situation involving an unfamiliar car parked in a neighborhood illustrates how stored information can be utilized. An inhabitant of the neighborhood noting its presence there may call the police. Later, if a crime is reported and that person learns of it, he or she may inform the authorities about previous suspicions. Sometimes a license plate number will be supplied with such calls; more often only the color, make, or type (e.g., van, hatchback, four-door sedan) is observed. Then, if a patrol officer a few days later submits a report on a traffic infraction and the description of the vehicle involved— data readily accessed from the computer—even partly matches the report on the unfamiliar parked car, the investigator has a potential lead (the driver's or owner's name).

As mentioned in a previous chapter, the capture of a group of alleged terrorists (who were subsequently convicted for a variety of felonies including murder, bombings, and robbery) was the direct result of a call to police. In this case, a woman became concerned about an unfamiliar van parked on her street. Not only had the vehicle attracted her notice, so had the behavior of the group of people (several men and one woman) gathered around it. Though dressed in sweat suits and jogging between the van and a nearby park, all held cigarettes in their mouths. Regarding this as unusual, she called the police and they were apprehended.

Data processing systems are not without problems. Difficulties arise when input depends on police officers filling out several page-long forms. Resenting the time required to complete them, many officers either fail to do so or are careless about verifying their facts. To cope with this problem, one large department altered its reporting format. They replaced the several different, separate forms for burglary, robbery, theft, sex offenses, and "miscellaneous" crimes with a single preliminary investigation form with a limited number of lines and boxes to be filled in, and ample space for a narrative report. Not only were department needs satisfied, so were the needs of its officers. In addition, the improvement made input more readily accessible from the computer.

CRIME PATTERN ANALYSIS

When a special unit is assigned to receive and analyze all available crime data, and to furnish or circulate the extracted information to operational units, the department is employing formal crime analysis. This is a good opportunity to apply information science to police operations, including criminal investigation. Most police departments engage in analysis to some degree, but according to George A. Buck, "There is an overall lack of the use of formal crime analysis."[2] Although published in 1973, this statement remains essentially correct today.

Crime data are collected from internal and external sources. Internal sources include patrol, detective, communications, and special units; external sources include crime victims, the courts, correction agencies, and probation and parole departments. Other governmental agencies may contribute, as well as private organizations such as crime commissions and *ad hoc* groups.

The storage of data may be manual or electronic; its analysis will depend on the sophistication of personnel and equipment. Modern computers facilitate the greatest extraction of useful investigative information. Some of the possibilities include:

1. Identifying possible suspects for a particular crime.

2. Listing crimes having a common offender.

3. Identifying crime trends and potential targets.

4. Preparing crime maps by type and location of crime, or by residences of known offenders.

The first two possibilities may be achieved by the use of a *modus operandi* file. The last two, because of a pioneering effort by university researchers and the Chicago Police Department, are feasible to a greater degree than in the past. This will be discussed later in the chapter.

MODUS OPERANDI

The identification of a suspect in a particular case is sometimes accomplished by examining how the crime was committed. Termed *modus operandi* (MO) by Atcherley in England, the concept was an early (1913) example of crime pattern analysis:

> . . . if the methods of known criminals can be classified so that the *modus operandi* disclosed in a new crime can be compared with the methods disclosed in previous crimes, it may be possible to establish the identity of the person who commits the crime. This realization led to the formulation of the MO system which seeks to analyze according to a given formula the ingredients of a crime, and then, by systematic comparison with analyses of other crimes, to establish the identity of the criminal.[3]

Atcherley's views are noteworthy for what would appear to be an overstatement, at least from the American perspective:

> Although it may be possible for a criminal to restrain his actions in the matter of leaving proof of his crime by finger impressions, no amount of restraint, or knowledge of the possibility of the results of his crime being recognized as his work, seems to deter the individual from so acting as to render himself unidentifiable by his *Modus Operandi*.[4]

However understandable Atcherley's enthusiasm, the experience of many police departments in the United States does not support such optimistic expectations. The MO system meets with more success when some unusual mode of committing the offense is noted. For example, if a convicted child molester moves to a new neighborhood soon after being released and reverts to old habits, he or she may be recognized as a possible suspect if the geographical area covered is sufficiently large and the way the child is lured remains essentially the same. Such recognition would be an example of *linkage*—the production of a list of suspects based on MO. Linkage also occurs when a common offender is identified as the individual responsible for a series of crimes.

The ViCAP (Violent Criminal Apprehension Program) (see Appendix 3) was set up by the FBI in 1985 to deal with serial murderers and other itinerant felons who commit violent crimes. In some respects it may be seen as an extension of the MO concept to the national level. The Gacy case points to the crucial need for a procedure that would prevent a killer (in this case, of more than 30 adolescent boys within a three-year period) from falling between the cracks of the criminal justice system. When reporting the unexplained disappearances of their sons to police, some parents had voiced suspicions about Gacy. However, because each investigator had many other cases, and because the data system was unequal to the task, the offender-victim connection was not recognized. The suspect was ultimately apprehended by a department that followed up on the investigation. Had an area-wide computer system been operational, the missing persons thought to be victims of foul play would have been in its data bank, and the name of one suspect (recurring in several of the cases) would have emerged sooner. Some of the jurisdictions involved subsequently installed a computer with this capability.

Crime pattern analysis depends on the sophistication of equipment and personnel, but any system—manual or fully automated—ultimately relies on those who design and operate it. Curiosity, imagination, and a willingness to experiment and be objective when appraising results are vitally needed to raise performance above the mediocre-to-adequate level, which unfortunately is a hallmark. The following examples demonstrate. An exceptional civil servant—inquisitive and energetic—wondered if there were valid driver's licenses in the hands of the legally blind. Entitled to special tax credits in that state, they were easy to trace. It was surprising, therefore, to find the names of about 120 people who, though legally blind, were licensed to drive. For crimes involving vehicles, the feature an eyewitness is most likely to observe is an automobile's color, yet less than half of the states in the United States require automobile color on license plate applications. If accompanied by other information about the vehicle, this detail would reduce the number of suspected vehicles. In as much as the cost of acquiring and storing the data is negligible compared to the benefits to be derived in hit-and-run homicide investigations alone, it is hard to fathom why this obvious step has not been universally adopted. (See Chapter 20 for more on the use of computers in criminal investigation.)

Organization of a Modus Operandi File

To improve efficiency, many police departments have coupled the MO file with the Rogues Gallery (mug shot file). The utility of the combined files rests to some degree upon the detective who interviews the complainant and eyewitnesses, and examines (or has a laboratory technician examine) the crime scene. Through these means it can be determined whether any feature, pattern, or trademark distinguishes the crime scene evidence or the behavior of the perpetrator. File utility also depends on how the file keeper subdivides the information furnished by the detective, and what he or she extracts from and enters in the file. Efficient processing and selection can also limit the number of mug shots that victims and witnesses are expected to examine. Burdening them with too many photographs could impair their ability to make an identification.

The most obvious basis for division of an MO file is by type of crime. With each indexed according to the behavior and peculiarities of the criminal, file subdivisions should be as specialized yet inclusive as possible. Experience with the crimes and criminals in a particular area should guide the selection of subclassifications. The advisability of assigning one specialist—or at most a few—to this duty has been demonstrated. Some detectives believe their on-the-job experience makes them better able to examine and enter data into the system—especially material from the narrative report. In any event, the following information will be sought: type of crime; when and where committed (time, day of week, and location); type of property targeted or persons victimized; ruse employed and tale told by perpetrator; miscellaneous idiosyncrasies; and photographs.

Type of Crime

As stated previously, a logical starting point in building a classification scheme for MO would be by type of offense. Criminals, at least in the United States, usually do not stick to one crime; they commit a variety of offenses, taking advantage of opportunities presented. Regardless of the type of crime, such criminals often employ the same or very similar MOs. For example, one offender ambushed his victims in apartment house hallways. If the victim was male, he would commit robbery; if female, he would stuff the washcloth he carried with him in her mouth, then rape and rob her. For taxonomy purposes, the distinctive features are apartment house hallways and the use of a washcloth. Robbery and rape are secondary for the purpose of MO.

Time, Day, and Location

The hour, the day (weekday, weekend, holiday), and the general area in which the crime was committed are other important aspects to be considered. Such information provides the basis on which a strategy for surveillance (including stakeouts and decoys) can be developed—or, should the criminal have been recognized from a broadcasted description, for putting a tail on the suspect. Also, should an intended victim's suspicions have been aroused by a criminal's behavior and the incident is reported, police may be able to match that behavior to an MO in the file. With a description and name provided, patrol car officers or detectives in an unmarked car may spot the suspect "working" the neighborhood and subsequently catch him or her in the act.

Type of Property or Persons Targeted

The property and person(s) commonly attacked include: gasoline stations, taverns or package liquor stores, 24-hour convenience stores and restaurants, druggists and doctors, bank messengers, occupants of apartment buildings or private homes, and cab drivers. However, information on such attacks may be of transitory value in identifying the MO of someone just commencing a career in crime. The individual who starts by robbing a bar after first having a drink may then repeat this in another bar a half-hour later a mile or two away. The MO having become obvious, radio and patrol cars can be alerted to the perpetrator's description, type of car used, and possibly its license number; if this pattern continues, the robber might be caught committing or fleeing from a subsequent crime in another bar. With experience, however, the criminal may shift from bars to gasoline stations or liquor stores. Therefore, MO information based solely on type of target does not necessarily characterize the perpetrator for any considerable period of time.

Building

What type of building was involved? Was it a loft, factory, condominium, single-family dwelling, or retail store? How was it entered? Did the burglar climb through a transom or exhaust fan opening, file through bars, cut through a roof, use a celluloid strip to slip the lock, or hide in a stairwell before closing time and then break in? These MOs are helpful in distinguishing burglars.

Object

Sometimes the property damaged or taken, or the person attacked, will indicate motive. It is often possible to determine whether the crime was "fingered" (i.e., it was an "inside job" requiring private knowledge about the person or object of the crime). Experienced criminals hesitate to leave "scoring" to chance; they tend to seek assurances that any attempt will be worth their time, and not be a poor risk. The number of people privy to inside information being limited, this insight helps to channel investigative efforts.

Ruse Used By Perpetrator ("Represented Self As")

Enterprising criminals may employ disguises that permit them to be in a locale without arousing suspicion. Accordingly, the following fairly common disguises warrant mention: house painter, telephone repair or store delivery worker, house-to-house sales representative, detective. Many of these ruses (of dress and possibly equipment) can account for a criminal's presence in an area. Required "credentials" can be forged. Whatever the pattern, the stratagem for gaining entrance characterizes the offender. Recognizing it helps to reduce the number of potential suspects that must be pulled from the MO file.

Tale Used By Perpetrator

Closely related to the way perpetrators represent themselves is the tale they tell to gain entrance to—or account for their presence in—the area. To succeed, this recital must be consistent with the role they are playing; when used, it is another characteristic of MO.

Miscellaneous Idiosyncrasies

For reasons not fully understood, criminals will sometimes do something unusual, something not related to the crime particularly, and which—like a trademark—brands them. For example, one man intent on rape repeatedly selected a pedestrian who was out early and ran her down with his car, apparently by accident. Then, offering to rush her to the nearest hospital, he would proceed instead to a deserted place for the assault. Although the MO was soon recognized, he was able to commit several more rapes in the same fashion until enough information from the victims could be pieced together. The alarm sent out at that point had sufficient facts to enable a patrol officer or detective to identify his car. Without this unusual MO, the connection between the rapes and vehicular accidents would not have been noted, nor would the assorted pieces of information from each victim have been assembled and directed toward apprehending one specific individual.

Peculiarities in MO are almost too numerous to mention. For example, there are: the burglar who, in addition to the customary objects of the crime (e.g., money and jewelry), will always take meat from the freezer; the robber who will offer the victim a cigarette; and the pyromaniac who will set two fires exactly six blocks apart on the first Friday of every month. Just as bizarre MOs can help to identify the criminal, so can unusual habits of dress: for instance, wearing a black beret in a neighborhood where such headgear is seldom seen. Again, before it is meaningful in a criminal investigation, odd behavior or dress must be observed, reported, and placed in the file.

Photographs

When a person is arrested for a serious crime, two bust-size photographs—one full face, one profile—should be taken in addition to a full-length photograph, mounted on a card containing the MO, and filed according to a scheme developed to meet the needs of the particular department (see Figures 7.1 and 7.2). To avoid viewer fatigue, the number of photographs shown to an eyewitness should be kept to a minimum. If the witness selects one that "resembles" the criminal, it is removed and returned covertly to the next group of photographs. If the eyewitness makes the same selection, greater reliance can be placed on the identification.

CRIME				CASE NO.	
DATE	TIME		DAY OF WEEK (If weekend or holiday—specify.)		
BUILDING (TYPE INVOLVED)					
ADDRESS					
WHERE ENTERED		MEANS OF ENTRY			
OBJECT ATTACKED		APPARENT REASON FOR ATTACK			
TALE (Use back side, if needed.)					
REPRESENTED SELF AS					
UNUSUAL BEHAVIOR (PECULIARITIES)					
NAME			ADDRESS		
AGE	HEIGHT	WEIGHT	EYES	HAIR	RACE
OCCUPATION			FINGERPRINT CLASSIFICATION		
ASSOCIATES: NAMES AND ADDRESSES					
FREQUENTS					

Figure 7.1
Modus operandi file card (front side).

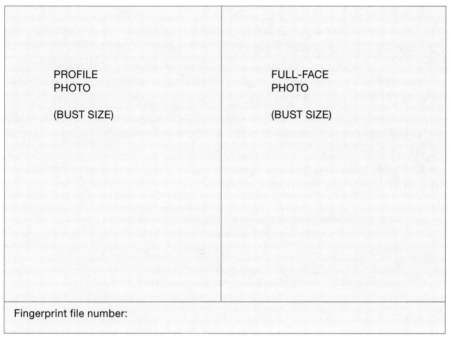

Figure 7.2
Modus operandi file card (rear side).

Electronic Data Processing

The advent of the computer—with its ability to store (and quickly retrieve) large quantities of information across jurisdictions—would seem to be the realization of Atcherley's dream of *modus operandi*. There are certain obstacles, however. To be functional, an MO database must cover a wide area, possibly comprising many jurisdictions. In Chicago, for example, it would mean extending the database to include the nearby cities of Milwaukee, Wisconsin, and Gary, Indiana. Admittedly a massive effort in data collection and analysis, it is a must if an effective MO file is to be built. Some additional obstacles to achieving Atcherley's vision in the United States are: budgetary considerations (because of the many governmental entities involved); responsibility for maintenance and operation; and sustaining voluntary cooperation across jurisdictions.

Microcomputers: Crime Mapping and Proactive Resource Allocation _____

An ambitious attempt to merge the needs of the police with the capacity of the microcomputer was reported by Maltz et al.[5] MAPADS (Microcomputer Assisted Police Analysis and Deployment System) produces maps that display an extensive array of information on crimes within a geographical area, ranging from an officer's beat to a radio car sector to an entire precinct. Data are entered daily from two sources: police incident reports and input from community organizations. The latter quickly become aware of local conditions that may not require immediate police response, yet are cause for concern. Community concerns include breeding spots for crime such as: a new locus for prostitution or the sale of narcotics, a gang taking over an abandoned building, a new site being used for loitering, or repeated, noisy parties where none were held before.

The computer can generate special reports and maps locating high criminal activity. MAPADS can also provide investigators with an overall picture of the crimes that have occurred since they were last on duty. This facilitates the recognition of a pattern that may be attributable to a particular offender and the development of a strategy to apprehend the offender. Meanwhile, of course, the department's crime analysis unit will be looking for trends and crime patterns using data that cover a larger area than a local precinct or district. The Maltz report states:

> Area 5 detectives were able to take advantage of the computer's ability to search through a large number of records. Finally, by combining mapping, fixed data (time, date, offense code, etc.), and free data (narrative), detectives were able to take advantage of the contextual information MAPADS provided, which their previous data-gathering procedures did not.[6]

The report then describes how an armed robber was recognized through clues from contextual information. This would not have resulted from fixed data alone.

> On January 7, 1985, due to the use of one map, Area 5 detectives found a pattern of armed robberies of cab drivers. All three robberies occurred within a block of each other, but may not have been detected by other means because:
>
>> One of the crimes was coded as a street robbery rather than a taxicab robbery, and detectives picked it up by reading the case narrative; and
>>
>> One of the victims walked into the District station to make the report, thus disguising the location of the incident on the incident report.
>
> The detectives submitted their information to the Crime Analysis Unit, which quickly issued a crime analysis pattern. Subsequently, on January 11, 1988, two more taxicab robberies were added to the pattern. On January 12 an arrest was made, based on and due to the use of MAPADS. The data display in the mapping system provided a view of the data that raised the suspicions of an experienced detective who discerned a pattern in spite of the inaccurate data. This is an example of the power steering concept: the computer system alone was misleading, but the detective was able to use experience and initiative to pursue the clues on the map and find a pattern which would not have been seen without the computer. Area detectives see MAPADS as providing a major improvement in their ability to detect patterns more rapidly and respond appropriately.[7]

The investigative value of MAPADS is only part of its usefulness in police work. Other benefits include managerial proactive measures that can increase the productivity of a patrol officer at the beat (or "post") level and provide for a two-way exchange of information between the police department and community organizations.

> In one instance, the police thought that residents' fear of crime had overcome their objectivity, and that their alleging that one busy corner was especially dangerous (particularly on weekends) was a clear error. But long-term data for the area, which community analysts were able to provide, and calls-for-service data, which were added to the mapped analysis, verified the accuracy of the community perceptions: relying on crime statistics alone gave a misleading picture of the corner's problems. This experience resulted in a vigorous response by the District Commander, and each party's respect for the other was solidified.

> These experiences, combined with the current (and we feel appropriate) development of problem-oriented policing strategies, have led us to conclude that a partnership can and should be developed and maintained between community organizations and the police—not just with respect to community tensions, as has always been the case, but with respect to fostering a working relationship that focuses on crime as an interest of mutual concern.[8]

If MAPADS fulfills its promise to nip crime problems in the bud, it will free up more time to investigate those crimes that could not be prevented through community input and crime mapping.

BUSINESS RECORDS

Business records, being numerous and widely distributed, are not readily available to the investigator. Indeed, if the search is likely to be protracted or costly, only a token effort, if any, may be undertaken by their custodians —who, in point of fact, are not obliged to furnish what is sought. Lack of cooperation was a key factor in a series of attempted bombing cases in the late 1940s and early 1950s. Early in the investigation it became apparent that the bomber's anger was directed at a particular company. The crime laboratory document examiner established that the letters taunting press and police about bomb placements were from the same individual who had planted bombs some 15 years earlier. Therefore, the contact appointed by the company (which was eager to cooperate) was orally requested to search company files for all annoying letters sent from 1930 on. The search produced some letters written in the late 1940s; it appeared there were none from the early 1930s. The explanation given was that the files had been purged of the earlier material.

This was the standoff between investigators and their contact until a series of open letters on the front pages of a New York newspaper elicited a response from the bomber. Police watched with growing interest as subsequent responses confirmed original suspicions: the grievance was directed at a particular company, and it began in the 1930s. Suddenly, the "purged" files were "found" in a warehouse. Because it would have been time-consuming to sift through the records and locate the letters, the contact had apparently concocted the tale about the emptied files. As it turned out, they contained the evidence that would have led to an earlier solution of the case. (A lesson learned: lack of cooperation can take many forms.) Somewhat similar to this case, the printing of the Unabomber's "manifesto" in two national newspapers led to a capture and arrest after 18 years of an unsuccessful search for the bomber's identity.

In summary, to acquire information from commercial establishments, the investigator must have a good idea of what the most common and useful business records are (see Chapter 5) and be aware of other systematic compilations. When tackling the ways and means to access records and files, he or she must first know what exists.

What Records Exist—Where to Find Them

Several books have been published that give extensive coverage to the sources of information available in public and private systems. *Where's What: Sources of Information for Federal Investigators* was written by an investigator for investigators.[9] Emphasizing the existence rather than the availability of recorded information, it points out what documents are available for inspection, the "educated guesses" that can be made about their contents, the conclusions to be drawn, and the information that may be disclosed.

Another publication, *Confidential Information Sources: Public and Private*, was written by an information scientist with experience in security matters. It discusses a wide range of sources, including credit-reporting agencies, medical records, and student records.[10] Its one-of-a-kind appendix (see Figure 7.3) deals with the probability of finding a particular item of information in records.

Directories in Print takes a general approach to other likely sources of business information and files.[11] Its purpose is to supply business and industry with lists of the many directories printed in the United States by business and reference book publishers, trade magazines, chambers of commerce, and federal, state, and city governmental agencies. Offering a means of locating the suppliers of products and services, the table of contents illustrates the extent of the areas and sources of information it can open up for the investigator. It includes descriptive listings in the following categories: General Business; Specific Industries and Lines of Business; Banking, Finance, Insurance, and Real Estate; Agriculture, Resource Industries, and the Environment; Law, Military, and Government; Science, Engineering, and Computer Science; Education; Information Sciences, Social Sciences, and Humanities; Biography; Arts and Entertainment; Public Affairs and Social Concerns; Health and Medicine; Religious, Ethnic, and Fraternal Affairs; Genealogical, Veterans, and Patriotic Affairs; Hobbies, Travel, and Leisure; and Sports and Outdoor Recreation.

The Encyclopedia of Associations rounds out this short list of comprehensive volumes.[12] This text may be described as a basic guide to information on specific subjects. Unique in this respect, the associations and professional societies it catalogs serve as "switchboards" connecting those in need of information to highly qualified sources. Earlier editions were limited to national nonprofit organizations, but later volumes have been expanded to encompass a wider variety. The encyclopedia provides pertinent information in the following diverse areas:

- Trade, Business, and Commercial Organizations
- Agricultural Organizations and Commodity Exchanges
- Legal, Governmental, Public Administration, and Military Organizations
- Scientific, Engineering, and Technical Organizations
- Educational Organizations
- Cultural Organizations
- Social Welfare Organizations
- Health and Medical Organizations
- Public Affairs Organizations
- Fraternal, Foreign Interest, Nationality, and Ethnic Organizations
- Religious Organizations
- Veterans', Hereditary, and Patriotic Organizations
- Hobby and Avocational Organizations
- Athletic and Sports Organizations
- Labor Unions, Associations, and Federations
- Chambers of Commerce and Trade and Tourism Organizations
- Greek and Non-Greek Letter Societies, Associations, and Federations
- Fan Clubs

The texts described above are veritable gold mines, with a scope and depth unmatched by other compilations of recorded information. Perusing their contents will suggest sources of which many investigators are unaware. They are indispensable when preparing for an undercover assignment.

Access to Records and Files

After the potential investigative value of a business file has been determined, obtaining it is the next step. One way to increase the likelihood of cooperation is to establish contacts with record custodians, particularly those who will be called on with some degree of regularity. Because people are generally more responsive to people they know, it is important to form a good working relationship from the start. A detective acting in an official capacity is usually able to secure records that can be adequately described; however, when a request lacks specificity or is merely a "fishing expedition" based on a likelihood that something might turn up, tracking it down can mean a long search. In either situation, to ensure a diligent search, the detective must pique the custodian's interest.

Individual Questions and Their Occurrence in Records

IDENTIFIERS AND LOCATORS

Question	Percent of Files
Name in Full	100
Residence Address (street and number or rural route)	100
Sex	100
Usual Signature	85
Date of Birth (DOB)	74
Residence Telephone Number	37
Place of Birth (municipality)	33
Social Security Number	22
Alias (AKA)	17
Citizenship	15
Height and Weight	11
Photograph	9
Physical Description (color of eyes and hair)	7
Port of Entry	4
Address to Which You are Moving	4
Fingerprint Card	4
Driver's License Number	2
Military Serial Number	2
Medical-Surgical Insurance Number	2
Hospital Insurance Number	2
Numbers of Previous Passports and Issuing Country	2
Welfare Account Number and Agency	2
Fingerprint Section Number	2
Place of Death (municipality)	2

EMPLOYMENT, EDUCATION AND SKILLS

Question	Percent of Files
Occupation and Title	61
Employer's Name and Address	43
Date of Employment	24
Education History (schools attended, dates, degrees or certificates earned)	20
Business Address	17
Business Telephone Number	13
Armed Forces Service History (country, branch, rank, dates, type of discharge)	7
School Marks (transcripts)	7
Language Spoken, Read or Written	4
Professional Organizations of Which You are a Member	4
Other Skills Possessed	4
Aptitude Test Scores	2
Apprenticeships Completed	2
Professional Publications of Which You Are an Author	2
Type of Employment Promised Upon Immigration	2

MARRIAGE AND IMMEDIATE FAMILY

Question	Percent of Files
Marital Status (married, never married, widowed, divorced, separated, common law)	39
Spouse's Name and Address	39
Dates of Children's Births	17
Names of Children	15
Number of Other Dependents (besides spouse and children)	15
Spouse's Employer (name and address)	13
Closest Relative (NOK)	13
Spouse's Salary	11
Spouse's Date of Birth	11
Names of Persons Unrelated to You Living in Your Home	9
Date and Place of Marriage	9
Number of Children	9
Date of Spouse's Employment	9
Places Where Your Children Were Born	9
Maiden Name of Wife	7
Names and Addresses of Other Dependents	7
Name and Address of Closest Relative not Living in Your Home	4
Parents-in-Law (name and addresses)	4
Previous Marriages (marital history)	4
Spouse's Business Telephone Number	2
Spouse's Occupation	2
Children's Schools or Occupations (names and addresses of schools or employers)	2
Previous Marital Status of Spouse	2
Dependents' Incomes	2
Incomes of Relatives Legally Liable for Your Support	2

FINANCIAL STATUS

Question	Percent of Files
Salary	31
Bank Accounts (institution's name and address and your balance)	22
Other Assets (describe and give value)	15
Bank or Other Loans Outstanding (institution's name and address and balance owing)	15
Other Debts Owed Including Liens	15
Insurance Policies (company, type, face value and cash surrender value)	13
Automobiles Owned (make, body style, year)	13
Stocks and Bonds Owned (description, value, and annual yield)	11
Real Estate Owned (description, and market value)	11
Accounts Payable (names and addresses of creditors)	9
Credit Cards	7

FINANCIAL STATUS (cont.)

Question	Percent of Files
Cash on Hand	7
Your Mortgage Payment (amount owing, name and address of institution)	7
Monthly Income	4
Monthly Living Expenses	2
Merchandise Inventory	2
Inheritances Expected	2
Assets to Follow Immigrant	2
Income Tax Form (copy required)	2

HEALTH STATUS

Question	Percent of Files
Physical Disabilities	20
Names of Hospitals and Medical Practitioners Who Have Treated You (address and permission to release medical records)	11
Results of Physical Examination Report	9
Vision Examination Report	2
Injuries or Surgical Procedures (names and addresses of hospitals and medical practitioners and permission to release medical records)	2
Psychiatric Report	2
Medical Details of Your Birth	2

HOUSING

Question	Percent of Files
Do You Own Your Own Home?	17
Number of Years at Current Home	9
Name and Address of Landlord	7
Previous Homes Owned or Rented	7
How is Your Home Financed?	4
Health Conditions in Home	4

LIFE HISTORY

Question	Percent of Files
Previous Employment and Dates (employment history)	8
Previous Addresses (residence history)	15
Criminal Convictions (date, court, and jurisdiction)	11
Foreign Travel (countries, dates, reasons for going)	6
Court Proceedings Pending Against You	4
Recent Transfers of Property	4
Annual Income the Last Full Year You Worked	2
Marital Status of Mother	2

LIFE HISTORY (cont.)

Question	Percent of Files
Length of Time in Country	2
Names of Natural Parents	2
Have You Ever Been on Welfare?	2
Previous Electric Utility	2
Names of Other Agencies Who Might Be Interested in Your Case	2
Record of Paying Bills (credit rating)	2
Automobile Accidents You Have Had in the Last 3 Years	2
Name and Address of the Previous Owner of Your Car	2

PERSONAL HABITS

Question	Percent of Files
Leisure-Time Activities	11
Purpose of the Loan (for which you are applying)	2
Pets Harbored	2
Do You Fly (other than as a paying passenger on scheduled airlines)?	2

ASSOCIATIONS

Question	Percent of Files
Personal References (names and addresses and length of time known)	7
Organizations (non-professional) of Which You Are a Member	4
Lawyer's Name and Address	

ANCESTRY AND RELIGION

Question	Percent of Files
Parents' Names (natural or adoptive mother and father; stepmother or stepfather; or legal guardians)	22
Religion	17
Parents' Ages	15
Parents' Birthplaces (municipalities)	15
Parents' Addresses	13
Parents' Religions	7
Maiden Name of Mother	7
Parents' Occupations (names and addresses of their employers)	7
Names and Addresses of Brothers and Sisters (natural, step- or half-siblings)	7
Father's Nationality	6
Citizenship History	2
Ethnic Origin	2

Figure 7.3

An appendix giving the probability of finding information in records. *(From* Confidential Information Sources: Public and Private, *2nd ed. Boston: Butterworth-Heinemann, 1991. Courtesy, Butterworth-Heinemann.)*

Several methods of gaining cooperation are possible. One would exploit the notion many people entertain—that they can unravel a mystery or be a sleuth. A second method would stress the value of the contribution, suggesting that without it the case might not have been solved. Activating latent aspirations ensures future cooperation. Another would be to thank the custodian personally and send a letter to his or her superior praising the employee's contribution to public safety and how it reflects on the company. Still another means would be to inform the employee of the outcome of the case, particularly if the information he or she provided helped to apprehend or identify the offender. In summary, treating a potential source of information with respect could be the basis for establishing and maintaining a good working relationship between record custodian and investigator.

REFERENCES

[1]   Robert J. Reider, *Law Enforcement Systems* (Springfield, IL: Charles C Thomas, 1972), vii.

[2]   George A. Buck, *Police Crime Analysis Unit Handbook* (Washington, DC: U.S. Government Printing Office, 1973), iii.

[3]   Llewelyn W. Atcherley, *Modus Operandi: Criminal Investigation and Detection*, rev. ed., G.C. Vaughn, ed. (London: Her Majesty's Stationery Office, 1937), 4.

[4]   Ibid.

[5]   M.D. Maltz, A.C. Gordon, and W. Friedman, *Mapping Crime in Its Community Setting: Event Geography Analysis* (New York: Springer-Verlag, 1991).

[6]   Ibid., 100.

[7]   Ibid., 100-101.

[8]   Ibid., xii.

[9]   Harry J. Murphy, *Where's What: Sources of Information for Federal Investigators* (New York: Quadrangle/New York Times, 1976).

[10]   John M. Carroll, *Confidential Information Sources: Public and Private*, 2nd ed. (Boston: Butterworth-Heinemann, 1991).

[11]   Gale Research, *Directories in Print*, 23rd ed. (Detroit: Thompson Gale, 2003).

[12]   Gale Research, *Encyclopedia of Associations: National Organizations of the U.S.*, 40th ed. (Detroit: Thompson Gale, 2003).

SUPPLEMENTAL READINGS

Carroll, John M. *Confidential Information Sources: Public and Private*. 2nd ed. Boston: Butterworth-Heinemann, 1991.

Gale Research. *Directories in Print*. 23rd ed. Detroit: Thompson Gale, 2003.

Gale Research. *Encyclopedia of Associations: National Organizations of the U.S.*. 40th ed. Detroit: Thompson Gale Research, 2003.

Murphy, Harry J. *Where's What: Sources of Information for Federal Investigators*. New York: Quadrangle/New York Times, 1976.

CHAPTER 8

Informants
Cultivation and Motivation

A BACKGROUND ON INFORMANTS

Anyone who discloses investigative information can be considered an informant. Today's journalists call their informants *sources*. (The two reporters who dogged the Watergate break-in would only identify their source(s) as "Deep Throat.") But whether the information is given to journalists or criminal investigators, when what is revealed is the result of a relatively close relationship between the informant and the one informed on, there is a certain repugnance attached to the activity. This is why unsavory names like stool pigeon, squealer, rat, fink, snitch, snout, informer, and *agent provocateur* have been coined to describe those perceived as betrayers. And yet, no religious faith holds this practice—as old as civilization itself—to be morally wrong. Neither does the judiciary: as Judge Learned Hand writes, "Courts have countenanced informers from time immemorial."[1]

A significant Supreme Court pronouncement on this issue is to be found in *Hoffa v. United States*. Defense counsel asked the Court:

> Whether evidence obtained by the Government by means of deceptively placing a secret informer [Partin] in the quarters and councils of a defendant during one criminal trial so violates the defendant's Fourth, Fifth and Sixth Amendment rights that suppression of such evidence is required in a subsequent trial of the same defendant on a different charge. . . .

The Court's answer:

> . . . we proceed upon the premise that Partin was a government informer from the time he first arrived in Nashville on October 22, and that the Government compensated him for his services as such. It is upon that premise that we consider the constitutional issues presented. . . .

I.

It is contended that only by violating the petitioner's rights under the Fourth Amendment was Partin able to hear the petitioner's [Hoffa's] incriminating statements in the hotel suite, and that Partin's testimony was therefore inadmissible under the exclusionary rule of *Weeks v. United States*, 232 U.S. 383. The argument is that Partin's failure to disclose his role as a government informer vitiated the consent that the petitioner gave to Partin's repeated entries into the suite, and that by listening to the petitioner's statements Partin conducted an illegal "search" for verbal evidence. . . .

In the present case, however, it is evident that no interest legitimately protected by the Fourth Amendment is involved. It is obvious that the petitioner was not relying on the security of his hotel suite when he made the incriminating statements to Partin or in Partin's presence. Partin did not enter the suite by force or by stealth. He was not a surreptitious eavesdropper. Partin was in the suite by invitation, and every conversation which he heard was either directed to him or knowingly carried on in his presence. The petitioner, in a word, was not relying on the security of the hotel room; he was relying upon his misplaced confidence that Partin would not reveal his wrongdoing.

Neither this Court nor any member of it has ever expressed the view that the Fourth Amendment protects a wrongdoer's misplaced belief that a person to whom he voluntarily confides his wrongdoing will not reveal it. Indeed, the Court unanimously rejected that very contention less than four years ago in *Lopez v. United States*, 373 U.S. 427. . . .

Adhering to these views, we hold that no right protected by the Fourth Amendment was violated in the present case.

II.

The petitioner argues that his right under the Fifth Amendment not to "be compelled in any criminal case to be a witness against himself" was violated by the admission of Partin's testimony. This claim is without merit. . . .

There have been sharply differing views within the Court as to the ultimate reach of the Fifth Amendment right against compulsory self-incrimination. . . .

But since at least as long ago as 1807, when Chief Justice Marshall first gave attention to the matter in the trial of Aaron Burr, all have agreed that a necessary element of compulsory self-incrimination is some kind of compulsion. . . .

In the present case no claim has been or could be made that the petitioner's incriminating statements were the product of any sort of coercion, legal or factual. The petitioner's conversations with Partin and in Partin's presence were wholly voluntary. For that reason, if for no other, it is clear that no right protected by the Fifth Amendment privilege against compulsory self-incrimination was violated in this case.

III.

The petitioner makes two separate claims under the Sixth Amendment, and we give them separate consideration.

A.

During the course of the . . . trial the petitioner's lawyers used his suite as a place to confer with him and with each other, to interview witnesses, and to plan the following day's trial strategy. Therefore, argues the petitioner, Partin's presence in and around the suite violated the petitioner's Sixth Amendment right to counsel, because an essential ingredient thereof is the right of a defendant and his counsel to prepare for trial without intrusion upon their confidential relationship by an agent of the government, the defendant's trial adversary. Since Partin's presence in the suite thus violated the Sixth Amendment, the argument continues, any evidence acquired by reason of his presence there was constitutionally tainted and therefore inadmissible against the petitioner in this case. We reject this argument. . . .

B.

The petitioner's second argument under the Sixth Amendment needs no extended discussion. That argument goes as follows: Not later than October 25, 1962, the Government had sufficient ground for taking the petitioner into custody and charging him with endeavors to tamper with the . . . jury. Had the Government done so, it could not have continued to question the petitioner without observance of his Sixth Amendment right to counsel. *Massiah v. United States*, 377 U.S. 201; *Escobedo v. State of Illinois*, 378 U.S. 478. Therefore, the argument concludes, evidence of statements made by the petitioner subsequent to October 25 was inadmissible, because the Government acquired that evidence only by flouting the petitioner's Sixth Amendment right to counsel.

Nothing in *Massiah*, in *Escobedo*, or in any other case that has come to our attention, even remotely suggests this novel and paradoxical constitutional doctrine, and we decline to adopt it now. There is no constitutional right to be arrested. The police are not required to guess at their peril the precise moment at which they have probable cause to arrest a suspect, risking a violation of the Fourth Amendment if they act too soon, and a violation of the Sixth Amendment if they wait too long. Law enforcement officers are under no constitutional duty to call a halt to a criminal investigation the moment they have the minimum evidence to establish probable cause, a quantum of evidence which may fall far short of the amount necessary to support a criminal conviction.

IV.

Finally, the petitioner claims that even if there was no violation—"as separately measured by each such Amendment"—of the Fourth Amendment, the compulsory self-incrimination clause of the Fifth Amendment, or of the Sixth Amendment in this case, the judgment of conviction must nonetheless be reversed. The argument is based upon the Due Process Clause of the Fifth Amendment. The "totality" of the Government's conduct during . . . trial operated, it is said, to "'offend those canons of decency and fairness which express the notions of justice of English-speaking peoples even toward those charged with the most heinous offenses'" (*Rochin v. California*, 342 U.S. 165, 169).

The argument boils down to a general attack upon the use of a government informer as a "shabby thing in any case," and to the claim that in the circumstances of this particular case the risk that Partin's testimony might be perjurious was very high. Insofar as the general attack upon the use of informers is based upon historic "notions" of "English-speaking peoples," it is without historical foundation. . . .

The petitioner is quite correct in the contention that Partin, perhaps even more than most informers, may have had motives to lie. But it does not follow that his testimony was untrue, nor does it follow that his testimony was constitutionally inadmissible. . . .[2]

The dissenting opinion written by Chief Justice Earl Warren stated:

At this late date in the annals of law enforcement, it seems to me that we cannot say either that every use of informers and undercover agents is proper or, on the other hand, that no uses are. There are some situations where the law could not adequately be enforced without the employment of some guile or misrepresentation of identity. A law enforcement officer performing his official duties cannot be required always to be in uniform or to wear his badge of authority on the lapel of his civilian clothing. Nor need he be required in all situations to proclaim himself an arm of the law. It blinks the realities of sophisticated, modern-day criminal activity and legitimate law enforcement practices to argue the contrary.[3]

In *Maine v. Moulton*, a case somewhat similar to *Hoffa*, the Court returned to the state's recruitment of an "insider" as an informant.[4] Colson, the informant and co-defendant with Moulton, was to learn of Moulton's threats and inchoate plans to murder a key prosecution witness (and other witnesses) in their upcoming trial. As the police wired his body with a transmitter, they warned Colson to "act natural," "not to attempt to question Moulton," and to "avoid trying to draw information out of Moulton."[5] Disregarding these admonitions and pretending memory lapse, Colson elicited incriminating facts concerning the event, as well as other joint criminal endeavors for which neither man had been indicted. On this evidence, additional felony charges were brought against Moulton, and he was convicted. He appealed on the ground that the admission into evidence of his statements to Colson violated his Sixth Amendment right to the assistance of counsel. In its decision affirming the conviction, the Court refers to and cites the Supreme Judicial Court of Maine, 481 A.2d 155 (1984):

. . . Regarding the admission of Moulton's recorded statements to Colson, the court agreed that there was "ample evidence" to support the trial court's finding that the police wired Colson for legitimate purposes, but held that [r]eference to the State's legitimate motive may be relevant to, but cannot wholly refute, the alleged infringement of Moulton's right to counsel." *Id.*, at 160. . . . the fact that at the time of the meeting Colson was "fully cooperating with the police and no longer stood in the same adversarial position as did Moulton," the (Maine Supreme) court held:

When the police recommended the use of the body wire to Colson they intentionally created a situation that they knew, or should have known, was likely to result in Moulton's making incriminating statements during his meeting with Colson. The police's valid purpose in investigating threats against witnesses does not immunize the recordings of Moulton's incriminating statements from constitutional attack. Those statements may be admissible in the investigation or prosecution of charges for which, at the time the recordings were made, adversary proceedings had not yet commenced. But as to the charges for which Moulton's right to counsel had already attached, his incriminating statements should have been ruled inadmissible at trial, given the circumstances in which they were acquired. *Id.*, at 161.[6]

In the text, *Constitutional Law*, Klotter summarizes *Moulton*:

Succinctly, the rule in this case is that when a defendant has been formally charged with a crime and has retained counsel, incriminating statements made to an undercover informant, *whose remarks prompted the statement*, are not admissible.[7]

USEFULNESS

The reasons individuals furnish information to an investigator can be laudable as well as nefarious. Whatever the reason, an informant is one who furnishes intelligence that may:

1. Prevent a crime that is planned but not yet committed;

2. Uncover a crime that has been committed but has not been discovered or reported;

3. Identify the perpetrator of a crime;

4. Locate the perpetrator of a crime or help to locate stolen property;

5. Exonerate a suspect;

6. Lower morale among criminals through apprehension (unanticipated by those involved in unlawful activity).

How such different results can be achieved from information supplied by informants is best understood by considering the types of informants and their motivations. Table 8.1 summarizes this material.

Table 8.1
Types of Informants; Information and Motivation

TYPE OF INFORMANT	OPEN		CONFIDENTIAL	
	TYPE OF INFORMATION	MOTIVATION	TYPE OF INFORMATION	MOTIVATION
VOLUNTEER	Observations of an eyewitness to a crime Facts on record or in a file Wife tells authorities about husband's gambling activities Income tax	Civic duty, vanity Official duty (one department to another) Monetary reward Revenge, gratitude	An investigator may receive, from time to time, details about almost any criminal activity Reports about vice activities Reports about suspicious behavior	Building a line of credit Friendship between informant and detective Fear, gratitude, civic duty Elimination of competition
PAID	Particulars about a specific crime or person Income tax matters	Monetary reward To make a "deal" with the police or prosecutor, i.e., plea bargaining Revenge, money from an informant fund	Income tax matters As above, information about almost any criminal activity	Monetary reward Payment from an informant fund Lenient treatment by authorities Revenge
ANONYMOUS	N/A	N/A	Precise information about a crime or its perpetrator Suspicious activities	Civic duty, fear, revenge, jealousy, repentance, gratitude Elimination of competition Money, reward

TYPES OF INFORMANTS

There are many types of informants. There are informants who volunteer information and those who expect some form of payment (which need not be, but most often is money). Either type may act openly or upon the condition that their identity not be revealed. Others remain anonymous, furnishing information via telephone or mail. Some informants are generalists; others, specialists. Some function but once; others, continuously.

Municipal police departments and federal agencies hold different points of view with regard to informants. In police departments, each informant will usually work with a particular detective. When that officer is reassigned, retires, or dies, the informant frequently is lost to the department. In federal agencies, informants are seen as belonging to the agency and are passed along from one investigator to another. At that level, the administrative controls that exist for dealing with informants are generally more elaborate than at the local level, and funds are available to purchase information.

The kinds of investigative information made available by informants are dependent on various factors: the informant's relationship to the person or activity being reported on; where they live, work, or hang around; what opportunities exist to observe an individual's or group's behavior or activity; and their motivation for providing the information. In other words, the contributory factors are opportunity and motivation.

MOTIVES FOR INFORMING

Basic motives include fear, revenge, jealously, repentance, gratitude, and concern with civic duty. Occasionally, individuals are prompted to act as an informant for venally self-serving and psychologically self-aggrandizing motives. An example of such mixed motivation is found in *The Informant.*[8] An engrossing tale of how a multi-motivated "insider," partly for psychological self-aggrandizement and partly for venal reasons, toppled his fellow corporate officers is superbly described in this book. A senior corporate insider looking to protect himself, but also out of civic duty, becomes an FBI informant. As the story unfolds, the agents recognize a shift in his motivation so that at the end, greed and betrayal emerge as motivating factors, while deceit and arrogance serve to meet deep psychological needs in carrying out his own agenda. Increasingly, the FBI agents are hard-pressed to control the destructive behavior of their informant while mindful that the case is threatened within by bureaucratic infighting about which branch of the Justice Department (the fraud division or the criminal division) was to prosecute and when it was to go to trial. The twists and turns encountered in this tale illustrate the difficulties that can arise in dealing with an informant who is disclosing a vast global conspiracy to fix commodity and other prices on the world market. Wearing a device to record the dialogue of the illegal meetings of top-level executives setting world market prices, the informant's recordings were viewed by investigators as almost too good to be true. However, government attorneys were less than pleased by them because the word "agreement" was not to be heard in the recordings although it was evident, on listening, that the conspirators were price-fixing. This points out the need to involve prosecutors early on, especially in complicated cases in which evidence is largely provided by an informant.

Self-Serving Reasons

Three kinds of self-serving (usually venal) motives are: cutting a deal, eliminating competition, and building a line of credit for future use.

Cutting a Deal

A deal is cut when a defendant agrees to impart what he or she knows about criminal activities in exchange for a promise (by a detective through a ranking departmental official) that a special recommendation for consideration will be made to a judge in a pending prosecution. By this means, informants may reduce or avoid altogether the punishment that would otherwise be expected on conviction. As a *quid pro quo* (something for something) arrangement, cutting a deal is in one sense a form of plea bargaining.

Elimination of Competition

In specialized crimes, particularly vice and narcotics (and, to some extent, arson and burglary), one lawbreaker may, most often anonymously, betray a rival to eliminate competition. This can occur when a new burglar invades the area and the rash of break-ins increases community pressure and police activity. By taking the competitor out of circulation, community anxiety will be kept at a level that does not provoke undue police response.

Building a Line of Credit

Uneasy pawnbrokers and secondhand dealers worry that police may one day discover stolen goods in their shops and accuse them of being receivers. Some will attempt to establish that they are not receivers by identifying those in the community who are fencing stolen goods, using this as a way to ingratiate themselves with authorities. For others on the fringe of the underworld, the ploy is to earn favors that could stay an arrest should they be apprehended for some law violation.

Mercenary Reasons

The old saying among investigators, "When the money ceases to clatter, the tongue stops the chatter," confirms what they well know; namely, that offering a reward for information is of fundamental importance. Merchants and farmers have long resorted to a bounty system; they will pay to find those responsible for stealing their merchandise or rustling their cattle. Law enforcement agencies budget ready monies (sometimes called "contingency funds") to buy information. The federal government is more lavish in this regard. Consider the case of three activists in the civil rights movement of the 1960s who disappeared after being released from a Mississippi county jail. Their burned station wagon was soon located, but not their bodies. What the following account makes plain is the efficacy of a pecuniary reward as perhaps the only means by which they could have been located:

> As it turned out, even if we had a thousand sailors and a thousand marines in Mississippi looking for those bodies, we never would have found them. They had been buried under thirty feet of earth. A huge hole had been dug a few days before the murders as part of a dam construction project, and the murderers took advantage of it by burying the bodies on the bottom a day or two before a bulldozer refilled the hole with hundreds of tons of earth. No one could have found them under that.
>
> We finally cracked the case with the help of an informant. We gave him about thirty thousand dollars to tell us who did the job and where the bodies were buried. . . . The bureau probably saved taxpayers hundreds of thousands of dollars worth of investigating hours by paying our informant thirty thousand.[9]

Without question this large sum is unusual. Even a few thousand dollars would be; 100 dollars (more or less, depending on the area of the country) is generally offered to obtain valuable information.

Self-Aggrandizement

Ordinary citizens as well as reformed criminals are motivated by vanity to provide information, believing it will win favorable attention from authorities. Employers, friends, and even the media in important cases may put them in the spotlight, making them instant celebrities. Because anonymity offers the best protection against retaliation, it is prudent that police safeguard such informants until public attention is directed elsewhere.

Emotions

Fear, revenge, jealousy, and repentance are among the emotions that often induce people to divulge what otherwise would remain unrevealed. When the information concerns criminal activity, it usually constitutes a major break in an investigation.

Fear

Fear is a powerful inducement to becoming an informer; however, protection must be negotiated with authorities. It may be fear for one's self or fear for one's family being killed, tortured, or harmed in some fashion. Fear of imprisonment will cause some people to seek a trade-off: information for *nol-prossing* an indictment (i.e., convincing the prosecutor to agree not to proceed any further with the action). When a gang member takes to heavy drinking, becomes sexually involved, and rashly starts to tell a new partner everything—or displays conduct that otherwise seems to threaten the security of the group—he or she will be told in no uncertain terms to change, "or else." For more than a few, the reaction would be to inform on the gang's activities.

Revenge and Jealousy

A grudge based on a perception of unfair treatment can provoke a desire for revenge. However hackneyed the expression "Hell hath no fury like a woman scorned," it still seems to speak for the pain of rejection. Indeed, any pain or distress induced by another can result in jealousy and the need for revenge, and turn a person to informing. The need to get even is deep in the human psyche.

Repentance

Just as those who have "got religion" will be led by a need for forgiveness and reestablishment in the community to furnish what they would not have disclosed before, so will the outcast make amends by informing on confederates in past crimes. The approbation of newly acquired peers is an especially strong stimulus.

Gratitude

Gratitude is not usually a major factor in prompting an individual to furnish information, but it can be potent at times. The story behind a big city mayor's exposure as a corrupt politician is a good example. The account illustrates how kindness was repaid. Owing to gratitude (on the part of a bank official who had been spared investigative demands when his family underwent the burdens of a serious illness), the investigator finally obtained the information that had eluded him during several months of effort. This led to the mayor's resignation before the governor had an opportunity to hear the charges and possibly have him removed for malfeasance and nonfeasance such as "to render him unfit to continue in office."[10]

Civic Duty

A significant motivating factor for informing is a sense of good citizenship. When an eyewitness tells police of observations made while a crime was being committed, or of suspicious behavior noted, that person carries out a civic duty.

OPPORTUNITY

Two kinds of opportunity must prevail if an individual is to function as an informant: one is to acquire useful information; the other is to reveal it without exposure to retaliation. Before an individual can function as an informant, the opportunity must exist to observe through sight, sound, or even smell, taste, or touch. Most often, it is provided by chance; the rest of the time, by propinquity of relationship or location (kinship or proximity furnishing more than a few opportunities for acquiring what may later be disclosed). Anonymous and confidential informants needing assurance that their identities will not be revealed may still want to be able to collect a reward if one is offered. With these needs in mind, two mechanisms have been developed: a widely-publicized special hotline telephone number and the anonymous-tip form. By calling police and obtaining a tip identification number, the informant can claim the reward should the tip lead to an arrest and indictment. Figure 8.1 illustrates an anonymous tip form, which can be printed at regular intervals in local newspapers.

Chief _____

c/o _____ Police Department

1234 High Street

Anytown, State, Zip Code

Tip Identification
Number _____

    I have a crime tip for the _____ Police Department.

I [do] [do not] wish to be contacted by the police.

_____

_____

_____

_____

_____

_____

_____

Name (optional):_____

Address (optional):_____

Telephone (optional):_____

Figure 8.1
Anonymous tip form.

CULTIVATION OF INFORMANTS

    The combination of opportunity and motivation required for a person to serve as an informant need not be left to chance. The experienced detective will recognize or create the opportunity to develop informants through an intimate knowledge of the neighborhood and the character of its inhabitants. Timing can be critical: thus, a falling out among thieves or between lovers, or the decision of a law violator to rejoin the community of the law abiding can be propitious for cultivating informants. To capitalize on such openings as they occur, the detective must remain assigned to the same geographical area.

    The itinerant nature of federal investigative assignments often forecloses the opportunities enjoyed by municipal, and to some extent, state investigators. This may partially account for the greater reliance at the federal level on money as the motivating factor in developing informants.

DEALING WITH INFORMANTS

    The following discussion is based on the collective experience of investigators in dealing with informants.

The Investigator-Informant Relationship

The relationship between investigator and informant can be fashioned in several ways. It might be a business arrangement in which the informant understands that the investigator associates with and employs him or her only to obtain information. The informant's motivation is often pecuniary, but another satisfaction such as revenge may serve as the inducement. A respectful relationship can be adopted with those motivated by vanity or civic duty. For the majority, a friendly relationship is probably the most useful. Although informants treated as equals may be eager to obtain the information needed, they nonetheless can be difficult to handle and may become a source of embarrassment. If the same results are otherwise achievable, informants should not be used.

Handling Informants

An informant who initially intends to furnish only limited information will often supply much more if properly handled. In light of this fact, the investigator should keep the following points in mind:

1. Meet the informant on neutral ground for the individual's protection and to preserve anonymity. Be careful to keep appointments.

2. Treat the informant fairly. Make promises with every intention of carrying them out; make none that cannot be fulfilled legally.

3. Treat the informant courteously. Never use offensive terms (such as fink, snitch, squealer, stoolie, double crosser). Describing an informant as a "confidential source" or "special employee" is acceptable.

4. The value of appealing to the reason that motivated the informant should not be forgotten.

5. Newly recruited informants must be clued in with respect to the information sought and the target(s) to be aimed at and reported on. While admonishing them to exercise great care in doing so, investigators should encourage them to organize and develop subsources.

6. Informants must be taught what constitutes entrapment; in dealing with any person (including a suspect), they must avoid the possibility or even the appearance of entrapment.

7. The importance of maintaining their "cover" must be stressed; otherwise, they may compromise their own security or that of the investigation.

8. Never permit informants to take charge of the investigation —to "run the show." Tact is necessary to keep them in line when, intentionally or not, they attempt to direct any phase of the investigation. (This can occur when the informant begins to like the notion of playing detective).

9. An informant may not, in general, be permitted to commit a crime in return for information. (See the Attorney General's guidelines later in this chapter).

10. In all financial transactions the investigator must be scrupulously exact. Except where necessary to keep an informant interested, payment should not be made until the value of the information has been verified; also, proof of payment should be obtained, if possible.

Interviewing Informants

There is a technique for interviewing informants that is made clear by the following suggestions:

1. After allowing them to state what they wish to report, subtly press for details. Take notes or otherwise record the information as soon as possible after the interview.

2. Be tactful: accept any information offered at its face value. Expressing appreciation for valuable information is an inexpensive form of encouragement that will be well received by the informant. Do not belittle worthless information.

3. To check on the informant's reliability, ask for information that is already known. Take great care to frame the questions so that what is known is not divulged.

4. Do not reveal to informants how their information differs from other information (if it does).

5. Be sympathetic about any difficulties the informant may be experiencing in attempting to secure information.

6. Avoid asking questions that may be embarrassing or that pry into the informant's private affairs. Avoid arguments.

7. Maintain control of the interview. Do not allow it to wander too far afield. Keep the focus on what is sought.

Potential Problems and Precautions

The early years of detective work involved a close relationship between criminals and police. Because many informants still come from the underworld, the potential for corruption exists. This is especially true today in the enforcement of those victimless crimes in which considerable money can be made. Thus, a distinction is drawn by Professor William P. Brown between the general investigator and the investigator who is limited to the conduct of investigations charged with a specific function, e.g., corruption or the use of informants:

> . . . general investigators need many contacts, criminal and non-criminal, and ordinarily have rather infrequent although often long-established relationships with their informants. . . . [Those who investigate narcotics, vice and gambling] rely much more heavily on information from informants in the criminal system. At the same time they generally assume it essential to establish close and continuous contacts with their criminal informants.[11]

In narcotics, vice, and especially gambling investigations, continues Brown:

> . . . Grossly illegal rewards for information have been paid. Police have cooperated in illegal activity and then received information from their partners in crime. They have paid substantial sums of money which were illicitly obtained. They have also paid in contraband, particularly narcotics.[12]

The purpose of Brown's working paper is to discuss:

> . . . a problem which has not generally been clearly visualized: that is, who should control the criminal informant, the individual investigator or the agency? Agency control is generally found at the federal level, sometimes at the state level, and at the municipal level only in dealing with issues of subversion and the superstructure of organized crime. At the municipal level for the great majority of cases the informant is the "property" of the individual investigator and known only to the investigator.[13]

Brown sums up:

> . . . The results of this analysis . . . [lead] to the conclusion that the development and processing of information about crime must remain in a crude and unproductive state so long as the individuals rather than investigative units or agencies control the investigation process.[14]

Similar Problems in Other Fields

It is illuminating to examine a similar problem in another field. In newspaper reporting, for instance, problems may arise when the identity of an informant (or "source") is not disclosed to the editor. When asked, reporters generally are required to divulge such information to their editor, but sometimes exceptions are made. For instance, those assigned to the Watergate story were permitted to use a confidential source that provided invaluable tips on the attempted cover-up. Another reporter on the same paper won a Pulitzer prize for a feature story describing a black youngster in the act of receiving heroin injections from a drug dealer as the child's mother watched. When the reporter claimed that the drug dealer had threatened to kill her if the source was disclosed, the editors again made an exception. The story later proved to be a hoax and glory quickly turned to notoriety. Commenting on the mess, the managing editor of another publication wrote: "The practice [of using blind sources] is valid if the source can help you expose criminal conduct. . . . It is not valid if the source is the person perpetrating the crime."[15]

Disclosure of a source of information becomes a matter of contention when a court or grand jury orders a news reporter to reveal the source. Because this issue is not covered by common law (as are privileged communications between attorney and client, for instance), it has come before state and federal courts with diverse results. For this reason, and in response to pleas from the journalistic profession, some state legislatures (but not the Congress) have passed laws to protect news reporters from being forced to divulge what they received in confidence. In the text, *Criminal Evidence*, Klotter summarizes the status of disclosure law:

> The United States Supreme Court has determined that, in the absence of statutes, communications to a newspaper editor or reporter are not privileged in federal courts. In states recognizing the privilege, some courts apply a balancing test that focuses on the need for the information and potential availability from other sources. If collateral sources make the information available, the news media privilege will likely prevail. Also, some states by statute have enacted news media privilege laws.[16]

Problems in Other Countries

Problems with informants are, in point of fact, ubiquitous. Consider an issue raised in England when a member of Parliament officially asked the Home Secretary:

> whether . . . he had considered the judgment in the Court of Appeal by Lord Justice Winn in the case of *Regina v. Macro and Others*; and whether he would institute an inquiry into the circumstances in which material information was withheld from the trial court by the police.[17]

The Home Secretary replied, in part, by stating:

> This case does however raise general issues about the procedure that is being followed when the police have warning from an informant of an intended offense in which he might participate. . . .[18]

This response was followed by a review of the current practice of having informants take part in crime. A set of principles was drawn up in consultation with representative Chief Officers of Police and the Director of Public Prosecutions. Stating that it was an operational police matter and that full details could not be disclosed, the guidance offered to Chief Officers of Police included the following points:

1. If society is to be protected from criminals the police must be able to make use of informants in appropriate circumstances. Informants, appropriately employed, are essential to criminal investigation and, within limits, ought to be protected.

2. Strict limits should be imposed on the extent of an informant's participation in a crime.

3. No member of a police force, and no police informant, should counsel, incite, or procure the commission of a crime.

4. The police should not embark on a course which will constrain them to withhold information from or mislead a court in order to protect an informant.

5.   There must be effective supervision by senior and experienced officers in the use of informants; and particular care must be given to the training of detectives in this subject. . . .[19]

GUIDELINES FOR THE USE OF INFORMANTS

In 1981 the Attorney General of the United States issued a set of guidelines on the use of informants and confidential sources by the FBI. More extensively formulated than those issued publicly by the Home Secretary, the two nonetheless cover much the same territory. For example, the introduction stated:

(1)   The courts have recognized that the government's use of informants and confidential sources is lawful and often essential to the effectiveness of properly authorized law enforcement investigations. However, use of informants and confidential sources to assist in the investigation of criminal activity may involve an element of deception, intrusion into the privacy of individuals, or cooperation with persons whose reliability and motivation can be open to question. It is proper for the FBI to use informants and confidential sources in appropriate investigations, but special care must be taken to carefully evaluate and closely supervise their use, and to ensure that individual rights are not infringed and that the government itself does not become a violator of the law. Though informants and confidential sources are not employees of the FBI, their relationship to the FBI can impose a special responsibility on the FBI when the informant or confidential source engages in activity where he has received, or reasonably thinks he has received, encouragement or direction for that activity from the FBI.

(2)   To implement these guidelines, the FBI shall issue detailed instructions to all Special Agents responsible for dealing with informants and confidential sources.[20]

The use of informants was then described under the following section:

General Authority

(1)   An informant or confidential source may be asked to provide information already in his possession, to provide information which comes to his attention, or to affirmatively seek out information concerning criminal conduct or other subjects of authorized investigative activity. An informant or confidential source may also be asked to provide operational assistance to the FBI, including furnishing resources or facilities.

(2)   The FBI may only use informants or confidential sources in furtherance of its authorized investigative activities and law enforcement responsibilities. Informants and confidential sources may not be used or encouraged to commit acts which the FBI could not authorize for its Special Agents.[21]

The guidelines also require that an informant or confidential source appear suitable for such a role. In making such a determination, the following factors should be weighed:

(a) the nature of the matter under investigation and the importance of the information or assistance being furnished;

(b) the seriousness of past and contemporaneous criminal activity of which the informant or confidential source may be suspected;

(c) the motivation of the informant or confidential source, including any consideration sought from the government for his cooperation;

(d) the likelihood that the information or assistance which an informant or confidential source could provide is not available in a timely and effective manner by less intrusive means;

(e) the informant's or confidential source's reliability and truthfulness, or the availability of means to verify information which he provides;

(f) any record of conformance by the informant or confidential source to Bureau instructions and control in past operations: how closely the Bureau will be able to monitor and control the informant's or confidential source's activities insofar as he is acting on behalf of the Bureau;

(g) the risk that use of informants or confidential sources in the particular investigation may intrude upon privileged communications, or inhibit the lawful association of individuals or expression of ideas; and

(h) any risk that use of informants or confidential sources may compromise an investigation or subsequent prosecution, including court-ordered disclosures of identity which may require the government to move for dismissal of the criminal case.[22]

As to the participation of an informant or confidential source in an activity that would be criminal under state or federal law, the guidelines define it as "otherwise illegal activity." It is justified when the benefits to be obtained outweigh the risks and it is necessary to:

(a) obtain information or evidence essential for the success of an investigation without such authorization [of otherwise illegal activity] or

(b) prevent death, serious bodily injury, or significant damage to property, and

(c) this need outweighs the seriousness of the conduct involved.[23]

Only designated supervisory FBI officials may authorize participation in otherwise criminal activity; and then only after a written finding that the above two conditions have been met.

LEGALITY OF EVIDENCE BASED ON INFORMANT-SUPPLIED INFORMATION

Legal issues can arise from the use of information furnished by an informant. Two issues have been raised by defense attorneys when evidence is seized or an arrest is made (with or without a warrant) on the basis of information supplied by an informant. One concerns the Fourth Amendment protection against unreasonable searches and seizures: based on an informant's tip, does probable cause exist to support an arrest or a seizure of evidence? The other concerns the Sixth Amendment right of a defendant to prepare a defense: must the identity of the informant be revealed, if sought for this purpose in a motion for a bill of particulars?

Probable Cause

The most difficult question regarding probable cause arises when the basis for establishing it depends on an unnamed informant's (hearsay) information. If a search warrant was approved by a judge, or the police made a warrantless search and arrest, will the evidence so obtained be suppressed on a defense attorney's motion? The objection rests on the propriety of using hearsay evidence to establish probable cause.

There are a number of Supreme Court decisions on this issue. In *Draper v. United States* the Court specifically approved the use of an informant's hearsay information to make a warrantless arrest.[24] In *Aguilar v. Texas* the Court reaffirmed previous decisions that the affidavit for an arrest warrant need not involve the personal, direct observation of the affiant, and that it may be based on hearsay information from an informant whose identity is not revealed.[25] The Court added, however, that the magistrate must be informed of the circumstances that caused the informant to conclude that a crime had, in fact, been committed. A few years later in *Spinelli v. United States* a two-pronged test was suggested to determine when an unnamed informant's information could be used to show probable cause.[265] The test would require: one, that the informant be reliable; and two, that the informant's information be credible.

After a decade and a half of experience with *Aguilar* and *Spinelli*, the Court abandoned them. Its next approach to evaluating an informant's hearsay evidence as a means of establishing probable cause was stated in *Illinois v. Gates*:

> . . . we conclude that it is wiser to abandon the "two pronged test" established by our decisions in *Aguilar* and *Spinelli*. In its place we reaffirm the totality of the circumstances analysis that traditionally has informed probable cause determinations. The task of the issuing magistrate is simply to make a practical common-sense decision whether, given all the circumstances set forth in the affidavit before him, including the "veracity" and "basis of knowledge" of persons supplying hearsay information, there is a fair probability that contraband or evidence of a crime will be found in a particular place. And the duty of a reviewing court is simply to ensure that the magistrate had a "substantial basis for . . . conclude[ing]" that probable cause existed.[27]

It is significant to note that in *Gates* an anonymous letter to police provided the basis for obtaining a search warrant. All of the facts (detailed travel plans of Sue Gates and Lance Gates to transport narcotics) alleged in the letter were verified through investigation, yet the Illinois Supreme Court sustained the trial court's suppression of the evidence. It reasoned that the letter failed both prongs of the *Spinelli* test. First, it provided no basis for determining the reliability and veracity of the informant. (Innocent people could well travel and behave as did the Gateses, without necessarily being involved in narcotics trafficking.) Second, the letter did not furnish the particulars (how the informant knew narcotics were actually present in the Gates's house) that would allow a magistrate to make an informed decision concerning probable cause. In place of a detailed analysis to determine if the warrant affidavit met each prong, the Court reaffirmed a "totality of the circumstances analysis," thereby permitting the magistrate to intertwine the facts. Despite this revisionary attempt at clarification, an investigator would be well advised to bear the two-pronged test in mind, recognizing that if one prong is weak, the other must be strengthened in the affidavit.

Preservation of Confidentiality

Informants run a potential risk that harm will befall them or their families should their identities become known to the criminal or the criminal's associates. More than one has borne witness to the old proverb "Dead men tell no tales." In light of this possibility, they often seek assurances of anonymity. Such a promise can be made when an informant provides a lead that the investigator must follow up independently to obtain sufficient evidence for conviction. On the other hand, there are numerous reasons for a defense attorney to move for disclosure in preparing for, or in the midst of, trial. Among them are:

1. To determine that the informant actually exists.

2. To determine the reliability of the informant.

3. To establish any differences between the police version of events and the informant's statements. (If the informant participated in the crime, is there a possibility of entrapment?)

4. To endeavor to have the charge dismissed by the court if the state refuses disclosure.

As to confidentiality, the Supreme Court decided in *Roviaro v. United States*:

> [A limitation on the applicability of the informer's privilege] arises from the fundamental requirements of fairness. Where the disclosure of an informer's identity, or of the content of his communication, is relevant and helpful to the defense of an accused, or is essential to a fair determination of a cause, the privilege must give way. In these situations, the trial court may require disclosure and, if the Government withholds the information, dismiss the action.[28]

At the same time the Court indicated that the rule regarding failure to disclose is not absolute with regard to reversible error.

> We believe that no fixed rule with respect to disclosure is justifiable. The problem is one that calls for balancing the public interest in protecting the flow of information against the individual's right to prepare his defense. Whether a proper balance renders nondisclosure erroneous must depend on the particular circumstances of each case, taking into consideration the crime charged, the possible defenses, the possible significance of the informer's testimony, and other relevant matters.[29]

A subsequent confidentiality case, *McCray v. Illinois*, involved an informant known by police to be reliable.[30] At a hearing to suppress, the defense requested but was denied the name and address of the informant. On conviction, the appeal was taken to the Supreme Court. Affirming the conviction, it held:

> When the issue is not guilt or innocence, but as here, the question of probable cause for an arrest or search, the Illinois Supreme Court has held that police officers need not invariably be required to disclose an informant's identity if the trial judge is convinced, by evidence submitted in open court and subject to cross-examination, that the officers did rely in good faith upon credible information supplied by a reliable informant.[31]

Elsewhere in the opinion, the Court went on to quote the New Jersey Supreme Court (*State v. Burnett*, 42 N.J. 377, 201 A. 2d 39 (1974)):

> We must remember also that we are not dealing with the trial of the criminal charge itself. There the need for a truthful verdict outweighs society's need for the informer privilege.[32]

One year later, the Supreme Court accepted *Smith v. Illinois*,[33] which directly concerned an unnamed informant who testified at a trial (rather than a hearing to suppress). Asked to identify himself, the witness claiming to be the informant offered a fictitious name, and the trial judge denied a request for his true name. The Court reversed the conviction on Sixth Amendment grounds, stating that without knowing the identity of the informant, cross-examination could not be conducted effectively. In another Illinois case a year later (*Shaw v. Illinois*), the Court reversed the conviction on the basis of *Smith*.[34] The distinction in *Shaw* was that the informant gave his name but refused to reveal his address. Now, it would appear, an informant who testifies for the state must disclose both name and address if asked.

Entrapment

If grounds exist to support it, *entrapment* is another issue almost certain to be raised by a defense attorney. Entrapment may occur when a police officer (or an informant with official concurrence) beguiles an innocent person into committing a crime. This can be used as an affirmative defense for the accused; having committed an act that would otherwise be a crime, he or she is, by statute, not held accountable in this particular case. Entrapment is perpetrated when the following conditions are met:

1. A law enforcement official (or a person cooperating with such an official);

2. for the purpose of instituting a criminal prosecution;

3. induces an individual;

4. to engage in conduct that constitutes a criminal offense;

5. by knowingly representing that such conduct is not prohibited by law; or prompting the individual who otherwise is not so inclined to act.

Even if all of these enumerated conditions are unambiguously met, some ethical and legal questions still pertain. For example, as the U.S. Eastern District Court of New York states in the *Myers* case (Part V—"General Discussion of Basic Legal Concepts"):

> Whenever government agents, in carrying out their law enforcement functions, assist criminals or participate with them in their criminal activity, questions arise as to the propriety or legitimacy of the government's conduct and as to whether the law should punish a person for engaging in governmentally instigated criminal activity. The answers must draw on considerations of philosophy, psychology, statutory construction, constitutional law, practical needs of law enforcement, and even undifferentiated visceral feelings about right and wrong. . . .

> Four Supreme Court decisions are central to the issue of entrapment. Sorrells, 287 U.S. 435; Sherman 356 U.S.369; Russell 411 U.S. 423; Hampton, 425 U.S.484, . . .

> Thus as the Court divided in *Hampton,* with Justice Stevens taking no part: three judges would make predisposition the only issue; three would eliminate predisposition entirely; and the decisive two concurring votes...indicate that predisposition is not only relevant but will be dispositive in all but the "rare" case where police over-involvement in the crime reaches "a demonstrable level of outrageousness."[35]

In other words, except when police encouragement and deception reaches a "demonstrable level of outrageousness" (i.e., conduct that grossly offends the sense of right and decency), an otherwise predisposed defendant can be convicted.

RETROSPECTIVE

"Detectives are only as good as their informants" was a truism in law enforcement circles during the first half of the twentieth century. At that time, informant information ranged from a cautious hint to an almost completed case. Modern standards for permissible tactics are higher. As a result, extracting a confession after the perpetrator's name is supplied by an informant is no longer tolerated or considered adequate. Today, an informant's information provides direction for the detective that can shorten and strengthen an inquiry.

The opportunity to learn of a criminal's activities is never greater than when a close personal relationship between a criminal and an informant has fallen apart. The effective investigator is always cultivating potential informants and motivating them at the opportune moment to share what they know. Information obtained in this manner can represent an important breakthrough in an investigation by simplifying the task and improving the end product.

REFERENCES

[1]   *United States v. Dennis*, 183 F.2d 201, 224 (2d Cir. 1950).

[2]   *Hoffa v. United States*, 385 U.S. 293, 295-311 (1966).

[3]   Ibid., 315.

[4]   *Maine v. Moulton*, 474 U.S. 159 (1985).

[5]   Ibid., 165, 183.

[6]   Ibid., 167-168.

[7]   John C. Klotter and Jacqueline R. Kanovitz, *Constitutional Law,* 7th ed. (Cincinnati: Anderson, 1995), 426.

[8]   Eichenwaldo, Kurt. *The Informant: A True Story* (New York: Broadway Books/Random House, 2000).

[9]   William C. Sullivan, with Bill Brown, *The Bureau: My Thirty Years in Hoover's FBI* (New York: Norton, 1979), 77.

[10]   Charles Garrett, *The LaGuardia Years: Machine and Reform Politics in New York City* (New Brunswick, NJ: Rutgers University Press, 1961), 77.

[11]   William P. Brown, "Criminal Informants" (working paper, School of Criminal Justice, State University of New York at Albany, 1968), 44.

[12]   Ibid., 25.

[13]   Ibid., 43.

[14]   Ibid.

[15]   Thomas Griffith, "Stuck with Labels," *Time*, 27 April 1981, 53.

[16]   John C. Klotter and Jefferson L. Ingram, *Criminal Evidence*, 8th ed. (Cincinnati: Anderson, 2004), 352.

[17]   Sir Dingle Foot (Ipswich), Oral No. 63 to the House of Commons, 20 February 1969.

[18]   Ibid.

[19]   Home Office, "Police Use of Informants," Press Notice, 15 May 1969.

[20]   Attorney General Benjamin Civiletti, "U.S. Attorney General's Guidelines on Criminal Investigations and Use of Informers," *Criminal Law Reporter* 28 (7 January 1981), 3032.

[21]   Ibid.

22   Ibid., 3033.

23   The Attorney General's Guidelines Regarding the Use of Confidential Informants, May 30, 2002. *<http://www.usdoj.gov/olp/dojguidelines.pdf>*

24   *Draper v. United States*, 358 U.S. 307 (1959).

25   *Aguilar v. Texas*, 378 U.S. 108 (1964).

26   *Spinelli v. United States*, 393 U.S. 410 (1969).

27   *Illinois v. Gates*, 462 U.S. 213 (1983). [Also see Klotter, ref. 7 above, Chapters 3 and 4.]

28   *Roviaro v. United States*, 353 U.S. 53, 58-61 (1957).

29   Ibid., 62.

30   *McCray v. Illinois*, 386 U.S. 300 (1967).

31   Ibid., 305.

32   Ibid., 307.

33   *Smith v. Illinois*, 390 U.S. 129 (1968).

34   *Shaw v. Illinois*, 394 U.S. 214 (1969).

35   *United States v. Myers,* 527 F. Supp. 1206 (E.D.N.Y. 1981).

Supplemental Readings

Anon. "Models for Management—Subject: Confidential Informants," *The Police Chief* LVII:1 (Jan. 1990), 56-57.

Brown, Michael F. "Criminal Informants: Some Observations on Use, Abuse and Control," *Journal of Police Science and Administration*, 13 (1985), 251-256.

Felkenes, G.T. *Constitutional Law for Criminal Justice*. Englewood Cliffs, NJ: Prentice Hall, 1988.

Gosling, John. *The Ghost Squad*. Garden City, NY: Double-Crime Club, 1959.

Harney, Malachi L., and John C. Cross. *The Informer in Law Enforcement*. Springfield, IL: Charles C Thomas, 1960.

Kleinman, David M. "Out of the Shadows and into the Files: Who Should Control Informants?," *Police* 13:6 (1980), 36-44.

Klotter, John C., and Jefferson L. Ingram. *Criminal Evidence*. 8th ed. Cincinnati: Anderson, 2004.

Klotter, John C., Jacqueline R. Kanovitz and Michael I. Kanovitz. *Constitutional Law*. 9th ed. Cincinnati: Anderson, 2002.

Morris, Jack. *Police Informant Management*. Orangevale, CA: Palmer Enterprises, 1983.

Singer, S., and M.J. Hartman. *Constitutional Criminal Procedure Handbook*. New York: Wiley & Sons, 1986.

PART C

FOLLOW-UP MEASURES: REAPING INFORMATION

When victim and eyewitness have been interviewed, laboratory findings reported, and records searched, the results must be assimilated, organized, and analyzed. They may be sufficient to identify and arrest the perpetrator or may suggest possible suspects to be investigated further. In either event, follow-up activity will depend on the facts on hand at that moment. If there is an eyewitness, an opportunity to scrutinize mug shots in the Rogues Gallery must be arranged without delay. If this is unproductive, an image of the offender should be developed by an artist, or from a composite image assembled with a facial-features kit or created by computer. Surveillance may be in order. When the end result is an arrest, additional action might require a lineup to see if a witness can make an identification. Finally, the suspect must be interrogated.

Understanding the theory underlying the methods provides a foundation. To become skilled in their use, on-the-job practice and experience are indispensable building blocks. (The police academy is well-suited to this purpose, as it can provide the requisite vicarious experience.)

Throughout an investigation the detective should be alert to potential clues that must be responded to and developed into evidence. This is a difficult process that calls for choices. In terms of resources and time, the choice must always be weighed against the likely yield of information—a *quasi*-cost/benefit consideration. The detective attuned to miscues and other unproductive leads conserves time and energy.

In summary, an alertness to unintentional hints, a healthy suspicion of everything said or observed, plus diligence, persistence, and thoroughness in follow-up efforts can serve as the cornerstone for promising, successful results.

CHAPTER 9

Surveillance

A Fact-Finding Tool—
Legality and Practice

Conducting a surveillance is generally expensive. Indeed to be successful, considerable resources in the form of work hours, equipment, and time (sometimes measured in months) must be invested. Given certain conditions, however, it may be the only means by which particular information can be obtained.

The lore of surveillance is based for the most part on three perspectives. One view is the result of the "private eye's" experience in divorce cases, in which a relatively simple, one-on-one observation is feasible. Another is that of the "street smart" detective who learns from tailing professional criminals of the elaborate precautions they take to shake off the police. The third and most sophisticated derives from the experience of investigators surveilling espionage agents who have been trained to detect and then lose anyone thought to be following them. The following treatment will reflect all three perspectives in varying degrees.

DEFINITIONS

To understand the literature or participate in a surveillance, the reader should be conversant with the terms and jargon of the field.

Surveillance:	the observation of a person, place, or thing, generally—but not necessarily—in an unobtrusive manner.
Subject:	the party under surveillance.
Surveillant:	the person conducting the surveillance.
Tail:	to follow and keep under surveillance; a surveillance.
Stakeout:	also called a *plant* or *fixed surveillance*; here, the surveillant remains essentially in one position or locale. (The term is derived from the practice of tethering animals to a stake, allowing them a short radius in which to move.)

Undercover: an undercover agent who often gets to know or work alongside the subject. The term *roping* describes this situation, and the under-cover agent is said to be *planted*.

Convoy: a countermeasure to detect a surveillance; a convoy, usually a person, is employed to determine whether a subject is under sur-veillance.

Shadow: to follow secretly; to place a person under surveillance.

Be made: to be detected or suspected of being a surveillant by the subject.

Burn the surveillance: when a surveillant's behavior causes the subject to surmise or know he or she is under surveillance.

Close surveillance: the subject is kept under constant surveillance. Also termed *tight surveillance*, the aim is not to lose the subject even at the risk of being "made." Example: an arsonist (known through an informant or a wiretap) who sets out to burn an inhabited building.

Fixed Surveillance: see *Stakeout*.

Moving Surveillance: the surveillant moves about in order to follow the subject.

Loose surveillance: a cautious surveillance; also termed *discreet surveillance* because the loss of the subject is preferred over possible exposure. Exam-ple: obtaining information about a subject through tailing his or her associates when there is reason to believe the subject suspects there is a surveillance. Another example: a burglary gang "casing" banks to select their next job.

Open Surveillance: a surveillance with little or no attempt at concealment; also termed *rough surveillance*, the subject is most likely aware of the sur-veillance, but must not be lost. Example: an important material wit-ness who has been threatened refuses police protection.

Mustard Plaster: a form of open surveillance; here, the subject is followed so closely that surveillant and subject are almost in lock step. It is tantamount to protective custody. See example for *Open Surveillance*.

Plant: see *Stakeout* and *Undercover*.

Tailgating: a form of open surveillance in which the subject's vehicle is closely followed.

Technical Surveillance: surveillance involving the use of scientific devices to enhance hearing or seeing the subject's activities.

Bugging: eavesdropping by electronic means, such as a hidden microphone or radio transmitter; *bug*: a device used for such eavesdropping.

Pen register: a device that records all numbers dialed on a telephone; it is gen-erally installed at the telephone company's central office.

Beeper: a battery-operated device that emits radio signals that permit it to be tracked (as it moves about) by a directional finder-receiver. Also called *beacon*, *transponder*, and *electronic tracking device*.

KINDS OF SURVEILLANCE

Surveillance may be conducted from a stationary or fixed position, such as a parked van or a room facing the subject's residence or workplace, or by posing as a street vendor or utility worker. The aim is to allow the surveillant to remain inconspicuously in one locale. Occasionally a *fixed surveillance* is conducted openly; for instance, by posting a uniformed officer in front of a bank before business hours start.

More often, however, just as the subject moves about, so must the surveillant. Several means are employed in a *moving surveillance*. Surveillance can be conducted from a vehicle (automobile, bicycle, helicopter); on foot (walking, running), or even underwater (when the expertise of frogmen is required). *Technical surveillance* involves electronic eavesdropping devices (wiretaps, pen registers), electronic tracking devices (beepers), and assorted visual and infra-red optical devices.

THE LEGALITY ISSUE

The issue of individual privacy (and possible harassment) has been invoked to confront the use of fixed and moving surveillances. Privacy and illegal search and seizure issues also have been used to confront the use of technical surveillance—employing as it does pen registers (to record all numbers dialed from a private phone); and wiretaps, electronic trackers (beepers), and telescopes or other optical devices (to listen, follow suspects, and peer into their homes or places of business).

Fixed and Moving Surveillance

A major case dealing with these kinds of surveillance involves Sam Giancana, who was alleged to be the Mafia boss of the Chicago "family" when he brought a civil rights action.[1] Giancana claimed that the FBI had anywhere from three to five motor vehicles posted in a 24-hour close surveillance outside his residence, and that agents used binoculars to look into his home, and cameras with telescopic lenses to photograph people coming and going. He also claimed that he was closely followed into restaurants, stores, golf courses, etc., and that the purpose of this was to embarrass, intimidate, and humiliate him in the eyes of his friends, neighbors, and associates.[2]

At the hearing for an injunction the judge stated:

> I suggest that the Bureau, and I think perhaps in order to give some force to it, that an injunction, a temporary injunction, be entered restraining the Bureau from having more than one car parked within a block of the plaintiff's house. This in no way is a restraining of having more than one car parked all over the neighborhood a block away. I feel that the parade of cars should be diminished to one car instead of three or four cars as the evidence heretofore indicates. I feel that one foursome should intervene between the plaintiff and his group, and those that are interested in determining what kind of game he is playing by following too closely.
>
> That I feel is as far as I can go without hampering the Bureau, and maybe that hampers them.[3]

Four days later the injunction was stayed. Later it was reversed on the ground that the federal district court judge lacked jurisdiction since Giancana had failed to allege damages of $10,000. On appeal, the Supreme Court denied *certiorari*, and there the matter ended.[4]

Technical Surveillance

Technical surveillance involves the use of electronic and visual enhancement devices to view or overhear suspects in the conduct of their daily affairs. Consequent legal issues are considered below.

Wiretapping

A 1928 Supreme Court decision concluded that wiretapping did not constitute unlawful search and seizure of messages passing over telephone wires and therefore did not come under the constitutional protection of the Fourth Amendment.[5] Undaunted, opponents turned to legislation. Their action to outlaw wiretapping is partially based on the *Olmstead v. United States* opinion written by Chief Justice Taft:

> Congress may of course protect the secrecy of telephone messages by making them, when intercepted, inadmissible in evidence in federal criminal trials, by direct legislation, and thus depart from the common law of evidence.[6]

Moving quickly on this suggestion, opponents thought they achieved relief through passage of the Federal Communications Act of 1934; Section 605 reads:

> ... [No] person not being authorized by the sender shall intercept any communication and divulge or publish the existence, contents, substance, purport, effect, or meaning of such intercepted communication to any person. ...[7]

Subsequent Supreme Court decisions held that the wording of Section 605 covered federal and state officials as well as private persons, and applied to both interstate and intrastate transmissions. Wiretapping proponents were not to be undone. In reading Section 605, they noted that a telephone communication had to be intercepted and divulged to come under its provisions. Divulgence, they argued, meant disclosure to those outside of government; for instance, using it as evidence in court. They claimed further that a conversation between one investigator and another, or one between an investigator and a supervisor, did not constitute divulgence. Hence, so long as both requirements (interception and divulgence) had not been met, wiretapping did not take place. Because the Department of Justice supports this view, no prosecutions for wiretapping by government agents have been brought. In 1968, Congress partially abandoned Section 605 by passing the Omnibus Crime Control and Safe Streets Act. For the first time, law enforcement personnel were authorized to wiretap and conduct other kinds of electronic surveillance.[8]

Each state is free to enact measures against wiretapping stricter than those of the federal government. Because most states have done so, legality varies widely throughout the country. Some states have outlawed all wiretapping—whether by law enforcement or private citizens; others permit it to law enforcement personnel with court approval, but outlaw private wiretaps. Thus, when considering the use of wiretaps, it is particularly important for an investigator to ascertain its legal status in the jurisdiction involved.

Bugs, Pen Registers, Beepers

There are other ways to obtain investigative information in addition to wiretapping. They include: bugs to eavesdrop on private conversations, pen registers to record all numbers dialed, and beepers attached—to a person, an automobile, or any wares being transported—to track the movement of a person or piece of merchandise. The Fourth Amendment's impact on these devices ranges from a total ban to outright approval.

Monitoring Conversations

Justice Tom C. Clark described eavesdropping as follows:

> At one time the eavesdropper listened by naked ear under the eaves of houses or their windows, or beyond their walls seeking after private discourse.[9]

Justice Hugo Black defined it another way:

> Perhaps as good a definition of eavesdropping as another is that it is listening secretly and sometimes "snoopily" to conversations and discussions believed to be private by those who engage in them. Eavesdroppers have always been deemed competent witnesses in English and American courts.[10]

It should be no surprise, however, that when it became possible to gather eavesdropping evidence through some kind of scientifically enhanced device, it would be challenged under the Fourth Amendment. When the first bugging case reached the Court in 1942, it was ruled that a detectaphone placed against a wall to listen to conversations in a neighboring office did not violate the amendment because there was no physical trespass upon the premises.[11] Two decades later, when a "spike mike" was inserted in an adjoining wall (making contact with a heating duct, "thus converting the [petitioner's] heating system into a conductor of sound"), the Court held it to be an intrusion of a constitutionally protected area—illegal search and seizure.[12] In another case of alleged trespass, the Court found no such transgression when, unknown to the suspect, a conversation inside his place of business was transmitted by one undercover agent "wired for sound" to another agent stationed outside to record it.[13]

Based on these cases, unless there is physical invasion of a constitutionally protected area, it would appear that electronic eavesdropping is permissible under the Fourth Amendment. But the *Katz v. United States* decision of 1967 alters this view.[14] In this case the suspect, placing a call from a public phone, had his conversation recorded by government investigators who had attached a listening device to the outside of the telephone booth. The Court held that the right to claim Fourth Amendment protection was not dependent upon a property right in the invaded place, but on a reasonable expectation of freedom from government intrusion.

> For the Fourth Amendment protects people, not places. What a person knowingly exposes to the public, even in his own home or office, is not a subject of a Fourth Amendment protection . . . but what he seeks to preserve as private, even in an area accessible to the public, may be constitutionally protected.[15]

By adding the idea of privacy, the Court expanded the potential reach of the amendment. This will be clear when the use of a beeper for surveillance purposes is considered.

Katz is important because it also ventilates the Court's view on what legitimates electronic surveillance.

> . . . It is apparent that the agents in this case acted with restraint. Yet the inescapable fact is that this restraint was imposed by the agents themselves, not by a judicial officer. They were not required, before commencing the search, to present their estimate of probable cause for detached scrutiny by a neutral magistrate. They were not compelled, during the conduct of a search itself, to observe precise limits established in advance by a specific court order. Nor were they directed, after the search had been completed, to notify the authorizing magistrate in detail of all that had been seized. In the absence of such safeguards, this Court has never sustained a search upon the sole ground that officers reasonably expected to find evidence of a particular crime and voluntarily confined their activities to the least intrusive means consistent with that end. Searches conducted without warrants have been held unlawful "notwithstanding facts unquestionably showing probable cause," *Agnello v. United States*, 269 U.S. 20, 33 . . . searches conducted outside the judicial process, without prior approval by judge or magistrate, are *per se* unreasonable under the Fourth Amendment—subject only to a few specifically established and well-delineated exceptions.[16]

Involving as it did a public telephone booth, *Katz* does not take up the issue of whether clandestine trespass to install a bug is permissible. This was resolved in 1979 by the Court in *Dalia v. United States*, when the constitutionality of Title III (Sections 2510-2520) of the Omnibus Crime Bill was challenged. (Title III permits courts to authorize electronic surveillance by government officers in specific situations).[17] In the *Dalia* case, around midnight, FBI agents pried open an office window to install a bug in the ceiling; six weeks later, when they ceased the electronic surveillance, they reentered the office to remove the listening device. Partly on the basis of the overheard conversations, Dalia was convicted of receiving stolen goods. As framed by the Court the two issues were:

> . . . First, may courts authorize electronic surveillance that requires covert entry into private premises for installation of the necessary equipment? Second, must authorization for such surveillance include a specific statement by the court that it approves of the covert entry?[18]

The first issue was disposed of:

> We make explicit, therefore, what has long been implicit in our decisions dealing with this subject: The Fourth Amendment does not prohibit per se a covert entry performed for the purpose of installing otherwise legal electronic bugging equipment.[19]

In resolving the second issue, however, the Court (going beyond the narrow issue posed) commented:

> The Fourth Amendment requires that search warrants be issued only "upon probable cause, supported by Oath or affirmation, and particularly describing the place to be searched, and the person or things to be seized." Finding these words to be "precise and clear" . . . this Court has interpreted them to require only three things. First, warrants must be issued by neutral, disinterested magistrates . . . Second, those seeking the warrant must demonstrate to the magistrate their probable cause to believe that "the evidence sought will aid in a particular apprehension or conviction" for a particular offense. . . . Finally, "warrants must particularly describe the 'things to be seized'," as well as the place to be searched.[20]

These remarks are followed by the observation that:

> . . . it is generally left to the discretion of the executing officers to determine the details of how best to proceed with the performance of a search authorized by warrant—subject of course to the general Fourth Amendment protection "against unreasonable searches and seizures."[21]

Finally, the Court settles the narrow issue posed:

> . . . the Fourth Amendment does not require that a Title III electronic surveillance order include a specific authorization to enter covertly the premises described in the order.[22]

Monitoring Telephone Usage

It is obvious that telephones can be used to plan a crime, to help carry it out, and following its commission, to confer about avoiding detection or apprehension. It is also obvious that recorded information identifying who called whom would be of value to an investigator—especially if home phones are involved. The *pen register*, a telephone company device, is the least costly way to obtain such data. Generally but not necessarily installed at the utility's central offices, the pen register neither overhears conversations nor indicates whether a call was completed, but by monitoring the electrical impulses produced by rotary or push button phones, it records all numbers dialed.

What if a utility with the appropriate technical assistance and facilities refused to cooperate in the belief that government lacks authority to order an installation of the device? This question was joined and settled in 1977 when the Court held:

> . . . The District Court had the power to authorize the installation of the pen registers under Federal Rule Crim. Proc. 41, that Rule being sufficiently flexible to include within its scope electronic intrusions authorized upon a finding of probable cause.[23]

It should be no surprise that the use of a pen register would also be contested on the ground that it constitutes a search and is thus subject to Fourth Amendment limitations that a warrant first be obtained. This issue was raised in *Smith v. Maryland.* The facts are fairly simple:

> The telephone company, at police request, installed at its central offices a pen register to record the numbers dialed from the telephone at petitioner's home.[24]

The Court went on to decide:

> We therefore conclude that petitioner in all probability entertained no actual expectation of privacy in the phone numbers he dialed, and that, even if he did, his expectation was not "legitimate." The installation and use of a pen register, consequently, was not a "search," and no warrant was required.[25]

As will be seen shortly, the concept of "expectation of privacy" will be used to its fullest by the Court in "beeper" and "plain view" cases.

Monitoring Movement of Vehicles and Items of Commerce

The beeper, a device that facilitates tracking the movement of contraband (items of commerce essential for criminal activity), in vehicles, or on persons suspected of or engaged in crime, can be of considerable help in an ongoing investigation. Of course the beeper must be secreted in advance on the subject to be tracked if it is to be followed and traced to its ultimate destination. Tracking a drum containing an organic solvent or other chemical (which may be purchased legally and then used to manufacture contraband, such as a narcotic or a bomb) may lead to a clandestine laboratory or terrorist's arsenal. If a search warrant is obtained, evidence may then be secured from the premises. Again it should be obvious that defense counsel would contest the use of a beeper:

> The presence of a beeper in effect transforms private property into an instrument of surveillance, a surrogate police presence, a use unintended by the original owner. Moreover, the continuing presence of the beeper is not a mere technical trespass, but an extended physical intrusion: they continually broadcast the message, "Here I am." In sum these "uninvited shadowers" pierce one's privacy of location and movement, as well as one's rights to protection of property against physical invasion.[26]

From another standpoint, law enforcement officials hold that the beeper merely facilitates surveillance: by substituting for the human eye, it reduces the danger of detection. Furthermore, it does not pinpoint location except when the receiver is very close; it would generally be too risky for an investigator to take up such a position.

In 1982 the Supreme Court addressed some of these issues for the first time in *United States v. Knotts*.[27] The facts are as follows: A beeper was installed in a five-gallon container of chloroform (a precursor chemical in the manufacture of illicit drugs), which was subsequently purchased by the suspect. Maintaining contact with visual surveillance and beeper signals, the officers following the transporting vehicle saw the container transferred to another automobile; again, it was tracked both visually and electronically. But during this part of the journey, the driver began to make evasive maneuvers, causing surveillants to call off their visual contact. At about the same time, the beeper signal was also lost. An hour or so later, with the aid of a monitoring device mounted in a helicopter, the beeper's approximate location was determined. Its resting place was next to a secluded cabin.

The officers secured a search warrant based on the foregoing experience and on additional information obtained after three more days of intermittent visual surveillance. Upon executing the warrant, they discovered a fully operable drug laboratory inside the cabin; outside, they found a chloroform container under a barrel. The defendant sought to suppress the evidence obtained from the *warrantless* monitoring of the beeper, but was denied. Later, his conviction for conspiring to manufacture a controlled substance and the imposed five-year prison sentence were appealed. When taken to the Supreme Court it ruled that:

> Monitoring the beeper signals did not invade any legitimate expectation of privacy on respondent's part, and thus there was neither a "search" nor a "seizure" within the contemplation of the Fourth Amendment. The beeper surveillance amounted principally to following an automobile on public streets and highways. A person traveling in an automobile on public thoroughfares has no reasonable expectation of privacy in his movements.[28]

Knotts appeared to be a victory for law enforcement, but it was a narrow one. The Court had approved the use of a beeper to monitor the movement of vehicles on public roads only. Before long, it again confronted the matter of beeper surveillance in *United States v. Karo*:[29]

> In this case, we are called upon to address two questions left unresolved in *Knotts*: (1) whether installation of a beeper in a container of chemicals with the consent of the original owner constitutes a search or seizure within the meaning of the Fourth Amendment when the container is delivered to a buyer having no knowledge of the presence of the beeper, and (2) whether monitoring of the beeper falls within the ambit of the Fourth Amendment when it reveals information that could not have been obtained through visual surveillance.[30]

The Court then ruled:

> We conclude that no Fourth Amendment interest of Karo or of any other respondent was infringed by the installation of the beeper. Rather, any impairment of privacy interests that may have occurred was occasioned by the monitoring of the beeper.[31]*

The Court subsequently returned to the substance of the decision and declared:

> We also reject the Government's contention that it should be able to monitor beepers in private residences without a warrant if there is the requisite justification in the facts for believing that a crime is being or will be committed and that monitoring the beeper wherever it goes is likely to produce evidence of criminal activity. Warrantless searches are presumptively unreasonable. . . . The primary reason for the warrant requirement is to interpose a "neutral and detached magistrate" between the citizen and "the officer engaged in the often competitive enterprise of ferreting out crime."[32]

Further along in *Karo*, another aspect of the warrant issue is treated:

> We are also unpersuaded by the argument that a warrant should not be required because of the difficulty in satisfying the particularity requirement of the Fourth Amendment. The Government contends that it would be impossible to describe the "place" to be searched, because the location of the place is precisely what is sought to be discovered through the search. . . . However true that may be, it will still be possible to describe the object into which the beeper is to be placed, the circumstances that led agents to wish to install the beeper, and the length of time for which beeper surveillance is requested. In our view, this information will suffice to permit issuance of a warrant authorizing beeper installation and surveillance. In sum, we discern no reason for deviating from the general rule that a search of a house should be conducted pursuant to a warrant.[33]**

Electronic Communications Privacy Act of 1986

The investigative practices permitted by *Knotts*, *Karo*, and *New York Telephone Co.* were subsequently limited by federal legislation enacted in 1986. Called the Electronic Communications Privacy Act, the law regulates (among other things) the use of beepers and pen registers.[34] The statute requires police to obtain a prior court order; any evidence resulting from a violation of its provisions is not admissible in court. It further provides for criminal and civil penalties.

---

*   Despite this holding, warrants for the installation and monitoring of a beeper will obviously be desirable since it may be useful, even critical, to monitor the beeper to determine that it is actually located in a place not open to visual surveillance. Such monitoring without a warrant may violate the Fourth Amendment.

** The United States insists that if beeper monitoring is deemed a search, a showing of reasonable suspicion rather than probable cause should suffice for its execution. That issue is not before us. . . . It will be time enough to resolve the probable cause-reasonable suspicion issue in a case that requires it.

Visual Enhancement Devices

Other technical devices can be used to observe a subject, vehicle, or other object unobtrusively. Some are quite simple (a pair of binoculars, a camera, a telescope); others are more intricate (an infrared snooperscope) and/or expensive (a helicopter or an airplane). As should be expected, there have been constitutional challenges to their use. Though not unobtrusive, even a flashlight has been challenged; however, unsuccessfully.[35]

An early (1952) Supreme Court decision, one of the few to confront the use of visual enhancement devices, is *On Lee v. United States*:

> . . . The use of bifocals, field glasses or the telescope to magnify the object of a witness' vision is not a forbidden search and seizure, even if they focus without his knowledge or consent upon what one supposes to be private indiscretions.[36]

In those early cases, the Court based its search and seizure decisions on a literal reading of the Fourth Amendment: "persons, housing, papers, and effects" are protected.[37] Thus, revenue officers who conducted a visual search without a warrant while trespassing on the defendant's land were not in violation because the amendment's protection "is not extended to open fields."[38] *Hester v. United States*, the so-called "open fields case," established that places and property were protected. It then was but a short step for the Court to extend the area protected by including the immediate vicinity of the dwelling (the open space, courtyard, or curtilage within a common enclosure and belonging to it). In *Katz v. United States* (1967), the Court indeed altered and expanded the scope of the Fourth Amendment. It went beyond that of a "constitutionally protected area" to embrace the idea of "privacy."

> . . . For the Fourth Amendment protects people, not places. What a person knowingly exposes to the public, even in his own home or office, is not a subject of Fourth Amendment protection. . . . but what he seeks to preserve as private, even in an area accessible to the public, may be constitutionally protected.[39]

Katz involved enhanced hearing, and questions involving enhanced observations soon arose. Would their use constitute a search requiring a warrant? Would the facts and circumstances (particularly in cases that entailed peering into premises) result in different judicial opinions as the venue changed? Would the use of a visual enhancement device to observe an open public area require a search warrant? Because enhanced observations usually provide the evidence that is the basis for probable cause—a search warrant prerequisite—such questions are crucial.

No case having yet reached the Supreme Court (in which a written opinion is rendered), relevant appellate court decisions must be consulted. Several post-*Katz* cases will illustrate. Before discussing them, it is important to note that "privacy" becomes qualified in these decisions. Appended to "expectation of privacy" are additional modifiers: justifiable, reasonable, legitimate. Many post-*Katz* cases involve the use of binoculars. In one, an FBI agent acting on a tip carried out the nighttime surveillance of a print shop suspected of turning out gambling forms for football games. Its high windows obstructing his view of the inside, the agent overcame the difficulty with a ladder, moving it some 30 to 35 feet from the building, well beyond the defendant's property. From this vantage, with the aid of binoculars, he could observe the print job. The Superior Court of Pennsylvania ruled:

> ... [This] case presents the situation in which it was incumbent upon the suspect to preserve his privacy from visual observation. To do that the appellees had only to curtain the windows. Absent such obvious action, we cannot find that their expectation of privacy was justifiable or reasonable. The law will not shield criminal activity from visual observation when the actor shows such little regard for his privacy.[40]

When the case was taken to the Supreme Court, *certiorari* was denied.[41] In other lower court cases, however, visually enhanced observations and the circumstances surrounding them were viewed as searches within the purview of the Fourth Amendment. Therefore, until the Supreme Court speaks definitively, it would be productive to summarize the constitutional concerns of the various courts when analyzing visually enhanced surveillance. The issues of some importance are:

1. The nature of the area. (Surveilling through enhanced viewing "within an individual's home," using such artificial aids as a telescope, requires a search warrant.)[42]

2. The kind of precautions taken by the suspect to ensure privacy.[43]

3. Whether, after having first made the observations with the naked eye, an enhancement device is needed to avoid detection of the surveillance.[44]

4. Whether the investigator must do something unusual to make the observation, such as climb a fence to be high enough to view the activity, or use a telescope.[45]

5. The distance between the officer and the behavior or activity under observation.[46]

6. The level of sophistication of the viewing device.[47]

In *United States v. Dunn* (1987) the Supreme Court reiterated that the area within the curtilage was protected by the Fourth Amendment.[48] In the *Dunn* case, drug enforcement agents crossed over the fence around the perimeter of a ranch, several interior barbed wire fences, then a wooden fence, to look into a barn located 50 yards from a house. Observing what they took to be a drug laboratory, and confirming its presence twice more the next day, they secured a warrant and arrested Dunn. Subsequently convicted, he won an appeal claiming that the trial court's denial to suppress all evidence seized pursuant to the warrant was in error because the barn was within the curtilage of his home.

In resolving what is inside (and outside) that curtilage (and what, therefore, should be placed under the home's "umbrella" of protection), the Supreme Court suggested the following four factors be considered:

1. The proximity of the area to the home itself;

2. Whether the area is within the enclosure surrounding the home;

3. The nature of the uses to which an area is put;

4. The steps taken by the residents to protect the area from the observations of passersby.

Applying these criteria to *Dunn*, the Court found:

1. The barn's substantial distance from the fence surrounding the house (50 yards), and from the house itself (60 yards), supports no inference that it should be treated as an adjunct of the house;

2. The barn was not within the fence surrounding the house; it stands out as a distinct and separate portion of the ranch;

3. The barn was not being used for the intimate activities of the home;

4. Little had been done to protect the barn area from observation by those standing outside, ranch fences were the type to corral livestock, not ensure privacy.[49]

For these reasons the Supreme Court reversed the decision of the California Court of Appeals, agreeing with the trial judge who had denied a motion to suppress.

In 1986 and again in 1989 the Court was engaged with the issue of surveillance (by means of an airplane or helicopter) to detect unlawful activity within the curtilage of a home; in one case (*California v. Ciraolo*), within the 2,000-acre "industrial curtilage" of a chemical manufacturing plant. In the Ciraolo investigation, police officers trained in the visual identification of marijuana were used. Based on an anonymous tip, they undertook in a private airplane at an altitude of 1,000 feet to detect with the naked eye (and photograph with a 35 mm. camera) marijuana allegedly growing in the defendant's back yard.[50] Based on the Fourth Amendment's protection of the curtilage, the defense attorney's motion to suppress the evidence was denied, and Ciraolo pleaded guilty. Agreeing that the back yard was part of the curtilage, the Court refused to require that a search warrant be obtained. It held:

> . . . any member of the public flying in this airspace who cared to glance down could have seen everything that the officers observed.[51]

In another (marijuana) curtilage case, *Florida v. Riley*, the Supreme Court went beyond *Ciraolo* in approving surveillance from a police helicopter flying at a height of 400 feet.[52] Riley's greenhouse 20 feet behind his home carried a "Do Not Enter" sign. Enclosed on two sides, it was shielded from public view by his mobile home; on two other sides were trees and shrubbery; on top, two corrugated panels, constituting about 10 percent of its roof, were missing. Based on a tip and by means of a helicopter, police verified that marijuana was being grown in the greenhouse. Obtaining a warrant, police seized the marijuana, and Riley was eventually convicted. As the case worked its way up the appeals ladder, the motion to suppress the evidence was sustained, denied, sustained, and ultimately denied. Again, the Court allowed that, even though the greenhouse was within the curtilage, Riley's expectation of privacy was unrealistic. Furthermore, the Court concluded, the flight was permitted under FAA regulations. Police use helicopters in all 50 states, and since there was no physical intrusion of the greenhouse, the fly-by observation was not a search within the meaning of the Fourth Amendment.[53] *Riley* was a 5-to-4 decision. Some dissenting opinions were prophetic. Justice Brennan's was punctuated with a remembrance of George Orwell's *1984*:

> In the far distance a helicopter skimmed down between the roofs, hovering
> for an instant like a bluebottle, and darted away again with a curving flight.
> It was the Police Patrol, snooping into people's windows.[54]

It would be beneficial for the law enforcement profession to consider seriously and debate the Brennan citation, and meanwhile, confine this kind of surveillance to serious cases.

In *Dow Chemical v. United States*, the Environmental Protection Agency (EPA) made aerial photographs of the 2,000 acres surrounding Dow's manufacturing plant. This action, taken without a search warrant, was in part based on the "open fields" doctrine.[55] Dow claimed the acreage to be within their "industrial curtilage" and under Fourth Amendment protection. The Court disagreed:

> . . . aerial photographs of petitioner's plant complex from an aircraft law-
> fully in public navigable airspace was not prohibited by the Fourth Amend-
> ment. . . . [and that] the open areas of an industrial plant complex . . . are
> not analogous to the "curtilage" of a dwelling. . . .[56]

In its 5-to-4 decision, the Court remarked in passing that only aerial photography and observation were involved. It went on to say, though, that had they made a physical entry, or used electronic eavesdropping or more sophisticated (satellite) cameras, a significant Fourth Amendment question might have been raised.

PRACTICAL CONSIDERATIONS

Surveillance is seldom the task of one person. Vehicles equipped with direct intercommunication systems are generally essential. Less expensive equipment, such as infrared optical devices and high quality binoculars, may suffice to locate suspects unobtrusively and to make a determination as to their (or an associate's) activities. These objectives, or a surveillance conducted to prevent a crime, may be realized without elaborate resources and staff. Although costly, sometimes a decision to invest whatever is necessary must be faced if an investigation is to progress. For the wary subject—the gang of interstate bank burglars, the espionage agent, or the terrorist—surveillance may require helicopters or even frogmen. Large departments will find it cost effective in the long run to train a group of specialists who, when given ample opportunity to work together, will develop coordination. Because small departments are able to commit only modest resources, there is some argument for having surveillance specialists available at the state level. As many state and municipal governments lack the ability to mount an elaborate surveillance, cooperation at all administrative levels will be essential if funds, personnel, and equipment are to be readily available.

Such an arrangement may be feasible in some states. Accordingly, because most police agencies in the United States employ fewer than 20 officers, forming a task force with other departments is often the answer when resources for such operations are limited or nonexistent.[57]

Some attributes considered desirable when selecting individuals for a surveillance team:

- exceptional common sense and good judgment

- an ability to operate both independently and as a team member

- a proven track record as to dependability and presence of mind in times of high stress

- 'street savvy,' a 'gift of the gab,' extreme patience[58]

Tactics

Strategic considerations govern the use of surveillance in a particular case. Tactical concerns determine its execution. A major problem that soon intrudes is how to weigh the possible loss of contact with a subject against the risk of being detected or exposed. A quick, believable response is called for when a subject takes some action to determine whether there is indeed a surveillance. It is easier to drop surveillance before being confronted than to respond to a confrontation by convincing the subject that he or she is mistaken.

Loose Surveillance

Loose surveillance is used when the objective is to locate a suspect by tailing his or her relatives and friends. The surveillant exercises great caution while observing the subject, preferring to drop the tail rather than risk detection or exposure. Whether for espionage, burglary, or terrorism, this tactic applies when a group's activities are under scrutiny to determine their contacts and intentions.

Close Surveillance

The aim of close surveillance is to avoid losing the subject—even at the risk of detection or exposure. When the goal is to prevent a crime or learn more about the subject's contacts, it is acceptable procedure. A subject who is naive or lacks experience in crime may panic and reveal valuable clues when the fact of the surveillance is realized. This may force that person's hand. It is particularly useful on those who are only peripherally connected with the subject or the crime. When a subject's behavior signals suspicion of the tail, it is said to have been *burned*. When the objective is to prevent an assault or other crime against an individual, the term *mustard plaster* (a variety of open surveillance) describes the tactic.

Loose and close surveillance are the two extremes. When a loose tail is the prudent choice, there is always the possibility of losing the subject; with close surveillance, the chance of being burned. In practice, a balance is sought between "being made" or losing the subject.

Planning

Never to lose a subject or to arouse suspicion is impossible, of course. When confronted with either decision, any vacillation is an additional hazard. Investigative momentum will be squandered if plans are not made in anticipation of such contingencies. Should a subject be lost, a viable method of locating him or her is often by educated guess—people being creatures of habit, doing the same things at about the same time each day. Prior surveillance reports on the case also can furnish insight. If wiretapping is legal in the jurisdiction, taps will provide additional information about the subject's movements. Indeed, the guarded language criminals employ to confound the officers on the tap may only become intelligible through the study of surveillance reports. When two people agree over the telephone to meet at "the same place as last time," it is itself of little value. Hand-in-glove with the surveillance report, however, the designated place may become known to the investigator and the subject picked up again. Seldom employing one technique at a time, the successful practitioner is one who, like a fine cook, knows when to season the effort with the correct amounts of each.

Preparation

The success of a surveillance depends on the degree of forethought and thoroughness given to the preliminary preparations. It is important to develop a plan of action for handling contingencies and to understand its objectives. Without such a plan, obvious, everyday matters—such as having a supply of coins and tokens available for transportation and telephone calls—can be overlooked. The major components of preliminary preparation are discussed next.

Familiarization

It is crucial that the surveillant(s) be certain of the identity of the subject, who should, if possible, be pointed out by one who knows him or her by sight. Though less satisfactory than direct "fingering," recent photographs are also acceptable. The surveillant must be familiar with details of the case, through discussion with others working on it and reading the previous surveillance reports. It is helpful to be familiar with the probable area of operations; for those working in unknown territory, preliminary inspections are worthwhile. Since many surveillances are conducted in cities (where most crimes occur) it is important to know about the type of people, the transportation facilities, street layout, public buildings, and other physical features. The investigator should be able to operate any technical equipment used. When teams of investigators are expected to work together a briefing session is appropriate.

Equipment

It hardly need be said that all technical equipment be serviced, checked, and ready to operate. Department policy should cover who is authorized to operate technical equipment. Before evidence derived from such equipment can be offered in court, a foundation must be laid. Even for such a simple device as a tape recorder, the following considerations govern the matter:

- the recording device was capable of taping the conversation

- the operator was competent to operate the device

- the recording is authentic and correct

- changes, additions, or deletions have not been made to the recording

- the recording has been preserved in a manner satisfactory to the court

- that the speakers are identified; and

- the conversation elicited was made volunatrily and in good faith without any kind of inducement.[59]

While being used, unmistakable police paraphernalia must be concealed or, when visible, disguised.

Some thought should be given to converting an enclosed, moderate-sized truck or van to suit the needs of lengthy, fixed surveillances. Disguises for an automobile include: extra sets of license plates (both in-state and out-of-state); window and bumper stickers; a set of props in the car's trunk such as: a shopping bag filled with groceries, a briefcase, and a few changes of outer clothing and headgear. The area of operation will suggest other props.

Night surveillance also requires that officers have appropriate equipment available. There are two types of night vision technology: infrared and image intensification.

> Infrared equipment detects heat variations among the objects in front of it and produces an image that looks like a black-and-white negative. . . . Image intensification uses a tube to gather existing light and amplify it thousands of times to create a fluorescent green image.[60]

Blending In

A surveillant must blend with the neighborhood of the operation. (A few props already have been suggested.) The aim is to play a role the locals will accept without question or suspicion. For example, on the west side of mid-town Manhattan, the investigator might assume the identity of a dock worker; in a rural area, that of a farmer. With ethnic groups, the problems become difficult: a white cannot be disguised as a black, the stereotypical Irishman as the stereotypical Italian, or a Slav as an Arab. In these situations another tack must be taken. Again, the aim is to be accepted in the neighborhood, not necessarily seem indigenous to it. Ubiquitous figures on the inner-city sidewalk, like the practical nurse, welfare worker, rent collector, and insurance adjuster, come to mind. Other practical matters also must be planned: providing relief for the surveillant's personal necessities and time off, and securing a supply of public transit tokens.

Discontinuing the Surveillance

Usually, a surveillance can be discontinued without repercussions, but should the subject directly or indirectly indicate that its existence is suspected, breaking off contact requires caution. It must be made certain that the investigator has not been placed under a counter-surveillance by the subject or an associate; accordingly, the investigator should not return directly to the station house until sure that no convoy was used. In the event of a direct challenge, it is important to be prepared with a response that has been thought through, rehearsed, and is almost instinctive for the surveillant. An improvised response would not ring true; it would only confirm the subject's suspicions. Neither should the investigator immediately deny being a police officer. It might be feasible to react with some irritation: impatient comments such as "you're bothering me" or "this is a new approach" might work. These suggestions are offered as practical responses in a given situation.

PROCEDURE FOR INTERCEPTION OF WIRE OR ORAL COMMUNICATIONS

Title III, Section 2518 of the Omnibus Crime Bill (as amended by the Electronic Communications Privacy Act of 1986) describes how to obtain an order from a judge authorizing the interception of a wire or oral communication. The detailed, comprehensive procedures resemble those traditionally employed to obtain a conventional search warrant. In federal cases, the application for an interception order must be approved by the attorney general (or a specific designee); in state cases, by the principal prosecuting officer of the state or its political subdivisions. The application must be in writing and sworn or affirmed to, then submitted to the appropriate federal or state judge for approval. The judge may issue an *ex parte order* authorizing the interception if it is determined, on the basis of the facts submitted by the applicant, that:

(a) there is probable cause for belief that an individual is committing, has committed, or is about to commit a particular offense enumerated in section 2516 . . .;

(b) there is probable cause for belief that particular communications concerning that offense will be obtained through such interception;

(c) normal investigative procedures have been tried and have failed or reasonably appear to be unlikely to succeed if tried or to be too dangerous;

(d) except as provided in subsection (11), there is probable cause for belief that the facilities from which, or the place where, the wire, oral, or electronic communications are to be intercepted are being used, or are about to be used, in connection with the commission of such offense, or are leased to, listed in the name of, or commonly used by such person.[61]

The order may not remain in effect longer than is necessary to achieve its objectives, and no longer than 30 days in any event. It must be executed promptly, minimizing any interference with communications otherwise not subject to interception, and must terminate upon attainment of the authorized objective. There is no limitation on the number of extensions that may be granted but, as in the original application, each must provide the requisite information and show probable cause. In executing the order the investigator must do all that is possible to avoid unnecessary intrusions upon innocuous communications, thereby respecting the right of privacy.

REFERENCES

[1] *Giancana v. Johnson*, 335 F.2d 366 (7th Cir. 1964).

[2] *Giancana v. Johnson*, No. 63 C 1145 (N.D. Ill. 1963).

[3] Ibid.

[4] 379 U.S. 1001 (1969).

[5] *Olmstead v. United States*, 277 U.S. 438 (1928).

[6] Ibid., 465.

[7] Ibid.

[8] Omnibus Crime Control and Safe Streets Act of 1968, ("Title III") 18 U.S.C. §§ 2510-2520 (1970).

[9] *Berger v. New York*, 388 U.S. 41, 45 (1967).

[10] Ibid., 71.

[11] *Goldman v. United States*, 316 U.S. 129 (1942).

[12] *Silverman v. United States*, 365 U.S. 505 (1961).

[13] *On Lee v. United States*, 343 U.S. 747 (1952).

[14] *Katz v. United States*, 389 U.S. 347 (1967).

[15] Ibid., 351.

[16] Ibid., 356.

[17] *Dalia v. United States*, 441 U.S. 238, 247 (1979).

[18] Ibid., 241.

[19] Ibid., 255.

[20] Ibid.

[21] Ibid., 257.

[22] Ibid., 258.

[23] *United States v. New York Telephone Company*, 434 U.S. 159, 160 (1977).

[24] *Smith v. State of Maryland*, 442 U.S. 735 (1979).

[25] Ibid., 745.

[26] *State v. Hendricks*, 43 N.C. App. 245, 253 (1979).

27   *United States v. Knotts*, 460 U.S. 276 (1983).

28   Ibid., 276.

29   *United States v. Karo*, 468 U.S. 705 (1984).

30   Ibid., 707.

31   Ibid., 713.

32   Ibid.

33   Ibid., 718.

34   Public Law No. 99-508, 18 U.S.C. ù 2510, *et seq.*

35   *Marshall v. United States*, 422 F.2d 185, 188 (1970); *United States v. Wright*, 449 F.2d 355, 357 (1971).

36   *On Lee v. United States*, 343 U.S. 747, 754 (1952).

37   *Hester v. United States*, 265 U.S. 57, 59 (1924).

38   Ibid.

39   *Katz, supra* note 15, 351.

40   *Commonwealth v. Hernley*, 263 A.2d 904 (1970).

41   *Hernley et al. v. Pennsylvania*, 401 U.S. 914 (1971).

42   *United States v. Kim*, 415 F. Supp. 1252 (D. Hawaii 1976).

43   Ibid., 1257.

44   *People v. Arno*, 153 Cal. Rptr. 624, 625 (1979).

45   *State v. Kender*, 588 P.2d 447, 449 (1978).

46   *United States v. Kim, supra* note 43, 1254; *Commonwealth v. Williams*, 396 A.2d 1286, 1290 (1978).

47   *People v. Arno, supra* note 45, 627.

48   *United States v. Dunn*, 480 U.S. 294 (1987).

49   Ibid., 294-295; 303-305.

50   *California v. Ciraolo*, 476 U.S. 207 (1986).

51   Ibid., 208.

52   *Florida v. Riley*, 488 U.S. 445 (1989).

53   Ibid., 844-845.

54   Ibid., 852.

55   *Dow Chemical v. United States*, 476 U.S. 227 (1986).

56   Ibid., 228.

57   Lois Pilant, "Achieving State-of-the-Art Surveillance," *The Police Chief,* 60(6), 25-34 (June 1993), 5.

58   Ibid.

59   Ibid., 30-31

[60]   Ibid., 26.

[61]   Omnibus Crime Control and Safe Streets Act of 1968 as amended by the Electronic Communications Privacy Act of 1986, Title 18, § 2518 (3).

SUPPLEMENTAL READINGS

Donner, Frank J. *The Age of Surveillance: The Aims and Methods of America's Political Intelligence System*. New York: Knopf, 1980.

Klotter, John C., Jacqueline R. Kanovitz, and Michael I. Kanovitz. *Constitutional Law*. 9th ed. Cincinnati: Anderson, 2002.

Marx, Gary T. *Undercover: Police Surveillance in America*. Berkeley, CA: University of California Press, 1988.

Motto, Carmine J., and Dale L. June. *Undercover*. 2nd ed. Boca Raton, FL: CRC Press, 1999.

Rule, James B. *Private Lives and Public Surveillance: Social Control in the Computer Age*. New York: Schocken Books, 1974.

Schlegel, Kip. "Life Imitating Art: Interpreting Information from Electronic Surveillance," in *Critical Issues in Criminal Investigation*, 2nd ed., edited by Michael J. Palmiotto. Cincinnati: Anderson, 1988.

Singer, Shelvin, and Marshall J. Hartman. Chapter 10 of *Constitutional Criminal Procedure Handbook*. New York: Wiley & Sons, 1986.

Westin, Alan F. *Privacy and Freedom*. New York: Atheneum, 1970.

Eyewitness Identification

Guidelines and Procedures

When a crime has been witnessed by a victim or another person, either might be able to identify the offender. This possibility must be exploited without delay. The first step is to arrange for both victim and eyewitness to scrutinize the mug shot files of the Rogues Gallery; then, if this effort is unsuccessful, to reconstruct an image of the offender with an artist's sketch, facial-features kit, or computer-generated sketch. The reconstruction should be distributed within the department and, to enlist the public's cooperation, in the vicinity of the crime. If an arrest is ultimately made, a lineup should be held to see whether victim or eyewitness can identify the suspect.

Clearly, the methods employed to identify an offender before an arrest differ markedly from those used after arrest. Just the same, the investigator must bear in mind not only the limitations of eyewitness evidence, but also the potential for misidentification. The following recommendations will help to minimize this potential.

THE ROGUES GALLERY

In many states the laws require the photographing and fingerprinting of anyone arrested for a felony or some of the more serious misdemeanors, such as possession of burglars' tools. Mug shots—a full-face and a profile photograph—are commonly made; a group photograph may be made as well, when more than one individual is apprehended for the same crime. A personal description is recorded: age, height, weight, place of birth, scars and tattoos, social security number, and fingerprints [classification and file (Bertillon) number]. In addition, nicknames and aliases as well as any peculiarities in *modus operandi* are noted. This information correlated with the mug shots provides the basis for an offender's Rogues Gallery file.

A file administrator must develop a system that permits only those photographs of likely offenders to be shown on demand to the case investigator and eyewitness. This could be accomplished with an ongoing set of mug shots classified by type of crime, object attacked, and method employed. For example, the following scheme would be practical:

ROBBERY—bank—gas station—armored truck—supermarket; and so on. Rape classifications might include: victim followed (from bus stop, subway station, supermarket); victim pulled into automobile from sidewalk; victim ambushed (in a parking lot, building elevator, when opening garage door); and so on.

To limit the number of mug shots that must be viewed, another scheme would be to divide the police jurisdiction into smaller areas appropriate to its geography and crime patterns. All mug shots of those who committed a particular type of crime would be organized by area so the victim would not be presented with such a profusion of images as to tire the eyes and brain. Exhaustion can be incurred fairly quickly with the result that every mug shot begins to look like another.

Regardless of the classification scheme devised, the choice of person to take charge of the Rogues Gallery file is vital to its success. Indeed this individual becomes a filtering resource who can recognize and pull appropriate material to show to the victim. The longer he or she remains at that post, the greater is his or her value for investigators. The file manager must deal with the difficult decision of what and when to cull—to remove photographs no longer likely to be useful and retain those which might still be of use. Leaner files are preferable in light of the issue of viewer saturation, with its attendant look-alike problems. Cost-effectiveness is another issue. Many police officials would choose to preserve every scrap of information despite the fact that even electronic storage by computer is expensive. This hoarding instinct is a factor to be reckoned with. The empirical knowledge the file manager acquires through long tenure can help to resolve the "retain versus discard" dichotomy, cut costs, and increase the efficacy of the file.

Computerized Mug Photographs

Looking to a future in which electronic data processing aids the investigator, in 1972 researchers at the University of Houston designed a program that retrieves photographs of potential suspects from the mug shot file (Rogues Gallery).[1] The following input is required to run the program:

1. An image of the suspect's face generated by an artist sketch or a facial composite kit[1*];

2. Descriptors such as sex, age, height, weight, and type of crime;

3. A photograph of the criminal taken during the commission of the crime (in check forgery or bank robbery cases).[2]

In what would seem a return to Bertillon's anthropometry (except that this software deals only with facial features), distances between predesignated features are measured. When loaded into the computer, the data are compared to corresponding facial feature ratios of mug shots on file. If agreement is found, the program ranks and selects possible "look-alikes," which are then examined by the witness and investigator to see if the perpetrator is recognized.[3]

---

* By the late 1980s, several software programs had been written to provide a composite image of an offender. In the form of a printout, the likeness is based on an interview with an eyewitness (see "Describing the Offender" in Chapter 6).

By 1990 three systems for the retrieval of photographs stored in a computer database or on a laser video disc had been developed for police use. These systems are expensive and usually only large police agencies can afford them, but if the history of the electronic industry is a guide, the price will drop over time. The computer's discriminatory capability is a major advantage over manual selection in a mug shot file. The more specific the information provided by an eyewitness (age, race, sex, hair color, scar, tattoo, type of crime and weapon, gang emblem or jacket, etc.), the fewer the mug shots that need be printed, thereby keeping viewer saturation to a minimum.

Using the Rogues Gallery File

When a witness agrees (and some will not) to come to the Rogues Gallery to view mug shots, several precautions must be taken to minimize the chance of a misidentification.

1. A reasonable number of randomly arranged photographs should be shown to the witness regardless of whether an identification is made immediately upon viewing but one or two of them. In *Simmons v. United States* the Supreme Court approved displaying only six photographs.[4] Many departments, however, require more. From an investigative standpoint, they find a higher number preferable.

2. A detective or other police officer must not offer an opinion as to which person in the mug shot display may have committed the crime. If a witness asks, it should be explained that this is not allowed because it is the eyewitness's unbiased opinion that is crucial.

3. Only one witness at a time should be permitted to view the mug shot display. Furthermore, one witness may not view photographs when another is present. All must act separately and out of earshot of each other.

4. After viewing a set of mug shots, a witness must not suggest by word or gesture to another witness that he or she has or has not made an identification.

5. When a positive identification is made and probable cause to warrant an arrest is thereby established, the remaining witnesses should not be shown more mug shots; instead the witnesses should be held in reserve to scan the lineup for the suspect.[5]

6. Whenever a positive identification results, a record should be made of all photographs shown, and the witness asked to initial and date any photographs found to identify an offender. When and where the procedure occurred and who was present should also be recorded. As soon as practicable, the investigator is to record anything the witness said upon making the identification.

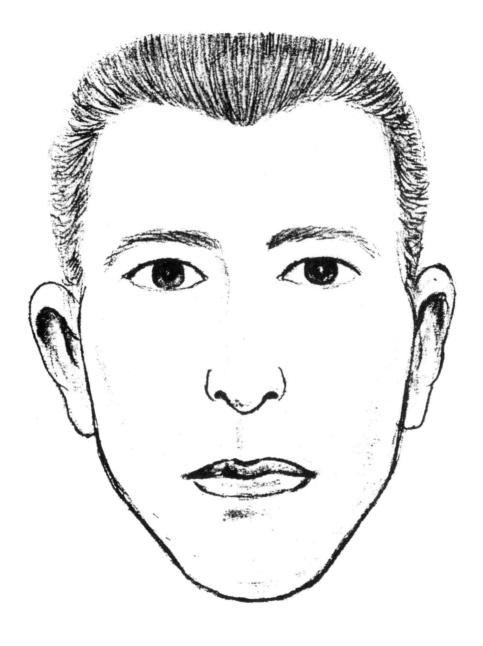

Figure 10.1
Police artist drawing of a suspect based on the description by the only nurse (out of nine) to survive a mass killing. *(Courtesy, Chicago Police Department.)*

Figure 10.2
Photograph of Richard Speck from the files of a maritime union hiring hall in Chicago, obtained the day after the artist's drawing was made. *(Courtesy, Chicago Police Department.)*

7. In general, the use of mug shot photographs to identify an offender is acceptable practice only when a live, corporeal identification—such as a lineup—is not feasible.

Taking these precautions ensures that the procedure will be fair and not subject to serious attack in court. Furthermore, the witness will have faith in any identification he or she made and will testify with greater confidence at trial.

SKETCHES AND COMPOSITE IMAGES

If viewing Rogues Gallery files does not produce an identification of an offender, the next step is the use of a police artist or composite image kits. The likenesses produced can then be distributed to the force and other police departments (see Figures 10.1–10.5). In important cases the public can be involved through the media (newspapers, circulars, television). Anonymity can be granted to those who wish it by means of a hotline telephone number.

A Rogues Gallery identification yields a greater quantity of information—name, fingerprint, arrest record, *modus operandi*, and so on—than does identification from a sketch or composite image, the latter being much more tenuous. Although the sketch or image may be recognized, no name or facts are necessarily known; rather, the investigator may be told only that the suspect is seen from time to time in one locality or has a woman friend in another, and so on. Thus, considerable follow-up is often required even when a good likeness is prepared, distributed, and recognized.

Using the Police Artist

Artists lend their talent for sketching facial images to the police. Such people are on the payroll of many departments, but civilian volunteers often serve equally well. Each develops a method of working with a witness. In one that has proved successful, the witness describes the offender and answers questions posed by the artist, who is then allowed to go to work free from interruption and, most important, without being observed by the witness. This prevents the witness from directing and shaping the artist's outlines. Consistent with Gestalt psychology, denying access to the image until its completion enhances viewer/witness perception of what changes are still needed. Typical comments evoked— "the eyebrows are bushier," "the eyes are closer together," "the lips are thinner," and so on—allow the artist to modify first attempts. This process is repeated until the witness is satisfied or the artist thinks the image cannot be improved.

If there are two or more witnesses, the others do not participate in this process. But they can be asked—separately—to view the end product. If either finds it a good likeness, further modifications are unnecessary; if not, the process can be repeated— using the same artist or a different artist—with the second witness.

Using Composite Kits

Composite kits for creating facial images are commercially available. Identi-Kit is well-known in the United States; another, developed in Great Britain and available here, is Photo-Fit Kit. Complete with instruction manuals, both offer front face and profile selections for a wide variety of racial and ethnic origins. For example, Photo-Fit has a "Caucasian-Afro-Asian Front Face Kit" as well as a "Male Caucasian Profile Kit," and there are supplementary kits for middle eastern features and those of North American Indians. The possible permutations and combinations offered in the "Female Caucasian Front Face Kit" and its accessories (age lines, eyeglasses, sunglasses, headgear) are claimed to be over 2 billion. It offers the following choices: 193 foreheads/hairstyles, 56 noses, 32 chins, 72 pairs of eyes, 80 mouths. Many of the features in the "Male Caucasian Profile Kit" are interchangeable with those of the "Female Kit," thus extending the range of possibilities. As with the Rogues Gallery file, it is best to allocate a limited number of personnel to deal with witnesses who are choosing and assembling facial features to form a composite image of the offender. In addition to traditional transparency kits, software programs can be used to create composites. Such software lets users create endless combinations of faces. Some computerized composite systems include Identi-Kit, Faces 3.0, ComPHOTOfit, and Compusketch. Because each feature selected is readily identified by code number, prompt transmission of the information to distant police departments is feasible.

LINEUPS

When a suspect is apprehended and there is an eyewitness to the crime, the appropriate next step is an investigatory lineup. In fact, it is preferred over any other eyewitness identification procedure. In contrast to the photo display, the lineup (in Britain, the "identification parade") is corporeal: the suspect is placed within a group of people for the purpose of being viewed by eyewitnesses. It is utilized most often, but not exclusively, for the crimes of rape, robbery, and assault. The following recommendations apply (with exceptions where noted) to investigatory lineups as well as lineups held after adversarial judicial proceedings have been initiated.

A lineup should be conducted as soon as possible after the apprehension of a suspect. Three reasons are: (1) the shorter the interval between the lineup and the commission of the crime, the more reliable the eyewitness's memory; (2) an innocent person can be released quickly; and (3) if the suspect is released on bond before a lineup is held, this could delay or frustrate the process. Accordingly, a procedure ought to be adopted for speedily contacting all eyewitnesses, obtaining nonsuspect participants, and arranging for an attorney's presence if necessary.

Figure 10.3
Police photograph of suspect
taken after apprehension.
*(Courtesy, Chicago Police
Department.)*

Figure 10.4
Identi-Kit composite of same
suspect, before apprehension.
(Courtesy, Chicago Police Department.)

Figure 10.5
Police artist's rendition of same
suspect. *(Courtesy, Chicago
Police Department.)*

Lineup Procedure

A properly operated lineup is important for two reasons. It bolsters the confidence of both eyewitness and investigator that the witness can, without help, recognize the offender in a group of apparently similar individuals, and helps to avoid subsequent legal challenges to its validity. Precautions need be taken to attain these ends.

Composition of the Lineup

The police must avoid any temptation to assist an eyewitness in making an identification. Though present at the procedure, they do not take part. The police must also exercise care in the selection of the participants and give consideration to such issues as: the number of participants in the lineup; the position the suspect selects; and the race, sex, physical characteristics, and type of dress worn by the participants.

Number and Position of Participants

Although some state courts have sanctioned a three-person lineup, the United States Supreme Court implicitly approved one comprising six people, including two suspects; that is, at least two nonsuspects for each suspect, a ratio of 2:1.[6,7] These numbers represent the minimum; they are acceptable only when additional nonsuspect participants cannot be located within a reasonable time. State courts generally require fewer participants for corporeal lineups than photographs for Rogues Gallery identification displays, based on the belief that a mug shot identification is less reliable.[8,9] Also, it is more difficult for police to find nonsuspect participants for a lineup than suitable photographs for Rogues Gallery identification.

As to position in the lineup, a suspect should be permitted to choose a spot and, after each viewing, to change to any other spot. This forestalls any charge that a suspect's positioning by a detective led to an identification or was otherwise suggestive. Sometimes, such elemental fairness has led suspects identified in a lineup to confess more readily if interrogated soon thereafter.

Outward Appearance of Participants

The participants in a lineup must not be too dissimilar in appearance. To facilitate this effort, the following factors must be considered.

Race and Sex: The apparent race and sex of all participants should be as identical as is practical. If the suspect is black or female, a lineup composed only of white males would clearly be improper.

Physical Characteristics: Attention must be paid to matching or being reasonably close to the suspect in such particulars as:

Age, height, weight, build or body type, light versus dark complexion
Hair—color, style, length, mustache, beard, sideburns

Type of Dress: If the offender was described as wearing eyeglasses or sunglasses, or such distinctive clothing as a leather vest or purple shirt, all participants (if possible) must be wearing this garb or none should be. Because finding a purple shirt (much less several of different sizes) would be inconvenient, some departments provide overalls. It also would be improper to have several police officers in a lineup wearing uniform trousers with business jackets, while a suspect was outfitted in a suit; in other words, no suggestion is to be made concerning who in the group might be the offender. The Supreme Court, however, has approved a suspect's being required to put on some distinctive accessory or article of clothing that distinguished him or her and was remembered by the victim (e.g., adhesive strips on the sides of the perpetrator's face).[10] The face of each nonsuspect must also be shown taped with adhesive or Band-Aids. Finally, if a suspect's unusual appearance makes it impossible to assemble a group of not-too-dissimilar people, a lineup would have no purpose and should not be held. A photo display can serve in its stead.

Conduct of Lineups

Lineup participants must be cautioned to behave similarly and avoid conduct that would set them apart from the suspect. For instance, it would be improper to put a glum suspect in the midst of participants in good spirits. When a viewer/witness requests that one in the group utter specific words, assume a particular pose, or make a certain gesture, then each must be required to do so in turn. One viewer/witness should be permitted in the lineup room at a time. Only when the process is completed and each has stated independently whether an identification was made are they to be allowed to converse with one another.

Suppressing Suggestions

All investigators, other officials, and even eyewitnesses must be warned about a natural tendency to offer any comment, casual or pointed, within earshot of another viewer/witness. This prohibition applies to gestures or actions that could single out the suspect from the rest of the lineup participants. An impropriety may be regarded as impermissibly suggestive and could "give rise to a very substantial likelihood of irreparable misidentification."[11] Though the Court's words bear upon a "pretrial identification by photograph," they should be regarded as applicable to lineups.

Recording the Procedure

The lineup procedure must be recorded. This includes written notation of such items as time, place, names of participants and others who were present, in addition to any statement by a viewer/witness or potentially suggestive remark made by anyone in the room. A color photograph—and when possible, sound and video recordings—serve to document how the lineup was conducted. Taking these precautions renders moot the fairness issue treated by the Court:

> . . . the defense can seldom reconstruct the manner and mode of line-up iden-
> tification for judge and jury at trial. . . . in short, the accused's inability effec-
> tively to reconstruct at trial any unfairness that occurred at the line-up may
> deprive him of his only opportunity meaningfully to attack the credibility of
> the witness' courtroom identification.[12]

In summary, a properly conducted, fully documented lineup can blunt unfavorable judgments and criticism. At trial, it will enhance the credibility of the witness's
identification.

Uncooperative Suspects

The suspect who refuses to participate in or threatens to disrupt a lineup can create a problem. To secure cooperation, a first step would be to inform him or her that no
constitutional right of refusal to be part of a lineup exists. It should also be made clear
that such refusal can be brought out in a criminal trial and its exact language will be preserved for this reason. If the outcome is an investigative standstill (i.e., the suspect continues to refuse to appear in a lineup), this can be remedied with a pictorial
identification—placing a photograph of the suspect among others of similar appearance.

Rɪɢʜᴛ ᴛᴏ ᴀɴ Aᴛᴛᴏʀɴᴇʏ

The law concerning the right to have an attorney present at each eyewitness identification varies with the procedure; for example, there are different requirements for
an investigatory lineup and one held after judicial proceedings are initiated.

Pictorial Identifications

The Supreme Court allowed a conviction to stand based on a pre-arrest display of
photographs in which no counsel was present, and held it to have been a valid procedure.[13] Subsequently, it ruled on a post-arrest photographic identification:

> . . . the Sixth Amendment does not grant the right to counsel at photo-
> graphic displays conducted by the government for the purpose of allowing
> a witness to attempt an identification of the offender.[14]

Accordingly, a suspect does not have the right to have an attorney present when an identification procedure—photo display, composite image, or sketch—is employed,
whether the attempt to effect an identification occurs before or after arrest.

Lineups

In 1967 the Supreme Court decided that a post-indictment lineup was a "critical stage" of the prosecution's case and that, therefore, a Sixth Amendment right exists for a suspect to have counsel present.[15] Five years later it refused (in *Kirby v. Illinois*) to extend the right to counsel in a pre-indictment case:

> The initiation of judicial proceedings is far from a mere formalism. It is the starting point of our whole system of adversary criminal justice. For it is only then that the government has committed itself to prosecute, and only then that the adverse positions of government and defendant have solidified. . . . It is this point, therefore, that marks the commencement of the "criminal pros- ecutions" to which alone the explicit guarantees of the Sixth Amendment are applicable.[16]

It is important to note that each state is free to exceed the constitutional requirements of *Kirby* (and *United States v. Wade*) in its own jurisdiction. Several have chosen to do so. The presence of counsel at a pre-arraignment lineup, while not required by *Kirby*, helps to ensure that due process standards are met.

Advising the Suspect

If a suspect has a *Miranda* or other right to an attorney, he or she also must be informed of the right to have a lawyer present at the lineup, that a lawyer will be provided free of charge should he or she be unable to afford one, and that the lineup will be delayed for a reasonable time in order for a lawyer to appear.

Waiver of Right

A suspect may waive the right to have an attorney at the lineup. The waiver may be oral or written, with the burden resting on the state—the police—to prove it was made knowingly and intelligently. At least one witness, preferably more, is needed to ver- ify the waiver.

ROLE OF THE SUSPECT'S ATTORNEY

The attorney should be allowed to consult with the suspect, make suggestions about the procedure, and observe the conduct of the lineup. At hand as an observer rather than an advisor, he or she must not be permitted to obstruct or control the process. However, any suggestion the attorney makes that is not adopted should be recorded in writing.

The attorney should be cautioned to remain silent during the lineup, and may be pre- sent when the witness informs the investigator whether or not he or she was able to make an identification. Only after this decision is conveyed and the lineup is concluded, and only if agreeable to the witness, may the attorney then speak to the witness.

ONE-ON-ONE CONFRONTATIONS (SHOW-UPS) _____

When a situation arises in which a proper lineup cannot be arranged quickly, a one-on-one confrontation or *show-up* may be utilized. As an identification procedure, confrontation frequently means bringing a suspect (within a short time frame) back to the scene or presenting a suspect to each eyewitness separately. (For further information, consult *People v. Manion*, 67 Ill. 2d 564, 367 N.E.2d 1313 (1977).)[17] Because the procedure is inherently suggestive, some compelling circumstance must be operative. For example, if a wounded eyewitness, suspect, or victim is in danger of death, a one-on-one confrontation may be set up when:

1. The permission of the physician in charge is obtained.

2. The time between the crime and the confrontation is limited—to within 20 minutes, preferably. (See the case law of the appropriate state; some states allow up to two hours.)

During a confrontation no comments or suggestions—such as "We found your wallet when we searched him" or "She confessed but we need your identification, too"—are to be made to a witness. An absence of incriminating commentary establishes the aura of impartiality that ought to characterize the procedure. Although there is no law or court decision that gives a suspect the right to have an attorney present at a one-on-one confrontation, it is prudent to keep a record of the procedure (as with a lineup). Later, if the case goes to trial and the investigator must respond to questions posed by the defense, the date, time, place, and statements made by the viewer or suspect will be available for ready reference.

RELIABILITY OF EYEWITNESS IDENTIFICATIONS _____

Eyewitness testimony has been studied by a number of behavioral scientists who belittle such testimony and believe that juries tend to overestimate the credibility of eyewitness accounts.[18–20] This outlook, however, is not shared by average citizens. Based on their own experience, they feel they can trust what they see with their own eyes. Jurors often transfer this credibility to the testimony of an eyewitness.

In the absence of forensic evidence, the two most compelling kinds of evidence presented to a jury are the signed confession and the identification of the defendant by an eyewitness. The Supreme Court has placed more severe limitations on obtaining and using a confession as evidence than it has on securing and using the evidence of an eyewitness. Significant eyewitness identification cases are listed in the references.[21-26] Also, Singer and Hartman cover this material in their handbook on constitutional criminal procedure.[27]

Jury Instructions on Eyewitness Identification

In a case involving damaging eyewitness testimony, the defense may ask a trial judge to give jurors special instructions to assist them in evaluating it. An explanation of jury instructions may help. First, readers should be aware that a defense attorney has this additional opportunity to protect a client's interests. Second, it is important that investigators be familiar with the contents of a carefully drafted set of jury instructions; then, they can spot and remedy any weakness before their evidence reaches the court.

In the appendix to his journal article, Sanders proposes an elaborate set of such instructions for an eyewitness identification case. He recommends they be read to the jury before the eyewitness is heard, and further, that each juror be given a copy before retiring to consider the evidence. They are as follows:

> [One of the most important questions] or [the only important question] in this case is the identification of the defendant as the person who committed the crime. The prosecution has the burden of proving beyond a reasonable doubt, not only that the crime was committed, but also that the defendant was the person who committed the crime. If, after considering the evidence you have heard from both sides, you are not convinced beyond a reasonable doubt that the defendant is the person who committed the crime, you must find him not guilty.
>
> The identification testimony that you have heard was an expression of belief or impression by the witness. To find the defendant not guilty, you need not believe that the identification witness was insincere, but merely that he was mistaken in his belief or impression.
>
> Many factors affect the accuracy of identification. In considering whether the prosecution has proved beyond a reasonable doubt that the defendant is the person who committed the crime, you should consider the following:
>
> 1. *Did the witness have an adequate opportunity to observe [see] the criminal actor?*
>
>   In answering this question, you should consider:
>
>   a. the length of time the witness observed the actor;
>
>   b. the distance between the witness and the actor;
>
>   c. the extent to which the actor's features were visible and undisguised;
>
>   d. the light or lack of light at the place and time of observation;
>
>   e. the presence or absence of distracting noises or activity during the observation;
>
>   f. any other circumstance affecting the witness's opportunity to observe the person committing the crime.
>
> 2. *Did the witness have the capacity to observe the person committing the crime?*
>
>   In answering this question, you should consider whether the witness's capacity was impaired by:
>
>   a. stress or fright at the time of observation;
>
>   b. personal motivations, biases or prejudices;
>
>   c. uncorrected visual defects;

d.   fatigue and injury;

e.   drugs or alcohol.

[You should consider also whether the witness is of a different race than the criminal actor. Identification by a person of a different race may be less reliable than identification by a person of the same race.]

3.   *Was the witness sufficiently attentive to the criminal actor at the time of the crime?*

In answering this question, you should consider whether the witness knew that a crime was taking place during the time he observed the actor. Even if the witness had adequate opportunity and capacity to observe the criminal actor, he may not have done so unless he was aware that a crime was being committed.

4.   *Was the witness identification of the defendant completely the product of his own memory?*

In answering this question, you should consider:

a.   the length of time that passed between the witness's original observation and his identification of the defendant;

b.   the witness's capacity and state of mind at the time of the identification;

c.   the witness's exposure to opinions, descriptions or identifications given by other witnesses, to photographs or newspaper accounts, or to any other information or influence that may have affected the independence of his identification;

d.   any instances when the witness, or any eyewitness to the crime, failed to identify the defendant;

e.   any instances when the witness, or any eyewitness to the crime, gave a description of the actor that is inconsistent with the defendant's appearance;

f.   the circumstances under which the defendant was presented to the witness for identification. [You may take into account that an identification made by picking the defendant from a group of similar individuals is generally more reliable than an identification made from the defendant being presented alone to the witness. You may also take into account that identifications made from seeing the person are generally more reliable than identifications made from a photograph.]

I again emphasize that the burden of proving that the defendant is the person who committed the crime is on the prosecution. If, after considering the evidence you have heard from the prosecution and from the defense, and after evaluating the eyewitness testimony in light of the considerations listed above, you have a reasonable doubt about whether the defendant is the person who committed the crime, you must find him not guilty.[28]

REFERENCES

[1] B.T. Rhodes, K.R. Laughery, et al., *A Man-Computer System For Solution of the Mug File Problem* (Houston, TX: University of Houston, 1977).

[2] Ibid., 2.

[3] Ibid., 7.

[4] *Simmons v. United States*, 390 U.S. 377, 385 (1968).

[5] Ibid., 386, note 4.

[6] *State v. Henderson*, 479 S.W.2d 485 (Mo. 1972).

[7] *Coleman v. Alabama*, 399 U.S. 1, 5 (1970).

[8] *Simmons, supra* note 4.

[9] *United States v. Ash*, 413 U.S. 300, 322 (1973).

[10] *United States v. Wade*, 388 U.S. 218, 220 (1967).

[11] *Simmons, supra* note 4, 377.

[12] *Wade, supra* note 10, 230-232.

[13] *Simmons, supra* note 4.

[14] *Ash, supra* note 9, 321.

[15] *Wade, supra* note 10, 237.

[16] *Kirby v. Illinois*, 406 U.S. 682, 689 (1972).

[17] *People v. Manion*, 67 Ill. 2d 564, 367 N.E.2d 1313 (1977).

[18] Elizabeth Loftus, *Eyewitness Testimony*. Txt. ed. (Cambridge, MA: Harvard University Press, 1980).

[19] Daniel Yarmey, *The Psychology of Eyewitness Testimony* (Riverside, NJ: The Free Press, 1979).

[20] Brian R. Clifford and Ray Bull, *The Psychology of Person Identification* (Boston: Routledge & Kegan Paul, 1978).

[21] *Wade, supra* note 10.

[22] *Gilbert v. California*, 388 U.S. 263 (1967).

[23] *Stovall v. Denno*, 388 U.S. 293 (1967).

[24] *Foster v. California*, 394 U.S. 440 (1969).

[25] *Neil v. Biggers*, 409 U.S. 188 (1972).

[26] *Manson v. Brathwaite*, 432 U.S. 98 (1977).

[27] Shelvin Singer and Marshall J. Hartman, *Constitutional Criminal Procedure Handbook* (New York: Wiley & Sons, 1986).

[28] Robin Sanders, "Helping the Jury Evaluate Eyewitness Testimony: The Need for Additional Safeguards," *American Journal of Criminal Law*, 12 (1984), 222-224.

Supplemental Readings

Boylan, Jeanne. *Portraits of Guilt*. New York: Pocket Books, 2000.

Clifford, Brian R. and Ray Bull. *The Psychology of Person Identification*. Boston: Routledge & Kegan Paul, 1978.

Cutler, B.L. and S.D. Penrod. *Mistaken Identification—The Eyewitness, Psychology, and the Law*. Port Chester, NY: Cambridge University Press, 1995.

Cutler, B.L., S.D. Penrod and T.K. Martens, "The Reliability of Eyewitness Identification," *Law and Human Behavior* 11 (1987), 233-258.

Klotter, John C., Jacqueline R. Kanovitz and Michael I. Kanovitz. *Constitutional Law*. 9th ed. Cincinnati: Anderson, 2002.

Loftus, Elizabeth F. *Eyewitness Testimony*. Txt. ed. Cambridge, MA: Harvard University Press, 1980.

Loftus, Elizabeth F. and Katherine Ketchum. *Witness for the Defense: The Accused, the Eyewitness and the Expert Who Puts Memory on Trial*. New York: St. Martin's Press, 1992.

Shapiro, P.N. and S.D. Penrod, "Meta-Analysis of Facial Identification Studies," *Psychological Bulletin* 100 (1986): 139-156.

Singer, Shelvin and Marshall J. Hartman. *Constitutional Criminal Procedure Handbook*. New York: Wiley & Sons, 1986.

Sobel, Nathan R. and Dee Pridgen. *Eyewitness Identification: Legal and Practical Problems*. 2nd ed. New York: Clark Boardman, 1981.

Wagenaar, Willem. *Identifying Man: A Case Study in Legal Psychology*. Cambridge, MA: Harvard University Press, 1988.

Wall, Patrick M. *Eyewitness Identification in Criminal Cases*. Springfield, IL: Charles C Thomas, 1965.

Yarmey, Daniel. *The Psychology of Eyewitness Testimony*. Riverside, NJ: The Free Press, 1979.

CHAPTER 11

Interrogation

Purpose and Principles

Today, many investigators believe that the sole purpose of interrogation is to get a confession. This may be in part a lingering heritage of English common law: in earlier times, its lack was often viewed as a serious deficiency in the Crown's case, enough to cause a judge or jury to acquit the accused. The weight given to confession as a means of solving a crime continues to the present day. Thus, the potential of the forensic sciences—especially criminalistics—as its partial replacement for establishing guilt is yet to be fully realized. In the United States, Supreme Court decisions have placed limits on the interrogative procedures that may be used to secure a confession (see the treatment of *Miranda v. Arizona* in Chapter 12); they reflect the importance it retains. In Great Britain, the Judges' Rules (formulated in 1912 and since modified) govern investigative behavior. The aim of judicial guidance in either country is to ensure that a confession is trustworthy and that it was made voluntarily—not under duress.

THE PURPOSE OF INTERROGATION

The purpose of interrogation is to elicit information from a suspect who may suppress the facts, or from people whose answers might be colored by close ties to a suspect. Though spouses, parents, accomplices, and friends will not often willingly divulge what could be damaging to a suspect's best interests, these sources may still provide potentially prejudicial information. Although obtaining information detrimental to the suspect's case is the primary goal of the interrogative process, other results may be achieved.

1. Establish the innocence of a suspect by clearing up facts that seem to point to guilt (Although a frequent, important result, this is ignored in much of the literature in the field);

2. Obtain from the suspect or relatives and friends of the suspect:

    The names of accomplices;

    The facts and circumstances surrounding the crime;

Follow-up leads provided unwittingly, or with ulterior motive, such as faking an alibi;

The location of stolen goods;

The location of physical evidence, such as documents, a weapon, or a burglar's tool.

3.   Obtain from the suspect alone:

An admission—an express or implied statement tending to support the suspect's involvement in the crime, but insufficient by itself to prove guilt;

A confession—an oral or written statement acknowledging guilt.

WHY PEOPLE CONFESS

An understanding of why it is possible to obtain a confession may be found in the works of Horowitz,[1] and Pavlov (as interpreted by Sargant).[2] The law enforcement community—academics as well as practitioners—has taken little notice of Horowitz's paper examining the psychology of confession (and virtually no social science research has ensued). Pointing to a problem as ancient as history itself he asks, "Why does it occur?":

> Why not always brazen it out when confronted by accusation? Why does a person convict himself through a confession, when at the very worst, no confession would leave him at least as well off (and possibly better off) from the point of view of the physical and social consequences of his act?[3]

Horowitz goes on to discuss how readily some college students suspected of cheating admitted their guilt when faced with strong evidence of collusion:

> . . . no accusations of an explicit nature were made [to the students]. There were no stern or frowning faces. All involved persons were simply and directly confronted with the evidence, namely, the coincidence of answers on adjacent papers, and asked if there was some explanation of the coincidence. The question was asked simply, calmly, and directly.

> When so confronted the involved persons confessed, much to the surprise of all. Clearly, cheating could not be proved in any accepted legal sense in these cases. Guilt was presumptive, only. Nevertheless, all did confess without being pressed. That pressure existed is nearly certain because of the nature of the situation. *But it was intrinsic in the psychology of the situation, and not induced* (emphasis added).[4]

This experiment demonstrates the powerful influence of evidence, particularly physical evidence, in building on the internal, self-generated, psychological pressure of a guilty person. Horowitz then notes that confession (even to offenses not committed) can be obtained through duress such as torture, brutality, and excessive or prolonged psychological pressure. But, he adds, this is unnecessary if the suspect is indeed guilty, and if certain other social-psychological conditions prevail.

Horowitz: Basic Concepts

An understanding of Horowitz's five social-psychological conditions will help to explain why a person confesses.

1. Accusation

The person under interrogation must be mentally or visually aware of an accusation. The accusation may be explicit—made directly at the start of an interrogation, or it may be implicit in the interrogator's attitude and demeanor—communicated by nothing more than a raised eyebrow. As a result, the person perceives that he or she has been accused or, based on guilt feelings, projects such a perception. According to Horowitz, whether the accusation is explicit or implicit makes *no essential difference* in the suspect's social-psychological situation.

Some consequences flow from the perception of accusation. One is the feeling that one's psychological freedom and movement are curtailed; another is being placed on unsure ground where the familiar clues governing behavior in normal situations are missing. Being interviewed for a job can produce a similar feeling. In either situation, the accused is largely supported by available ego defense responses. There is

> . . . no role if you will, that he can utilize in this situation. He must behave, then, in stereotyped and compulsive ways. He feels that he has been personally attacked, hemmed in, constricted. This perception of accusation to the guilty person must inevitably produce defense for an attacked ego. Indeed even innocent persons frequently *feel* guilty when falsely accused.[5]

Whether guilty or innocent, the individual is in a difficult position. Feeling cornered, freedom is the main concern, but the route appears blocked. The strength of the perception of accusation is subjective; it is "a function of the person rather than a function of the objective strength of the authority itself."[6]

2. Evidence is Available

The first response, especially of the guilty person, to the realization of being accused is to become worried and psychologically unsettled.

> [The accused's] . . . perceptual structure is unstable. This is so because he does not know exactly how much is actually known to the accuser. Perhaps the accuser is bluffing, in which case one might brazen it out. Perhaps the accuser knows all, in which case one is better off to ask for sympathetic treatment or to argue for extenuating circumstances. Most usually, the truth lies between these extremes but the accused doesn't know exactly where.[7]

An accusation in and of itself implies that a certain amount of evidence is indeed available. When hard evidence is produced, any logical person will infer at some point in the interrogation that he or she "is caught with the goods." Their psychological position becoming precarious, freedom is even more threatened. It is not essential, however, that hard evidence be produced—*believing* that it is available may suffice. The accused may "read into what may be innocent things in reality, portents which need not be there."[8] Hence, failing a lie detector examination often leads to confession (though the failure is not admissible as evidence in court—except by stipulation). Hearing that an accomplice is "just starting to talk" or that crime scene evidence has been taken to the laboratory may reinforce natural anxiety and provoke a confession. Indeed, the considerable potential of physical evidence is not taken advantage of by many investigators, owing to a lack of training and education in understanding crime laboratory results. This point has been made before, and probably will be again; it is worth reemphasizing. Playing one co-offender against the other (using the revelations of each on the other) is an additional means of indicating that "evidence is available." Also useful is framing a question to imply that its answer is already known (e.g., "You bought the gun, not your partner—is that correct?")

Motive is not normally thought of as evidence, but if it has been determined—especially for crimes in which it is particularized rather than universal, as in homicide—this information can be put to good use during interrogation. The victim may be able to suggest a motive. Sometimes it can be surmised by the shrewd investigator from facts developed during the investigation or from similar cases. Since suspects believe that motive has evidentiary value, they often believe that it has furnished evidence by providing a reason for the crime.

3. Forces—Friendly and Hostile

It should be obvious from the foregoing that any factors contributing to psychological uneasiness will also be conducive to confession. Accordingly, any legally permitted action that either reduces the forces friendly to the accused, or increases the hostile forces, can enhance the likelihood of a confession:

> . . . the suspect must perceive . . . that the total hostile array of power exceeds the total array of friendly power that he can martial [*sic*]. . . . In short, the person must believe he is alone, or nearly alone. He is cut off from succor. His situation is such that salvation lies only in him.[9]

This is why an interrogation is not conducted in the comfort of the suspect's living room, convivial drinks in hand, surrounded by supportive family members. On the contrary, the characteristically dreary police station house unintentionally minimizes forces friendly to the suspect.

4. Guilt Feelings

> It should be equally clear that if a person does not feel guilt he is not in his own mind guilty and will not confess to an act which others may regard as evil or wrong and he, in fact, considers correct.[10]

Confession, therefore, is rare when the "hit man" in a gangland killing is apprehended and questioned. The code of silence (*omerta*) among these criminals acknowledges that death is the rightful punishment for those who break it. The assignment to execute anyone is a clear indication of gangland trust; the execution carried off, a path to advancement. From this perspective, there is little if any reason for the gunman to feel guilt. The killer was "only carrying out orders" or "the punk had it coming." Hard empirical evidence, therefore, confirms that admissions of or confessions to gangland killings are rare, even when police know the killer's identity and interrogate him or her. Horowitz's statement on guilt feelings helps to explain this phenomenon.

Ordinarily, most people feel guilt as a consequence of wrongdoing, their sense of right conduct having been violated. When it moves beyond mere self-reproach, the feeling becomes strong enough to cause the person's inner peace to crumble. Then other factors—an accusation, physical evidence, or both—have a cumulative effect by generating psychological stress. As stated at the onset, Pavlov also studied this process. Understanding his theory (explained below) can increase the chances of obtaining a confession. Although his study considers how stress was induced in dogs, it may apply to humans as well.

5. Confession: The Way Out

Under interrogation, people are aware of their vulnerability and weakness when accused by "an authority with a high ratio of power compared to the forces [they] can martial [*sic*]." Perceiving "that there is good evidence of [their] guilt," they feel guilty, are mindful of loneliness, inner ferment, and the need for relief.[11] At this point in the process, investigators should make them aware that confession is the path to deliverance and mental freedom. Meanwhile, it must be made easy for the person to confess. A crowd of onlookers—police chief, captain of detectives, district attorney, reporters—is not conducive to this end. This is why privacy and anonymity are the rule in religious and psychiatric practice. Confessing may well be "good for the soul," but a person about to do so must be made to feel comfortable. Any residual hesitancy must be removed with assurances that their emotions are at least understood, if not shared. Sentiments that could convey this might include: "Tell me about it, and you will feel better," "I've heard what you're going to tell me before," "You're not the first to do this, and you're probably not the last," or "Lots of people have had the same idea." Minimizing the ethical considerations and seriousness of their conduct makes it easier for a person to confess.

Pavlov: Basic Concepts

Pavlov, a Russian scientist, won the Nobel Prize in 1904 for research on digestion and the nervous system. Working with dogs, he found that an artificial stimulus or signal (the sound of a bell) could, by repeated association, be substituted for a natural stimulus (the taste of food), to cause a physiological response (salivation). Pavlov called this response the *conditioned reflex*. By varying the artificial stimulus or signal, he could estimate the extent of stress created from the amount of saliva produced by the animal.

Assuming that dogs and humans react to stress in a somewhat similar fashion, Pavlovian theory is of service to investigators in fathoming why a confession may be obtained. Sargant explains that four sources of stress were studied; they will be treated in greater detail immediately following these abstracts:

> The first was simply an increased intensity of the signal to which the dog was conditioned. . . . (Intensity of Signal)

> The second . . . was to increase the time between giving the signal and the arrival of food. . . . (Anxiety Waiting)

> Pavlov's third . . . was to confuse them by anomalies in the conditioning signals given—continued positive and negative signals being given one after the other. . . . (Alternate Signals)

> A fourth . . . was to tamper with a dog's physical condition by subjecting it to long periods of work, gastrointestinal disorders, fears, or by disturbing its glandular balance. (Physical Condition)[12]

1. Intensity of Signal

Though humans have *not* been deliberately conditioned, a signal is nevertheless received when a suspect realizes that incriminating evidence exists. The process is similar to Horowitz's results: the stronger the evidence, the stronger the signal; the greater the threat to freedom, the greater the stress. For example, the questioning of relatives or associates may reveal some apparently innocuous details about a suspect's past. If, during a subsequent interrogation of the suspect, the investigator picks up on them, the suspect may suppose that his or her life is an open book. The guilty person might then jump to conclusions, infer that their participation in the crime is also known, and confess. Though an innocent person is unlikely to be similarly affected, a guilty person may well receive an increased signal and feel greater stress when the authority making the accusation is a chief of detectives or a district attorney specifically called in to handle the interrogation.

2. Anxiety Waiting

Pavlov's observations seem applicable to human behavior. For example, it is a common experience for an individual to become tense while remaining in readiness, expecting something to happen—especially if the anticipated result is of some concern. Thus, a suspect awaiting an alibi check may become anxious because of the time it entails (particularly if the alibi proffered cannot bear checking); as may, to a lesser extent, a person who is forced to wait for an investigator to complete other business after being brought to the station house for questioning. Sometimes, it is productive to ask an individual who has denied involvement with a crime to "think it over" and "come back tomorrow." The effect on a guilty person will be prolonged tension. Except for the inconvenience, the innocent should be relatively unaffected.

3. Alternate Signals

In Pavlov's experiments, positive and negative conditioning signals were given to the dogs consecutively. Because suspects are neither positively nor negatively conditioned, this means of inducing stress is not applicable to human beings. Yet the concept seems to throw light on the efficacy of the "good cop/bad cop," or "friendly/unfriendly," interrogation method whereby a friendly signal may be regarded positively and an unfriendly one negatively.

4. Physical Condition

The means Pavlov employed—subjecting animals to long periods of work, inducing gastrointestinal disorder and fever, and disturbing glandular balance—are not even remotely permissible with humans. Indeed, they are unthinkable in countries owing their allegiance to traditional Anglo-Saxon jurisprudence. Yet, a misuse of the finding that lowered physical condition is conducive to confession has been documented by Solzhenitsyn.[13] Even from the perspective of the worst days of the "third degree" in the United States, it is difficult to imagine subjecting suspects to the torture this former Russian political prisoner describes. The Wickersham Commission revealed in 1931, however, that the "third degree," which it defined as "the extraction of confessions through police brutality," was a "widespread, almost universal practice."[14] It is not administered today, certainly, but for those curious about just how far civilized methods of interrogation have come, the Wickersham Reports are recommended reading.[15]

Occasionally, however, an opportunity may present itself to obtain a confession from a suspect who is exhausted. When serial killer Ted Bundy escaped from a Colorado court house while in sheriff's custody, he was able to hide out for five days in the mountains before being captured. Mike Fischer, a district attorney's investigator, was asked if he

> . . . thought he could ever get Bundy to talk—to confess or make any incriminating concessions at all. "I doubt it," replied Fischer, "unless you catch Theodore when he's really down. When he's all in pieces, ragged as hell. Now that could happen. If, y'know, he gets caught here—without being shot—and he's all exhausted. He'll be really, really down. Maybe then."

> Fischer confided that he had gotten a promise from Sheriff Kienast. "If Theodore's caught, then the first thing that happens is "I'm gonna hit him with questions. Not about his goddamn escape, that's what he'll be expecting. We're just going to talk about Caryn Campbell's murder.

> "I think he's still up those goddamn mountains somewhere," Fischer continued, "and he can't handle those mountains. They're just awesome if you're not familiar with them. When we get him, he's going to be pitiful. He's gonna be way down. And we'll just talk about that murder.

> . . . The look on his (Fischer's) face told it all. The sheriff had reneged on the promise. Fischer wasn't getting first crack at questioning Bundy—about murders. The sheriff was draining all the details from Bundy about his escape. That was the sheriff's political priority at the moment.

Later when Fischer finally had the opportunity to talk with Bundy, he opened with: ". . . Ted, I want to talk with you about the Caryn Campbell murder."

Bundy smiled, his eyes were confident. Fischer knew that the fleeting moment when Bundy might be caught with his defenses down had passed.[16]

The two lead detectives who questioned O.J. Simpson provide another example of interrogators failing to exploit a suspect's weariness. In the book *Evidence Dismissed,* they state:

that they planned to run the interview until Simpson, who appeared tired from his trip to and from Chicago, became "agitated enough to ask for his attorney or until he simply runs out of juice."[17]

If, instead of pressing Simpson further, they had led him to believe that in his situation salvation lay with himself, they would have shown him a way out of inner torment, thereby making it easy to confess. Their account of events, however, suggests that a question lingered in their minds as to whether they were interviewers or interrogators. Four days after his questioning, Simpson's inner turmoil is still manifest in both a suicide note and an escape-suicide attempt in a Ford Bronco during which he held a gun to his head and threatened to pull the trigger.[18, 19] Subsequently, after the detectives coaxed him out of the car, they again did not take advantage of the fatigued individual they were handling (see Pavlov's "Physical Condition").

WHY SOME DO NOT CONFESS

By now the reader will understand that obtaining a confession is not a simple matter. After all, Horowitz's experiments involved a noncriminal, rather homogeneous group of people; Pavlov's, a group of dogs. Investigators know quite well that all guilty persons—particularly those facing severe sanctions—are not as ready to confess as one might assume, even when Horowitz's five basic conditions have been met. There are several reasons why even a guilty person will not acknowledge, much less confess to, involvement in a crime:

- Some suffer no pangs of conscience and have no need to relieve guilty feelings.

- Some are fearful of the consequences if they betray their accomplices;

- Some have learned (having been through the mill) that only by talking do they dig their own grave.

- Under *Miranda*, it would require an unusual set of circumstances for an attorney to fail to advise a client to remain silent.

CONCLUSION

Just as an understanding of Horowitz and Pavlov can improve an investigator's ability to conduct an interrogation, so can it ensure that the process be humane. No investigator wishes to have an innocent party confess to a crime. A crude test might be to judge from experience just how much stress would fall short of eliciting a confession from the innocent person, yet cause many of the guilty to cave in under the pressure of conscience.

In any event, evidence beyond the confession should also be sought as a means of corroborating guilt. For example, shortly after a confession is obtained, it may be possible to have the suspect lead investigators to the fruits of the crime, or to physical evidence such as the weapon or tool used. Sometimes the suspect will agree to reenact the crime, and in the process mention a fact to which only the guilty party would be privy. A confession may be therapeutic, provoking the need to "tell all" (including other crimes committed by the suspect). Two important reminders should be considered: one, that a written confession should be limited to the crime under investigation—any mention of others being prejudicial to the defendant; and two, though confirmation of confession is highly desirable, it has all too often been ignored in practice.

REFERENCES

1   M.W. Horowitz, "The Psychology of Confession," *Journal of Criminal Law, Criminology, and Police Science* 47:2 (1956), 197-204.

2   William W. Sargant, *Battle for the Mind: A Physiology of Conversion and Brainwashing* (New York: Doubleday, 1957; Springfield, IL: Greenwood Press, 1975).

3   Horowitz, *op. cit.*, 197.

4   Ibid., 198.

5   Ibid., 200.

6   Ibid., 201.

7   Ibid., 200.

8   Ibid., 202.

9   Ibid.

10   Ibid., 203.

11   Ibid.

12   Sargant, *op. cit.*, 35-36.

13   Aleksandr I. Solzhenitsyn, *The Gulag Archipelago: An Experiment in Literary Investigation*, Thomas P. Whitney, trans. (New York: Harper & Row, 1974), chap. 3.

14   President's Commission on Law Enforcement and Administration of Justice, *The Challenge of Crime in a Free Society* (Washington, DC: U.S. Government Printing Office, 1967), 93. [Commissioned by Lyndon Johnson.]

15   National Commission of Law Observance and Enforcement, *Report on Lawlessness in Law Enforcement, No. 11* (Washington, DC: U.S. Government Printing Office, 1931). [One of 14 reports of the Wickersham Commission appointed by Herbert Hoover in 1929.]

16   Richard W. Larsen. *Bundy: The Deliberate Stranger* (Englewood Cliffs, NJ: Prentice Hall, 1980), 187-190.

17   Tom Lange, Philip Vannatter, Dan E. Moldea, and E. Friedrichsmeyer, *Evidence Dismissed: The Inside Story of the Police Investigation of O.J. Simpson*. (New York: Pocket Books, 1997), 67.

18   Marsha Clark, *Without a Doubt*. (New York: Viking, 1997), 49, 52.

19   Lange and Vannatter, *op. cit.*, 154, 159, 163.

SUPPLEMENTAL READINGS

Hess, John. *Interviewing and Interrogaiton for Law Enforcement*. Cincinnati: Anderson, 1997.

Merloo, Joost A.M. *The Rape Of The Mind*. Universal Library edition. New York: Grosset & Dunlap, 1961.

Rabon, Don. *Interviewing and Interrogation*. Durham, NC: Carolina Academic Press, 1992.

Reik, Theodor. *The Compulsion to Confess*. New York: Farrar, Straus & Cudahy, 1959.

Rogge, O. John. *Why Men Confess*. New York: Da Capo, 1975.

Royal Commission on Criminal Procedure. *Police Interrogation*. Research Studies Nos. 1 and 3. London: Her Majesty's Stationery Office, 1980.

Sargant, William W. *Battle for the Mind: A Physiology of Conversion and Brainwashing*. New York: Doubleday, 1957; Springfield, IL: Greenwood Press, 1975.

Wicklander, Douglas E., and David E. Zulawski. *Practical Aspects of Interview and Interrogation*. New York: Elsevier, 1991.

CHAPTER 12

Interrogation of Suspects and Hostile Witnesses

Guidelines and Procedures

)⦿⦿⦿⦿⦿⦿⦿⦿⦿⦿⦿⦿⦿⦿⦿⦿⦿⦿⦿⦿⦿⦿(

The practice of criminal interrogation in the United States has been significantly affected by decisions of the Supreme Court, most significantly by *Miranda v. Arizona* in 1966. This being so, it is essential to consider the guidelines laid down in *Miranda* before the procedure involved in conducting an interrogation can be treated.

MIRANDA GUIDELINES

The *Miranda* doctrine spells out the constitutional rights and procedural safeguards, including the waiver of those rights, that must be conveyed to a person before any interrogation may be undertaken. Chief Justice Warren delivered and summed up the opinion of the Court as follows:

> Our holding will be spelled out with some specificity in the pages which follow but briefly stated it is this. The prosecution may not use statements, whether exculpatory or inculpatory, stemming from custodial interrogation of the defendant unless it demonstrates the use of procedural safeguards effective to secure the privilege against self-incrimination. By custodial interrogation, we mean questioning initiated by law enforcement officers after a person has been taken into custody or otherwise deprived of his freedom of action in any significant way.[1]* As for the procedural safeguards to be employed, unless other fully effective means are devised to inform accused persons of their right of silence and to assure continuous opportunity to exercise it, the following measures are required. Prior to any questioning, the person must be warned that he has a right to remain silent, that any statement he does make may be used as evidence against him, and that he has a right to the presence of an attorney, either retained or appointed. The defendant may waive effectuation of these rights, provided the waiver is made voluntarily,

---

* This is what we meant in *Escobedo [v. Illinois]* when we spoke of an investigation that had focused on an accused.

knowingly and intelligently. If, however, he indicates in any manner and at any stage of the process that he wishes to consult with an attorney before speaking there can be no questioning. Likewise, if the individual is alone and indicates in any manner that he does not wish to be interrogated, the police may not question him. The mere fact that he may have answered some questions or volunteered some statements on his own does not deprive him of the right to refrain from answering any further inquiries until he has consulted with an attorney and thereafter consents to be questioned.[1]

The words of the Court also spell out what the police must do to comply with the *Miranda* ruling.[2]

THE RIGHT TO REMAIN SILENT

At the outset, if a person in custody is to be subjected to interrogation, he must first be informed in clear and unequivocal terms that he has the right to remain silent. For those unaware of the privilege, the warning is needed simply to make them aware of it—the threshold requirement for an intelligent decision as to its exercise.

ANYTHING SAID CAN BE USED AGAINST THE INDIVIDUAL

The warning of the right to remain silent must be accompanied by the explanation that anything said can and will be used against the individual in court. This warning is needed in order to make him aware not only of the privilege, but also of the consequence of forgoing it. It is only through an awareness of these consequences that there can be any assurance of real understanding and intelligent exercise of the privilege. Moreover, this warning may serve to make the individual more acutely aware that he is faced with a phase of the adversary system—that he is not in the presence of persons acting solely in his interest.

RIGHT TO COUNSEL

The circumstances surrounding in-custody interrogation can operate very quickly to overbear the will of one merely made aware of his privilege by his interrogators. Therefore the right to have counsel present at the interrogation is indispensable to the protection of the Fifth Amendment privilege under the system we delineate today.

Accordingly we hold that an individual held for interrogation must be clearly informed that he has right to consult with a lawyer and to have the lawyer with him during interrogation under the system for protecting the privilege we delineate today. As with the warnings of the right to remain silent and that anything stated can be used in evidence against him, this warning is an absolute prerequisite to interrogation. No amount of circumstantial evidence that the person may have been aware of this right will suffice to stand in its stead. Only through such a warning is there ascertainable assurance that the accused was aware of this right.

If an individual indicates that he wishes the assistance of counsel before any interrogation occurs, the authorities cannot rationally ignore or deny his request on the basis that the individual does not have or cannot afford a retained attorney.

An individual need not make a pre-interrogation request for a lawyer. While such request affirmatively secures his right to have one, his failure to ask for a lawyer does not constitute a waiver. No effective waiver of the right to counsel during interrogation can be recognized unless specifically made after the warnings we here delineate have been given. The accused who does not know his rights and therefore does not make a request may be the person who most needs counsel.

COUNSEL FOR THE INDIGENT

In order fully to apprise a person interrogated of the extent of his rights under this system then, it is necessary to warn him not only that he has the right to consult with an attorney, but also that if he is indigent a lawyer will be appointed to represent him. Without this additional warning, the admonition of the right to consult with counsel would often be understood as meaning only that he can consult with a lawyer if he has one or has the funds to obtain one. The warning of a right to counsel would be hollow if not couched in terms that would convey to the indigent—the person most often subjected to interrogation—the knowledge that he too has a right to have counsel present. As with the warnings of the right to remain silent and of the general right to counsel, only by effective and express explanation to the indigent of this right can there be assurance that he was truly in a position to exercise it.

THE WISH TO REMAIN SILENT

Once warnings have been given, the subsequent procedure is clear. If the individual indicates in any manner, at any time prior to or during questioning, that he wishes to remain silent, the interrogation must cease. At this point he has shown that he intends to exercise his Fifth Amendment privilege; any statement taken after the person invokes his privilege cannot be other than the product of compulsion, subtle or otherwise. Without the right to cut off questioning, the setting of in-custody interrogation operates on the individual to overcome free choice in producing a statement after the privilege has been once invoked. If the individual states that he wants an attorney, the interrogation must cease until an attorney is present. At that time, the individual must have an opportunity to confer with the attorney and to have him present during any subsequent questioning. If the individual cannot obtain an attorney and he indicates that he wants one before speaking to police, they must respect his decision to remain silent.

WAIVING ONE'S RIGHTS

If the interrogation continues without the presence of an attorney and a statement is taken, a heavy burden rests on the government to demonstrate that the defendant knowingly and intelligently waived his privilege against self-incrimination and his right to retained or appointed counsel.

An express statement that the individual is willing to make a statement and does not want an attorney followed closely by a statement could constitute a waiver. But a valid waiver will not be presumed simply from the silence of the accused after warnings are given or simply from the fact that a confession was in fact eventually obtained.

Moreover, where in-custody interrogation is involved, there is no room for the contention that the privilege is waived if the individual answers some questions or gives some information on his own prior to invoking his right to remain silent when interrogated.

ADMISSION OF STATEMENTS

The warnings required and the waiver necessary in accordance with our opinion today are, in the absence of a fully effective equivalent, prerequisites to the admissibility of any statement made by a defendant. No distinction can be drawn between statements which are direct confessions and statements which amount to "admissions" of part or all of an offense. The privilege against self-incrimination protects the individual from being compelled to incriminate himself in any manner; it does not distinguish degrees of incrimination. Similarly, for precisely the same reason, no distinction may be drawn between inculpatory statements and statements alleged to be merely "exculpatory." If a statement made were in fact truly exculpatory it would, of course, never be used by the prosecution. In fact, statements merely intended to be exculpatory by the defendant are often used to impeach his testimony at trial or to demonstrate untruths in the statements given under interrogation and thus to prove guilt by implication. These statements are incriminating in any meaningful sense of the word and may not be used without the full warnings and effective waiver required for any other statement.

In dealing with statements obtained through interrogation, we do not purport to find all confessions inadmissible. Confessions remain a proper element in law enforcement. Any statement given freely and voluntarily without any compelling influences is, of course, admissible in evidence. The fundamental import of the privilege while an individual is in custody is not whether he is allowed to talk to the police without the benefit of warnings and counsel, but whether he can be interrogated. There is no requirement that police stop a person who enters a police station and states that he wishes to confess to a crime, or a person who calls the police to offer a confession or any other statement he desires to make. Volunteered statements of any kind are not barred by the Fifth Amendment and their admissibility is not affected by our holding today.

Congressional Action[3]

In 1968, two years after *Miranda*, Congress (as part of a crime control bill) passed a law that applied only to federal prosecutions. The intent was to get around *Miranda* and allow voluntary confessions to be admitted into evidence. In 1997, Attorney General Janet Reno directed federal prosecutors not to argue that *Miranda* warnings can be disregarded, and in a letter to Congress, she stated that the 1968 law was unconstitutional. In 1999, however (31 years after *Miranda*), the 4th Circuit U.S. Court of Appeals permitted the resurrection of the 1968 law that had never been invoked. In a 2-1 ruling, it reaffirmed the admissibility of voluntary confessions. In *United States v. Dickerson*,[4] the defendant had voluntarily confessed to a series of bank robberies, but it was only later that he was read the *Miranda* warnings. Because Justices Scalia and Thomas have expressed doubt about *Miranda*, this case may well be appealed and a reconsideration will result. It will be interesting to see how the Supreme Court deals with the following statement in *Miranda* (see above):

> "Volunteered statements of any kind are not barred by the Fifth Amendment, and their admissibility is not affected by our holding today."

IMPLEMENTING THE MIRANDA WARNINGS

As a means of compliance with the *Miranda* decision many police departments have cards printed that spell out the constitutional rights of the individual (see Figure 12.1). One of these cards may be given to the person in custody, but the officer also must verbally inform the individual of each right. If necessary (owing to some difficulty in language, hearing or intelligence), or if requested, the rights should be explained further to the individual.

WAIVING ONE'S RIGHTS

The concern, first expressed by the police after *Miranda*, that no one would agree to be interrogated is not supported by experience. Fewer individuals exercise their rights than do those who waive them. It is incumbent on the investigator to prove that the person voluntarily and knowingly waived his or her *Miranda* rights and decided to answer questions posed by the investigator. The language of *Miranda* is significant on this point:

> Whatever the testimony of the authorities as to waiver of rights by an accused, the fact of lengthy interrogation or incommunicado incarceration before a statement is made is strong evidence that the accused did not validly waive his rights. In these circumstances the fact that the individual eventually made a statement is consistent with the conclusion that the compelling influence of the interrogation finally forced him to do so. It is inconsistent with any notion of a voluntary relinquishment of the privilege. Moreover, any evidence that the accused was threatened, tricked, or cajoled into a waiver will, of course, show that the defendant did not voluntarily waive his privilege. The requirement of warnings and waiver of rights is a fundamental with respect to the Fifth Amendment privilege and not simply a preliminary ritual to existing methods of interrogation.[5]

1. You have the right to remain silent. This means you do not have to answer any questions.

2. If you answer any question, anything you say can be used against you in court.

3. You have the right to legal counsel. This means you may secure the services of a lawyer of your own choosing and seek his or her advice. You may also have him or her present with you while you are being questioned.

4. If you cannot afford to hire a lawyer, one will be appointed to represent you before any questioning takes place, if you so wish. This will be done without any expense to you.

5. If you decide to answer questions now without a lawyer present, you retain the right to stop answering at any time. At that time you still have the right to seek the advice of a lawyer before continuing to answer questions.

Figure 12.1
Miranda warning form.

Fortunately the Court indicated in its decision that an "express statement that the individual is willing to make a statement and does not want an attorney, followed by a statement" may serve as proof for the waiver of the individual's rights.[6] In practice there are two ways to accomplish this. One is to ask the individual the following questions, each of which must be answered affirmatively:

1. Do you understand each of the rights which has been explained to you and which you have read?

2. Keeping these rights in mind, do you now wish to talk and answer questions regarding _____?

The second method is to obtain a signed, witnessed "waiver of rights" form as shown in Figure 12.2. These should be available in several languages.

INTERROGATION IN PRACTICE

To conduct an interrogation it is important to establish its purpose and be familiar with the underlying principles (as discussed in Chapter 11). In addition, the investigator must be prepared to evaluate the responses throughout the questioning. Finally, if the outcome is a confession, the results must be documented for possible later use in court. Since, on occasion, others besides a suspect are interrogated, the term *subject* will be used below to describe the person being interrogated.

I have had my rights explained to me and have read a statement of them. I understand what my rights are. I do not want an attorney at this time. I know and understand the consequences of what I am doing. I am willing to answer questions and to make a statement. No threats have been made to me. No coercion of pressure of any kind has been exerted against me. No promises have been made to me.

DATE: _____   _____
                                    (Signature)

TIME: _____

LOCATION: _____

WITNESS: _____ DATE: _____

                                          TIME: _____

WITNESS: _____ DATE: _____

                                          TIME: _____

Figure 12.2
"Waiver of rights" form

Preparation

The success of an interrogation rests on several factors, among which preparation is one of the most important. Accordingly, a diligent investigator will:

1. Personally visit the crime scene in important cases, or refresh memory by reviewing the crime scene photographs.

2. Review the entire file so as to be thoroughly familiar with all the details of the case.

3. Be aware of how any physical evidence that was discovered is useful in reconstructing the crime or in connecting a suspect to the crime scene or victim.

4. Learn as much as possible about the subject from his or her family and friends. If the subject's name appears in the records of the department, the facts and circumstances of each and every incident recorded in the files should be studied. Anyone in the department who knows or has had contact with the subject should be queried for any helpful insights they might be able to provide. In addition, anything that is of concern or interest to the subject should be learned. This would include such matters as: What job does he or she hold? Is he or she of a religious bent? Does he or she have hobbies and other interests—such as specific sports played or watched?

5. Ascertain which elements of the crime can be proved by the existing evidence and which still need to be proved. Any possible incriminating facts disclosed by the subject should be followed up, particularly when they relate to those elements still to be proved.

The aim at the outset of such preparation is to get the subject to talk (see Item 4 above) and keep talking. This permits the investigator to question the subject in a logical fashion with the purpose of arriving at the facts, particularly those not yet known (or proven) about the crime.

The Setting

The conduct of an interrogation is best served if the barriers to communication are minimized. The amount of privacy and time, the room arrangement, and the tone set by the investigator can significantly influence the conduct and progress of an interrogation. These and related matters are considered next.

Privacy

A subject in a criminal investigation usually does not wish to be queried in public. Also, as pointed out in Chapter 11, a person is unlikely to confess unless it is made easy to do so. Thus, a private, one-on-one conversation in a setting free from interruption and distraction is especially suitable. Recognizing the need and importance of privacy in "going to confession," the Catholic Church temporarily isolates priest and parishioner in small enclosed stalls called confessionals. It would behoove the police to learn from such time-tested wisdom.

The Room

The room in which an interrogation is conducted should contribute to its success rather than provide distractions that defeat it. Unfortunately, many police departments ignore the importance of having a proper room available for this purpose. A proper room has a decor that precludes distractions of sound or sight. Thus, a sparsely furnished, relatively sound-proof, windowless room with bare walls and subdued light would help to keep the questioning focused and on track.

Seating Arrangements

The arrangement of furniture can facilitate or hamper communication. For example, a judge's bench or that of a desk officer in a police station enhances the superior-subordinate relationship by its elevation, the separation it provides, and its ornateness and spaciousness—thus hampering communication. Even a plain table set between two persons is considered to be a barrier—physical and psychological—to communication. Accordingly, some practitioners believe the furniture in an interrogation room should consist of two chairs, and absolutely nothing else.[7] Others disagree, claiming it would be ridiculous to have a room with just two chairs in it.[8] The chairs should be plain, unpadded, and straight-backed with no arms, with the interrogator's chair four to five inches higher and easily moved. The subject's chair, placed with its back to the door, should be anchored to the floor or otherwise made difficult to move by employing rubber tips on the leg ends.[9]

The purpose is to allow the interrogator to move closer and closer to the suspect as the latter's guilt feelings develop to the point of wanting to confess. Propinquity creating a more intimate relationship, it is easier for the subject to confess.

Viewing, Listening, and Recording Devices

Although the perception of privacy is paramount if a confession is to be obtained, the need to have others witness the interrogation can be met by installing a two-way mirror and a listening device. Having others who are involved in the case observe and listen to the interrogation is a form of insurance that some clue is not missed or not followed up thoroughly by additional questioning. These and other suggestions made to the interrogator during a break (taken for personal and humane reasons) can be invaluable and contribute to an effective interrogation.

Two-Way Mirror: This is a mirror that functions in a normal fashion but also permits viewing through its back side as though it were a pane of glass. By installing it in a medicine chest over a small sink on the side of the room it may go unnoticed and not be a distraction.

Listening Device: A concealed, sensitive, nondirectional microphone, if permitted by law, can be installed to overhear (and record) the conversation in the interrogation room.

Recording Device: There are many methods of recording an interrogation. These will be treated later in this chapter under "Documenting the Interrogation."

Creating the Tone

It is important at the outset to create an atmosphere that will govern the interrogation. This is done with several objectives in mind: to make it easy for the subject to talk (and confess); to establish that you are in control of the questioning; to avoid distractions that allow the subject's mind to stray from the matter at hand; and to prevent interruptions that break the continuity of the narrative description or thought pertaining to the event under investigation.

The importance of the room setting in achieving some of these objectives has already been described. The manner in which the investigator carries and conducts himself or herself is another significant factor in creating the tone that will govern the interrogation. For example, consider the following aspects of an investigator's behavior and how they may influence the outcome of an interrogation.

Dress and Appearance

A decently groomed, conservatively dressed investigator creates a businesslike appearance and a first-impression respect that helps to set the tone of the inquiry. On the other hand, display of police equipment—gun, handcuff, billy club, and the like—

is likely to be counterproductive because of its distractive potential. Similarly, flashy clothing and sloppy appearance are discouraged because of the credibility problem that they may create.

Diction

One's manner of speech and choice of words also have influence over the tone of a conversation. Although good diction is important in many situations, it may be a barrier to communication if the subject comes from a deprived economic class or a different culture. This not-uncommon situation calls for a knowledge of street language, current jargon, and even the argot of professional criminals if the investigator is to understand and be understood. Often it is advisable to soften the terms and words critical to establishing the elements of the crime. Thus the subject "went into" rather than "broke and entered" the apartment. They "took" the television set rather than "stole" it. They are asked "to tell the truth," not "to confess." Employing euphemisms to diminish any harshness that attends the description of the individual's action or crime makes it easier for that person to admit it.

Mannerisms

Any distinctive trait or habit of the investigator that may cause the subject's attention to become unfocused or his or her mind to wander is to be avoided. Blinking the eyes or waving the hands excessively, twitching of the mouth or limbs, doodling, pacing the floor—all are examples of mannerisms that can be counterproductive because they are a source of distraction during interrogation.

Attitude

It is important to establish at the start of the investigation that your job is to investigate the complaint. It is as much your job to prove that a subject was not involved as it is to prove that he or she was. This then is the subject's opportunity to tell his or her story. If a wrong accusation has been made by an accomplice, now is the time to "get the facts out on the table and clear the matter up." Open-mindedness, a willingness to be convinced, and a concern that an innocent person not be unjustly charged are attitudes that should be conveyed by word and deed. With experience, vicarious or personal, an investigator should be able to mention cases in which, though it looked bad in the beginning for a subject, the matter was ended when a little checking established that he or she was telling the truth.

Taking Command of the Situation

An investigator must at all times be in control of the interrogation. It can be lost if the investigator succumbs to his or her emotions (temper, frustration, etc.), has to grope for questions to ask, or allows the subject to take over the session by asking questions in place of answering them. Indeed, it is in just this manner that some subjects are able to ascertain whether the evidence against them is weak or strong. They may also try to defeat the purpose by giving unduly long answers or offering extraneous information. An investigator keeps control not by intimidation (which would be illegal) but rather by "selling" himself or herself to the subject, being on top of the investigation, and using clear thinking that keeps the questions and answers focused on the purpose of the interrogation. Utilizing those factors that are important in creating the tone of the interrogation also helps to establish the investigator as person who is in command of the situation.

Conducting the Interrogation

Preliminaries

Prior to beginning an interrogation, a few preliminary precautions must be observed. The first is concerned with the capacity of the subject to understand and respond rationally to questions. If a subject is intoxicated, under the influence of drugs, or exhibiting any abnormal emotional reactions, there is good reason for not commencing (or continuing) the interrogation. In these circumstances, the advice of a physician may be needed to determine when, and if, the process may begin (or continue) with assurance that the subject's responses will be rational and intelligent.

The second precaution pertains only when the person to be interrogated is a suspect. Surprisingly, there are those who will respond affirmatively if asked whether they committed a particular crime. Captain Robert Borkenstein, as the commanding officer of the Indiana State Police Laboratory—before administering a lie detector test—asked a suspect who had been transported several hundred miles for the test if he was guilty. The response was a quick "yes." Further inquiry by Borkenstein as to why the suspect had not told the investigators who had been with him all day and questioned him earlier evoked a reply that is as surprising as it is instructive: "They didn't ask me." There are more than a few such persons who merely need to be presented with an opportunity to admit their guilt at the outset. Good practice requires that this opportunity be provided for them.

Beginning the Interrogation

After *Miranda* warnings have been given and the suspect has agreed to be questioned, the first few inquiries are directed toward establishing that the suspect can remember, is in touch with reality, and responds rationally. Questions such as the following can be used to accomplish this:

- What is your full name?
- Where are you now?
- What time is it?
- Where do you live?

- Do you have a job?

- What day is it?

- Where do you work?

- Do you know my name?

- Do you know my occupation?

If the answers to these questions indicate that the suspect knows what is going on, he or she should (generally) then be informed of the crime about which he or she is to be questioned, the location and time it happened, and the identity of the victim(s).

The Body of the Interrogation

If a *res gestae* statement implicating the suspect was uttered by the victim, witness, or even the suspect, it is appropriate (usually at the beginning) to make use of it during the interrogation. One may commence by allowing the suspect to offer, without interruption, a statement of his or her involvement or noninvolvement. Ample opportunity must be given the suspect to advance any explanation he or she cares to express. The tack to be taken will vary depending on what has been said and how it squares with the information developed independently during the investigation. If there is a complete denial of having been in contact with the victim or of having been at the crime scene, it is important to establish whether the denial is valid. If a claim is made that there was some previous contact with the victim or the scene, it is important to ascertain when and under what circumstances. If the possibility of a prior contact is denied, the suspect is forestalled from later offering a credible explanation for any evidence—tangible or from an eyewitness—that places him or her at the scene or in contact with the victim. If in making the denial the suspect fails to mention any of the following, it is appropriate to inquire further as to:

- His or her whereabouts at the time of the crime;

- Who he or she was with at the time;

- What he or she was doing at that time;

- Whether there was anyone who had an opportunity to observe him or her at that time, and who they are.

These responses must be verified or determined to be inaccurate. If accurate and they exculpate the suspect, it is appropriate to reevaluate the individual's "suspect" status at this point. If inaccurate, however, the suspect should be asked to explain each discrepancy. For a guilty person this will be difficult to accomplish, and sooner or later it becomes apparent that there is "evidence available against him or her." (See Horowitz, Point 2, in Chapter 11.)

Evaluation of Responses

Throughout the interrogation the manner of response as well as the answers must be evaluated. A talent for good analytical thinking, an ability to read *body language* (i.e., to recognize nonverbal cues), and the knowledge and experience needed to recognize signs of lying—these provide the means for detecting whether a subject is telling the truth, stretching it, or lying. The physiological symptoms of lying are known to many because almost everyone has had the experience of telling a lie. Even for a minor falsehood, some persons blush, develop sweaty palms, experience an increased heart rate, have trouble looking the other person in the eye, or display signs of uneasiness such as a twitching of the cheek or licking of the lips. A major lie exacerbates these symptoms and adds at least three others:

1. Just as experiencing an intense emotion can give one a "lump in the throat" so can a lie affect the larynx or "Adam's apple", causing it to move up and down excessively.

2. The carotid arteries in the neck stand out and can be noticed throbbing.

3. The mouth becomes dry, apparently by inhibiting the salivary glands. To relieve this condition the subject may try to wet the lips, work cheeks and tongue to produce saliva, or ask for a glass of water.

It hardly requires mention that these symptoms do not constitute legal evidence. It should also be pointed out that, perhaps with the exception of mouth dryness, these symptoms to a lesser degree can be caused by nervousness. Because most persons suspected of a crime and being interrogated about it are likely to be nervous, there is a question as to the degree of manifestation of the symptoms. With experience, an investigator often can detect the difference between the signs of "normal" nervousness and those caused by "guilty knowledge."

An invitation to take a lie detector (polygraph) test may be appropriate at the point when these symptoms appear or perhaps after the subject has been caught making contradictory statements that have been pointed out but remain unexplained.

The "Break"

Although not a part of Horowitz's analysis of why people confess, it is appropriate to discuss what in police circles is called "the break." The symptoms of lying (already described) may be part of the *break*, i.e., the point in the interrogation at which the investigator recognizes that the person is about to confess. Such recognition is the result of experience but it manifests itself in several ways. Some early signs include the cessation of denial of involvement in, or commission of, the crime, and the repetition of phrases like "not that I remember." Such behavior might be followed by "What if" questions such as "What if a person didn't intend to _____?" or "What if this is the first time?" or "I have never been in trouble before; wouldn't that be taken into consideration?" Other signs consist of a display of uneasiness: shifting the body in the chair frequently; chain smoking when otherwise a light smoker; casting the eyes on the floor; and so on. It is at this point that the individual needs to be shown gently that confession is the way out (Horowitz, Point 5).

Documenting the Interrogation

On the assumption that Horowitzian and Pavlovian principles have been employed where appropriate and a confession has been made, it is important to document that it was not obtained as a result of coercion or duress, that it was freely and voluntarily made, and that it is trustworthy.

Recording the Confession

Perhaps the most suitable means for demonstrating that an interrogation was conducted using civilized police practices and that the confession is trustworthy and voluntary is to record the session with video-sound tape. Advances in television equipment (e.g., a camcorder) and reusable tape, have made this technologically and financially feasible. As yet, however, not many police departments have adopted this practice.

Another method is to record the interrogation by means of an audiotape recorder. Both videotape and audiotape must be treated in the same fashion as any other physical evidence, i.e., their identification and custody must be considered. In order to introduce such evidence in court there are additional requirements as to how the tape is made. These may be found in some state court decisions. The following guidelines cover the key points:

1. The tape recorder must be capable of recording conversation; a camcorder must be able to record visually in addition to recording conversation.

2. The operator must be competent.

3. The recording must be authentic and correct.

4. No changes, additions, or deletions may be made in the tape.

5. The operator should state at the beginning of the tape the time it began running and the recorder should be left on at all times during the interrogation. The time when the tape ends (or stops) must also be stated for the record. Compliance with this recommendation, however, is not always feasible. For example, some suspects state to detectives that they will not confess while the video camera (or tape recorder) is running.

6. If the tape breaks during the recording, it should not be spliced. A new tape should be started, with a new time of beginning and ending.

Concern has been expressed about individuals who were put on trial and found guilty by a jury but, then, years later had their convictions overturned when a court ruled they had been falsely accused and convicted. Just as false (often coerced) confessions play a major role in these cases, so does DNA evidence, but to impugn the confession and throw out the conviction.

A *Chicago Tribune* editorial, "False Confessions Don't Solve Crimes," elucidates:

> Three murder cases have been dismissed in Cook County in the past two weeks, amid allegations of police brutality and coerced confessions. . . .
>
> The latest to be dismissed involves [L.G.], 17 years old at the time of his 1997 arrest for murder. The heart of his case was a confession that he alleges Chicago police detectives beat out of him.
>
> . . . county prosecutors dropped murder charges against [R.J.], who had been sentenced to death in 1989 also largely on the basis of an allegedly coerced confession. [He] is the twelfth person in as many years in Illinois to be sentenced to die and later cleared. . . .[10]

An apparent solution to the confession problem is offered in another *Tribune* editorial:

> From now on, the state's attorney's office and the Chicago police will videotape confessions, but only in homicide cases and with the suspect's permission.[11]

That the solution proposed is not as plausible as it would seem is evident in the evaluation of videotaping in criminal investigation commissioned by the National Institute of Justice (NIJ).[12] NIJ's preliminary report (issued in 1993) covered the following:

Types of cases videotaped

Overt vs. covert taping

Full interrogation vs. recaps

Videotaping and the quality of interrogation

      —Suspects' willingness to talk

      —Type of information obtained

      —Interrogation techniques

      —Claims of misconduct

Effects of videotaping on charges

Case preparation and plea negotiations

      —Prosecutors' views

      —Defense attorneys' views

      —Prosecution and defense access to tapes

Procedural issues of videotaping

Videotapes in the courtroom

A consensus favoring videotaping[13]

The first and last of these findings will be elaborated on.

Types of Cases Videotaped

Although 57,000 criminal cases involving videotaped suspects' statements were examined, an endnote cautions: "As a result, the findings of this national survey . . . must be taken as preliminary."[14] Even so, the results disclose that 83 percent of agencies videotaped statements in homicide cases. The practice is also utilized in many other crime cases, but usage decreases as seriousness decreases; for example: rape (77%); aggravated battery or assault (71%); armed robbery (61%); drunk driving (59%); unarmed robbery (45%); burglary (44%); and other property crimes (34%).[15]

A Consensus Favoring Videotaping

Geller states that on the basis of this exploratory study, videotaping appears to be a distinctly useful tool. "It is seen as simultaneously furthering the criminal justice system's pursuit of disparate objectives. . . . a striking 97 percent of all departments that have ever videotaped suspects' statements continue to find such videotaping, on balance, to be useful. Likewise, agencies visited were asked, knowing what they know of videotaping now, if they would do it again. Every agency said yes."[16]

Reducing the Confession to Writing

If the interrogation and confession have not been recorded according to these guidelines, it is wise to obtain, if possible, a confession written in the suspect's hand. Although less desirable, it can also be dictated to a stenographer. If dictated it must be typed and signed, or if the suspect is unwilling to sign the document, acknowledged by the suspect as his or her statement before a witness.

Prior to *Miranda,* many recommendations were made by textbook writers that involved the investigator in structuring the confession statement. In the post-*Miranda* era, these older practices are considered to be undesirable because they may affect the credibility of the document. Jurors, for example, may find it difficult to believe that in a free and voluntarily statement a person is likely to ensure that he or she has covered each and every element of the crime in his or her narration. Similarly, there is criticism of the use of the question-and-answer form of confession. Some believe there is too great a possibility of controlling the suspect's story and influencing the suspect's answers through suggestive questions.

Witnessing the Confession

After a confession acknowledging guilt, many persons experience a quieting effect and peace of mind. By the time a statement is put in writing, a witness to its signing can often be brought in without objection from the suspect. If possible, for reasons of credibility, it is best to have a disinterested citizen serve as witness; if not, a civilian member of the department should be used. As a last resort, another sworn member in addition to the investigator may serve as a witness to the signing.

It is important that the address of the witness and a typed (or printed) spelling of their name be obtained in addition to a signature. Sworn members of the force may use title, badge number, and assignment in lieu of a street address.

Time and Personal Needs Register

The time an interrogation commenced and any recesses taken to attend to the personal needs of the suspect should be recorded. Personal needs include such things as food and drink, use of the toilet, telephoning, and smoking. If interrogation sessions are taped, this information should automatically be made part of the tape recording. Some departments also use a "Time and Personal Needs Register" to refute an allegation of coercion or duress that might be raised subsequently. If food and drink are purchased for the suspect, it is advisable to obtain a receipt for the purchase and to ask the cashier to write on it the name of the purchaser and the person for whom it is being purchased, together with the restaurant and cashier's name, the date, and the time.

REFERENCES

1   *Miranda v. Arizona*, 384 U.S. 436 (1966) at 444.

2   Ibid., 467-478.

3   *New York Times*, Feb. 11, 1999, A, 1:1.

4   *United States v. Dickerson*, 166 F.3d 667 (4th Cir. 1999).

5   *Miranda, op. cit.*, 476.

6   *Miranda, op. cit.*, 475.

7   Richard O. Arther and Rudolph R. Caputo, *Interrogation for Investigators* (New York: William C. Copp and Associates, 1959), 7.

8   Clifford H. Van Meter, *Principles of Police Interrogation* (Springfield, IL: Charles C Thomas, 1973), 56.

9   Arther and Caputo, *op. cit.*, 8-9.

10   *Chicago Tribune*, 24 May 1999, 14.

11   *Chicago Tribune*, 3 October 1998, 22.

12   William A. Geller, *Videotaping Interrogations and Confessions.* (Washington, DC: Dept. of Justice, National Institute of Justice) March1993.

13   Ibid., 2-10

14   *Loc. cit.*, note 1.

15   *Loc. cit.*, 3.

16   *Loc. cit.*, 10.

SUPPLEMENTAL READINGS _____
Interrogation

Aubry, Arthur S., Jr., and Rudolph R. Caputo. *Criminal Interrogation*. 3rd ed. Springfield, IL: Charles C Thomas, 1980.

Fisher, Ronald P. *An R.E. Geiselman Memory-Enhancing Technique for Investigative Interviewing; the Cognitive Interview*. Text Ed., Springfield, IL: Thomas, 1992.

Gudjonsson, Gisli H. *The Psychology of Interrogations, Confessions, and Testimony*. Text Ed., New York: Wiley, 1992.

Hess, John E. *Interviewing and Interrogation for Law Enforcement*. Cincinnati: Anderson, 1997.

Inbau, F.E. *Criminal Investigation and Confessions*. 3rd ed. Baltimore: Williams & Wilkins, 1985.

McDonald, Hugh C. *The Practical Psychology of Police Interrogation*. Santa Ana, CA: Townsend, 1963.

Macdonald, John M., and David L. Michaud. *Criminal Interrogation,* Rev. & Enl. ed. Denver: Apache Press, 1992.

Rabon, Don. *Interviewing and Interrogation*. Durham, NC: Carolina Academic Press.

Royal Commission on Criminal Procedure. *Police Interrogation*. Research Studies, Nos. 2 and 4. London: Her Majesty's Stationery Office, 1980.

Zulawski, David E., and Douglas E. Wicklander, eds. *Practical Aspects of Interview and Interrogation*. Boca Raton, FL: CRC Press, 1993.

Nonverbal Communication

Archer, Dane. *How to Expand Your Social Intelligence Quotient*. New York: M. Evans and Company, 1980.

Kuhlman, Merlin S. "Nonverbal Communications in Interrogation." *FBI Law Enforcement Bulletin* 49:11 (November 1980), 6-9.

Detection of Deception

Ekman, P., and M.V. Friesen. "Leakage and Clues to Deception." *Psychiatry* 32 (1969), 88-106.

Ferguson, Robert J. *The Scientific Informer*. Springfield, IL: Charles C Thomas, 1971.

Lykken, David T. *A Tremor in the Blood: Uses and Abuses of the Lie Detector*. New York: McGraw-Hill, 1981.

Matte, J.A. *Art and Science of the Polygraph Technique*. Springfield, IL: Charles C Thomas, 1980.

Murphy, J.K. "The Polygraph Technique: Past and Present," *FBI Law Enforcement Bulletin* 49:6 (June 1980), 1-5.

Nizer, Louis. "How to Tell a Liar," in *Reflections Without Mirrors*. Garden City, NY: Doubleday, 1978.

Reid, John E., and F.E. Inbau. *Truth and Deception: The Polygraph Technique*. 2nd ed. Woburn, MA: Butterworth, 1977.

SECTION II

APPLYING THE PRINCIPLES TO CRIMINAL INVESTIGATION

Most working detectives hold that their work is unique, that few tasks even come close. The authors of this text, on the other hand, maintain that the criminal investigator's job is simply another kind of inquiry—a reconstruction of the past. Because others with a similar concern for the past (ranging from historians to geologists) employ the scientific method in their endeavors, so too must the detective. Section II, therefore, opens with a general treatment of methods of inquiry, the use of induction and deduction in scientific reasoning, and the sources of information available for reconstructing past events. The section deals with the investigation of some of the more common penal law crimes (i.e., those against the person, those against property). Categorizing crimes in this way may well be useful for didactic reasons, but the distinction fades when subjected to more careful analysis: a burglar's aim is to steal property of value in order to then pawn or sell it, yet a person feels not only its loss but also a sense of having been violated; likewise, arson adversely affects individuals directly or through increased insurance rates, just as homicide seriously affects individuals as well as their loved ones.

When perusing the chapters in this section, the reader will quickly note that motive is very important to the development of suspects. For some crimes, however, ascertaining motive can be difficult. For instance, arson is generally committed for several reasons; therefore, in any treatment of criminal investigation, it is necessary to expand on the motivation a perpetrator might have had for committing the crime. Despite the fact that it can often be the key to the solution of crimes, motive is seldom treated in criminal investigation texts, except with regard to the informant looking for monetary or other compensation from the police.

There are two kinds of motive: general and specific. A general motive is one that applies to most—if not all—offenders; for example, the burglar or robber looking for profit with the least effort. A specific motive is one that relates the offender to the victim or object of the crime, which has been selected for a specific reason. An example might be the owner of a business who has lost customers to a competitor and "arranges" to burn down the rival's building.

With a specific motive established, a list of potential suspects can be compiled through the process of deduction. Using this as the generalization, the particulars (a list of individuals perceived to have such a motive) can be compiled. The list may then be shortened by determining who had the opportunity with respect to time and place, and who possessed the temperament to commit the crime or arrange for its commission. Although motive is not an element that must be proved in court, juries feel more comfortable about convicting a defendant who can be shown to have one. Consequently, establishing a particularized motive has both investigative and probative significance.

Without a particularized motive, the investigation of crimes having a universal motive (for example, rape and robbery) is rendered more difficult. A compensation, however, is the fact that these crimes often have an eyewitness. Except in cases of date rape, this is apt to be more useful in proving guilt than in identifying and apprehending the perpetrator.

This section emphasizes investigative activities that point to likely suspects, to the honing of any list developed, and to the search for additional evidence. Depending on what any new evidence supports or fails to support, the original hypothesis regarding the suspect(s) is either enhanced, downgraded, or rejected.

Considerably more space is allotted to homicide than to other crimes because:

1. It has a greater impact on a community than does any other felony; the public expects this crime to be handled competently and expeditiously.

2. It is the ultimate challenge to an investigator, demanding the highest professional standards if the case is to be proved in court.

3. Success in solving homicide requires familiarity with all possible investigative moves; each new development calls for an evaluation of the next step to be taken.

4. The skills acquired in solving a homicide can serve well when applied to other crimes.

CHAPTER 13

Reconstructing the Past

Methods, Evidence, Examples

METHODS OF INQUIRY

It brings insight to divide the principal methods of inquiry into two broad, distinct categories: those that reconstruct the past and those that discover or create new knowledge. The first is the method of the historian, archeologist, epidemiologist, journalist, and criminal investigator; the second, that of the scientist in general (as well as the creative artist). Although usefully stated as a dichotomy for the sake of a conceptual distinction, these methods finally fuse in the minds of the better thinkers and practitioners, for the reconstruction of the past often makes use of the scientific method, while science and art build on and digress from the past. Further reflection suggests that any thorough inquiry employs techniques common to both. This certainly applies to the best practice in criminal investigation. Disciplines as diverse as geology, physical geography, physical anthropology, forensic medicine, statistics, and criminalistics can make a contribution. Indeed, the discrete methods they employ may be seen as a continuum, with the ideal drawing on history, science, and art in varying proportions depending on the subject under probe. Therefore, just as the model investigation must utilize both principal methods of inquiry, so must the model investigator. This is not to say that a unique investigative technique may not be developed to deal with a specific problem, and be helpful with others as well. For testing the authenticity of a confession for example, the tools of psycholinguistics could be put to use. That they have not (thus far) indicates the wide range of resources yet to be tapped by criminal investigators.

As the work of Sanders[1] and Winks[2] indicates, scholars are aware of the extension of their methods to criminal investigation. They see the parallels between the ivory-towered inquirer and society's more familiar figure, the detective: both study human behavior and both employ information-gathering practices such as interviews and observations. Sanders recognizes that the sociologist can learn from the detective, among other things, how to combine several methods of inquiry (or research) and sources of information (or data) into a single inquiry. Winks's selection of essays by writers and historians reveals how scholars penetrate rumors, forgeries, false accounts, and misleading clues to unravel old mysteries. Not only do the essays "point up the elements of evidence within them to emphasize leads and clues, straight tips, false rumors, and the mischief wrought by time," they demonstrate that the historian and detective are on common ground when confronting the techniques and pitfalls of dealing with evidence.[3]

> The historian must collect, interpret, and then explain his evidence by methods which are not greatly different from those techniques employed by the detective, or at least the detective of fiction. . . . Perhaps the real detective trusts more to luck, or to gadgetry, or to informers than does the fictional hero. . . . Much of the historian's work then, like that of the insurance investigator, the fingerprint man, or the coroner, may to the outsider seem to consist of deadening routine . . . yet the routine must be pursued or the clue may be missed, the apparently false trail must be followed in order to be certain it is false; the mute witnesses must be asked the reasons for their silence, for the piece of evidence that is missing from where one might reasonably expect to find it is, after all, a form of evidence itself. . . . We are all detectives, of course, in that at one time or another we all have had to engage in some genuine deductive routine. Each day we do so, if only in small ways. By the same token, we are all historians, in that we reconstruct past events from present evidence, and perhaps we build usable generalizations upon those reconstructions.[4]

Attention will now be turned to the scientific method; then to the means for reconstructing the past.

The Scientific Method

Evolving from the efforts of many workers over the course of several thousand years, the scientific method is a way of observing, thinking about, and solving problems objectively and systematically. As the prestigious nineteenth-century student of science Thomas Huxley emphasized, its use is not limited to scientists. A lesson Huxley learned early was "to make things clear," and his easy, plain-talking style in the opening paragraphs of this piece serves well as an introduction to the scientific method.

> The method of scientific investigation is nothing but the expression of the necessary mode of working of the human mind. It is simply the mode by which all phenomena are reasoned about, rendered precise and exact. There is no more difference, but there is just the same kind of difference, between the mental operations of a man of science and those of an ordinary person, as there is between the operations and methods of a baker or of a butcher weighing out his goods in common scales, and the operations of a chemist in performing a difficult and complex analysis by means of his balance and finely graduated weights. It is not that the action of the scales in the one case, and the balance in the other, differ in the principles of their construction or manner of working; but the beam of one is set on an infinitely finer axis than the other, and of course turns by the addition of a much smaller weight. You will understand this better, perhaps, if I give you some familiar example. You have

all heard it repeated, I dare say, that men of science work by means of induction and deduction, and that by the help of these operations, they, in a sort of sense, wring from nature certain other things, which are called natural laws, and causes, and that out of these, by some cunning skill of their own, they build up hypotheses and theories. And it is imagined by many, that the operations of the common mind can be by no means compared with these processes, and that they have to be acquired by a sort of special apprenticeship to the craft. To hear all these large words, you would think that the mind of a man of science must be constituted differently from that of his fellow men; but if you will not be frightened by terms, you will discover that you are quite wrong, and that all these terrible apparatus are being used by yourselves every day and every hour of your lives.

There is a well-known incident in one of Molière's plays,* where the author makes the hero express unbounded delight on being told that he had been talking prose during the whole of his life. In the same way, I trust, that you will take comfort, and be delighted with yourselves, on the discovery that you have been acting on the principles of inductive and deductive philosophy during the same period. Probably there is not one here who has not in the course of the day had occasion to set in motion a complex train of reasoning, of the very same kind, though differing of course in degree, as that which a scientific man goes through in tracing the causes of natural phenomena.

A very trivial circumstance will serve to exemplify this. Suppose you go into a fruiterer's shop, wanting an apple—you take up one, and, on biting into it, you find it is sour; you look at it and see that it is hard and green. You take up another one, and that too is hard, green, and sour. The shopman offers you a third; but, before biting it, you examine it, and find that it is hard and green, and you immediately say that you will not have it, as it must be sour, like those that you have already tried.

Nothing can be more simple than that, you think; but if you take the trouble to analyze and trace out into its logical elements what has been done by the mind, you will be greatly surprised. In the first place, you have performed the operation of induction.[5]

Definitions

Before proceeding to an example of the scientific method in criminal investigation, several terms require definition. They are: induction, deduction, classification, synthesis, analysis, hypothesis, theory, *a priori*, and *a posteriori*.

Induction is a process of reasoning based on a set of experiences or observations (particulars) from which a conclusion or generalization is drawn. It commences with the specific and goes to the general. As to the result secured, however, care must be exercised. This warning is implicit in Huxley's "sour apple" lesson. For another illustration, consider the man who notes that of the 10 species of bird he has observed, all are able to fly. When he induces from this observation that all birds fly, he will be incorrect. Though not

---

*Le Bourgeois Gentilhomme

always recognized as such, the penguin is a bird. At one time, its short paddles covered with hard, close-set feathers served as wings. Now, it moves swiftly and gracefully through water, having over the eons become adapted to this medium; the penguin does not fly. The ostrich is another example of the fallacious conclusion that all birds fly. The wings of this huge bird, formed like those of its flying ancestors, are extended when running, but because their length-to-body weight ratio and flight muscles are insufficient, the power of flight has been lost. Induction, therefore, can lead to probabilities, not certainties. When integrated over a lifetime, however, inductive experience is an important component of the so-called common sense which supposedly governs human behavior.

Deduction is a process of reasoning that commences with a generalization or a premise and by means of careful, systematic thinking moves to a particular fact or consequence. For example, if one begins with the statement that "All persons convicted of a serious crime are felons," (the major premise) then adds the fact that "Jack was convicted of a serious crime" (the minor premise), that "Jack is a felon" (the conclusion) may be deduced. This is a syllogism, a form of deductive reasoning that moves from the general to the specific. If the original premise is valid, the logical consequences must be valid. In logic (the science of correct reasoning), deduction leads to certainties and not to probabilities; in criminal investigation, the generalization cannot be so precisely formulated as to always be relied upon as valid. Only in fiction is a Sherlock Holmes able, after a quick glance at the mud on the butler's shoe, to state unequivocally that it originated from but one meadow. In the real world, the criminal investigator cannot mouth certitudes while an awed partner (like Dr. Watson) stands by and accepts them on faith. Because of the illogical, often perverse quality of human behavior, deduction does not necessarily lead to certainty.

Classification is the systematic arrangement of objects into categories (groups or classes) based on shared traits or characteristics. The objects in each category, having one or more traits in common, are chosen to suit the classifier's purposes. They may be natural (in accord with the observed order of things), logical, or even purely arbitrary. The science of classification is called *taxonomy*. Biology has developed a taxonomy to classify organisms; chemistry, to analyze compounds; law enforcement, to file fingerprints, bullets, laundry marks, dry cleaner marks, a wide range of typefaces, and automobile paints.

Synthesis is the combining of separate parts or elements. For purposes of criminal investigation, those elements that, when combined, provide a coherent view of the crime and its solution, are: the evidence provided by witnesses, forensic examinations, and the facts disclosed by records.

Analysis starts with the whole (whether a material substance, thought, or impression), and then involves an effort to separate the whole into its constituent parts for individual study. Hence, on being assigned to investigate a crime, the investigator seeks relevant information from three separate sources—people, records, and the physical evidence found at the crime scene.

A *hypothesis* is a conjecture that provisionally accounts for a set of facts. It can be used as the basis for additional investigation and as a guide for further activity. Since it is an assertion or tentative guess subject to verification, the pursuit of more evidence is required of the detective (or scientist). Along the way, the hypothesis may have to be adjusted, causing the investigation (or inquiry) to change direction depending on whether the original conjecture is substantiated or disproved as new facts are uncovered. As corroborating data accumulate and are analyzed, the hypothesis moves toward the next phase of proof—a theory.

A *theory* is a somewhat verified hypothesis, a scheme of thought with assumptions chosen to fit empirical knowledge or observations. As a theory becomes more solidly based and evidence accumulates, it evolves into a methodical organization of knowledge applicable to any number of situations. It should predict or otherwise explain the nature of a specified set of phenomena. The ultimate theory presents a grand conceptual scheme that both predicts *and* explains, while keeping assumptions as few and as general as possible. In science, the ultimate is often achieved; in criminal investigation, a less decisive "somewhat verified hypothesis" is the best that can be expected at the present time.

A *priori* (Latin for "from the previous cause") is defined: from a known or assumed cause to a necessarily related effect; from a general law to a particular instance; valid independently of observation. In some instances, *a priori* conclusions are reached through reasoning from assumed principles, which are regarded as self-evident. Thus, it is deductive and theoretical rather than based on experiment or experience.

A *posteriori* is a term denoting reasoning from empirical facts or particulars (acquired through experience or experiment) to general principles; or, from effects to causes. It is inductive.

Problem Identification

The first step in reconstructing the past or unraveling the mysteries of the universe is to identify the problem. Although the techniques and methods for problem-solving have been systematized as the scientific method, the state of affairs regarding problem identification—namely, recognizing what it is, precisely—is less than satisfactory. Indeed, operational research, which is concerned with correctly stating the problem to be studied, was conceived of in England by scientist J.D. Bernal when he solved a problem submitted by the military during World War II. Informed that his solution did not work, Bernal investigated further only to find that although he had solved the problem given him, it was not what was actually troubling the military. Painstakingly, he was obliged to reformulate and restate the problem for them before the solution could be applied.

Texts dealing with public relations reveal that problem identification is a major concern. It begins with an interview of the client to ascertain what the problem is believed to be. Then, a search of the literature is made to learn more about the apparent issues. Finally, there is an attempt to restate the problem. This procedure is the basis on which an effective public relations program can be developed.[6] Although problem identification is seldom the concern of the criminal investigator, the problem statement pertains to two situations in the criminal justice system. One occurs when a crime is committed on the borderline of two jurisdictions; the other, when it is difficult to determine what crime was committed. If it is a question of jurisdiction, an investigator may either seek to obtain the case, or convince the investigator working the other jurisdiction to accept it. The choice can depend on several factors: Is the case likely to be publicized? Is it inherently interesting or important? Is there a chance to make a "good arrest"? As to determining what crime was committed, this is usually quite simple because the elements of major crimes (burglary, robbery, murder, manslaughter, assault, rape, and arson) are well-known to the experienced investigator. The advice of legal counsel is advisable, however, when the determination is a complicated one: Is it a case of extortion or third-degree robbery? In crimes involving consent, was consent granted or withheld? Does the mere scorching of the paint on a house, without fire, satisfy an element of arson?

SCIENTIFIC REASONING APPLIED TO A CRIMINAL INVESTIGATION

The use of the scientific method in criminal investigation is illustrated by the following situation, based on an actual case. A detective, called to the scene where a young woman had been murdered in her apartment, found the table set for two. There were melted-down candles, wine, supper still warm on the serving cart, and a radio softly playing. Finding no evidence of forced entry or struggle, the detective hypothesized that the woman admitted the killer into her home, probably as her dinner guest. In subsequent questioning of the victim's family, friends, and business associates, one name, that of her former lover, continually surfaced; indeed, several people indicated that his earlier behavior during a quarrel had been forgiven, and that this was to have been a reconciliation dinner.

The hypothesis that the killer was an invited guest is somewhat verified by the facts obtained through interviews. Needing additional information, however, the investigator must consider the following possibilities: Can the friend be located at his place of business, home, or other usual haunts? Is flight indicated? If so, is any clothing or other item such as a prized trophy or razor missing? Did the suspect cash a large check or withdraw money from his bank the day of or on the morning following the homicide? If affirmative answers are obtained and applied inductively, the weight of evidence in support of the hypothesis is even greater. The former lover may now be considered the prime suspect (the generalization). An inductive result, however, is not necessarily a certainty: flight may be evidence of guilt, but it is not proof. The suspect could have innocently gone on a vacation at what would, in retrospect, have been an inopportune time. Assuming that information from relatives and friends has failed to trace him, the homicide investigator must now discover his whereabouts.

The next logical step in the investigative process is deduction. The characterization of the lover as the prime suspect (the generalization) leads to the question: "Where would he be likely to flee?" (answers to which are the particulars). Possible locations are suggested by such considerations as: Where was the suspect born? Had he lived for a time in some other area? Has he a favorite vacation spot? With additional facts or details elicited, investigative activities will seek answers (again, particulars) to other questions, such as: What else might he do to earn a living? Who might he write or telephone? Will he try to collect his last pay check either by mail or other means? Will he continue to pay union dues? Will he change his driver's license? A sufficient amount of acquired and utilized facts (particulars) should allow the investigator to come to a generalization through the process of inductive reasoning. The generalization about the likely whereabouts or location of the subject permits the investigator to deduce the particulars (such as addresses) needed to apprehend the suspect. Again, reasonable premises (e.g., that suspects will turn up at their usual haunts) may prove to be invalid because of the illogical, often perverse aspects of human behavior.

In summary, the cyclical process of scientific reasoning—moving from induction to deduction, and vice-versa—is applicable to criminal investigation as a means of reconstructing past events. A noted philosopher of science, Hans Reichenbach, recognized the similarities in the thought process shared by scientist and detective:

> I should like to mention the inferences made by a detective in his search for the perpetrator of a crime. Some data are given such as a blood-stained handkerchief, a chisel, and the disappearance of a wealthy dowager, and several explanations offer themselves for what has happened.
>
> The detective tries to determine the most probable explanation. His considerations follow established rules of probability; using all the factual clues and all his knowledge of human psychology, he attempts to arrive at conclusions, which in turn are tested by new observations specifically planned for this purpose. Each test, based on new material, increases or decreases the probability of the explanation; but never can the explanation constructed be regarded as absolutely certain.[7]

RECONSTRUCTING THE PAST: SOURCES OF INFORMATION

The information needed to reconstruct the past is available through three sources: people, physical evidence, and records. Historians' efforts to shed light on the distant past are largely confined to researching records. Art and epic poems (physical evidence) and folk tales (people) are also researched. Criminal investigators, more concerned with the immediate past, often put all three sources to use. Table 13.1 summarizes and compares the sources of the historian and the criminal investigator.

People

As long as general, specific, or intimate knowledge concerning an individual endures, it can be acquired by those who know how. People are social beings, and information on them can usually be found in the possession of family and relatives, work or business associates, and others who share their recreational interests. It can also be picked up accidentally through those who were witness to, or the victim of, a crime. The careful investigator identifies and exploits all potential sources. Some people will talk willingly; some will be reluctant to disclose what they know. Investigators must learn how to overcome resistance and retrieve facts that were overlooked, forgotten, or thought not important enough to mention. Meanwhile, they must guard against deliberate distortions or attempts to mislead, thwarting such maneuvers through skillful questioning. Talking with people and unobtrusively observing them and the places they frequent may be useful. In addition to surveillance, tips or decisive information furnished by informants can be significant in moving an investigation toward a conclusion.

Source of Information		Ancillary Disciplines Available to Assist In the Study of a Past Event	
History	Criminal Investigation	History	Criminal Investigation
Physical Evidence		**Physical Evidence**	
1. Fossils 2. Bones 3. Human remains	1. Impressions (finger, tool, tire, shoe) 2. Narcotics 3. Paint 4. Bullets 5. Blood 6. Flora	1. Paleontology 2. Geology 3. Zoology 4. Physical Anthropology 5. Archaeology	1. Criminalistics 2. Chemistry 3. Physics 4. Immunology 5. Botany
Records and Documents		**Records and Documents**	
1. Memoirs 2. Letters 3. Official documents 4. Manuscripts 5. Books 6. Paintings, other artwork 7. Coins 8. Epic poems	1. Fraudulent checks 2. Threatening notes 3. Kidnap letters 4. Miscellaneous documents	1. Paleography 2. Art History 3. Linguistics 4. Numismatics 5. Information theory—storage and retrieval	1. Criminalistics 2. Questioned document expertise 3. Photography
People		**People**	
1. Folklore 2. Cultural survivals	1. Victim 2. Eyewitnesses 3. Suspects 4. Others related to victim, suspects, and crime scene	1. Cultural Anthropology 2. Ethnology	Techniques rather than disciplines are available. 1. Questioning 2. Surveillance 3. Use of informants

Table 13.1
**History and Criminal Investigation as Methods of Study of Past Events:
Sources of Information Common to Both; Available Ancillary Disciplines**

Physical Evidence

Any object of a material nature is potential physical evidence. The scientific specialties that undertake most examinations of physical evidence are forensic medicine and criminalistics. Their purpose being the acquisition of facts, the following questions arise: What is this material? If found at a crime scene, can it be linked to, or help exonerate, a suspect? Can it be used to reconstruct what happened (especially when witnesses give conflicting accounts)? In a homicide, what was the cause of death?

In the conduct of everyday affairs, people employ physical evidence in decisionmaking, but few note this fact. For example, when looking for a house they will examine the condition of the paint, plaster, and plumbing; determine its location relative to transportation, schools, and churches; then inspect the surrounding neighborhood. The ultimate decision is based to a large extent on this kind of evidence; indeed, it is the way many day-to-day decisions are made.

Records

Records are a form of physical evidence. They receive separate treatment in this text, however, because they are widely scattered, voluminous, and have specialists devoting full time to their storage and retrieval. Modern society relies on paper records by storing the information collected day in and day out. Later this can prove useful in a criminal investigation. For example, telephone company records of toll calls can establish that two people who deny any relationship had indeed been in communication. Records need not be printed or handwritten. They may be stored on film, tape, or computer disc or hard drive; for example, the White House tapes that provided the "smoking gun" evidence in the Watergate cover-up.[8] This case clearly demonstrates the power of physical evidence over verbal testimony. In this light, it is difficult to understand the federal government's failure to support teaching and research in the forensic sciences (through the Law Enforcement Assistance Administration), despite having well over a billion dollars to spend for "law and order" in the first decade of LEAA's brief existence.

Innovative Applications

History and archeology are academic disciplines that reconstruct the past through information from people, physical evidence, and records. Some unusual investigative efforts employing classical techniques have gained attention in the press as well as in scholarly literature. They demonstrate that the means for reconstructing the remote past are applicable to the immediate past. Hence, criminal investigation is not unique; it shares the approaches sanctioned by scholars in established disciplines. The following examples will illustrate.

Industrial Archeology

Uncovering traces of an ancient civilization in a temple or amphitheater sounds more romantic than finding what remains of an old factory. Yet the classical techniques of archeology are now being used

> . . . to discover and record how American industry moved from colonial cottages to the vast mechanized and automated complex it is today. Although the industrial revolution began in the U.S. only about 200 years ago, there already are tremendous gaps in the knowledge of how it occurred.
>
> Records and artifacts of entire industrial processes, including some in use as recently as the 1920s, either have been lost or, often, were never made. And the machines and buildings that would give clues to how an industry evolved are rapidly being destroyed or buried by parking lots, housing developments and new factories. If Patterson (New Jersey) is any indication, American cities are being buried several times faster than ancient Troy; the archaeologists in Patterson found foundations barely a century old at depths of eight to twelve feet. . . . It took over 5000 years for fifty feet of debris to build up over ancient Troy.[9]

Lest such behavior be thought of as that of a few eccentric archaeologists, it is significant that Rensselaer Polytechnic Institute has set up the Institute of Industrial Archeology, and the first book on the subject was published in 1972.[10]

Garbage-ology

Another contemporary form of archeology is *garbage-ology*, the "science of rubbish" or the study of garbage, in which the University of Arizona began to offer credit courses in 1971.[11] Discarded material can be revealing when analyzing present-day consumer trends. So too are the different facets of a family's shopping habits better disclosed through the study of its trash than through buying surveys alone. There is, however, the issue of an individual's right to privacy, even though refuse left on a sidewalk is abandoned property and its removal not theft. The journalist who took five plastic bags of trash left in front of a celebrity's home unwittingly gave fresh meaning to Shakespeare's lines: "Who steals my purse steals trash; 'tis something, 'tis nothing," for Iago, knows only too well that the trash will indeed "filch . . . [his] good name."[12] Whether from contemporary rubbish or the ruins of antiquity, reconstructing the past can reveal how people live(d).

Theological Detective Work

Candidates for sainthood in the Catholic Church undergo an investigation that has been described as "theological detective work."[13] To be declared a saint, a candidate must ". . . have to be responsible for two miracles, specifically medical miracles."[14] Scrutinizing such candidates involves performing archival searches; sifting through diaries, poems, and letters; and interviewing people. Because an important goal is to find a stain on the candidate's character, theological detective work is akin (in the reverse sense) to criminal investigation wherein the protection of the innocent has an equal claim. As a process of inquiry, beatification is always exhaustive and expensive. Like criminal investigation, it has its share of critics who claim there are better ways to spend time and resources.

This brief survey of a few novel examples of inquiry suggests that the study of criminal investigation is not one of narrow vocational interest; instead, it lies within the educational tradition that produces generalists rather than narrow specialists. Because industrial archeology, garbageology, and the process of canonization share the same purpose—that of reconstructing the past—the astute student will perceive that what is learned through the study of criminal investigation can be applied to a broad range of theoretical and practical problems.

FURTHER COMMENTARY ON THE INVESTIGATIVE PROCESS

Peripheral issues surface from time to time regarding the investigative process. They involve such questions as: Is luck important to the outcome of an investigation? Is a skeptical attitude of value to an investigator? Is there such a thing as an investigative mindset? Some cases and examples are provided below to illuminate these issues.

Luck or Creativity

Rather than merely an exercise in objective, systematic thinking, criminal investigation is believed by experienced detectives and some scholars of the investigative procedure to involve an element of luck.[15] As careful analysis will suggest, it is not good fortune alone. It is "chance which can be on our side, if we but stir it up with our energies, stay receptive to its every random opportunity, and continually provoke it by individuality in our hobbies and our approach to life."[16] William Beveridge devotes an entire chapter to this matter, which he summarizes as follows:

> New knowledge very often has its origin in some quite unexpected observation or chance occurrence arising during an investigation. The importance of this factor in discovery should be fully appreciated and research workers ought deliberately to exploit it. . . . Interpreting the clue and realizing its possible significance require knowledge without fixed ideas, imagination . . . and a habit of contemplating all unexplained observations.[17]

The unknown factor of chance and the way experienced investigators can interpret and deliberately exploit it, thereby opening up new knowledge and discovery, are exemplified in the next two cases.

The first case involves an aged widow, a recluse living in an apartment-hotel. Her meals delivered daily, the evening tray would be placed in her locked foyer by the night shift elevator operator. After he left she would retrieve the tray, and upon finishing, replace it in the foyer to be picked up several hours later. Occasionally, the night shift operator had an opportunity to talk with the woman, but then only briefly. When the evening tray had not been replaced even by breakfast time, and the morning tray had remained untouched, the day shift operator notified the building manager. Using a pass key, the manager found the woman apparently dead on the bedroom floor; on the kitchen table were the remains of the evening meal of the previous day. The medical examiner established that she had been strangled. It was a case of criminal homicide. The day shift operator was questioned but could supply no useful information; other tenants had not seen or heard anything suspicious. Checking out the victim's background, friends who visited, and other possible leads occupied the investigators for the remainder of the day. They then focused their questions on the night shift operator who had delivered the last tray of food she had touched. Except for her failing to replace it, he observed nothing unusual, he said, adding that even this had not surprised him, because it was not the first time it had occurred. Asked to account for his own dinner hour, he reported that it had been meatloaf as usual at the corner cafeteria; after that, a smoke on the street outside the restaurant.

To the detectives assigned to the case it looked like a protracted investigation. Returning to the station house close by, and passing the cafeteria, one of the two suggested, "Let's check on the operator's story, and see if anybody remembers seeing him last night." The slight possibility that he had not had dinner there was dashed when the cashier, the owner's wife, stated unequivocally that she had seen him: "He always comes in when he works. He likes our food and prices." The detective probed further, inquiring about the meatloaf served the previous night. The cashier's reply was a surprised, "It's odd that you ask. Yesterday we had trouble with the ovens and the cook couldn't bake. It's the first time in more than a year that meatloaf was not our Thursday night special." Needless to say, the detectives did not continue on their way back to the station house; instead, they quickly returned to the hotel to conduct an intensive interrogation of the night shift operator.

Was it chance or was it thoroughness that prompted the check on the man's story? Had chance prompted the inquiry about the meatloaf? Had experience suggested the most trivial of statements be verified?

The second case started innocuously enough when a U.S. Army .45 automatic pistol disappeared from a tavern in a small university town. The detective who responded to the report made proper notifications (within the department and to other law enforcement agencies) pertaining to gun theft, but did little else. A month later, however, an armed robbery occurred in a bank 20 miles away; the weapon the robber brandished, a U.S. Army .45 automatic. The disappearance of the pistol from the tavern still unsolved, and there being no clues except for the eyewitness descriptions of the bank robber, the federal agent assigned to the case decided to follow up on the uncleared gun theft.

The agent's diligence uncovered the information that a carpenter had been working in the back of the tavern during the time the gun disappeared. On the outside chance that the carpenter had seen or heard something, the agent made an appointment for an interview at his home. Arriving early and invited in by the carpenter's wife, he observed a photograph on the piano. Its smudged surface had caught his eye. "Is that a picture of your husband?," he inquired. Walking over to it, she answered, "Yes it is. And you know, he did a dumb thing a few days ago. He ruined it trying to see how he would look with a mustache. He never had one before. Then he tried to erase the marks, and now look what he's done!" It was not surprising that the woman saw only the damage done a cherished possession. But to an investigator who had acquired the habit of scrutinizing seemingly trivial details and contemplating unexplained observations, the implications of her husband's need for a disguise were clear. Until then the man in the photograph had not even remotely been a suspect. When placed in a lineup, there was an eyewitness identification of the carpenter; this, followed by an interrogation, led to a confession.

Beveridge drew on Pasteur's well-known aphorism, "In the field of observation, chance favors only the prepared mind," when he wrote:

> It is the interpretation of the chance observation which counts. The role of chance is merely to provide the opportunity and the scientist has to recognize it and grasp it.[18]

The Prepared Mind

In any investigation it is easier to perceive clues or hints when the mind is prepared through interest or experience. As already suggested, a creative, albeit critical, nature is also helpful for suspecting potential or actual criminality. The next case illustrates suspicious behavior that went unnoticed during an inquiry; it is an example of just the opposite. Had the unwitting signals been recognized and interpreted correctly (rather than missed, and ignored even when pointed out), the outcome would have been different and much grief prevented. Although the present focus is on the need for a prepared mind that sees and recognizes clues and hints, this case also demonstrates how an investigation can fall between the cracks when there is dual jurisdiction between state and federal governments.

A Case of Unheeded Warning Flags

This case involved one Billie Sol Estes, an alleged wheeler-dealer who took advantage of U.S. Department of Agriculture regulations affecting ammonia fertilizer tanks, grain storage facilities, and acreage allotments for the growing of cotton. The following are excerpts from a news article on the developing investigation:

> . . . Discoveries so far seem to add up to a pattern of confusion, in which the left hand of Federal or state government was often unaware of what the right hand was doing, and in which many a red warning flag was ignored.

> *SLOW RESPONSE TO WARNING*

> Moreover, even when . . . caution signals finally were heeded, the response was so clumsy that. . . . It took a newspaper exposé in February to stir up enough momentum, finally resulting in the arrest of Mr. Estes.

> *Items*

> At one point four sets of Federal and State officials—the Federal Bureau of Investigation, the Agricultural Department's cotton division and grain storage supervisors, and the Texas Department of Public Safety—were scrutinizing pieces of the Estes puzzle, each without knowing what the others were doing. . . . Even red flags vigorously waved faded out of Governmental vision. A Pecos physician, Dr. John Dunn, worked up a massive memorandum on the matter of the non-existent mortgaged fertilizer tanks, buttressing a recital of his suspicions with about 14 pages of official records on mortgage transactions. . . . [T]his information was placed in the hands of FBI agents in El Paso, and in subsequent conversation Dr. Dunn told them more about the phantom tanks and about the finance companies that were trying to find them.

> Yet no action was taken . . . [and] no high official of the department even became aware of it. What happened?

> The official explanation, shapes up thus: The FBI took what it dug up to [the] Special Assistant U.S. Attorney in El Paso. . . . he decided that the case

should be dropped—on his conclusion the charges were based on hearsay evidence and he could spot no violation of Federal banking law. The FBI field office then forwarded a routine 2-$1/2$ page report to FBI headquarters in Washington. A carbon was given to the fraud section of the criminal division of the Justice Department, where a lawyer confirmed in August that the file should be closed.

Justice Department spokesmen note that . . . Mr. Fuller, who decided the case . . . knew he would be leaving office and who did leave in September. . . . [T]he headquarters lawyer who received . . . [it recalled that the] memo was buried in a mass of seemingly similar material; about 4,000 such reports are referred to the criminal division each month.

OTHER PATHS TRIED

When it became apparent that the Justice Department was dropping the case, Dr. Dunn says he went to the Texas Department of Public Safety. . . . Homer Garrison, director of this Department—a wide-ranging outfit having under its command the State Highway Patrol, the Texas Rangers and a batch of investigators—confirms that its inquiry began nearly a year ago but says that it hasn't yet ended. . . . This arm of the State government did not, however, work with the State Attorney General's office on this case, as it often does on others. . . .

SIZE OF BOND DISPUTED

At the U.S. Department of Agriculture, a caution light was flashing during negotiations between its career officials and Estes over the size of the surety bond he was required to post as a storer of Government grain surpluses. Despite the fact that [he] was the millionaire head of a vast farm empire and one of the biggest grain warehousemen in the nation, he flew to Washington in January 1961, to protest a proposed bond increase that would cost him only a few hundred dollars.

Yet, this unusual concern over an inconsequential sum apparently raised no alarm in the mind of the man who fixed the bond, Carl Miller, a 25-year employee of the department. Estes' recounting of his rags-to-riches rise, his philosophy of life, his church work—embellished with strategically dropped names of Washington political figures—persuaded Miller to leave the bond unchanged, as he was quite entitled to do under departmental rules.

In congressional testimony Miller declared that he had no reason to suspect Estes, and was at a loss to explain why Estes went to such effort to hold down his bond. [The] Texas Attorney General claimed the West Texan feared exposure if the bonding company audited his jerry-built empire in order to put up a larger bond.

BONDING COMPANY REBELLED

Therein lies another seemingly ignored caution light. At the time of the Estes-Miller confrontation, [the] Aetna Casualty and Surety Co., was refusing to back a higher bond. . . . Agriculture Department officials say, [this] reluctance merely reflected company policy and "did not cast suspicion on Estes' financial position." Miller did insist that to avert a bigger bond, Estes had to furnish an independent audit of his net worth; the higher the net worth, the lower the storage bond required by department rules. W. P. Jackson, a Texas certified public accountant, has testified he prepared this audit. . . . But added a disclaimer. "By reason of the limitation of the scope of our examination as to inventories," he declared, "no opinion may be expressed as to the fairness of presentation in the accompanying balance sheet of the financial position of Billie Sol Estes." Miller, who is not a certified public accountant, discounted an "inventory" item of $942,701.13 and accepted the rest. Jackson, however, says an experienced accountant would have thrown his statement "in the wastebasket . . . because any time you cannot get a CPA to express an opinion, you cannot depend on the audit work or what was done to establish the figures." The Agriculture Department now concedes Miller's job requires an accountant. . . .[19]

In summary, the Billie Sol Estes scandal reveals how clues that would be evident to a skeptical investigator were missed. It also demonstrates the importance of coordination and consultation when several agencies have jurisdiction over an investigation. Attention is now turned to investigative "mind-set," another example of the prepared mind; the purpose, to consider how this capability can be improved.

Investigative Mind-Set

Just as hindsight brings clear vision, so does investigative *mind-set* provide foresight, and possibly insight, to the creative investigator. The terms *mind-set* and a *set mind* are antithetical; one should not be mistaken for the other. A set mind is scarcely useful to the investigator, the cerebral faculty being neither developed nor strengthened by an inflexible outlook. Investigative mind-set on the other hand, is to some extent a gift at birth. It can, however, be developed through practice and experience. More than mere suspicion, it is doubt or misgivings based on experience that, in combination with a critical faculty, often perceives a connection between two apparently unrelated items or bits of data, and looks for what does not fit the situation. What exactly is wrong? Is there anything out of place? Unusual? If so, why? Two maxims speak to the practical value of a skeptical outlook: such old proverbs as the Latin "Believe nothing and be on your guard against everything," and the Persian "Doubt is the key to knowledge." The philosopher René Descartes developed a theory of knowledge based on doubting everything—including his own existence. He said, "I think, therefore I am," employing the aphorism to show how the doubt had been resolved to his satisfaction. Examples of investigative mind-set are found in the Watergate affair,[20] the Lloyd Miller miscarriage of justice,[21] and the World Trade Center case. The last apprises us of how the investigative mind-set of two FBI officers was tragically ignored.

Watergate

Of the millions of televiewers, how many recognized the investigative significance of John Dean's testimony about the president's strange behavior in taking him to a corner and lowering his voice? Even committee investigators, Democratic appointees, failed to follow up on the implication that the president was taping normal conversation in the room; instead, a member of the Republican staff asked Nixon's appointment secretary, Alexander Butterfield, if there was reason for Dean's concern.[22] Fearful of perjury, he was responsive, disclosing the installation of a recording system in the Oval Office, the cabinet meeting room, and other locations the president used. By providing unassailable evidence of Nixon's involvement in the cover-up of the Watergate burglary, the tapes ultimately led to the resignation of the president and the trials of several close subordinates. Perhaps Dean's clue should not have been missed by the bright young staff lawyers; however, legal training is no substitute for education in methods of inquiry and the investigative process. To those possessing the investigative mind-set that characterizes many seasoned investigators, the failure to follow through on the hint is hard to understand. Had Dean's clue not been exploited, albeit by chance, the reconstruction of Watergate and the president's involvement might not have been accomplished.

The Lloyd Miller Case

Another example of the failure to follow up on a clue is found in W.J. Lassers's account of the Lloyd Miller story.[23] A pair of men's shorts, discovered under circumstances that seemed to corroborate Miller's involvement in a homicide, was instrumental in his conviction. On appeal many years later (at issue, an alleged bloodstain) and not until then, was an inquiry forthcoming as to whether the shorts fit the defendant at the time. Having gained weight and his former size therefore unknown, a definitive answer was feasible only if original investigators had required their suspect to try on the underwear. Unaccountably, the issue had not been raised by defense counsel at the original trial. This obvious source of information was overlooked or ignored when it could have been useful in establishing Miller's innocence or possible guilt.

As an example of a miscarriage of justice, the Miller murder case requires thoughtful consideration. An incompetent criminal investigation can have grave consequences. When an innocent person is incarcerated, respect for the individual is diminished in the concrete as well as the abstract sense; the democratic process being impaired. Some lawyers believe an inept investigation is a constitutional issue, tantamount to a denial of due process. If they are correct, it would have a significant impact on criminal investigation.

The World Trade Center

The terrorists who leveled the World Trade Center on September 11, 2001, were, in retrospect, able to enter, leave, and explore the country for potential opportunities that would allow them to accomplish their villanous goals. One prospect was to enroll as students in pilot flight training schools. They showed little interest in learning how to take off and land; rather, they wanted to learn how to pilot a commercial jet while airborne. Anyone with an investigative mind set would regard this behavior as suspicious. Two FBI agents did so. One, on July 10, 2001, sent a communication to headquarters "outlining links between a group of suspected Middle Eastern terrorists and the Embry-Riddle Aeronautical University . . . The agent (Kenneth Williams) . . . suggested that the FBI should canvass U.S. flight schools for information on other Middle Eastern students. He speculated that bin Laden might be attempting to train operatives to infiltrate the aviation industry.[24] The other agent, Coleen Rowley, a Minneapolis field office lawyer, sent a 13-page letter to the newly appointed Director of the FBI warning him, among other things, how "instructors at the Pan Am flight school near Minneapolis-St. Paul had phoned the FBI the previous day reporting that a student, in bad English, had showed up asking for instruction how to fly a 747."[25] When FBI agents arrived at the student's motel, they asked for his immigration papers. "[W]hen the documents showed evidence of a possible visa violation, agents from the Immigration and Naturalization Service arrested (Zacarias) Moussaoui on charges of overstaying his visa."[26] Despite evidence obtained from French intelligence that Moussaoui "was not only operational in the militant Islamist world but had some autonomy and authority as well,"[27] Rowley's request for permission to obtain a search warrant to study the contents of (Massaoui's) laptop was denied by a superior at headquarters. "Only after September 11, 2002, did the FBI successfully obtain a warrant to search Moussaoui's belongings; among other things the search turned up crop dusting information . . . and a notebook that contained an alias eventually traced to the roommate of hijacker Mohammed Atta."[28]

It is perhaps relevant to remark at this point on the relationship between criminal investigation, which is a reactive endeavor, and intelligence, which is a proactive endeavor.

> It was old-fashioned interrogation and eavesdropping that first led U.S. agents to the Qaeda [sic] plotters. In the summer of 1998, only a couple of weeks after bin Laden operatives truck-bombed two U.S. Embassies in Africa, the FBI got a break: one of the Nairobi bombers had been caught. . . . (He) was supposed to have killed himself in the blast. Instead, he got out of the truck at the last moment and fled. He was arrested in a seedy Nairobi hotel, . . . (and) questioned by the FBI, . . . Among the information he gave agents was the telephone number of a Qaeda [sic] safe house in Yemen . . . U.S. intelligence agents began listening in on the telephone line of the Yemen house, described in government documents as a Qaeda [sic] 'logistics center,' where . . . the African bombings and later the Cole attack in Yemen—were planned. . . . [I]ntercepted conversations on the Yemen phone tipped off agents to the January 2000 Kuala Lumpur summit [meeting]. . . . After the meeting, Malaysian intelligence continued to watch the condo at the CIA's request, but after a while the agency lost interest. Had agents kept up the surveillance, they might have observed . . . Zacarias Moussaoui."[29]

These details about intelligence gathering suggest that some attributes are shared by criminal investigators and intelligence agents, even though one is reacting to a crime already committed, while the other is trying to fathom future activities of a targeted person. These shared characteristics include:

- Investigative mind-set

- Interrogation methods

- Surveillance capabilities—including technical means

- Perseverance

- An ability to "think outside the box"

The Development of Mind-Set

In day-to-day reading, a news story occasionally triggers the mind to question its details and reflects a developing investigative mind-set. If articles are clipped and files maintained as stories unfold, original suspicions may be confirmed or denied. (The Vinland Map incident described below required nine years.) As the reader's ability improves through practice, more validations and fewer misjudgments will occur.

Conscientious students will find that the study of old newspaper and magazine files in libraries helps stimulate those intuitive responses that characterize investigative mind-set. A great deal of time may be required to find suitable case examples, but with patience—a primary investigative attribute—there is intellectual gold to be mined. The Vinland Map episode and the Edgar Smith homicide are recommended as starters.

The Vinland Map Episode

Columbus Day was chosen by Yale University Press in 1965 to publish *The Vinland Map and the Tartar Relation*. Containing a newly authenticated map, the first to depict any part of the Western Hemisphere before the voyage of Columbus, this book received media coverage seldom accorded a scholarly publication. Selected examples follow:

> The map throws further doubt on the legend that Columbus was sailing into completely mysterious and unchartered seas when he set out with his fleet in 1492. . . .

> Proudly put on display this week by the Yale Library, the map and its accompanying text have been annotated and explicated in a scholarly book . . . which describes the eight years of elaborate detective work that were needed to date and authenticate it.[30]

A Yale University librarian called the map

> about the most exciting single acquisition of the Yale Library in modern times, exceeding in significance even Yale's Gutenberg Bible and its Bay Psalm Book.[31]

Elsewhere it was stated: "The testimony of the paper, handwriting, style and binding is undeniable"[32] creating "a presumption of authenticity so strong as to be difficult, if not impossible, to challenge."[33]

Yet, throughout the *Time* and *Newsweek* accounts there are elements that a reader with investigative mind-set will find unsettling. After reading both accounts, serious students should ask themselves whether they recognized any circumstances or clues to suggest that the map's authenticity was open to question.

Scholarly interest in the map continued with a conference in 1971 in Washington, DC,[34] and a seminar in 1974 in London, with both proceedings published.[35] A month before, however, Yale University announced that its prized map had been found to be an elaborate, skillful modern forgery, the basis for repudiating its authenticity resting on the study of its ink.[36, 37] Although Yale had first proposed an ink examination in 1968, not until 1972 were ultramicro sampling techniques developed to permit the use of instrumental methods of analysis. For example, X-ray diffraction (XRD) of the ink pigment disclosed the presence of titanium dioxide in the form of anatase, which has been available in the observed form only since 1920 (at the earliest, 1917). This remarkable demonstration of the definitiveness of physical evidence is documented in *The Geographical Journal* by W.C. McCrone and L.B. McCrone.[38]

Apparently, there were some who disagreed with the claim that the map was a forgery:

> After languishing in disrepute for almost a decade, the map was again analyzed in 1985 . . .
>
> The findings were entirely different from those of McCrone. After analyzing all of the ink and parchment (physicists at the University of California at Davis) found only trace amounts of titanium and determined it was not a major constituent of the map.
>
> Further studies on other medieval documents, including a Gutenberg Bible, revealed that the map's composition was comparable to theirs, and that it contained less titanium than some.
>
> The accumulation of new evidence supporting the Vinland Map's authenticity, from the nature of the ink to the map's similarity to other medieval documents, prompted Yale to reissue "The Vinland Map and the Tartar Relation . . ."
>
> George D. Painter, the sole survivor of the original team of expert's who studied the map and prepared the first edition of the book, still takes great umbrage at the fact that their work was initially rejected.
>
> In an essay at the beginning of the new edition, Painter concludes with the confident assertion that the Vinland Map "is a true voice from the past, which still lives, and need never be silent again."
>
> McCrone, for his part, remains unapologetic and defiant. "The Vinland Map is a highly skilled forgery," he wrote to Yale's Ryden earlier this month. "It was produced in a way that announced to a microanalyst the intention of fooling the world into believing it to be more than 500 years old."
>
> While the dispute will probably never be definitively resolved, the Smithsonian Institution's Wilcomb E. Washington, who convened the 1966 conference, notes in the introduction to the new edition that "those who have been charging forgery must now assume a defensive role and respond to those previously on the defensive."[39]

From a criminalist's viewpoint this new evidence does not undercut McCrone: he argues that anatase (one of two crystallined forms of titanium dioxide, and not commercially available before 1920) was present in the ink on the document. The issue is the kind of titanium dioxide and not the quantity of "titanium."

The fact that it was both a qualitative and quantitative impossibility for anatese to be a constituent of thirteenth-century ink leads to the conclusion that, ergo, the document is a forgery. Moreover, its provenance, the circumstances of its discovery, and the manner by which it was brought to public attention raise serious questions regarding authenticity.

The study of medieval documents that "revealed that the map's composition was comparable to theirs" means, at best, that it may be partially genuine (because of the parchment), but not necessarily authentic (because of the ink). Furthermore, the use of the misleading phrase "was comparable to" is reminiscent of forensic scientists' "is consistent with." (See page 327-329 for an example of how incorrect interpretation can result.)

Studies as recent as 2002 conclude that while the parchment may be old the ink appears modern. In July 2002, a University College London study upheld the belief that the map is a fake, again pointing to the presence of anatese. In August of the same year, a Carbon-14 dating analysis supported that the parchment was made around 1434.

The Vinland Map story holds an important lesson for the criminal investigator. Genuine materials, combined with something obtainable only at a much later time, were used to create a spurious authenticity. If the technology is available, it is possible to expose such a counterfeit; indeed, the well-staffed forensic science laboratory should welcome requests for the analysis of uncommon physical evidence. So much for the ideal world. In reality, a pioneering spirit is seldom fostered in the bureaucracy of government. Therefore, not only must criminal investigators know what the laboratory is capable of, but also how to recognize potential physical evidence, then collect and preserve it. With such expertise, they will know when a request is met perfunctorily or with imagination and interest, the difference being success or failure in their endeavors.

The Edgar Smith Case

This case, involving the homicide of a 15-year-old cheerleader, will help students interested in testing their mind-set capability. The most concise account is provided by D.G.M. Coxe; his thesis: Edgar Smith should not have been found guilty.[40] During 14 years on death row, Smith constantly claimed he was innocent, but from reading Coxe's report of events surrounding the girl's death, anyone possessed of investigative mind-set should have a strong sense that Smith was the likely perpetrator. Others, however, came to an opposite conclusion as a result of the books and briefs Smith produced from prison.[41, 42] With his release in 1971 having been obtained through a complicated legal ploy, and considering the exemplary character of the people working to free him, it was reasonable to assume that a genuine miscarriage of justice had occurred in his case. Yet Smith was again arrested (and convicted in 1977) and the *modus operandi* (method of operation) of that crime was similar to the earlier one. The conviction was partly the result of his witness-stand admission. On the same witness stand, he admitted to the 1957 murder.

Investigative mind-set capability can indeed be tested by this case, in which an intelligent, successful attempt was made by the guilty party to mislead and confuse more than a few citizens who cared about justice. It should be recognized, however, that a mere notion ensuing from mind-set does not constitute evidence under the criminal law. Just as fundamental discoveries in science and mathematics have developed from hunches and surmises, so will they in criminal investigation if investigators are willing to make the follow-up efforts suggested by such conjectures. What evidence and proof consist of in science, law, and criminal investigation are the subject of the next section. Table 13.2 summarizes this information.

EVIDENCE AND PROOF

A chance observation, such as a detective's noting the marred surface of a photograph (as in the case of the U.S. Army pistol theft), represents an investigative opportunity. It does not constitute evidence of probable cause. Sometimes chance may raise a mere suspicion, a sense that the nature or quality of what is observed presents "interesting possibilities" worthy of follow-up. To be of further value to the investigator, it must be supplemented by an apperceptive noting and recording of facts—seen and understood in the light of past experience. The chance observation and apperception coming together in this process inductively provide grounds for a hypothesis or a belief that leads to a tentative generalization. For example, a detective's attention was called to a vehicle parked across the street from a bank, the bank president having observed it there several times in the past month. Additional suspicion was aroused when it was again seen an hour or so before opening time on one day, and just before closing time the following day. A check of its license plate revealed that the car was not stolen; its registered owner was a local resident with no police record. Despite this, the detective, acting on a sense of "interesting possibilities" in the nature of what had been observed, briefed the radio car patrol covering the car owner's residence about the bank's uneasiness. A week later the sector car patrol officer spotted an out-of-state vehicle parked in the driveway of the house. A check disclosed that the vehicle was registered to an individual with a bank burglary record, whose *modus operandi* was to burn around the dial of a safe with an acetylene torch.

By now, the detective's thinking had moved by degrees from the mere suspicion or intriguing possibilities stage to one that at the very least called for some follow-up measures. Official interest was still based on speculation however, with additional facts needed to prove that the bank was indeed to be "hit." Local welding equipment suppliers were alerted and provided with photographs of both individuals. As prearranged, when a customer resembling either one came in for a tank of acetylene, police were alerted and surveillance of the purchaser—now a suspect—was begun.

It is clear from the foregoing that evidence consists of a number of facts that point to a conclusion. In this case, if the bank is broken into, that fact would prove intent to commit burglary, but if the detective waits for the suspect to emerge, loot in hand, it would provide sufficient evidence to support and prove the charge of burglary. The number and kind of facts, together with the ambiguity or doubt associated with each fact, dictate the

Table 13.2
Evidence and Proof: In Science, Law, and Criminal Investigation[a]

CATEGORY	I	II[b]	III[b]
DEGREES OF PROOF	INTUITIVE	SPECULATIVE	PROBABLE CAUSE
EVIDENCE Kind	Guess; hunch; gut feeling.	Impression; surmise.	Facts that a reasonable, prudent person would accept as a basis for decisionmaking.
Quantity	Virtually none that can be identified and articulated to another person.	Not sufficient to be convincing.	*Prima facie:* presumptive but rebuttable.
Degree of uncertainty	Considerable.	Apparent.	Less than apparent but still quite possible.
USAGE IN Science	Discovery and hypothesis formulation		Basis for theory development through testing of hypothesis.

Law (in the US)	Exercise a peremptory challenge in jury selection.
	
	Defense may move to suppress this kind of evidence.
			Satisfies requirement for an arrest or issuance of a warrant for search and seizure of evidence.
			   Basis for going on to the next stage of a legal proceeding.
			   If no defense is made *prima facie* evidence for every element constitutes a *prima facie* case that is sufficient to support a conviction in criminal cases.

Criminal Investigation (in the US)	Useful during the first stages of investigation. Basis for decisions on what to monitor, what to investigate, and what direction—at least initially—an investigation should take.		Obtain a search warrant or an arrest warrant.

a Although depicted as seven categories for didactic reasons, such a division may also (and should) be viewed as a continuum.

b Reasonable Suspicion. A category of proof that is less than probable cause but more than speculative, it was invoked by the managers for the House of Representatives in the impeachment and trial of President William Jefferson Clinton. This category of proof is not recognized in science.

c The U.S. Supreme Court has not looked favorably upon attempts to define "beyond a reasonable doubt" because it found the words themselves sufficiently descriptive. (Consult *Miles v. United States,* 103 U.S. 312 (1981). "Beyond a shadow of a doubt" is a colloquial term that falls between Categories VI and VII. Proof "beyond a shadow of *any* doubt" falls into Category VII.

d Circumstantial evidence falls into Category III-VI. It is evidence not bearing directly on the fact in dispute, but on various attendant circumstances from which a judge or jury may logically infer the occurrence of the fact in dispute. It is indirect evidence by which a principal fact may be arrived at inductively. It is far more common than direct evidence, i.e., eyewitness testimony or a confession.

e This standard of proof was invoked in the political impeachment of President Richard Milhous Nixon.

IV	V	VI[c]	VII[c]
PREPONDERANCE OF THE EVIDENCE	CLEAR AND CONVINCING	BEYOND A REASONABLE DOUBT	SCIENTIFIC CERTAINTY
Additional facts, increasingly supportive, obtained through eyewitness testimony, or the examination of documents and other physical things—fingerprints, toolmarks, bullets, tape recordings, and so on. A forensic scientist may be required to interpret and evaluate the significance of this evidence for legal use.[d]			Factual data and details arrived at by methods of analysis of known precision and accuracy.
Over 50 percent of the facts are in support.	Only slightly less than proof beyond a reasonable doubt.	Sufficient to preclude every reasonable hypothesis except that which it tends to support.	Overwhelming but still probabilistic.
Some is permitted.	A little may remain.	Almost none.	Essentially none.
Basis for theory development through continued testing of hypothesis.		Theory.	Scientific law that accounts for the known, observed facts.
Basis upon which most civil cases are decided. Suggests need to plea bargain in criminal cases and offers to settle in civil cases. Meets burden of proof such as under RICO. Revocation of probation, conditional discharge, and supervision.	A U.S. President may be impeached (accused).[e] A mentally ill person may be committed involuntarily. Supports a decision in a civil case involving moral turpitude and fraud.	Basis upon which a criminal case is decided or a U.S. President removed from office.	Seldom achieved.
Obtain an admission or confession by pointing out the evidence against the suspect as part of the questioning. Induce a suspect who is a potential informant to talk. Verifies investigation is proceeding in the proper direction. May suggest use of civil processes rather than criminal prosecution in a given case.		Satisfies the quantity of legal proof required to convict in a criminal case.	Seldom achieved.

level of evidentiary value. When enough facts are available, proof becomes possible depending upon the purpose, criteria, and requirements of the discipline in which the proof is offered. As pointed out earlier, Beveridge suggests discoveries result when attention is paid to the slightest clue. A certain attitude of mind (capable of a quantum leap from limited evidence) is required for the discovery stage; whereas the unquestioned proof stage has distinctly different evidentiary requirements. In criminal investigation, similarly, there are two standards of proof: "probable cause" for a legal arrest and "beyond a reasonable doubt" for a conviction. In civil cases the standard is "a preponderance of the evidence"; the House Judiciary Committee in its impeachment deliberations proposed as the yardstick "clear and convincing" evidence.[43] Although each standard seems discrete, it should be viewed as a continuum of evidence and proof .

Evidence, then, is the means by which a fact is established. When the number of facts collected and confirmed is sufficient, depending on whether it is a civil or criminal matter, the point in question is proved. (In civil law, a preponderance of the evidence is required; in criminal law, it must be "beyond a reasonable doubt" (see Table 13.2).

Investigation—Art or Science?

The concept of continuous succession—a continuum—is helpful in understanding other aspects of the investigative process; specifically, to examine two polar views: investigation as an art versus investigation as a science. But if art and science are part of a continuum, where does the separation point lie? Further reflection suggests it is determined by the subject under consideration: for the physical and biological sciences, it is far to one side; for culinary creativeness, it leans toward the arts (since any chef can read a cookbook and follow directions). For criminal investigation, the separation point is moving by degrees toward science. The field is becoming a focus of academic study and research, one in which the impact of forensic science is felt more and more.

SUMMARY OF THE SCIENTIFIC METHOD AND ITS APPLICATION TO CRIMINAL INVESTIGATION _____

The steps involved may be summarized as follows:

SCIENTIFIC METHOD	*CRIMINAL INVESTIGATION**
1. State the problem.**	1. What crime was committed? In what jurisdiction?
2. Form the hypothesis.	2. Hypothesize as to possible suspects based on information known about the victim or gathered from witnesses, physical evidence at the crime scene, and motive (if determined).

3. Collect data by observing and experimenting.	3. Seek out pertinent records. Continue effort to locate and interview additional witnesses. If possible, obtain from each potential suspect's person (home or automobile) exemplars for comparison with physical evidence discovered at the crime scene. Interview witnesses again, if necessary, based on information acquired after initial interviews.
4. Interpret the data as a test of the hypothesis.	4. Review and evaluate the evidence so far available relative to making a case—for and against—each suspect. Focus the investigation on the most likely suspect. After *Miranda* warnings, interrogate the suspect.
5. If the data support the hypothesis so far, continue to collect additional data (as a logical consequence of the hypothesis).	5. Seek additional evidence (possibly through follow-up measures) that supports (or disproves) the hypothesis that the suspect was the offender.
6. Draw conclusions (which, if the data are sufficiently supportive, may lead to a theory).	6. If evidence amounting to probable cause has been developed, arrest suspect. Continue seeking evidence to support or refute the guilt of the defendant.

* Criminal investigation generally commences as an inductive process with deductive reasoning integral to it.

** Problem recognition precedes this stage and is, perhaps, the driving force leading to an investigation of the problem. As part of the process, the issue must be clearly formulated by "stating the problem."

REFERENCES

1   W.B. Sanders, ed., *The Sociologist as Detective* (New York: Praeger, 1974).

2   Robin W. Winks, ed., *The Historian as Detective* (New York: Harper & Row, 1969).

3   Ibid., XXIV.

4   Ibid., XIII, XVII, 4.

5   Thomas H. Huxley, *Collected Essays*, Vol. II: Darwiniana (London: Macmillan, 1970), 363-365.

6   E.L. Bernays, *The Engineering of Consent* (Norman, OK: University of Oklahoma Press, 1956), 9 ff.

7   Hans Reichenbach, *The Rise of Scientific Philosophy* (Berkeley: University of California Press, 1951), 9 ff., 232.

8   "The Republicans' Moment of Truth," *Time*, 29 July 1974, 10.

9   J.E. Bishop, "Industrial Evolution," *The Wall Street Journal*, 26 June 1975, 40.

10   R.A. Buchanan, *Industrial Archeology in Britain* (London: Penguin Books, 1972).

[11] J. Beck, "Study of Garbage Threatens Privacy," *Chicago Tribune*, 18 July 1975.

[12] "Trashy Journalism," *Time*, 21 July 1975, 40.

[13] L.R. Gallese, "The Good Fight: American Saint's Cause Took Century of Work, Millions in Donations!," *The Wall Street Journal*, 25 June 1975, 1, 19.

[14] Ibid.

[15] Charles E. O'Hara and Gregory L. O'Hara, *Fundamentals of Criminal Investigation*, rev. 5th ed. (Springfield, IL: Charles C Thomas, 1973), 22.

[16] J.H. Austin, "The Roots of Serendipity," *Saturday Review World*, 2 November 1974, 64.

[17] William I. Beveridge, *The Art of Scientific Investigation*, Modern Library rev. ed. (New York: Random House, 1957), 55.

[18] Ibid., 46.

[19] J. Western, "The Unheeded Warning Flags," *The Wall Street Journal*, 13 January 1962, 26 ff.

[20] Bob Woodward and Carl Bernstein, *All the President's Men* (New York: Simon and Schuster, 1974).

[21] W.J. Lassers, *Scapegoat Justice: Lloyd Miller and the Failure of the American Legal System* (Bloomington, IN: Indiana University Press, 1973).

[22] B. Sussman, *The Great Cover-Up: Nixon and the Scandal of Watergate* (New York: Crowell, 1974), 252-253.

[23] Lassers, *loc. cit.*

[24] Barton Gellman. "Dots That Didn't Connect," *The Washington Post National Weekly Edition*, May 27-June 2, 2002, 10.

[25] R. Ratnesar and M. Weisskopf. "How the FBI Blew the Case," *Time*, 3 June 2002, 28.

[26] *Loc cit.*, col. 2.

[27] *Loc cit.*, col. 3.

[28] Ibid., 31, col. 3; 32, col. 1.

[29] M. Isikoff and D. Kaidman. "Terrorists Who Got Away," *Newsweek* 10 June 2002, 24, 25.

[30] "Map of History," *Time*, 15 October 1965, 120.

[31] Ibid., 123.

[32] *Newsweek*, 18 October 1965, 103.

[33] R.A. Skelton, T.E. Marston, and G.D. Painter, *The Vinland Map and the Tartar Relation* (New Haven and London: Yale University Press, 1965), VI.

[34] Wilcomb E. Washburn, ed., *Proceedings of the Vinland Map Conference* (Chicago and London: University of Chicago Press for the Newberry Library, 1971).

[35] H. Wallis, et. al., "The Strange Case of the Vinland Map," *The Geographical Journal*, 140: 92 (1974), 183-214.

[36] *Chicago Tribune*, 26 January 1974.

[37] *Report to Yale University Library: Chemical Analytical Study of the Vinland Map* (Chicago: Walter C. McCrone Assoc., 1974).

[38] Walter C. McCrone and L.B. McCrone, "The Vinland Map Ink," in H. Wallis, et. al., *op. cit.*, 212-214.

39 Farquhar, Michael, "Nordic or Forged? New Wolrd Map Sunders Scholars," *The Washington Post,* 26 February 1996, Col. 2-5, p.3.

40 D.G.M. Coxe, "The Strange Case of Edgar Smith," *National Review,* 25 (1963), 273-278.

41 Edgar Smith, *Brief Against Death* (New York: Knopf, 1969).

42 Edgar Smith, *Getting Out* (New York: Coward, McCann, and Geoghegan, 1973).

43 U.S. Congress, House Committee on the Judiciary, *Hearings on H. Res. 803,* 93rd Cong., 2nd sess. "Summary of Information," 19 (July 1974), 5. "Debate on Articles of Impeachment," 24, 27, 29, 30 (July 1974).

Supplemental Readings

Barzun, Jacques, and Henry F. Graff. *The Modern Researcher.* 5th ed. New York: Harcourt Brace Jovanovich, 1992.

Berkman, Robert I. *Find It Fast: How To Uncover Expert Information On Any Subject.* Rev. ed. New York: Harper & Row, 1993.

Cohen, Morris R., and E. Nagel. *An Introduction to Logic and Scientific Method.* Boston: Routledge and Kegan Paul, 1949.

Copi, Irving M., and Carl Cohen. *An Introduction to Logic.* 9th ed. New York: Macmillan, 1993.

Davidson, James West, and Mark H. Lytle. *After the Fact: The Art of Historical Detection.* 3rd ed., 2 vols. New York: McGraw-Hill, 1992.

Fischer, David. *Hard Evidence.* New York: Simon and Schuster, 1995.

Hockett, Homer C. *The Critical Method in Historical Research and Writing.* Westport, CT: Greenwood Press, 1977.

Joyce, Christopher, and Eric Stover. *Witnesses From the Grave: The Stories Bones Tell.* Boston: Little, Brown, 1991.

Kerr, Harry P. *Opinion and Evidence.* New York: Harcourt Brace & World, 1962.

Kukura, Thomas V. "Trash Inspections and the Fourth Amendment," *FBI Law Enforcement Bulletin* 60:2 (Feb. 1991), 27-32.

Lance, Peter. *1,000 Years for Revenge: International Terrorism and the FBI—The Untold Story.* New York: Harper Collins, 2003.

Macaulay, David. *The Motel of the Mysteries.* Boston: Houghton Mifflin, 1979.

Myren, Richard A., and Carol H. Garcia. *Investigation for Determination of Fact: A Primer on Proof.* Pacific Grove, CA: Brooks/Cole, 1988.

Rose, Louis J. *How to Investigate Your Friends and Enemies.* 2nd ed. Rev. printing. Edited by Robert Byrne and Lawrence Fiquette. St. Louis: Albion Press, 1983.

Ruchlis, Hy. *Discovering Scientific Method: With Science Puzzle Pictures.* New York: Harper & Row, 1963.

Sanders, W.B. *Detective Work: A Study of Criminal Investigations.* New York: The Free Press, 1977.

Shafer, Robert J. *A Guide to Historical Method.* 3rd ed. Homewood, IL: Dover Press, 1980.

Woodward, Kenneth L. *Making Saints: How the Catholic Church Determines Who Becomes a Saint, Who Doesn't, and Why.* New York: Simon and Schuster, 1990.

Winks, R.W., ed. *The Historian as Detective.* New York: Harper & Row, 1969.

CHAPTER 14

Homicide

INTRODUCTION

One of the most feared crimes is murder—it can completely immobilize a community hit by a series of localized killings. A case in point is the climate of fear created by the Boston Strangler; the elderly were afraid to answer the door, much less attend evening church services. A cherished right—freedom of movement—had been curtailed by the acts of a single individual in much the same way a terrorist can hold a sovereign nation hostage.

The removal of such offenders following a competently conducted investigation is not only a gratifying result for the investigators and officials who direct it, but for the general public as well. Hence, due to its impact on the community, and because the investigator skilled in handling homicide cases should then be capable of managing other felony investigations, the reader will find that this crime receives more comprehensive treatment than the other crimes covered in this text.

Definitions

Homicide is the killing of one human being by another. All homicides are not criminal: they may also be justifiable or excusable. (Self-inflicted death is treated by the police as homicide until it can be established as suicide.)

Justifiable homicide involves the intentional but lawful killing of another. The state commits justifiable homicide in carrying out a death sentence handed down by a judge after conviction. Justifiable homicide is also committed when a police officer kills a bank robber who shoots at the officer while attempting to escape; or when an individual, believing his or her life is being threatened with a weapon, kills in defense of self or family. In the last example, should the weapon used to threaten—a gun, perhaps—subsequently prove to be an imitation, it would, even so, remain a case of justifiable homicide.

Excusable homicide involves one person killing another by accident without gross negligence and without intent to injure; for example, the hunter who honestly mistakes another person for game. The following scenario is another example: around 2 A.M. a police officer pursues a suspected burglar fleeing down a dead-end alley. He orders the suspect to halt, put up his hands, and not move; instead, the suspect turns around. The officer, observing a shiny object in the suspect's hand and believing it to be a weapon, fires and kills the suspect. The questions that will inevitably be raised are:

- How much light was available?

- Did the suspect whirl and crouch, or turn slowly?

- Did the suspect say anything?

- Was there a shiny object? Was it a gun or other weapon?

When the circumstances are determined, the issue of whether a case is excusable homicide can be settled.

Suicide is the taking of one's own life. Although not deemed a crime, suicide is considered a grave public wrong in many jurisdictions throughout the world.

Criminal homicide is the unlawful taking of a human life. There are two kinds of criminal homicide: murder and manslaughter.

Murder is the unlawful killing of another human being with malice aforethought (premeditation). Killing a person during the commission of a felony also constitutes murder—even when the killing is unintentional. Most murder convictions are for felony murder rather than for premeditated murder.

Manslaughter is the unlawful killing of another without intent—expressed or implied—to effect death.

Further classifications of unlawful homicide—such as first-degree (in police/prosecutor jargon: "murder one") versus second-degree murder; voluntary manslaughter (heat of passion) versus involuntary manslaughter (reckless or vehicular); and so on—are to be found in the penal laws of the states. The annotated statutes of the state in which the crime was committed must be consulted to determine which category of homicide fits a particular case (see Chapter 23). The term homicide will be employed throughout this chapter without further reference to the subcategory into which it legally falls.

Corpus Delicti

The *corpus delicti* is the collection of basic facts establishing that a crime has been committed and that some person is responsible. Regardless of the classification of an unlawful homicide, the investigator must marshal evidence for each element of the *corpus delicti* in order for the prosecutor to obtain an indictment or for the judge to hand the case over to a jury. The elements for unlawful homicide are:

1. The death was not the result of suicide, natural causes, or accident, thus establishing that it was a homicide. (This is the province of the forensic pathologist.)

2. Some person was responsible for the unlawful death. (Establishing the identity of the person is the province of the investigator, evidence technicians, and criminalists.)

The circumstances surrounding the death will determine whether the charge will be murder or manslaughter.

Demographics

Of all crime statistics, those on homicide are probably the most reliable. This is because two agencies of government—the police and the medical examiner (or coroner)—have jurisdiction, file separate reports, and compile data. The Uniform Crime Reports (UCR) disclose the number of murders and non-negligent manslaughters in the United States for each calendar year. Although the numbers increase or decrease from one year to another, three peaks (based on homicides per 100,000 population) have been noted for the twentieth century. The first occurred in 1933 when there were 9.7 homicides per 100,000; then the number fell to a low in the late 1950s and early 1960s.[1] The second peak, in 1980, hit 10.2 per 100,000. After a period of decline, the homicide rate peaked again in 1991 at 9.8 per 100,000.[2] The homicide rate has slowly decreased to its 2001 rate of 5.6 per 100,000.[3] Some perspective may be gained on UCR data if they are juxtaposed against statistics for another country or another time. For example, present-day Canada's low annual homicide rate remains under 2 per 100,000,[4] whereas Oxford, England's medieval-era rate of 110 per 100,000 is appalling even for those times.[5]

In absolute terms, more than 15,000 murders are reported in the United States each year—most occurring in large metropolitan areas, frequently in July and December, on weekends or holidays, at night. By region, southern states account for more murders than do states in other parts of the country; by gender, male victims outnumber female victims about 3 to 1. Approximately 10 percent of murders are interracial, but usually victim and killer are of the same race. In proportion to their numbers, blacks are more often victims than whites. About one-third of all murder victims are in the 20–29 age bracket; the most commonly used weapon is a firearm.[6] In general, studies show a prior relationship between victim and killer in about 80 percent of the cases. There has been a significant drop in the clearance rate* for homicide, probably because stranger-to-stranger killings are on the increase. In these cases, ascertaining the particularized motive (if any) and working from motive to murderer is very difficult. Because many robbery and narcotics cases also have a generalized motive (and some develop into homicides), particularized motive is of little help as an investigative aid.

It is commendable that among serious felonies, homicide has a high clearance rate, and that in the last decade of the twentieth century it is declining in absolute numbers. A potentially more important development with regard to homicide was the appearance in 1997 of *Homicide Studies*, an interdisciplinary international journal. Its goal is to bridge the gap between academician and practitioner as well as between different disciplines, and ultimately to assist in the formation of more effective public policies and programs. Such interdisciplinary research can help us understand the causes of homicide so that we may learn how to reduce and perhaps even prevent it.

OVERVIEW OF INVESTIGATIVE ACTIVITIES

A broad survey of homicide investigation is presented in this section. Outlining what needs to be done in apparently logical order creates an impression that there is a step-by-step procedure to be followed, but adhering to a prescribed course of action is often not feasible (see Chapter 27). Rather, the investigator must be prepared to seize upon any development that seems important and see that it is followed through and fully exploited, while remaining watchful for other developments to emerge. One should record the date and time any tactical maneuver is taken in response to new information, as preparation for a "when" question from defense counsel during a trial or other hearing. There are risks involved in such jumping around—other aspects of the investigation may be eclipsed, ignored, or overlooked. Hence, a comprehensive checklist will not only preclude this unfortunate result, it will serve as a reminder of the fundamentals that are part and parcel of a thorough investigation. Later, when preparing to testify in court, the investigator will find the list invaluable.

Recording the crime scene (with sketches and photographs), interviewing, and examining records were covered earlier in the text. Other procedures, such as ascertaining motive and assessing its value, are dealt with for the first time and treated here at some length.

Assuming the crime was committed in the investigator's jurisdiction, the following procedure is in accordance with normal practice:

---

* The term "clearance rate" as used by police is determined by the number of cases in which an arrest was made for a crime (e.g., robbery), divided by the number of incidents (in this example, robberies) reported. Clearance rates as reported by the state's attorney include cases that are plea bargained or prosecuted successfully (far fewer cases falling into the latter category). Hence, the prosecutor's clearance rates are generally higher, partly because a state's attorney can be selective with regard to the cases he or she chooses to plea bargain or prosecute. The apparent difference in competence merely reflects the inherently more difficult task assigned to the police.

INVESTIGATIVE ACTIVITIES IN A HOMICIDE

1. Record crime scene (photographs, sketches, notes).

2. Recognize, collect, and preserve all physical evidence.

    To facilitate reconstruction of the crime.

    To link a suspect to the victim, crime scene, or both.

    To identify a substance (poison, narcotic, blood, semen), or an object (bludgeon, gun) in order to locate its source and trace its owner.

3. Identify the victim.

4. Establish the cause, manner, and time of death.

5. Ascertain the motive for the crime.

    From the way the crime was committed—using evidence at the scene, and trauma inflicted on the victim for psychological profiling.

    From those who had knowledge of the victim's activities (social, familial, business).

    From documents written by or sent to the victim—diaries, letters, or documents relating to financial or business dealings of the victim.

6. Seek additional information.

    Interview people to check on the background and activities of the victim; obtain leads from those who knew the deceased; seek a possible informant; consider surveillance in some cases.

    Examine records to ascertain business interests of the victim; trace source of murder weapon through manufacturer's records or firearms registration records.

    Review intradepartmental electronic communications on a daily basis. Scan the police information network for possibly related criminal activity in other jurisdictions. Check on previous arrests to compare *modus operandi.*

    Obtain exemplars from any suspect (or from his or her home, garage, vehicle, etc.) for comparison with similar physical evidence discovered at the crime scene.

7. Question suspects (after administering *Miranda* warnings).

    Allow suspects to make any statement they wish, including those that are exculpatory. Check any statement in regard to suspect's knowledge of what happened in order to compare it against facts revealed through reconstructing the event, using available autopsy and physical evidence. The forensic pathologist can be very helpful in reconstructing the event; this should be attempted early in the investigation, preferably within the first 48 hours in a conference involving all investigators and technical personnel. Obtain an admission or a confession. During questioning, make use of forensic laboratory reports and other evidence of guilt that link the suspect to the crime.

PARTITIONING RESPONSIBILITIES

The investigation of a homicide can involve several persons—a crime scene evidence technician, criminalist, forensic pathologist, and detective or investigator. The responsibility for investigative activities in most cases can be partitioned as follows. [Numbers correspond with those used in "Investigative Activities in a Homicide" in preceding section.]

Individual	Activity-Responsibility
Evidence Technician	• recording crime scene (1) • recognizing, collecting, and preserving physical evidence (2)
Criminalist	• recognizing, collecting, and preserving physical evidence (2) *Sometimes responsible for:* • recording crime scene (1)
Forensic Pathologist	• identifying the victim (3) • estimating the time of death (4) • establishing the cause and manner of death (4) *Sometimes contributes to:* • recognizing, collecting, and preserving physical evidence (2) • ascertaining the motive for the crime (5)
Forensic Anthropologist	• recognizing, collecting, and preserving physical evidence (2) • identifying the victim (3)
Detective (Investigator)	• recording crime scene (1) • recognizing, collecting, and preserving physical evidence (2) • ascertaining the motive for the crime (5) • seeking additional information (6) • questioning suspects (7) *Develops authentic information for:* • identifying the victim (3)

MOTIVE

Importance

Motive is an important factor in pointing to possible suspects in a homicide. Often there is a personal relationship between victim and perpetrator that, if subjected to stress, may impel one of them to kill the other. If the underlying cause can be found, deductive reasoning may lead the investigator back to the one who logically might have been so motivated. Further investigative efforts are then required either to develop additional evidence of guilt or to eliminate the suspect entirely. Because it will provide some focus to the investigative process, it is useful to understand the most common motives for homicide.

The following classification treats ostensible motives as they appear to detectives initially, or as they are alleged by offenders after apprehension. Usually, deeper psychological motivations are not considered; in the absence of a psychiatric study of the killer, they are generally unknown. But psychological profiling can be of help in solving some cases.

Categorizing Motives

The following list covers most of the apparent reasons that impel one person to kill another. Sometimes it can be a combination of motives:

- Financial gain
- Sexual gratification
- Apparently sex-connected homicides
- Emotional factors
- Self-protection
- Removal of an inconvenience or impediment
- Apparently motiveless crimes

Financial Gain

Killers prompted by the expectation of financial gain include: the beneficiary of a will or insurance policy of a spouse or relative; the surviving spouse in a community property state; the merchant who stands to profit from the death of a business associate; the so-called "Lonely Hearts" killer and the poisoner (see section on multiple killings).

When financial gain is the precipitating factor, deductive reasoning from motive to possible suspect(s) is often fruitful. There are exceptions, however. In robbery cases when the victim resists and is killed, the motive is seldom particularized; then, the answer is to solve the felony utilizing techniques appropriate to that felony. This would pertain to a burglary/homicide. The motive of a "Lonely Hearts" killer or poisoner is also financial gain, but in these cases a paper record of financial transactions connecting killer and victim is more likely to remain. Such transactions might include signing the home ownership deed over to the killer, opening a new checking or savings account in the name of the victim and killer, or even using a credit card.

Sexual Gratification

The classic example of sex as a motive for homicide is lust. Wanting a new or younger mate has led to the murder of a spouse, particularly in community property states where husband and wife own equal shares in their accumulated wealth (and the survivor need not settle for half the estate—as would ordinarily be the case with divorce). Both motives of sex and financial gain offer clues as to who might profit from the victim's death.

Apparently Sex-Connected Homicides

The psychological motivations for crimes of this kind are quite different. The killing of homosexuals and of young boys and girls (particularly girls) by older men appears to be of sexual origin. However, this is unlikely to aid in the identification of a suspect unless the slayer's *modus operandi* is on record.

Sadism—obtaining sexual satisfaction by inflicting pain on others—generally is not carried out to the point of death, yet there are some who do cross the threshold into homicide when not satiated by cruelty alone. Biting and mutilating may precede or follow the actual killing. There often is no prior connection between offender and victim, so motive is not helpful in leading back to the killer. On the other hand, a psychological profile may be constructed using inductive reasoning. It would begin with the recognition and interpretation of the evidence at the crime scene, including the trauma inflicted on the victim. According to the type of offender described, the profile would suggest the most beneficial interrogative approach. Additional data generated (according to FBI literature) might include: the murderer's sex, race, age bracket, employment history, socioeconomic status, sexual adjustment, past record of offenses and, in some cases, a prediction as to whether the individual will strike again. Psychological assessment and the details needed for constructing a profile are given more extensive treatment in Chapter 4.

Some murders are committed simultaneously with or immediately after the sex act, as a concomitant of sexual gratification. In other cases, gratification is achieved through the act of killing rather than through the act of sex; the assertion of power over the victim is the primary motivation—any sexual gratification is secondary. If these cases are initially perceived as ostensible sex homicides, the result may be a misdirected investigative effort. The inaccurately assessed crime scene can allow serial murders to escape detection for long periods of time. (See the discussion of ViCAP later in this chapter.)

Along with a study of the crime scene and the victim's body, interviews can provide important information by questioning those who might have been present when the victim and perpetrator were likely to have met (in a tavern or a school yard, for instance). A description of the offender and possibly of an automobile may be obtained from such eyewitnesses.

In some homicides thought to be sex-connected, peers or bar companions may know a good deal about the suspect: where he or she lives; if he or she is a recent arrival, where he or she comes from, occupation, and so on. Informants, surveillance, and canvassing are often employed in solving these cases. In child homicides, canvassing the neighborhood in the vicinity of a school yard or playground may produce a partial identification of a suspect or an automobile. Surveillance would then be worthwhile, with surveillants positioned to observe a subsequent effort to lure another victim.

Emotional Factors

Strong emotions—anger, jealousy, revenge, envy, hatred—can provoke a person to commit manslaughter or premeditated murder. A typical case of manslaughter is the lover or spouse caught in *flagrante delicto* and killed in the heat of passion. On the other hand, if the aggrieved partner plans and carries out the killing, it is premeditated murder.

Broken nuptial engagements, domestic quarrels, and altercations in general can escalate and lead to homicide when they exceed the bounds of dispute. As a rule, homicides motivated by strong emotion are readily solved, many being manslaughter cases with witnesses present. But even premeditated murder permits potential suspects to be identified deductively once motive is established.

Killings that involve the working out of emotional fantasies are called fantasy murders; they are sex-related as a rule, but not always sex-dominated. Some serial killings fall into this category.

Self-Protection

Self-protection as a reason for homicide should be recognized as a feasibility in specific situations. One example would be the criminal (caught in the act of committing a crime) whose escape is interrupted or hampered by the victim. Another would be a murder committed as a result of the realization of the eventual danger that would be posed by an eyewitness should the offender become a suspect. Another example, perhaps more frequent in occurrence, is that of an offender known to the victim (often a child or teenager) who kills to silence the victim. In such situations, self-protection is the motive for the removal of the eyewitness as a potential informant.

Interrupted Crimes

Home burglaries in particular are sometimes interrupted by the unforeseen return of the resident; if the burglar's escape is hampered, a homicide can ensue. An important early step in this kind of investigation would be to trace the movements of the victim just prior to the time of death.

In one case, the victim told a friend she had to go back home for papers needed for an appointment with the family lawyer. When she failed to keep the appointment, a concerned relative went to her apartment and found her murdered. No signs of a forced entry could be detected, but a partial palm print was developed on a bedroom lamp that had been moved from its usual place. A few months later, a young hardware store employee and lock specialist was apprehended for the burglary of a nearby sporting goods store; again, there were no signs of forced entry. A review of unforced entry cases in the area, coupled with the hardware store record of the employee's lock work, disclosed that in both cases he had changed the locks shortly before the burglaries (and homicide) occurred. Palm print evidence established that the hardware store employee handled the woman's bedroom lamp, located far from the hall door on which the lock work was done. When questioned about the woman's death, the intruder admitted that her unanticipated early return had surprised him, and that a struggle ensued which ultimately led to her death.

Eliminating an Eyewitness

The killing of an eyewitness (as a secondary homicide) may immediately follow the primary homicide. When homicide-suicide has been ruled out, the case is viewed as a dual criminal homicide. The chance that one of the victims was an eyewitness to the first (primary) homicide should also be considered. Checking on the background of each victim often determines who was most likely the intended victim and who the potential eyewitness (or secondary victim). Investigative efforts then can be concentrated on solving the initial (primary) homicide.

Slaying a Potential Informant

When the motive for a secondary homicide is the silencing of a potential informant, it will have investigative value only if some connection existed between killer and secondary victim that made the victim privy to the activities of the killer. Since the secondary victim could have incriminated only a limited number of individuals, the investigator must discover who they might be, and who among them had the opportunity (as to time and place) to commit the secondary homicide. Furthermore, if the suspect in the secondary homicide and the motive for the primary homicide are congruent, the hypothesis asserting the suspect's guilt is reinforced. Additional investigative effort will be necessary, but the result will be doubly satisfying if the case is made.

Removal of an Inconvenience or Impediment

A blackmailer, an unwanted child, a feeble parent blocking the takeover of a family business—each is an example of an obstacle to be removed. Once an investigator perceives that the very existence of the deceased was a major inconvenience or impediment to another person, the prospects of solving the homicide are enhanced. Records and people are important sources of information in such cases; they can support the hypothesis that the removal of an obstacle was the motive. Depending on how the crime was committed, physical evidence may link the victim or crime scene to the killer; for instance, a weapon could be traced to the offender's household.

Apparently Motiveless Crimes

There are two distinct kinds of homicide that appear motiveless or senseless: those of stranger killing stranger and those in which a person other than the intended victim is killed.

Stranger Killing Stranger

Although far less frequent than killings involving friends or acquaintances, this kind of homicide is on the increase in the United States. The adolescent male acting on a dare or the gang member asserting manliness (machismo) shoots to kill the first stranger he encounters. Encountering the stranger isn't always necessary; such shootings come from high-rise buildings as well as from passing cars. Nor is it necessary to be male; adolescent girl gangs are proliferating. Alcohol and other drugs often play a role in these senseless crimes, the fundamental cause of which is probably low self-esteem. The solution of such crimes is frequently based on information obtained through a neighborhood canvass, from informants motivated by a substantial community reward, from pawn shop records, and from people who saw or heard the discharge of a firearm and reported it.

Mistaken Identity

Infrequently, a homicide will appear to be without motive, and—after a thorough check on the victim's background—quite senseless. Though the time or site may suggest the killing was intentional, no reason can be found. For example, a businessman was shot upon emerging from his apartment house at about 6:30 A.M., apparently by two men who just before that were observed loitering outside the building. The deceased's business and social background furnishing no possible motive, the case remained unsolved. Several months later, in the vicinity of the first homicide, another man was shot at the same time of day as he emerged from a building bearing the same house number but on a different street. When apprehended and questioned, the perpetrators confessed that they were hired killers. The first slaying had been a case of mistaken identity; the second was committed to rectify the mistake: this time they got both house and street number correct.

The very absence of motive is, in itself, significant. Here, it enabled investigative activities to concentrate on a neighborhood canvass and to find in both cases that the various bits of evidence matched: descriptions of victims and loiterers; occurrences at same time of day and same day of the week; two targets in the same neighborhood, in similar kinds of buildings with identical numerical addresses; and so on.

In another homicide, that of a Kansas farm family (see the Clutter case in the section on multiple deaths), the possibility of a mistake was considered. Investigators were about to fan out over several states and check everybody who had ever worked for the family. Before this exhaustive plan could be implemented, an informant changed the course of the investigation and led to a solution. The informant, a prison inmate who once worked for the Clutters, had shared everything he had learned about Mr. Clutter's way of doing business (where he kept his files, his cash flow, etc.) with his former cellmate. The news of the massacre overcame the prison-culture tenet to tell authorities nothing; he offered information to investigators implicating his former cellmate as one of the killers.

Homicides like those of the businessmen previously mentioned occur when a criminal tracks down the wrong person. Another example concerns an Ohio man who thought he was shooting his ex-wife and the man with whom she had fled to Florida. Instead, he had broken into the home of a family whose car in the driveway had a "vanity" license bearing the initials of the man he was pursuing. Upon arriving in Florida, the woman—knowing she had made a narrow escape and still fearing for her life—reported to local police the threats her husband had made. When they investigated the break-in and murder, the police recalled her report. The detectives making inquiries at the mobile home park brought along the photograph she had provided of the husband; and employees readily identified him as the man who had been looking for a couple newly arrived from the north. As this case demonstrates, people are an important source of information. To prove guilt in court, however, it is necessary to collect all available physical evidence—here, the key piece of evidence was a firearm found in the trunk of the killer's vehicle. It is important to note that even when the motive seems apparent, it is still a hypothesis to be proved or discredited. Clinging tenaciously to what is ultimately the wrong motive can be hazardous; not only is precious investigative time lost, an offender is given the opportunity to eliminate any trail leading to him or her.

Determining Motive

In addition to understanding the motivations for homicide, it is necessary to be acquainted with how motive may be ascertained. Three major sources of information—crime scene, people, and records—serve this purpose.

Crime Scene

In addition to physical evidence, there are other kinds of evidence from which to surmise motive. As pointed out elsewhere in the text, the experienced homicide detective may be able to form a "crime picture" of the offender based on familiarity with similar crimes. This approach has been refined and to some extent codified. For some homicides, therefore, a psychological profile of the offender may help to ascertain motive (see Chapter 4).

People

The most productive source for determining motive is people—family, friends, business associates, and others who had more than a passing acquaintance with the deceased. As indicated above, several reasons can prompt one person to kill another: some involve premeditation; some, a heat-of-the-moment impulse. With regard to the latter, a certain amount are for trivial reasons; for others, however, the reason can be enormous, deep-seated, and compelling. A thorough background check on the deceased may provide insight into a likely motive for the homicide. From this determination, a list of people harboring such a motive can be compiled, and then narrowed, by considering who had the opportunity, means, and temperament to commit the crime. If victim and potential suspect come from a culture in which face-saving or male dominance is the norm, and the victim is female, then interpersonal relationships must be examined. What might merely be a lack of courtesy may be, in another culture, perceived as an insult to be repaid; such a confrontation often escalates—with lethal results.

Records

Records are also of help in suggesting motive. Financial gain may be indicated if a large insurance policy was issued or a will changing beneficiaries was signed just prior to the homicide. Records might reveal a history of "sharp" business practices or debt default, of family quarrels or disturbances requiring police response, or of filing for separation or divorce—any of these can leave a paper trail to the person motivated by anger, hatred, or the need to retaliate.

THE CRIME SCENE AS THE FOCUS OF THE INVESTIGATION

In homicide cases particularly, the crime scene can be a rich source of physical evidence—if care is taken to recognize it. To reconstruct how the crime was committed, or determine what actually happened, physical evidence must be recognized before it can be recorded, collected, and preserved. Moreover, there may be but one chance to accomplish this. In fact, legal requirements can limit the crime scene search to a single opportunity, should the property owner refuse to allow a second search. Other reasons for a thorough initial search include the possibility that the scene may be damaged by weather conditions (rain, snow, temperature), building construction in (or the tearing down of) the premises housing the crime scene, or other factors.

Another consideration arises when a dead body is in plain view. Because decency and dignity obligate investigators to shield it from public gaze, a cover must be carefully selected. This may create a problem; for example, investigators in the Nicole Brown Simpson/Ronald Goldman double-murder case used an old blanket from the home of the suspect's former wife (one of the murder victims). Because the accused had been a frequent visitor there, defense counsel maintained that fibers and hairs found at the scene could have dislodged from the blanket only to fall on the victims' bodies. Had a vinyl shower curtain or a new (painter's) drop cloth been selected, any potential for adding evidence to the crime scene would have been mitigated.

At the outset of the homicide investigation, the crime scene is the center point around which important questions revolve:

- Is this an unlawful homicide?

- Is this a homicide disguised as a suicide?

- Who is the deceased?

- What was the motive for the killing?

- Is there physical evidence present that may link the killer to the crime scene or the victim or could be useful in reconstructing the crime?

- What happened and/or how was the crime committed?

A somewhat different and complementary perspective was promulgated in late 1997 by a National Medicolegal Review Panel consisting of 144 highly experienced professionals from across the country.[7] Almost 60 percent of the reviewer network had medical backgrounds, in contrast to 31 percent who had law enforcement backgrounds. The title of its research report, *National Guidelines for Death Investigation*, suggests the difference between death and homicide investigation.

The purpose of the report was to identify and delineate the "set of investigative tasks that should and could be performed at every death scene.[8] To this end, coroners (especially in rural areas) and medical examiners can be assured that they now have the "means for substantially enhancing performance in fulfilling their far-ranging responsibilities."[9] Furthermore, adherence to the guidelines "may also serve to prevent innocent people from being accused of criminal activity when, in fact, a crime was not committed or the person suspected was not involved."[10]

The benefits of conforming to these guidelines stand in sharp contrast to the situation that existed before they became available:

> . . . With no "official training" required for elected coroners, it is difficult for the elected coroner to know what should be done in investigations. Most elected coroners have begun their jobs with little or no knowledge as to how and what they need to do. Having a set of national guidelines for medicolegal death investigation would ensure that at least the elected coroner would have a "cookbook" to follow and would have some idea of what is expected of him/her in every case.[11]

The guidelines cover in considerable detail the following: investigative tools and equipment, arriving at the scene, documenting and evaluating the scene, documenting and evaluating the body, establishing and recording decendent profile information, and completing the scene investigation.

Is This an Unlawful Homicide?

One element of murder or manslaughter that must be proved in court is whether the death was a result of an action or an omission that is neither excusable nor justifiable. This task being the responsibility of the medical examiner's or coroner's office, the forensic pathologist provides expert testimony on the cause and manner of death. This matter is given more extensive treatment in the next section, "The Body as the Focus of the Investigation."

To the investigator coming upon a crime scene it is important to point out that appearances are not always what they seem; cause of death is not necessarily obvious from viewing the body. In one case, an observant police officer saw a man leave an apartment house with a newspaper-wrapped package under his arm, return to the building, and re-emerge 10 minutes later with another package from which some apparently human toes protruded. On accompanying the man back to his apartment, the officer was confronted with the sight of a dismembered female body, a blood-splattered kitchen and bathroom, and what would appear to be an open-and-shut case of criminal homicide.

But not necessarily. The chain of events started the night before when the man in question met the woman at a bar, and after some heavy drinking took her to his apartment, then passed out. Waking in the morning to find a dead woman in his bed, he assumed he had killed her before blacking out. His attempted cover-up—dismembering and disposing of the body—had been exposed by the observant officer. The autopsy determined the death was from natural causes.

Is This Homicide Simulated as Suicide?

Simulating (or staging) a crime to cover up another crime is fairly rare, but it is not unheard of: to cloak homicide, arson and automobile accidents are the most common expedients; to conceal larceny—especially when an inventory is imminent, burglary may be used. Such crimes are detected because the simulation is often "overstaged" by an offender who is too anxious that investigators not miss the point.

Books that graphically detail how to terminate one's life open up the possibility of such information being misapplied (e.g., simulating a suicide to cover up a murder). Geberth, the author of a well-known work on homicide investigation, claims that "there are a significant number of such suicides occurring throughout the country."[12] He discusses three case histories of cases that were classified as suicides due to the similarities between the case and the information in the book *Final Exit*. Each was on file as a suicide because of the similarities between the death and the preparatory steps taken in the suicide: a plastic bag over the victim's head, a copy of the book *Final Exit* found beside the body, a note or letter(s) encompassing the recommendations prescribed in the book.[13]

The investigator must bear in mind how relatively easy it would be to gather such props in order to make a criminal homicide appear to be a suicide. To determine whether an apparent suicide falls into that category, Geberth provides a checklist.[14] Following is a checklist modified for the purpose of this text: an asterisk is placed next to those steps that, if followed, should help to differentiate a criminal homicide from a *Final Exit*-type suicide:

INVESTIGATIVE CHECKLIST

1. Is *Final Exit* at the scene?

2. Is there any underlining, written entry, or other markings in *Final Exit* related to what is observed at the scene, i.e., did the highlighted part(s) of the book serve as a model for the act of self-deliverance?

3. Is there other evidence for an act of self-deliverance, i.e., a suicide note (or other letters), perhaps accompanied by a Living Will and/or a Durable Power of Attorney for Health Care?

*4. Care must be exercised when touching or handling the suicide note (or other document) until it has been examined for fingerprints. To assess any latent prints that may be developed, the finger and palm prints of the deceased and all persons who were present at the scene or who are considered to be close to the deceased, must be obtained for comparison purposes.

*5. If there is a plastic bag over the head of the deceased (or if one is present at the scene) it must be examined for fingerprints. Any latent print that is developed must be compared with the known prints, as suggested above. A print present on the plastic bag (other than that of the deceased) must be evaluated against any explanation offered for its presence, taking into consideration the account given before the print was developed.

*6.   Is the substance of the suicide note (or letter) expressed at the literacy level of the deceased? Or does the "last letter or note" duplicate almost exactly what is suggested in *Final Exit*? An illiterate (or semiliterate) person may copy the words out of the book, but it should give rise to some suspicion if a literate person did so.

*7.   If the note or letter is handwritten, its authenticity must be established. Is the handwriting (or hand printing) that of the deceased? If typed, was the instrument—typewriter or computer—available to the deceased? Was the deceased able to type or use a computer?

*8.   All medicine containers must be gathered—including those that are empty. If a label bears the name of any of the drugs mentioned in *Final Exit* as useful for self-deliverance, any remaining contents should be analyzed. From the label (which shows the quantity dispensed) and the Drug Dosage Table in *Final Exit,* determine if a lethal dose was available to the deceased. If an autopsy and a toxicological analysis were carried out, check the results against the content of the containers.

Any information at variance with what might be expected should be followed up until any discordant or jarring results are clarified or a criminal homicide is settled upon.

Who is the Deceased?

Victim identification is of singular importance in homicide cases; otherwise, the crime will rarely be solved. The experience of numerous investigators bears witness to this assertion, for only after an identification has been made can a motive for the killing be established and then utilized to generate potential suspects. Correctly identifying the victim, therefore, is crucial. In addition to its investigative value, the identification is part of the *corpus delicti;* thus, it has probative value as well.

In many homicide cases identification is easy. It is speedily accomplished by relatives, friends, neighbors, and business associates who have known the victim for some time and can be relied upon to perform this function. On the other hand, if the victim was known casually or for a short time—as the new roomer by a landlady—an identification based on such limited acquaintance is considered a "presumptive ID" and not deemed reliable.

Confirming an identification by independent means is therefore advisable. Identification by two unrelated persons who knew the victim well or by one person and a document (such as a driver's license) in the victim's possession with matching description or photograph is adequate for a "positive ID." Jewelry, although not in itself sufficient for an identification in a criminal homicide, can make a contribution if it is engraved or of unusual design.

Fingerprints, useful perhaps 10 percent of the time, nevertheless should be checked—especially if the body is not readily identified. (Of course, this is fruitless if the victim has not been previously fingerprinted.) Missing persons records should be reviewed. The victim's clothing should be examined; if a laundry dry cleaning mark is found (either visually or by ultraviolet light) and a laundry file is maintained, it must be checked. A photograph of the victim (and laundry mark, if not identified) can be distributed in the community, and a public appeal made through newspapers and television. The roles of medical and dental evidence are discussed later in the text.

What Was the Motive?

To be of investigative value, it is vital that any psychological evidence suggestive of the killer's motive be recognized at the crime scene and interpreted. An informed effort to estimate what kind of a person could have committed the crime is called *psychological profiling* (see Chapter 4). Apt to be useful in homicides involving sex, sadistic torture, disembowelment, or genital mutilation, a psychological profile may enable investigators to choose among those likely suspects whose aberrant behavior has been noted in the community and who appear capable of committing such a crime. Follow-up is obviously necessary to prove or disprove clues provided by this means.

The lack of apparent motive in a homicide raises the possibility of a mistake. A neighborhood canvass should be undertaken in search of a living individual whose description and behavior are consistent with those of the deceased; then a background check made on that individual. If a motive is found to explain why his or her sudden demise would be desirable, there is some chance that the motiveless crime was a case of mistaken identity.

An interesting twist on lack of motive manifested itself in the case of the murder of Jennifer Levin (the Central Park preppie murder case) when Prosecutor Linda Fairstein informed FBI profiler John Douglas:

> We know who the killer is, but we don't have a motive. Can you try and reverse the process for me? We don't have to prove motive in court, but everybody's going to be asking why he did it, and it'll be easier to get a conviction if we can explain it to them.[15]

This is a reversal of the normal course of events: this investigation moved from suspect to motive, rather than from motive to suspect.

Is There Associative Evidence Present?

Evidence that can link the perpetrator to the crime scene or victim is of two kinds: (1) evidence brought to and left (often unintentionally) at the scene; and (2) evidence taken deliberately or accidentally from the scene. Examples of the first kind are: fingerprints; spent bullets and cartridge cases; and blood, hair, and fibers from the person or clothing of the perpetrator. Examples of the second kind include: easily carried loot such as small appliances; rug and clothing fibers; broken glass particles imbedded in clothing or in the rubber heel of a shoe; smeared fresh paint or blood spattered on clothing; and so on. A mutual transfer of evidence is also feasible—clothing fibers, blood, or hair—from victim to killer during a struggle, and vice versa.

The covering employed to protect the privacy of the deceased could contain associative evidence. As mentioned previously in this chapter, investigators in the Nicole Brown Simpson/Ronald Goldman double murder case took a used blanket from the home of Nicole Brown Simpson. Because the accused (O.J. Simpson) had been a frequent visitor there, defense counsel maintained that fibers and hair found at the scene could have been dislodged from the blanket onto the victims' bodies. A different selection of coverings (e.g., a drop cloth or shower curtain) would have mitigated any potential for adding evidence to the crime scene.

The sources of associative evidence suggest what might be looked for at the crime scene; they are:

- Traces of the person
  Finger and palm prints
  Blood, semen, saliva, hair
  Bare footprints
  Other skin patterns such as ear prints and lip impressions
  Teeth marks

- Traces of wearing apparel
  Shoe prints
  Weave pattern and stitching of clothing and gloves
  Clothing accessories

- Impressions left by
  Weapons—firearms, cutting or stabbing devices
  Tools—jimmies, metal cutters, hammers, metal punches
  Shovels—used to bury a body or weapon (Some types of soil, such as clay, retain striation marks left by the digging edge of a shovel.)

The discovery, preservation, and investigative value of physical evidence are treated extensively in Chapters 2 and 3.

Reconstructing What Happened

There are scientific means available to reconstruct the crime; that is, to determine how it was committed and what happened. The purpose is to allow any account of the event advanced by a suspect or witness to be compared with the reconstructed facts. Therefore, before anything is moved it is vital that the initial appearance of the crime scene be faithfully recorded through notes, sketches, and particularly photographs—including video pictures.

The kinds of clue materials most frequently involved in the reconstruction of a crime are firearms and blood evidence. Other determinations might include: estimating the time needed to perform an act; pinpointing the exact time of a telephone call; making a theoretical analysis of a certain phenomenon; or conducting experiments. For example, how does a particular coffee table topple when struck during a struggle? Does it land on its side or turn upside down? A theoretical calculation of its center of gravity by a physicist, coupled with controlled experimentation by a qualified scientist, will provide a more reliable answer than an investigator's rudimentary tests at the scene.

Unexplained, significant differences between the facts disclosed through scientific reconstruction of evidence, and facts alleged by a suspect or witness, can be put to good use in subsequent interrogations (see Chapter 2 on crime reconstruction and Chapter 11 on confessions.) Owing to its serendipitous nature, physical evidence may, when least expected, bring to light what actually happened. For example, though human hair seldom serves this purpose, when the need arose to determine which of two inebriated individuals was the driver of a car that killed two people in an unwitnessed accident (with each accusing the other), examination of the hair imbedded in the damaged windshield on the passenger side provided an indisputable answer.

The major contribution of the forensic pathologist to homicide investigation rests on the autopsy. Should a pathologist respond directly and promptly to the crime scene, he or she may also assist by offering an opinion as to the kind of weapon used in the killing. This information will facilitate a search for the weapon in the surrounding area and along possible escape routes.

THE BODY AS THE FOCUS OF THE INVESTIGATION

When examined by properly trained forensic scientists the victim's body can provide evidence of investigative and probative value. The testimony of the forensic pathologist figures significantly in this endeavor; it is required to prove one of the elements of homicide—that death was the result of a criminal act. In addition to shedding light on the cause and manner of death, he or she may be able to testify about some of the circumstances surrounding the event, thus permitting a reconstruction of the crime—how and when it was committed. An experienced forensic pathologist can provide facts useful in constructing a profile of the killer, for instance, a description of the blows—their number and location—and the way they were inflicted. Other forensic scientists (e.g., odontologists, radiologists) may be able to identify the victim through the study of evidence obtained from the body—by X-rays of the teeth, for example.

Who is the Deceased?

In general, the most common means of identifying the victim are successful in permitting investigators to move on to other pressing matters. But sometimes body and facial features are unrecognizable (or missing if the body was dismembered), and clothing or jewelry is not present. In these circumstances, the forensic pathologist and forensic odontologist may be able to identify the body through a comparison of skeletal and dental X-rays, or through unique features such as a surgically repaired organ, spinal cord defect, scar, birthmark, or tattoo (see Figure 14.1). An exemplar, a medical and dental record, or photograph of the feature taken before death is required for such a comparison to be successful (see Figure 14.2).

Figure 14.1
Body tattoos can be important in the identification of the deceased. *(Courtesy, Office of the Medical Examiner, Cook County, Illinois.)*

Establishing the Cause and Manner of Death—The Autopsy

A death may be from natural causes, accident, suicide, or criminal act. When the first three are ruled out, it falls under the criminal law. The forensic pathologist, using medical autopsy, determines the cause and manner of death, and also evaluates the circumstances of the death. In gunshot cases for instance, cause and manner are determined in part by the circumstances surrounding the discovery of the body. Answers to the following questions, therefore, can reveal whether a death was suicidal, accidental, or criminal.

- Are there signs of a struggle?

- Could the injuries have been self-inflicted? The location of the entrance wound, the powder pattern, and the trajectory of the bullet in the body are important to this determination.

- What was the location of the weapon (or other object) that inflicted the injury or injuries?

- Is there a suicide note? Is it in the deceased's handwriting or printing?

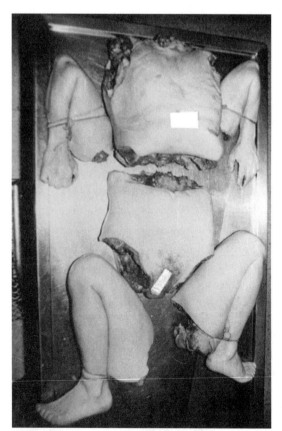

In addition to its probative value, in the event that death was the result of a criminal act, the autopsy reveals detailed information. This affords the investigator, assisted by the pathologist, an opportunity to reconstruct the crime (should that be necessary).

Autopsy did not become a widely accepted, integral part of homicide investigation until the nineteenth century. Before that and continuing to this day, its principal purpose is the study of disease, particularly terminal disease. A medicolegal autopsy is a postmortem, scientific and systematic, internal and external examination of a corpse by a physician, the forensic pathologist. Involving as it does the practice of medicine, confidentiality must be maintained, albeit the patient is deceased.

Figure 14.2
Unidentified dismembered body. Neither fingerprints (criminal or civil) nor medical records could be found; homicide remains unsolved. *(Courtesy, Office of the Medical Examiner, Cook County, Illinois.)*

The External Examination

The external examination of the corpse is a significant part of a total medicolegal autopsy. The pathologist will also want to see the clothing of the deceased, and the weapon (see Figure 14.3). Yielding details (such as scars or tattoos) that facilitate an identification, the external examination also provides what is necessary to reconstruct inductively the circumstances of the death—what happened, how and when it happened, and whether the body was moved after death.

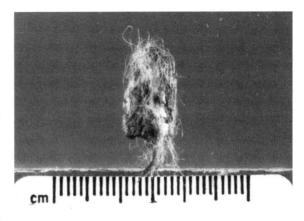

Figure 14.3
Clothing fibers on bullet retrieved from body. Warning: Do not wash bullet and destroy evidence. Fibers are important in garment identification. *(Courtesy, Office of the Medical Examiner, Cook County, Illinois.)*

The Internal Examination

The internal examination of the cadaver involves making incisions (generally of the scalp, chest, and abdomen) to remove organs, tissues, and fluids. Following a gross visual inspection, samples are taken for further study under the microscope and for chemical analysis by a toxicologist. The test results and the external examination allow for the formation of an expert opinion on the cause and manner of death. Sometimes, however, the cause of death cannot be determined.

Reconstructing the Crime

Answers to the following questions arising from autopsy evidence and its interpretation will help the investigator to reconstruct a homicide: Was the body moved after death? What occurred, and how did it occur? How much time would it take to inflict the injuries?

After committing a crime, a killer may move the victim's body to create the appearance of accidental death. To accomplish this, other aspects of the crime scene will have to be staged. In one case, asphyxiating the victim with a pillow in a drunken rage before blacking out created a problem for the murderer on regaining consciousness in the morning. Taking some time to think, he decided to carry the body to a full bathtub, place an electric hair dryer in the water, and turn on the current. The fact that the body had been moved was immediately apparent to the investigator, and the simulated electrocution was rendered a failure (see *postmortem lividity* below).

If there are two victims, the perpetrator may arrange the bodies to make it appear that they killed each other or that it was a murder-suicide. Another reason for moving a victim's body is to limit the scope of the investigation; a sudden disappearance can look like a missing person case instead of a homicide. Serial killers sometimes bury their victims in remote, unfrequented places to avoid detection. Another compelling reason for moving a body from the site of a homicide is the perpetrator's realization of the close connection between himself or herself and the crime scene.

Investigators have some means for determining whether a body has been moved from the site of the killing. One involves the circumstances surrounding the discovery and the place of the discovery; another, the phenomenon known as *postmortem lividity.*

Circumstances and Where Found

The appropriateness of the deceased's clothing, considered in conjunction with the place of discovery of the body, may suggest that the crime was committed elsewhere. For instance, a dead woman found in a garbage dumpster clothed in a nightdress more than likely was killed somewhere else. The chances of solving such cases are improved if the site of the murder can be determined. If the site is under private control or ownership, and there is a known connection between the controller and the victim, questioning that individual is in order. If the site is theoretically open to the public but seldom used, the investigator should determine who knew the victim and who had access to that locale and would feel safe from detection while committing the crime.

Postmortem Lividity

Liver mortis (*postmortem lividity*)[16] is a reddish, purplish-blue discoloration of the skin due to settling of blood, by gravity, in the vessels of the dependant areas of the body. In dependant areas pressed against a hard surface, the vessels are mechanically compressed by the pressure and blood cannot settle in them. This gives these areas a pale coloration. Lividity can be evident within 30 minutes of death and, because of clotting (which may take up to three to four hours), it will remain where it started, even if the body is subsequently moved. If signs of lividity can be seen on the top and side surfaces of the body, the inference can be drawn that it was moved after death.

Forensic Entomology

Entomology is the branch of zoology dealing with insects. The kind of insect(s) found on a body may prove it was moved, there being "city flies" and "country flies." In one case, such proof was provided when a cadaver discovered in a rural area was found to be infested with "city flies." The environment—indoor versus outdoor—influences the kind of insect species to be found on decomposing bodies.

> Some species of insects were restricted to remains discovered indoors; others were associated with remains in outdoor situations. Knowledge of the species associated with different habitats may serve to provide information concerning the history of the remains.[17]

When the entomologist fails to find insects on a body, this may indicate that the body was indeed moved, and that the suspect's denial is false. Entomologists study where a body is discovered as an ecological problem, then interpret their findings in terms of locality (i.e., is the body's insect population consistent with that of the environment of its discovery?). If it is not, then one can surmise that the body was moved from somewhere else. When a body has been moved, locating the site of the homicide can be critically important. Investigators may have a candidate site in mind:

> In an investigation of this sort the entomological examination will have to be conducted on that area, rather than on the body itself. This is because the presence of the body may affect the species composition of the soil beneath it, and these changes will remain detectable after the body has been moved. In indoor situations, the presence of certain corpse-associated insects will reveal the fact that a body had been placed there at some earlier time. There are even cases in which it was shown that murder victims were transported from place to place in a particular car.[18]

Similarly, investigative interest sometimes centers on who or what frequented a certain area:

> Very small insects and other organisms can be inadvertently collected on the clothes or in cars and other vehicles. The presence of these insects can often show that the person or vehicle frequented a particular locality. . . . Again, this kind of associative evidence has largely been overlooked, in spite of its great potential.[19]

Other information entomologists may be able to provide include answers to:

1. How did the death occur?

   When the body is in an advanced state of decay, it may be possible to offer an opinion.

2. Was the body mutilated after death?

   Insect secretions or bites sometimes seem to have a pattern, appearing to have been inflicted by a handmade tool. If a similar pattern were observed in another homicide shortly thereafter, investigators might infer that a disturbed person was involved. Clearly, this would be an unproductive effort if the mutilation pattern is that of insects.

3. Was this animal, especially a species protected by law, killed illegally?

   A conflict regarding time of death—(1) as "told" to an entomologist by studying the insect population and (2) the story told by a suspect as to where or when the carcass was discovered—can have significance for an investigator.[20]

Entomological information is most effectively utilized in the interrogative stage of an investigation, by invoking Horowitz's "Evidence is Available" principle looking toward a confession.

What Time or Times are Involved?

It is often important to know the time of death. Some reasons include:

- To question the individual who appears (from initial interviews) to be the last one to have seen or talked with the victim.

- To look for flaws in a witness's account when it is in conflict with the forensic pathologist's estimated time of death.

- To protect the innocent—often, one person immediately seems the likely suspect, and the sequence of events relative to the homicide can have inculpatory or exculpatory consequences.

Last Person to See the Victim Alive

The last person to see the victim alive (besides the killer), not realizing that he or she possesses information of value, may have useful clues that remain undiscovered unless sought by the investigator. Hence, it is important to allow witnesses to recall the last contact with the victim in their own way, after which the investigator can follow up with questions that ensure disclosure of all potential information:

- What was the state of mind of the victim?

- Were there any signs of agitation or nervousness?

- Was there anything unusual in the behavior of the victim?

- Was anything said that, upon reflection, now seems important?

- If the witness is being re-interviewed after the investigation is underway, were facts developed independently that now suggest additional questions?

Checking a Witness's Story

It is important to check a witness's story. For instance, the establishment of time of death in the following case caused an individual to become a suspect. The victim had told a business associate of an after-dinner appointment—naming the individual to be met, but not the place or purpose of the meeting. As the last person to see the victim alive, this individual was questioned. He claimed, however, that the appointment was never kept, that he had waited more than an hour before leaving for another engagement, and that his first inkling of the crime came from the morning news.

If the pathologist's estimated time of death was substantially the same as the appointment time, the man who was to be met should be considered a potential suspect.

Developing a motive involving this suspect would support the hypothesis that he was the killer, and indicate the need for a thorough follow-up to generate evidence that confirms (or refutes) the hypothesis.

Time of Death

Time of death is more accurately determined in manslaughter cases (witnesses often being present) than in murder cases. In the absence of a witness, the forensic pathologist estimates time of death, basing it on as many factors as possible. Rigor mortis, body temperature, and other factors are used for this purpose.

Rigor Mortis[21]

Rigor mortis, the stiffening of the body after death, is the result of chemical changes within muscle tissue. Evident at first in the small muscles of the hands and jaws (in two to four hours), it becomes more obvious in the larger muscles (in four to six hours), and is fully developed in 12 hours, where it remains until postmortem decomposition begins. Decomposition is affected by extremes of heat and cold; it occurs very slowly in cold weather, more rapidly in hot weather. Clearly, the extent of rigor mortis can be useful in establishing the approximate time of death.

Body Temperature[22]

The live body is able to maintain a constant temperature of about 98 degrees Fahrenheit regardless of weather and type of clothing. After death, its temperature falls to that of the surrounding medium. The rate of fall can be affected by a number of factors; for instance, how the deceased was dressed or covered or the surface on which it is lying may influence heat loss. However, when a clothed adult body is in a room with normal heat, the formula below allows for an estimate of the interval between time of death and time of recording of rectal temperature. It assumes an average drop in temperature to be 1.5 degrees Fahrenheit per hour, that the ambient temperature was about 70 degrees Fahrenheit, and that the deceased had a normal body temperature of 98.6 degrees Fahrenheit at death.

$$\frac{98.6 - T}{1.5} = N$$

Where: T = body rectal temperature in degrees Fahrenheit
        N = number of hours elapsed since death

Several factors can affect the cooling rate; thus, the results have greater validity in the first 12 hours than after a longer interval. If no thermometer is available, feeling the body can yield a more subjective estimate: if the armpits are warm to the touch, death most likely occurred within the last few hours; if the body overall is cool and clammy, the elapsed time since death is approximately 18 to 24 hours.

Other Factors

In addition to bodily changes (postmortem lividity, rigor mortis, heat loss), other factors that can also help in estimating time of death include stomach content, insect growth, and external factors.

Stomach Content:[23] As part of the autopsy, the stomach and small intestines are examined for undigested food. This procedure was developed by twentieth-century pathologists as one of the factors that might suggest time of death. Unlike other postmortem markers, digestion comes to a complete end at death. It provides two important pieces of information—what the deceased ate for the last meal and how long ago it was eaten. When "what" is coupled with "where"—the victim's home or a restaurant he or she frequented—the information obtained can affect the outcome of the investigation. In theory, at least, a medical examiner who knows the approximate time and quantity of the victim's last meal should be able to extrapolate time of death based on the rate that food might be expected to pass out of the stomach into the intestine.

Insect Growth:[24] There are other scientists besides the pathologist whose expertise can be useful in estimating time of death: the forensic entomologist (of which there are few) studies insects from egg laying and larvae growth to fully developed adulthood. Entomologists regard the human cadaver as an ecosystem in which certain insects appear and depart on a predictable schedule; they know, for example, that the eggs of houseflies hatch into maggots in 24 hours. Specific knowledge about the time required for each growth stage permits the specialist to estimate time of death for a body on which insect specimens were observed, recorded (by color photography if possible), and collected. If practicable, the entomologist should visit the crime scene to collect specimens, and do so at the autopsy as well. For such evidence to be reliable, the life cycles of the specific insects obtained from the cadaver must be replicated. Insect evidence in the form of eggs and larvae can sometimes be difficult or impossible to identify, but DNA now permits formerly difficult specimens to be identified.

External Factors: Clues from the victim's residence and personal habits can be of assistance in estimating time of death. Gathering this information is the function of the investigator who then shares it with the pathologist.

Victim's Residence

Neighbors are often able to state when the victim was last seen alive. Additional information can be gleaned from such observations as: any food on the table, dishes in the sink, newspapers or mail not picked up, blinds or shades drawn or open, electric lights on or off, or a watch or clock stopped by its having been damaged (possibly from a struggle).

Personal Habits

If the deceased habitually performed certain daily tasks (e.g., walking the dog, leaving the house to buy cigarettes, going to work, picking up the mail, telephoning friends and family—or receiving calls from them), failure to do so establishes boundaries for estimating time of death.

Time Sequence

In some homicides the time available to the killer to carry out the crime can become an important issue; in others, there may be evidence that the killer delayed in leaving the scene. In either event the investigator should appreciate the implications of the time factor.

Accuracy

Forensic pathologists cannot pinpoint time of death; rather, based on when the victim was last seen alive and when the victim was found dead, they can state the interval of time during which death could have occurred. When the time span is great, the forensic pathologist may be able to narrow these limits—by utilizing insect growth, for example.

Was There Sufficient Time?

The sequence of events surrounding a homicide can be of great importance in fulfilling the obligation to protect the innocent. The investigator should ascertain whether the interval of time was sufficient for the suspect to inflict the injuries. An example will clarify this:

A young man returned home early one evening to find that his mother had been viciously assaulted and left for dead. Instead of dialing 911, he called the friend with whom he had spent the evening and was advised by his friend's father to call the family doctor. As the doctor was out of town, his wife suggested that the young man call an ambulance. Not long thereafter, the friend, an ambulance, and police arrived.

Now a potential suspect, the young man was asked by the police to strip. Investigators found no evidence of involvement in the struggle that had obviously taken place: no blood was on his body or clothing; a minor injury to a knuckle was accounted for (the suspect claiming it resulted when repairing his car); and no physical evidence was found to tie him to the homicide. Just the same, the fact that he was slow to summon assistance was viewed as peculiar, as was his failure to weep or display any other emotion. Along with the fact that he was the first to discover the crime, these particulars made the young man a prime suspect.

Initially, little investigative effort was put into establishing the time of each event surrounding the homicide; subsequently, important differences developed. Had there been sufficient time to commit the crime? This issue was resolved when the friend's father recalled in an interview that the telephone call from the young man had coincided with the fire engine sirens from the firehouse across the street. From this fact and the time the suspect was last seen, the pathologist could answer in the negative: there had not been sufficient time for the brutal murder—including as it did the breaking of several large bones and mutilation of the body.

Delayed Departure—Its Significance

Homicides have been made to appear incidental to an interrupted burglary. This deception is more likely in a manslaughter case, but it can materialize when a premeditated murder plan goes awry. The perpetrator, knowing that he or she will be suspected will sometimes take jewelry and valuables as a way to avoid this possibility.

In one case, a watch was removed from the victim's wrist. She had suffered a brutal beating and blood had seeped through the watchband and dried, leaving an outline of its design on her wrist. It, however, would be a rare burglar-turned-killer who would linger long enough for this to happen; the natural impulse is to escape. Thus, evidence that an offender delayed leaving the scene of a homicide should be a red flag to the investigator, suggesting a connection between victim and killer—a killer who felt secure from interruption while devising and executing a plan to throw investigators off the track.

Time Line

Defense investigators, particularly in cases involving several witnesses, now utilize the time line flowing from witnesses' stories. The purpose is to pick up inconsistencies or impossibilities regarding when the event occurred. For example, if a wife claims to have been with her husband four days ago, and forensic entomological evidence establishes that the victim was not alive four days ago, a case may be opened or its investigation intensified.

In the Nicole Brown Simpson/Ronald Goldman murder case, time of death assumed great importance in answering whether O.J. Simpson had the opportunity to commit the killings. Unfortunately, no forensic pathologist was summoned to the crime scene until so many hours had elapsed that the estimate of the time of death would no longer be of any value.

The suspect (Simpson) was last seen (before the crime) at his residence at 9:36 P.M. He was seen there again at about 10:58 P.M., but was not seen at any time in between (although a cell phone call was made from his vehicle at 10:03 P.M.). The time between 10:58 P.M. and the time the crime was committed determines whether he had the opportunity to carry it out. The last verifiable time that Nicole Brown Simpson, one of the victims, was alive was 9:43 P.M., when she telephoned and spoke with the other victim, Ronald Goldman. A more speculative time marker involved the uncontrollable barking and plaintive wails of her dog. One of the "dog witnesses" estimated that those sounds were heard between 10:15 and 10:30 P.M.

When answers to the quaternary issues (opportunity, means, motive, and audacity) are forthcoming, the investigation is off to a good start. Establishing a time line is helpful with regard to opportunity.

What Occurred?—How Did It Occur?

What occurred in a homicide may be determined from the kind of injury inflicted on the victim. Trauma results when violent or disruptive action causes physical injury or when a toxic substance is introduced into the body. A bullet, a bludgeon, and a sharp weapon produce visibly different injuries. To understand an autopsy report, the terms must be defined:[25]

Abrasion   a superficial, scraped surface area of tissue produced by friction. The result of a blunt force (see Figure 14.4).

Contusion   a hemorrhage beneath the skin; a bruise. If blood vessels are ruptured and considerable bleeding occurs, it is a hematoma.

Fracture   a break or crack of a bone or cartilage. A fracture with the skin broken—an open wound, perhaps with the bone exposed, is a compound (or open) fracture. A simple (or closed) fracture is one in which there is no break in the skin.

Incision   a relatively clean cut that results when a sharp instrument or force is applied to a small, limited area of tissue.

Laceration   a tearing of tissue, generally with ragged edges, caused by stretching the tissue beyond its ability to rebound. The result of a blunt force.

Wound   the result of a blunt or a sharp force. A wound is an injury—especially one in which the skin is pierced, cut, torn, or otherwise broken; however, a wound need not necessarily have open skin. A hematoma (a localized collection of blood, usually clotted, in tissue) is a wound.

Trauma   the result of any force—blunt, sharp, or penetrating. A hit-and-run automobile accident can result in lacerations, fractures, and on occasion, abrasion. A knife or ice pick produces incisions; even a dull axe leaves an incision but its opposite end will produce a laceration. All of these incidents result in trauma.

If the pathologist is able to state with some certainty what kind of weapon was used, the investigator can search for it along the paths the perpetrator may have taken in fleeing the crime scene. When a suspect is developed, his or her home, garage, and automobile can be searched for the weapon. The search and seizure laws must always be kept in mind; otherwise, the evidence may not be admissible. This could materially damage a case since a weapon can serve to link an offender to the crime.

Gunshot wounds are of particular interest; from them it may be possible to determine how and what occurred. They are an important source of information which the forensic scientist interprets for the homicide detective.

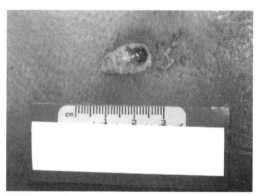

Figure 14.4
Gunshot wound of entry (at oblique angle) showing abrasion on the lateral side of the entrance. *(Courtesy, Office of the Medical Examiner, Cook County, Illinois.)*

Gunshot Wounds[26]

A gunshot wound is the result of the discharge from the barrel of a gun—flame, hot gases, smoke, partially burned and unburned powder particles, and the projectile itself (bullet, wad, or shot). The nature of the wound inflicted is a function of the distance between victim and muzzle at the time of discharge (assuming no object—such as a cigarette lighter in a shirt pocket—was struck by the bullet in flight between weapon and

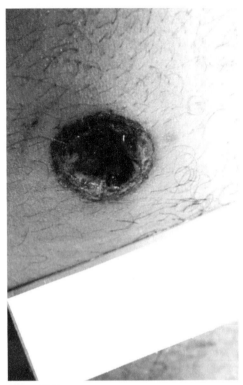

Figure 14.5
Shotgun contact wound. *(Courtesty, Office of the Medical Examiner, Cook County, Illinois.)*

wound), and of the characteristics of the weapon itself (see Figures 14.5-14.7). Both entry and exit wounds can be observed on a body. Distinguishing between them may allow the crime to be reconstructed, as may any blood spatter pattern produced—especially when the victim is shot at close range.

Entrance Wounds— Firing Distance

There are three kinds of entrance wounds: contact, near discharge, and distant discharge. A *contact wound* results when a small weapon is fired while in contact with the skin (a closed wound) or up to a distance of two or three inches from the body (see Figure 14.8), or a large caliber weapon (or rifle) is fired up to a distance of six inches from the body. A *near discharge wound* is the result of firing at a distance of six to 24 inches for handguns, and six to 36 inches for rifles. In reconstructing the possibility of suicide, the near discharge distance cannot exceed the deceased's arm length (unless there is some mechanical contrivance rigged to allow firing the weapon from a distance). A *distant discharge wound* results when a weapon is fired from a distance greater than 24 to 36 inches, respectively, for handguns and rifles (see Figure 14.9).

Characteristics of Entrance and Exit Wounds

Entrance wounds (assuming the bullet is not tumbling or misshapen at the time of entrance) are round or oval in appearance (see Figure 14.10); their edges form an "abrasion collar" with the skin surface inverted—depressed and crater-like. Contact wounds inflicted over thick bone structure have an irregular, stellate (star) shape; their edges are everted—pushed outward. The tearing of the tissue surrounding a contact wound results from the gases that, having entered the wound, seek to reverse direction and escape (see Figure 14.8). The laceration is irregular in appearance; it may be oval-shaped with no abrasion around the edges, but it can and usually will have an abrasion.

An exit wound results when a bullet, emerging from the body, splits the skin. This skin will exhibit greater tearing if the bullet emerges when it is no longer spinning on its axis—wobbling in its passage through the body. This can happen after striking a bone; if the emerging bullet carried bone splinters with it (and possibly some large pieces of bone), the wound may be mistaken for a laceration caused by a blunt force.

Figure 14.6
X-ray of body shows pellets dispersed after striking bone. *(Courtesy, Office of the Medical Examiner, Cook County, Illinois.)*

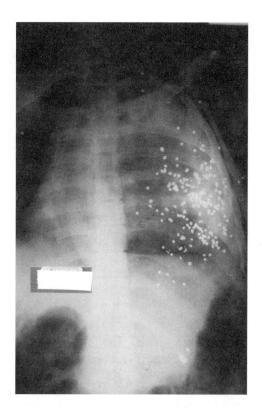

Figure 14.7
An example of stippling (tattooing). Firing distance approximately six inches. *(Courtesy, Office of the Medical Examiner, Cook County, Illinois.)*

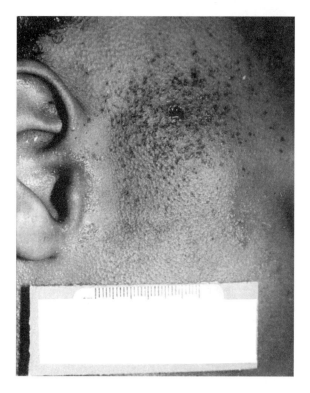

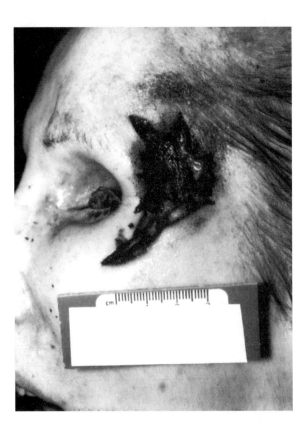

Figure 14.8
Close contact wound of the head with splitting of the skin. This is a suicide. Splitting of skin is due to gaseous discharge from weapon. *(Courtesy, Office of the Medical Examiner, Cook County, Illinois.)*

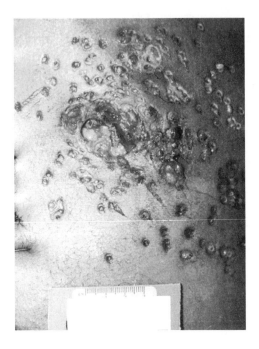

Figure 14.9
Shotgun entrance wound showing satellite wounds from pellets. Firing distance approximately six to eight yards. *(Courtesy, Office of the Medical Examiner, Cook County, Illinois.)*

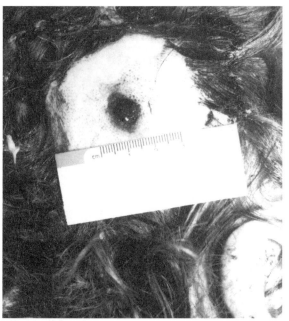

Figure 14.10A
Bullet entrance wound of head.

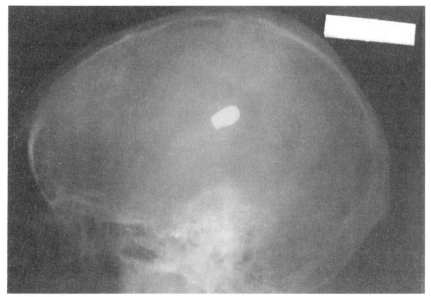

Figure 14.10B
X-ray of head showing lodged bullet.

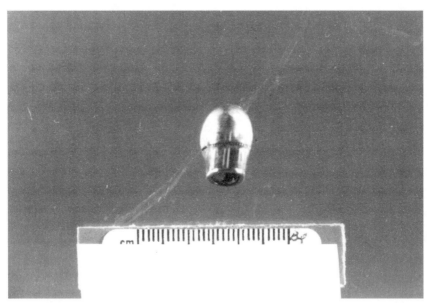

Figure 14.10C
Copper-jacketed bullet removed from head.

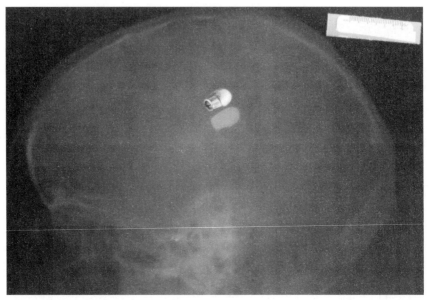

Figure 14.10D
Comparison of bullet with X-ray of lodged bullet. *(Figure 14.10, Courtesy, Office of the Medical Examiner, Cook County, Illinois.)*

Once in the body, bullets have been known to behave erratically. There are several reported instances of a bullet entering a limb and following a blood vein back to the heart to be deposited in an upper chamber; or lodging between the skin and the skull, sometimes traveling between the two (see Figure 14.11). In at least one instance a bullet entered the victim's temple, traveled between the skin and skull around the head, and exited at the other temple.

Figure 14.11
Bullet lodged underneath the skin above ear. Exit wound next to it at left. This illustrates the eccentric behavior sometimes observed of bullets as they pass through the body. *(Courtesy, Office of the Medical Examiner, Cook County, Illinois.)*

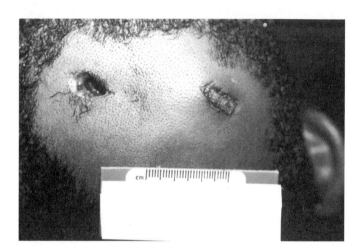

Number of Wounds

When the number of entrance and exit wounds is the same, it is evident that all bullets that entered the body exited as well. Should the entrance number be greater than the exit number, one bullet (or more) remains in the body to be retrieved as potential evidence. Whether a particular wound is an entrance or an exit wound is best determined by the pathologist. If the distinction is of significance in reconstructing the crime and expert testimony is required, a forensic pathologist must make this determination.

Cutting and Stabbing Wounds

Although a wound may appear to the casual observer or untrained police officer to be the result of cutting or stabbing, in fact it is often difficult to determine cause (see Figures 14.12-14.15). For instance, a penetrating stab wound can be mistaken for a bullet wound; a gunshot wound may resemble cleavage by a knife or axe; a laceration on the scalp (from falling on a smooth hard surface such as a table or floor) can resemble a dull knife wound. These determinations often require the expert opinion of the forensic pathologist.

Accidental deaths from cutting or stabbing are relatively rare, but examples might include: being impaled on a picket fence, sliding from a hayloft onto a pitchfork, or tripping onto the teeth of a rake. The circumstances surrounding the death as well as the practices and habits of the deceased will help the medical examiner/coroner decide. Deaths from cutting or stabbing are generally suicidal or homicidal.

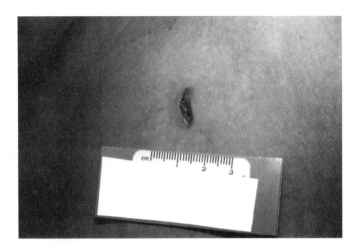

Figure 14.12
Stab wound.
*(Courtesy, Office of the
Medical Examiner,
Cook County, Illinois.)*

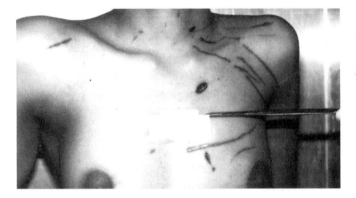

Figure 14.13
Stab wound of chest
with knife slash wounds
of upper anterior chest.
*(Courtesy, Office of the
Medical Examiner, Cook
County, Illinois.)*

Figure 14.14
Multiple incised wounds,
of which only four or five
are stab wounds. *(Cour-
tesy, Office of the Med-
ical Examiner, Cook
County, Illinois.)*

Suicidal Wounds

In feudal times, stabbing oneself or falling on one's sword was a more common way to commit suicide. Today, suicides by stabbing or cutting are more likely to involve a knife or razor, a broken bottle, glass, or other sharp-edged instrument. Seldom the result of one deft incision, usually a number of short superficial cuts are inflicted before the wounds are fatal (see Figure 14.15). These slight, often shallow cuts, known as *hesitation marks,* typify suicide and suicide attempts. (Even when a gun is used, there may be evidence that hesitation shots were fired.)

The parts of the body usually assaulted in such attempted suicides are the wrists, the throat, and sometimes the ankles. If the attempt is successful, the victim is usually found where the act took place. In some unsuccessful suicides by cutting or stabbing, the individual may decide to seek help, leaving the scene of the initial assault and a trail of blood behind.

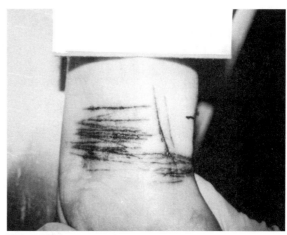

Figure 14.15
Hesitation slash marks on wrist of a suicide. *(Courtesy, Office of the Medical Examiner, Cook County, Illinois.)*

Homicidal Wounds

Stabbing (not cutting) is often the cause of a homicidal wound—even when the weapon is a knife (see Figure 14.16). Because victims will instinctively try to defend themselves, the forearm may bear slash marks, or if a knife grasped in self-protection is pulled away by the attacker, the palm and fingers will be cut deeply. These are known as defense wounds (see Figure 14.17). The upper parts of the body—most often the chest but also the side and back of the neck—suffer wounds that result in death. An autopsy can track the internal path of a stab wound. An upward thrust is normally (but not necessarily) indicative of homicide. It is easier to stab oneself with a downward or horizontal thrust; such a track usually points to suicide. Criminal homicide, however, cannot be ruled out; in such a case, blood will often be found scattered throughout the area of conflict— evidence of the victim's attempts to ward off the attacker and escape. The absence of a cutting weapon at the scene suggests homicide, but the experienced investigator knows that such evidence is often taken from the scene by the first person to discover the body.

Blunt Force Wounds

Wounds that are the product of neither a penetrating nor a cutting instrument are termed *blunt force wounds.* Various weapons are able to produce such wounds: a hammer, a stout branch, a two-by-four, an iron pipe, a brick or large stone, or an automobile. Blunt force wounds can be caused merely by falling from a height and striking the

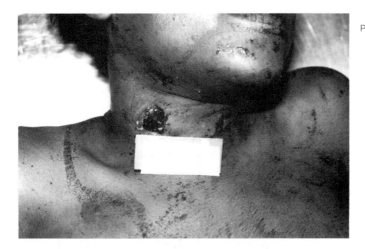

Figure 14.16A
Perforating stab wound
of the neck, showing
entrance and exit.

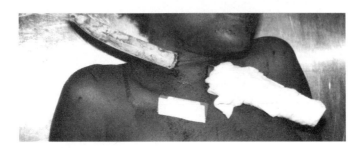

Figure 14.16B
Same through-and-
through stab wound,
with knife in place.

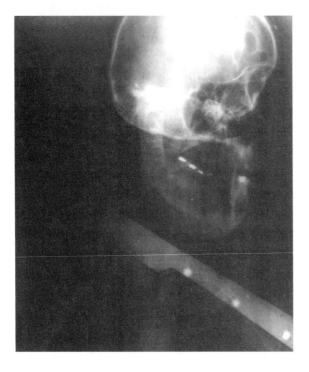

Figure 14.16C
X-ray from front.

Figure 14.16D
X-ray from side. *(Figure 14.16, Courtesy, Office of the Medical Examiner, Cook County, Illinois.)*

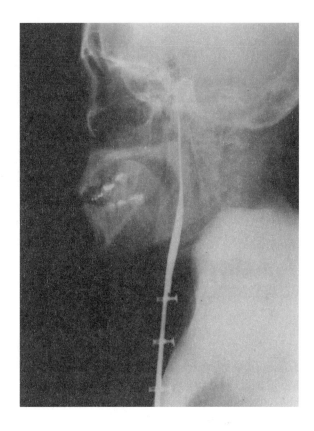

Figure 14.17
Defense incised wound. *(Courtesy, Office of the Medical Examiner, Cook County, Illinois.)*

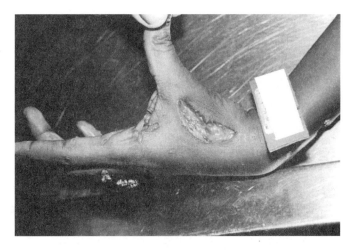

head, or landing feet-first on a hard surface. The injuries vary from lacerations, bruises or contusions, bone fractures, internal bleeding, and severe crushing wounds, most often to the head, neck, chest, and abdomen. The wound may not necessarily be the same size and shape as the crushing weapon. Despite this, a forensic pathologist often can suggest the kind(s) of weapon(s) used, thereby allowing the homicide investigator to conduct a search for the weapon. If found, it might bear traces of the victim's skin, blood, hair, clothing fibers—evidence that can have probative value.

Blunt impact weapons may also produce blood spatter which, if properly interpreted, can help to reconstruct the crime and determine what happened (see Chapter 2). Should this interpretation not agree with the suspect's explanation, the investigator can take full advantage of the difference by informing the suspect that contradictory evidence is available (one of Horowitz's principles of interrogation; see Chapter 11.)

Asphyxiation

The medical term *asphyxiation* describes death caused by interference with the supply of oxygen to the lungs. Although the cause may be accidental (e.g., from food lodged in the windpipe, or drowning), of greatest interest to the homicide investigator are deaths from smothering, strangulation, hanging, poisoning, and drowning. Some drownings that appear accidental may be attempts to cover up criminal homicide; hanging and poisoning deaths, on the other hand, often are mistaken for criminal homicide when in reality they are suicides or accidents.

Smothering

Deaths from smothering are frequently encountered in infanticide, in which it is sufficient to place a hand over the infant's mouth and nose. Adults can also be killed deliberately by smothering. The assailant in these cases is usually more powerful than the victim and uses a pillow, cloth, or plastic pressed tightly over the face. It is not uncommon to use greater-than-necessary force; thus, scratches and bruises from the struggle will remain on the body. Their interpretation, together with autopsy findings, are best left to the forensic pathologist.

In most of these cases, the offender has a close relationship with the victim. A consideration of who had motive, opportunity, and the nerve to follow through should lead to some possible suspects. Because in these cases the offender is not a hardened criminal, any evidence provided by the pathologist and family members that is raised during the interrogation is (again in accordance with the principles of Horowitz) likely to result in an admission or confession.

Strangulation

A person may be strangled manually or with a ligature such as a clothesline, electric lamp wire, belt, necktie, nylon stocking, scarf, and so on. The external signs of manual strangulation on a corpse are different from those left by a ligature. In both types of strangulation, however, the internal signs are hemorrhage and damage to the interior structure (bones and cartilage) of the neck, throat, and larynx. They are disclosed through an autopsy.

Manual: Suicide by manual self-strangulation is virtually an impossibility; accidental throttling is also relatively rare. When the death is sudden and the injury slight and apparently unintentional, accidental strangulation is indicated. If, however, the signs of injury are obvious and severe, it is unlikely that the death was accidental. When death clearly resulted from manual strangulation, there is a strong presumption of felonious homicide. It may be surprising to learn that the hands are not commonly used to strangle; for one reason, it is difficult to throttle a healthy adult—a male especially—unless the attack is by stealth, or the victim is stunned by a blow or under the influence of alcohol or drugs.

Following rape or attempted rape an assailant may try to eliminate the victim/eyewitness by choking. During a quarrel, one person may seize another by the throat to stifle an outcry for help. If this causes death, the attacker's intent would be a decisive factor as to whether it is murder or manslaughter. Witnesses should be queried about any spontaneous utterances made before or during the altercation, particularly by the assailant. If the intent was to silence the victim's call for help, murder is an appropriate charge.

Reconstructing some manual strangulations may reveal how they happened. The reconstructions are based on the probability that the force required to asphyxiate will leave an external pattern of finger marks (including fingernail marks) on the victim's neck. If the assault is from behind, the assailant generally uses both hands; if a frontal assault, one hand. The physical evidence may or may not square with the offender's account; if it does not, the discrepancy can be put to good use for interrogative purposes.

Ligature: Some strangulation deaths are caused by a broken wire, machine belt, or other ligature wrapping itself around the victim's neck. The nature of the circumstances together with eyewitness accounts of the incident should attest to its being accidental and not a crime. The intentional use of a ligature as a means of homicide is rare (except for lynchings and official executions), but when one is committed, a horizontal groove or furrow cut by the ligature is often visible on the throat, and normally is about the width of the ligature, and is located (on a male) at a level with or below the Adam's apple (see Figure 14.18). Signs of bruising and blood congestion just above and below the furrow indicate the victim was alive when it was

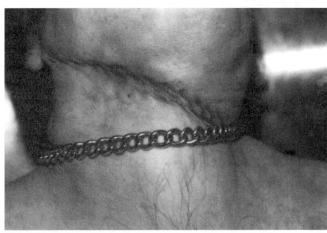

Figure 14.18
Strangulation by hanging—chain ligature showing patterned abrasion. *(Courtesy, Office of the Medical Examiner, Cook County, Illinois.)*

applied. Since attempts are made to cover up a homicide by simulating suicidal hanging, these contusions have investigative and probative significance.

The pathologist will also examine the inside of the eyelids and the facial skin for another sign of strangulation: pinhead-sized red dots that are minute hemorrhages called *petechiae*. It is also not uncommon to find that the victim has bitten the tongue.

If a ligature is knotted, photographs (including one-to-one size) should be taken before it is removed; and a cut made as far as possible from the knot, with the cut ends carefully and securely tied together and labeled as such. Although rather unusual as evidence, the use of an unconventional knot can suggest a vocation (or hobby), and examining the victim's recent experience with anyone in that occupation may provide investigative insight.

Figure 14.19
Suicidal hanging—note feet are on the floor. *(Courtesy, Office of the Medical Examiner, Cook County, Illinois.)*

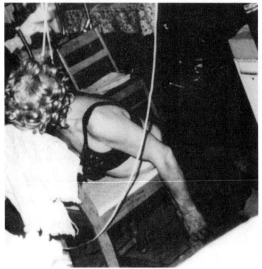

Figure 14.20
Autoerotic death by strangulation. *(Courtesy, Office of the Medical Examiner, Cook County, Illinois.)*

Hanging: Although a form of strangulation, some hangings require separate treatment. The majority are intentional and thus suicidal (see Figure 14.19), but occasionally there are attempts to cover up criminal homicide by making it appear that the victim committed suicide by hanging. If the autopsy is competent, this ruse should fail. Autoerotic deaths, a form of hanging, are indeed accidental. Being unfamiliar with eroticized death, the relatives and friends of the victim—and even a few detectives—will almost invariably insist that the hanging was a case of murder.

Autoerotic deaths occur when an individual—usually, but not necessarily, a young male—engages in a solitary, sex-related activity whereby he or she is asphyxiated accidentally. There is some physiological support for the belief that oxygen deprivation to the brain intensifies sexual arousal. When there is too much oxygen deprivation, however, the person loses control of the autoerotic exercise and dies of asphyxiation by being suffocated or hanged. The body may be found with the head covered by a plastic bag or with a ligature around the neck. If male, the decedent is often nude, or sometimes dressed in women's clothing (see Figure 14.20), his limbs shackled in a form of bondage with a mirror positioned for self-observation; if female, erotic paraphernalia such as an electric vibrator or dildo may be present. There is no evidence of suicidal intent such as a note.

Of the two modes of death—suffocation and hanging—hanging is a more common effect of autoeroticism. A bit of cloth or other material is often found wrapped around the ligature; its purpose, to prevent marking of the neck which would require some explaining to inquisitive relatives or friends, should the exercise turn out as expected—providing enhanced sexual arousal with no fatality. If this was a frequent practice, parallel rope marks (and possibly rope fibers) on an overhead pipe or top edge of a door (used as support) are likely to be present. They should be looked for after any suspected autoerotic fatality.

If most of the accompanying clues described are not present and the young victim is thought to be normal and well-adjusted, a ruling of accidental death rather than murder will almost certainly be incomprehensible to relatives. Treating the grieving family sympathetically will help to alleviate their anguish, and eventually lead to an acceptance of the autoerotic death finding.

Poisoning[27]

Carbon monoxide, is a colorless, odorless gas that is produced when any carbon fuel is incompletely burned. It is the primary cause of death due to inhalation injury. Familiar sources are coal and gas appliances such as stoves, refrigerators, hot water heaters, furnaces, and automobiles. The exhaust pipe fumes of an automobile are all too often seen as a convenient way to commit suicide.

Defective home gas appliances are responsible for accidental deaths by carbon monoxide asphyxiation. Very small concentrations—one part per 1,000 parts of air— breathed for about an hour cause headache, nausea, dizziness, and confusion. Carbon monoxide accumulates in the blood, so that even smaller concentrations—one part per 10,000—have similar effects if breathed overnight. Awakened by headache and realizing something is amiss, the sufferer often will try to open a window or leave the room, but disorientation makes this impossible. Frequently, the victim stumbles and hits a radiator, table corner, or other hard object, opening a head wound that bleeds profusely. The floundering will make the room look like a battle occurred. In many cases, the victim will die before reaching fresh air and the accidental death will have signs of a felonious homicide.

Young children, owing to their high metabolic activity, succumb more readily to carbon monoxide poisoning than do adults; however, it is possible for all the people sleeping at one residence to die from carbon monoxide leaking into a home with its windows sealed shut.

Carbon monoxide turns blood to cherry red and produces a patchy, pinkish color in the lividity of the corpse. Armed with this knowledge, together with what can be learned from relatives and neighbors about the circumstances surrounding the death(s), the investigator can focus on the source of the gas and see that it is no longer a danger. The autopsy and toxicological analysis will confirm cause of death to be carbon monoxide, and with its source identified (generally a defective gas-burning appliance), establish a case of accidental death rather than criminal homicide.

Drowning[28]

Drowning causes approximately 8,000 deaths in the United States each year. Most deaths from drowning are accidental; a few are suicidal. A large number of drowning deaths involve young children. Adults who drown in bathtubs are usually found to have contributing factors such as natural disease or toxicological abnormalities. Criminal homicide by drowning is largely limited to infants and small children, but adults can be overpowered and drowned. Usually, however, this requires accomplices. Attempts have been made to cover up a criminal homicide by placing the corpse in a bathtub filled with water to simulate a drowning. This ploy is called for when the connection between victim and killer is obvious and the latter will almost immediately be suspected. The manifestations of a true drowning (or other type of asphyxiation) and those of putting a dead body into water are sufficiently distinct to be differentiated by autopsy. The medical examiner/coroner, of course, determines whether the death is accidental, suicidal, or criminal.

Burns[29]

The very young and the very old are at greatest risk from burn accidents. In all fire deaths, the forensic pathologists should attempt to determine:

- The positive identity of the deceased, especially if the body is charred beyond visual recognition.

- Whether the deceased was alive prior to ignition of the fire, or whether the fire was set and the body burned in an attempt to conceal a homicide.

- The cause and manner of death.

- Whether contributing factors are present, such as alcohol/drug intoxication.

Suicide by burning is quite rare in this culture; rarer still is burning a victim with the intent to kill. Accidental death resulting from burns is more common, particularly among the young and the elderly. A burned corpse may be of interest to the homicide detective because attempts have been made to cover up criminal homicides by making them appear to have been the result of smoking in bed. Hence, the question of accident versus cover-up needs to be considered whenever human remains are discovered at the scene of a fire. The medical examiner/coroner office can be helpful in furnishing answers to the following concerns:

- Are the remains those of a human being?

- How is the body to be identified?

- Was the deceased alive or dead when the fire started?

- Who was the deceased? Sex? Age? Height?

Are the Remains of Human Origin?

A partially consumed body poses no problem as to its human origin. On those rare occasions when all flesh has been destroyed, the skull, skeletal bones, and especially the teeth, are likely to remain. The latter are most indestructible by fire; they generally can be recognized as human (see Figures 14.21 and 14.22). The issue of the origin of a bone or bones is raised occasionally when skeletonized remains are discovered outdoors in a sparsely settled area. They may be a mix of human and animal bones, or bones of animal origin only. Should there be any question, a forensic pathologist is consulted. In some cases, the pathologist may wish to seek the opinion of a forensic anthropologist before arriving at a definitive answer.

The Victim—Alive or Dead When the Fire Started?

In attempting to cover up a homicide by having it appear that the victim died as a result of a fire, the killer often makes a serious error based on ignorance. Though it is not common knowledge, two relatively simple procedures can determine if a person was dead or alive before the fire. The first is by autopsy of the air passageway to the lungs and the lungs themselves, inspecting for the smoke deposits that will be present only if the victim was breathing when the fire was started. The second method is a toxicological analysis of the blood for carbon monoxide. Because red blood cells combine preferentially with carbon monoxide (rather than oxygen), the gas will be found in the blood of a victim who was alive at the time of the fire. The absence of smoke deposits and carbon monoxide signifies that the individual was already dead, killed by another means.

Antemortem and Postmortem Injuries

In reconstructing a crime, it is sometimes important to know whether an injury was sustained before or after death. Cover-ups have been attempted by claiming an injury occurred after death, when it was actually inflicted before (and was the cause of the) death. The perpetrator's obvious intention is to corroborate the account he or she gave to investigators. Differentiating between an antemortem and a postmortem injury can be difficult when the injury

Figure 14.21
Charred remains from a house fire/arson. Note pugilistic attitude of arms, a characteristic of death by fire. *(Courtesy, Office of the Medical Examiner, Cook County, Illinois.)*

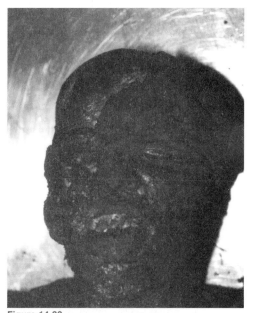

Figure 14.22
Face no longer recognizable, identification was made by comparing teeth with antemortem X-rays. *(Courtesy, Office of the Medical Examiner, Cook County, Illinois.)*

occurred within minutes of—or very close to—the time of death; a longer time span makes it easier for the pathologist to estimate when an injury was inflicted. This pertains whether it was before or after the death. It is a matter for the expert to decide.

PEOPLE: THOSE WHO KNEW THE VICTIM

The most obvious persons to be interviewed are family members, close associates, co-workers, and social acquaintances of the victim. Some seek out the investigator to impart what they know and believe to be of value; others, either not realizing that they have relevant information or feeling reticent about any contact with police, do not come forward. Still others, not being especially close to the victim, may refrain from becoming involved in a homicide investigation; if reassured, they might cooperate. The competent investigator will cultivate and explore all of these potential sources (see Securing Cooperation in Chapter 6).

Information that may be elicited by interviewing a victim's associates includes:

1. The suggestion of a motive for the crime.

2. The naming of a suspect or suspects and providing the reasons for such charges or beliefs. (At this point immediate follow-up may be required if the suspect is likely to flee the area).

3. Describing the usual activities and habits of the deceased permits his or her movements to be traced at the time of, and just before, the death. The last person to see the victim alive may provide valuable insights: Was the deceased's state of mind apparently normal? Did he or she seem depressed, anxious, or agitated? Does the last person to talk with the victim recall any pertinent remarks or expressions of concern?

Canvassing

Canvassing as a tactic in the search for witnesses is generally confined to the immediate crime scene area. In homicide investigation, the various places and locations visited by the deceased on the fatal day should also be revisited with the purpose of identifying anyone who was in contact with the victim. Follow-up will depend on all the facts generated through the canvass and other investigative efforts. To enlarge upon any hints or bits of information that might have been gleaned, it would be appropriate to place an individual under surveillance, or seek the help of an informant.

Informants

There are a number of homicides in which perpetrators appear to have successfully avoided detection, but after the initial fear of apprehension passes, they will relax their guard and talk, finding gratification in bragging about their exploits. At this point informants can provide what was overheard (often in a neighborhood bar). Various factors motivate informants. They may be out for a monetary reward, currying future favors, or trying to make a deal with the police—either seeking leniency in connection with a matter currently under investigation or being prosecuted, or looking for revenge on one of the perpetrators.

Follow-up measures include surveillance of the suspect (by wiretaps where permitted); review of the physical evidence discovered at the crime scene; and ultimately, interrogation.

Questioning Suspects

A suspect may be interviewed or interrogated, depending on the evidence. If, for instance, a person has been named as a possible suspect but no supporting reasons are cited, or a charge is based on mere suspicion, the proper procedure is an interview; its purpose, to learn what the individual knows about the crime and where he or she was at the time of death. The information must then be checked out. This might involve cross-checking with other people or require a reconstruction of the event, utilizing the physical evidence at the scene. When (and if) sufficient evidence is gathered and the investigation has shifted from a general inquiry to one focusing on a particular suspect, the interrogation process begins and *Miranda* warnings are in order.

The purpose at this juncture of the interrogation is to determine what the suspect is willing to disclose about the crime, and what connection (if any) exists between the suspect and the crime scene. Whether exculpatory or incriminating, a statement must still be checked against the alleged facts. This is true for all facts developed during the investigation—including those divulged by a reconstruction. Ultimately, if the case against the suspect continues to build, with support increasing for the hypothesis of guilt, the purpose of the interrogation shifts toward obtaining an admission or confession.

THE VALUE OF RECORDS IN HOMICIDE INVESTIGATION

Records can be an important source of information: providing insight into the motive for the crime, allowing the fatal weapon to be traced to its source or ownership, and documenting previous activities of the victim or suspect (which relate the motive to the killing). Special efforts must be expended to discover the existence of records, particularly those not maintained for law enforcement purposes.

Insight into Motive

Who Benefits?

A person who stands to gain from a criminal homicide as the beneficiary of an insurance policy, a will, or other inheritance may become a suspect. Individuals may also become suspects if it is learned that their former friendly relations with the deceased had soured to the extent that police were called to restore peace, or the deceased filed a civil suit. A person may also become a suspect if he or she was very recently made a beneficiary and had the means, nerve, and opportunity to commit the crime.

Diaries and Letters

If diaries or letters exist, they may reveal or hint at a motive for the crime (and even name the perpetrator), or disclose a hostile business or personal relationship. Unlike records that are routinely maintained and accessible to law enforcement, diaries or letters must be hunted down. They may be withheld by family members because of their intimate nature, or because their potential value to the investigator is not fully appreciated. Careful interviewing of close friends of the deceased is required if such evidence is to be located and made available.

Tracing Ownership

An item of physical evidence—whether discarded when fleeing from the crime scene or brought to and left there by the perpetrator—represents an opportunity to trace its ownership. For example, the Mannlicher-Carcano rifle used to assassinate President Kennedy and found in the Dallas book depository was soon traced to Lee Harvey Oswald through business records and Oswald's post office box in that city. On the other hand, 54,000 records had to be checked for the owner of a pair of eyeglasses, a crucial piece of physical evidence in the Loeb-Leopold case discussed later in this chapter. When it was determined that the glasses found near the body were not the victim's, the optical firm that sold them was traced through a faint, diamond-shaped mark on the lenses. The unique hinges on the eyeglass frames were a new item of manufacture dispensed to but three customers. Only the third customer—Leopold—failed to produce his pair upon request, and this brought him into the network of suspects.

In another homicide case, it took hours of library research just to identify an item of physical evidence, whose purpose was not obvious or known to anyone who examined it. It was a fabricated piece of metal, found in a lover's lane frequented by college students. Library reference books listing trade associations that might be of assistance were consulted. Photographs of the evidence were then mailed to a number of possible manufacturers. The piece of metal was finally identified as a part for a stove, itself a new item dropped from production because it did not sell. The stove's former manufacturer was located in a state more than 1,000 miles from the college town where the evidence was found. A check of college registration records turned up the name of one student from the distant state. The human blood on his car's front seat fabric was the break needed in the case. Records were also crucial in tracing the ownership of the contents of the bundle discarded by Martin Luther King Jr.'s killer (see Chapter 5). VIN (Vehicle Identification Number) records helped trace the van used to transport the explosives set off in New York's World Trade Center. The individuals who rented the van were on record with the rental agency.

Previously Recorded Activities

In addition to files maintained routinely to aid in criminal investigation, other police and judicial records should be probed. For example, there could be telephone calls to police complaining of a disturbance of the peace—a family quarrel or a noisy party. (Some even may be recalled by a member of the uniformed force before they are retrieved from the tapes.) There will also be court records when a person is put under bond not to interfere with the victim or when a divorce petition involving the victim is on file. Such records can suggest who to interview, and may also disclose:

- Unpaid bills
- Status of loans (including any mortgages)
- Credit problems
- Bank accounts (any significant movement of funds)
- Employment (job changes and reasons for them)
- Recent business transactions (Were they legal? Who was involved?)
- Safety deposit boxes (Were they recently purchased, used, or closed?)
- IRS records (Was more money reported than accounted for, indicating illegal activity?)
- Insurance policies (Who were the beneficiaries? Was policy of recent origin? Is there a double indemnity clause?)
- Wills (Who were the heirs? Is the estate in a healthy financial condition? Who is the executor? When was the will made?)
- Other records, if obtainable, should include:
    Medical records
    Psychiatric records
    Military records

Follow-Up Action

Through police computer information networks, current knowledge of investigative activities within a department (or in other departments) can be exchanged. The extent of the sharing varies among departments within a state. Computerized systems often employ acronyms: LEADS stands for Law Enforcement Automated Data System; PIMS for Police Information Management System; and NCIC for the National Crime Information Center (operated by the Federal Bureau of Investigation).

The utility of crime information systems is enhanced when the reporting of major crimes or arrests is accurate, and when it is done promptly and routinely. Thus, in a homicide investigation, useful information may be obtained through daily perusal of the computer printouts. For example, computer reports describing bank robbery/homicide perpetrators may help investigators recognize a potential suspect based on the *modus operandi* of a robbery. Pooling the information developed might help to clear more than one crime.

Other useful law enforcement files for follow-up having been treated elsewhere in the text, only a few need be mentioned in passing: arrest records, "moniker" (nickname) and fingerprint files, firearms evidence files, and so on (see Chapters 5, 7, and 20).

TYPES OF HOMICIDE INVESTIGATIONS

Definitions

In the vernacular of detectives (at least in some jurisdictions), homicide investigations are categorized as: a *grounder,* a *mystery,* or an *in-between.* A *grounder* is a case that is easily solved—the proverbial "smoking gun" is quite evident. Other expressions synonymous with grounder are: *platter, dunker,* and *meatball.* A *mystery* (or *who-done-it case*) is one in which no apparent solution is readily perceived; thus, time and effort are in order. Major, difficult cases (i.e., those that have the entire community agitated) are sometimes called *red balls.* An *in-between* is a homicide that appears to have a solution but will require some effort. Examples of each kind of homicide investigation follow.

A Grounder Case

> A husband returning unexpectedly found his wife in bed with another man. In a rage, he tried to strangle her while fighting off her lover, who was momentarily knocked out in the struggle. The wife was able to keep her husband at bay and defeat his attempt to choke her to death; however, when the kick she aimed at his groin missed, he ran down a long hallway to the kitchen for a knife. Meanwhile, regaining consciousness and recognizing the danger, the lover left via the fire escape while the enraged husband finished off the wife and left for parts unknown.

The major issue in this case, a grounder requiring little effort to solve, is whether the charge against the husband should be manslaughter or murder. The latter would rest on the premise that his dash to (and from) the kitchen for the knife allowed sufficient time for reflection. A conclusion that it had would mean a charge of premeditated murder.

A Mystery: The Leopold-Loeb Case

Though more than a half-century old, this landmark case from 1924 is chosen for discussion because the investigation itself represents a solid, imaginative effort; because its solution involves physical evidence, people, and records; and because the use of physical evidence was remarkable, considering that crime laboratories were yet to be born in this country. Even today, the case would call for the conferral of many an accolade on the Chicago Police Department. The following is a brief account of the crime and the investigative activities that resulted.

Leopold and Loeb were young, bright college students with IQs of 160 and 210. Their parents were wealthy. Petty fraternity house thefts launched their criminal careers, and before long they graduated to more serious transgressions. Eventually, they felt the need to experience the ultimate thrill—to commit the perfect crime. Dilettantes and students of the fine art of murder think "the perfect crime" means circumventing the established hazards by concealing the motive, disguising the crime, and avoiding the consequences. This pair would succeed only in concealing the motive. Though Leopold came into the investigation early on, the demand for ransom and his family's wealth were perceived as incompatible elements in the case; therefore, he was eliminated as a potential suspect—at least the first time around.

Planning the Crime

The first step in planning the crime was to choose the place to dispose of the body. Capitalizing on Leopold's familiarity with the woods he roamed as an amateur ornithologist, Leopold and Loeb studied the terrain while escorting a troop of boy scouts there a week or so before the planned crime. They found the burial site, a culvert beneath hardly used railroad tracks. Should they be seen in this vicinity or leave any traces behind, the scout trip would provide an alibi. To preclude a hitch when the time came, they reserved a hotel room under an assumed name to establish credit; rented a car for a "dry run" (going so far as to select the victim by observing children leaving school at the end of the day); and, after typing the ransom notes and envelopes to be sent to the victim's family on a portable Underwood typewriter, discarded it in a park lagoon nearby. Next, they concocted an elaborate scheme for collecting the ransom. It comprised a series of steps to be taken by the boy's parents which could be monitored by the kidnappers to determine if the police had been notified. The person paying the ransom was to throw the ransom parcel from a moving train, acting on a signal from alongside the track.

Despite the best laid plans, the body, rather than remaining hidden in the culvert, was not only discovered, but identified. The criminals instantly recognized the danger and the need for a more detailed alibi, but they quarreled over when to use it: Loeb insisting it not be used at all unless they were arrested within a few days, Leopold wanting to use it regardless of when they were picked up. Settling this point by agreeing not to invoke the alibi unless arrested within seven days of the time of the crime, they failed to establish what was meant by "the time of the crime." To Loeb it signified the time of the murder (about 5:00 P.M. on Wednesday); to Leopold it meant the time of the last telephone call to the victim's family (about 3:30 P.M. on Thursday). Apprehended the following Thursday, and believing the seven-day period was over, Loeb did not use the alibi. Contacted by detectives on the same day (Thursday)—at 2:30 P.M., one hour before the deadline—Leopold did use it. This divergence contributed significantly to their downfall. Only when a college newspaper reporter unwittingly served as a conduit and brought Leopold's message to Loeb was there congruence in their alibis.

The Crime

Except for one hitch, the crime was carried out as conceived. The problem was that the intended victim did not leave school as usual. The perpetrators viewed this as a minor inconvenience leaving them with two alternatives—abandon the plan for that day or select another victim. They chose the latter; the new target was 14-year-old Bobby Franks. This meant the ransom envelopes had to be readdressed. Mr. Franks' name, street address, and (in lieu of Chicago) "City" were hand-printed because they had already disposed of the typewriter. Believing that block lettering made identification by handwriting experts impossible, they used it for the envelopes.

The victim they enticed into the rented car was killed almost immediately. The killers drove about, then left the body in the car while they had dinner. Finally, they hid it in the preselected culvert after throwing acid on the face and genitals to render it unrecognizable. The very next day, it was noticed by railroad laborers working a handcar on the tracks above the culvert; from that vantage, the workers realized what they had discovered. They climbed down to the immediate area, looked about, and noticed a pair of horn-rimmed eyeglasses, which one man picked up, intending to keep them for reading.

They carried the body to a funeral home nearby and called the police. An officer arriving in due course asked the usual questions about the circumstances surrounding the discovery. One question would prove to be of critical importance: Had they seen or found anything at or near the crime scene? The man who had the glasses replied in the affirmative and, overlooking the fact that they constituted physical evidence, the officer placed them on the victim's chest in the funeral home.

On the evening of the kidnapping, the Franks family had a telephone call—the message: "Your boy has been kidnapped. He is in safe custody. You will hear from us in the morning." On the following day, the father received a letter; it read: ". . . this is an extremely commercial proposition. . . . your son will be safely returned to you within six hours of our receipt of the money." The $10,000 ransom demand stipulated old 20 and 50 dollar bills. When Jacob Franks was informed by the police of the discovery of an unidentified boy's body, he refused to view it. Sustained by the kidnapper's assurances that the boy would not be harmed and the fact that his son did not wear eyeglasses, Franks remained hopeful that his son was still alive. Only to be certain was an uncle sent forth; as it turned out, to make the identification of his nephew. Shortly thereafter, when a paper boy's hawking of a special edition carried the news to them, the killers realized the urgent need for an alibi for the preceding day.

The Investigation

At this point in the investigation, the police had a young, unclothed, male homicide victim on which an attempt had been made to render identification impossible or at least difficult; a pair of eyeglasses; a typewritten letter in a block-printed envelope; and no suspects.

A typewriter expert was sent for and soon identified the kind of typewriter (a portable Underwood) used for the ransom note. Teachers of the victim believed to be homosexual were asked to block print the name and address of the victim's father. The eyeglasses were traced. The forester employed in the woods where the body was found was asked for the names of those he knew to frequent the area. Although Leopold's name appeared on this list, he was not considered a suspect; after all, his father's secretary was authorized to write checks up to $2,500 upon his son's request—at a time when such an amount exceeded the average yearly family income in America. Yet Leopold's name was indeed on the list. For that reason and because of a lull in the investigation, reporters assigned to the story surmised that he constituted a lead worth pursuing. Since the victim's family lived in the Hyde Park area, home of the University of Chicago where Leopold studied law, two news reporters took advantage of the slack period to interview his student friends. They learned he was one of a small group that met weekly to study, type "dope sheets," and prepare for examinations. The reporters sought out group members in order to obtain typewriting specimens from the machine in the Leopold house; in one effort, they acquired typed notes that seemed different. They were examined and compared with the ransom notes by a typewriter expert, who found three letters—*m, t,* and *i*—to be defective both in the exemplars (the study group notes typed earlier on Leopold's machine) and in the questioned (ransom) documents. His conclusion: both were from the same machine.

Leopold (now a suspect) denied owning a portable Underwood, and despite painstaking searches, it was not to be found in the house. Eventually, a diver located it at the bottom of a nearby marina where the perpetrators had dropped the incriminating evidence.

During this time, diligent efforts were ongoing to find the owner of the eyeglasses. They led investigators to a Chicago optical firm that identified its product and provided a list of purchasers. This list could be pared down, since the glasses found near the body had unique hinges, a new type supplied to but three customers. When Leopold—the only one unable to produce his glasses—was questioned specifically about this, he equivocated by claiming that he must have lost them while bird watching.

Police learned that Leopold was a close friend of Loeb, so Loeb too was brought in for questioning. The young men were questioned separately; each presented a different version of his activities on the day of the murder (Loeb calculating that it was now outside the seven days agreed upon). Investigators intensified their efforts to learn what other people recalled. Upon being interviewed, the family chauffeur unwittingly contradicted the suspects' version of events, which essentially claimed that Leopold and Loeb picked up two girls in Loeb's car on the day of the murder, went to a park, had a few drinks, and fooled around; failing to reach an "understanding" with the girls, the group broke up and all went home. The chauffeur, on the other hand, recalled that brake repairs had kept the car in the garage all that day. Asked if he was certain about the date, the man remembered interrupting his work to have his child's prescription filled. On the medicine bottle was the date of the murder. Confronted with this evidence, Loeb cracked and unfolded details of the plan and crime to the state's attorney. Leopold was then confronted with facts known only to the perpetrators; informed of Loeb's confession, he too confessed.

This case was chosen because it illustrates how the three sources of information—records, physical evidence, and individuals—dovetailed and supplemented each other in the solution of this crime.

An In-Between Case: The Case of Fred Teal

Fred Teal, a wealthy 51-year-old executive, called his friend Dr. Bealler and asked the doctor to come to his home immediately. Arriving in about 15 minutes, the doctor examined the executive's wife, Joan, and pronounced her dead.* About 20 minutes later, Teal called the police and said, "I believe my wife is dead." The detectives who responded to the scene, and later the coroner, noted five bullet wounds in the chest and abdomen of the deceased. Two bullets were lodged in the body; three more were found in the room; all five entered from the front. Asked what happened, the husband gave the following account:

> A card was received from out-of-state friends telling of the friends' plans to divorce. After hearing it read to her, his wife (Joan) remarked that she should have divorced him (Fred) years ago. She then demanded to know if he still planned to "get out of the house tomorrow" as had been agreed. He informed her that he did, adding that he was leaving on a business trip to Mexico by automobile. He did not say he was also planning to take along his 24-year-old stepdaughter, Sarah Dunne, as an interpreter. Sarah, Joan's child by a former marriage, taught Spanish at the local high school and lived with them. Joan inquired whether he intended to take Sarah with him and threatened to kill him if he did. Turning toward her, he saw she had pistol; he lunged for it and in the struggle, the gun went off several times.

From an investigator's perspective, the following circumstances are significant:

- A quarreling couple on the brink of divorce.

- The deceased's threat to kill her husband should he take her daughter (his 24-year-old stepdaughter) along on a business trip to Mexico by car.

- A victim (the wife) with five bullet holes in her body, allegedly after a struggle over a firearm.

Inductive reasoning would lead an investigator to conclude that *Miranda* warnings were in order. Additional follow-up steps should include:

1. Reconstructing the facts of the crime based on physical evidence.

    A. When did the shooting occur (time of death)? How much time elapsed before the police were notified? (Evidence of a significant time lag can be important information to use in interrogation.)

---

* Such behavior may seem strange, but affluent people will often telephone their lawyer (or physician) before notifying the police of a crime they may have witnessed or been involved in. Similarly, young people, homebodies, and others inexperienced in the ways of the world may call a friend for help or advice before reporting a crime.

      B.   What was the distance from gun muzzle to victim?

      C.   Were all bullets fired from the suspected weapon?

2.   Interviewing: Dr. Bealler; Sarah Dunne; close friends of the couple who knew the degree and length of their estrangement; professionals they may have consulted—marriage counselor, psychiatrist, spiritual advisor, etc.; and any others whose names crop up during these interviews and who may be willing to talk.

3.   Reviewing records such as:

      A.   Gun registration file to establish ownership as well as place and time of purchase;

      B.   Arrest record file to learn about any previous arrests;

      C.   Court records to learn whether a divorce petition had been filed, and if so, what allegations were made by each party; and if there were court orders prohibiting one party from visiting, threatening, or abusing the other;

      D.   Financial records, such as checking and savings accounts, brokerage accounts, credit cards to find evidence of recent unusual activity—scrutinizing them for the transfer of a significant sum from a joint account to a single name account; or for large purchases made by Fred and sent to a third party (particularly a female).

Based on information thus developed, and from following up on leads (from crime laboratory findings, interviews, and disclosures from pertinent records), an investigator can prepare a strategy of interrogation. Clearly, success will depend on the quality and completeness of the information and evidence developed, how effectively it is utilized during interrogation, and whether the principles of Horowitz and Pavlov—as to why people confess—are borne in mind.

COVER-UP ATTEMPTS

Sometimes, a killer makes an effort to disguise a crime. Several means are employed to make the death appear accidental or explainable, to misdirect the efforts of investigators (diverting them to someone else or persons unknown), or to conceal the perpetrator's own involvement.

Accidental Means

A relatively common means used to cover up a homicide is to make the death appear accidental—the result, for example, of driving into a ditch or cleaning a gun. Not so common but worth noting are arson and poisoning.

Vehicles

Inspecting a motor vehicle that has caused a death can determine if it has been tampered with; for example, a brake line nut loosened to allow fluid to leak with each application of the brake, or an accelerator made to stick in the feed position. Another kind of cover-up is the use of an automobile to run over the victim's bicycle or motorcycle to make it appear that the damage was caused by striking a telephone pole, curb, or other fixed object. To detect the deception in such cases, the services of a forensic scientist (physicist, engineer, or pathologist) and a mechanic are needed. They will ask: Is the damage to the vehicle or trauma to the victim consistent with that known to be sustained when striking or being struck by such an object? If not resolved satisfactorily, the issues raised by these questions can be significant in any subsequent interrogation.

Firearms

In supposedly accidental gun deaths, the deceased's occupation, hobbies, and interest in weapons should be checked out. They can be consequential when interpreting the tests to be discussed here. The crime laboratory can sometimes determine muzzle-to-victim distance through examination of gunpowder residue on fabric, a garment, or the body itself; then, based on a comparison with test firings of the suspect weapon at known distances, the information can be used to reconstruct the crime. The suspect's account of what happened should be checked against the laboratory finding, and any discrepancy utilized later in interrogation.

The detection of significant levels of barium and antimony (primer residue) on the back and thumb web of the firing hand, when there is little or no residue on the nonfiring hand of the victim, is considered evidence that the deceased discharged a firearm. Primer residue is easily removed from the skin—intentionally, unintentionally, or by natural absorption. Since there is no barium and antimony in most .22 rimfire cartridges, a lack of these substances on the victim's firing hand does not warrant a conclusion that he or she did *not* discharge the weapon.

Fire

Setting fire to a mattress to make it appear that the victim was careless about smoking in bed has been used as an attempt to mask criminal homicide. This matter is given further treatment in the arson chapter; here, it will suffice to note that forensic pathology plays a key role in proving a victim was dead before the fire. The use of apparent homicide to cover up insurance fraud is another twist; insurance investigators are confronting a flood of cases in which intense fire consumes the victims and makes identification difficult or impossible. Often the insured is found to be a recent arrival—sometimes from a third-world country in which scant fingerprint, medical, or dental records exist. It is comparatively easy under these circumstances to substitute the body of a countryman or vagrant to serve as the victim of an "accidental" fire.

One case involved a newcomer in a community who, early on, let neighbors know that his hobby was tinkering with cars. Then, to set the stage for accidental death from a gasoline fire, he said he needed to borrow pliers to fix a leaking carburetor. The stratagem worked; the burned body was assumed to be that of the newcomer. However, when investigators juxtaposed the facts with the probabilities in the case—a recently issued life insurance policy carrying an exorbitant death benefit and the likelihood of a tinkerer having to borrow a simple tool—the facts became clues which, by induction, led investigators to uncover the sham.

Poisons

Some poisoners, when caught, will claim that they put the poison in a medicine capsule with the intention of committing suicide, only to find that the victim took it accidentally. Rather than report the death immediately (the normal response to an accidental death), they will hide the body and claim the person is missing; then, if it is discovered, allege they acted out of fear of not being believed. In such cases, they take shelter under a second cover-up to account for the first.

Explainable Means

Two common cover-ups are employed to make a crime explainable: (1) simulating a felony (motor vehicle homicide, burglary, robbery, or kidnapping) to account for death; and (2) claiming self-defense. Another ruse (developed further in the section on missing persons) is to provide inquisitive neighbors with a plausible reason for the absence of a spouse or live-in companion.

Simulated Felony

Most people have neither the knowledge nor the ability to stage the scene of a crime with a fair degree of verisimilitude. The experienced investigator is often able to recognize a poorly conceived and executed scenario. When a suspect is questioned, any nervousness (from having committed the crime) or anxiety (because an explanation might be implausible) hints at a cover-up. Reconstructing the event and checking the results against the suspect's account can pay dividends if a cover-up has been attempted.

One case example concerns the motor vehicle homicide of an elderly woman much beloved in her neighborhood. There was a severe thunderstorm on the night of the murder, the prolonged downpour washing away any broken headlight glass or other debris (such as damaged grillwork) that could link a vehicle to an accident scene. At about 11:00 the same night, just after a change of shift, a factory employee came to the police station to report that his car was stolen while he was at work. Remarking that he had heard of the death, he wondered aloud if the thief might have hit the woman after stealing his car. The detective, noting the remark as curious, asked why he thought so; the man offered no reason for the notion, only expressed his need for the car and the hope that he would soon have it back.

The abandoned vehicle was discovered later that night by patrol car officers. The damage to its windshield and two side windows seeming excessive for a break-in and theft, the detective's first step was to call the mobile crime laboratory. Evidence technicians quickly determined that the break-in had been simulated, the windows having been broken from the inside and the windshield as well as front side windows cracked. Their experience indicated that the simulation of theft had been carried too far: the extensive damage making visibility nil, it would have been difficult if not impossible to drive the car. The laboratory noted a broken headlight lens, but because of the storm no accident scene glass was available to link the vehicle to the scene of the homicide. Evidence technicians also noted that hood damage was consistent with striking a person.

The police decided not to notify the car's owner of its recovery and the crime laboratory's examination, but to leave it in place. Inductive reasoning had led the detective to conclude: (1) that the car had not been stolen; and (2) that it might have been involved in the homicide. When the man reported finding his car the next morning, the conclusion was given support, for stolen vehicles are rarely recovered by their owners.

As part of the case follow-up, the detective also learned that a ladder placed against the perimeter wall of the plant where the car owner worked (which was fenced in, with access allowed only to those with proper identification through the front gate) permitted workers to have a drink at the local tavern while the time clock punch card would indicate they were on the job. Utilizing the facts in the interrogation—simulated theft, atypical recovery of the car, and the freedom to leave the plant and return—the investigator required little time to elicit a confession from the factory worker.

Self-Defense

The following case illustrates the use of a claim of self-defense to cover up a killing. In his statement to the police, a husband claimed he had called his estranged wife on the morning of the shooting to ask that she come to pick up her mail and sign an insurance check. He said he expected her in the late afternoon after work; instead, she showed up at midday. He also claimed that, after she had signed the check, he reached for it and the pen only to look into a pointed gun and to implore her, "No, no, don't shoot, Jenny!" He stated that he then turned sideways to reach for a gun hidden under a cushion; his wife fired once and missed, the bullet lodging in the couch; and only then did he pull the trigger of his gun, killing her.

Ballistics tests determined that the bullet retrieved from the couch had been fired by his weapon. The autopsy disclosed that the victim had been shot twice: once in the side of her body, once in the back of the head. The number of shots did not comport with his claim of self-defense; neither did the location of the head wound. These facts, in addition to the strained marital relation, led the jury to convict him of second-degree murder.

Diversionary Means

Several ways have been used to deceive an investigator; they are as follows:

First Person to Report the Crime

Some people believe that if they discover or are the first to report a crime they will not be suspected—that the mere fact they came forward will be construed as showing honesty and integrity. Such credence is misplaced; many a criminal has come to regret this naïve assumption. Therefore, recognizing a potential diversionary tactic for what it may be, experienced investigators customarily consider and check out the person who discovers the body or first reports the crime.

Contrived Alibi

Another diversionary tactic is to contrive an alibi. For example, a man murdered his wife and children at about 7:00 P.M.; at about 8:30 P.M., just after calling his brother-in-law ostensibly to discuss a matter of mutual interest, he left on a business trip. Arriving some 150 miles away, he put in a long-distance call to his home through the motel operator. Receiving no response, he surmised, presumably for the benefit of the motel operator, that his wife and children must be sound asleep. He asked to be awakened at 7:30 A.M. so he could place another call to his family. Again, his call was unanswered. Expressing concern to the operator, he asked that a call be placed to neighbors to look in on his family. It was shortly thereafter that he claimed to have first learned of the tragedy.

In her contacts with the guest, the motel operator received the impression of a person who was not being straightforward and whose nervousness and anxiety were excessive. A background check on the family, the forensic pathologist's estimate of time of death, and the operator's suspicions led to an interrogation and later to an indictment.

Ruse

This case example of a cover-up by misdirection involves an attempt to have it appear that two women had engaged in a "cutting match"; this term and the following scenario were suggested by the man in whose apartment the double homicide took place. A background check on him and the victims disclosed that he and one woman had lived together for years, while the other woman was his new lover. The bodies were side by side; a carving knife was found next to each victim. Blood spatter patterns and the distribution of two types of blood in the patterns led investigators to reconstruct an event quite different from that suggested by the male who rented the apartment—the first person to report the crime. Investigators later learned from his confession that somehow the women had met, discovered his "double dealing," and confronted him. The ensuing quarrel led to the murders and the attempted cover-up.

Other red herrings can be put out to mislead an investigation. One is to report a person missing in order to cover up a homicide. This is discussed in the section on missing persons. Another is to fake kidnapping—including leaving a ransom note, a jimmied door, or a broken window.

Partial Cover-ups

Some killers attempt a partial cover-up instead of taking the stronger measures already described. Realizing that the police are looking for them, or at least soon will be, they go into hiding or take flight. Some conceal or destroy incriminating evidence such as a weapon, stained clothing, letters, or records; some think an adequate expedient is to remove bloodstains. Partial cover-up measures are more likely when the homicide is not premeditated.

Flight, the assumption of a false name, or the concealment or destruction of evidence are interpreted in the investigative phase as consciousness of guilt. Having raised the possibility that a particular individual is the offender, the investigator should seek additional evidence to support the hypothesis. If the circumstances surrounding the flight, the destruction of evidence, and so on are carefully explained to a jury, they can have probative value at trial.

MISSING PERSONS

Missing person cases are treated in this chapter because of the fear commonly expressed by relatives that the vanished family member has been the victim of a homicide. From the police viewpoint there are two kinds of missing persons cases, each having different consequences with regard to law enforcement follow-up. One kind is voluntary: the missing person has created circumstances suggesting an abduction, suicide, or accidental death. The other is involuntary: the missing person was abducted and is being held captive or is in fact dead, the victim of a criminal homicide. The murderer accounts for the disappearance by telling inquisitive neighbors that the victim is caring for a sick relative or friend living some distance away. The murderer may even attempt to mislead the police in this way, should pressure from family or friends precipitate official inquiries. Almost immediately after the police leave, the killer takes off for parts unknown.

Apparently Involuntary Disappearances

Most families believe that the disappearance of a relative, especially a child, is not voluntary. Some adolescents in a rebellious stage run away from home; such disappearances, of course, are voluntary. Just as the reasons for a child, adolescent, or adult to suddenly vanish will vary, so do the appropriate investigative efforts.

Children

Conventional police wisdom on missing children cases dictates that some disappearances are not cause for official concern; thus, a "24-hour rule" often governs the response. However, the rule is not invoked when there are signs of foul play or when a very young child abruptly vanishes. These circumstances call for an immediate, intensive search. Although police quickly recognize the potential for harm to the very young, as social science research suggests, the basic assumption that runaways are not at risk is ill-founded. Moreover, abuse and neglect can be involved even when a child has been abducted by a parent.

A linkage is believed to exist between the violence of a criminal and a childhood marred by physical, psychological, or sexual abuse. It has led to the development of a comprehensive multistate network for the exchange of information on missing or abducted children. Known in Illinois as the I-Search Program (Illinois State Enforcement Agencies to Recover Children), it defines a missing child as one whose whereabouts is unknown. Several states having joined the program, a jurisdictional issue should no longer permit cases to slip through the cracks of the criminal justice system—to remain uninvestigated and unsolved.

LEADS (Law Enforcement Automated Data System), a further refinement, improves the means for locating missing children and preventing their abduction. LEADS is connected to the FBI's National Crime Information Center (NCIC); hence, descriptive physical data and dental records can be entered into NCIC, making it possible to determine if the missing child was found dead elsewhere. Should a child be found subsequently, either dead or alive, a comparison can be made with data in the National Unidentified Person's File.

Another effort is the National Center for Missing and Exploited Children, which was federally funded in 1985. Authorized by the Missing Children's Assistance Act of 1984, it was responsible in its first two years of existence for locating about 5,300 missing children: runaways comprised 71 percent, about 2 percent were abducted by strangers, and more than 25 percent were abducted by a family member or friend.[30] The Center estimates that 20 percent of missing child cases are not reported to law enforcement agencies, considerably diminishing the chances of recovery.[31]

According to the National Incidence Studies of Missing, Abducted, Runaway, and Throwaway Children (NISMART), in 1999 there were 203,900 children abducted in family abductions, and of those, 98 percent were located. In comparison, there were 58,200 non-family member abductions in 1999, with a 99 percent return rate. Consider these additional kidnapping statistics for 1999.[32]

- 115 children were kept overnight and either held for ransom or killed (60% released safely; 40% killed)

- 61 percent of missing child cases were reported to a law enforcement agency.

- 48 percent of all missing child cases can be attributed to runaway/throwaway cases.

Recognizing that "missing children investigation is a somewhat neglected and under-developed area," the National Center for Missing and Exploited Children has addressed this problem by publishing a manual[33] and classifying each case according to definitions provided by the Office of Juvenile Justice and Delinquency Prevention (OJJDP):

Family Abduction: When a family member (1) takes a child in violation of a custody agreement or decree; or (2) in violation of a custody agreement or decree fails to return a child at the end of a legal or agreed-upon visit, with the child being away at least overnight.

Non-Family Abduction: The coerced and unauthorized *taking* of a child into a building, a vehicle, or a distance of more than 20 feet; the *detention* of a child for a period of more than an hour; or the *luring* of a child for the pur-poses of committing another crime. *Stereotypical kidnappings* are non-fam-ily abductions in which (1) the child is gone overnight; (2) is killed; (3) is transported a distance of 50 miles or more; (4) is ransomed; or (5) in which the perpetrator evidences an intent to keep the child permanently. The per-petrator needs to be a stranger.

Runaways: Children who have left home without permission and stayed away overnight, or children who are already away and refuse to return home—depending on their age and amount of time away.

Thrownaways: Children who (1) have been directly told to leave the house-hold; (2) have been away from home and a caretaker refused to allow the child back; (3) have run away but the caretaker has made no effort to recover the child or does not care whether the child returns; or (4) have been abandoned or deserted.

Lost, Injured or Otherwise Missing: Children, missing for various periods of time (from a few minutes to overnight), depending on the child's age, dis-ability, and whether the absence is due to an injury.[34]

Various checklists of service to investigators of missing children can be found in Appendix 4. They will probably need modification as they are tested in practice.

A special problem with young children missing for several years is the change in their appearance as they mature. Medical illustrators at the University of Illinois have identified 48 facial landmarks that change with some degree of predictability between the ages of six and 18. It takes about 20 hours to draw a facial illustration by hand. The computer, however, has been put to effective use in creating a color representation of a child's face as he or she grows older.

Commercial enterprises (dairy, telephone, direct media companies) have attempted to help develop information about missing children. By distributing computer-updated photographs of the maturing child coupled with a toll-free "800" telephone number, they hope to involve the general public. Other official efforts include legislation to require county and school district clerks to notify police of requests for an abducted child's birth certificate or school records.

Another innovation is the AMBER (America's Missing: Broadcast Emergency Response) Alert program, which was created in 1996 as a legacy to 9-year-old Amber Hagerman, who was kidnapped and brutally murdered while riding her bicycle in

Arlington, Texas. Residents contacted radio stations in the area and suggested they broadcast special alerts over the airwaves so that they could help prevent such incidents in the future. In response, the Dallas/Fort Worth Association of Radio Managers teamed up with local law enforcement agencies in northern Texas and developed this innovative early warning system to help find abducted children. CodeAmber.org went live on August 23, 2002. On April 30, 2003, President George W. Bush signed the Prosecutorial Remedies and Other Tools to End the Exploitation of Children Today (PROTECT) Act of 2003 into law. This Act codified the national coordination of state and local AMBER Alert programs, including the development of guidance for issuance and dissemination of AMBER Alerts and the appointment of a national AMBER Alert Coordinator.

In child homicide cases, death can either be caused by another child or an adult. If the latter, the slaying is often sex-related; this motivated serial murderer John Gacy to kill more than 30 prepubescent and adolescent males in the Chicago area. Leads may be provided by law enforcement records on recently released sex offenders; these files have information on *modus operandi,* location, and so on. Leads may also come from a canvass of the victim's playmates, individuals who were able to observe the child's movements and activities, or those who frequent his or her environment (school, playground, after-school haunts). Because the perpetrator may have to entice at least a few children before succeeding in tempting one, a partial description of the individual or vehicle, as well as the MO, may be learned. If a suspect is developed, surveillance is in order.

Death at the hands of another child is difficult for most people to comprehend. At one extreme, it happens almost accidentally as the outcome of child/adolescent exploration; at the other extreme, it may be the result of the pleasure derived from the excitement and thrill of killing. Within the psyche of a child-killer in the latter cases there often are pain, rage, and a sense of ineffectiveness. Killing seems a way out; circumstances becoming unbearable, a child may strike out against the one perceived responsible, even if it is another child.

Family and playmates usually provide the key to solving homicides committed by children. They may not volunteer a name or a motive, but interviewing them separately about various aspects of family life might produce insights. Confronting one interviewee with the statements of another during requestioning is often a fruitful exercise. Given the relative unsophistication of the child-turned-killer, obtaining an admission or confession is fairly simple.

Adults

The investigator should be mindful that the unexplained disappearance of an adult is a frightening experience for family and friends; in general they fear foul play. It is important to note, however, that an adult may lawfully leave home, job, and normal haunts without notice, provided the family does not become a community burden.

There are males, usually middle-aged, who disappear to take up a new life, as often as not with a younger mate. To soften the impact and account for the departure, they contrive an explanation. Some will leave evidence of apparent suicide—for example, arranging for their car to be found parked on a bridge over a large river running to the ocean, with an article of their clothing on the railing. Some will simulate an accident. In one such case, a father took his small son to the ocean for a day at the beach. When other bathers noticed the child playing alone and unminded at the water's edge, they notified the police. Later that day, when husband and child had not returned, the wife reported them missing. It was assumed the husband had drowned; this was the contrived explanation.

An experienced investigator will sense that something is wrong. The situation has the earmarks of a simulated missing person's case, employing a relatively common stratagem, e.g., a disappearance near a large body of water (an ocean, gulf, or sea). This lends plausibility; the perpetrator is relying on the fact that not all bodies are recovered under such circumstances.

Another fairly common deception is making it appear that the missing person has been the victim of a felony. A robbery and abduction might be simulated; sometimes the "missing" person's empty wallet will be left in a conspicuous place. Again, the experienced detective will be distrustful. An examination of the personal and business affairs of the missing person may produce support for the suspicion that the disappearance was contrived.

Obviously, missing persons cases are not always criminal homicides, but persons reported missing may indeed be homicides. Generally in a true homicide case, the disappearance is sudden and mysterious and the victim often is a female. The age factor should be significant to the investigator. When a young woman in her twenties at a social gathering leaves to go to the lavatory or refreshment stand and vanishes, leaving no trace, the likelihood of a serial murderer like Ted Bundy must be considered. If the victim is older and lives alone—single or widowed—a "Lonely Hearts" killer is more likely. The investigation of these kinds of cases is treated later in this chapter.

Adolescents

Police usually treat the missing adolescent as a runaway who is sure to turn up sooner or later, but this is not always so. In the Gacy case, a missing teenaged boy's family insisted he was not a runaway and that the circumstances surrounding the disappearance called for more than routine police action. Finally, because the case fell within the jurisdiction of a relatively small police department, it was investigated vigorously. Gacy became an immediate suspect when it was noted that different parents reporting disappearances under similar circumstances had previously provided his name to other police departments; this had not been shared among the several jurisdictions involved. After his arrest, however, remedial steps were taken; now, such information enters the law enforcement computer network. It should no longer be lost between the cracks of the criminal justice system.

Misleading Reports

In the event of a misleading report, there is generally a connection between the individual making the fictitious report and the "missing" person; hence, the need for a cover-up. The possibility of homicide must be considered if there is an unusual delay in making the report. More than a day would be unusual unless a satisfactory explanation is offered. By interviewing family and friends, conducting a neighborhood canvass, and making a thorough background check, the investigator will often discover a motive and strengthen the suspicion that the report is a diversionary effort.

MULTIPLE DEATHS

Serial murders are frequently the subject of television and newspaper reports; this fuels public awareness and curiosity. The term, however, has become a common refrain, with the result that the incidence of serial murder is greatly exaggerated. Media speculation also makes this crime seem a modern phenomenon, which it is not. The reader who recalls "Jack the Ripper" in England or "Bluebeard" (real name: Giles de Rais) in fifteenth-century France knows that multiple homicides by a single killer have been around for years. All the reporting, however, does have its "up" side; on-the-spot coverage enables law enforcement agencies to recognize similarities in homicides committed over time and in wide-ranging areas (see the discussion of ViCAP later in this chapter).

All multiple killings are not the work of serial murderers. A Charles Whitman who indiscriminately shoots from the University of Texas tower is not a serial murderer, but a mass murderer. Other useful distinctions can be made among those responsible for multiple deaths. As a consequence, the investigation and solution of a case will differ depending on the classification into which the particular case falls. For example, most mass murderers either commit suicide, are killed by the police while committing the crime, or are taken into custody following negotiations at the scene.

Before police agencies can coordinate their efforts, serial killings must first be recognized as the work of one individual. "Lonely Hearts" cases and crime spree killings differ from serial murders, though less careful analysis may put them into one category. The following section treats multiple homicides according to whether they were all part of one episode or were a series of events spread over a period of days, months, or even years. It discusses the differences and nuances involved, while keeping the focus on the investigative measures employed to solve each kind of case.

Several Mortalities—All Part of One Event

Double homicide is the most common kind of multiple death. Less frequent, and often involving more than a few victims, is family slaughter by one of its own members; or the murder of all persons in a household by an intruder bent on robbery, burglary, or rape. The least frequent kind of multiple death, random mass murder, usually accounts for the greatest number of fatalities per event.

Double Homicide

The most common kind of double homicide is criminal homicide followed by suicide. For example, chronic ill health or financial worry can cause a married pair to decide to end their lives together. The forensic pathologist can provide considerable help in establishing which death was a homicide and which a suicide. (There may be insurance, as well as legal, implications to these findings, e.g., determining which last will and testament governs.) A background check of family and friends will often provide a reason. Sometimes a note is left behind; not infrequently, there is a pact between the victims. It would be worthwhile to find out if any prerequisite steps were taken, like purchasing a weapon, medicine, or poison. Such evidence, when coupled with the medical examiner's findings, can obviate further investigative effort by indicating that the perpetrator took his or her own life.

Another somewhat common double homicide is the shooting of a retail store clerk and a customer during a robbery. Here, the disposition rests on solving the robbery. From time to time, an individual is murdered merely for happening to be with the target, being an unwitting witness who must be eliminated. In such cases, the luckless bystander is peripheral to the solution of the case.

If the killings are the work of mobsters, statistics suggest that even when the motive is ascertained, solution and conviction are unlikely. If not of gangland origin, motive provides an important lead requiring exploration and follow-up on people, physical evidence, and records.

Family/Residence Murders

The scene of some multiple deaths is the victims' home. There are three kinds of perpetrator: a family member; an ex-family member—husband, or former lover or friend; or a stranger (who invades the residence to commit a felony). When perpetrated by a family member, the case is usually amenable to solution, but solution is considerably more difficult when an unknown factor such as a home invader is responsible.

Intrafamily Killings

In family killings, an adolescent son rather than a daughter or parent is more likely to be the guilty party. The fact that there are no signs of forced entry suggests the crime was committed by someone with access to the premises. Intruders, however, can gain entry simply by ringing the doorbell and then pointing a weapon at whomever responds. Hence, a lack of evidence of forced entry does not necessarily rule out an intruder.

Initial investigative steps include a background check of all family members and a neighborhood canvass. A psychological profile should also be considered. Disclosure of any odd behavior or significant change in lifestyle, such as unanticipated flight or other uncharacteristic act of a family member, obviously warrants investigation. All are signals suggesting involvement; they call for a check on the whereabouts claimed by the individual at the time the crime was committed.

It might be productive to inquire whether anyone would profit from the death of the victim(s), or whether there are hints or suspicion of interest in the occult or demonology (satanism). Such information, if obtained, might turn a "mystery" into a "grounder."

The weapon used offers another investigative opportunity: Who had a familiarity with it? Owned it? Had access to it? Knew where it was kept?

Home and Workplace Invasions

In most cases, homes are invaded for the purpose of carrying out a felony—robbery, rape, or burglary (for money, jewelry, narcotics, sex, weapons). The workplace or public building is generally invaded for a different reason: often there is a perception of injustice or a need to vent anger. For instance, a disgruntled discharged postal worker invaded the Edmund, Oklahoma, post office in 1986 and indiscriminately shot 14 former coworkers (see Table 20.1). Three cases of home invasion are discussed below.

Home Burglary-Turned-Homicide: This first case began as a burglary, then became a double homicide when a sleeping teenager awakened. The struggle that ensued aroused her brother and resulted in the deaths of both young people. Nothing of value was stolen from the premises.

Consideration was given to the fact that after midnight the intruder had climbed through an open bedroom window overlooking the backyard. Investigators speculated that he cased the neighborhood for ground floor windows left ajar. To apprehend the suspect, an innovative fixed surveillance was felt to be justified.

The strategy and tactics of the surveillance employed were as follows: Four unmarked cars were assigned to the area and ordered to respond promptly to every prowler call after midnight. Instead of proceeding to the immediate vicinity, they were to park one block away—one each to the north, east, south, and west—and wait two hours while observing any movement on the street. Following a call months later, detectives watched an individual walking rapidly for several blocks and moving between houses located in the middle of the block as if looking for an opportunity to commit burglary.

When the walker was intercepted, it was learned he did not reside in the area; rather, he lived four miles away. He was dressed all in black and wore tennis shoes though the temperature was below freezing. The pawn tickets in his wallet inducing them to believe he was a burglar, investigators asked to search his home. He granted permission readily—probably to keep official focus off murder and on burglary, and to establish himself as cooperative. Should there ever be questions about the double homicide committed nine months earlier, his denials, he believed, would be accepted at face value.

A search of the suspect's flat produced numerous television sets and other small electrical appliances; this confirmed the suspicion that a burglar had been caught. The suspect's cooperation was unflagging; he tried to identify the source of each stolen item shown him. When a certain flashlight with its reflector cavity stuffed with orange-colored paper (recovered at the scene of the double homicide) was presented, he exclaimed "Where did you get that? I couldn't remember where I put it." The memory lapse and admission of ownership were unfortunate for him; the intruder had dropped the flashlight at the scene of the double homicide.

The suspect confessed and agreed to reenact the crime. At the scene, his spontaneous comments about the placement of furniture (which had since been moved) bore witness to his presence there on the night of the killings. Also useful in corroborating his confession was the physical evidence—hair, blood, and the twig of a cherry tree.

In some break-ins, robbery or rape is intended rather than burglary. Either crime may motivate artisans or delivery/repair personnel, who in the course of their work spot people who are well off or particularly vulnerable. At some later time, perhaps bolstered by alcohol, they make their move. Occasionally, traces of the intruder's occupation are left behind: by a fuel delivery man, an odor of oil; by an upholsterer, an upholstery cord (used to tie up the victim while searching for a safe); etc. Usually, though, such evidence will not be present. Nevertheless, a fruitful avenue of inquiry may be opened up by checking on recent (within the last six months or so) repairs or deliveries for which a stranger had to come into the home.

The Clutter Case: This home invasion started as a robbery and ended as a quadruple homicide. A well-publicized case, it is recounted in Truman Capote's nonfiction novel *In Cold Blood.* Seemingly without motive, using a 12-gauge shotgun and a knife, the killers slaughtered the Clutters and their teenaged son and daughter; the only family survivors were two elder daughters living away from home. There were no signs of struggle; the victims, gagged with adhesive tape and tied hand and foot with cord, were found in different locations through the house. Based on these facts, investigators speculated that at least two persons had invaded the farmhouse that night.

Robbery was discounted as a motive because two rings remained on the woman's fingers; however, a pair of binoculars and a gray Zenith portable radio were missing. No shotgun shell cases were found (it was learned after their apprehension that the intruders had been careful to remove them). The physical evidence unknowingly left behind, a potential link to the suspects, was a bloody "Cat's Paw" half-sole impression found on a cardboard box in the basement. Also, when the enlarged crime scene photographs were printed, investigators saw the imprint of another shoe not visible to the naked eye, one with a diamond-shaped pattern on its sole.

People who knew the family were questioned and records were checked. Meanwhile, other information was developed; for example, Mr. Clutter had taken out a large, double indemnity insurance policy just eight hours before his death—its beneficiaries, the surviving daughters. The father had raised objections because of religious differences to his (now deceased) daughter's steady boyfriend. (An interrogation and subsequent lie detector test eliminated the youth as a suspect.) Other promising leads had to be ruled out. A farmer who tied rope with knots identical to those that bound the victims was in another state on the fatal night. A piece of information that seemed incriminating and important—a month before the crime, an alcoholic father and son who had had a confrontation with Mr. Clutter over a minor business deal were heard to say, "Every time I think of that bastard, my hands start to twitch. I just want to choke him!"—was also rendered useless by good alibis.

It was feasible, thought investigators, that they had a case of mistaken identity. Had the intended victim been another rancher, spared because a hired killer took a wrong turn on unfamiliar roads? Just as this line of inquiry proved fruitless, so too were all efforts to locate the stolen binoculars and radio in pawn shops throughout several states. (As it would later turn out, a need for cash forced the killers—who, meanwhile, had fled to Mexico City—to sell both items to a police officer there, thus placing the stolen property out of reach.)

Meanwhile the former cellmate of one of the killers remained in the penitentiary, the man who—having once worked for Mr. Clutter—had talked so freely about the thousands of dollars expended each week to operate the ranch. Knowing he bore some responsibility for the reports of the massacre being broadcast over the prison radio, this prisoner's need to tell somebody was overwhelming, yet prison culture made it quite clear that inmates did not inform on each other. However, he opened up to a fellow prisoner with a religious bent who persuaded him to talk. The warden arranged to have him "called out" of his cell.

Conscience or civic duty aside, the cynic might speculate on the roles played by the reward and the possibility of parole. Needless to say, the authorities were interested in what the informer knew. Having worked for Mr. Clutter, he had told his former cellmate (now the killer) about the $10,000 turned over at the ranch each week. This led to extensive questioning by the cellmate: Where was the ranch? How did one get there? How was the house laid out? Was there a safe and where was it kept? Ultimately a plan unfolded; there was talk of robbing and then killing Mr. Clutter to leave no witnesses. The informant told authorities of having heard about another prisoner who shared in the plan. When "sprung," both were to "score big."

Primed with this information, along with descriptions and photographs of the two suspects, investigators decided not to go public. This strategy, they believed, would facilitate locating the killers by allowing them the delusion that they were scot-free. It proved a wise course. On their return from Mexico, the suspects threw caution to the wind, electing to "hang paper" (i.e., pass bad checks). Needing cash, they purchased merchandise for pawn. It worked until a television salesperson had the foresight to jot down the license number and make of their car on the back of a check. These facts found their way into investigators' hands long after the suspects had left the area for Las Vegas. On arrival, their intention was to pick up a general delivery parcel, pass more checks, and leave in 24 hours. By this time, however, a description of their car and license had been shared by police departments over many states. As it pulled away from the post office, the wanted vehicle was spotted by police officers in a patrol car. The parcel they had collected contained two pairs of boots: one sole bore the "Cat's Paw" trademark; the other, a diamond-shaped pattern.

The four detectives sent by the Kansas Bureau of Investigation to question the suspects deferred any mention of the Clutter murders. Interrogating them separately, they employed the strategy of "anxiety waiting" (see Chapter 11). When the evidence and the lies each had told were massed against them, confessions were elicited.

As the old maxim has it, "chance favors the prepared mind." The role played by luck is discussed in Chapter 13, but in the Clutter case it might well be argued that luck struck twice: first, when the killer's cellmate decided to become an informer; second, when they were apprehended after—and not before—picking up the boots. The first argument suggests that the case would have gone unsolved had the cellmate not come forward; however, to move the stalled investigation, a canvass of all those who had worked for Mr. Clutter was being considered. Since most of these people were scattered through Kansas (and elsewhere), this would have been a formidable task—no wonder British police call the canvass "intensive inquiry"—but carried through it would have led to the cellmate who probably would have told his story to investigators.

As to the second argument. It was, admittedly, sheer chance that the package containing the physical evidence linking the killers to the crime scene did not languish in the dead-letter office. This result would have come to pass had the suspects been picked up as they arrived at the post office to claim it—rather than afterward.

The Speck Case: The second well-known case represents what newspaper headline writers might term "a murder-sex orgy." Forcing his way into a dormitory, the intruder fatally stabbed and strangled eight student nurses. Tying their hands behind them with palms out to prevent their working themselves free, he marched all eight victims one by one into other rooms where he methodically killed them; some he mutilated. A ninth survived by crawling under a bed; she was able to provide a description of the murderer. Trying to account for the crime, psychiatrists speculated that it was motivated by a hatred of women or another twisted emotion. They also suggested that the criminal would not soon strike again; instead, he would spend some time to cover his tracks and throw off suspicion.

Detectives, meanwhile, were canvassing the neighborhood. They learned from a gas station operator that a man fitting the survivor's description of the offender had left two bags of clothing there to be picked up later. Based on the contents of the bags, the way the victims' hands were bound (palms out), and how the knots were tied, investigators inferred that the killer might be a seaman. Note was also taken of the maritime union hiring hall virtually next door to the nurses' residence. When the hall's files were searched for recent job applicants, investigators found a photograph of Richard B. Speck, whom the survivor identified as the killer. After latent fingerprints developed in the nurses' residence were found to match those of Speck in the union's files, the problem remaining was to locate and apprehend the suspect.

Up to this point, the case could serve as a model for how an investigation should be handled. Later, however, in the 67-hour hunt for the fugitive, police had two contacts with Speck, yet they failed to recognize him. In the first contact, they were called to a shabby hotel because of a complaint that a roomer had a gun. The roomer identified himself as Richard Speck and claimed the weapon belonged to a prostitute with whom he had spent the night. Instead of taking proper police action, the responding officer merely confiscated the .22 caliber revolver. The mistake was realized, but Speck had left the hotel just 30 minutes before it could be rectified. In the second contact, Speck attempted suicide in another "sleazy" hotel. Again police were called; again Speck went unrecognized. When Speck arrived in the emergency room with a slashed arm and wrist, the ward duty doctor noted the similarity between his patient and the artist's sketch in the newspaper, and a cleaning of the blood-caked arm exposed the tattoo, "Born to raise hell," purported to be on the wanted man.

This case demonstrates the need for improving the distribution of information within departments and for closely supervising routine police duties.

Mass Murders

There are two kinds of mass murder—those resulting from a crime spree spread over a period of time, and those in which all deaths occur in one (generally random) shooting event. The latter kind is by far the easier to handle.

Random Shootings—All Victims Die in One Event

Many of the perpetrators of these massacres are misfits unable to cope in society. Often "loners" with few emotional ties and some bottled-up anger, they seek relief by killing total strangers (in most instances), generally by gunfire. Largely a twentieth-century phenomenon, this kind of mass murderer may be trying to exert control over a world that seems out of control. (See Table 14.1.)

Table 14.1
Mass Murders—Random Killings—All Victims Die in One Event

DATE	NAME	NUMBER OF VICTIMS	LOCATION	OUTCOME
Sept. 6, 1949	UNRUH, Howard	13 killed 4 wounded	On the street in Camden, NJ	Committed to a mental hospital.
July 15, 1966	SPECK, Richard F.	8 killed	Student nurse dormitory of Chicago community hospital	Sentenced to electric chair. Now serving a life sentence.
Aug. 1, 1966	WHITMAN, Charles J.	16 killed 33 wounded	Fired rifle from observation tower on the campus of the U. of Texas at Austin, TX	Slain by the police.
Sept. 25, 1982	BANKS, George A state prison guard	13 killed 1 wounded	Wilkes-Barre, PA	Convicted of murder.
Feb. 19, 1983	NG, Benjamin Kin MAK, Kwain Fai (Willie) NG, Wai Chiu (Tony)	13 killed	Wah Mee Social (Gambling) Club, Seattle, WA	B.K. Ng and K.F. Mak convicted for murder. W.C. Ng disappeared.
April 15,1984	THOMAS, Christopher	10 killed	Palm Sunday Massacre, Brooklyn, NY	Convicted for manslaughter.
July 18, 1984	HUBERTY, James Oliver	21 killed 15 wounded	At a McDonald's Restaurant in San Ysidro, CA	Killed by the police (SWAT Team).
Aug. 20, 1986	SHERRILL, Patrick H.	15 killed 6 wounded	In the Post Office at Edmund, OK	Suicide at end of rampage.
April 23, 1987	CRUSE, William B.	6 killed 10 wounded 3 held hostage	At two shopping centers in Palm Bay, FL	Convicted of murder.
Jan. 17, 1989	PURDY, Patrick Edward	5 killed 30 injured	Schoolyard in Stockton, CA	Suicide at end of rampage.
March 13, 1996	HAMILTON, Thomas	17 killed (16 children, 1 adult) 14 wounded (12 children, 2 adults)	Dunblane Primary School Dunblane, Scotland	Suicide at end of rampage.
April 20, 1999	HARRIS, Eric KLEBOLD, Dylan	13 killed 12 students, 1 teacher	Columbine High School Littleton, CO	Suicide at end of rampage.

In general, cases of one random shooting event are easily handled: the offender is killed by the police in the act of mowing down his (or her) victims, commits suicide, or is taken into custody (after negotiations). There is also an abundance of supplementary information available—e.g., eyewitness accounts, physical evidence (firearms), records (weapon sales, mental health), which allows evidence to be developed with little difficulty.

Multiple Killings—Separate Events Spread Over Time

In addition to crime spree mass murderers (see Table 14.2), three other types of killers are responsible for multiple deaths—serial murderers, "lonely hearts" killers, and poisoners. Motive is usually an important factor in the solution of murder, but it contributes little to the solution of mass murders and serial killings. Motive plays a more significant role in solving homicides committed by "lonely hearts" killers and poisoners.

Table 14.2
Mass Murders—Crime Spree Killings—Victims Die in Several Events Spread Over Time

DATE	NAME	ASSOCIATED CRIMES	NUMBER OF VICTIMS	LOCATION	OUTCOME
1958 (9 days)	STARKWEATHER, Chas. FUGATE, Carol		11 killed	Nebraska and Wyoming	Convicted of murder. Starkweather—executed; Fugate—life sentence. but released in 1977
1971-72 (8 months)	McCRARY, Sherman McCRARY, Carolyn McCRARY, Danny TAYLOR, R. Carl TAYLOR, Ginger	Robbery Kidnapping Murder	22 killed (at least 10 are connected by ballistics tests)	Texas; Wyoming; Florida; Kansas; Missouri; Oklahoma; Nevada; Utah; Colorado; Oregon; California	S. McCrary and R. Carl Taylor convicted of murder
1982	HENDERSON, Robt. D.	Rape Kidnapping Murder	12 killed "execution style"	Ohio; South Carolina; Georgia; Florida; Mississippi	Convicted of murder
1982	COLEMAN, Alton BROWN, Debra		7 killed	Wisconsin; Illinois; Indiana; Ohio	Convicted of murder
1987	SIMMONS, Ronald G.	Incest Spouse abuse Murder	14 family, 2 acquaintances killed, 4 wounded	Dover, Arkansas; Russellville, Arkansas	Surrendered to police. Convicted of killing two relatives and later tried for other murders
2002	MUHAMMAD, John Allen MALVO, Lee Boyd	Murder 6 wounded	13 killed	Virginia; Maryland; Georgia; Alabama; Louisiana; Washington, DC	in November 2003, Muhammad was found guilty of committing a murder in an act of terrorism, conspiracy, and use of a firearm in the commission of a felony. In December 2003, Malvo was found guilty of 9 counts of capital murder and using a firearm in the commission of a crime. More trials to come.

Crime-Spree Mass Murders

Although crime-spree mass murder cases occur infrequently, they are generally solved:

1. when they are recognized as the product of a crime spree—often motivated by robbery and rape—that results in the deaths of victims who are generally unknown to the killer;

2. when the public, becoming involved through media coverage, reports sightings of the wanted criminal. This may ultimately lead to apprehension—if police surveillance and other follow-up activities have not succeeded. Many reports will be erroneous; just the same, each must be followed up quickly—such killers depend on mobility to avoid capture. Should flight take them back to where they formerly lived (as is often the case), the likelihood of their being recognized and reported is increased.

Serial Murders

The serial murderer almost without exception is a male who is prompted by a sexual or aggressive drive to exert power through killing. Since each serial murderer has the same motivation, the value of motive in solving such homicides is nullified. An added hindrance is the general lack of any previous connection between victim and killer.

An exception is found in the case of serial killer Judias Buenoano.[35] Over a 12-year period, she murdered her son, his father, her second husband and a (common law) husband in order to collect their insurance. Subsequent attempts to kill her latest boyfriend—first by poisoning and then blowing-up his car—were unsuccessful. The discovery that she had insured him for $500,000 without his knowledge led to an investigation and a reexamination of the above-mentioned deaths. Three separate trials for each victim resulted in three convictions—one carrying the death sentence.

In general, the serial killer is intelligent. When brains and a good appearance are combined with a beguiling (albeit superficial) charm, winning a victim's confidence is not difficult. What differentiates serial killers from other murderers, however, is that they know right from wrong; what they lack is a conscience impelling them to do right. These criminals genuinely relish their victim's terror; for them, murder is the ultimate thrill, and this distinguishes them from the "average" killer. Not driven by conventional motives, therefore, they select their victims at random: perhaps some physical or mental attribute galvanizes them into action, or they are attracted by the seductive prospect of a corpse with its promise of erotic pleasure. Necrophilia can be defined as:

1. A morbid liking for being with dead bodies

2. A morbid desire to have sexual contact with a dead body, usually of men to perform a sexual act with a dead woman.[36]

Serial killers, therefore, present the investigator with an additional burden in both quality and degree: their mobility, the absence of any prior association with the victim, and their use of remote burial sites all represent some of the difficult obstacles to be overcome. Indeed, the difficulty in solving serial murders may account for the drop in the homicide clearance rate from about 82 percent before World War II to 68 percent in 1989.[37]

When a serial murderer continues to operate in the same locale, disposing of the bodies becomes a problem. Serial murderers Wayne Williams and John Gacy dumped some victims from a bridge into a river. When a river or stream casts up murder victims, it is possible with technical help to estimate from which bridge they were thrown so that it can be placed under fixed surveillance. Although expensive in terms of personnel, surveillance has the potential for solving such homicides. It can become a tedious assignment, requiring close supervision of the surveillants to assure alertness and compliance with its special demands. See Table 14.3 for information on some notorious serial murders.

Table 14.3
Some Notorious Serial Murders

DATES	NAME	LOCATION/ NUMBER OF VICTIMS	KIND OF VICTIM	MANNER OF KILLING	TRADEMARK	OUTCOME
The 1940s Arrested March 1949.	FERNANDEZ, Raymond BECK, Martha "The Lonely Hearts Killers"	New York, Michigan, Minnesota and various other states. At least 3 killed. Many attempts; number of successes unknown.	Widows and spinsters who seem to be well-off.	Strangulation. Dismember-ment.	Found likely vic-tims through correspondence in reply to a column in a "lonely hearts" magazine.	Convicted of murder in the Borough of Queens, NYC, in 1949. Electrocuted in 1952.
1962-1964	DE SALVO, Albert Henry "The Boston Strangler"	In and around Boston, MA. 13 killed.	Mostly old women, but some young; all single.	Strangulation. Stabbing. Beating.	Tied an item of clothing—a stocking or bra—around the neck of the victim.	Life sentence in Walpole State Prison.
1963; 1970-1971	KEMPER, Edmund	California, (San Francisco Bay area and Santa Cruz). 8 killed.	Family (grandpar-ents, mother). Young women hitchikers.	Strangulation. Shooting. Knifing.	Dismember-ment of victims' bodies. Necrophilia.	Life sentence.
1970-1971	CORONA, Juan	Yuba City (Sutter County), Cal-ifornia. 25 killed.	Migrant farm workers.	Stabbing. Slashing of face, neck, and scalp.	Chop wounds inflicted by machete (or thin metal cleaver). Victim buried in a shallow grave.	Convicted of murder (1973). On appeal ordered retried (January 1978). Convicted of murder again in 1982. (Trial lasted 7 months and cost an estimated $7 million.) Life sentence.
1971-summer of 1973	HENLEY, Elmer Wayne CORLL, Dean	Houston, TX and vicinity. Yorktown, Lake Sam Rayburn, and High Island, TX. 27 killed.	Boys between age 13 and 18.	Strangula-tion. Shoot-ing. Blows with a blunt weapon. Kicking.	Rape. Torture. Castration of some victims.	Convicted of murder and sentenced to 594 years in prison. Con-victed again after a new trial in June 1979.

Table 14.3
Some Notorious Serial Murders (cont.)

DATES	NAME	LOCATION/ NUMBER OF VICTIMS	KIND OF VICTIM	MANNER OF KILLING	TRADEMARK	OUTCOME
1971- 1973	BUENOANO, Judias "The Black Widow"	Florida, Colorado. 5 victims— 4 killed; 1 survived.	Relatives or boyfriends .	Arsenic poisoning, drowning.	Insured victim for large sums.	Sentenced to death in electric chair. Electro- cuted in Florida (March 30, 1998).
1974- 1978	BUNDY, Theodore (Ted) "The Love Bite Killer"	Washington, Utah, Colorado, Florida. 36+ killed.	Young women with blond or light brown hair parted in the mid- dle.	Crushing skull with a club. Strangulation with nylon stocking or pantyhose. Stabbing.	Ingratiated self through smooth talk—using the name Ted. Faked injury (arm in a sling or leg in cast) and asked for help. Entered victim's bed- room in early morning or after midnight. Young women dissappear suddenly; body not found until much later (if at all) in isolated area. Butchered some.	Electrocuted in Florida (January 24, 1989).
1975- 1978	GACY, John Wayne (Jack)	Illinois (Chicago and its suburbs). 33 killed.	Adolescent boys.	Choking. Strangulation by rope.	Tricked victims into being handcuffed. Buried bodies in crawl space beneath his home. Also dumped vic- tims into Des Plaines River.	Convicted of murder (1980). Executed by lethal injection in Illinois (May 10, 1994).
1975- 1983	LUCAS, Henry Lee "The Hands of Death"	A drifter, he confessed to killing 188- 336 persons in 26 states— mostly Florida and Texas. Later repudi- ated many of his claims.	Men, women, and children, often picked up as hitch- hikers.	Bludgeoning. Stomping. Shooting. Hanging.		Sentenced to 75 years in prison.
1976- 1977	BERKOWTIZ, David "Son of Sam"	NYC boroughs: Queens, Bronx, and Brooklyn. 5 killed, 7 injured.	Young women, but some young men.	.44 caliber revolver.	Victims gener- ally shot late at night in sup- posedly safe neighbor- hoods, often while seated in a parked car.	Pleaded guilty to second degree murder. Sentenced to 365 years in prison.

Table 14.3
Some Notorious Serial Murders (cont.)

DATES	NAME	LOCATION/ NUMBER OF VICTIMS	KIND OF VICTIM	MANNER OF KILLING	TRADEMARK	OUTCOME
1977-1979	BIANCHI, Kenneth BUONO, Angelo "The Hillside Stranglers"	Los Angeles, CA; Washington state. 12 killed.	Females, often prostitutes, who were unknown to them; age range: 17 to 30.	Strangulation —manually or by ligature.	Discarded bodies on a hillside (or a roadside) for all to view their handi-work.	Bianchi—sentenced to 6 life terms in prison. Buono—life sentence with-out parole.
1978-1981	SUTCLIFFE, Peter "The Yorkshire Ripper"	England. 13 killed, 7 other attempts.	Prostitutes.	Used a hammer to bludgeon and a screwdriver to stab and mutilate victims.	Striation marks on the bodies of victims left by the screw-driver.	Found guilty of murder. Sentenced to life imprison-ment, orderd to serve at least 30 years.
1979-1981	WILLIAMS, Wayne	Atlanta, GA. 28 killed.	Black males— teenagers and young adults.	Asphyxiation— usually by strangulation. Blows to the head.	Attracted victim by offer of a role in a movie or money for a homosexual act. Dumped victims into a river from the bridge above.	Sentenced to death for murder (1984).
1982-1984	EYLER, Larry	Indiana, Illinois, Kentucky, Wisconsin. 23 killed.	Young men and boys, ages 14 to 28. Many street people with connections to homo-sexual community. Many picked up as hitchhikers.	Stabbing with knife or ice pick. Sometimes severed head of victim or dismembered body, throw-ing parts into dumpster.	Discarded bodies in out-of-the-way areas. Victim was partially dressed with pants pulled down to ankles.	Sentenced to death for mur-der (1984). Died of AIDS in 1994 before execution.
Sept.-Oct. 1982	"The Tylenol Killer"	Chicago, IL, and its suburbs. 7 killed.	Chance pur-chasers of Tylenol.	Cyanide poisoning.	Added cyanide to Tylenol cap-sules in commercial establish-ments.	Unapprehended.
1984-1987	HARVEY, Donald (dubbed "The Kiss of Death" by cowork-ers.)	Ohio, Kentucky. 21 killed in Cincinnati; 9 others killed else-where.	The elderly and the critically ill.	Poisoning of a drink or dessert with cyanide, rat poison, or petroleum distillate.	Used his position as a nurse's aid or orderly in a hospital to administer the deadly concoction.	Two consecutive life sentences.

Table 14.3
Some Notorious Serial Murders (cont.)

DATES	NAME	LOCATION/ NUMBER OF VICTIMS	KIND OF VICTIM	MANNER OF KILLING	TRADEMARK	OUTCOME
1978-1991	DAHMER, Jeffrey	Milwaukee, WI.	Young men and boys (mostly African-American or Hispanic)	Drugged victims, strangled or dismembered them, cannibalized some.	Lured victims to his apartment for a drink or to take pictures.	16 consecutive life sentences. Bludgeoned to death in prison in Portage, WI. Sole suspect: a fellow inmate.
July 15, 1982-1998	RIDGWAY, Gary "The Green River Killer"	Northern Oregon and the Seattle-Tacoma areas of Washington state. 49 killed.	Young women, mostly prostitutes.	Strangulation.	Dumps bodies in river, in ravines in the mountains, along logging trails, and in urban sites such as the back of a Little League field. Conceals bodies to prevent their being found quickly. When and where contact has been made, the victim is unknown.	Arrested for the murders in November 2001. Confessed to 48 murders on November 5, 2003, in exchange for a life sentence without possibility of parole.

The Violent Criminal Apprehension Program (ViCAP)

The Tenth Amendment to the United States Constitution retains for the states the enforcement of criminal laws. The fact that law enforcement is a local responsibility in the United States undoubtedly contributes to the ability of serial murderers to commit so many homicides and remain at large. Whenever the criminal moves to a new locale, the prospect of apprehension is reduced; the greater this distance, the smaller the likelihood that the work of a transient killer will be detected. Not to be overlooked is the lack of cooperation between different police departments. Although not common, "bad blood" does exist between departments—perhaps the result of a previous experience in which one agency felt its public image was damaged by the other.

This has led to the development at the national level of the Violent Criminal Apprehension Program (ViCAP). Located at the Federal Bureau of Investigation Academy in Quantico, Virginia, it became operational in June 1985. To be effective, the program must receive reports on homicides within the jurisdictions of local and state police departments. As might be expected, the ViCAP Crime Report Form had to be modified based on practical experience with its use. The primary purpose of the form was to recognize and match cases having an apparently common perpetrator; initially, however, it asked for too many details. A review and validation of a revised form were then undertaken. Now in checklist format, it requires far less time (15 to 20 minutes) to complete. The current model is reproduced in Appendix 3.

Not every homicide is suitable for consideration by the ViCAP program. Criteria for submission and acceptance are:

> **Homicides:** solved, unsolved, attempted (particularly if an abduction is involved); appear to be random, motiveless, or sexually oriented; suspected or known to be part of a series.

> **Missing Persons:** if the circumstances indicate a strong possibility of foul play and the victim remains missing.

> **Unidentified Dead Bodies:** if the manner of death is known or suspected to result from criminal homicide.

Submission criteria and suggestions regarding how a police agency recognizes when it may have a serial-killer problem are essentially the same.[38] The decline in the homicide clearance rate (93 percent in 1961, 67 percent in 1990) may in part be attributed to serial killers for two reasons: (1) "their habit of extensive interstate travel"; and (2) the fact that they are generally not known to their victims.[39]

When a case is solved by a local authority before submission to ViCAP and the offender is known or has been arrested, a Crime Report Form should still be forwarded; cases in ViCAP's files may then be compared against the facts supplied. The aim is to find a match between the known offender and unsolved cases. When separate homicides are linked, the detectives in the different jurisdictions are informed of each other's interest; to coordinate efforts, their respective telephone numbers are exchanged.

It should be noted that ViCAP can only be as good as the data supplied. As a national law enforcement resource, it can increase the likelihood that violent criminals—especially serial murderers—are recognized early, identified, and ultimately apprehended.

The Role of Routine Police Work in Solving a Serial Murder

Several notorious serial murderers have been apprehended as a result of routine police work: preventive patrol (Bundy); responding to a domestic disturbance involving a bizarre fire setting attempt, and following through on a ticket for illegal parking ("Son-of-Sam"); checking for required tax stamps or stolen plates on a vehicle ("Yorkshire Ripper"); and following up on the last known contact of a missing teenager who disappeared after a job interview (Gacy). (See Table 14.4.) Most of these cases were the subject of intensive investigation; before being solved, they required sizeable resources: forensics, personnel, and computers. The case of the Yorkshire Ripper is an example. Absorbing more than five years of official effort, it cost about $8 million. Police received three letters and a tape cassette signed "Jack the Ripper"; the letters promised more murders and taunted them for incompetence. Considerable effort was spent analyzing material subsequently found to be a hoax.

Table 14.4
Circumstances Leading to the Solution of Some Serial Murder Cases

CASE	ROUTINE POLICE WORK	BEHAVIOR OF SUSPECT
BERKOWITZ, David "Son of Sam"	Following up on tickets issued for illegal parking in Brooklyn, Berkowitz's car was the only one not belonging in the neighborhood, i.e., it was registered in another county. Following up some days later in the Bronx, an army duffel bag with a machine gun protruding from it is observed in his car parked on the street outside his apartment.	Berkowitz is suspected by neighbors of shooting two dogs for no apparent reason. A fire is set in another neighbor's doorway and Berkowitz is suspected.
BUNDY, Ted	Checking on restaurant after closing time, patrol officer observes unknown vehicle prowling the area. Officer makes a U-turn and follows suspicious car, which then attempts to speed away. When stopped, driver produces a stolen credit card for identification.	Assaults officer and attempts to escape.
GACY, John Wayne	Adolescent momentarily left his pharmacy job near closing time to talk about summer work with a contractor outside in the parking lot. Not returning, his disappearance is reported to the police. John Gacy is observed in the pharmacy that day at 6 P.M. and 8 P.M. Gacy is verified to be a contractor.	Gacy, realizing he is under surveillance, slows down, speeds up, and after pulling into a restaurant parking lot, invites investigators to have a cup of coffee with him.
LUCAS, Henry Lee	Arrested on a weapons charge. (Inspection of a driver's license and a vehicle—with owner's consent—of what is in plain view can result in the discovery of an item or material that suggests further investigation may be necessary. Obtaining the voluntary consent of the individual to accompany the officer to the station house legitimizes questioning, even though insufficient evidence for probable cause exists.)	When stopped by police when driving, Lucas walks back to the officer's car, regardless of whether he had anything to hide at the moment, in order to keep police away from his car.
SUTCLIFFE, Peter "The Yorkshire Ripper"	Officer observes known prostitute entering automobile. Discovers in license check that plates are not registered to vehicle. Driver is brought to police station for further investigation. Suspect's need to use the toilet shortly after relieving himself is noted and viewed as suspicious. Toilet is searched and possible murder weapon found. Follow-up search in the vicinity of site of apprehension leads to discovery of additional incriminating evidence.	At site of arrest, and shortly thereafter at station house, suspect asks for permission to relieve himself.
WILLIAMS, Wayne B.	Several missing children's bodies found floating in stream. Suspect's auto license noted through surveillance of a bridge from which victims were thought to have been thrown.	Suspect is observed with each of several victims shortly before they disappear.

Cases receiving inordinate media coverage cause an equally inordinate quantity of misleading and vexatious information to pour in to the police. Most, if not all, are shams. Just the same, on the outside chance that a real tip may have been provided, everything must be investigated. This means that precious resources will be squandered. In New York, for instance, the "Son of Sam" investigation required 200 detectives to be assigned exclusively to the case, the expenditure of $5 million, and about a year of investigative effort before David Berkowitz was identified and apprehended. A letter Berkowitz wrote to reporter Jimmy Breslin (published in the *Sunday Daily News*) brought on a flood of telephone calls to the police "hot line." Local precinct switchboards also were jammed by callers, all naming their suspect. For several days, more than 300 separate investigations per day were needed to follow up on ultimately useless information.

The ViCAP program offers the prospect of reducing the need for such extensive investigations by:

- Recognizing serial murders earlier than heretofore possible.

- Pooling the clues from each case and—once a series of unrelated homicides is perceived to be the work of a serial murderer—compiling and narrowing the list of possible suspects by induction.

- Clearing up other unsolved murders when an arrest is made.

"Lonely Hearts" Killings

The term "lonely hearts" killers describes murderers who prey on lonesome people. They examine the personal columns of newspapers, magazines, and perhaps Internet chat rooms with great care, select prospective victims, and then correspond with them (or with those who reply to their own notices in personal columns). Starting off as pen pals, they follow up with telephone calls, and eventually arrange a meeting. By means of charm, a reassuring voice and manner—whatever it takes—they finally are able to learn whether the prospective victim has bank accounts or other assets. If they deem the potential reward worth the effort, attention is then lavished on the victim-to-be, with marriage or promise of marriage the ultimate bait. At this stage, they may take out an insurance policy on the life of the intended victim. "Lonely hearts" killers are most often males who work alone, but sometimes they work in pairs, perhaps with a female posing as a sister.

A famous case is that of Raymond Fernandez and Martha Beck; together they killed female spinsters, often burying the bodies in the victims' own basements. Indeed, disposing of and accounting for the disappearance of the slain individual are two major problems facing the "lonely hearts" killer. Explaining to friends and neighbors that he and his new wife (the victim) intend to visit distant relatives or perhaps resettle enables the killer to take off. He can transport the body in a large trunk without arousing suspicion, and bury it before departing. Although friends and neighbors might regard this as strange behavior, not until some time has passed—when no letters, calls, or Christmas cards have been received—do they suspect foul play and report it to police.

By this time, the killer's trail is faint and difficult to track. Sometimes, though, a victim refuses to turn over control of her assets, and her signature must be forged after she is murdered. Such documents can link the killer to the crimes of forgery and homicide. There is little doubt that some "lonely hearts" killers have gotten away with murder. Yet others have been tripped up by those who became skeptical and reported their suspicions to police. In such circumstances, the VICAP program will allow more such offenders to be recognized and apprehended.

Poisonings

This section deals with mass poisoners and with those who, like most murderers, intend to kill just once. Homicide by poisoning is relatively rare today. Those who employ it to seize their victims' assets are somewhat akin to "lonely hearts" killers. They often befriend their prey and become live-in companions; in this way, they assure a supply of victims. Another method is to run a boarding house for the elderly living on private pensions or social security. Should boarders need help with everyday problems—shopping, errands, picking up parcels, and so on—they are easily persuaded to have their checks cashed as well. This practice becomes routine, and it need not cease after the poison victim dies. When finally disposed of, the victim is replaced by a new paying guest. Poisoners must use care when selecting their victims—those without relatives or friends can disappear with no questions asked.

In the past, multiple homicide by poisoning was not uncommon.[40] In 54 A.D., Nero became emperor of the Roman Empire after his mother (Agrippina the Younger) poisoned, among others, her husband and uncle—the emperor Claudius. By the Middle Ages, poisoning had flowered into an art form. Those who practiced the poisoner's art were Catherine de Medici, and Cesare and Lucrezia Borgia (though modern writers say of Cesare's half-sister that "she was a lady much maligned."[41]) In 1709 Mme. Toffana furnished the white arsenic (to make "Agua Toffana"); it killed more than 600 people. Food tasters became a royal prerequisite, and during the reign of Henry VII, poisoners were boiled to death in England. In those days, conviction rested solely on circumstantial evidence, such as the onset of symptoms or any malicious intent attributed to the suspect. Not until 1781 did Plenck observe what is considered obvious today, i.e., the only certain sign of poisoning is the identification of the poison itself in the organs of the body; however, ". . . it remained for the rise of scientific methods in modern times to make the practice more risky for poisoners."[42] To put this in perspective, it should be noted that in 1831 Marsh developed the definitive test for arsenic—historically, one of the most widely used poisons. This is an example of the early interaction of science with criminal investigation in furnishing credible evidence that can be offered as proof in court.

A poison is a substance which, when taken in small doses, causes an individual to sicken or die. It generally works by affecting a major organ—liver, kidney, brain, lungs—or the autonomic nervous system. Symptoms can be mistaken for those of a natural illness: acute bacterial food poisoning (so-called ptomaine poisoning) and acute arsenical poisoning resemble each other. Hence, if a toxicological examination is not conducted when a sudden onset of symptoms and death follow the ingestion of food or drink, a criminal homicide may not be recognized and a poisoner could go free. (See Table 14.5 for effects of some poisons after and before death.)

If several people had the same food or drink, and only one became ill but did not die, a bungled poisoning is a possibility. Owing to inexperience, many poisoners believe that too much poison will be detected. They hold back, causing sickness but not death, then must increase the doses until the desired result is achieved. Some poisons act cumulatively: each dose precipitates acute symptoms until a lethal level is reached. Thus, if a person were to have repeated symptoms (a week, a month, or even several months later) with no prior record of such symptoms and is otherwise in good health, the death should be regarded as suspicious. At the very least, a toxicological analysis of the body organs and fluids should be performed.

The symptoms manifested before death are of utmost importance, as are the appearance and odor of the body after death. All can offer clues to the kind of poison that might have been used.

Table 14.5
Effects of Some Poisons After and Before Death

MANIFESTATION AFTER DEATH	POSSIBLE POISON
Pupil of eye—contracted	Opiates
Pupil of eye—dilated	Atropine (Belladonna), Scopolamine
Skin is cherry red in color	Carbon monoxide, cyanide
Skin of face and neck is quite dark (compared to normal complexion of the victim)	Aniline, hypnotics, nitrobenzene, strychnine
Burns—mouth, lips, nose	Strong acid—nitric, hydrochloric, sulphuric Also oxalic and carbolic acids Strong bases—sodium or potassium hydroxide, i.e., lye or caustic potash
Odor of peach pits	Cyanide
Odor of garlic	Oxalic acid, phosphorous
Odor of disinfectant	Carbolic acid (or other phenol)
MANIFESTATION BEFORE DEATH	**POSSIBLE POISON**
Diarrhea (severe and unexplained)	Metallic compounds of arsenic, mercury, copper, antimony, lead, sodium fluoride
Vomiting and/or abdominal pain	Metallic compounds, food poisoning, sodium fluoride
Convulsion	Strychnine, nicotine, sodium fluoride
Sudden, quick death after ingestion	Cyanide
Abdominal pain	Metallic compounds, food poisoning

Investigating a Suspected Poisoning

Not every suspected poisoning case is necessarily a criminal homicide. There is no felony involved in at least three situations in which a poison causes a death:

1. accidentally taking an overdose (particularly a narcotic);

2. accidentally taking the wrong medicine;

3. deliberately taking poison.

When poisoning is suspected, it is crucial that the source and kind of substance be determined. The following investigative steps should be taken:

1. Interview the family, the physician (if any), and any others who have had recent contact with the deceased.

2. Examine the premises where the death occurred and collect all potential evidence relating to the possible substance used. Who brought it in the house? Why?

3. Transmit the evidence to the laboratory for examination by a toxicologist.

4. Check records of the pharmacy that filled the prescription and other possible commercial sources of the poison.

Among the facts to be ascertained by initial interviews are:

1. The date and time of death. When was the victim found and by whom?

2. The time the victim's last meal was eaten. What was eaten?

3. The date and time the deceased was last seen alive. Was the deceased in his or her usual state of health? Was he or she behaving normally? If not, when did the change in appearance or conduct occur?

4. A complete description of the victim's physical symptoms and behavior prior to death. Was any odor detected? (This information can help in distinguishing between acute and chronic poisoning situations.)

Significance of Acute and Chronic Symptoms: The symptoms of acute versus chronic poisoning are:

Acute	**Chronic**
The person is in apparent good health, when the symptoms (including death) appear shortly after drinking, eating, or taking medicine; or several persons are afflicted at the same time after eating or drinking the same food or beverage.	The individual appears to suffer from a persistent malaise or chronic ill health, and the cause is difficult to diagnose or otherwise understand. When the person leaves his or her usual setting (most often by leaving home for a vacation or other trip), the condition improves but recurs upon returning home.

Mass poisoners normally use substances that produce acute symptoms; for example, several victims (unconnected to each other) living scattered throughout an area will exhibit similar symptoms, then sicken and die in a short time. Running a thorough background check will usually reveal what, if anything, they shared in common. For instance, in the Chicago area in 1982, it was found that just before a quick death from cyanide poisoning, each victim had taken newly purchased over-the-counter medicine (Tylenol).

Mass poisoners are usually motivated by revenge, hate, discontent, and even extortion (by threatening to poison a company's product). They often see themselves as having been unfairly treated—in life generally or in the business world particularly. If the motive can be learned, the investigation has taken a significant turn. Sometimes the poisoner will volunteer crucial information through a letter to the media or a note planted at the scene, or a public appeal will induce the poisoner to share the reasons for the discontent. The appeal may be coupled with an offer (perhaps from a well-known newspaper columnist) to address the concerns of the offender. Written communications obtained in this way are valuable physical evidence; handwriting and typewriting specimens as well as finger or palm prints (if any) may tie a suspect to the crime.

Chronic symptoms of poisoning are more likely when the criminal is inexperienced and unfamiliar with the amount of poison required. Insufficient dosages are often administered since the victim must fail to detect the poison when eating or drinking.

A variation in type is the poisoner with the so-called Florence Nightingale complex. Here, each of several individuals is administered poison on separate occasions. As each victim becomes sick, the poisoner, having previously let out to neighbors that he or she is a nurse, is called in to restore the person to health; and does so. It is only when a death occurs (rather than a restoration of health through the ministrations of the nurse) that the police are likely to become involved. "Nurse" poisoners who "help" their victims are like arsonists who see themselves as heroic when they "save" people from fires they themselves set. The investigator who learns from friends and neighbors of the deceased about similar sudden illnesses and restorations to health—by a neighbor/nurse—should be alert to the possibility of poisoning and to the fact that this individual needs to be checked out.

Physical Evidence at the Scene of Death: In cases of suicide—an accidental overdose or prescription medicine taken by mistake—the suspected substance is generally located with little difficulty (often on a night table or chair). The substance, together with any illicit drugs, hypodermic syringes, and needles that may be found, must be marked, preserved, and transmitted to the proper laboratory for analysis. The hypodermic needle requires special handling: the tip must be inserted carefully and securely into a cork stopper.

> *Medicine Cabinet:* The entire contents of the medicine cabinet should be collected for examination and analysis.

> *Food:* In addition to any uneaten food present at the scene, condiments, sugar, flour, baking powder, and so on, should be collected for analysis later; also any food in garbage containers.

> *Beverages:* Milk, fruit juices, beer, wine, liquor, or any unsealed container of liquid that might have been consumed should be collected and refrigerated for possible analysis. An alcoholic beverage is often employed to administer a poison; it helps to mask the taste of the toxic substance. Any cup, glass, or other vessel the victim might have used should be seized.

> *Other Sources:* Possible sources of poison within a household are rat and roach powders, ant traps, and garden insecticides. They should be looked for and collected.

> *Body Excretions:* Diarrhea and vomiting are symptoms of poisoning. Accordingly, vomit and fecal matter must be collected separately in containers, then sealed to preserve any volatile poison present.

Transmission of Evidence: For identification and security against tampering, it is important that physical evidence be handled to meet the requirements of both the lawyer and the toxicologist. Its transmission to the laboratory is part of the chain of custody. The forensic pathologist should submit the appropriate organs obtained by autopsy to the toxicological laboratory for analysis.

Checking Records: If a prescription medicine appears to be the source of the poison—either by overdose or mistaken ingestion—the records of the dispensing pharmacy should be checked and the physician who wrote the prescription interviewed. When the medicine has been identified by the toxicologist, the results must be compared with what was ordered and dispensed. Any serious disparity—for example, poison substituted for medicine—must be investigated.

Records are sometimes kept on toxic compounds, supplying the date, to whom furnished, and the amount obtained. A follow-up inquiry can determine if the individual who bought the material (or any suspect) performed work requiring the use of the toxic material.

When a possible known source of the poison is established, a sample should be obtained to determine the trace (chemical) elements present as impurities and contaminants. A similar analysis should be made of the suspected poison discovered at the scene or in the home of the suspected poisoner. Depending upon the qualitative and quantitative results, especially if both specimens have the same combinations of unusual trace elements, it may be possible to identify the known source of the fatal poison. If access to the source is limited, the investigator's task is much simpler.

DYING DECLARATIONS [43]

A dying declaration (also known as an *antemortem statement*) is hearsay evidence. Though generally not admissible in court, it is allowed into evidence in homicide cases in certain jurisdictions. When allowed (as an exception to the rules of evidence), the dying declaration has proved persuasive although it is neither supported by the oath of the victim nor subjected to cross-examination. The underlying reasoning behind its credibility is the belief that human beings about to "meet their Maker" are strongly motivated to tell the truth. When close to death, supposedly, people do not lie.

An investigator's testimony on a dying declaration is subject to cross-examination. If the following recommendations are adhered to, few if any problems should be encountered when introducing the dying declaration on the witness stand.

The value of a dying declaration is illustrated by the successful prosecution of a homicide on New York's waterfront, which was accomplished largely because a dying declaration was used to convict three defendants of the murder of a dock boss. Because homicides on the waterfront are not often solved, and successful prosecution is even more infrequent, this case was well-known as the first in many years to lead to a conviction.

Obtaining a Dying Declaration

To be admissible as evidence, a dying declaration must meet several conditions:

1. The victim must believe he or she is about to die.

2. The victim must have no hope of recovery.

3. The victim's declaration must:

    Identify the person responsible for his or her condition.

    State the circumstances and manner by which the mortal injuries were inflicted.

4. The victim must be rational and competent.

5. The victim must die from the injuries received.

The last two conditions are met through the testimony of the investigator and forensic pathologist. The first three are met by asking the victim to reply to the following questions:

*   What is your name?

*   Where do you live?

*   Do you now believe that you are about to die?

*   Do you have any hope of recovery?

*   Are you willing to make a true statement as to how and why you were injured?

The dying declaration may be oral, but it should be taped on a tape or digital recorder, if possible. It also may be written, either by the victim or the investigator, and signed by the victim. It is useful, though not required, to have the declaration witnessed by a member of the public. A video is ideal, but unworkable in many cases; very often a dying declaration is made in an ambulance bearing the victim to a hospital.

CONCLUDING COMMENTARY

This chapter illustrates how the three sources of information—people, physical evidence, and records—are employed to solve homicides. It includes crimes with no apparent motive in which the killer seems to have escaped undetected (cases that confront the detective with a true mystery), and other kinds of homicides more easily handled by the trained, perceptive investigator. As the most serious of all crimes, it is fortunate that there are significantly fewer homicides than other major offenses. Several reasons account for the high rate of solution:

1. The resources that departments are willing to invest are greater than those allocated for other crimes. Large departments can assign personnel from other units to check out all leads as they develop in the course of an investigation. Smaller departments arrange to pool investigative talent, drawing from nearby communities.

2. For most homicides a particularized motive exists that prompted its commission. When ascertained, a list of suspects can be developed and honed by considering who among them had the opportunity, the means, the ability, and the necessary backbone to commit the crime. Investigative efforts can then concentrate on proving or disproving a suspect's involvement.

3. Physical evidence inadvertently left at the crime scene (e.g., a fingerprint, fired bullet, etc.) or taken from it (blood of the victim, fibers, etc.) may be available to link a suspect to the scene or the victim.

4. More than in most crimes, considerable physical evidence may be at hand to permit a reconstruction. The details revealed thereby can be checked against those provided by a suspect and possibly used in an interrogation aimed at obtaining a confession.

5. Investigative effort seeking to identify the perpetrator also may produce the evidence needed to prove that the defendant was the killer. The forensic pathologist provides the evidence—that the death was not natural or accidental, but criminal.

REFERENCES

[1] *Historical Statistics of the United States, Colonial Times to 1970,* Bicentennial Ed., Part I (Washington, DC: U.S. Bureau of the Census, 1975), 414.

[2] U.S. Department of Justice, Federal Bueau of Investigation, *Uniform Crime Report 1975-2001* (Washington, DC: U.S. Government Printing Office).

[3] Ibid.

[4] The Daily, *Statistics Canada* (2001). Homicide Statistics, 2000.

[5] Ted R. Gurr, *Violence in America,* Vol. I (Newbury Park, CA: Sage, 1989), 28.

[6] U.S. Department of Justice, Federal Bureau of Investigation, *Uniform Crime Reports* (Washington, DC: U.S. Government Printing Office, 1975-2001).

[7] Clark, Steven C. *National Guidelines for Death Investigation.* (Washington, DC: U.S. Dept. of Justice, Office of Justice Programs, 1997).

[8] Ibid., 1.

[9] Ibid., xx.

[10] *Loc. cit.*

[11] Ibid., xxii.

[12] Vernon J. Geberth, *Practical Homicide Investigation: Tactics, Procedures, and Forensic Techniques,* 3rd ed. (Boca Raton, FL: CRC Press, 1996), 379-388.

13   Ibid.

14   Ibid.

15   John Douglas and Mark Olshaker, *Obsession*. (New York: Scribner, 1998), 117.

16   Dominic J. DiMaio and Vincent J.M. DiMaio, *Forensic Pathology* (New York: Elsevier, 1989), 21-25.

17   M. Lee Goff, "Comparison of Insect Species Associated with Decomposing Remains Recovered Inside Dwellings and Outdoors on the Island of Oahu, Hawaii," *Journal of Forensic Sciences*, 36:3 (1991), 748-753.

18   Y.Z. Erzinclioglu, "Forensic Entomology and Criminal Investigations," *Police Journal*, 41(1), 5-8 (Jan. 1991), 7.

19   Ibid., 8.

20   Ibid., 6-8.

21   Vincent J. DiMaio and Suzanna E. Dana, *Handbook of Forensic Pathology* (Austin, TX: Landes Bioscience, 1998), 21-22.

22   Ibid.

23   Ibid.

24   Ibid.

25   DiMaio and DiMaio, *op. cit.*, 87-107, 171-206.

26   Vincent J.M. DiMaio, *Gunshot Wounds: Practical Aspects of Firearms, Ballistics, and Forensic Techniques* (New York: Elsevier, 1985), 67-77, 103-121.

27   DiMaio and Dana, *op. cit.*, 169-171.

28   Ibid., 187-191.

29   Ibid., 161-173.

30   J. Spencer, "Custody Wars," *Chicago Tribune*, 8 December 1986, sec. 5:2.

31   Anon., "Center Needs Clippings About Missing Children," *AARP News Bulletin* 26:8 (Sept. 1985), 9.

32   National Incidence Studies of Missing, Abducted, Runaway, and Throwaway Children, *NISMART-2* (Washington, DC: Office of Juvenile Justice and Delinquency Prevention, 2002).

33   Stephen E. Steidel (ed.), *Missing and Abducted Children: A Law Enforcement Guide to Case Investigation and Program Management*, 2nd ed. (Alexandria, VA: National Center for Missing and Exploited Children, 2000).

34   David Finkelhor, Gerald Hotaling, and Andrea Sedlak, *Missing, Abducted, Runaway, and Thrownaway Children in America, Executive Summary* (Washington, DC: U.S. Department of Justice, Office of Juvenile Justice and Delinquency Prevention, 1990).

35   Chris Anderson and Sharon McGeheen, *Bodies of Evidence: The True Story of Judias B. Buenoano: Florida's Serial Murderess* (New York: Lyle Stuart, 1991).

36   *Mosby's Medical, Nursing, and Allied Health Dictionary*, 5th ed. (St. Louis, MO: Mosby, 1998).

37   U.S. Department of Justice, Federal Bureau of Investigation, *Uniform Crime Reports 1975-2001* (Washington, DC: U.S. Government Printing Office).

38   Terrence J. Green and Jane E. Whitmore, "ViCAP's Role in Multiagency Serial Murder Investigations," *The Police Chief*, 60(6), 38-45 (June 1993), 42.

[39] Ibid., 38

[40] Louis J. Casarett and John Doull, *Toxicology: The Basic Science of Poisons* (New York: Macmillan, 1975), 4-9.

[41] Baron Corvo [Frederick Rolfe], *A History of the Borgias* (Westport, CT: Greenwood Press, 1975), 204.

[42] Casarett and Doull, *op. cit.,* 6.

[43] Ronald L. Carlson, *Criminal Justice Procedure,* 5th ed. (Cincinnati: Anderson, 1995), 160.

SUPPLEMENTAL READINGS

Homicide Investigation

Geberth, Vernon J. *Practical Homicide Investigation: Tactics, Procedures, and Forensic Techniques.* 3rd ed. Boca Raton, FL: CRC Press, 1996.

Hughes, Daniel J. *Homicide Investigative Techniques.* Springfield, IL: Charles C Thomas, 1974.

Crime Scene Investigation

Bevel, Tom, and Ross M. Gardner. *Blood Stain Pattern Analysis: With an Introduction to Crime Scene Reconstruction.* Boca Raton, FL: CRC Press, 1997.

DeForest, Peter R., R.E. Gaensslen, and Henry S. Lee. *Forensic Science: An Introduction to Criminalistics.* 2nd ed. New York: McGraw-Hill, 1995.

Dix, Jay, with Mary Fran Ernst. *Handbook for Death Scene Investigators.* Boca Raton, FL: CRC Press, 1999.

Fisher, Barry A.J. *Techniques of Crime Scene Investigation.* 6th ed. Boca Raton, FL: CRC Press, 1995.

Lee, Henry C. *Crime Scene Investigation.* Taoyuan, Taiwan (Republic of China): Central Police University, 1994.

Osterburg, James W. *The Crime Laboratory: Case Studies of Scientific Investigation.* 2nd ed. Eagan, MN: West Group, 1982.

Rynearson, Joseph M., and Wm. J. Chisum. *Evidence and Crime Scene Reconstruction.* 3rd ed. Redding, CA: National Crime Investigation and Training, 1993.

Medico-Legal Investigation

Adelson, Lester. *The Pathology of Homicide.* Springfield, IL: Charles C Thomas, 1974.

Baden, Michael M. *Unnatural Death: Confessions of a Medical Examiner.* New York: Random House, 1989.

Curran, William J., and E. Donald Shapiro. *Law, Medicine, and Forensic Science.* 3rd ed. Boston: Little, Brown, 1982.

DiMaio, Dominick J., and Vincent J.M. DiMaio. *Forensic Pathology.* Boca Raton, FL: CRC Press, 1993.

DiMaio, Vincent J.M. *Gunshot Wounds: Practical Aspects of Firearms, Ballistics, and Forensic Techniques.* 2nd ed. Boca Raton, FL: CRC Press, 1999.

Parikh, C.K. *Parikh's Textbook of Medical Jurisprudence and Toxicology: For Classrooms and Courtrooms.* Elmsford, NY: Pergamon, 1980.

Spitz, Werner U. *Spitz and Fischer's MedicoLegal Investigation of Death: Guidelines for the Application of Pathology to Criminal Investigation.* 3rd ed. Springfield, IL: Charles C Thomas, 1993.

Forensic Odontology

Cottone, James A., and S. Miles Standish, eds. *Outline of Forensic Dentistry.* Chicago: Year Book Medical, 1982.

Rogers, Spencer, L. *The Testimony of Teeth: Forensic Aspects of Human Dentition.* Springfield, IL: Charles C Thomas, 1988.

Stinson, Paul G., and Curtis A. Mertz (eds.). *Forensic Dentistry.* Boca Raton, FL: CRC Press, 1997.

Miscellaneous Topics

Anderson, Chris, and Sharon McGehee. *Bodies of Evidence: The True Story of Judias Buenoano, Florida's Serial Murderess.* New York: Lyle Stuart, 1991.

Carey, Arthur. *Memoirs of a Murder Man.* New York: Doubleday, Doran, 1930.

DiMaio, Vincent J.M. *Gunshot Wounds: Practical Aspects of Firearms, Ballistics, and Forensic Techniques.* New York: Elsevier, 1985.

Douglas, John, and Mark Olshaker. *The Anatomy of Motive.* New York: Scribner, 1999.

Egger, Steven A. *Serial Murder: An Elusive Phenomenon.* Westport, CT: Praeger, 1990.

Fisher, Jim. *Fall Guys: False Confessions and the Politics of Murder.* Carbondale, IL: Southern Illinois University Press, 1996.

Fromm, Erich. *The Anatomy of Human Destructiveness.* New York: Holt, Rinehart and Winston, 1973.

Godwin, John. *Murder USA: The Ways We Kill Each Other.* New York: Ballantine, 1978.

Hazelwood, Robert R., Park Elliot Dietz, and Ann W. Burgess. *Autoerotic Fatalities.* Lexington, MA: Lexington Books, 1983.

Hickey, Eric W. *Serial Murderers and Their Victims.* Florence, KY: Brooks/Cole, 1991.

Holmes, Ronald M. *Profiling Violent Crimes: An Investigative Tool.* Newbury Park, CA: Sage, 1989.

Holmes, Ronald M., and James DeBurger. *Serial Murder.* Newbury Park, CA: Sage, 1988.

Keppel, Robert D. *Serial Murder: Future Implications for Police Investigations.* Cincinnati: Anderson, 1988.

Kolarik, Gera-Lind, with Wayne Klatt. *Freed to Kill: The True Story of Larry Eyler.* Chicago: Chicago Review Press, 1990.

Kozenczak, Joseph, and Karen Henrickson. *A Passing Acquaintance.* New York: Carlton Press, Inc., 1992.

Lester, David. *Serial Killers: The Insatiable Passion.* Philadelphia: Charles Press, 1995.

Levin, J., and J.A. Fox. *Mass Murder: America's Growing Menace.* New York: Plenum, 1985.

MacHovec, F.J. *Cults and Personality.* Springfield, IL: Charles C Thomas, 1989.

Magee, Doug. *What Murder Leaves Behind: The Victim's Family.* New York: Dodd, Mead & Co., 1983.

Masters, Brian. *Killing for Company: Inside the Mind of a Mass Murderer.* New York: Random House, 1993.

Mones, Paul. *The Dramatic True Story of the Detective Who First Used DNA Testing to Catch a Serial Killer.* New York: Pocket Books, 1995.

Morse, Dan, Jack Duncan, and James Stoutmire, eds. *Handbook of Forensic Archeology and Anthropology.* Pub. by editors, 1983.

Norris, Joel. *Serial Killers.* New York: Doubleday, 1988.

Ressler, Robert K., Ann W. Burgess, and John E. Douglas. *Sexual Homicide: Patterns and Motives.* Lexington, MA: Lexington Books, 1988.

Schechter, Harold, and David Everitt. *The A-Z Encyclopedia of Serial Killers.* New York: Pocket Books, 1996.

Sullivan, Terry, with Peter T. Maiken. *Killer Clown: The John Wayne Gacy Murders.* New York: Grosset & Dunlap, 1983.

Tritt, Howard. "Missing Children: What the Investigator Needs to Know." In *Critical Issues in Criminal Investigation,* 2nd ed., edited by Michael J. Palmiotto. Cincinnati: Anderson, 1988.

von Hentig, H. *Der Nekrotope Mensch.* Stuttgart: F. Enke Verlag, 1964.

Wilson, Anna Victoria (ed.). *Homicide: The Victim/Offender Connection.* Cincinnati: Anderson, 1993.

CHAPTER 15

Robbery

INTRODUCTION

Armed robbery has strong psychological and social implications within the community. Robbery affects millions of Americans every year. Not only do victims suffer, but relatives and friends also must cope with the trauma of a loved one's victimization. Robbery involves either violence or the threat of violence, and the theft of property. It confronts the victim with a high probability of physical injury, emotional trauma, and frequently a feeling of helplessness.

Today, we know much more about robbery than we did 10 years ago. However, much of this information relates to sociological and demographic variables, and is less than helpful in aiding in its investigation. However, with regard to victimization, there have been several important studies about offenders and specific types of robberies that can aid the well-versed investigator in developing an investigative plan. Robbery investigations employ all the elements involved in criminal investigation: people (victims and witnesses), method (*modus operandi*), physical evidence, crime analysis, and records. It is a confrontational crime, thereby placing the victim in position to be an eyewitness—even if the suspect is disguised.

Robberies have considerable impact on the community. They engender fear and reduce the quality of life in a neighborhood, and political pressure is often brought to bear on the police department to solve them. For these reasons, supervisors will, if possible, assign their most trusted and capable investigators to robbery cases.

Robberies on streets or highways accounted for more than 40 percent of the robbery offenses during 2001. Robberies of commercial establishments accounted for an additional 26 percent, and those occurring at residences, 12 percent. The remainder were miscellaneous types.[1]

Victimization studies indicate that slightly more than one-half of all robberies were reported to the police. The reported rate of robbery victimization in 1998 was 4.2 per 1,000 persons. In 2001, there were 2.8 robberies per 1,000 persons.

Males are more likely to be victims of robbery, with persons between 25 and 34 victimized most frequently. For victims 50 years of age and older, robbery rates are generally lower than for younger persons.

Minorities and the poor are more likely to be victims of robbery than others. The robbery victimization rates for whites was 3.8 per thousand whereas for blacks and Hispanics it was 7.4 and 7.3, respectively, from 1994 to 1997.[2]

In almost 90 percent of robberies, the suspects are male. Not surprisingly, most robberies occur in metropolitan areas. Black males tend to be robbed at twice the rate of black females and at two and a half times the rate of white males. In more than one-half of the cases, the suspects use weapons, with guns being the weapon of choice in 40 percent of the weapons cases. Statistics also indicate that offenders using guns have a higher probability of carrying out the robbery than do those using other weapons. These statistics provide a background for the investigator and a frame of reference as the investigation proceeds.[3]

Almost 7.8 out of 10 robberies are committed by a stranger—about one-half of these by more than one offender. Most armed robberies and assaults occur on the street after dark. Most victims do not perceive that they are about to be robbed. The actual event usually takes place in a relatively short period of time.[4] In such cases, the victim may tend to perceive things that did not occur, and care should be taken to walk the victim through a reconstruction of events. This may prove helpful in developing an MO and in searching through files for similar cases.

The investigator should be aware that victimization studies indicate that about one-half of all robberies are never reported to the police. This fact can be important because the investigator may want to use the media and other community resources to ask victims who have not reported the crime to come forward in order to develop information about suspects and their description.

Definitions

Generally, robbery involves the taking of property from a person by the use of force or the fear of force. The Model Penal Code offers the following definition:

> A person is guilty of robbery if, in the course of committing a theft, he or she:
>
> (a) inflicts serious bodily harm upon another; or
>
> (b) threatens another with or purposely puts him in fear of serious bodily injury; or
>
> (c) commits or threatens to commit any felony of the first or second degree.
>
> An act shall be deemed "in the course of committing a theft" if it occurs in an attempt to commit theft or in flight after the attempt or commission.[5]

Robbery is generally defined for statistical purposes as:

> The unlawful taking or attempted taking of property that is in the immediate possession of another, by force or threat of force.

Because theft or attempted theft is an important element of robbery, the investigator should be familiar with the definitions of theft and related offenses. The definitions from the Model Penal Code provide general information. However, the investigator must be thoroughly familiar with the definitions of the jurisdiction in which he or she works.

PEOPLE

Victims and Witnesses

Robbery victims come from all walks of life. Robbers run the gamut from unsophisticated juveniles to experienced career criminals. Males are victimized more than twice as often as females (3.8 per 1,000 males versus 1.7 per 1,000 females); persons between the ages of 12 and 24 have a higher probability of victimization than those who are older (9.0 per 1,000 between 12 and 15; 9.9 per 1,000 between 16 and 19; 6.5 per 1,000 between 20 and 24; and 4.3 per 1,000 between 25 and 34). One-half of all robbery victims were 26 years of age or younger. Blacks are victimized at a higher rate than whites (7.4 per 1,000 for blacks; 5.3 per 1,000 for whites), while Hispanics are victimized the most frequently (10.5 per 1,000). People making less than $7,500 are victimized more than three times as much as those making more than $35,000.[6]

Types of robberies include street robberies; residential robberies (usually termed "home invasions"); robberies in schools; bank and armored car robberies; and other commercial robberies. The most common commercial robberies involve convenience stores, gas stations, liquor stores, drug stores, cab drivers, and other businesses or activities that frequently operate during evening hours and involve cash transactions. (See Table 15.1 for one year's breakdown of robberies by type of target.) Significant increases in so-called "carjacking" offenses has made this a "high priority" crime in many jurisdictions.

Not surprisingly, the probability of victimization is related in large measure to where individuals live, their occupation, and their "availability" as targets.

Most victims do not make good witnesses because the incident occurs quickly, a high degree of stress is involved, it is often dark—at least in street robberies—and the suspects often wear masks. Facial identification is frequently difficult for this reason. However, a good investigator working carefully can elicit information that may be buried in the victim's subconscious. Police artists, various identification kits, and more recently, computer imaging systems can be used to help create a drawing of the suspect.

The investigator should be aware that facial identification, while important, is not the only source of information. Clothing, physical marks (e.g., a scar) or characteristics (e.g., a limp), type of weapon, and words (i.e., "tale") used by the perpetrator to convey that robbery is intended can be invaluable. The robber's tale is extremely important in establishing an MO.

Table 15.1
Robbery, Percent Distribution, 2000

	United States	North-eastern States	Mid-western States	Southern States	Western States
Total	100.0	100.0	100.0	100.0	100.0
Street/highway	46.0	59.0	51.0	40.3	43.7
Commercial house	13.9	8.5	11.1	14.7	17.4
Gas or service station	2.9	2.5	3.5	2.6	2.8
Convenience store	6.4	6.3	4.4	7.7	5.9
Residence	12.2	9.7	9.7	16.2	9.2
Bank	2.1	2.1	2.0	1.8	2.8
Miscellaneous	16.5	11.9	18.4	16.7	18.3

From *Crime in the United States* (2001), Washington, DC: U.S. Department of Justice, Federal Bureau of Investigation, 1999. Because of rounding some percentages may not add to total.

When investigating robberies committed by juveniles, one should be aware that perpetrators may continue to wear the clothing worn during the robbery and/or use the same weapon again. Determining where and when the robbery took place also can be important in developing a profile and for crime pattern analysis.

Keeping in mind that the victim is likely to be traumatized by the event, the investigator should take care in conducting the interview. Initially, interviews should be conducted individually when there is more than one victim. The victim should first be asked to describe in his or her own words what actually took place. The investigator should attempt to obtain answers for the questions: who, what, when, where, how, and why. During this stage careful notes of the specifics should be taken. After the victim has explained what happened, the investigator should begin to work carefully through specific items of information. Some departments provide a checklist that is useful in obtaining specific information. The investigator should recognize that victims are prone to inadvertently giving inaccurate information; for example, height and weight are difficult to estimate accurately and are often reported incorrectly.

Robberies fall into categories based on the kind of force or threat employed:

Armed robbery involves the use of a weapon such as a firearm, knife, or other dangerous weapon. Other terms for this include: *holdup*, *stickup*, *heist*, and *hijacking*.

Strong-arm robbery involves the use of physical force to commit the robbery. Other expressions for this include: *mugging* and *muscle job*.

There may be more than one victim and there may be more than one suspect. In more spectacular robberies involving some degree of planning—such as a bank or armored car robbery—there usually will be witnesses, and every effort must be made to locate them.

The detective handling a robbery investigation must isolate the victim and witnesses and then interview them separately. He or she also must quickly identify and protect the crime scene. This aspect of the investigation is frequently overlooked or handled poorly, largely because the crime scene may actually be in more than one place (e.g., within a building where the robbery took place and outside where a getaway vehicle was parked). There is also a tendency to want to interview witnesses too quickly, which may result in a loss of information or varied accounts based on misconceptions.

In many instances the initial phase of the investigation is handled by the patrol force and there is a desire to broadcast a physical description of the robbers and vehicle as soon as possible, and even to remove the victim from the scene to accompany patrol officers in a search for the suspect. Such actions, though understandable, can complicate the investigation. In some cases it is almost impossible to preserve the crime scene because so many curious bystanders have entered the area. If not kept separated, witnesses also may influence each other in providing descriptive and other information.

The increasing use of closed-circuit television monitoring systems in businesses, apartment buildings, elevators, and other locations should not be overlooked. Cameras may also be located in parking lots or other areas away from the crime scene.

Robbery investigations depend on the ability to reconstruct the event, to develop physical descriptions and, perhaps most important, to establish the *modus operandi*. Because individuals are creatures of habit, they are likely to say or do similar things in different acts. The ability of the investigator to identify these "calling cards" can go a long way toward solution of the crime.

The investigator who bases a case solely on eyewitness testimony is endangering the case and the possibility of a conviction. The investigator should carefully develop an interview plan, both in terms of the sequence of individuals involved and the sequence of questions asked. All too often investigators "feed" information to individuals being interviewed.

Victims and witnesses generally fall into categories based on physical and emotional/psychological factors. These categories help determine the interview plan, the validity of the information, and the direction in which the investigation will head.

Physical Factors
Age
Sex
Race
Stature
Eyesight or other physical infirmities
Injury

Emotional/Psychological Factors
Degree of distress
Whether or not a prior victim
Ego
Attitude toward police
Attitude toward race

In addition to interviewing victims and witnesses, the investigator should remember that important information may also be gleaned from officers who arrived on the scene, as well as secondary witnesses who, though they may have arrived after the event took place, may have seen or heard something that was overlooked in the preliminary investigation.

Individuals—including the officers who handled the preliminary investigation—should not be permitted to hear or take part in the initial interviews of others. At a later time it may prove worthwhile to conduct group interviews, but this should be done only after everyone has been interviewed alone and after the investigator has compared notes with any partners or assistants.

Ideally the victim should be interviewed first and witnesses interviewed in descending order on the basis of those who appear most reliable. A classic mistake often made during interviews is grouping individuals in the same location as they await the interview, or permitting those who have been interviewed to mingle with those who have not.

Victim and witness perceptions may vary considerably. Short individuals, for example, will likely perceive the suspect as being taller than will witnesses who are tall. Elderly witnesses may have varying perceptions of age. Young witnesses may be able to provide more information on specific types of details, such as automobile descriptions, types of clothing, and mannerisms. When a victim has been robbed before, he or she may be able to provide details resulting from that unique frame of reference.

Sometimes victims (particularly males) experience ego problems because they did not act as they felt they should. Care should be taken to assure the individual that a lack of action or resistance was a wise course.

In addition to information provided by victims and witnesses, the investigator should identify and gather any physical evidence. All too often there is an assumption that the rapidity of the event precludes the possibility of physical evidence being present, but such a possibility should never be ruled out.

The Robbery Suspect

In 2001, persons under 25 years of age accounted for 62 percent of all robbery arrests. Younger suspects tend to operate within a geographical radius of two miles from their residence. While males are overrepresented in robbery arrest statistics, making up 89 percent of all offenders, the racial breakdown has changed significantly over the past decade. Whites now represent 53.8 percent of all robbery offenders, with blacks and other races representing 44.5 percent and 1.7 percent, respectively. For the most part, these offenders are also likely to commit street and commercial robberies with relatively little advance planning. They also are likely to commit multiple offenses in a relatively short period of time, frequently under the influence of alcohol or drugs. In 2001, about one-fourth of all robberies were cleared. Sixty-two percent of those arrested were under the age of 25, and 89 percent were males.[7]

Most robberies involve more than one offender operating against a single victim. About one-third of robberies involve three or more offenders. The number of offenders is usually age related. Young robbers tend to act in groups, whereas older robbers frequently operate alone or with a partner.

Investigation of youthful robbers will focus largely on patterns and *modus operandi*. Although these suspects may have prior arrest records, they may be difficult to retrieve because they were handled in a juvenile court and are unobtainable. Nevertheless, the frequency of events is in the investigator's favor. Information should be sought from youth investigators, informants, beat officers, neighborhood residents, and others who have access to possible suspects.

Professional robbers are more likely to be older and to have a prior arrest record. Frequently they have been convicted of a crime. According to the 2001 Uniform Crime Reports, juveniles comprised only 14.4 percent of robbery clearances.[8] Older offenders are more likely to plan the act, but the plan is sometimes no more than "casing" the location. Well-planned and well-executed robberies will usually be obvious to the investigator and will involve large sums of money or merchandise. The professional robber is also much more likely to operate over a wide geographic area, in some cases across jurisdictional boundaries and even state lines. he or she is also more likely to use firearms, automobiles, masks or disguises, and lookouts. In some instances, professionals use hand-held radios for communication and monitor police radio frequencies.

The professional robber represents a different challenge than the so-called opportunist robber who selects victims by chance. Because this type of robbery is executed less frequently and over a wider geographic area, it is much more difficult to establish a pattern or useful MO. In these cases the investigator must resort to the use of records, physical evidence, and robbery analysis techniques to be successful.

Conducting the Investigation

Physical Evidence

General crime scene protection and search measures should be observed at the robbery scene and in other key locations, such as a vehicle recovered after use in the crime.

Some specific types of physical evidence should be considered at robbery scenes:

1. Footprints may be present.

2. Fingerprints may be left in proximate locations. For example, the suspect in a store robbery may have handled merchandise prior to carrying out the robbery; in a bar there may be fingerprints on the glass or bottle used; in a handbag snatching in which the item is recovered there may be fingerprints on the handbag or its contents, or footprints where it was recovered. There may also be fiber traces on recovered material.

3. Saliva may be present on discarded facial masks.

4. Body secretions, fiber evidence, or other trace materials may be present on the victim's clothing if there was a scuffle or the use of force.

5. When a suspect has been identified or apprehended, trace material may be present on the suspect's clothing that will link him or her to the victim or the scene.

6. Physical evidence may be available where a weapon is recovered. Blood samples, skin or tissue residue, or even "tool marks" should not be overlooked. In one robbery-homicide case the perpetrator struck the victim with a serrated hammer. The blow was struck with such force that an impression that matched the weapon was left on the skull.

7. Fingerprints or trace evidence can be left on the articles recovered. A watch taken during a robbery, which was later pawned and recovered by police, produced a partial print that helped convict the suspect. In a rape/robbery, a suspect was identified more than a year later when a fingerprint recovered from the victim's handbag was run through the computerized fingerprint system known as AFIS (Automatic Fingerprint Identification System) when the suspect was arrested for another crime.

Records and Other Sources of Information

A robbery suspect will probably have a prior arrest record. The manner in which records are used may determine the success or failure of the investigation. By a process of elimination it may be possible to narrow the range of suspects considerably. In departments that use a computerized record system it may be possible to initiate "blind" searches. Some of the variables that can reduce a list of suspects include:

- Sex
- Race
- Age (although this can be deceiving)
- Color of hair
- Specific descriptors (such as a tattoo)
- Clothing (particularly hats or jackets)
- Type of weapon
- Geographic location
- Type of vehicle used
- Number of subjects involved

This partial list of variables provides an indication of the ways in which a potential list of suspects can be developed and then reduced.

Most robbery suspects will commit more than one crime. If, over time, it is possible to link crimes to one person, a more accurate profile can be developed and used to plan a strategy for apprehension. In addition to police department records, consideration should be given to other records, including:

1. Court records

2. Prison records (particularly recent releases)

3. Other law enforcement agency records (including federal, state, and local)

4. Other agencies (unemployment offices, schools, housing offices, drug rehabilitation programs, etc.)

5. Credit card companies (particularly when cards were taken in the robbery)

6. Motor vehicle bureau records

Numerous other sources of information may be pursued. These include:

1. Other investigators

2. Information from patrol officers

3. Informants

4. Individuals arrested in other cases

5. Stores where particular types of weapons may be purchased

6. Closed-circuit television tapes recovered at the scene

FOLLOW-UP ACTIVITIES

Successful robbery investigations depend heavily on the ability of the investigator to recognize significant variables that can be used to research past crimes as a measure of identifying and locating suspects. When all leads have been exhausted with reference to the immediate investigation, the solution will frequently lie in past crimes.

Recognizing patterns, geographical locations, the types of victims, and the number and characteristics of associates should be a high priority in the follow-up sequence of the investigation. By putting this information together it is frequently possible to add to the information about suspects. Having accomplished this, the investigator should begin to review arrest records of individuals who fit the composite *modus operandi* and physical characteristics.

Where this fails, the investigator should relay information to other jurisdictions, requesting their cooperation in crimes of a similar nature, or those in which potential suspects may have been arrested.

Research concerning robbery indicates that most street robberies are not well-planned, and the choice of victim is based on both circumstances, usually associated with time of day and location, and the perceived vulnerability of the victim. More sophisticated or professional robberies, on the other hand, generally display varying degrees of preparation. All of these factors should be a part of the robbery investigator's store of knowledge. The literature in this area is rich with information that can be of assistance. The National Criminal Justice Reference Service in Washington, DC, can provide a comprehensive annotated bibliography which should not be overlooked.[9]

REFERENCES

[1]   U.S. Department of Justice, Federal Bureau of Investigation, *Uniform Crime Reports 1975-2001* (Washington, DC: U.S. Government Printing Office).

[2]   U.S. Department of Justice, Federal Bureau of Investigation, *2002 National Crime Victimization Survey* (Washington, DC: U.S. Government Printing Office, 2003).

[3]   See Bureau of Justice Statistics (BJS) *<www.ojp.usdoj.gov/bjs>*

[4]   U.S. Department of Justice, Bureau of Justice Statistics, *2002 National Crime Victimization Survey* (Washington, DC: U.S. Government Printing Office, 2003).

[5]   American Law Institute Model Penal Code, 1895. As adopted at the 1952 Annual meeting of the American Law Institute at Washington, DC, 24 May 1962, 145.

[6]   U.S. Department of Justice, Bureau of Justice Statistics, *2002 National Crime Victimization Survey* (Washington, DC: U.S. Government Printing Office, 2003).

[7]   U.S. Department of Justice, Federal Bureau of Investigation, *Uniform Crime Reports 1975-2001* (Washington, DC: U.S. Government Printing Office).

[8]   Ibid.

[9]   The National Criminal Justice Reference Service (Washington, DC) can be reached at 800/851-3420.

SUPPLEMENTAL READINGS

Banton, M.O. *Investigating Robbery*. Brookfield, VT: Gower, 1986.

Bureau of Justice Statistics. "Carjackings in the United States." March 1999.

Wright, Richard T., and Scott H. Decker. *Armed Robbers in Action: Stickups and Street Culture*. Boston: Northeastern University Press, 1997.

CHAPTER 16

Rape and
Other Sex Crimes

INTRODUCTION

The investigation of rape and other sex crimes represents a significant challenge for the criminal investigator. The manner in which the investigation is conducted can have an impact not only on a successful conclusion in court, but also on the psychological and social well-being of the victim. Sex crimes, more so than many other forms of criminal activity, are likely to leave an emotional scar that can last a lifetime.

The focus of this chapter is on the crime of rape. However, it is important to recognize that virtually all sex-related offenses demand special attention. To begin with, interviewing victims, witnesses, and even offenders requires a high level of compassion and skill. One of the fastest growing types of crimes todayis the general category of Internet-related crimes.

The success of the investigation will also depend frequently on the collection of physical evidence. The nature of proof in sex offenses, unlike most other crimes, traditionally has required some corroboration other than the victim's testimony. Sex crimes also arouse the concern of the community, and there is likely to be political and public pressure on the police to solve the case. If not handled properly, this pressure can contribute to a faulty and hasty investigation. Rape is also the felony that is least reported to the police.

In 2001, rape victims accounted for approximately 0.7 per 1,000 households, with the probability of victimization being higher in metropolitan areas.[1] Statistically, we know that most rapes are committed by a single individual acting alone; almost one-third occur in or near the home; one in four occur in a public area or garage; almost three-fourths occur between 6:00 P.M. and 6:00 A.M.; and about one-half of the victims are under the age of 18. According to victimization surveys, between 30 and 60 percent of rapes are never reported, and in more than 50 percent of the cases the perpetrator is known to the victim.

Many law enforcement officials feel that even these figures are low. Divorced or separated women are victimized more frequently than those never married (3.2 rapes per 1,000 divorced and separated, and 4.2 per 1,000 never married). Less than one in 1,000 married women is a rape victim. Statistically, lower-income women are more likely to be raped. Rape offenders are more likely to be young, between the ages of 14 and 19; individuals between 25 and 34 represent the second largest grouping.[2]

Understanding the definition and elements of the various kinds of sex crimes is important, for in many cases the offender maintains that the victim consented to the act.

Definitions

Sex crimes cover a multitude of offenses ranging from indecent exposure to forcible rape. The issue of mutual consent is frequently a key defense contention. However, it should be noted at the outset that the concept of mutual consent is not well defined in the law, and what may be perceived as consent may not in fact be the case. A prostitute can be raped. An individual under the influence of liquor or drugs may not be in a position to psychologically (and legally) consent. Minor children cannot generally give consent. Plus, the phenomenon known as "date rape" has generated new case law.

Within the rubric of mutual consent lies a number of acts that may involve full consent between the parties, but that nevertheless are illegal within a particular jurisdiction. Examples of these include prostitution, adultery, homosexual acts, and other sex acts, such as anal intercourse. These crimes are rarely handled by investigative units and are not discussed in this chapter.

The most serious sex-connected crime from the perception of the public is forcible rape or sodomy, coupled with murder. It is important to recognize, though, that all rapes and serious sexual assaults must have a high priority in the investigative universe. They are frequently difficult to prove in a court of law and offenders have gone free because of a lazy or sloppy investigation.

Corpus Delicti

The legal definition of rape generally involves the following elements:

A. Sexual penetration, however slight, of the victim's vulva;

B. By a person or persons without the victim's consent;

C. Or with a minor child.

Sex crimes include other forms of aberrant behavior with which the investigator should be familiar. These include:

1. Sexual assault

2. Child abuse and molestation, also known as pedophilia

3. Some forms of pornography

4. Indecent exposure

5. Incest

6. Stalking

STALKING

Very little research has been done on stalking, which generally involves conduct that is directed at a specific person or persons, that seriously alarms, annoys, intimidates, or harasses the person(s), and that serves no legitimate purpose. Stalking may involve telephone calls, notes or letters, confrontations, and following a person or persons. It may be instituted for a variety of reasons.[3] Two types of stalkers have been identified by New York homicide detective Vernon Geberth: the Psychopathic Personality Stalker, and the Psychotic Personality Stalker[4] (see Table 16.1).

Understanding the reasons for stalking behavior is a critical part of the investigation. In the case of love-scorned and domestic stalkers the suspect is usually known. He or she often may be known in the case of celebrity stalkers. In cases involving lust, contract murder, and political stalkers, the suspect is usually not identified. In the absence of letters, phone calls, or other warnings, the victim may tell the investigator that he or she "feels" they are being watched.

Table 16.1
Types of Stalkers

The Psychopathic Personality Stalker	Usually a male from a dysfunctional family, who is likely to use violence as a form of control over a former girlfriend or wife, and who frequently displays homicidal behavior. This is the most common form of stalker.
The Psychotic Personality Stalker	A male or female who becomes obsessed with a particular person, such as an unobtainable love subject.
Celebrity Stalker	Follows someone who is famous, usually an entertainment or sports figure.
Lust Stalker	Usually involves desire for sexual (rape) gratification, or psychological gain or power over a stranger.
"Hit Man" Stalker	A professional killer who stalks his or her victims.
Love-Scorned Stalker	Involves prior personal relationship between the stalker and the victim.
Domestic Stalker	Involves anger against a spouse.
Political Stalker	Focuses on a political figure, usually not personally known to the attacker.

Adapted from V. Geberth, "Stalkers," *Law and Order* (October 1992) and R. Holmes, "Stalking in America: Types and Methods of Criminal Stalkers." *Journal of Contemporary Criminal Justice* (December 1993).

When telephone calls are being made, a pen register may be placed on the phone with the cooperation of the telephone company. This identifies the phone from which a call is being made. In the case of mail, leads may be developed by looking at postmarks to determine where the letter was posted.

The U.S. Secret Service maintains an extensive file on potential political stalkers or assassins, and the FBI maintains a sexual offender file that may be of assistance in cases involving lust stalkers.

In a study of more than 120 stalkers, Holmes found that, with the exception of love-scorned stalkers, most had the intent to commit murder. In the case of love-scorned stalkers, while they do not usually intend to murder the victim, they do have a propensity for violence, and many of these cases have resulted in a murder.[5]

PEOPLE

Two aspects of sex crime investigation must receive priority handling. The first is seeing that the victim receives proper medical attention and a physical examination that can establish rape or sexual assault. The second is protection of the crime scene and, if a suspect is apprehended immediately or shortly thereafter, the collection and protection of his clothing—particularly undergarments. In addition, efforts should be made to locate witnesses who, although they may not have seen the crime, can place the suspect with or in proximity to the victim.

The attitude and demeanor of the investigator is crucial during these initial stages. A progressive law enforcement agency will have developed relationships with hospital emergency rooms and victim support groups that can be of great assistance. The medical practitioner conducting a rape examination is expected to follow a set of standard procedures that are a part of the case during its investigative and trial stages.

In rape cases there may be more than one crime scene requiring protection. For example, the victim may have been abducted and taken by car to another location and held there, or assaulted in one location and then taken to yet another location where she was released.

Because there might not be any other witnesses, it is necessary to establish an evidentiary link between the perpetrator and the victim that will serve to corroborate the victim's allegation. Even where the suspect admits that he was with the victim, but denies that a rape took place or says that the victim consented, it may be possible through physical evidence to attack the suspect's statements. For example, the presence of semen in the vagina may be used to refute an allegation that intercourse did not take place; and trace or fingerprint evidence may be used to show that the suspect was at a location where he denied being, such as the bedroom.

After the victim has received medical attention, a follow-up interview should be conducted. In many jurisdictions this interview is conducted by a female investigator if one is available. Under ideal circumstances it is prudent to have a psychologist who is familiar with sex crimes advise the investigator as questioning proceeds (this is not usually done in the presence of the victim). The psychologist should not take part in the interview, although in some cases it may be advisable to permit a representative from a victim support group to be present. This will depend on the emotional state of the victim and her desire to have an outsider present.

In practice, the first officer on the scene will likely conduct a preliminary interview. These interviews are critical; patrol officers should be trained in handling them. (A second officer or investigator should immediately be assigned to canvass the area or neighborhood for potential witnesses.) Also, the time, manner, and nature of the interview may be affected if considerable time passes before medical authorities permit the victim to be interviewed by the investigator. For example, if there is serious physical or emotional trauma, the doctor may not permit an immediate interview. In such a case, the investigator must depend on the information from the initial interview. Also, because there may be a tendency to "block" or subconsciously forget information because of trauma, the initial interview may be used later to help refresh the victim's memory.

Victims and Witnesses

The preliminary interview should address the physical description of the offender, where the act occurred, and the circumstances surrounding it. The interview should be conducted in private, preferably with an impartial observer such as a nurse or female officer. Generally, the officer with the most experience should conduct the interview. However, circumstances may dictate otherwise—for example, if the victim is more comfortable with a female officer with less experience.

At this stage, the victim is frequently highly traumatized and may be hysterical. It is not necessary to focus on physical details of the act. If the victim alleges a rape, the officer should assume that one has occurred and operate on this assumption. It is usually advisable to let the victim tell her story uninterrupted and to take good notes. If time permits, the next stage of the interview should attempt to build on the victim's statements, taking care not to challenge or question statements. The officer should studiously avoid accusatory statements such as "Why were you in the bar?," "Why were you out late at night?," "Why did you go with him?," or "Why were you wearing that clothing?"

The interview should take into account such factors as age, psychological state, willingness to cooperate, and special circumstances. This involves an ability to "size up the situation." The officer should avoid leading questions and should respond to statements by nodding or asking, "Then what happened?" Confusion, disorientation, or fear may create inconsistencies in statements. Inconsistencies do not mean that the victim is lying. She may be avoiding certain items of information because she is psychologically traumatized, severely embarrassed, or worried about the reactions of a spouse, boyfriend, or some family member.

The goal of the preliminary interview should be to establish:

1. a physical description of the offender or offenders;

2. the location or locations where the crime took place;

3. the identification of possible witnesses (Remember that even the fact that a witness can place the victim with an offender could be important. The fact that they "saw nothing" should not be a reason to dismiss them, or to refrain from obtaining their addresses and phone numbers.);

4. specific actions of the offender that are volunteered by the victim;

5. circumstances leading up to the attack;

6. information on any weapon or vehicle that may have been used;

7. specific information on the actual location of the assault (bedroom, back of a vehicle, etc.).

During the preliminary interview the officer must take care to be supportive and understanding. This is as important for female officers as it is for males. It is not unusual, subconsciously, to provide the victim with visual cues that indicate skepticism, disbelief, disapproval, or even hostility.

Unless there are very unusual circumstances, the interview should never be conducted in the presence of the husband, boyfriend, or other family member. In some cases the victim may insist on having a close friend in attendance. Again, this generally should be avoided unless a determination has been made that this will aid in the interview process.

The officer should refrain from telling individuals that the victim does not want them present; instead he or she should politely tell them that their presence is not advisable at this point and assure them that they will have an opportunity to speak to the victim as soon as possible. In some cases the victim may be afraid to face a husband, boyfriend, or parents who may be accusatory. An effort must be made by the investigator to be present, if at all possible, when the victim first meets with persons close to her after the assault. A victim-assistance counselor or psychologist can be of great assistance at this stage.

FOLLOW-UP INTERVIEWS

Follow-up interviews will usually be conducted by the investigator, and in some cases by the prosecutor. If the victim has recovered sufficiently to talk, this stage involves the development of specific information that will form the basis for a legal case. A trained rape counselor (many of whom have been victims of rape) with experience in handling and counseling rape victims can be of assistance in reassuring the victim. The use of counselors should be countenanced by department policy. Ground rules should be established for their utilization. The task of a counselor is not to conduct the interview; it is rather to lend support.

Ideally, the interview setting should be comfortable for the victim. Generally, the police station is to be avoided. The interview should be conducted with only the necessary people present—the investigator, the victim assistance counselor or psychologist, and perhaps the prosecutor. In some cases a stenographer may be needed. Doctors, nurses, police supervisors, and of course, reporters are excluded; the fewer people the better.

The investigator should ask the victim to tell his or her story from the beginning, apologize for having her repeat it, and explain that some questions may be asked again—not because the investigator does not believe her but because it will help later in conducting the investigation, arresting the perpetrator and, most importantly, gaining a conviction. The investigator should explain that the more information the police have, the greater the likelihood that the case may not have to come to trial. The defendant is likely to plead guilty in cases where the prosecutor has a lot of information.

The victim should be allowed to tell the story in her own words with minimal interruptions while the investigator makes notes of the areas in which more information is needed. The investigator should establish the basic points of information: who, what, when, where, how, and why. The elements of the crime must be established. Taking care not to "lead" the witness, the investigator should move from the general to the specific. If the victim appears uncomfortable providing the details of the commission of the crime, she should be allowed to come back to them later.

Many victims will have difficulty explaining certain sex acts. Questioning will be governed in large measure on the experience and comfort of the victim in providing graphic details. While taking care not to appear like a voyeur, the investigator should exhibit a sense of comfort in discussing the case.

In establishing the acts of the perpetrator, language familiar to the victim should be used. Terms such as "coitus," "fellatio," and "cunnilingus" may be alien to the victim. The investigator must not assume that the victim understands what has been said to her just because she nods agreement or says yes. She should explain what happened in her own words. If there are multiple acts, they should be identified and categorized in chronological order.

Because consent is a common defense against rape, care must be taken to determine the "mind-set" of the victim when the crime was committed. The actions of the perpetrator and the victim, including statements made and physical actions taken at that time, must be ascertained. The psychological state of the victim may have prompted her to acquiesce out of fear even though on the surface it may not appear that a threat was present. The victim's actions and words may be crucial to a conviction and must be carefully recorded.

Some victims may be reluctant to use profanity and may hesitate to repeat the words an offender used. Even some novice investigators have been known to omit profanity from reports even though it was used in a verbatim account of the crime.

The so-called "experience" or moral character of the victim may also be used against the victim during a trial, and the investigator should establish in detail what in the victim's mind constituted a lack of consent, and how or why the victim may have acquiesced. The fact that a suspect is unarmed and said to the victim, "I want to fuck you," and she acquiesced does not preclude rape if the victim felt she was being coerced. The fact that she had sexual intercourse with other men is immaterial.

In many cases there is a victim-suspect relationship, but this does not preclude forcible rape. In one case, the victim, who had been drinking, had sexual intercourse with one individual willingly, after which his friend entered the room and held her down and copulated with her, despite her protests and physical attempts to stop him. This is rape.

In recent years "date rape" has come to be a serious problem, one frequently ignored by authorities in the past. Greater recognition and sensitivity to this issue in society has prompted concern and action by law enforcement. In such cases the investigator must take special care in the interview phase to obtain information that establishes the sequence of events. The exact statements of the victim, witnesses, and the suspect may be crucial for prosecution. For this reason, it is important to try to record interviews.

The actions of the suspect after the act should also be determined if possible. Remarks initiated by the offender may constitute part of his MO. For example, phrases such as "I'll bet that's as good as you've had it" or "You liked it, didn't you?" reflect an inner need that is likely to be repeated with subsequent victims. Because the *exact* words used vary from rapist to rapist, phrases can characterize an MO and help to tie two or more rapes to one perpetrator. The victim may be able to provide other information that makes it possible to collect physical evidence linking the suspect to the scene. The suspect in one case went into the bathroom and discarded his and the victim's underwear in the toilet. The underwear was later recovered and used against him. In another case a suspect left a dress shirt in the garbage pail at the scene. He was linked to it through the laundry marks on the collar.

In developing a physical description of the offender, the investigator should make every effort to have the victim identify distinguishing marks or characteristics such as scars or tattoos—particularly those that are normally not visible. The investigator should ask if the offender was circumcised, and should be sure that the victim understands what circumcision is and what it looks like. If she does not know or is unsure, this should be noted, because the defense may try to lead the victim into a trap on this issue.

Interviews with the victim should be kept to a minimum; repeated interviews can cause trauma. On the other hand, the investigator must feel confident that all the necessary information has been collected. This may mean holding two or more sessions.

Interviews of witnesses in rape cases fall into two categories: (1) those who can testify that the offender was with the victim, and (2) those who may be able to testify to specific acts. Hostile witnesses may claim that the victim gave her consent; others may be ashamed at what they saw and might not want to cooperate.

With hostile witnesses efforts should be made to gather as much detail as possible. What they perceive as acquiescence may not be. In addition, if they are lying to help a friend, it may be possible to develop conflicting statements or descriptions of the actions. Such witnesses should be handled carefully; the investigator must not lead them in their responses.

Interviewing Children

Interviewing children requires great sensitivity and, unless there is an immediate necessity, these interviews should be conducted with the assistance of trained professionals.

Where there is an indication of rape or sexual abuse of a child, the offender is frequently known to the child. The investigator must keep in mind that the child may have been victimized by a parent. It is important to maintain eye contact, and to observe physical movements and the relationship between parent and child.

The preliminary interview may involve parents who have discovered that a crime has taken place. Often the suspect is known. In most cases where such an allegation is made, the reporting officer need not conduct an interview immediately. It is better to wait for an investigator trained in such matters.

When a case of forcible rape or sexual abuse has just occurred, it may be necessary to conduct a preliminary interview. The child should be allowed to explain what happened in his or her own words. The investigator should try to secure an identification or physical description of the offender. Trained investigators, children's advocates, or counselors who are familiar with this type of investigation should be summoned immediately. The crime scene must be protected and the victim's garments obtained after taking the victim for medical attention.

CONDUCTING THE INVESTIGATION

The investigation of sex-related offenses requires sensitivity. The investigator must be aware that the lives of victims, as well as alleged suspects, can be ruined through carelessness.

The crime scene and the collection of physical evidence represent an important part of the initial phase of the investigation.

Physical Evidence

In general the collection of physical evidence in rape and sexual abuse cases should follow the recommendations outlined in Chapter 5. A Sex Crimes Investigation Kit should also be available to the investigator. These kits are designed to help in the collection and preservation of evidence, especially by medical personnel (see Figure 16.1).

The investigator should recognize that sex crimes may occur in multiple locations. Care should be taken to quickly identify multiple crime scenes and immediate steps should be taken to protect them.

The goal of the crime scene search is to locate evidence that will:

1. link the victim and the offender to the crime scene;

2. establish that sexual relations took place;

3. establish that force was used; and

4. establish the offender's role or activity.

Establishing a link between the victim, offender, and crime scene may be necessary in cases in which the offender denies being present or claims that the victim was not present. This link has great investigative and probative significance. Rapid advances in DNA technology make establishing a link to the victim easier, especially where the suspect claims he was not present. In addition to fingerprint evidence, the investigator should look for evidence that may establish a DNA link. Cigarette butts, saliva, or blood, for example, can be especially important if the perpetrator used a condom.

In order to establish rape it is necessary to prove that penetration, however slight, took place. This is usually accomplished through a medical examination, which may show that intercourse took place. However, laboratory analyses may be hampered if the victim has taken a shower or douche. Analysis also can be impeded if the victim had intercourse with another individual prior to the rape, or was attacked by more than one person. In one case (mentioned earlier) a victim had sexual intercourse with her boyfriend willingly, but awoke later to find that one of his "friends" had entered her room after her boyfriend left and forced her to have sexual relations. The offender maintained that he had not had sexual intercourse, but instead merely had sat on the bed, propositioned the woman, and been refused. A crime scene search produced the victim's undergarments, which contained traces of semen. When examined to determine

Figure 16.1
Sex crimes evidence collection kit. *(Courtesy, Sirchie Finger Print Laboratories.)*

its blood group, the blood group found matched that of the accused, but differed from that of the victim and the boyfriend. When confronted with this evidence the man confessed. Because it is more specific, modern DNA technology is even more helpful than blood grouping in resolving such an issue.

The use of force be established through the recovery of weapons or material used to tie the victim down, or by showing the marks left through the use of force in restraining the victim. In one case involving a homicide, the rope fibers on a tree established that one of the victims had been tied to the tree.

Establishing the offender's actions or role can be accomplished in several ways, ranging from an analysis of the scene (such as moved furniture) to trace evidence and bloodstain patterns in different locations. In the case mentioned above, the offender denied being present at the scene. However, drops of his blood from a cut received in a struggle with one of the victims left a trail that not only established his presence, but also showed his movements and direction. It was established that he had not only been at the scene, but had moved to his vehicle and then returned to the scene.

Dale M. Moreau provides a list of some of the types of physical evidence that the investigator should be aware of and the means of collection and preservation that should be used with them.[6] These include:

Clothing	All clothing worn by the victim should be obtained and packaged in a sealed, secure condition. Each item must be packaged separately to avoid transfer of evidence from one item to another. Sections of manila-type wrapping paper or sturdy paper bags can be used for packaging purposes.
Head Hair Combing/Brushing	The head hair region of the victim should be combed or brushed for evidence. This requires an uncontaminated comb or brush used for the head area only. The comb or brush and adhering materials are then packaged and sealed.
Known Head Hairs	An appropriate amount of hair (one to two dozen hairs from each region sampled) to represent color, length, and area variation must be obtained. Hairs should be pulled whenever possible. Known hairs should be acquired after the head hair combing or brushing procedure is completed. These hairs are then separately packaged and sealed.
Pubic Hair Combing/Brushing	The pubic region of the victim should be combed or brushed for evidence. This requires an uncontaminated comb or brush for the pubic area only. The comb or brush and adhering materials are then packaged separately and sealed.
Known Pubic Hairs	An appropriate amount of pubic hair (one to two dozen hairs) to represent color, length, and area variation should be obtained. Hairs should be pulled whenever possible. Known pubic hairs should be acquired after the pubic hair combing or brushing procedure is completed. These hairs are packaged separately and sealed.
Combing/Brushing of Body Hair Regions Other Than Head and Pubic Area	In the event an individual is observed to have excessive body hair, a separate, uncontaminated comb or brush and appropriate packaging material can be used to collect any trace evidence that may be present.
Vaginal Swabbings	The vaginal cavity should be swabbed to detect the presence of spermatozoa or seminal fluid. An unstained control sample of the gathering medium must be retained and packaged separately.
Oral Swabbings	The oral cavity should be swabbed to detect the presence of spermatozoa or seminal fluid. An unstained control sample of the gathering medium is retained and packaged separately.

Anal Swabbings	The anal region should be swabbed to detect the presence of spermatozoa or seminal fluid. An unstained control sample of the gathering medium is retained and packaged separately.
Microscope Slides of Smears Made from Vaginal, Oral, and Anal Swabbings	Any such slides prepared for the examination of spermatozoa should be retained along with the swabs used to prepare the smears.
Penile Swabbings	The penis should be swabbed to detect the presence of blood or other evidence. An unused control sample of the gathering medium is retained and packaged separately from the swab used to obtain the penile sample.
Vaginal Aspirate	In addition to vaginal swabbing, the vaginal vault should be irrigated with saline solution. Spermatozoa not obtained through the swabbing procedure may be recovered in this manner. The aspirate solution is placed in a separate tube or small vial. A control sample of the irrigation fluid is also retained and packaged separately.
Oral Rinse	The mouth of the person examined can be rinsed in order to remove spermatozoa not collected via the swabbing procedure. The rinse is expectorated into a tube or vial. A control sample of the rinse is retained and packaged separately.
Nasal Mucus Sample	This type of sample is acquired by having the individual being examined blow his or her nose on cloth. The mucus may contain spermatozoa that were deposited in the mouth or the facial area. An unstained portion of the cloth is needed as a control sample.
Fingernail Scrapings	Using appropriate materials (such as a flat wooden toothpick), the areas underneath the fingernails should be scraped for significant debris such as hairs, fibers, blood, or tissue. The gathering implement is retained. It is suggested that each hand be scraped individually and the resulting debris packaged separately.
Miscellaneous Debris Collection	Evidence substances not included in the previous discussion can often be observed during the examination of a person. Several individually packaged swabs or sections of cotton cloth should be available to collect such items as blood or semen found on the skin. Additionally, several separate containers should be included to collect debris taken from the clothing or body of the individual.

Known Blood Blood should be drawn (by medical personnel) into a sterile test tube for blood grouping purposes. A minimum of 5 milliliters is recommended—preferably without the inclusion of a chemical anticoagulant or preservative.

Known Saliva Saliva should be sampled from the person to assist in the determination of secretor status. An unstained control sample of the gathering medium is retained and packaged separately.

"Catch" Paper/Cloth A section of paper or cloth should be provided on which the person (victim and suspect) can stand while undressing. Additionally, a separate piece of paper or cloth can be used to cover the examining table to collect any evidence that is dislodged during the examination. Such paper or cloth is carefully folded, marked, and sealed in a suitable container.

Physical evidence plays an important role in the prosecution of sexual assault cases. It helps establish the credibility of the victim and may be used to negate or support an offender's contentions. How the physical evidence is used will depend on the various elements of the case as it is being prepared. For example, fingernail scrapings from the victim may be used to tie the offender to the victim. Scrapings from the suspect may be used to place the suspect in a particular location as well as link him to the victim. Blood can be grouped and examined for its DNA pattern.

Some important considerations play a role in the use of physical evidence in both investigation and prosecution:

Blood Modern blood-testing techniques make it possible for the laboratory to provide much more information than in the past. DNA (deoxyribonucleic acid) analysis determines the genetic code that is unique to that individual; only identical twins will have the same genetic codes (see Chapter 2). Using this technique it may be possible to "individualize" the sample. Care must be taken in the collection of blood samples; efforts should be made to ensure that there is no mixing of body fluids.

Semen Microscopic examination of semen may help determine if the sexual activity was recent. (Recent sexual activity will be indicated by live, mobile spermatozoa.) In most cases the crime laboratory deals with dead sperm because of the passage of time prior to examination. For this reason, if possible, a microscopic examination of a sample should be conducted as soon as possible. This is usually done in the hospital by a physician or trained medical microscopist. Semen can also provide evidence of blood type. More recent research indicates that it may be possible to identify an individual's genetic code by examining semen. Collecting semen samples from the victim will generally be handled at the hospital where rape "kits" should be available for use by a physician or nurse (see Figure 16.1). The investigator or crime scene technician should collect the clothing of the victim and the suspect whenever possible. Each item should be handled as a separate piece of evidence; under no circumstances should the garments be put in the same container. Care should also be taken with garments containing dried semen samples so that it does not flake off. They should not be folded as the semen sample may then crumble and be lost. In searching for semen samples it is common to use ultraviolet light because semen fluoresces. This is not a conclusive indication of semen, but it marks the area that should be handled carefully and protected.

Saliva   Saliva samples may be used to identify blood group and can also be used to identify genetic codes. Saliva is found less frequently than blood and semen; the properties of saliva make it look like water. Nevertheless, it may be possible to obtain a saliva sample from cigarettes, food, chewing gum, or bed sheets. It also may be present in bite marks on the victim. In collection, care should be taken not to touch the saliva directly as secretions on the fingers can contaminate it.

Hair   Hair can be taken from the head, chest, legs, or pubic area. Facial hair is less likely to be present unless the individual has a beard or mustache. An individual's DNA can be determined from a hair if the root is present.

Fibers   Fibers obtained from the suspect's clothing or from other material, such as rope or cord used to tie the victim, may be useful evidentiary material. (Guidelines for the collection of fibers appear in Appendix 1.) Here again, it is important to note that each collection should be handled separately and clearly identified as to location.

Markings   Tool or weapon markings may be used to link the weapon or tool to the scene or victim, particularly if it is recovered in the possession of the suspect. For example, a screwdriver or other tool used in a forced entry may leave distinctive marks on the door or window. When a knife or other instrument is used as a weapon, it may be possible for a victim to identify, especially if it has any unusual characteristics.

When collecting or identifying physical evidence at the scene, particular care should be taken to note clearly where each piece of evidence is located. Do not rely on memory: use sketches, photographs, and notes.

Records and Other Sources of Information

The use of records and information in sex crimes cases follows the general pattern described in earlier chapters (see Chapters 5 and 7). However, a number of additional sources of information should be pursued.

The initial inquiry should be addressed either to the records department or crime analysis unit. A sex offender may have a prior arrest record, although not necessarily for rape. If another crime accompanied the rape, such as burglary or robbery, it is possible that the perpetrator committed the sex offense as a "target of opportunity."

A computerized record system may be able to assist the investigator in identifying possible suspects based on physical description, prior arrests, or MO. The crime analysis unit may help by recognizing similar cases that can be compared to the present one. This effort should include queries to surrounding jurisdictions and, if the information obtained provides additional details, it is wise to follow up by querying other jurisdictions as well.

Unlike most other crimes, the sex offense may have a "specific" motive known only to the perpetrator. Do not assume that it was solely for sexual gratification. Rape is rarely associated with sexual gratification, and is more likely associated with a need for power.

The nature of the attack may also provide valuable clues. The type of weapon, geographical location, time of day, and the suspect's actions can all link him to other crimes or to past activities. In addition to law enforcement records, the investigator may want to explore other sources (see Chapter 5).

Profiling Offenders

In recent years emphasis has been placed on the development of rape offender profiles. Much of this research was pioneered by the Federal Bureau of Investigation's Behavioral Science Unit, part of the National Center for the Analysis of Violent Crime located in Quantico, Virginia. The methodology employed by the FBI in profiling violent offenders through the ViCAP program involves information collected from police departments, interviews with convicted offenders, and research results published by social scientists.

The FBI will assist local agencies on request. These requests usually should be made through the Profile Coordinator at the local FBI office. Police departments are asked to complete the ViCAP forms on offenders, which are then computerized at Quantico. (Appendix 3 contains the instrument used to collect profile information.) The rape offender profile is based on the theory that an individual displays unique characteristics in personality, crime scene behavior, and method of operation.

The investigator should be aware that many of the commonly held assumptions about rape and rapists are inaccurate. Many rapists are married; they are not necessarily oversexed, they are not necessarily women-haters. Most are employed—but some are not, and their intelligence levels vary significantly. On the other hand, there are likely to be clues in the crime itself that can assist the investigator and that are believed to be subject to profiling.

The majority of rape offenders are not psychotic, but virtually all of them have deeply rooted psychological problems. According to A. Nicholas Groth, a psychologist who specializes in the study of sexual assault:

> Some men who ordinarily would never commit a sexual assault commit rape under very extraordinary circumstances, such as in wartime, but the likelihood of such a person's being a repetitive offender is very low. There are other men, however, who find it very difficult to meet the ordinary or unusual demands of life, and the stresses that we all learn to tolerate are unendurable and overwhelming to these individuals. The extent to which they find

most life demands frustrating, coupled with their inability to tolerate frustration and their reliance on sex as the way of overcoming their distress, make the likelihood of their being a repetitive offender very high. Furthermore, they constitute an immediate and ongoing threat to the safety of the community.[7]

The investigator may find that a profile of the offender will assist in reducing or narrowing the range of potential suspects through identification of age, and social and demographic characteristics.

In a study of 170 men who were convicted of sexually assaulting adults and 178 who were convicted of sexually assaulting children, Groth identified the following patterns for various types of rape:[8]

1. *Gang Rape.* In 9 percent of the cases in the study the sexual offense involved more than one assailant. Most of these cases (90 percent) involved one victim; 77 percent involved offenders between the ages 17 and 27.

2. *Elderly Rape.* In 18 percent of the cases the suspect sexually assaulted a woman who was significantly older; in 12 percent women over the age of 50 were attacked. Offenders were most likely to be young, white, single males, ranging in age from 12 to 38; 43 percent were in their twenties. All of the offenders showed life adjustment difficulties beginning with adolescence.

3. *Child Rape.* The individual who rapes children is likely to come from a disadvantaged background. He is usually relatively young and is rarely beyond age 40. Rape of children appears to be more class-related, the act is frequently devoid of a sexual or emotional involvement, and the suspect attacks different victims.

In their pioneering work on sexual homicide, Robert K. Ressler, Ann W. Burgess, and John E. Douglas developed a model for the criminal profile generating process (see Figure 16.2).[9]

Profiling aids a reasoned, systematic process for the investigation of rape and reduces the possibility of investigative error. In sex-related homicides there is a good possibility that the offender will strike again or that he has committed other crimes. Although the techniques for investigating a sex-related homicide are similar to those in any homicide investigation, this type of crime has unique characteristics that should be considered. The motivation of the offender may or may not have been homicide, but in most cases the perpetrator set out to commit a sexual assault. An exception to this is a sex-related homicide during a burglary or robbery in which the offender rapes and kills merely because a victim is present.

Of particular importance is the length of time the perpetrator remains at the scene. The longer he is there, the higher the probability of leaving trace evidence and other information that may assist in developing background information. Moreover, because the offender is likely to commit more than one attack, it is possible to bring together information from other crimes to develop a composite database.

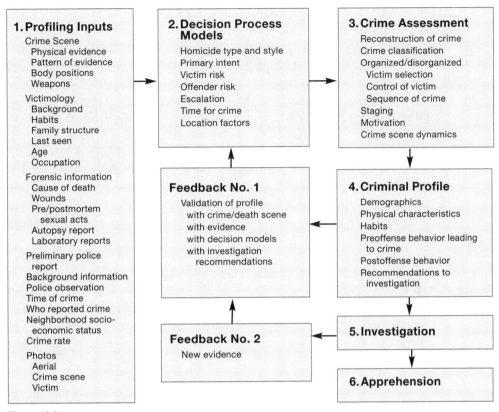

Figure 16.2
Criminal profile generating process. Reprinted with permission from *Sexual Homicide: Patterns and Motives,* by Robert K. Ressler, Ann W. Burgess, and John E. Douglas, p. 137. Copyright © 1988 Jossey-Bass Inc., Publishers. First published by Lexington Books. All rights reserved.

Hazelwood and Warren, in a study of 41 serial rapists, found that:[10]

76 percent had been sexually abused as children
71 percent had been married at least once
54 percent had generally stable employment
52 percent scored above average on intelligence tests
51 percent had served in the armed forces
36 percent collected pornography

The mobility of American society makes it possible for an offender to commit crimes in many different states. Thus, every attempt should be made to share information with other jurisdictions.

FOLLOW-UP ACTIVITIES

The investigation of sexual assault requires an objective, reasoned approach. A sympathetic understanding of the trauma of the victim should be combined with an unemotional attitude toward the suspect. The investigator should not judge or let personal emotions interfere with the investigation. His or her primary task is to identify the perpetrator and build a case for prosecution. However, the emotional factors involved in such investigations create a greater probability of making mistakes.

When a suspect has been identified, the investigator should carefully check out the alibi and any other items of information that might serve to support the suspect's statements.

The use of police sketches, Identi-Kit images, or computerized graphics can be of particular use if the victim or witnesses can provide detailed descriptive information. However, the investigator should recognize that eyewitness identification frequently is flawed. For this reason, identification through sketches, photographs, or even lineups should be considered with caution. All too often there is a tendency to couple an eyewitness identification with a prior record as a basis for prosecution. Such evidence, though valuable, should be combined with a thorough investigation that endeavors to tie the suspect to the crime scene, to link him or her to the victim, and to counter any defense contentions of mistaken identity.

In many cases the offender will say that the victim actually induced the crime. Such claims may be difficult to prove in court; it is the investigator's responsibility, however, to explore all contentions, keeping in mind that the victim's background or reputation does not have any bearing on whether she was assaulted. Although interviews are an important part of this phase of the investigation, there are other ways in which an individual's statements can be verified or disproved. Contradictory statements, errors of fact, and descriptive comments should be explored during interrogation. For this reason it is important to keep good notes and to record statements if possible.

As the case progresses and more information becomes available, the investigator should maintain a set of cross-referenced files for ease of access and comparison. Further, because there may be information available from other cases or from prior records, information management is particularly important.

In cases in which a suspect has a prior record, it is frequently useful to review court records or case and investigative reports for information. Information on *modus operandi*, accomplices, weapons, locations, and statements may all prove important.

It is important that photographic evidence be reviewed carefully. The investigator should scrupulously review crime scene sketches, laboratory reports, and witness statements. The review of evidence is particularly important in preparing the case for prosecution.

REFERENCES

1   U.S. Department of Justice, Federal Bureau of Investigation, *2002 National Crime Victdimization Survey* (Washington, DC: U.S. Government Printing Office, 2003).

2   Ibid.

3   Ronald M. Holmes, "Stalking in America: Types and Methods of Criminal Stalkers." *Journal of Contemporary Criminal Justice,* December, 1993.

4   Vernon Geberth, "Stalkers." *Law and Order,* October, 1992.

5   Ronald M. Holmes, "Stalking in America: Types and Methods of Criminal Stalkers." *Journal of Contemporary Criminal Justice,* December, 1993.

6   R. Hazelwood and Ann Wolkert Burgess, eds., *Practical Aspects of Rape Investigation: A Multidisciplinary Approach*, 2nd ed. (Boca Raton, FL: CRC Press, 1995).

7   A. Nicholas Groth, with Jean Birnbaum, *Men Who Rape: The Psychology of the Offender* (New York: Plenum Press, 1979), 7.

8   Ibid., 110-192.

9   Robert K. Ressler, Ann W. Burgess, and John E. Douglas, *Sexual Homicide: Patterns and Motives* (Lexington, MA: Lexington Books, 1988), 137.

10   Robert R. Hazelwood and Janet Warren, "The Serial Rapist: His Characteristics and Victims," *FBI Law Enforcement Bulletin* 58:1 (January, 1989), 10-17.

SUPPLEMENTAL READINGS

Douglas, John, and Mark Olshaker. *The Anatomy of Motive*. New York: Scribner, 1999.

Forcible Rape: A Manual for Sex Crime Investigators, G.P.O. Stock No. 027-000-00621-3. [Also available in Microfiche (free) from: WCJRS Microfiche Program, Box 6000, Rockville, MD 20850.]

Gregory, Jeanne, and Sue Lees. *Policing Sexual Assault*. New York: Routledge, 1999.

Hazelwood, Robert R., and Ann Wolbert Burgess. *Practical Aspects of Rape Investigation: A Multidisciplinary Approach*. 2nd ed. Boca Raton, FL: CRC Press, 1995.

Holmes, Ronald W. *Profiling Violent Crimes: An Investigative Tool*. Newberry Park, CA: State Publications, 1989.

Parrot, Andrea, and Laurie Bechhoffer. *Acquaintance Rape: The Hidden Crime.* New York: John Wiley & Sons, 1991.

CHAPTER 17

Burglary

INTRODUCTION

Burglary is a difficult crime to investigate. Success depends in large measure on the actions of the initial officer on the scene, the efforts of crime scene technicians and the crime lab and fingerprint analysts, and the dogged determination of the investigator in using interviewing skills, crime pattern analysis, and available records to identify a suspect. Burglary is a crime that affects all strata of society. Losses range from relatively small amounts to millions of dollars; burglary suspects can have widely varying degrees of skill and expertise. In 2001, losses due to burglary were estimated to be $3.3 billion.[1] All burglaries violate someone's physical space, and for this reason even the most simple burglaries must be taken seriously, particularly those that occur in private residences.

All too frequently, and particularly in the inner city, burglaries are given short shrift by the police, who may be deluged with large numbers of violent crimes against the person. Although burglary is viewed as a property crime in Uniform Crime Reports, it has a direct impact on the victims who frequently feel violated by the offense. In many cases, although the burglary may not appear serious in terms of its dollar value, it may deprive a family of its most valued possessions.

Burglary affects a large segment of society. It is estimated that more than 70 percent of all households will be burglarized at least once over a 20-year period, and almost one-half of all urban residences will be victimized two or more times. According to the Bureau of Justice Statistics, the probability of being a household burglary victim is higher in the central city, in homes headed by younger people, in residences where six or more people live, and in homes in which the head of the household is black. According to the FBI Uniform Crime Reports, there were about 2.1 million burglaries in 2001, a 14.3 percent decline from 1997. However, it is estimated that almost one-half of all burglaries are not reported to the police.

Two of every three burglaries in 2001 were residential in nature. A little more than 63 percent of all burglaries involved forcible entry, 30.2 percent were unlawful entries (without force), and 6.5 percent were forcible entry attempts. Burglary occurs more often in the summer months, with the majority of residential burglaries occuring in the day and most nonresidential burglaries taking place at night.[2]

The National Crime Victimization Survey has indicated that many rapes, robberies, and aggravated and simple assaults in the home occurred during an illegal entry. Burglary is also a seasonal crime, occurring more frequently in the summer months.[3]

Although difficult to investigate, burglary usually offers a relatively large number of clues. The expanding capabilities of single-digit fingerprint systems, such as AFIS, and breakthroughs in DNA analysis offer significant tools in burglary investigations. Research indicates that the preliminary analysis of a burglary case can provide "solvability factors" that make it possible to focus on those cases with the highest probability of being solved.[4] Burglary investigation can bring a high degree of satisfaction to the person who is truly interested in the elements of solving a mystery.

Definitions

The Model Penal Code of the American Law Institute defines burglary as follows:

> A person is guilty of burglary if he enters a building or occupied structure, or separately secured or occupied portion thereof, with purpose to commit a crime therein, unless the premises are at the time open to the public or the actor is licensed or privileged to enter. It is an affirmative defense to prosecution for burglary that the building or structure was abandoned.[5]

The Uniform Crime Reporting Program defines burglary as the unlawful entry of a structure to commit a felony or theft. The use of force is not required to classify an offense as burglary.[6]

Although burglary is generally considered a property crime, it is important for the investigator to recognize that a theft need not be committed to establish a burglary charge.

PEOPLE

Victims

Burglaries take many forms and affect victims in different ways. The homeowner who loses a personal heirloom or other personal property —which may have little monetary value—may be more devastated than the business person who loses millions of dollars worth of insured goods.

Understanding the type of burglary, the characteristics of the offense, and the demographic characteristics of the victim can provide insight into the suspect and his or her background. For example, burglaries of middle-class or poor residences are more likely to be committed by juveniles, and the probability increases in cases in which entry is through a broken window, and again when the search appears to have been haphazard and the property taken is varied rather than specific. Burglaries in hotels are more likely to be committed by an older, more experienced professional. In a residential burglary, the method of entry and exit, as well as the type of search, will provide information about the suspect. (More experienced burglars will frequently unlock all the doors and even windows in a residence in order to exit quickly in case the owner returns.) The more professional burglar searches methodically (e.g., emptying drawers on the bed one at a time, then pulling the contents off after sifting through each one; see Figure 17.1); uses a specific type of tool for entry; takes only valuable property; and concentrates on wealthier victims. As one burglar put it, "You'll do time for a big job as well as a small job, so why increase the risks with a lot of small scores?"

With the exception of the small store, most commercial or business burglaries require a greater degree of expertise and frequently more planning than a residential burglary. Nevertheless, many burglars operate with very little planning or "casing" of the target and the victim. In burglaries involving large amounts of merchandise or very valuable property there is likely to be an inside informant working with the burglar. This is especially true in businesses that have a high employee turnover; it is important to ask the victim about employment records.

In addition to providing information about property stolen, the victim should be asked to review the past few weeks and recall any unusual events or the presence of individuals who seemed out of the ordinary. Other questions that might produce information of interest include:

- Is there anything unique about the timing of the burglary (e.g., valuables were there only on certain days, such as payroll money)?

- Have there been prior attempts or successful burglaries?

- Who knew about the property and its location?

- Is the property unique, including items such as art objects?

- Have there been similar burglaries?

- Did any publicity appear in local newspapers (e.g., notification of a wedding indicating that people won't be at home)?

The Public

Although conventional wisdom holds that there are few witnesses to burglaries, in reality there are likely to be many more than one might suspect. In most cases the police make a cursory or half-hearted attempt to locate witnesses. A careful canvass of the immediate area should be made as soon as possible with a view to identifying or developing descriptions of potential suspects. If some time has passed since the burglary occurred, it may be worthwhile to interview persons who might have been on the scene at or near the time of the burglary. For example, in residential burglaries, besides neighbors, the canvass might also include the mail carrier, delivery persons, utility meter readers, and telephone company workers, among others. Residents should be asked if they observed any other individuals or suspicious vehicles in the vicinity.

Figure 17.1
Two crime scenes, typical of residential burglaries. *(Courtesy, Chicago Police Department.)*

One should also keep in mind that persons who are "out of place," such as juveniles during school hours, or "strange" vehicles and unusual activity at the burglary site may not be thought important by witnesses at first. Careful questioning can uncover this information.

In addition to witnesses at the scene, there will also be witnesses at the point where the property is disposed. Although these witnesses are not likely to be cooperative, pointing out that linking the stolen goods to the burglary could result in a charge of receiving stolen property and will frequently elicit their cooperation. Of course, without adequate property identification this avenue is less hopeful.

Informants or petty criminals on the fringe of illegal activity in a neighborhood also can be a source of information. Most good burglary detectives have a good informant network, and are tied in with other sources of information, such as beat patrol officers, bartenders, truant officers, playground attendants, and other individuals who pick up information on illegal activities. Cultivating such sources is an important component of the investigator's work.

The Burglary Suspect

Professional burglaries represent different challenges. When large amounts of merchandise or warehouse goods are taken, identification of the truck or other vehicle used is important. Here again, witnesses may have seen the truck at or near the scene. The vehicle may even have received a traffic citation. Witnesses should be asked about vehicles that were out of place, such as a van where tractor trailers usually park, or whether there was an inordinate number of people on the truck. Usually, a truck only has a driver and loader on it.

A sympathetic and unhurried approach to questioning the victim is important, not only because it helps alleviate much of the stress associated with victimization, but also because details provided about what has been stolen, the *modus operandi* of the burglar, or other aspects of the case may become critical as the investigation proceeds. Stolen items overlooked in the initial report may provide the link that helps solve the case; items with serial numbers or individual marks, custom-made jewelry, or original artwork, documents such as checkbooks or stocks, and even keys or personal tools taken by the burglar may be recovered later. In most cases the burglar will dispose of stolen items through a fence or even directly on the street, but some items may be kept for personal use.

In addition to stealing property, the offender may do things at the scene of the crime that can help identify or link him or her to the scene of the crime at a later date. One burglar thought it clever to leave disparaging notes on the walls of his victims' homes. When he was eventually apprehended he was surprised to learn that handwriting analysis helped add several years to his sentence because the prosecution was able to charge him with multiple crimes. Other burglars may take food from the refrigerator, use the victim's facilities (perhaps to make phone calls), or display other forms of aberrational behavior that help establish a *modus operandi*.

Harry O'Reilly, a former New York City burglary detective who is something of a legend for his ability to solve cases, identified some of the more common techniques used by burglars to gain entry:

Figure 17.2
Burglar's tools: on the left, a pry bar or jimmy; on the right, a lock and chain cutter. *(Courtesy, Chicago Police Department.)*

Prying: The use of a jimmy, screwdriver, tire iron, pry bar, or knife to force a door, window, or lock. The perpetrator may leave tool impressions on the point of entry (see Figure 17.2).

Picking: Using a knife or professional locksmith's picks to open the cylinder of a lock.

Pulling: Using an auto body repair tool called a dent puller or "slap hammer" to pull the cylinder out.

Smash and crash: Simply breaking a window to gain entry, and in the case of a store, reaching in and grabbing articles on display.

Cutting glass: Using a glass cutter to make a hole in order to reach in and open a lock or unfasten the latch. A small suction cup may be used, such as a toy dart, to keep the glass from falling inside and making noise. After the cut is made around the suction cup, the burglar simply pulls the glass out.

Slipping lock or "loiding": Originally celluloid strips were used, hence the term *loiding,* but they are frequently replaced now by credit cards and pocket knives (the knife may be filed down to make it narrower) or other thin objects, such as nail files, that are less identifiable as a burglar's tools. The card is slipped between the lock and the door jamb where there is no "dead bolt" or other latch.

Brute force: Kicking, breaking, or forcing a door with the body or an instrument. Where a door has been kicked in, the perpetrator may leave shoe or sneaker impressions.

Removing door panel: Kicking in or breaking the door panel, or unscrewing the panel on an aluminum door.

Entry through windows: Entry through windows is usually accomplished by breaking a hole through a pane and removing the broken glass so that the latch can be reached. In order to minimize the noise from falling glass, the burglar may press a rag against the window; sometimes adhesive tape may be used. In some cases, the burglar may remove the entire window pane by removing the putty holding the glass in place. Entry may also be gained by forcing in a tool to push back a window latch. In such cases, tool marks should be looked for and samples of wood and paint should be taken for comparison if a tool is later found. A prybar, screwdriver, or other tool is also sometimes used in forcing a window.

Entry through doors: A burglar usually opens a door by using a prybar and jamb around the lock until either the bolt can be pushed back or the bolt is actually freed from the striker plate. This may be done by mere pressure from the body or by inserting a jack horizontally across the door frame. The lock might also be made accessible through a hole that is drilled, sawed, or broken in a door panel. Far too many doors are fitted with glass that is simply broken so that the lock may be reached. Entry can also be gained by cutting the hinge pins off by means of a bolt cutter. More commonly, however, the pins are simply knocked out with hammer and chisel or screwdriver.

Entry through basement windows and skylights: These windows are forced in the same manner as ordinary windows, but the investigator should pay special attention to the possibility that the burglar's clothes may have become torn and cloth fragments or fibers may have been left behind.

Entry through walls: Walls are either broken by tools or by explosives. A brick wall is easily broken by a hammer and chisel or a sledge hammer. In blasting, a hole is usually chiseled between two bricks and the charge is inserted. Small hydraulic jacks may be used to force holes into a wall.

Entry through floors: This method of entry is often preferred in the case of warehouses or other buildings that have a crawl space underneath. The burglar usually drills or saws a hole in the floorboards large enough to crawl through. Entry through walls and floors is also made when the criminal suspects or knows that the premises are protected by burglary alarms on doors and windows.

Safe cracking: A very specialized form of burglary that may involve burning, blasting, punching (see Figure 17.3), chopping (through the bottom) ripping, cutting, or peeling a safe.

"Second-story" job: Gaining entry to warehouses, factories, and other businesses through upper floor windows or roof.[7]

This is only a partial list of burglary techniques, but it is important to recognize that it contributes in large measure to efforts to determine *modus operandi*. In addition to technique, a burglary typology can serve as a frame of reference for the investigator. Figure 17.4 is a matrix that may be useful in this effort if completed at the start of the investigation and compared with similar forms on file for previous burglary cases. If some common thread, such as an MO, is recognized, clues from the crimes can be pooled in an attempt to develop a suspect.

In burglaries of businesses, particularly where entry may have been gained through an adjoining wall or over a roof, it is likely that the perpetrator cased the location on a prior occasion. Employees should be asked about persons who either acted strangely, or asked questions about the building, or lingered for a long time.

Figure 17.3
Broken safe, opened by punching through its dial. *(Courtesy, Chicago Police Department.)*

	RESIDENCE Apartment/house	BUSINESS Office/Factory	OTHER Tractor trailer/ warehouse etc./ recreation vehicle, boat, etc./hotel, etc.
1. Occupied Not occupied			

2. Day (Dawn to dusk)
   Evening
   (Dusk to midnight)			

3. Night (Midnight to dawn)			
4. Actual time			

5. Entry through:
   Door
   Window
   Roof
   Wall			

6. Means
   (See list of techniques
   in text.)			

7. Victim type
   Poor
   Middle-class
   Wealthy
   Shop owner
   Business/corporation			

8. Search method
   Haphazard
   Specific area
   Methodical overall			

9. Characteristics in
   addition to theft:
   Property damage
   Murder/assault/rape
   Eat food
   Graffiti
   Other MO suspects			

10. Number of offenders
   Single
   Two
   More than two			

Figure 17.4
Burglary typology and method matrix.

In questioning burglary witnesses it is difficult to develop good physical descriptions unless the burglar had a distinguishing facial feature, such as a mustache. Because most witnesses will probably not be able to identify the suspects, this effort may serve mainly to develop general descriptions or other items of information. In such cases, the smallest details put together over several burglaries may help to develop a composite that leads to identification of the suspect.

CONDUCTING THE INVESTIGATION

Repetition is a predominant characteristic of burglary. Burglaries are generally committed over and over again until eventually the suspect is caught. Unfortunately, in most cases, very little information from one burglary to another is exchanged by investigators, which makes it difficult to clear cases. One of the best sources of information on prior cases is the patrol force. Officers collect a great deal of information, but even over a relatively small geographical area there may be five or more officers working during a seven-day period. When one considers the number of officers in a city or county, it becomes clear that much information is lost for lack of collation or analysis. Few burglary reports are designed to collect the unique elements of information that make it possible for the investigator to link prior cases. Fortunately, there has been significant progress over the past decade in this area. A number of forms now collect information that can help solve the crime rather than simply report it. However, the value of a report is only as good as the information collected. Patrol officers should be trained and supervised properly, and proper credit should be given to them when they provide information that helps solve a case.

Because the vast majority of burglaries are residential, and because research suggests that many of these are committed by juveniles, a good deal of information may be found on the street. In addition to the patrol force, juvenile courts, youth squads, and other youth service agencies may be of assistance.

Investigation of large professional burglaries, which may involve multiple jurisdictions, requires communication with other agencies. Major case squads will frequently be established and information on their activities and sources of contact should be available. In some jurisdictions, such units meet periodically to discuss ongoing or unusual cases.

Professional associations and business groups, particularly those affiliated with the insurance industry, also can be valuable to the burglary investigator. In addition to providing information on specific groups, such associations can provide the investigator with other helpful information—such as burglary techniques being used, types of property most frequently attacked, and kinds of merchandise in greatest demand.

Research on burglary and burglars provides some information that will help the burglary investigator better understand the dynamics and career patterns of the crime. Generally, burglary offenders begin their careers at a young age, acting with other juveniles in break-ins or burglaries. In 2001, 31 percent of burglary arrests were of juveniles, with 11.7 percent under the age of 15.[8] Some offenders turn to more violent forms of crime, but career burglary patterns usually emerge, and some individuals develop specialties in certain types of acts, such as safe or art burglaries.[9]

Wright and Decker interviewed 105 burglars, finding that more than 50 percent had committed 50 or more burglaries during their criminal careers.[10] An analysis of parole violators by the Bureau of Justice Statistics reveals that 73 percent of burglars are rearrested, 60 percent are convicted again, and 56 percent are reincarcerated. About 70 percent of the time whites are arrested for burglary offenses, although these figures differ significantly in urban areas. About 74 percent of burglary arrestees under the age of 18 were white; about 11 percent were female.[11] Table 17.1 illustrates how a burglary career develops over time.

Table 17.1
The Burglar's Career Path

Burglar	Juvenile offender	Late teens / early 20s	Mid-20s / early 30s	Career burglar
Activity Range	Usually close to home.	Wider pattern; use of vehicle for trans- portation.	Operates over a broad area; crosses jurisdictions.	May operate anywhere.
Burglary	Not planned well.	Better planned, but usually target of opportunity.	Selects targets; some planning.	Well-planned and researched; or uses a set MO.
Type	Residential.	Residential, or easy business target.	Business, some residential.	Corporations, larger businesses; specific wealthy targets.
Property Stolen	Anything in the open or easily taken.	Money, jewels.	Specific types of property or valuables, e.g., computers.	Very specific valuable targets.

Juvenile burglars commonly operate with an accomplice, and are even more likely to work in groups of three or more. More sophisticated burglars may operate in pairs, but research on them is inconclusive. The professional burglar will frequently operate with a lookout, and may use walkie-talkies to communicate.

Most burglaries are not well planned. The choice of target is likely to be based on whether the perpetrator views it as an easy mark. An easy mark would be a place such as an unlighted residence, or one with high hedges, old windows, or easily opened doors. A small percentage of thrill-seeking perpetrators, commonly called "cat burglars," enter homes when residents are present, usually at night, and try to accomplish the crime without arousing the occupants.

In recent years there has been an increase in home invasions, in which a residence is entered while an individual or a family is present. These are usually carried out by groups or gangs, who may often commit crimes such as robbery, assault, rape, or murder. The viciousness of these crimes often defies imagination, and makes home invasions a high investigative priority. For the most part, though, burglars are looking for quick cash or goods they can fence. Tracking stolen property offers another avenue of investigation.

Many burglars are drug addicts who can frequently be identified by the types of property they take. They usually fall into the second or third category of burglars listed in Table 17.1, but exhibit less sophistication in their activities. These burglars commonly steal television sets and other easily disposable items.

Many burglars turn to robbery (the taking of property from a person by force) as they get older. Relatively few become professional burglars, but those who do develop a high level of expertise in planning and carrying out their crimes.

Physical Evidence

For purposes of identifying perpetrators and making a case that will hold up in court, a wealth of physical evidence is usually available. Unfortunately, for a variety of reasons, crime scene searches are conducted in only a few cases, usually only where there has been a large loss, or where another serious crime such as assault, rape, or homicide is involved.

Research indicates that most crime scenes contain much more physical evidence than is discovered. Fingerprints are the most common form of evidence sought in a crime scene search, and other items of trace evidence and materials are often overlooked. Trace evidence can establish a link between the perpetrator and the crime scene. Blood, saliva, footprints, hair, and fibers may be present. The suspect may also leave behind items such as cigarettes, matchbooks, tools, clothing, or handwriting.

Successful crime scene processing begins with the initial officer on the scene. Even though a decision may be made not to call in an evidence technician, a crime scene search can and should be conducted. (See Chapter 3 for a method of conducting a crime scene search.)

Bear in mind that what may seem trivial at first may later prove to be a key piece of evidence. In one case, a matchbook containing no more than a woman's name in it enabled an investigator to clear up a string of burglaries. The matchbook had come from a local bar. The investigator located the woman, who said she had written her name on it for a guy she met there. This information, coupled with a sole print on a kitchen floor from an athletic shoe, tied the suspect to the scene. He also had a habit of eating food at the residences, which linked him to other crimes. The chipped screwdriver with which he forced doors provided further evidence when investigators went back to the scenes. Confronted with the evidence, the suspect admitted to more than 100 residential burglaries. The case was solved by an investigator who followed up a lead that some might have disregarded.

The search for physical evidence at a burglary scene will frequently require the assistance of the victim, who can be very helpful in identifying what has been moved or what does not belong. Often overlooked are tool marks, personal items such as discarded cigarettes and matchbooks, and footprints outside the house (e.g., below windows).

One of the more promising advances in scientific criminal investigation has been the Automated Fingerprint Identification System (AFIS), which makes it possible to search criminal records for a single latent print.[12] This technological breakthrough is of particular value to burglary investigations, in which latent prints generally represent the most common form of physical evidence available. The utilization of evidence technicians at burglary crime scenes increases the probability of collecting latent prints.

AFIS technology is based on the ability to electronically scan and identify fingerprint characteristics and store them in digital form in a computer. Using ridge endings and bifurcations it is possible to create a digitized representation of the print, which can be stored in the computer (see Chapter 2).

Although frequently overlooked, latent fingerprints represent a potential source of information that should not be ignored. Unlike for most other crimes, the suspect is usually in the house for some period of time and, because he or she is looking for things, objects are touched. In addition to the more common locations processed by crime scene technicians, other areas should be examined:

- beer and soda cans in the garbage

- items in the refrigerator that may have been touched, moved, or bitten— leaving a print or a bite mark

- toilet seat and the nearby wall

- the bottoms of dresser drawers that may have been removed for searching

- window locks that may have been opened from the inside as a means of escape in the event that the owner returned

- documents that may have been handled

On a rolled inked print, usually obtained from a prior arrest, it is possible to find 90 or more points on each finger, making the print distinguishable from all other single-digit prints. When a latent (partial) print is recovered at the crime scene, it can be run through the system for a match. Even a poorly developed partial print may provide enough information to conduct a successful search. It takes just minutes to accomplish a 10-print search in a file of about 5,000 records, although it may take a half-hour or longer to search for a match to a partial, single print. The ability of the investigator to provide the names or record numbers of potential suspects can help reduce the search time.

Records and Other Sources of Information

The uniqueness of burglary investigation rests in large measure on the use of records and information about the stolen property. In even the smallest burglary there is likely to be something taken that has a number or mark that individualizes it for identification purposes. In the age of computers and other forms of technology, it is much easier to track items, to communicate and cooperate with other agencies, and to work closely with companies and businesses that may be able to assist. This chapter focuses on sources and information unique to the crime of burglary. Obviously, police records will contain information on possible suspects, reports leading to the recognition of crime patterns and MO, and property data. The key here is in knowing how to use department records to search for information.

External information from manufacturers, businesses, and trade associations may also provide valuable assistance. For example, most manufacturers include identification numbers and other information on merchandise, such as where it was sold and additional details that may facilitate identification. Sometimes the investigator will have a load of stolen merchandise but will not have a victim. Tracing its sales point may indicate where, and possibly to whom, it was sold.

Some of the sources with which the investigator should be familiar include:

1. The National Crime Information Center (NCIC), a national database that is particularly useful in tracing weapons and items with serial numbers.

2. The National Auto Theft Bureau (NATB), which provides information not only on stolen vehicles, but also on property taken from trucks.

3. Credit card companies, which can provide information on the use of stolen credit cards, thus providing clues to a suspect's movements, sometimes helping to produce eyewitness descriptions by sales clerks (when the burglar has used the card).

4. Chambers of commerce, which may assist in the investigation of certain types of crimes against businesses.

Today, using scanners and bar codes, it is also possible to more clearly identify merchandise. It is now possible for police departments to scan reports into the computer, making it much easier to retrieve information about specific items of property. Further, more sophisticated databases allow investigators to search for information using *strings* (groups of characters entered for computer searches), thereby making it easy to look for records of stolen property that cannot be identified by numbers. For example, assume a suspected burglar or fence is caught with an IBM computer, a Hewlett Packard printer, and a microwave oven. Although there is a high probability that these are the proceeds of an office burglary, the lack of identification numbers (which may have been removed or were not recorded by the owner) would necessitate sifting through hundreds, if not thousands, of burglary reports. Using a database program it would be possible to query the computer using a string such as: "Search (all reports for past year) for IBM and/or Hewlett Packard printer and/or microwave." In this configuration, the computer can find reports that fit these criteria. Such searches can be conducted relatively quickly and are a powerful resource for burglary investigation. The information on items can be combined with geographical information, such as zip codes (e.g., IBM and 60607), which would provide all reports with IBM and the 60607 designator in them. These are relatively simple examples, yet they serve to illustrate just how powerful computers are in criminal investigation. (See Chapter 20 for more on computer applications for criminal investigation.)

FOLLOW-UP ACTIVITIES

The investigation of burglary involves several stages:

1. Investigating the crime scene and collecting and preserving any available physical evidence.

2. Interviewing potential witnesses.

3. Using informants.

4. Examining records.

5. Tracing property.

6. Identifying suspects.

The successful conclusion of a case will frequently depend on the investigator's ability to handle a large amount of seemingly unrelated pieces of information in an analytical way.

Most burglars are known to the police. Most have prior arrests, and a large percentage are drug users. Most are young males. Generally, burglars must commit a relatively large number of crimes in order to meet their needs. They usually operate within a specific geographic area, but there are some signs that this is changing. Many burglars steal cars to carry out the crime. Distinguishing marks—such as method of entry, type of property taken, or method of search—are often left behind. All of these factors lend themselves to crime analysis. Computers, if used properly, are an important investigative tool. Even in large cities, where burglaries are relatively common, the investigator or crime analyst can frequently "sort out" burglaries committed by one or more individuals.

The computer also can be used in tracing property. The initial and follow-up reports must be as specific as possible in the identification of property. Brand names, specific marks, and serial numbers are important. Burglary investigations can generate a vast amount of information. Information overload can be avoided if one handles the information effectively.

As computers become more available to investigators, there must be an effort to screen and sort information and cases in the most efficient way possible. Some investigators use only 3×5 cards; even more rely on memory. In today's environment, this is generally ineffective.

Under ideal conditions, some form of case screening will help. With a case-screening approach, individual investigators are assigned cases with common characteristics; some will work on residential, others on business cases—some on juvenile cases, others on professional jobs.

Another effective but seldom used approach is the daily or weekly case review in which investigators meet to describe their cases and to identify common characteristics of burglaries and burglary suspects.

In one major city, a string of burglaries was solved when an investigator attended a regional training seminar where he spoke to a colleague about a peculiar cat burglar who always drank a glass of milk at the scene and then washed the glass. The colleague named the suspect immediately. The burglar had moved from one jurisdiction to another after he was released from prison. Unfortunately, most cases are not solved that easily. Both luck and the prepared mind factor into it, and investigators help make their own breaks.

Having mastered the information concerning burglary types and career patterns, the investigator has taken a long stride toward developing expertise. Putting the aforementioned information together with an investigative plan is the initial step.

A short description prepared for the case report should emphasize the differences in burglaries. It should begin with the type of burglary and proceed to include the finer details. An example of this might be:

> Residential burglary of middle-income, single-family house. Entry through broken rear window between 9:00 A.M. and 3:00 P.M.
> Property taken:
>
> 1. One 13" portable television (Zenith)
>
> 2. Approximately $20 in currency
>
> 3. Unknown amount in coins from jar in bedroom
>
> Search haphazard, left large television and other electronic goods. Suspect wrote "Thanks" on bedroom mirror with lipstick.
>
> The follow-up investigation reveals:
>
> Blood found on broken glass. No crime scene search conducted, but glass marked and maintained as evidence. Investigator lifted single fingerprint from mirror in bedroom. Sent to fingerprint section.
>
> Interviews with neighbors. A neighbor, Mary Smith (address) states that a male, white, 14-16 years old, knocked on her door at approximately 1300 hours and asked if "Joey" lived there. Suspect description: M/W/14-16 years/5' 4"/110 lbs./wearing black leather jacket.

The investigator can now ask the juvenile courts for a records check. Although it is unlikely that the television set will turn up as fenced property, the investigator can add this to his or her list of items when checking pawn shops, informants, or other outlets for stolen goods.

There are enough individual items in the report to assist in the continuing investigation. By keeping the case "alive," it is possible that a break will come. "Filing" it will mean less likelihood that it will be remembered. If a suspect is turned in—either through records, informants, or other information—there is physical evidence that may be brought into play. Although this is a relatively simple case, it is not an uncommon one.

For a more sophisticated burglary, a similar, although more detailed, investigative plan may be developed. The plan need not be written out for each case, but it should be considered, used as a guide, and referred to especially when a case stalls. Time management is a critical factor in the investigation because most investigators may be working on dozens of cases at one time. Keeping a written summary is important.

"Solvability factors" have been adopted by a number of police departments as a means of screening cases to identify those with the highest probability of solution. Originally pioneered in the Rochester Police Department in the 1970s, this approach employs a research-based "weighted" checklist that helps the supervisor select cases for assignment. The approach represented a major breakthrough in burglary investigation which, when combined with advances in computer technology, should move the field even further forward.

A burglary checklist developed by Harry O'Reilly and Mark Ronaldes, a criminal investigator with the Granby (Connecticut) Police Department, is in use in many departments (see Figure 17.5). The form is useful for both patrol officer and investigator.

1. Determine location of building—street and house number, street name, nearest proximity of homes, escape routes, etc. (residential—industrial—commercial).

2. Determine description of building—size, color, type, height, shrubbery, multi-family, one-story/two-story, wood frame, brick, etc.

3. Determine date and time (hour) of entry.

4. Determine date and time location was last known to be secure—estimate time of break.

5. Determine who reported burglary and how it was discovered.

6. Determine where the occupants were at the time of burglary—when did they leave?, were all doors and windows secure?, were keys available?

7. Determine upon arriving at scene the state and condition of the location—lights on, curtains drawn, windows open, doors ajar, furniture moved, etc.

8. Determine if location had recent visitors—strangers, servicemen, peddlers, tradesmen, lights/telephone/gas, etc.

9. Check other burglars in same section for similar *modus operandi.*

10. Determine point and manner of entering—measure distances and heights; diagram crime scene.

11. Determine manner (means) of entry—pass key, jimmy, saw, drill, pry bar, hammer, axe, wrench, etc. Compare tools with marks found on building, doors, windows, etc.

12. Photograph crime scene—exterior/interior, tool marks, evidentiary objects, place of entry/exit, injuries if any, etc.

13. Determine stolen property—compile list of stolen property, detailed description and marks of means of identification, approximate values, serial numbers, etc.

14. Determine if identifiable laboratory clues exist—fingerpints, footprints, tire marks, blood, fibers, etc. Photograph/diagram evidence prior to removing or lifting.

15. Determine names of any persons showing interest in stolen items. Were such persons familiar with location of stolen items?

16. Determine if burglar did anything other than steal—help self to food, ransack house, confine them to one specific area, etc.

17. For boarding house or apartment burglars, check all occupants and past occupants within reasonable time back, particularly any who took keys or had access to dwelling.

18. Conduct canvass to detemine possible suspect information.

19. Contact pawnshops and secondhand dealers for stolen property. In addition, notify surrounding departments of property stolen and *modus operandi* of criminal.

Figure 17.5
Burglary checklist. *(From* Practical Burglary Investigation, *by Harry T. O'Reilly. Courtesy, Office of Security Programs, University of Illinois at Chicago, 1990.)*

REFERENCES

1   U.S. Department of Justice, Federal Bureau of Investigation, *Uniform Crime Reports 1975-2001* (Washington, DC: U.S. Government Printing Office, 1998).

2   Ibid.

3   U.S. Department of Justice, Bureau of Justice Statistics, *Report to the Nation on Crime and Justice,* 2nd ed. (Washington, DC: U.S. Government Printing Office, 1988).

4   John Eck, *Managing Case Assignments: Burglary Investigation Decision Model Replication* (Washington, DC: Police Executive Research Forum, 1979).

5   American Law Institute a Model Penal Code. As adopted at the 1962 Annual Meeting of the American Law Institute at Washington, DC, 24 May 1962, 142.

6   U.S. Department of Justice, *loc cit.*

7   Harry O'Reilly, *Practical Burglary Investigation* (Chicago: Office of Security Programs, University of Illinois at Chicago, 1991).

8   U.S. Department of Justice, *loc cit.*

9   Barry Fisher, *Techniques of Crime Scene Investigation*, 6th ed. (Boca Raton, FL: CRC Press, 2000).

10   Richard T. Wright and Scott H. Decker, *Burglars on the Job: Streetlife and Residential Break-ins* (Boston: Northeastern University Press, 1994).

11   *Report to the Nation on Crime and Justice,* 2nd ed. (Washington, DC: Bureau of Justice Statistics, U.S. Department of Justice, 1988). See also, *Criminal Victimization in the United States: National Crime Victimization Survey, 1998.*

12   U.S. Department of Justice, Bureau of Justice Statistics, "Automated Fingerprint Identification Systems: Technology of Policy Issues," pamphlet (Washington, DC: U.S. Government Printing Office).

SUPPLEMENTAL READINGS

Cromwell, Paul F., James N. Olson, and D'Aunn Wester Avary. *Breaking and Entering: An Ethnographic Analysis of Burglary.* Newbury Park, CA: Sage, 1991.

Shover, Neal. *Great Pretenders: Pursuits and Careers of Persistent Thieves.* Boulder, CO: Westview Press, 1996.

Wright, Richard T., and Scott H. Decker. *Burglars on the Job: Streetlife and Residential Break-ins.* Boston: Northeastern University Press, 1994.

CHAPTER 18

Arson

IIIIIIIIIIIIIIIIIIIIIIIIIIIIIIIIIIIIIIIIIIIIIIIIIIIIIIII

INTRODUCTION

In the 1970s and early 1980s, arson was the fastest growing crime in the United States. Although it has slowed down some, it remains very costly in economic and human terms, as indicated by the following data on the estimated number of intentionally set structural fires:[1]

Year	Number of Fires	Number of Civilian Deaths	Direct Property Loss (in dollars)
1980	92,000	590	1.16 billion
1985	68,500	455	1.59 billion
1990	58,500	565	875 million
1995	57,500	570	981 million
2000	45,500	375	792 million
2001*	45,500	330	1 billion

An estimated 3 to 6 percent of all structural fires in the United States are incendiary (i.e., intentionally set) or of suspicious origin. Many go undetected. Of those recognized as arson, about 20 percent result in arrest, yet the conviction rate is only 1 to 2 percent. This poor showing is inevitable, given the limited number of trained investigators.

Among the arson cases cleared by arrest in 2001, 50 percent of the perpetrators were under 18 years of age. In fact, arson was the criminal offense with the greatest percentage of juveniles in the arrestee population. Between 1997 and 2001, the juvenile arrest rate decreased by 6 percent, marking a decided decrease from the peak number of arrests in 1994. Among the juveniles arrested for arson, the majority were under 15 years of age; a significant amount of those children are age 12 or younger.[2]

In many areas of the country, authority for arson investigation is in the hands of state and local fire marshals, and in some, the police have concurrent jurisdiction. A fire has

---

*This figure does not include events of September 11, 2001, which resulted in 2,451 civilian deaths and property loss valued at $33.4 trillion.

to be investigated, in certain cases extensively, *before* there is proof that a crime was committed—that the fire was of incendiary origin. Some unusual aspects of the crime of arson contribute to the difficulty of obtaining evidence to convict. They are:

1. The fire may consume all traces of its incendiary origin, especially if detecting and extinguishing it were delayed.

2. Rather than remaining undisturbed until recorded properly and the physical evidence collected, the crime scene may be hosed down with powerful streams of water, or its contents moved outdoors.

3. The perpetrator can use a timing device to delay the start of the fire, thus allowing an interim for an alibi.

4. Falling debris or the collapse of a building may cover or destroy evidence of the fire's having been set.

5. Freezing weather makes searching for evidence more difficult; if everything becomes caked with ice, search and recovery are further delayed. Extremely hot weather can evaporate volatile accelerants.

Definitions

The elements of the crime of arson differ more from state to state than do the elements of any other crime. Such words borrowed from the common law as "willful," "malicious," and "intentional" appear in combination or separately in the various statutory definitions of arson. More recently, some states have included "the use of explosives to injure property"; and, rather than having to rely on a charge of "attempted arson," they added "the preparation of a building for burning" to the arson statute per se. The degree of arson is keyed to the endangerment to life; as deadly as any gun, arson is a weapon against people as well as property. The fire started at night is considered more life-threatening than one set when most people are awake or unlikely to be present. Therefore, the question is asked: When the fire was started, was a person in the structure, or was it reasonable to expect anyone to be?

Corpus Delicti

The *corpus delicti* of arson has three elements:

1. That a fire or burning occurred in a structure or property (including vehicles, in many states) protected by law. To meet this requirement, the case law of a particular jurisdiction must be consulted to determine whether charring or merely scorching is sufficient to meet this requirement; or whether there must be an actual physical change in the material.

2. That the fire or burning was intentional: neither accidental nor attributable to negligence or natural causes, but the result of a criminal act.

3. That someone set the fire, caused it to be set, or otherwise furthered the act.

WHY IS ARSON SUSPECTED? _____

In strictly legal terms a fire is considered to be of accidental origin unless proved otherwise. But as firefighters know very well, it is not unusual to be unable to make out a case for arson, even when experience strongly suggests the fire was not accidental. Their reaction (as described by one fire chief) is akin to that of the police when an officer is killed in the line of duty; in the performance of the firefighter's duties, arson has the potential to kill. Hence, when the police have the primary responsibility to investigate a fire, they should exploit the firefighters' eagerness to put their suspicions to the test; when the arson issue is raised, the first step toward proving the *corpus delicti* is taken.

People are usually responsible for questioning the source of the fire. Not only the victim, but customers, tenants, and business rivals may express the belief that the fire in question was most timely or convenient. This should open up reservations as to its origin. Physical evidence also can strongly suggest arson; for instance, when two distinctly separate fires are encountered at the same time in the same premises. Records are least likely to be of immediate service, but later in the investigation they may be invaluable in establishing a motive; for example, a large insurance policy taken out shortly before the fire occurred; or, over time, the same owner having several fires in different locations.

Rather than prejudge any fire or explosion, the investigator should question all information until it is verified. To minimize the loss of evidence, every fire scene should be treated as a potential crime scene; any conclusion as to its incendiary or accidental cause must be based on the totality of the evidence gathered. The investigator must then sort it, form a "working hypothesis" and, testing new information against that hypothesis, modify it as needed. If the data collected continues to support the hypothesis, the end product should fit the facts—that is, answer all challenges.

PEOPLE AS A SOURCE OF INFORMATION _____

Besides the firefighters who extinguish the blaze, other people can add to the pool of information collected through interviewing. They are: the person who discovered the fire; the owner or manager, and the tenants of the burned structure; company employees; business associates and business competitors; insurance and financial personnel; and TV camera technicians.

Who Discovered the Fire?

The person who discovered the fire can report on which part of the building was ablaze when he or she first noticed it. This helps to determine the point of origin. Additional information from residents and bystanders might include observations on how quickly it spread, whether the color and volume of smoke were unusual, and descriptions of people or vehicles seen in the area shortly before the fire.

Firefighters

Firefighters are able to pinpoint the origin of structural fires (in contrast to forest or grass fires) almost 50 percent of the time. Based on past experience, they are often the first to suspect arson and quick to recognize the unusual. Giving voice to their suspicions, they will note: flame height; how rapidly the fire expanded; smoke density, and any odd color of the smoke; odor redolent of organic accelerants; fire doors that are open but should be shut; and boxed merchandise blocking passageways and doors.[3] They will recall having responded previously to alarms from the same location, and whether a fire benefitted the owner. A failed fire alarm or sprinkler system certainly will give firefighters pause (later, the investigator should have such equipment checked to see whether it was tampered with).

Owner or Manager of the Structure

The owner or manager of the destroyed property may be questioned twice: first, soon after the fire and before arson is suspected; then, when evidence obtained from people, the scene, and records supports a case for arson. The second round of questioning may be an interrogation.

During the first session of questioning, information should be sought concerning the interviewee's knowledge of the fire, e.g., how and why it started. It is important for the investigator to establish the expected fuel load (what was purported to be in the building—including any recent additions to or removal of stock or furniture) for later comparison with the amount of physical remains. The whereabouts of the interviewee at the time the fire started should be ascertained, as well as how he or she learned of the blaze. Questions concerning insurance coverage are also in order and the responses should be placed in the record. Suspicion should be aroused if the individual can produce a fire insurance policy on the spot when no other policies are immediately on hand; or if he or she can account quite readily for his or her whereabouts at the start of the fire and cite eyewitnesses, yet remain hazy concerning the hours just prior to the fire. When a case can be made for arson, especially arson-for-profit, a second round of interviewing is in order. At this point the investigator must be fully prepared to conduct an interrogation.

Employees

Employees of a commercial enterprise possess potentially useful information, which will be divulged if they are interviewed properly. They may tell what they know of any recent changes in business practice or (by repeating office gossip) offer a perspective on the firm's financial health that differs markedly from management's. Although such information does not constitute evidence in and of itself, it can give direction to a line of inquiry that otherwise might not be pursued by the investigator. For example, the owner's reputation as a gambler or womanizer suggests a need for ready cash. If accounts receivable records were destroyed in the fire, the clerical staff should be asked if a change in their overnight storage had been made. Employees (and tenants) should be questioned about the contents of the building: How was it distributed? Where was the stock? Where were the furnishings? They should be asked about any recent changes: Was new stock added or substituted for old stock that was moved or removed? Employees may report having observed fire hazards that management ignored. Any recent laxity requires a follow-up to find any connection between the hazard and the spread of the fire or its initial site.

Insurance and Financial Personnel

When insurance fraud is believed to have motivated the arson, the following people must be interviewed: the insurance agent who sold the fire policy to the owner, the claims adjuster, the insurance company's arson investigator, and the owner's creditors and bankers. In almost all cases, the insurance company will be conducting a parallel investigation to protect its interests in potential civil litigation. Frequently, the company's investigator, whether in-house or independent, has much more latitude than the public sector criminal investigator, as insurance contracts generally require a building owner to allow company investigators on the site as often as they reasonably demand access. A criminal investigator, however, must either have a search warrant or permission from the owner, who thereby waives Fourth Amendment rights. Within the terms of the contract, the insured can be required to submit to examinations under oath, and may not refuse to answer any questions without jeopardizing his or her right to collect on a claim. Hence, cooperation (without collusion) is feasible between the public and private sectors. Public sector employees have access to criminal and other records not available to the private sector investigator. On the other hand, if an insured has invoked his or her Fifth Amendment rights with the criminal investigator, the company can be notified of this fact, and an exploration conducted under the auspices of the civil investigation. By disclosing any financial situation that could have prompted the arson, such inquiries can be useful in any subsequent interrogation.

Business Competitors

Business competitors can provide information on the economic health of the industry in general and the arson target in particular. If financial problems are manifest, this can be cited during interrogation to reinforce a supposition about the motive for setting the fire.

Other Possible Witnesses

Spectators at the scene, neighbors and tenants of commercial buildings, news media staff, and those unearthed by neighborhood canvassing are other potential sources of information not to be overlooked.

Spectators at the Scene

For residence fires that occur during normal sleeping hours, occupants will generally be found out on the street. Any spectator not dressed appropriately for that time—that is, wrapped in bedclothes, street clothes thrown over nightdress, and so on—should be asked for identification. If one is a stranger to the neighborhood, how they came to be there should be ascertained. Suspicious behavior to be looked for among spectators at the scene includes: anyone making light of the situation, laughing, moving about constantly, or talking to other spectators (the investigator should find out just what was said), as well as the so-called eager beaver who provides unsought information or "helps" the firefighters with more enthusiasm than the situation warrants.

Neighbors and Tenants

Neighbors or tenants in the same building or one nearby should be questioned because they may have observed unusual activity immediately before the fire was reported. Unusual activity would include a vehicle speeding from the scene just prior to the fire. In cases of insurance fraud, it would be the removal of such valuable merchandise as high-quality men's suits, and their replacement with suits of low quality. If the shift was made during regular business hours, it would probably be noticed by other tenants (especially if the elevator was inconveniently tied up); if one was made after hours, it would be even more suspicious (at least in retrospect). In residential fires the removal of guns and electronic appliances, especially TVs, is common. Irreplaceable possessions like the family bible, photographs, trophies, or certificates also are frequently removed prior to the setting of a fire.

News Media Camera Technicians

News media reporters and photographers covering the fire may photograph the crowd gathered to watch. Photographs and films taken of bystanders at recent fires should be scrutinized to determine if the same individual appears at several fires, or whether a suspect generated subsequently was a spectator. Videotapes made by professionals as well as amateurs have proved invaluable in documenting the course of large fires and the actions taken during their suppression.

Fortuitous Witnesses

Depending on the time and location of the fire, the investigator must consider the potential eyewitnesses who, during the course of each day, pass by the place routinely. If the target is on a bus route, there should be bus drivers, passengers, and people waiting for transportation. There also may be service deliverers (U.S. Postal Service, United Parcel Service, trash pick-up, laundry, food, etc.); pedestrians on errands or walking their dogs; and motorists driving by or sitting in parked automobiles. Considerable time and effort would be needed to ferret out witnesses from among so many people. Yet it may be worth it, as they can fall into the category of fortuitous witnesses (that is, people who fail to report the valuable information they possess—what they saw or heard—simply because they do not realize its worth).

CONDUCTING THE INVESTIGATION

The motives for committing arson are numerous, but can be summarized as follows: profit, spite, and revenge; vandalism; and pyromania. Generally, motive is quite personal (that is, secret and having a particular purpose). When tentatively identified, it may send the investigator to search records, or require a surveillance, neighborhood canvass, and/or additional interviewing of those who might confirm or dispute the motive attributed to the suspect. This topic will be considered again, following the discussion on how the investigator obtains information from people and physical evidence.

PHYSICAL EVIDENCE

The purpose of examining the scene and attempting to recognize and collect physical evidence in a case of suspected arson is threefold: first, to determine where the fire started (only when the origin is known can possible causes be searched for and eliminated); second, to establish whether the fire was intentionally set, thereby proving an element of the crime; and third, if the fire is determined to have been set, to connect the arsonist to the crime scene. However, the task of locating and recognizing physical evidence is a different one for arson than it is for most other crimes: some physical evidence may be destroyed by flames and heat, or washed away by pressure hoses. Despite this, telltale signs of where the fire started may remain, but the investigator must be capable of reading them. To do so, the following very elementary knowledge of the chemistry and physics of fire is needed.

Combustion[4]

Three components are required for fire: burnable material (a fuel); oxygen; and a heat source (which raises the temperature of the fuel to its kindling point). The relationship is expressed in the equation:

$$\text{FUEL} + \text{OXYGEN} + \text{HEAT SOURCE} = \text{COMBUSTION}$$

The first two components coexist all the time with no threat of fire. Only when the third—a heat source—is present can fire occur. The temperature of the heat source must be greater than the ignition (or kindling) temperature of the fuel; also, the heat source must be able to raise the fuel to its ignition point by direct contact, or by transferring the heat through radiation, conduction, or convection. Because each component can play a role in proving or disproving that the fire was set intentionally, it is important to understand the function of each.

Fuels[5]

All fuels have an ignition temperature, meaning that when raised to that point, they start to burn. The temperature of the heat source must be higher than the fuel's ignition temperature. Most fuels are organic (i.e., they are carbon compounds), as are the many products used in constructing and furnishing buildings, such as wood, paint, and fabrics used in rugs, draperies, upholstery, and bedding.

When burning, carbon combines with oxygen to form carbon monoxide and carbon dioxide, releasing heat in the process:

ORGANIC (CARBON) COMPOUNDS + OXYGEN =
CARBON MONOXIDE + CARBON DIOXIDE + HEAT

Oxidation is the term used by chemists to describe the reaction of a chemical compound with oxygen. A compound such as linseed oil (a drying oil found in paints) combines at room temperature with oxygen and releases considerable heat as part of the oxidation process. Should linseed oil be left on rags that are piled up or dropped in a heap, thereby preventing the air currents from carrying away the heat, fire can break out. What may appear initially to be a suspicious fire will actually have been caused by spontaneous combustion, a result of the careless disposal of paint-waste rags. Most petroleum products—oils, greases, kerosenes, and gasolines—are not drying oils and thus do not pose a spontaneous combustion risk.

When arson is employed to cover up a homicide, investigative use can be made of the fact that carbon monoxide is one of the by-products of combustion. Its absence in the blood of a dead person who apparently fell asleep while smoking in bed may unmask a cover-up attempt—a supposedly accidental death may be revealed to be a criminal homicide. A living person breathing carbon monoxide retains it in the blood because hemoglobin forms a stronger chemical bond—about 200 times stronger—with the deadly gas than it does with oxygen. A dead person's blood is no longer circulating; accordingly, carbon monoxide is not taken up by the body even though it is exposed to it.

Soot is another by-product of combustion. Its presence or absence in the respiratory passages of an alleged victim of a fire indicates whether he or she was alive or dead at the time of the fire. Soot will be detected only in those who were breathing at that time. The absence of soot in the windpipe and lungs of the deceased could indicate that a death first believed accidental—from falling asleep while smoking in bed—may actually have been homicide.

Oxygen

The earth's atmosphere, approximately 21 percent oxygen, remains constant through the cyclical processes of combustion (best described for living matter as oxidation) and photosynthesis. The carbon dioxide produced by combustion is used by green plants and trees for the photosynthesis of organic compounds and the simultaneous release of oxygen into the atmosphere, thereby maintaining the earth's oxygen supply at the 21 percent level. Fire requires at least 16 percent oxygen content to continue; concentrations between 16 and 21 percent promote heavy smoke production.

Investigative interest is aroused when a fire extinguishes itself through a shortage of oxygen (a level below 16 percent), and by the carbon dioxide and carbon monoxide produced. This situation arises only under certain conditions; for instance, when a fire is ignited in a building so tightly sealed and unventilated that it does not allow the oxygen to be replaced as it is consumed by the burning fuel. By extinguishing itself before it has consumed the structure, the fire may leave evidence of combustible material placed to spread the fire (see Trailers below).

Heat Sources[6]

It is the temperature and size of the heat source that matters, fires usually being small at the beginning. If circumstances are favorable—a flammable gas or vapor, or a finely divided, solid material such as kapok is present—a mere spark can be the ignition source. A spark was all it took to set fire to the ocean liner *Normandie*, being refitted as a troop carrier during World War II. Naturally, sabotage was suspected. An immediate investigation, however, revealed that an acetylene torch had been used in disregard of such a known fire hazard—the proximity of highly flammable kapok. The ship was quickly engulfed in flames and the volume of water ultimately needed to quench the flames sank the liner at her berth in New York harbor. Because the welder could testify about how and exactly where it began, the initial site of the fire was readily determined. In the meantime, a thorough background check on the welder ruled out sabotage.

Accidental Heat Sources

In cases of suspected arson, the initial site of the fire may be determined from the physical evidence and traces remaining after it is extinguished. Whether its origins were accidental or natural, some evidence of the cause will usually be found at its source. The most common accidental causes include:

Heating/Cooking Systems: Sparks from a fireplace, dirty chimney, overturned space heater, exploding or leaking kerosene oil stove, or overheated greasy frying pan. Radiant heat from boilers, stoves, furnaces, faulty chimneys, or overheated equipment—motors, gear boxes with dry bearings. Vents and exhaust systems that allow flames or hot gases to escape and come in contact with combustibles.

Heating systems are the most common cause of fires, especially in the southern states where they tend to be portable (electric or liquid fueled). Cooking accidents are the most common cause of injuries resulting from fires.

Electrical System (Equipment and Appliances): Deterioration because of: worn insulation; misuse (overloaded circuits); improper installation (loose connections—especially with aluminum wire); defects (shorted circuits through a faulty switch, causing sparking or arcing); overheating caused by a loose connection; and any of the above coupled with neglect (grease collected in stove vents and hood filters).

Smoking: Careless use or disposal of cigarettes, cigars, or pipes, especially in bed and in living areas is the cause of many fires, and the most common cause of death by fire. Ignition can be delayed up to 12 hours when smoking materials are improperly discarded (see Figure 18.1).

Figure 18.1
A common scene—a burned, overstuffed chair possibly ignited by a smoldering cigarette dropped between cushion and arm. *(Courtesy, John DeHaan.)*

Figure 18.2
The same chair from the side. Heaviest charring is seen on the outside of the chair frame, indicating the fire started exterior to the chair. The remains of a plastic trash bin (lower left) show heavy damage. Fire was started in newspapers in bin, and spread to chair. *(Courtesy, John DeHaan.)*

Matches: Fumes or vapors, virtually impossible to ignite with a glowing cigarette, are ignited easily with a spark from a match or a flame. Matches and lighters—with their exposed flames—probably are responsible for more fires than are the glowing embers of tobacco, if fires started by children playing with matches are counted. Though accidental fires do not result every time a child plays with matches, they can be a consequence of such activity. The investigator should look into the child's past behavior, which is not likely to have escaped the family's notice. Asking the family if precautions were taken to keep matches safe and asking the child whether he or she was able to obtain them would also be appropriate.

Natural Heat Sources

Occasionally, nature is responsible for starting a blaze. Some natural causes are: spontaneous combustion, which can make flammable material smolder and then burst into flame; lightning (especially in remote areas), which can start fires in structures (such as silos or barns) but more frequently causes forest fires; and—although a rare cause—sunlight, which can be concentrated on combustible material by the lens effect of a water-filled glass container or a concave mirror. Witnesses can help to establish whether conditions were right for such an occurrence: Was it a hot, sunny day? Was lightning seen in the area? How long had the fuel been there—hours, days, weeks?

Investigative Significance

Making a fire appear to have been the result of an accidental or natural cause may look like an easy cover-up to an arsonist. Investigative efforts must make certain that the cause was not so simulated. Cover-up attempts are usually associated with insurance fraud or with fires meant to conceal other crimes such as homicide or theft. Motive, especially pecuniary, can be an important factor in deciding to press on with the inquiry rather than accept the ostensible cause. The absence of (1) a natural cause, or (2) an accidental cause leads to an assumption of arson. If both are eliminated after a thorough investigation by a qualified expert, one element for a charge of arson—the fact that the fire was set willfully or maliciously—is sustainable.

Additional factors to be considered include: the nature of the fuel present; its physical form; whether the suspected source could provide enough energy to ignite a fire; and whether normal ventilation was tampered with, which otherwise would have cooled off the fuel faster than it could be heated.

Accelerants

A number of commercially available volatile liquids are used to start fires and help them spread more rapidly. Known as *accelerants* in the field of arson detection, some examples are: gasoline (or gasoline blended with diesel fuel, a precaution sometimes taken by arsonists); kerosene; lighter fluids; paint thinners (turpentine, mineral spirits, acetone); and toluene. All carry a high potential for danger, the greatest attaching to the most common accelerant by far—gasoline. If gasoline and other extremely volatile fuels are ignited at concentrations between 1.5 and 6 percent, gasoline vapors may pro-

Figure 18.3
Low pressure, low velocity explosion damage, with exterior sooting and scorching, from a gasoline vapor explosion. *(Courtesy, John DeHaan.)*

duce an explosion that shatters windows, pushes out walls (see Figure 18.3), and scorches the skin and clothing of the arsonist, who may be burned acutely on the back while making a hasty exit. By notifying hospitals, emergency clinics, and doctors of the need to report all cases of extensive burns, particularly back burns, the arson investigator may locate a likely suspect—certainly if the patient with severe back burns claims they resulted from having lighted a gas oven. In reality, an exploding gas oven would cause more frontal burns and less severe back burns. If the suspect is a hired professional, paid to torch the structure for the benefit of the owner or someone with a grudge against the owner, follow-up is obviously necessary. A possible ploy, which often succeeds with a novice or a youth, would be to inquire into the amount contracted for, feign surprise, and then let on that the going rate is higher. Feeling cheated, the inexperienced arsonist may blurt out the name of the individual who did the hiring.

Point of Origin

In the investigation of any structural fire, it is critical first to determine its point of origin. There are two reasons for this. The primary one is to establish cause, because arson becomes probable should both accidental and natural causes be ruled out. The second reason is germane to the kind of debris remaining at the site: if an accelerant was used, some residue can be retrieved for laboratory analysis; if a fire-setting mechanism was employed, its parts can be collected as evidence.

Locating the Initial Site

Three sources of information can help to determine where a structural fire originated.[7] The first source is provided by the burn patterns visible on partially consumed combustible material. In this age of high technology it may be surprising to learn that the prosaic shovel is a must if burn patterns are to be made visible, for a huge quantity of debris is the inevitable consequence of fighting a fire. Indeed, it is not uncommon for arson experts called to the scene to find a foot of rubble covering much of the site. The distorted shapes and other effects of intense heat on such objects as light bulbs or furniture springs are the second source of information (see Figure 18.4). The third source, one that may lead to the point of origin, was noted earlier in the chapter: the observations of the person(s) who first noticed the fire.

Burn Patterns[8]

The intensity and duration of a fire can, with some confidence, be inferred from the burn patterns that can be observed on combustible material not completely consumed. When wood is the fuel, a blister or alligator-like pattern is usually present. Even on a noncombustible surface, such as a cement block wall, a pattern may be visible. Fire usually burns upward (by convection), then outward (by radiation and conduction). By examining where things are burned and where they are not, the investigator establishes the pattern of the burning. Surfaces exposed to oncoming flames are always burned more than surfaces not

Figure 18.4
Drawing of light bulb exposed to heat from oncoming fire. Gas pressure in bulb causes blow-out, which points toward the fire.

exposed—protected, on the lee side. Beveling takes place; this and the "V" pattern resulting from the flow of the fire (see below) are used to reconstruct its path.

Pour Patterns: The kind of burn pattern that results from pouring an accelerant onto the floor of a room is particularly important. A pour pattern is clear, demonstrable evidence of the use of an accelerant (see Figures 18.5-18.7).

Alligatoring: Anyone who has observed the partially burned residue of a campfire is familiar with how the blisters on the logs resemble the skin of an alligator. The size of the alligatoring or checking is not useful to the investigator, for it is dependant on the type of wood and its cut rather than on exposure to the fire. The single exception is the flat, baked appearance caused by low intensity heating over a long time (see Crazing below).

"V" Pattern: Fire, if unobstructed, will shoot upward and fan out, often registering as a "V" or a cone pattern left after the fire is put out (see Figure 18.8). When the "V" is distinct, the bottom of the cone sometimes points to where the fire started, or to where the fuel was burning. An ignition or fuel source may be found at the base of a "V" pattern. The action of interior structural fires, however, is not always this simple. Obstructions can prevent a fire from spreading; strong drafts from stairwells and elevator shafts can distort the "V"; and broken or open windows and doors can create drafts that dramatically alter the way the fire spreads and, therefore, the configuration of its burn pattern.

Figure 18.5
Evidence photograph of cleaned floor—showing char where accelerant was poured and the undamaged surrounding area. *(Courtesy, Brooksville Fire Department, Brooksville, Florida.)*

Figure 18.6
Pour pattern on floor in corner protected by carpet. A pour pattern area—in this case, near the wall and baseboard—is a good place to take samples. *(Courtesy, Brooksville Fire Department, Brooksville, Florida.)*

Figure 18.7
A pour/drip pattern visible on carpet. Fire spread from room to room. *(Courtesy, Brooksville Fire Department, Brooksville, Florida.)*

Figure 18.8
Burn pattern on both walls extends upward in a "V" from chair, the initial ignition site. Note secondary ignition of bookcase by radiant heat from chair fire. *(Courtesy, John DeHaan.)*

Figure 18.9
Charring as an indicator of fire travel and point of origin. It is clear from the charring that the fire traveled from left to right. *(Courtesy, Brooksville Fire Department, Brooksville, Florida.)*

Charring: The charring of wood inevitably is observed in structural fires and can be an indicator of fire travel and point of origin (see Figure 18.9). Many arson investigators believe that the deeper the charring, the longer the fire burned at that spot. Because the longest burning time must be at the point of origin, observing the depth of char at various places can help them to trace the fire back to that point. This may be true sometimes, but too many complicating factors interfere with accuracy. One area, for instance, may be drenched by the fire hoses (and cooled), and an adjacent one completely missed. An accelerant itself may burn more intensely than the materials on which it was splashed, leaving a darker, recognizable char pattern of its own. Even when thrown on a vertical surface (such as a door), the resulting burn pattern indicates where the fluid was applied. Heavy charring in a corner of a room, which would otherwise be difficult to fathom, may have resulted because the accelerant flowed there across an uneven floor.

From an investigative viewpoint, the most useful facts relative to charring may be summed up as follows:

1. the depth of char is proportional to the intensity of the fire (if short in duration) and to the length of burning if the fire burns slowly for a long time;

2. those places where intensity was greatest—directly over a fire, or where ventilation or drafts "fan" it—will have deeper charring;

3. the relative depth of char around a room may help locate sources of fuel or ventilation.

Heat Distortion

Direct flames or atmospheric heat build-up can distort objects, thereby impressing telltale signs on materials (especially plastic) that partially melt, fuse, or crack when exposed to intense heat. Even without flames and charring, the direction of fire travel may be established through the deformation of some objects by heat.

Light Bulbs: The glass housing of a light bulb can be partially melted, and the distorted form that results will point in the direction of the oncoming fire (see Figure 18.10).

Figure 18.10
Light bulbs melt first on side facing oncoming fire. Gas pressure in bulb causes blow-out to point toward heat source (fire). *(Courtesy, John DeHaan.)*

Spalling:[9] Although noncombustible, cement can show exposure to intense heat through spalling. The signs that indicate spalling are surface discoloration, chipping, crumbling, or a flaky, chalk-like appearance. Most often it results from exposure to radiant heat from a large, established fire. Brown-black stains on the cement around the spalled area suggest the use of an accelerant, although experiments reveal it is very difficult to produce spalling with a liquid accelerant. A pattern or trail of spalling can be read like a burn pattern on any surface (see Figure 18.11).

Crazing: A pattern or network of fine, irregular lines in glass and wood are termed craze lines. In glass and ceramic material they may be the result of rapid, intense heat, possibly because of the use of an accelerant. Craze lines on wood, found on the baked, flat surface of a board are the result of relatively low heat over a long period of time.

Significance of Finding Point of Origin

When all relevant information sources (people, burn patterns, heat distortion) on the fire have been exploited, the fire's point of origin may be found at or close to the low point of the burned-out area. Multiple low points, signifying possible multiple origins, are highly suspicious. They signal an intentionally set fire. Questionable sites include: a closet, bathroom, attic, crawl space, the area beneath stairs—because accidental fires in such locations are rare. An unusual burn is another suspicious sign: the fire burning down instead of up, or fire developing as a result of a flashover when normally there would not be enough fuel on hand for this to occur. Flashover is a phenomenon that occurs when, in the growth of a fire, all the fuel in a room is ignited and flames flash over the entire area. Whenever arson is suspected, the point of origin, once located, must be examined for all possible sources of ignition and for any remaining traces of accelerant.

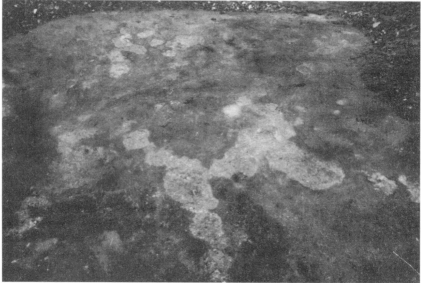

Figure 18.11
Concrete spalling may indicate the use of a liquid accelerant. Look for patterns of discoloration around the spalling, and have a laboratory analyze samples of concrete or absorbent powder that has been allowed to stand on the concrete for about an hour. *(Courtesy, John J. Lentini, Applied Technical Services, Marietta, GA.)*

Ignition Sources

Once an area of origin has been established, the investigator can then turn to a search for ignition sources. Flame from a match or a cigarette lighter is the most common source for an incendiary fire, but except through exclusion, the use of either will not be apparent in a case of arson. In other words, only when no other possible source of heat can be found at the point of origin—no electric or gas outlet in the area; no spark, friction, or chemical source of heat; no child having access to the area or to matches; and no stored rags that could have undergone spontaneous combustion—is such a source indicated. The presence of an electrical outlet or appliance near or at the point of origin requires checking out, as does the possibility that overheating, or an arc (or spark) may have caused the fire. If such causes are to be eliminated, an expert is needed to perform these tasks.

Although less common as an ignition source, it is important to ascertain whether any mechanical (frictional), chemical, or natural source was present at the point of origin to account for the fuel's having reached ignition temperature. When all are eliminated, an inference that the fire was deliberately set is warranted.

Plants (Sets)

Arson investigators employ the term *plant*, or arson *set*, to describe a device that ignites the first fuel, or assists the initial flame to build in intensity. A timing mechanism may be included as part of the device. In addition, a *trailer* may be used to spread the fire to other parts of the structure.

Timing Devices: Arsonists employ timing devices to delay the start of a fire and allow them to establish an alibi. By this means, witnesses can be produced to attest to their presence in another place at the time of the blaze. The simpler the timing device, the more difficult it is to prove one was used, and the less likely it is to malfunction. The more complicated and clever the device, the fewer the people with the ability or the means to design, test, and build it.

Matches, Candles, Cigarettes, and Other Timing Devices: A simple but effective ignition and timing device involves the use of matches with a burning candle wrapped in excelsior or other readily flammable material (see Figure 18.12). Generally, a candle three-quarters of an inch in diameter burns at about one inch per hour, making possible a few hours' delay. Blasting safety fuses and cannon/pyrotechnic fuses make shorter delays feasible (up to 10 minutes), by burning at a predictable rate of 24 to 60 inches per minute. Another means of causing ignition in a short time is the use of a matchbook and a burning cigarette. Candles may be used in combination with other fuels for delayed ignition. Another device, the road accident flare, is also easily obtained. A mattress or some readily combustible material may be placed near or wrapped around any ignition/timing device.

Phosphorus, a chemical element that ignites upon exposure to air, has been employed to start a delayed fire. When dissolved in a solvent that evaporates slowly, combustion is postponed until it is exposed to the air after the solvent has evaporated. Alternatively, phosphorus may be coated with paraffin, sewn inside the shoulder pad of a garment, then sent to a dry cleaner where the cleaning fluid dissolves the paraffin, exposing the phosphorus to the air. Dry cleaning shops involved in labor disputes or fighting a competitor have been burned out by this technique.

A lighted cigarette dropped accidentally or placed deliberately between upholstered chair cushions may smolder and incubate for three-quarters of an hour to four hours before bursting into flame (and may never go to open flame). A fire started within an upholstered chair will heavily char the chair's insides as well as the floor. The chair's coil springs will usually collapse, then be hardened by rapid cooling from the water doused on them. A fire started from the outside and engulfing the same chair would do more exterior than interior damage; the springs and floor underneath may remain virtually undamaged. Light bulbs or hot appliances wrapped in cloth rags or cotton batting will cause smoldering after several minutes, and later, flaming combustion.

Other more esoteric devices have been constructed. To time the start of a fire, the electric, telephone, or gas utility system can be altered. Electronic timers, alarm clocks, and other mechanical devices are also used, and can be set off by remote control—telephone or radio signal. As a general rule, some physical trace of a timing device (if one was employed) is likely to be found in the debris remaining at the point of origin—provided that the point of origin is located and thoroughly examined.

Figure 18.12
Candle on plastic boxes and newspaper with a suspended toy balloon containing a small quantity of gasoline (see arrow) make an effective short-delay ignition device. *(Courtesy, John DeHaan.)*

Trailers: *Trailers* (or *streamers*) are used to extend the fire from the plant (or set) to other parts of the structure. Sometimes they lead from the starter plant to one or more secondary plants from which other trailers emanate. A wide variety of materials can be utilized for this purpose: newspapers, waxed paper, toilet paper, rags twisted into rope and doused with accelerant, gunpowder, certain motion picture film, and such flammable liquids as a mix of kerosene and gasoline, or a mix of gasoline and fireplace ashes.

In using trailers, the amateur arsonist might not make allowances for the replacement of oxygen in a relatively air-tight building that has no source of ventilation to restore the oxygen consumed by the fire. This causes the carbon dioxide and carbon monoxide (generated by combustion of the fuel and simultaneous reduction of the oxygen) to snuff out the fire. Left behind is visible evidence of the streamers and plants, photographs of which should convince a jury that arson was intended (see Figure 18.13).

Accelerants

Gasoline (the most common accelerant), turpentine and kerosene are readily identified by their distinctive odors. When searching the crime scene for an accelerant, a shovelful of debris—ashes, wood flooring, carpeting, or upholstery, for instance—must be lifted, then sniffed. The sense of smell, however, is easily fatigued or dulled; it is not always reliable. Several attempts (perhaps by more than one person) may be necessary before an odor is detected; when it is, the debris must be collected and preserved for transmission to the laboratory.

Figure 18.13
Trailer across counter and into open cabinets failed to ignite contents. *(Courtesy, John DeHaan.)*

The distinctive odors of many accelerants come from the impurities remaining after petroleum, pine tree wood, or other natural products are distilled. With care and some expense, they can be removed. This process yields a relatively odorless, flammable liquid which, when objections are raised about the fumes of ordinary oil house paints, serves as an acceptable paint thinner. Such products can also be used by the arsonist to mask the use of an accelerant. In such a case, some method other than lifting and sniffing must be found to discover the presence of an accelerant.

Detection Methods—For Use at the Crime Scene: Accelerants can sometimes be detected at the scene of a suspected arson by visual inspection, by odor, or by means of instrumental devices.

Visual Observations
In addition to a pour pattern, other visual evidence of the use of an accelerant can be found when heat intensity is sufficient to melt, twist, or oxidize metals used in the construction of a building or piece of furniture. Figure 18.14 shows the aluminum threshold of a doorway in which the metal was melted by the intense heat.

Figure 18.14
Melted aluminum in a low area (such as door sill in photograph above) is a good indicator of intense heat—as from a flammable liquid. A wooden door charred on the bottom edge is a strong indicator that an accelerant burned on the floor underneath the door. *(Courtesy, Brooksville Fire Department, Brooksville, Florida.)*

Detecting by Scent [10]

The human olfactory nerve can be sensitive. A few people are capable of recognizing one part of gasoline in 10 million parts of air; the majority require a concentration of about 10 parts per million. Trained dogs have been successful in detecting gasoline at fire scenes; their sensitivity also is on the order of one part per million. Chemical dyes and instrumental means also can establish the presence of a flammable hydrocarbon in the debris at a crime scene. The "rainbow" effect to be observed on pools of water, caused by contamination from the oily residue found in many commercially available volatile fluids, suggests the presence of an accelerant, but may also be the result of naturally occurring decomposition (pyrolysis) products.

Dye Color Test

If sprinkled over a suspected area, dyes soluble only in organic solvents can change to red or another color (depending on the dye). They are easy to use and low in cost. But just as dyes are the least sensitive detection method, they are the least specific: they may turn color even when no accelerant is present. Their low cost does make detection of odorless accelerants feasible. Thus, samples should be collected for the crime laboratory in which sophisticated equipment is available for analysis.

Instrumental Devices

Well over a dozen instruments are available for the detection of accelerants. Costing from a few hundred to a few thousand dollars, they vary widely in price as well as sensitivity, specificity, and portability. Underlying their operation is a broad range of scientific principles—from flame ionization and gas chromatography to infrared spectrophotometry and catalytic combustion/resistance analysis (see Chapter 2). Known as a *sniffer* in the jargon of arson investigators, the catalytic combustion device is the most common means employed to detect flammable vapors. Specificity to hydrocarbon accelerants being impossible with field devices, some false positive results will occur; therefore, any positive reading must be confirmed by collecting and submitting samples for further laboratory analysis.

Collection and Transmission: The volatility of accelerants requires that crime scene debris suspected of harboring flammable material be sealed tightly in new, quart- to gallon-sized metal paint cans or glass jars. Polyethylene or polystyrene containers are unsuitable for collecting accelerants; they are deteriorated by, or are permeable to petroleum products. The cans or jars should be filled until they are 80 to 90 percent full. They should not be exposed to the heat of the sun or left in a closed automobile or trunk during hot weather. To prevent the escape of flammable vapor, expeditious delivery to the laboratory is crucial. There, the evidence can be sampled (using head-space or charcoal trap concentration) and then analyzed by gas chromatography. A fresh cellulose sponge, gauze, or cotton batting can be used to soak up small quantities of liquid, and then stored in a small, tightly covered glass jar or can. Flour, diatomaceous earth, or calcium carbonate can be spread on a wet concrete surface to absorb traces of gasoline or other petroleum distillate. The absorbent should then be sealed in a can to await analysis.

MOTIVE

After a fire has come under suspicion (based on information obtained from people and crime scene evidence) a knowledge of the wide differences both in motive and *modus operandi* of arsonists facilitates the search for the individual responsible. Property owners looking to collect insurance want everything completely burned down. They often take measures to ensure the fire's spread to all parts of the premises, and do so with little fear of being in the building since they are in control of it. Hence, a disabled alarm or sprinkler suggests the arsonist is an owner or holds another financial interest. Those looking for thrills rarely go to such lengths; it is sufficient that they see the flames and hear the fire engines. The kind of person whose name would crop up on a list of individuals seeking to collect insurance is unlikely to resemble the thrill-seeker in age and business background. Likewise, an attempt to make the cause of a fire seem accidental is not expected when the motivation is vandalism, spite, revenge, or hatred; rather, it suggests insurance fraud. Because the nature of a fire can provide clues to motive, the following discussion is designed to enhance the investigator's understanding and skill in dealing with this crime.

Financial Gain

Arson can result when a business or person gains financially, for example, by eliminating competition, through insurance fraud, or through welfare fraud (following the destruction of home and possessions). Obviously, the greatest benefit accrues from swindling an insurance company.

Insurance Fraud

Liquidating a large inventory of unsold or obsolete merchandise—"selling" it to the insurance company by means of a set fire—is most likely when the goods are seasonal or produced by an industry that has suffered a severe downturn. Other scenarios include the need for: extensive renovation to meet new safety standards; costly retooling, or replacing of an outmoded plant, in order to remain competitive; capital that is tied up (e.g., in a long-vacant building, whose sale would mean taking a great loss). In cases in which insurance fraud is suspected, the careful inspection of business, personal, and especially financial records is an obvious first step. If a thorough inventory of the firm's assets was kept, it will often become apparent why arson was seen as a solution.

Elimination of Competition

A strategically timed fire can undoubtedly benefit a surviving firm when its competitor is forced out of business by arson. For example, many companies rely on Christmas buying to ensure adequate annual profits. If, as the season is launched, its inventory is received and then destroyed by a set fire, the business may be hard put to survive. Arson is intimidating at any time, but especially so for a struggling new business. When arson is suspected or proved, the victim more likely than not is able to suggest who might benefit. Because fire setters are often hired professionals, a list of the calls—local, and particularly long distance—charged to a suspect's business and residence telephones can be very useful to the investigator. If the records of several months prior to and following the fire are studied, a particular number may be noted that appears abruptly, then vanishes. Next, a background check on the recipient may turn up an individual with an arrest record or reputation as a fire setter. Since professionals usually demand ready money, cash is the most likely form of payment; therefore, an investigator's failure to examine bank statements for cash withdrawals and checks written is inexcusable. Surveillance may be called for; if the suspect is subsequently caught red-handed, a confession should be obtained for the first fire.

Moving and Resettlement Allowance

People who do not live below the poverty line cannot know the hardships endured by those who live on the edge. For the middle class a home fire is regarded as a calamity, the emotional impact of which is partially offset by insurance coverage. For the poor a fire may be seen as a way out. Possessions good for the junk heap can be replaced and the rundown house left behind. With the homeless given priority for public housing, and charitable organizations helping families to resettle, arson is sometimes seen as a viable option. It is resorted to from time to time, therefore, and should not be ruled out. When there is evidence to prove that the fire was set, and the family agrees to be interrogated, a confession is extremely likely.

Intimidation

Arson has been used to:

1. instill fear regarding the safety of one's person or family;

2. threaten economic loss; or

3. effect a desired change in government or business policy.

Fear for Safety

The threat of arson has caused individuals to fear for their safety. It may be used either to prevent or force them to do something. Witnesses may be threatened with the torching of their home or business should they come forth with testimony in an upcoming criminal trial. Sometimes, owing to racial hostility, a home is burned when a new family moving into the neighborhood is not welcomed by the dominant group. In the event of witness intimidation, the motive is clear after a threat has been made. Before the fire is set, surveillance of the targeted property, the suspect, and associates is an effective strategy. Although there might seem to be too many suspects in a racially tense neighborhood, if the property and those who seem capable of disregarding the civil rights of others can be kept under surveillance, the offender(s) could be caught in the act.

Threatened Economic Loss

Arson has been used to intimidate management in labor disputes, especially when the settlement of a strike seems unlikely. Mobsters have sometimes extorted money from business concerns by torching a company vehicle as a signal that more serious repercussions will take place should compliance not be forthcoming.

Change of Policy

Arson has been used to press for a change in governmental policy. During the Vietnam war, government and quasi-military installations were set afire or bombed. It also has been used to induce action for the alleviation of other problems: for example, banks believed to be "redlining" a community (not approving mortgage loans for housing in the area) have received arson threats. In these cases informants can be helpful by indicating promising suspects to be placed under surveillance.

Emotional Reasons

Jealousy, spite, revenge, and hatred are strong enough to cause some individuals to resort to arson to relieve the malaise produced by these emotions. In such arson cases, the victim usually is aware of the aggrieved individual and can provide the investigator with the name of the likely perpetrator.

Jealousy

Jealousy can cause a jilted sexual partner to resort to arson, by setting the property of the former lover or new lover afire. It is not uncommon for an unrequited lover to throw a Molotov cocktail against the front door of the person who has rejected him or her. Although similar to jealousy, envy is less useful in suggesting a possible suspect.

Spite

Domestic quarrels and feuds between neighbors are often marked by arson. Some property of value to the other party to the conflict is burned. In rural areas a barn may be targeted; in cities, a vehicle.

Revenge

A relationship between employer and employee also can become so embittered as to cause the firm's business or equipment to be set afire. Family feuds and gang warfare provide excuses for revenge fires as well.

Hatred

Hatred is another strong emotion that sometimes is relieved through arson. The target may be the commercial property, automobile, or residence of the intended victim. Those so motivated have probably let others know of their feelings, or the victim may be aware of the animosity and furnish the names of possible suspects. The list can be pared down if necessary by considering who had the opportunity and who might be foolhardy enough to commit arson.

Dislike of an assigned task (a mild form of hatred) has caused arson to be employed as a diversionary tactic. The disruption, it is hoped, will eliminate the need to fulfill an obligation. For example, to force the postponement of a test, a student may start a diversionary fire in a dormitory or classroom. Such fires usually are set with material readily available—pages torn from a phone book, curtains, draperies, upholstered cushions, a waste basket. If a series of small fires (sometimes the first one or two will not be reported) is extinguished before they do extensive damage, an analysis of the time, day of the week, and the period separating them may be profitable. In one case, a chemistry class held a monthly examination, always on a Thursday; over a three-month period, several fires were set late at night on the Wednesday preceding the test. After the pattern was recognized, a course list of students who were faring poorly was obtained. Questioning each one separately led to a confession.

Concealment of Another Crime

Sometimes arson serves to conceal a homicide, account for an inventory shortage, destroy incriminating records, or distract police from another felony being committed simultaneously in the area. When the investigator realizes that arson was put to such use, heed should be given to whomever may have had a motive to commit the other offense.

Homicide

Attempts have been made to conceal a criminal homicide by having it appear that a person fell asleep while smoking and then died. Such attempts are doomed if a proper autopsy is conducted. The carbon monoxide level, soot inhalation, and burn patterns on the body must be consistent with the hypothesized reconstruction. The possibility of suicide by fire must not be overlooked; fires and even explosions have been set in structures and vehicles as a means of self-destruction.

Larceny

Sound business practice requires that an inventory count be taken regularly to ferret out theft. An employee who is periodically stealing from a firm can attempt to conceal a shortage through an apparent destruction by fire. When a fire occurs shortly before inventory time, the possibility that arson was a cover-up for larceny must be considered. When the resale value of a residence has dropped, owing perhaps to market conditions, a home owner may decide to "sell it" to the insurance company through arson. To maximize the reimbursement, expensive items are replaced by cheaper ones. An arson investigator must check to verify that the remaining contents (and ashes) are what would be expected from the inventory provided by the insured (see Figures 18.15 and 18.16).

Fraud, Forgery, Embezzlement

These crimes generally involve documents, some of which are needed to prove the *corpus delicti*. If such documents are unavailable because they were destroyed in a fire, crucial evidence will be missing and the prosecution made more difficult.

Other Crimes

A substantial fire requires the presence of the police to redirect traffic and see to it that spectators do not interfere with firefighters and are kept at a safe distance. With police so preoccupied, the criminal or an accomplice, having set the fire, is at liberty to commit another crime—a burglary or robbery, for instance—elsewhere in the jurisdiction.

Figure 18.15
Inventory of rooms may reveal fraud by substitution or removal of contents. After the fire, hangers, buckles, zippers, springs, and hardware will reveal the amount and quality of clothing or furniture in the room. Rooms empty of furniture or stock may indicate insurance fraud. *(Courtesy, John DeHaan.)*

Figure 18.16
The same room as in Figure 18.15. Even though heavily damaged, the remains of the sofa, clothing, and floor covering are identifiable and can be checked against owner records. *(Courtesy, John DeHaan.)*

Pyromania

Pyromania is defined as an irresistible impulse or compulsion to start a fire or set something on fire. Even though excitement or sensual gratification makes the motive clear, this kind of arson may be considered motiveless from an investigative viewpoint. In any event, because all pyromaniacs have the same inner drive, the term pyromania is too general to be useful in identifying an offender.

Modus operandi, however, can be a telltale sign; the investigator armed with this information can take the necessary steps to apprehend the pyromaniac. The arsonist motivated by profit wants to do maximum damage by penetrating deep inside the structure to set the fire. The pyromaniac, a creature of impulse who seldom forms any plans, must make do with material on hand: old newspapers, garbage chute refuse, the mattress from a baby carriage standing in a hallway, trash underneath a staircase, etc. In other words, the fire is set wherever the fuel is found. When, for instance, many such fires occur in urban areas in the late evening hours when neighborhood bars are emptying, a pattern may be recognized: Are the fires set on the same day of the week? About the same time of night? Is there a linkage between them and payday? What local bars are within walking distance of the fire? Is the same kind of structure being attacked—apartment building, factory, garage, barn? Are they along the same route; if so, how does this relate to the locations of the local bars? If a fire setting pattern becomes clear, the use of surveillance—fixed (of possible targets) and moving (of possible suspects)—is an obvious strategy, albeit an expensive one, in terms of work hours.

Recognition as a Hero

Some arsonists will set a fire in order to "discover" it and then "save" the inhabitants or contents. These so-called heroes tend to fall into certain, not necessarily exclusive, classes: volunteer firefighters, babysitters, volunteer librarians, night watch personnel. True heroes certainly exist—people who risk their own lives to save others, but when an individual manages to make a second heroic rescue not too long after the first, it is feasible that he or she is an arsonist. Questioning the suspect, then homing in on the details of the "discovery/rescue" during requestioning, will expose discrepancies and ultimately produce an admission or confession.

Vandalism

Run down or vacant buildings in deteriorating neighborhoods can become the target of adolescent gangs looking to vent anger or simply to relieve monotony. A set fire is good for a certain amount of excitement. Sometimes gang members "graduate" to setting fires for landlords of rent-controlled properties; having driven the tenants out, the owners realize increased revenues by subdividing the large flats. Motives varying widely in these situations, it would facilitate the investigation if a suspect gang member can be turned into an informant.

Churches and schools are vandalized and even torched from time to time. Often the individuals responsible are (or were) closely associated with the institution or congregation. But just as often, they are mischievous or malicious juveniles. Some are people who, feeling they have been unfairly treated, vandalize to redress a slight or recover self-esteem. The investigator must follow all leads, even those that seem trivial. When religious property is the target, bigotry and hatred are usually the underlying motives, especially of older offenders; on the other hand, neo-Nazis, a younger group, also vandalize to express bigotry. Identifying the culprits can be difficult at best, unless an informant can be developed or an extensive surveillance conducted to catch them red-handed. A reward offered by church members may be helpful.

RECORDS

Some motives that drive a person to commit arson—intimidation, policy differences, emotions—may have been the consequence of an earlier provocation or quarrel requiring that the police be called. Depending on the circumstances, the altercation could be a matter of a formal police record or merely a note in the memo pad of the uniformed officer who responded. In either event, the investigator must be diligent in following through to determine if any recorded evidence exists to support a motive for arson. Other law enforcement records to be checked out include those on recently released prisoners who were convicted of arson, with special attention paid to their *modus operandi* and the kinds of targets involved.

Fire Records

As part and parcel of an arson suppression program, some fire departments have recognized the value of the computer to store and retrieve data on suspicious or deliberately set fires. A complete Fire Incident Report should include the following information:

- Location of the incident
- Time and day of the week that the incident occurred
- Name of the occupant(s) of the premises
- Name and address of the owner of the premises
- Area of fire origin
- Source of heat-causing ignition
- Type of material ignited
- Damage: whether it is restricted, or extends beyond confines of the structure
- Estimated damage in dollars

When such data are collected and stored routinely at the state level, it will be more difficult for "fire-prone" owners and those convicted of arson-for-profit to avoid detection of their previous behavior by keeping on the move. The investigator should know that the insurance industry in this country maintains a Property Insurance Loss Register that records the prior fire loss history of individuals. Although most of the data in the Fire Incident Report is obtained easily, an owner's name and address may not be (see section on "Straw Owners"). Many states have instituted immunity laws to promote sharing of insurance company records with criminal investigators. Such legislation would allow an interchange without penalizing the insurers for releasing client information.

Straw Owners

In arson cases, especially arson-for-profit, uncovering hidden ownership or financial interest in the burned property can be a formidable task. It is complicated by the incidence of *straw ownership*, whereby the individual or business entity on record (i.e., the *straw owner* or *straw*) is a front for the real owner. If not set up for illegal purposes, straw ownership is lawful; however, the arrangement often seems questionable—bordering on "sharp" or shady business practice. By seeking answers to the following questions, the real owner may be discovered:

- Who owns the building in which the "straw" lives?

- For whom does the straw work?

- What attorney, management company, notary public, contractor, or tax advisor does the straw hire? Are any of these people also hired by the straw's boss (at work) or landlord (at home)?

- Who collects the rents for the burned building? (It is often the real owner in the guise of the collector who does so instead of the straw, who may be unknown to the tenants).

Of those persons developed by the above line of inquiry, is there anyone whose financial affairs appear to be bordering on insolvency? Beacon signals to look for are:

- Bills that are not paid soon enough to qualify for the discount offered for prompt payment.

- Accounts receivable that are pledged to secure a loan or are sold at a high discount (20 to 40 percent) prior to their collection in the ordinary course of business.

- Taxes on (or collected by) the business that are not being paid as required by law (liens for unpaid taxes usually being a matter of public record).

If the business affairs of the suspect (who appears to be connected to the straw) seem in a state of potential insolvency, this obviously requires a follow-up. One approach would be to identify an employee who may feel insecure because of the downturn in the firm's financial strength, or who may otherwise be sufficiently disgruntled to be turned into an informant.

FOLLOW-UP ACTIVITIES

The investigation of arson—especially arson-for-profit—is a demanding task. The technical assistance of auditors, accountants, tax lawyers, real estate agents, and credit and financial managers will often be needed to get past the roadblocks set up to hide ownership of the property and the identity of the individual responsible. In such cases, circumstantial evidence may provide the basis upon which prosecution is possible. It can result from an admission that two separate fires in the premises occurred simultaneously; or from a finding that the door was locked, the occupant was present or in possession of the only key, and therefore had exclusive opportunity to start the fire. Opportunity may be established through canvassing: the suspect might have been seen in the area about the time the fire was first noticed.

Arson cases are also solved by direct evidence: the investigator observes the arsonist preparing to commit, or actually committing, the crime. To accomplish this, surveillance is obviously necessary. Undercover efforts can be effective. Posing as a jobless vagrant, for instance, allows the investigator to be ignored while observing the suspect entering or leaving a likely target just before the fire breaks out.

CASE ILLUSTRATION: INVESTIGATING ARSON

An apartment house fire killed two residents and injured many more. The criminal case that ensued comprises all the elements of a good arson investigation. The two investigators, responding within minutes of the early morning alarm and having had considerable experience uncovering evidence of arson, soon discovered a doormat soaked with gasoline lying before a ground floor apartment. This incriminatory finding permitted the area to be designated a crime scene. The street having been roped off and made secure, the injured awaiting ambulances on the sidewalk were questioned. Asked if she had any enemies, the female occupant of the target apartment suggested her former fiancé who was angry about their broken engagement and her refusal to return the ring.

With a motive provided and a potential suspect named, additional facts could now be sought to prove or disprove the hypothesis that the fiancé was the arsonist. When investigators learned that he lived within a short driving distance of the building, opportunity as well as motive could be considered. Piece by piece, their canvass of the fiancé's neighborhood gathered more information: a hardware store employee identified him from a photograph as the man who had purchased some gallon metal containers; and a service station attendant remembered (and identified) the individual who had filled cans with gasoline and the green Ford van in which the cans were placed.

Meanwhile during questioning the suspect continued to deny leaving home the night of the fire. Even though the relatives with whom he lived admitted he could have left without waking them, they had not heard him do so. The suspect also maintained that an unreliable fuel gauge in his van necessitated carrying extra gas. Investigators then questioned everyone who took part in the routine life of the street, including people making regular deliveries and those using it at odd hours. During the first neighborhood canvass, every doorbell had been rung and every resident interviewed; in the second canvass, any resident whose lights remained on after 1:30 A.M. were checked again.

As there were no witnesses who could place the suspect at the scene of the fire around the time it started, the only recourse for investigators was a stakeout of the street. Not until several days into the stakeout was their persistence rewarded: around 2:00 A.M. a young couple parked close to the arson scene and turned off the lights. The detectives waited approximately 10 minutes before tapping on the car's window. At first the car's occupants were reluctant to talk, then the woman responded to the nonthreatening form of the questions and the appeal for help in apprehending the criminal who had set the fire. The woman, having kept a wary eye on the street while parked there that night, remembered a green Ford van parked outside the apartment and its hurried departure just before flames flashed forth. This recollection not only placed the suspect at the scene, it established that he had the opportunity to commit the arson.

This case illustrates the value of proceeding with all speed to ascertain whether a fire was intentional. Motive was established by questioning the victims, causing one particular individual to emerge as the one responsible for setting the fire. This permitted investigators to channel their efforts, and by appropriate follow-up measures (canvass and surveillance), to determine if the suspect had the means and the intent to commit the crime. Means and intent were established by the newly purchased containers that were subsequently filled with gasoline. Opportunity was established through a stakeout of the crime scene area; maintained over several days, it finally produced an eyewitness. This case points to the importance of canvassing and surveillance, despite their costliness in time and salaries.

REFERENCES

1   *Sourcebook of Criminal Justice Statistics*, online. Table 3.178 <*http://www.albany.edu/source book/1995/pdf/t3178.pdf*>

2   *Juvenile Arson, 1997: OJJDP Fact Sheet, No. 91.* Washington, DC: U.S. Department of Justice, Office of Justice Programs, Office of Juvenile Justice and Delinquency Prevention, 1997.

3   J.D. De Haan, *Kirk's Fire Investigation*, 3rd ed. (Englewood Cliffs, NJ: Prentice-Hall, Brady Books, 1990), 106.

4   Ibid., 6-33.

5   Ibid., 34-66.

6   Ibid., 67-92.

7   J.D. De Haan, "Determining the Point of Origin—Diagnostic Signs and Laboratory Analysis," *Fire and Arson Investigator* 36 (June 1986).

8   De Haan, *Kirk's Fire Investigation, op. cit.,* 109-119.

9   D.V. Canfield, "Causes of Spalling of Concrete at Elevated Temperatures," *Fire and Arson Investigator* 34 (June 1984).

10   De Haan, *op cit.*, 135.

SUPPLEMENTAL READINGS

Carroll, John R. *Physical and Technical Aspects of Fire and Arson Investigation.* Springfield, IL: Charles C Thomas, 1983.

Carter, Robert E., and A.J. McKechnie. *Arson Investigation.* Beverly Hills, CA: Glencoe, 1978.

Cook, R., and R. Ide. *Principles of Fire Investigation.* Leicester, England: Institute of Fire Engineers, 1985.

DeHaan, John D. *Kirk's Fire Investigation.* 3rd ed. Englewood Cliffs, NJ: Prentice Hall (Brady Books), 1990.

Karchmer, Clifford L., James Greenfield, and Marilyn E. Walsh. *Enforcement Manual: Approaches for Combating Arson-for-Profit Schemes.* Washington, DC: U.S. Department of Justice, Law Enforcement Administration, 1980.

McCarney, William P., and Robert James Fischer. "Arson Investigation: One Means of Preventing Future Fires," in *Critical Issues in Criminal Investigation*, edited by Michael J. Palmiotto. Cincinnati: Anderson, 1988.

Noon, Randall. *Engineering Analysis of Fires and Explosions.* Boca Raton, FL: CRC Press, 1995.

O'Connor, John J., and David R. Redsicker (eds.). *Practical Fire and Arson Investigation.* 2nd ed. Boca Raton, FL: CRC Press, 1997.

Roblee, Charles L., and Allen J. McKechnie. *The Investigation of Fires.* 2nd ed. Englewood Cliffs, NJ: Prentice Hall, 1988.

Yallop, H.S. *Explosion Investigation.* Harrogate, North Yorkshire, UK: Forensic Science Society Press, 1980.

Yereance, Robert A. *Electrical Fire Analysis.* Springfield, IL: Charles C Thomas, 1987.

SECTION III

SPECIALIZED INVESTIGATIONS

This section considers some crimes that have shown an upsurge in recent times. To be investigated successfully, they will require sizeable resources, and may involve several law enforcement agencies. A satisfactory outcome depends on cooperation and coordination between all parties, best achieved if the parties have worked together in the past and gained mutual respect and trust.

Modus operandi, particularly in terrorism cases, has proved to be useful in establishing responsibility. Because the terrorist use of a bomb leaves physical evidence behind, diligent follow-up of such trace material can identify the offender (see pp. 52-53, the case of Pan Am Flight 103). For crimes involving computers, it is necessary to acquire considerable familiarity with this technology.

Some instructors may choose to deal with but one of these crimes; or perhaps none. If criminal investigation is taught as a two-semester course, then time should permit a discussion of all the chapters in Sections III and IV.

CHAPTER 19

Terrorism

INTRODUCTION

Terrorism investigations differ markedly from more traditional types of investigations, and the events of September 11, 2001, marked a significant change in the world's attitude toward political violence. Although a great emphasis has been placed in recent years on international terrorism, it is important to recognize that in the United States there continues to be a "home-grown" threat. Generally, terrorism falls into one or a combination of typologies. The more commonly accepted forms of terrorism include:

Violent political movements—These are generally separatist movements or efforts to destabilize governments. In many cases, such efforts may also be linked to religious or economic factors.

Single-issue or special-interest movements—These movements focus on a specific issue, such as anti-abortion, ecology, animal rights, or personal vendettas, usually against government agencies.

Racial or religious movements—These generally involve conflicts between religious, racial, or ethnic groups.

Global-economic movements—These include a newly emerging form of violence tied loosely to protests against international economic institutions and the disparity between rich and poor nations.

Hate group movements—This is a long-standing form of terrorist violence based upon the hatred of individuals of different racial, ethnic, or religious minorities. In recent years, there has emerged growing concern about the influence of immigrants.

There may be considerable overlap between these types of individuals or groups, but from an investigative standpoint it is important at times to be able to distinguish between the baseline motives of the principal actors involved in perpetrating violence. It is also important to recognize that in virtually all of these typologies there are likely to be large numbers of individuals who may be sympathetic to a cause but who do not do anything more than provide vocal support or participate in peaceful demonstrations. In a free society, freedom of speech and the right to protest are protected unless a law is broken. Undoubtedly, this may present some obstacles to an investigation, but this is an inherent right that must be protected. History has shown that one of the most significant reasons for individuals to embrace a movement is the abuse of police power.

Two aspects of terrorism should be of interest to the investigator. First is the recognition that terrorist activity has the capability to kill or injure large numbers of people. Second is the fact that the most effective investigations of terrorism are actually aimed at preventing the act from occurring (proactive). In most criminal cases, investigators are responding after a crime has been committed (reactive), and it is rare that investigations are mounted without some advance warning, usually in the form of intelligence analysis—a tip from an informant or an undercover operative.

Terrorist-related investigations should focus on those cases for which a proactive approach can work (before the incident occurs approach) and then deal with those cases after an incident occurs. Given the potential for widespread violence, as evidenced by the 2001 attacks on the World Trade Center in New York and the Pentagon in Washington, DC, the need for a proactive approach has become a high priority for law enforcement.

OVERVIEW

Prior to the September 11 attacks, the American public was lulled into the belief that terrorism was largely a problem that existed overseas. There was, of course, recognition by federal agencies and the intelligence community that the terrorist threat was greater than what was being reported in the media. The FBI, which had national responsibility for investigating domestic terrorism, focused efforts largely on internal groups and individuals who were believed to have ties to external terrorist organizations. Following the attacks on the World Trade Center and the Pentagon, the FBI and other agencies, such as the Central Intelligence Agency (CIA), were criticized for not sharing information as well as for a lack of cooperation in monitoring threats. The 2002 Joint Inquiry into Intelligence Community Activities Before and After the Terrorist Attacks of September 11, 2001, concluded that:

> While the Intelligence Community had amassed a great deal of valuable intelligence regarding Osama bin Ladin and his terrorist activities, none of it identified the time, place, and specific nature of the attacks that were planned for September 11, 2001. Nonetheless, the Community did have information that was clearly relevant to the September 11 attacks, particularly when considered for its collective significance.[1]

The most immediate response to 9/11 has been a complete reorganization of security efforts and the establishment of the Department of Homeland Security. As part of this massive national reorganization, greater awareness of the importance of state and local policing emerged, and millions of dollars have been expended at the state level to upgrade the capabilities of law enforcement at the local level. These endeavors had begun prior to the September 11 attacks with so-called "first responder training," but little effort had been devoted to information gathering and investigative efforts. Although major terrorist investigations continue to rest at the federal level, much is being done to involve local law enforcement.

Another component of the terrorist threat involved a greater awareness of the serious dangers of weapons of mass destruction, commonly referred to as the radiological, chemical, biological, and nuclear (RCBN) dimensions. When these are added to the more traditional tactics of terrorism, it is apparent that terrorist violence poses a major threat to global stability.

Figure 19.1 illustrates the types of attacks against American interests between 1981 and 2002. While the loss of life and injuries represent the most immediate concerns of government, 9/11 and several other recent incidents have illustrated the economic and quality-of-life threats posed by concerted terrorist activities. In this regard, the 9/11 experience has emerged as a guidebook or manual for future terrorist activity, illustrating the vulnerability of a free society to such threats.

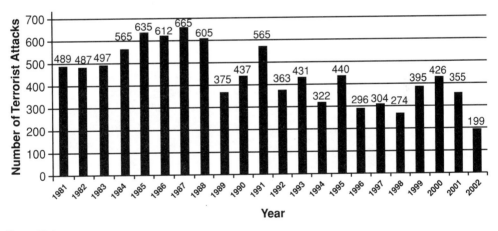

Figure 19.1
Total Terrorist Attacks 1981-2002

Over the years, the tactics, technology, and weapons used by terrorist groups have also changed. Although explosives continue to be the most frequently used weapons in the terrorist's arsenal, greater levels of sophistication (such as the use of aircraft in the 9/11 attack), the use of new timing and detonation devices, and the advent of more powerful explosives have increased the danger. In addition to this growing threat of radiological, chemical, biological, nuclear weapons, one must consider the impact of the Internet as a means of attacking or disabling both public- and private-sector computers. There is an emerging array of technology and sophisticated weaponry that is readily available to the committed terrorist group.

It is important to recognize that terrorism, like any other social phenomenon, has changed over the years. Much of the earlier research on terrorism and terrorists is outdated. For example, in the past, terrorist groups were quick to take credit for an act and seek media attention. Groups today are less likely to take credit for fear of being identified by investigators. Terrorists of the past also were likely to be college-educated, upper-middle-class youths. Such profiles are useless today, for involvement in terrorism covers a broad spectrum of society. In the past, there was likely to be a formal organized structure utilizing "cells" directed by a central authority. Today, most terrorist attacks in the United States are carried out by a small group, or even one or two individuals, whose ties to a formal organization are likely to be weak and whose acts are "individualized" and not part of a larger plan, except insofar as their views are consistent with those of a larger (usually law-abiding) organization. This is commonly referred to as "leaderless resistance."[2]

Modern-day or contemporary terrorism in the United States has its roots in the 1960s and 1970s during the Vietnam War, when a relatively few left-wing groups and political activists chose to use violence as a means of ending American involvement in the war. Internationally, modern-day terrorism is generally viewed as beginning with the terrorist attack on the Munich Olympics in 1972. Throughout the 1980s and 1990s, public perceptions of terrorism focused on events in the Middle East and Europe, although statistically the largest number of terrorist activities actually occurred in countries in South America.

Figure 19.2
Osama bin Laden, photographed in 1998, is the primary suspect in the attacks on the World Trade Center and the Pentagon. As a mastermind of the past decade's most barbaric acts of terrorism, he tops the FBI's most wanted terrorist list. Since the collapse of the Taliban regime, under whose protection he had been living in exile, he has been in hiding. *(AP Photo)*

As the nature and tactics of terrorism have changed over the years, so have the investigative approaches. The bombings of the World Trade Center in New York City in 1993 and the Alfred P. Murrah Federal building in Oklahoma City in 1995 should have served as warnings to the American people that large-scale destruction and loss of life through terrorist activities represented a clear threat for the future. Prior to these and the September 11 attacks, terrorism in the United States was largely attributed to fringe or splinter groups with a specific aim. Animal rights groups, anti-abortion attacks, militia movements, and hate crime violence perpetrated by so-called skinheads or right-wing extremists were the primary focus of investigators in the United States. Violence perpetrated against Americans and American interests abroad represented an international focus, but such attacks were generally not of concern in terms of domestic investigations.

Today, the United States faces new threats organized by international terrorists operating alone or in cells, sometimes supported by rogue governments, or by wealthy private individuals from countries friendly to the United States (e.g., Saudi Arabia). Perhaps the most notorious of such individuals is Osama bin Laden, who is accused of funding and organizing terrorist attacks against American interests abroad through a loose confederation of global terrorist groups tied to his al Qaeda network.

In 1999 there were 21 Joint Terrorism Task Forces (JTTFs) throughout the United States, consisting of federal agents and state and local law enforcement officers working together with other elements of the criminal justice system to investigate and prosecute a broad range of criminal activities that fall under the umbrella of terrorism. Today the

Figure 19.3
Investigators sift through the rubble on the ground at the Alfred P. Murrah Federal Building bombing site in Oklahoma City. Reports indicate that the April 1995 truck bomb blast killed 168 people and injured 599. The destructive effects of this explosion were obvious. Less obvious has been the meticulous detail and investigative expertise involved in bringing the perpetrator to justice. *(AP Photo/John Kuntz.)*

number of task forces has more than tripled to 66. They are found in every large city in the country. A National JTTF was established in 2002 in Washington, DC, which includes representatives from nearly 30 different agencies. A Foreign Terrorist Tracking Task Force (FTTTF) and the Office of Law Enforcement Coordination were established in 2001 and also play significant roles in terrorist-related investigations.

Defining Terrorism

Although there are a number of definitions of terrorism, each includes in some way the phrase, "the use of force or the threat of force to achieve a political end." In recent years this has been modified in some sectors to read "to achieve a political or criminal end." So-called narco-terrorism (drug traffic–related terrorist acts), gray-area phenomena, and various forms of extortion are embraced in this broader definition. International terrorism in the United States directed against citizens and interests from abroad was brought about by groups that committed crimes in an effort to change American policies. Some of these acts have been supported by representatives of foreign governments.

There are many definitions of terrorism that, from an investigative standpoint, are virtually meaningless because they are vague and do not provide a clear *corpus delicti* for the crime. For purposes of this text, terrorism can be defined as the use of force or the fear of force to achieve a political or criminal end. Another definition, offered by the Vice President's Task Force on Combating Terrorism, provides some further clarification:

> [Terrorism] is the unlawful use or threat of violence against persons or property to further political or social objectives. It is generally intended to intimidate or coerce a government, individuals or groups to modify their behavior or policies.[3]

These definitions currently provide a framework that encompasses relatively new legislation that includes more traditional types of crime under the Patriot Act and other legal entities in the Homeland Security framework. Local law enforcement's investigative activities may be more likely to focus on the more traditional crimes. The most common types of crimes in this area include:

- Conspiracy

- Murder (assassination)

- Kidnapping

- Hijacking (skyjacking)

- Bombing/arson

- Robbery

- Extortion

- Manufacturing or possessing radiological, chemical, biological, or nuclear weapons or the materials necessary to make them.

- Raising funds for terrorist groups as designated by the Secretary of State

Ultimately, media exposure and world events have contributed to greater public awareness of terrorism as a public policy issue. The investigation of terrorist activity has increasingly become a concern to law enforcement. Responsibility for crime scene protection and preliminary investigations rests largely with local law enforcement because they are the first to respond. Successful investigations depend on a high degree of cooperation between local, state, and federal officials, as well as cooperation between geographic jurisdictions and, in some cases, countries.

What makes terrorism crimes different than others is that they are frequently carried out by groups or individuals within a group, the motive for them is not usually monetary gain (except as a means to support the movement), they are frequently well-planned, and the acts themselves are designed to achieve some political aim.

Narco-terrorism, a relatively new criminal activity, is an exception to the general rule that monetary gain is not a motivation. Although narco-terrorism is more closely associated with criminal cartels in Central America and South America, there is an increasing use of violence related to illegal drugs in the United States. The difference between drug-related violence and narco-terrorism lies in the fact that the latter involves the use of terror to achieve a political aim. In Colombia, for instance, the goal of the drug cartels has been to try to force the Colombian government to stop extradition of criminals to the United States. In the United States, gangs and other groups involved in drug trafficking use violence to intimidate communities or eliminate witnesses.

LEGAL ASPECTS

Over the years, the U.S. Congress has passed legislation that relates specifically to terrorism. Most recently has been the so-called USA Patriot Act. (HR 3162) Among other things, this legislation makes it a federal crime to:

- Hijack or destroy a foreign aircraft outside the United States and take refuge in the United States.

- Use violence against any passenger on board a civilian or government aircraft.

- Commit a crime against a federal official.

- Travel interstate or use foreign transportation to commit murder or assassination.

- Train foreign nationals in the use of firearms, munitions, or explosives.

- Murder a hostage.

- Kidnap, assault, or murder a United States citizen outside the country, if the suspect is returned to the United States.[4]

The U.S. Congress also passed the Public Health Security and Bioterrorism Preparedness and Response Act of 2002 (HR 3448), which places greater controls on protection of food and water, enhances controls on biological agents and toxic substances, and establishes new powers for several levels of government, including the Department of Agriculture and the Food and Drug Administration.

There is no international convention on the prevention and suppression of terrorism as a whole, but conventions do exist to address related issues. An initiative titled the International Convention for the Suppression of the Financing of Terrorism was introduced by the United Nations in 2000. In order for it to go into effect, at least 22 nationals must have signed and ratified it. The convention is designed to ask governments to freeze the funds of terrorist groups and prohibit arguments that criminal acts committed by groups are justified on political, racial, ethnic, or religious grounds. It also calls for the extradition of persons found guilty of handling financial services for terrorist groups.

In general, there are two categories of conventions:

1. Specialized conventions, focusing on certain types of offenses, such as:

    A. The 1973 New York Convention, which addressed diplomats and other protected persons.

    B. The 1979 New York Convention, which addressed the taking of hostages and defined hostage-taking as:

    > To seize or detain and threaten to kill or injure another person in order to compel a third party to accomplish an act or abstain from doing it.

C.   Conventions on air piracy, including:

- The 1944 Chicago Convention on International Civil Aviation.

- The 1963 Tokyo Convention on Offenses and Certain other Acts Committed on Board Aircraft.

- The 1970 Hague Convention for the Supression of Unlawful Seizure of Aircraft.

- The 1971 Montréal Convention for the Suppression of Unlawful Acts against the Safety of Civil Aviation.

2.   Regional conventions that may cover terrorism, including:

- The 1952 Extradition Convention adopted by the League of Arab Countries.

- The 1971 Convention adopted by the Organization of American States designed to prevent and punish terrorism

- The 1977 European Convention of the Suppression of Terrorism, adopted by the Council of Europe.

The United States has federal legislation that calls for extraterritorial jurisdiction for terrorist acts abroad:

1.   The Comprehensive Crime Control Act of October 12, 1984, USC 18 par. 1203, relates to hostage taking.

2.   The Omnibus Diplomatic Security and Antiterrorism Act of August 27, 1986, USC 18, par. 2331, provides for:

> Federal jurisdiction in certain offenses (murder, involuntary manslaughter, physical violence, conspiracy) committed outside the United States if the offense was to "coerce, intimidate, or retaliate against a government or civilian population."

3.   Uniting and Strengthening America by Providing Appropriate Tools Required to Intercept and Obstruct Terrorism Act of 2001 (the USA Patriot Act). (Pub. L. 107-56, 115 Sat 272 [effective October 26, 2001])

> This act greatly broadened powers of the government to conduct electronic wiretaps, mail covers, monitoring of foreign nationals, and other investigative tools in the investigation of terrorism.

The federal government continues to endeavor to pass new legislation designed to strengthen laws related to terrorism. Many other countries have also passed legislation related to terrorism that enables greater cooperation, communication, and intelligence gathering between nations.

Constraints on Intelligence-Gathering Activities

In the early 1970s, Congress (as well as various individuals and organizations) expressed concern about domestic security investigations. In an effort to curb the overzealous efforts of some investigative personnel, several United States Attorneys General have issued guidelines to regulate domestic intelligence gathering. Some federal district courts have entered judgment orders (consent decrees) for the same purpose. The fundamental concern is the threat to First Amendment rights posed by domestic intelligence operations. The problem is finding a way to separate those who are legitimately protesting or dissenting from those who go outside the law by carrying out the threat of violence or inciting others to do so. A "reasonable suspicion" standard is applied to determine whether an investigation may be undertaken to gather evidence concerning suspected criminal conduct that has occurred, is occurring, or is about to occur. Reasonable suspicion may be defined as "the belief of a reasonably prudent person, based on specific, articulate facts, that an investigation is justified to determine if 'probable cause' exists to issue a warrant, or to support some other appropriate police action."[5] By specifying the criteria used to select the targets of the investigation, criticism of proactive investigations can be softened or eliminated.

The USA Patriot Act authorized a broader approach to the interception of electronic information than had been in force before. Cases involving terrorism investigations permit disclosure of more noncontent information than is permissible in other types of criminal investigations. The Act, which applies to Internet service providers, "can force the disclosure of a subscriber's name; address; local and long distance telephone connection records, or records of session times and duration, length of service (including start date and types of service utilized; telephone or instrument number or other subscriber number or identity, including any temporary assigned network address; and means and source of payment for such service of a subscriber."[6]

Court Proceedings

Terrorist planning and tactics have become more sophisticated with regard to the American legal system, and both domestic and foreign terrorists have used the courts to further propaganda, as well as to use various legal strategies and disruption of proceedings to hamper prosecution efforts. For this reason, it is extremely important that investigators pay particular attention to rules of evidence, maintenance of detailed records, and procedural requirements in case preparation.

William Dyson, a former FBI agent with more than 20 years of experience in supervising terrorist investigations, notes that:

> Investigators should be well prepared when they testify in court. They should not be surprised if they are asked about aspects of the Constitution or about their "Oath of Office. They should also not be surprised if they are asked if they have committed any illegal activities during the course of the investigation. If an officer has acted in an undercover capacity during the case, he will probably be questioned in detail about entrapment issues.[7]

In some cases, defendants have refused to accept the legal system and have disrupted proceedings, frequently supported by followers. In others, they have filed civil actions against officers. In still others, they have used the courts to gather information about investigative methods, undercover operatives or informants, and a variety of legal tactics. Stalling procedures are not uncommon.

TERRORISM INVESTIGATIONS

Terrorism investigations have a number of unique characteristics that set them apart from more traditional approaches. To begin with, the investigator assigned to such investigations must have a high tolerance for lengthy stakeouts and surveillance, be mindful of minor details and seemingly insignificant information, and be willing to shun publicity. He or she must recognize the importance of teamwork and cooperation, be thoroughly familiar with technology and the use of computers, and have an appreciation for detail. Terrorist investigations are usually lengthy and may involve months or even years of painstaking effort.

The success of a terrorist investigation depends largely on intelligence and analysis. It is likely to involve numerous individuals operating over large geographic areas, who are usually suspicious and watchful of surveillance. The investigator must take copious notes and keep detailed records, which may prove crucial not only in making a case but also in developing a successful prosecution. Unlike most criminal investigations, if at all possible, a case must be made before the criminal act is carried out. The successful investigation will result in charges of conspiracy (if more than one person is involved) and charges for an *attempted* crime, such as attempted murder. The point at which an arrest is made may well depend on circumstantial evidence, which will no doubt complicate prosecution. For this reason, physical evidence (i.e., explosives or receipts of purchase) and record keeping are important. The investigator must be able to explain why or how actions of a suspect can be linked to the crime charged. For example, the fact that a person says he wishes someone is dead, and then goes out and purchases bomb-making equipment, follows a potential victim or "cases" a location, and purchases a one-way ticket to Timbuktu may well establish a *prima facie* case.

When an investigation takes place after a crime has been committed, it is important to identify the group that is responsible right away. Frequently, there are a number of groups that take credit for an act, so efforts must be made to sort out prank calls or those of imposter groups. Incidents involving known groups or suspects necessitate reviewing all of the information that is available both in police files and from other sources. Many radical groups now have Internet web sites, which should be routinely monitored.

At the scene of a terrorist incident, care should be taken with regard to secondary devices that may be planted to explode after the police arrive in response to the first explosion or call. Crime-scene investigators should also be aware that "booby traps" might be planted. Once a crime scene has been secured, it is important to conduct a thorough search. Because there is a high probability that there will be another incident, reconstructing the event may be very important. For example, one should ask: where was the explosive device planted, how was it delivered, was there a warning, and was it designed to inflict personal injury or property damage? Some terrorist groups will give the police a "code word" that can be used in future communications to convince authorities that they are the actual perpetrators. It is important to try to open and maintain communication in whatever form possible. This may include telephones, mail, the Internet, or even uninformed messengers.

The actual investigation of an incident will frequently include different agencies or organizations. Accordingly, a central command office should be established. Most large cities now have command and control facilities that are well equipped. Of particular importance is the availability of telephones, computers, and peripheral equipment (e.g., scanners). Personnel trained in the use of databases and who are familiar with ways to draw information from computerized databanks should also be available. It is imperative that all information collected in the investigation be centralized in some manner. Because the investigation may involve more then one incident, the ability to conduct comparative computer data analyses is vital.

Terrorist Suspects

The primary difference between terrorist-related investigations and more traditional investigations is in the use of intelligence. Because individuals involved in terrorist acts are likely to be part of a larger group, and their activities are more likely to range over large geographical areas (between states or even countries), there is a strong need for communication and coordination between organizations and governments. Thus, intelligence represents a key element in the investigative process.

Further, because different individuals may be involved in specific criminal acts of the group, the *modus operandi* associated with a particular crime may vary from act to act. For this reason, it becomes important to know about:

1.   a group's stated goals;

2.   its organizational structure;

3.   its membership;

4.   its tactical approach;

5.   its means of communication;

6.   its methods of raising funds; and

7.   its propensity for violence.

It is, of course, important to know who is in the group. It is essential, though, to be aware that this can create special problems. There are restrictions on keeping records concerning innocent people who may be supportive of the group's aims but who are opposed to criminal activity.

In order to develop a file on an individual or a group, it is generally necessary to establish a *prima facie* case establishing the probability that a crime has occurred or is about to occur, or that there is a conspiracy among specific individuals to commit a crime. An exception to this is when the investigative action is less restricted.

Successful investigation of terrorist groups requires patience, skill, and cooperation. For this reason, the task-force approach offers the highest probability of success. Teams working together can compile a considerable amount of information and, when aided by an analyst, can do much more than a single individual or a group of individuals acting independently.

If a group has been identified as a criminal organization, every effort should be made to collect as much information as possible about the group and its members. A fine line must be observed. For example, a great many people are involved in the animal rights movement, yet only a few are committed to violence. How then does the investigator make a distinction between legitimate protest and criminal activity? First, one must be familiar with aims and goals of the group and, even more importantly, with the tactics it espouses to carry out its aims. If the literature of the group calls for illegal acts, such as destruction of property or injury to persons, there are reasonable grounds to investigate further. One must keep in mind that it is not illegal to espouse the overthrow of a government. It is, however, illegal to support and conspire to commit an illegal act in an attempt to carry out that goal.

Observing the behavior of individuals in a group can be productive. Rather than focusing on everyone in the group (an approach sometimes used in the past), attention should be given to individuals who go beyond mere protest and civil disobedience. Individuals involved in domestic terrorism in the United States will frequently display a pattern of activity that begins with protesting, moves on to civil disobedience, and escalates to committing assaults or other significant crimes, such as destruction of property. Often acting out of frustration with their inability to sway the political process, such individuals are likely to progress to more serious crimes. In many cases, this will mean more extensive destruction of property, usually without the intent to injure. In the final phase of their transition, they justify murder to accomplish their goals. The point at which a person moves beyond civil disobedience is the stage at which further investigation is warranted.

When an individual or group becomes the subject of an investigation, an effort must be made to understand the psychological dimensions involved. A background investigation can provide information on an individual's arrest history, psychological makeup, friends and acquaintances, technical skills (such as the use of weapons or explosives), military service, prior experience or employment, geographical movement, and economic status. Observation of the individual will provide information of daily habits, contacts, employment, knowledge of the city or community, and commitment to the group or cause.

Investigations involving foreign nationals may prove more difficult because the background of a foreign subject is more difficult to determine and, in the case of state-sponsored terrorists or those belonging to a known terrorist group, they may be trained to avoid detection. In such cases, the investigative team frequently must depend on information from the community, other law enforcement agencies, or informants or undercover operatives. Most immigrants and foreign nationals living in the United States have no desire to support terrorists. However, they may have a fear of cooperation with law enforcement because of negative experiences with police in their country of origin. Developing informants is thus an important but difficult task.

Although informants are helpful, the investigator should be aware that such individuals may have their own motives for cooperating. Paid informants may give false information in order to stay on the payroll; criminal informants may give false information to protect themselves or others.

Undercover operatives working in other areas, particularly narcotics, organized crime, or gunrunning, frequently will have information on potential terrorists. For this reason, it is important to maintain good contacts with other units within the local police organization, as well as with federal and state authorities working in this area. Drug Enforcement Administration (DEA) and Alcohol, Tobacco, Firearms, and Explosives (ATF) agents, customs officers, postal inspectors, and immigration officials all can be helpful.

The investigation of foreign nationals also suffers because of language differences. An investigative team working against Middle Eastern terrorists, for example, is at a great disadvantage if members of the team do not speak Arabic. Similarly, a team investigating Puerto Rican terrorists will not be very effective if no team member understands Spanish. Information often comes from members of a specific ethnic community, most of whom are wary of police and/or do not have a strong command of the English language. When language skills are absent or poor, an effort should be made to identify individuals who can speak more than one language. Maintaining a department "skills index" is useful.

In addition to knowing the language used in a group, the investigator should understand the culture of the individual or group under investigation. Although this may be obvious with regard to foreign nationals, it is important to recognize that there are a great many cultural differences in the United States that are not necessarily ethnically based. These range from regional differences, to neighborhood, racial, occupational, and educational differences.

Some international terrorist groups will cooperate with each other in matters such as recruit training and information sharing. Some will even join forces to carry out a particular deed, or one group may act on behalf of another. Similarly, effective action against international terrorism requires the coordinated efforts of the central governments of nations and the cooperation of law enforcement agencies in each country. They will be assisted by INTERPOL, the international, voluntary organization of police agencies headquartered in France. INTERPOL's purpose is to assist and improve police cooperation and the exchange of information between 181 member countries. With the capability of working in four languages—French, English, Spanish, and Arabic—messages and inquiries are received and transmitted to the proper authorities, data is computerized, and text may be retrieved in English. INTERPOL routinely files requests for help in tracing passports; identifying weapons, explosives, and vehicles; and identifying persons, whether victims or criminals. Additional services include establishing links between cases; obtaining information about suspected terrorists, their criminal records, and proper identification; and circulating warning notices about suspects who have committed or are likely to commit terrorist activities.

Another potential source of information is the patrol force that works in the community every day. However, it is important to brief the beat officers on things to be aware of and watch for. A progressive training program will address the collection of information by the patrol force and other investigators.

When a terrorist event has taken place, the preliminary investigation should make every effort to identify potential witnesses, particularly people who may have been in the vicinity prior to the event. In many cases, the perpetrators of terrorist acts will survey the area prior to the incident. Their actions may have been observed by witnesses, who frequently may be located through a canvass of the neighborhood after the crime. Security cameras both inside and outside of the buildings have become so commonplace that a canvass of such security devices should be made in the vicinity. They may have recorded the terrorists as they "cased" the target or as they actually perpetrated the crime.

Physical Evidence

One of the most important components of terrorist-related investigations is the collection and preservation of physical evidence. A terrorist attack necessitates careful analysis and examination not only of the immediate crime scene but of the surrounding area and locations where the suspects may have conducted surveillance or used as a hideout or a safe house (a rendezvous point free of surveillance or used for illegal activities such as making bombs). Meticulous examination of the debris from the 1993 bombing of the World Trade Center resulted in the discovery of a piece of the rear frame rail that bore the vehicle identification number (VIN) of the suspect vehicle, which led to the first break in the case.

Because terrorist activities are usually carried out by more than one individual, it may prove important to establish each individual's activities or whereabouts through physical evidence. In some cases, one individual will carry the explosives or weapon to the scene, another may place the explosives or carry out the attack, and yet another may detonate the bomb or, if necessary, remove the weapon. Still another may leave the communiqué or otherwise make the claim.

The collection of physical evidence is covered in general in Chapter 3. However, it should be noted that in terrorist investigations items that appear to have no relevance may prove to be critical at a later time. During the investigation of the Baader-Meinhoff gang in Germany, the Bundeskriminalamt (BKA) (which is similar in many ways to the FBI in the United States) made it a policy to record every item collected at the scene of a crime or from a safe house used by terrorists. This evidence was entered into a computer, making it possible to compare and recognize similarities and variations among locations. These painstaking efforts over time made it possible to track the movements, identify the habits, and establish the presence of individuals. The presence of a can of cocoa commonly used by one of the terrorists at one scene made it possible to identify the individual who used it. By tracing the manufacturer's code to identify the town and eventually the store where it was bought, investigators were led to the safe house occupied by the suspects. A similarly thorough examination of the crime scene where the Irish Republican Army (IRA) attempted to murder England's Prime Minister Margaret Thatcher resulted in the identification of a small piece of trace evidence that eventually helped convict one of the offenders. Investigators literally sifted through the ruins of the demolished hotel. In yet another case, the minute examination of the scattered debris and particularly the detonating device left from the bombing of a Pan American flight over Lockerbie, Scotland, made it possible to help identify the most likely perpetrators.

Most terrorist acts involve bombing, kidnapping (hostage taking), or assassination. Each of these acts provides different forms of physical evidence. The following review focuses on terrorist activities and should be reviewed along with other chapters on physical evidence—particularly Chapters 2 and 3.

Bombings

When a threatened or actual bombing is reported, an after-the-fact investigation is begun in reaction to the incident. More often than not, however, the perpetrators are not arrested. A proactive approach has proved more productive in arresting and convicting those responsible for terrorist bombings. Both kinds of investigation—reactive and proactive—will be used to illustrate how physical evidence, people, and records contribute to solving such cases.

Explosives

Several types of explosives are used by terrorists. In the United States the most common explosive has been a pipe bomb using black powder. The materials necessary to make a pipe bomb are readily available in most countries and can be purchased in drug stores, hardware stores, and construction supply stores (see Figure 19.4). In the 1993 World Trade Center explosion, a urea nitrate bomb was used. In Oklahoma City, the bomb consisted of a mixture ammonium nitrate and fuel oil (called Anfo). Although homemade bombs have been used frequently, the availability of other types of explosives—particularly dynamite, TNT, and hand grenades—makes their use in the future more likely. Some types of explosive devices include:

> SEMTEX—A yellowish plastic explosive, SEMTEX is about one-third more powerful than a similar amount of TNT. It has a texture like clay putty or clay, and can be molded. It is easy to transport because it will not explode without a detonator. SEMTEX has been manufactured in Czechoslovakia with equal parts of RDX and PETN.

> C-4—Similar to SEMTEX, C4 is a plastic explosive (which can be manufactured in solid or powder form) made in the United States and used by the U.S. Army and many allies, as well as by mining companies. It explodes at 26,400 feet per second.

> HME (Home Made Explosives)—Home-made explosives usually involve the use of fertilizer. See Ammonium Nitrate.

> Pipe Bomb—A pipe bomb is a device built with a length of pipe stuffed with explosive (usually black powder) and shrapnel, such as nails or BBs, sealed at both ends and fitted with a detonator.

Plutonium-229— Plutonium-229 is radioactive material that, when of weapons-grade quality, can be used in the making of nuclear bombs.

TNT (Trinitrotoluene)—TNT is approximately twice as powerful as common dynamite, It has a lower explosive velocity than plastic explosives. It is made of nitric and sulfuric acid, and toluene. It is readily available in the United States and is usually produced in half-pound and one-pound sticks.

Ammonium Nitrate—Ammonium nitrate is a common fertilizer that when mixed with diesel fuel has an explosive velocity of 3,600 feet per second. The bomb is "triggered" by a detonator, which is used to introduce an electrical charge, which causes the explosive to ignite. Detonation may be achieved in a number of ways, including using a timing mechanism, electronically or by a fuse—all of which complete an electric (usually battery-operated) circuit in some way.

Detonation of an explosive device results in three primary effects: fragmentation, blast pressure, and fire. Fragmentation bombs produce shrapnel and are designed to be used against people. Homemade fragmentation bombs include such items as nails, steel ball bearings, or other materials that spread out over the blast area. The blast from any explosive is capable of killing; the greater the amount of explosive used, the greater the damage. In addition, the very placement of the bomb can be designed to create a fragmentation explosion. A car bomb, for example, will create shrapnel from the metal parts as the vehicle is torn apart.

Figure 19.4
A typical pipe bomb, a type of explosive commonly used by terrorists. *(Courtesy, Cmdr. Joseph Grubisic, Bomb Squad, Chicago Police Department.)*

Some explosives can be traced through markers that are placed in the material by the manufacturer, making it possible to trace the source of the explosive. However, this identification is limited largely to dynamite or TNT, and the large quantity used for industrial purposes may hamper tracing.

Some common types of bomb attacks include:

Car bombs: *Car bombs* are used to kill the occupants of a vehicle, to kill individuals in close proximity to the vehicle, or as so-called "suicide" bombs in which a driver runs a vehicle into a facility or crowd of people or parks the vehicle near a target.

Fragmentation bombs: As noted earlier, fragmentation bombs are designed to kill or maim people. Like homemade bombs, hand grenades, mines, and other antipersonnel devices, they are becoming more common.

Letter bombs: Letter bombs consist of a relatively small amount of explosive but enough to kill or maim. The explosive is placed in an envelope or package and is wired to detonate when it is opened. A bomb of this type killed a federal judge in Alabama in 1989.

Aircraft bombs: Aircraft bombs are usually designed to explode when the aircraft is in the air, ideally over water, which makes evidence recovery difficult. Various means (air pressure, timing, suicide bomber, etc.) may be used to detonate the explosives.

It is not uncommon for terrorists to plant a second explosive device designed to kill police or military officials who respond to the scene. Great care must be taken in responding to and protecting the scene. An investigator should never try to process a bomb scene until trained bomb disposal technicians have cleared the area.

Figure 19.5
The "Jony" bomb, used by Tamil Rebels in Sri Lanka, is an example of a simple pressure-sensitive device placed in roadways or outside doors. The mine explodes when stepped on. More than 1,000 soldiers and police officers have had their legs blown off by this device.

Missiles

In addition to the typical types of bomb attacks, the availability of various forms of military hardware poses an increasing threat. An RPG (rocket propelled grenade) or shoulder-mounted missile, such as the Stinger, can bring down a plane or can be fired into a building from a distance. Because these devices are usually fired from discardable tubes, fingerprints and other trace evidence may be available.

Weapons of Mass Destruction

Nuclear

The prospect of a terrorist organization acquiring a nuclear device, or even radiological material, is one of the most frightening scenarios for which law enforcement must prepare. Even a low-level nuclear attack (for instance, a 30-pound nuclear warhead detonated in a suitcase) would have yields as low as 50 tons (high explosive equivalent) to tens of kilotons, several times the size of the first nuclear weapons that were dropped on Hiroshima and Nagasaki.

In a nuclear terrorist event, the hazards are thermal radiation, blast or shock effect, and nuclear radiation. Obviously, the most protective measure is to be as far away from the blast or burst as possible. For nuclear radiation, both distance and shielding help for the initial radiation, which consists of penetrating gamma and beta radiation. Residual nuclear radiation is commonly referred to as fallout; it consists of particles dangerous to inhale or get on the skin (gamma, alpha, and beta particles). Individuals who survive a blast will be immediately affected by radiation poisoning and will experience the following symptoms: fever, nausea, vomiting, lack of appetite, bloody diarrhea, hair loss, subcutaneaous bleeding, sores in their throat or mouth (nasopharyngeal ulcers), and decay and ulceration of the gums about the teeth (necrotic gingivitis). High rates of radiation exposure often result in death.

It is important to point out that the likelihood of a terrorist organization employing nuclear terrorism is relatively low. This is because terrorists are generally rational actors that are seeking to accomplish a political goal rather than killing for the sake of killing. Further, the logistical support needed to acquire, transport, and detonate a nuclear device is substantial, and most terrorist organizations would be unable to accomplish this without a state sponsor. It is unlikely that a state would be willing to risk facing a full military reprisal if it supported a nuclear attack on the United States.

Biological

There are many advantages for terrorists who would like to use biological weapons, namely the availability of biological agents and the ease with which they can be transported. Unlike with nuclear devices, technical knowledge necessary to use biological agents is practically nonexistent. There are no technical experts or high-technology laboratories required, and the costs would be minimal. When one considers the public panic that followed the October 2001 anthrax letters*, it appears likely that the resulting panic caused from a coordinated biological weapons attack will increase the impact of the operation as well as the reputation of the terrorist organization. The four main types of biological agents are:

- *Anthrax*—An acute infectious disease caused by the spore-forming bacterium *Bacillus anthracis*. Anthrax most commonly occurs in wild and domestic lower vertebrates (cattle, sheep, goats, camels, antelopes, and other herbivores), but it can also occur in humans when they are exposed to infected animals or tissue from infected animals.

- *Ricin*—Ricin is a poison that can be made from waste left over from processing castor beans. It can be in the form of a powder, a mist, or a pellet, or dissolved in water or weak acid. Death from ricin poisoning could occur within 36 to 48 hours of exposure, whether by inhalation, ingestion, or injection. Exposed people who live longer than five days without complications will probably survive. In February 2004, three Senate office buildings were closed because ricin was found in a mailroom. A tiny amount of ricin can be deadly, but unlike anthrax, it is very difficult to spread through the air.

- *Botulism*—There are three main kinds of botulism. Food-borne botulism is caused by eating foods that contain the botulism toxin. Wound botulism is caused by a toxin produced from a wound infected with *Clostridium botulinum*. Infant botulism is caused by consuming the spores of the botulinum bacteria, which then grow in the intestines and release toxin. All forms of botulism can be fatal and are considered medical emergencies. Food-borne botulism can be especially dangerous because many people can be poisoned by eating a contaminated food.

---

* Several letters containing anthrax were received in the United States in October 2001, resulting in some illnesses and deaths from inhalation anthrax. The identified source letters were mailed in late September or the first week of October.

- *Smallpox*—Smallpox s contagious and sometimes fatal. A virus called *variola* causes smallpox. Smallpox spreads slowly, usually by face-to-face contact for an hour or more with a contagious person. It can also be spread by contact with inanimate objects (such as clothing, towels, linens), but this is uncommon.

Chemical

Although deadly chemical attacks have not been used in the United States, they do pose a threat. In 1995, a poison gas called Sarin was used in Tokyo subway system, killing 11 people and injuring hundreds more. Sarin and Tabun are nerve agents that kill by short-circuiting the nervous system. Odorless and colorless, they enter the body by inhalation or through the skin. Symptoms include intense sweating, lung congestion, dimming of vision, vomiting, diarrhea, and convulsions. Death comes in minutes or hours. An atropine sulphate injection can counter the respiratory paralysis of nerve gas. Along the same lines, butyric acid, which gives off a noxious odor and is difficult to remove, has been used in attacks on abortion clinics. Mustard gas causes sores on the skin and sears damp surfaces, eyes, lungs, and open sores. It can kill in a short period of time at very high doses or can maim a victim. Evidence recovered in Afghanistan indicated that the Taliban and al Qaeda were experimenting with chemical agents, and such an attack cannot be ruled out in the future.

PROACTIVE INVESTIGATIONS

A proactive investigation focuses on the gathering of evidence that proves (or disproves) the involvement of a suspected perpetrator in a crime. In most proactive investigations, the subject has a criminal record with several convictions for the same crime. Terrorism by bombing in the United States as yet has seen few persons convicted, much less released, who may be the subject of a proactive investigation. Nevertheless, there are organizations whose members are capable of terrorist bombings. The problem facing those directing a proactive investigation is frequently trying to determine which members should be the subjects of the investigation.

Because at least some members of a terrorist organization are likely to be known, painstaking surveillance can result in identifying others who may not be known. Accordingly, for this and other reasons, terrorists generally employ counter-surveillance measures—an activity generally unknown to (and certainly not practiced by) the average citizen. For example, terrorists may commit repeated traffic violations (going through a red light, driving the wrong way on a one way street, speeding, and so on) coupled with other counter-surveillance techniques (turning into a cul-de-sac) in order to detect surveillance. Such activity, combined with behavior such as using disguises or taking two hours to make a trip that should require less than 20 minutes, indicates that the subject under surveillance, as well as those people whom he or she is in contact, is worth following. Observing other suspects engaged in similar conduct will aid in the construction of a terrorist group or cell profile.

A person who is close to the members of the suspected organization, or who has been arrested for terrorist activities or another crime, can sometimes be turned into an informant. This type of person is often able to provide information that assists in further developing a profile of a terrorist bomber. By placing suspects who fit this profile under surveillance, it is possible that the investigator will finally be led to the safe house or bomb factory. If the location is an apartment building or other multi-party residence or building, further delicate investigation is required to determine which unit is being used without scaring the neighbors or warning the terrorist. The person who pays the rent and utility bills may serve in that capacity only or may be involved somehow in constructing the bombs.

At some point in the investigation, it may be necessary to persuade a judge that there is probable cause to issue a warrant for placing a listening device in the suspected premises. Because terrorists engaged in making bombs have been known to pass written notes rather than speak to each other, it may become necessary to seek a warrant to install a video camera in the suspected premises (see Chapter 9 on surveillance). The evidence obtainable through such intrusion can be overwhelming and may provide the proof necessary for an arrest and ultimately a conviction.

REACTIVE INVESTIGATIONS

Traditionally, after-the-fact investigations of a bomb explosion focus on the site of the detonation in order to recover as many parts of the bomb or its carrier as possible. Similarly, if a telephoned bomb threat is received and the bomb is discovered before it was set to go off (or if it was defective and failed to explode), considerable investigative effort is required. Following through on collecting and examining this valuable evidence can yield important results:

1. A part of parts of the bomb may be traced to the source (manufacturer down to retailer). Similarly, a VIN from the vehicle used to carry explosive to a bomb site may be discovered following detonation by examining each piece of metal found at and near the scene.

2. If a series of bombings has occurred, they may be linked to show a common origin. Clues from each event then may be pooled to further the investigation.

3. Bomb parts recovered at the scene can be compared to similar parts or materials found in the bomb factory if and when one is finally located.

4. Extensive research over the past decade on the characteristics and properties of different types of bombs has led to the creation of data banks designed to aid investigators. The Energetic Materials Research and Testing Center (EMRTC) at New Mexico Institute of Mining and Technology (New Mexico Tech), which conducts counter-terrorism studies, have carried out much of this research. Such research frequently makes it possible to determine the amounts and types of explosives used, their relationship to other physical evidence, and their origin.

Individuals who might possess useful information become known to the investigators through diverse sources.

1. An organization may lay claim (through a telephone call or a letter distributed by the mass media) to having placed the bomb. The same organization is likely to be known to the police (whose presence at such events is necessary to preserve order) if it has been active in the past in any of

the following ways: (1) disruptive picketing, (2) harassment of speakers who are discussing current social or political issues, or (3) distribution of inflammatory pamphlets supporting or opposing an issue.

2. When an item of physical evidence is traced to the place where it was bought, an identification of the purchaser may result from a record of the transaction (sales slip, invoice, credit card slip, etc.). If the record bears no name or a fictitious name was used, but an organization has claimed responsibility or has been established by other means, photographs of its members can be shown to the salesperson to ascertain if a member of the group is recognized as the purchaser.

3. An informant—especially an average citizen who reports observing some unusual, suspicious behavior to the police—can point to a suspect. A disaffected member of the terrorist group may also turn (or be turned into) informant and provide very useful information.

Depending upon the facts developed during the investigation, interviews and surveillance can produce further information that must be followed up—ending either in interrogation or when an impasse is reached.

One of the longest investigations on record involves the case of Ted Kaczynski, also known as the Unabomber, who eluded law enforcement for almost two decades. The break in the case came largely as a result of the release of the Unabomber's writings to the media, which resulted in recognition of the suspect's writing by a family member. The Federal Bureau of Investigation was able to tie to the suspect hundreds of small items of information and evidence collected over the years—including physical evidence, travel records, eyewitness reports, and writing samples. The investigation involved a suspect profile (which proved to be quite accurate), a study of the victims to determine relationships to each other as targets and how they might have been selected, reviews of various types of records of possible suspects, and the investigation of an estimated 10,000 suspects. Although the Unabomber was not classified as a terrorist by traditional definitions, his activities represented a new form of terrorism apparently carried out by a single individual.

Figure 19.6
An artist's sketch of convicted Unabomber Theodore Kaczynski, listening to his defense attorney during his sentencing hearing. Seen in the background are his brother, David Kaczynski, left, and his attorney. David Kaczynski went to the authorities after adding up geographic connections between his brother and the Unabomber and recognizing familiar phrases and misspellings in the Unabomber's "manifesto" in *The Washington Post*. *(AP Photo/Vicki Behringer)*

ECOLOGICAL TERRORISM

Ecological terrorism, sometime called *ecotage*, involves efforts by groups to protect the environment. Driving spikes into trees to prevent lumbering, pouring sand into the gas tanks of vehicles, and other forms of sabotage have been used, many resulting in severe injuries.

ASSASSINATION

Assassination attempts are often made through bomb attacks. In the United States, however, the trend in political assassination has involved firearms. When an attempt is made with a handgun and the perpetrator is apprehended immediately, the evidentiary requirements can be handled in a relatively routine fashion. Attacks using a rifle or automatic weapon represent a greater problem. Perhaps the most infamous assassination in the United States was the murder of President John F. Kennedy in Dallas, Texas. Although the crime scene in the Texas Book Depository from which Lee Harvey Oswald fired was protected, a number of items were overlooked in the initial crime scene search. Perhaps more important was the failure to protect other potential sites where later speculation suggested there may have been a second or even a third gunman. The way in which this case was handled has created a national mystery that leaves unanswered questions in the minds of many Americans (see the Firearms section in Chapter 2).

Assassination attempts carried out by terrorist groups are generally planned in advance. In almost every case, the scene has been analyzed and avenues of escape have been plotted. The crime scene may actually be in several locations, and the investigator in making the initial assessment should take time to explore the various possibilities that may exist. The terrorist will frequently try to disguise or mislead in a variety of ways. This may involve the employment of a ruse or diversionary action, more than one attack location, or even a hostage to gain access to a particular location. Tracing the activities of the suspects as soon as possible may lead to knowledge of various locations and ultimately to additional physical evidence, but the investigator must take care not to form a hypothesis immediately or jump to conclusions.

KIDNAPPING

The investigation of kidnapping is difficult. Combined with a terrorist act, it becomes even more troublesome. The complexity of this type of investigation requires a thorough understanding of the use of the crime scene search to develop evidence that may lead to suspects and the location where the victim is held. Most terrorist-related kidnappings involve a high degree of planning. This planning effort may provide clues to determine when the suspects are careless.

At the outset, it is important to determine the reason for the kidnapping, which may be for monetary ransom, to force a political concession, or to bring a specific individual under the custody of the kidnappers for a "revolutionary trial." The initial crime scene will usually be the refuge where the victim is taken, but it may shift quickly to other locations as the case develops. Each individual location where it can be ascertained that any action took place should be treated as an individual crime scene. Some areas to consider are:

- Scene of the actual kidnapping
- Telephone booths
- Vehicles used
- Safe houses
- Locations where victim was held
- Victim's residence
- Victim's place of work

Beyond the normal evidence collected, some of which focuses on prosecutorial needs, the kidnapping scene may provide other information that will assist in the investigation. For example, dirt, clay, or other trace material that might adhere to shoes may, on occasion, offer a clue as to approximately where the offenders have been. Tire tracks may provide information on the type of vehicle or may link the vehicle to the scene. Items such as cigarettes, candy and chewing gum wrappers, articles of clothing, and other materials may help determine the number of perpetrators and even who they are. Bullets and shell casings may help determine if the weapon was used in another crime, which in turn may provide geographical information. Even books, magazines, and other reading materials may help identify potential suspects.

Evidentiary material collected at terrorist crime scenes should be compared with databases compiled for other intelligence purposes. The Bundeskriminalamt (BKA) developed extensive profiles on individuals in the Baader-Meinhoff gang by means of such data-collection efforts, even though they did not know the exact identities of the individuals they were seeking. In one case, police knew that one of the male suspects always wore a raincoat, and that he would cut the pocket of the coat out to that he could reach for his weapon. This seemingly insignificant information not only saved the life of the police officer but also made it possible to identify various locations where the suspect had been hiding out.

In addition, information regarding the names used to register for utilities or other services at safe houses made it possible to develop patterns for alias. For example, many individuals will use their own first name or initials in selecting an alias. These names may

Figure 19.7
The attacks on the World Trade Center and the Pentagon on September 11, 2001, marked a turning point in efforts to combat terrorism. *(Photo courtesy Bureau of Alcohol, Tobacco, Firearms, and Explosives.)*

appear on bills, letters, or other documents at a safe house. Maps obtained as safe houses should not be overlooked. They should be examined for marks on the document that identify targets, fingerprints, marking, or residue from handling certain parts of the map. (See Chapters 5 and 27 on the assassination of Dr. Martin Luther King, Jr.)

Regarding vehicles, careful attention should be given to the trunk (in which the victim may have been carried) and under the dashboard and seats (where weapons may have been stowed). Fragments of rope or fabric (including fibers) used to bind the victim may also prove valuable. The exterior parts of the vehicle must also be examined. Mud, dirt, or other debris located on the undercarriage may help identify locations where the vehicle has been. It is also not uncommon to use stolen plates on a vehicle. An examination of the vehicle from which the plates were stolen may provide latent prints. This is an avenue frequently overlooked by investigators.

When a victim has been found, he or she may have traces of evidence on clothing or body parts. It is important to ascertain whether the victim owns the clothing he or she is wearing when found.

Physical evidence can be extremely useful in kidnapping cases. The investigator should be aware of the value attached to such material and should work closely with evidence technicians and the crime laboratory.

STRATEGIC INITIATIVES

Because terrorist cases frequently involve more than one act and sometimes many individuals, the follow-up investigation requires particular care. Because these cases generally produce a large volume of paperwork, the use of a computer as a means of storing, analyzing, comparing, and retrieving information should be considered. Several computer programs are available to assist in this effort. In a major case involving the Irish Republican Army, in which two soldiers had been killed at the funeral of an IRA member, the Royal Ulster Constabulary (RUC) put together an elaborate reconstruction of the crime by combining television coverage, surveillance films, and photographs. A computerized analysis made it possible to isolate virtually every one of the more than 100 persons at the scene. By analyzing the pictures from different angles it was possible to follow individual actions and determine who was actually responsible for the assault when a victim was dragged from his vehicle. The effort was also valuable in presenting what was a very complicated case to the court.

In another case, in which an individual attending another IRA funeral had thrown hand grenades at the mourners, the police were able to show that the individuals had ties to a "Loyalist" group. Although this appeared to be an isolated incident at first, a computer analysis of thousands of "vehicle stop" reports produced evidence that the suspect has been at another location months before with a known member of a Protestant terrorist group. This link furthered the investigation.

Of singular importance is the timely use of intelligence and any other information collected. After a terrorist incident, the police may receive hundreds of anonymous phone calls from numerous sources. Entering this information into a computer makes it possible to correlate variables that may allow a determination of which calls are valid, and may even lead to identification of the caller.

As noted earlier, terrorist investigations usually involve many investigators collecting large quantities of information. Because of the volume, it is frequently difficult to correlate data without assistance. Computer analysis helps to identify the areas that require additional follow-up, the relationship between crimes and persons, and a wealth of other clues that heretofore might have been impossible to review and analyze.

Because individuals involved in terrorist acts are likely to have arrest records or other confrontations with authority, careful attention should be paid to records. Some areas that may prove valuable include:

1. arrest records;

2. reports of similar crimes or crimes that may have a link to the investigation, such as stolen vehicles, weapons, or explosives;

3. military records;

4. employment records, particularly of the victimized business or individual (for example, in "casing" the location for the crime, an individual may seek employment within an organization at that location; accordingly, employees who work for only a brief period that began shortly before and ended shortly after the crime should be investigated);

5. driver's licenses;

6. vehicle records of sales or rentals; the VIN on the demolished can used to transport the explosive device to the New York World Trade Center led to the individual who had rented the van in another state;

7. weapons and explosives dealers;

8. businesses that may have sold particular items (Chapter 27 illustrates the types of evidence collected in the investigation of the murder of Dr. Martin Luther King, Jr., and their value to the investigation);

9. school records;

10. bank records;

11. airline records;

12. car rental records;

13. credit bureau information;

14. applications for loans, credit cards, insurance, etc.

In addition, other law enforcement agencies may have specific information of value. The Secret Service maintains files on individuals who make threats against political leaders; custom records may provide information on imported goods; the Immigration and Naturalization Service (INS) can provide information on individuals entering and leaving the country; the Bureau of Alcohol, Tobacco, Firearms, and Explosives (ATF) maintains records on weapons; the U.S. Marshals Service maintains records on fugitives; the U.S. Postal Inspection Service may assist in matters related to the mails; and the Federal Bureau of Investigation (FBI) may have information because they have primary jurisdiction in terrorist-related cases.

On the local level, police departments frequently maintain individual photo or "mug" files, alias files, business indexes, *modus operandi* (MO) files, victimization records, and crime patterns. In addition, court records, probation and parole files, and other municipal records (e.g., utilities) may prove valuable. Records of businesses, such as telephone and electric companies, may also be helpful.

Surveillance and stakeouts are important components of terrorist investigations. These activities may require various forms of electronic surveillance, including wiretapping, eavesdropping, automobile locator systems, videotaping, and photography. Such efforts may require assistance from other agencies. The investigator should be familiar not only with the use of such equipment, but also with the laws surrounding their application. The investigator must know when a court order is necessary for the use of electronic surveillance. In no case should an investigator use extralegal means to secure information. The lessons of the 1960s should not be forgotten.

REFERENCES

[1]   Report of the Joint Inquiry into the Terrorist Attacks of September 11, 2001—By the House Permanent Select Committee on Intelligence, and the Senate Select Committee on Intelligence, 2002. <http://www.gpoaccess.gov/serialset/creports/911.html>

[2]   Dyson, William. *Terrorism: An Investigator's Handbook* (Cincinnati: Anderson, 2001, 30).

[3]   *Report of the Vice President's Task Force on Terrorism* (Washington, DC: U.S. Government Printing Office), 1986, 2.

[4]   The USA Patriot Act, Pub. L. 107-56, 115 Sat 272 (effective October 26, 2001).

[5]   *Terry v. Ohio*, 392 U.S. 1, 88 S. Ct. 1968.

[6]   Cogar, Stephen W. "Obtaining Admissible Evidence from Computers and Internet Service Providers." *FBI Law Enforcement Bulletin* (Washington, DC: U.S. Department of Justice, 2003, 15).

[7]   Dyson, *op. cit.*, 308.

SUPPLEMENTAL READINGS

Anti-Defamation League. *Explosion of Hate: The Growing Danger of the National Alliance.* New York: The League, 1998.

Burke, Robert J. *Counter-Terrorism for Emergency Responders.* Boca Raton, FL: CRC Press, 1999.

Dyson, William. *Terrorism: An Investigator's Handbook.* Cincinnati: Anderson, 2001.

Hill, Sean (ed). *Extremist Groups: An International Compilation of Terrorist Organizations, Violent Political Groups, and Issue-Oriented Militant Movements* (Huntsville, TX: Office of International Criminal Justice, 2003).

Levitas, Daniel. *The Terrorist Next Door: The Militia Movement and the Radical Right.* New York: St. Martin's Press, 2002.

Miller, John and Michael Stone with Chris Mitchell, *The Cell: Inside the 9/11 Plot, and Why They Failed to Stop It.* New York: Hyperion, 2002.

CHAPTER 20

Information Technology

INTRODUCTION

Crimes linked in some way to computers or other forms of information technology (IT), such as cell phones or the Internet, are among the fastest growing criminal activities in the world. Frequently referred to as "cybercrime," the use of information technology in many forms has become a specialized area of criminal investigation. Each year brings new ways in which clever individuals adapt new forms of old crimes, such as fraud or child pornography, to technology. The full impact of IT crimes has yet to be realized, largely because this is an area in which rapid changes continue to take place. Some of the more troublesome types of criminal activity cut across borders and jurisdictions, further complicating investigative and legal action.

On the other hand, it is important to recognize that IT has also had a positive impact on law enforcement in any number of ways, not the least of which is criminal investigation. The growing numbers of computer applications in the investigative field have been enhanced by the use of relational databases that are beginning to play a major role in handling large amounts of information. With these changes has come a new form of investigator, sometimes referred to as the cyberdetective. Cyberdetectives are specialists who bring a new dimension to the field of crime investigation. Like advances in forensic science, their contributions are becoming increasingly important. Nevertheless, it is probably safe to say that law enforcement is behind the curve in knowledge of information technology and crime.

Today more than one-half of the homes in America have at least one computer, and a new generation of technology-savvy individuals has now arrived. Overall, only a small percentage uses IT for criminal purposes. Because of the power of today's computers and the Internet, the impact of these criminals can be much greater than that of more traditional criminals. Some of the more common types of crime using information technology that an investigator should be familiar with include:

Child pornography and exploitation

Economic-related fraud

Electronic stalking and harassment

Extortion

Gambling

Identity theft

Illegal drug activity

Money laundering

Prostitution

Software theft

Telecommunications fraud

Terrorism

The National Institute of Justice's *Electronic Crime Scene Investigation: A Guide for First Responders* is an important publication that should be of interest to all investigators. Material for this chapter was culled from this NIJ guide, as well as other publications. This chapter focuses on IT from the crime perspective and in relation to its use by law enforcement.

CYBERCRIME: INFORMATION TECHNOLOGY AND CRIMINAL ACTIVITY

It is virtually impossible to determine the monetary amounts of various types of IT crime, but costs and losses easily run into billions of dollars and may be close to reaching a trillion dollars. Child pornography and identity theft are just two types of crime that cross national and international borders and involve thousands of individuals, both as perpetrators as well as victims. Telecommunications fraud is estimated to cost telecommunications providers between 3 and 5 percent of their annual revenue. Current statistics point to a global loss of $55 billion per year, making telecommunications fraud a bigger business than international drug trafficking.[1]

There was a time when it was generally possible to profile cybercriminals, but this has changed over the past decade. Profiling in this area is now related more to the type of computer crime perpetrated. For example, individuals involved in economic fraud are more likely to be older than those involved in "hacking" or software piracy; child pornographers cut across international dimensions that may involve persons from two or more countries; identity theft is usually an individual criminal activity; and terrorist web sites may involve numerous persons. Enterprise and organized crime groups have taken to using various forms of technology to elude detection and foster communication.

Investigations following the September 11, 2001, terrorist attacks revealed a global computer network used by terrorists to communicate. It was also found that the terrorists used computers to gather information about targets as well as to research everything from bombs to building layouts and vulnerabilities.

Emerging databases and search engines on the Internet will enable individuals to gather information on virtually any subject, as well as biographical data on millions of individuals. Not only has storage capacity increased dramatically, but today it is possible to carry as much as one gigabyte (1,000 megabytes) of information on a hard drive the size of a pack of chewing gum. These portable storage devices allow a person to carry as much as 2,000 pictures (at 500KB each) or more than 10,000 pages of text in their pocket, plugging it into a computer only when needed.

Figure 20.1
Some memory keys are capable of storing up to one gigabyte of information in digital form. Such keys can make it easier for criminals to elude detection.

Cell phone technology has also increased to the point where it is possible to store and send images, access the Internet, and perform many of the functions that once required a computer. Handheld personal digital assistants (PDAs), electronic organizers, and memory cards may also be used to store information that may be of interest to investigators.

In addition, smart cards and other small devices may contain their own microprocessors that enable a card to hold and change information, such as fund balances (e.g., debit cards). Removable storage devices come in many different forms, ranging from early floppy disks, to Zip disks, CDs and DVDs, and tape drives, to name a few.

A further complicating factor in cases involving various forms of electronic technology involves case preparation and the presentation of evidence for court. Because this is a relatively new area in which lawbreakers frequently know more about the technology than investigators or the courts, there is always the danger of not being able to present a case that can be understood by a jury. Everything from initial investigations to the collection, presentation, and admissibility of evidence is important.

Electronic evidence is, by its very nature, fragile. It can be altered, damaged, or destroyed by improper handling or inappropriate examination. For this reason, special precautions should be taken to document, collect, preserve, and examine this type of evidence. Failure to do so may render it unusable or lead to inaccurate conclusion.[2]

Systemic Components

At the heart of virtually all information technology lies a computer system or central processing unit (CPU). Generally, these systems contain a data storage component and a hard drive that is programmed to run the system. The computing power of today's technology is enormous, enabling the user to run a broad range of programs, commonly referred to as software, in conjunction with the hard drive.

The computer contains a number of files that are connected to different types of software, such as word processing programs, spreadsheets, databases, e-mail servers, or Internet web sites. Some of these programs, such as dictionaries and directories, may not be alterable. User-created files generally prove to be the most valuable from an investigative standpoint. One major exception, however, involves downloaded images or documents that may be used in developing a prima facie case, for instance, of child pornography.

Some of the more important files that an investigator should be familiar with include:

- Address books
- Audio or video files
- Bookmarks
- Calendars
- Databases
- Documents or correspondence files
- E-mail files
- Favorite sites
- Images and graphics
- Indexes
- Spreadsheets
- Voicemail

Scanners and Copiers

The development of high-quality scanners and printers has opened further opportunities for the criminal element to expand illicit activities, including counterfeiting, various types of fraud, child pornography, and identity theft.

Other forms of technology that can be involved in cybercrime include answering machines, audio and photo devices, digital cameras, digital watches (that can store information), intrusion devices, fax machines, and global positioning systems (GPSs). GPS technology (GPS) was originally developed by the military to aid in navigation. It operates when a network of satellites reads the signal sent by a user's unit (which emits a radio signal). A GPS unit can provide information on location, velocity, bearing, direction, and track of movement.

LEGAL ISSUES

In many ways investigation involving various forms of technology, especially computers and the Internet, are complicated by a myriad of legal issues, court decisions, and policy issues of organizations. Because case law in this area is relatively new, there are times when the investigator may be operating in an uncharted area or facing newly designed computer programs or criminal activities. Moreover, because many of the laws and policies may be based on individual state laws, they may not be applicable from one state to another. For this reason, when in doubt, the investigator should consult with appropriate legal counsel.

On the federal level, there has been a steady stream of decisions by circuit courts that serve to better clarify the procedures that must be followed by investigators. A search warrant is generally required to conduct an investigation of a computer's contents or to gather information from an Internet source (e.g., either e-mail or Internet service providers—ISPs). A suspect may give permission for an investigator to conduct a search of his or her computer, but it is advisable to get this permission in writing. Courts have become more involved in Fourth Amendment issues related to the search and seizure of computers and data culled from ISPs.[3]

Figure 20.2
Media representatives learn about computer disk splicing from a computer forensic lab examiner during a 1999 tour of the new Department of Defense Computer Forensic Laboratory in Linthicum, Maryland. Designed for fighting computer crimes, the lab aids investigators in tracking hackers through cyberspace, unscrambling sensitive data, and rebuilding floppy disks that have been destroyed. *(AP Photo/John Gillis.)*

The primary issue in computer-related cases centers on an individual's right to privacy regarding information stored in a computer. The primary areas from which information can be obtained are:

- the home
- the workplace
- Internet service providers
- "chat" rooms
- web sites

Home Computers

Home computers fall under the Fourth Amendment of the U.S. Constitution, which protects citizens from unreasonable searches and seizures. Thus, it is necessary to obtain permission for a search warrant to gain entry to a residence and any computers therein. The warrant must include a statement as to what technological equipment (computers, storage devices, cameras, printers, etc.) is to be searched, what is to be sought, and why the warrant is requested. The investigator must show probable cause for the search, which may be based on a variety of circumstances, such as prior knowledge based on the experience of the investigator, the past criminal record of the suspect, or information from informants and victims.

In circumstances in which a home or computer is shared by another person, that person may give permission to search the computer, but not access to password protected files.[4]

Workplace Computers

Workplace searches present a somewhat different issue. Here it has been held that an employee does not necessarily have a right to the expectation of privacy.[5] However, in determining an individual's expectation of privacy, Stephen W. Cogar suggests that the following questions should be considered:[6]

- Is the employee's office shared?

- Is the hard drive password protected?

- Is the computer physically locked?

- Is the office locked, and if so, who has access?

- Can the files be accessed remotely through a network program?

- Is there an employee policy in place regarding computer usage that states that files can be searched or monitored?

- Is the policy enforced uniformly?

- Is there evidence that the employee was aware of the policy?

- Is software used to monitor computer use, and are employees aware of the practice?

- Do workstations contain a message when the computer is accessed that the computer can be monitored?

In many instances, employees may contend that they were not aware of company policy, which may negate permission given by the employer to conduct a search. For this reason it is advisable to seek a search warrant whenever possible.

Internet Service Providers

In cases in which a suspect may be anonymous, using a screen name or other form of e-mail address, the best source of identification is likely to be an Internet service provider, such as America Online (AOL), Microsoft (MSN), Juno, NetZero, or Earthlink. Although the content of information may be protected under the Fourth Amendment, the Courts have held that the identity of the subscriber is not protected.

While under certain circumstances a person may have an expectation of privacy in content information, a person does not have an interest in the account information given to the ISP in order to establish an e-mail account, which is noncontent information.[7] This includes: name; billing address; home, work, and fax telephone numbers. The Stored Wire and Electronic Communication and Transactional Records Act (SWECTRA) requires ISPs to disclose noncontent information to the law enforcement community pursuant to legal authorization.[8]

Cases involving terrorism investigations permit disclosure of more noncontent information that is permissible in other types of criminal investigations. The USA Patriot Act "can force the disclosure of a subscriber's name; address; local and long distance telephone connection records, or records of session times and duration, length of service (including start date and types of service utilized; telephone or instrument number or other subscriber number or identity, including any temporary assigned network address; and means and source of payment for such service of a subscriber."[9]

Figure 20.3
A view of the NetDex website hacked by "Analyzer," a mysterious Israeli who is allegedly behind cyber-attacks on Pentagon and university computers. This photo was taken from the World Wide Web on March 6, 1998. Deputy Defense Secretary John Hamre stated that this was "the most organized and systematic attack the Pentagon has seen to date." *(AP Photo/HO/AntiOnline.)*

Chat Rooms

Internet chat rooms have become a common place for individuals to meet in cyberspace and discuss any number of issues. For the most part, chat rooms provide a harmless means of communication, which has resulted in people making contacts and friends throughout the world. Some chat rooms are devoted to specific issues and play an important role in helping to further research. Of importance to law enforcement, however, are the relatively few individuals who use chat rooms for illicit purposes, frequently involving sex crimes and the exploitation of women and children.

A number of law enforcement agencies currently use chat rooms as a means of identifying potential criminal activities, especially child abuse. In such cases, it is important to avoid entrapment, which is a common defense.

Web Sites

Today there are thousands of web sites, making it possible to gather information on almost any subject. Some of these are nothing more than propaganda sites, devoted to fostering ideological positions, racism, ethnic hate, and dissatisfaction with the government. Free speech protects these sites, and many of them draw a fine line between what is legal and what is illegal. The fact that an individual visits a web site is not a crime, and the investigator must take care regarding how such information is used. In cases involving pedophiles, the fact that they subscribed to or visited web sites may serve as circumstantial evidence when a sex crime is involved.

Web sites also serve as one of the largest libraries in the world, providing information about people, places, and things. A number of federal agencies monitor the web sites of suspected violent groups, largely as a means of keeping track of potential criminal activity. However, care must be taken in attempting to develop cases based on information from a site. Many web sites are also targets for hackers tying to disrupt an organization.

INVESTIGATING HIGH-TECH AND IT CRIME

A thorough discussion of investigative methods involving high-tech crime is beyond the scope of this chapter, but it is important to have a basic understanding of the type of crimes that an investigator may come across. Because computers have become so common in everyday life, it is important to recognize that a vast amount of information can be obtained from what appears to normal record keeping. This may include address and telephone records, bank account records, e-mail transactions between suspects, and other personal data.

The investigator facing a crime scene involving computers should protect the area and call for a component service technician. However, there may be situations in which this is impossible. For example, if a computer "virus" has been introduced or a self-destruct system implanted by an intruder, it may be necessary to take preliminary action to preserve the equipment.

In other cases, the investigator may be seizing or protecting a computer that has been or is being used in the commission of a crime. In such cases, the suspect may have built systems into the computer designed to destroy the evidence necessary for proving that a crime has been committed using the equipment. Thus, the investigator must have some basic familiarization with the types of criminal activity he or she might encounter, how they are generally carried out, and the procedures necessary for the safeguarding of evidence and preliminary investigations. The investigator also should be familiar with those agencies or organizations that might be able to assist in such investigations. A number of federal agencies, such as the FBI and the Secret Service, now have cybercrime experts located in major field offices.

Because cybercrime and other forms of high-tech crime may involve multiple jurisdictions, or involve a federal offense, it is important to communicate with appropriate agencies or organizations early in the process. For example, fraud involving interstate communication by electronic communication is likely to fall under the jurisdiction of the U.S. Postal Service. The use of a computer to transmit child pornography—much of which actually originates abroad—may involve multiple jurisdictions; it is extremely important that a detailed record be kept of all actions taken during the investigation. This may prove helpful when it is necessary to reconstruct events or design a particular strategy and may be very important when such cases reach the trial stage.

At the outset, the investigator must be extremely careful not to destroy evidence that may be on a computer, a disk, or other electronic storage mechanism. Sophisticated criminals using computers are likely to use passwords or other program methods that are designed to erase data if not properly accessed. It may be possible, though, for experts to recover data that appears to have been erased. Thus, unless an investigator is thoroughly familiar with this type of investigation, it is best to leave the equipment untouched until an expert can be called. One should turn the computer off or on—and the suspect should not be asked to assist unless an expert is present.

Most experts agree that training and education of investigators must increasingly include a basic knowledge of computers and how they can be used in criminal activities. In many cases, the investigator will have to rely on the victim to explain how a crime was carried out and what damages may be attributed to the offender. The investigator, frequently in cooperation with legal counsel, will be faced with determining what crime took place and the legal standards and jurisdiction involved.

Of the crimes that are predominantly carried out using various forms of technology, child pornography and exploitation, electronic and economic fraud, identity theft, and gambling are quite common. The following illustrations and case studies provide an overview of the more common methods employed.

Child Pornography and Exploitation

Unfortunately, the computer and the Internet have become notorious tools for pedophiles, child pornographers, and other child sex abuse perpetrators. A base international network of child pornography providers and users involves hundreds, if not thousands, of sites on the Internet. The U.S. Customs Department, the Postal Inspection Service, and the Federal Bureau of Investigation generally investigate international providers. Depending on how information comes to authorities, federal, state, and local law enforcement agencies may handle local investigations of users. Users of child pornography may also be pedophiles that are active in recruiting children for photos or in using chat rooms to entice children to meet them.

Figure 20.4
University of Illinois at Chicago Professor Michael Maltz, working with a computerized crime analysis and prediction program he helped develop in cooperation with the Chicago Police Department.

A growing number of states have expanded or initiated child exploitation units. Units usually include a computer specialist who is familiar with the methods used by suspects who make contact with young people though chat rooms as a means of luring victims to a prearranged location. When a parent or other person makes a complaint, the investigator should be thoroughly familiar with local laws relating to the solicitation of a minor. Generally, it must be proved that the suspect was aware that the individual was a minor, and in most cases it will be necessary to prove that something more than a meeting was planned. For this reason, prior communications are important to obtain. If a meeting is arranged, it must be proved that the suspect was actually going to make contact and that a positive identification of the suspect has been made.

The Cook County Sheriff's Department in Illinois and the Texas Attorney General's criminal investigation unit have been successful in drawing out numerous pedophiles who believed they were communicating with a minor. One key to success has been the ability to establish and build cases that have not been viewed as entrapment. By studying the ways in which young people communicate on the net, law enforcement agents have been successful in getting the suspect to communicate freely. When arrested, suspects frequently are found to have other incriminating material in their residences.

The U.S. Postal Investigative Service has stopped about 500 child molesters and convicted more than 250 persons for child sexual exploitation since 1997. Their research indicates a high correlation between child molesters and people involved in selling, purchasing, and trading child pornography. The Postal Inspection Service is an excellent source for assistance in cases involving the Internet or mail.

A more common problem for local law enforcement is use of the computer to stalk or harass individuals. In most cases, the sender is anonymous. The section in this chapter on "Legal Aspects" outlines the procedures involved in gaining access to the identity of an individual who is using the computer or telephone for illegal purposes.

Economic Crimes—Fraud, Embezzlement, and Identity Theft

There are a great many types of economic-related fraud, including business fraud and embezzlement. Perhaps the largest of these was the Enron case in Texas, which involved a broad range of criminal activities. A major component of this scheme involved computer usage for money transfers and communication. The sale of products that are not delivered and misrepresentation by sellers have become a growing problem, and investigations may involve multiple jurisdictions and countries.

Keeping transactions within the computer allows the suspect to destroy information rapidly. However, in many cases, transactions may have been sent to one or more other computers or organizations with which the suspect is conducting business. For example, in the case involving former Panamanian leader Manuel Noriega, authorities were able to trace many of Noriega's financial transactions through other banks or financial institutions. They compiled a fairly complete record of the way in which he moved funds associated with alleged drug activity and payoff. Further, with the development of small storage devices that can hold enormous amounts of data, it will be increasingly common for criminals to maintain suspect records separate from the computer.

One of the more common types of electronic fraud involves the use of stolen or forged credit cards. Despite efforts by companies to create "safer" credit cards using photos and fingerprints, this problem continues to grow, due in some measure to the ability to order products over the Internet. Identity theft is one of the fastest growing crimes in the United States. Criminals use a variety of means to secure information. They then use this information to commit fraudulent purchases, acquire others forms of false identification, receive large cash advances, and establish fraudulent lines of credit in the forms of loans and other credit cards. Additionally, a number of organized crime groups, frequently with Nigerian or Asian connections, have developed sophisticated fraudulent credit card rings. Investigations of these types of activities must be handled quickly because perpetrators are likely to move frequently to avoid apprehension. Unfortunately, in many cases, the victim whose number or card has been stolen is not aware of the crime until he or she receives a statement.

On a higher level, fraudulent wire transfers, bank fraud, telecommunications fraud, and money laundering have also become commonplace. In many instances, the illegal activities are carried out across national and state borders and will involve multiple jurisdictions. Electronic funds transfers have made it possible for individuals to move funds to off-shore accounts, to gain entry illegally into funding institutions and make transfers, and to embezzle large amounts of money.

Economic espionage has also become a major problem. Although little attention is paid by law enforcement to the issue of economic espionage, or the stealing of trade secrets, this is an area in which the amount of criminal activity has been growing steadily. In many cases, the companies being victimized are unaware of the problem or do not have procedures for reporting or investigating such activities. A 1998 survey of intellectual property losses by the American Society for Industrial Security (ASIS) indicated that the annual misappropriations (usually by trusted employees) of United States companies may amount to more than $250 billion.

Computer Hacking/Cracking and Sabotage

One of the more pervasive ways to illegally use a computer is hacking or cracking, which generally involves entering a computer system illegally or without knowledge of the victim. The terms "hacker" and "cracker" generally refer to individuals who enter computer systems illegally, with the term "cracker" used more often to describe a person who attempts to destroy, change, or steal programs or information. Often undertaken as what hackers refer to as an "intellectual challenge," the practice has become a major problem in both the public and private sectors. A growing number of individuals and "clubs" have been involved throughout the world in developing methods to break codes or find ways to enter a system, and they have frequently been successful in "crashing" web sites, altering information, and introducing viruses. Figure 20.5 illustrates some of the terms involved in economic related criminal activity.

Professional crackers are involved in garnering classified or sensitive information that they can sell to others. In recent years, governments have also been involved in using the computer to steal or pass information. In 1999, the so-called "Chinese spy case" involved the theft of military secrets from a number of top-secret military research sites. Investigations of this nature require sophisticated knowledge of the computer and should not be attempted without consulting a technical advisor.

Closely related to hacking is computer sabotage, which may involve the actions of a disgruntled employee to destroy an employers' database or make an external attack on a computer database.

Figure 20.5
Computer Terminology

Clipper chip	A computer chip for encryption as a means of protecting computerized information.
Encryption	A means of protecting communication and electronic commerce. Can be used by organized crime or terrorist groups to conceal illegal activities.
Logic Bomb	A virus that is dormant until a particular time (which can be days, months, or years) or when a particular command is entered in the computer.
Pinging or Spamming	A form of vandalism, or sabotaging, which involves bombarding an e-mail address with thousands of messages using automatic remailer tools.
Remailer	A program that makes it possible to send thousands of messages to an e-mail address.
Trapdoor	A means for bypassing the security controls of a computer mainframe system (usually installed by programmers to permit them to enter the system to check when things go wrong).
Trojan Horse	Software embedded in a popular and trusted computer software program (maybe unknown to the user) that is stealing secrets or modifying the database, or deleting specific items of information. It is not usually considered a virus because it does not replicate itself and does not spread.
Virus	A program designed to attach itself to a file, reproduce, and spread from one file to another, destroying data, displaying a message, or otherwise disrupting computer operations.
Worm	Software that works its way through a single computer system or a network, changing and destroying data or codes.
Packet Sniffer	A program that examines all traffic on a section of network to find passwords, credit card numbers, and other information of value.
SATAN	A security loophole analysis program designed for use by system administrators (and abused by electronic intruders) to detect insecure systems.
File Infector	Computer viruses that attach to program files and spread when the program is executed.
Boot Sector Virus	A computer virus that infects the sectors on a disk that contain the data a computer uses during the boot process. This type of virus does not require a program to spread, and may cause the destruction of all data on a drive.
Macro Virus	A computer virus that infects the automatic command execution capabilities (macros) of productivity software. Macro viruses are typically attached to documents and spreadsheets.
Cracking	The process of trying to overcome a security measure

Figure 20.5, *continued*

Black Hat	A term used to describe a hacker who has the intention of causing damage or stealing information
Cracker	A person who breaks into a computer system with intent to damage files or steal data, or who is driven to hack highly secure systems.
Denial of Service Attack	An attack that causes the targeted system to be unable to fulfill its intended function
IP Spoofing	An attack where the attacker disguises himself or herself as another user by means of a false IP network address
Letterbomb	An e-mail containing live data intended to cause damage to the recipient's computer
Phreaking	The process of hacking telephone systems, usually for the purpose of making free phone call
Phracking	The process of combining phone phreaking with computer hacking
Trap and Trace Device	A device used to record the telephone numbers dialed by a specific telephone
War Dialer	Software designed to detect dial-in access to computer systems

Illegal Drug Activity

Drug traffickers have taken to using the Internet for distribution of drugs, communicating between groups, and keeping records of transactions.

Telecommunications Fraud

A number of schemes involving telecommunications fraud have developed with the increase in the number of cell phones available throughout the world. The most common usage involves stolen cell phones to make large numbers of calls.

Terrorism

Although this subject is covered in more detail in Chapter 19, it is important to recognize that terrorist groups use the Internet as a primary means of communication. They also use the Internet to gather information about individuals, possible targets, and ways of making explosives or other weapons.

COMPUTER CRIME INVESTIGATION AND THE ELECTRONIC CRIME SCENE

Beyond the methods discussed above and in Chapter 3 on managing the crime scene, there are a number of considerations that should be observed when dealing with a high-tech crime scene. The National Institute of Justice (NIJ) Guide stresses the importance of documentation in detail. This includes:

- Observing and documenting the physical scene, such as the position of the mouse and the location of components relative to each other (e.g., a mouse on the left side of the computer may indicate a left-handed user).

- Document the condition and location of the computer system, including power status of the computer (on, off, or in sleep mode). Most computers have status lights that indicate the computer is on. Likewise, if fan noise is heard, the system is probably on. Furthermore, if the computer system is warm, that may also indicate that it is on or was recently turned off.

- Identify and document related electronic components that will not be collected.

- Photograph the entire scene to create a visual record as noted by the first responder. The complete room should be recorded with 360 degrees of coverage, when possible

- Photograph the front of the computer as well as the monitor screen and other components. Also take written notes on what appears on the monitor screen. Active programs may require videotaping or more extensive documentation of monitor screen activity.

COMPUTERS AS AN AID IN LAW ENFORCEMENT

The computer has come of age in law enforcement as departments and other agencies develop applications through which this technology can benefit the field. In many cases, the technology and the application software—the programs used to handle and manipulate the data—exist in various forms but require modification for law enforcement purposes. In other cases, software is available (frequently through hardware vendors) that has been designed specifically for police work. Included in this category are programs ranging from relatively simple data storage programs to extremely complex systems for tasks such as imaging (for storing photographic images on the computer) and optical scanning (for storing fingerprints for later retrieval).

Figure 20.6
Michigan State Police personnel check a computer report. The system stores cross-indexed information on wanted persons, wanted vehicles, and criminal histories. *(Courtesy, UNISYS Corporation.)*

In the field of criminal investigation, the computer has not yet come close to the potential it offers as an investigative tool. Although one reason for this is a lack of sufficient funding, other considerations also limit computer utilization—for example, concern about the right to privacy, a lack of trained technicians, and an entrenched resistance by officers who have little understanding of the computer's capabilities.

Nevertheless, as a new generation of computer-literate personnel moves into the law enforcement profession, there is likely to be growing trend toward acceptance. Many federal agencies have begun to develop and adopt computer-based systems that go far beyond mere data storage and retrieval. The Federal Bureau of Investigation, for example, will virtually revamp its computer system in the first decade of the twenty-first century. A number of police departments—including those in Chicago, Los Angeles, and Houston—have invested millions of dollars in automated fingerprint identification systems (AFISs) and are seeing their value in the investigative function. Illustrative of this potential value is a case involving a forcible rape in which a latent fingerprint was lifted from the handbag of the victim. Fingerprint analysis provided no suspects. However, more than a year later, a suspect arrested in a burglary was surprised to learn that, despite the passage of time, his prints identified him as the rapist. (At the time of the rape he had been too young to be fingerprinted, despite his long record as a juvenile offender.) This illustrates the capability of technology to solve what in all likelihood would have remained an unsolved case.

Computers also are being used: for developing crime patterns (see Figure 20.7), for sophisticated data manipulation using a concept known as "artificial intelligence," and using a technique known as imaging for storing online mug shots of suspects and photographs of stolen artwork or other valuable collections.

Figure 20.7
International cooperation through expanded computer networks continues to grow. Representatives of the Attorney General's office in Sri Lanka participate in a training program at the Office of International Criminal Justice at the University of Illinois at Chicago with Officer Thomas Moran.

Perhaps the most important innovation in programming software in the past decade has been the development of relational databases for law enforcement purposes. A relational database makes it possible to combine a large number of individual databases into a system that makes it possible to link a broad range of disparate variables for search and profiling purposes. The Chicago Police Department's CLEAR program makes it possible to link millions of records from different sources (including other police departments) to provide a powerful tool for investigators. The program utilizes artificial intelligence, photographs, images, and geographic mapping in addition to text-based records. Some of these include:

1. Nickname database

2. MO file

3. Informants file

4. Business locator index with emergency phone numbers for business owners

5. Case file indicating which cases are assigned to which investigator

6. Skills index listing the names of those who can assist with specific needs, such as language skills, scuba divers, technicians, etc.

7. Intelligence file offering a source for various bits of information that can be pieced together to form a clearer picture of suspects or crime patterns. (This file, which usually requires the expertise of an analyst or other individual familiar with the technology, represents one of the more significant changes appearing in the field of criminal investigation.)

8. Stolen property files

9. Building layouts and schematics

10. Tattoo files

11. Gang symbols and descriptors

12. Motor vehicle records

13. Victimization files

On an individual basis, investigators can use laptop or personal computers (PCs) to maintain their own data sources, address and telephone files, and case information, as well as for numerous other applications.

Rapid Start Team

The FBI's "Rapid Start Team" is an elite unit with responsibilities for assisting federal and local law enforcement with a rapid mobilization capacity for the investigation of serious crimes. Utilizing laptop computers, which can be linked to the Bureau's mainframe and more than 1,000 public databases, it is possible to handle thousands of field and case investigation reports as the investigation proceeds. For example, records of motor vehicles, licensees, or data can be culled from most of the states. The FBI provides training to local police in ways to use their database and the expertise of the Rapid Start Team.

Figure 20.8
Rapid Start Team

If a picture is worth a thousand words, imaging technology offers immerse possibilities. The most obvious use today is through computer-based identification kits, which make it possible to prepare a composite of a suspect relatively easily. However, the quality and color of newer monitors and systems make it possible to have a four-color, instant-access mug shot book readily available. Indeed, coupled with search technology, the investigators can feed in information on modus operandi, physical descriptors, type of victim, and so on, to call up groups and individuals in various categories for the victim to view on the scene.

Electronic surveillance takes many forms and is being used more frequently in terrorism and organized crime investigations. Some of these (most of which require a court order) include:

- Telephone wiretap
- Electronic intercept of oral conversation
- Voice paging
- Digital display paging
- Cellular telephone intercepts
- Pen register
- Internet or computer communications intercept

Information technology offers investigators one of the most important advances in law enforcement and is a major new area of development. Most federal agencies and many police departments are now employing crime analysts, that is, specialists schooled in this technology who can serve as an important source of support to field investigators. Additionally, there are also a great number of sources on the web that are available to investigators. They include:

American Society for Industrial Security, International—Private organization providing training and information on matters related to industrial security. *http://www.asisonline.org/*

Center for Education and Research in Information Assurance and Security (CERIAS)—One of the world's leading centers for research and education in areas of information security that are crucial to the protection of critical computing and communication infrastructure, CERIAS is unique among such national centers in its multidisciplinary approach to problems such as intrusion detection and network security. *http://www.cerias.purdue.edu/*

CERT Coordination Center (CERT/CC)—Located at the Software Engineering Institute (SEI) at Carnegie Mellon University, the Center is charged with coordinating communication among experts during security emergencies and to help prevent future incidents. *http://www.cert.org*

Critical Infrastructure Assurance Office (CIAO)—Responsible for the federal government's initiatives on critical infrastructure assurance. The CIAO's primary areas of focus are to raise issues that cut across industry sectors and ensure a cohesive approach to achieving continuity in delivering critical infrastructure services. *http:// www.ciao.gov/index.html*

FBI Awareness of National Security Issues and Responses (ANSIR) Program—Provides information related to national security such as terrorism, espionage, and foreign intelligence. Contact ANSIR Coordinator at local FBI field office. *http://www.fbi.gov/hq/ci/ansir/ansirhome.htm*

FBI Child Abduction and Serial Killer Unit (CASKU) and Morgan P. Hardiman Task Force on Missing and Exploited Children—Quantico, VA; 800/634-4097; 540/720-4700.

Federal Computer Incident Response Center (FedCIRC)—The federal civilian government's focal point for computer security incident reporting, providing assistance with incident prevention and response. *http://www.fedcirc.gov/*

Financial Crimes Enforcement Network (FinCEN)—A financial center maintained by the U.S. Treasury Department that provides information and technical assistance in the area of financial crime. *http://www.fincen.gov*

Forum of Incident Response and Security Teams (FIRST)—A consortium of computer security incident response teams from government, commercial, and academic organizations, FIRST aims to foster cooperation and coordination in incident prevention, to prompt rapid reaction to incidents, and to promote information sharing among members and the community at large. *http://www.first.org*

ICAT Metabase—A searchable index of computer vulnerabilities, ICAT links users into a variety of publicly available vulnerability databases and patch sites, thus enabling one to find and fix the vulnerabilities existing on their systems. *http://icat.nist.gov/icat.cfm*

InfraGard—A partnership between Private Industry and the U.S. government (represented by the FBI), the InfraGard initiative was developed to encourage the exchange or information by the government and the private sector members about securing the nation's electronic infrastructure. *http://www.infragard.net*

Internet Fraud Complaint Center (IFCC)—A partnership between the FBI and the National White Collar Crime Center (NW3C) to address fraud committed over the Internet. For victims of Internet fraud, IFCC provides a convenient and easy-to-use reporting mechanism that alerts authorities of a suspected criminal or civil violation. For law enforcement and regulatory agencies at all levels, IFCC offers a central repository for complaints related to Internet fraud, works to quantify fraud patterns, and provides timely statistical data of current fraud trends. *http://www.ifccfbi.gov/index.asp*

INTERPOL—The International Police Organization now has field offices in each of the 50 states and can be of assistance in cases involving individuals from other countries. Queries within states should be made through a local office when possible. *http://www.interpol.int*

National Counterintelligence Center (NACIC)—Coordinates U.S. government response in the areas of foreign counterintelligence and U.S. economic security. *http://www.nacic.gov*

National Infrastructure Protection Center (NIPC)—The Department of Homeland Security's clearinghouse for information related to the Nation's infrastructure protection apparatus. *http://www.nipc.gov*

U.S. Department of Justice Computer Crime and Intellectual Property Section (CCIPS)—A division of 40 lawyers who focus exclusively on the issues raised by computer and intellectual property crime. Section attorneys advise federal prosecutors and law enforcement agents, comment upon and propose legislation, coordinate international efforts to combat computer crime, litigate cases, and train all law enforcement groups. Other areas of expertise possessed by commerce, hacker investigations, and intellectual property crimes. *http://www.usdoj.gov/criminal/cybercrime/index.html*

U.S. Postal Investigative Service—Provides a broad range of information and investigative assistance in crimes involving the mail and Internet. *http://www.usps.gov/postalinspectors/welcome2.htm*

SUMMARY

The rapid advancement of information technology has been one of the most positive developments in law enforcement, especially in the field of criminal investigation. Unfortunately, these advancements have also spawned new types of crimes that are far more complex and require highly technical and specialized knowledge to perpetrate and investigate. Criminal justice agencies are beginning to take the initiative in hiring and training investigators, analysts, and researchers in these technologically enhanced fields. Practitioners at all levels must become aware of the changing legal issues and recognize that law enforcement must consider an individual's right to privacy now more than ever before. The most important resource for criminal justice professionals is the wealth of information available electronically through the Internet.

REFERENCES

[1]   Jacobs, R. (2003). *Telecommunications Fraud: The Single Best Cause of Revenue Loss for Telecommunications Providers*. Dimension Data White Paper. [Electronic]. *<http://www.didata.com/services/white_papers/Fraud_White_Paper.pdf>*

[2]   Technical Working Group for Electronic Crime Scene Investigation, *Electronic Crime Scene Investigation* (Washington, DC: U.S. Department of Justice, Office of Justice Programs, National Institute of Justice, 2001), 2.

[3]   Cogar, Stephen W. "Obtaining Admissible Evidence from Computers and Internet Service Providers. *FBI Law Enforcement Bulletin* (Washington, DC: U.S. Department of Justice, 2003), 11.

[4]   *Trulock v. Freeh*, 275 F.3d 391 (4th Cir. 2001).

[5]   *United States v. Simons*, 206 F.3d 392 (4th Cir. 2000).

[6]   Cogar, *op cit.*

[7]   *United States v. Hambrick*, 225 F.3d 656 (4th Cir. 2000).

[8]   Cogar, *op cit.*, 14.

[9]   Ibid., 15.

Casey, Eoghan (ed.). *Handbook of Computer Crime Investigation: Forensic Tools and Technology* (San Diego, CA: 2002).

U.S. Department of Justice, *Electronic Crime Scene Investigation: A Guide for First Responders* (Washington, DC: National Institute of Justice, July 2001).

SUPPLEMENTAL READINGS

Blitzer, Herbert L. and Jack Jacobia, *Forensic Digital Imaging and Photograph*. Academic Press. San Diego, CA. (2002)

Kovacich, Gerald L. and William C. Boni. *High Technology—Crime Investigator's Handbook: Working in the Global Information Environment*.Butterworth, Heinemann: Boston. (2000)

U.S. Department of Justice, *Electronic Crime Scene Investigation: A Guide for First Responders*. National Institute of Justice: Washington, DC. (July 2001)

U.S. Postal Service, *A Law Enforcement Guide to Postal Crimes*. Washington, DC. Publication 146, December 2000.

CHAPTER 21

Enterprise Crime
Organized, Economic, and White-Collar Crime

INTRODUCTION

The changing nature of organized crime prompted some criminologists to redefine, or at least bring under one heading, a phrase encompassing the broad range of crimes including but not limited to organized and white-collar crime, corruption and economic crime, organized drug trafficking, and other illicit activities of societal concern. Known as *enterprise crime*, this form of criminality includes a much broader range of criminal activity than what is commonly thought of as traditional organized crime; it is characterized by criminal networks and illegal relationships. The primary goals of individuals involved in enterprise criminality are:

1. Propagation of the group.

2. Financial or economic gain.

3. The advancement of power and influence.

In order to achieve these goals the group may engage in both legal and illegal activities, be willing to corrupt or intimidate, and—in the case of many groups—to use extreme violence or the threat of violence.

PEOPLE

The Enterprise Criminal

Enterprise criminals differ from traditional lawbreakers in several ways. They represent a greater threat to society, are much more difficult to investigate and bring to trial and conviction, and are usually self-perpetuating. The criminal groups are usually hierarchical in nature with an exclusive membership, and operate within their own code of behavior.

Within this context we can identify numerous groups throughout the world, including the Mafia or *la Cosa Nostra* (traditional organized crime in the United States); Asian gangs in the United States (offshoots of the Triads in Hong Kong and Taiwan, and more recently in mainland China); the Yakuza in Japan; the United Bamboo Gang in Taiwan; the Colombian drug cartels; the drug "Warlords" in Myanmar; and black and Hispanic gangs in America. Numerous other organizations are involved in enterprise crime, though they frequently are smaller and less well identified. Such newer groups are more likely to be involved in various aspects of white-collar and economic crime, and do not usually evidence the traditional organizational structure common to gangs. Nevertheless, their influence is pervasive and their danger to society can be immense. The growing influence of Russian enterprise criminality in the United States is notable. It is one of the newest forms of crime being carried out by well-organized and frequently violent groups.

CONDUCTING THE INVESTIGATION

Investigation of the criminal activity associated with enterprise crime involves greater coordination and cooperation than for the more traditional forms of crimes. Experience has shown that all components of the criminal justice system—police, prosecution, courts, and corrections—must be well-trained and prepared to be flexible, innovative, and committed to joint efforts.

At the outset, one must recognize that not all investigations can be handled in the same manner, and that prosecution may require greater knowledge than currently exists within most investigative units. For example, it is difficult to investigate or prosecute computer fraud unless one knows something about how computers work (see Chapter 20). In cases in which a group is working transnationally (between countries), it is imperative that there be positive working relationships with investigators representing the other countries involved. Today, it is not uncommon for a criminal enterprise to plan a crime in one country, carry it out in another, escape to a third country, and keep the proceeds in a fourth country.

Enterprise crime, however, is not necessarily an international activity; most organized criminal activity of interest to the United States will occur within its borders. In some cases it will be necessary to pass new laws and develop new procedures for the control of enterprise crime, but this cannot be done without a full understanding of the problem. One of the most effective laws of recent origin involves *asset forfeiture*, which makes it possible for police to seize assets of criminals that are being used in criminal enterprises.

Investigating enterprise crime involves five primary areas of interest:

1. The organization and structure of the group.

2. The membership of the group

3. The sphere of influence of individuals the group works with or controls.

4. The goals or purpose of the group.

5. The means by which the group attains its goals

Organization and Structure

Not all groups are organized in the same way. Most groups are hierarchical, with individuals serving in the roles of leader, supervisors or managers, and workers. This is common in virtually all traditional organized crime groups. In some of the newer groups, however, investigators are finding shared leadership, sometimes involving a loose confederation of groups working together to commit crimes where particular expertise or contacts are necessary. For example, a group may be involved with one group for purposes of drug trafficking, another for prostitution, and so on.

Some of the newer international groups have committee structures similar to boards of directors, each with its own operating group. The Medellin and Cali cartels in Colombia, for example, are known for their disparate structure.

Because law enforcement throughout the world has had some success in fighting enterprise crime, many groups have now introduced new "layers" of people to pass decisions on or carry out street-level activities. In the United States, for example, some states have passed laws imposing a mandatory life sentence on drug sellers; as a result, criminals have been recruiting children under the age of 15 (who as minors are not subject to such a sentence) to deliver drugs to customers.

In some criminal groups a person will be utilized between the leader and the criminal activity, so that the leader is not caught instructing someone to carry out a crime. Many big-time criminals use this approach today. In very large criminal enterprises the organization may be specialized for certain types of business, such as drugs, gambling, or prostitution. Regarding other groups, such as some Russian organizations, investigators are still learning about structures, one of which appears to be extensive use of the Internet for communications.

Membership

In the more traditional groups, membership is strictly controlled; it may take years before an individual is fully trusted. Groups tend to develop elaborate recruiting procedures, including using young children as runners who "graduate" slowly to more difficult and challenging assignments. At the center or core of the leadership one usually finds old friends and frequently family members. Many of the newer groups are built around family relationships, which makes control much easier for the group and infiltration difficult for law enforcement.

In some criminal gangs, especially in the United States, new members are recruited from prisons. This lessens the possibility of infiltration and—because the person has a criminal record—ensures that his or her credibility is in question in the event he or she becomes an informant.

Most established criminal enterprises employ high-priced lawyers who are not actually members of the group but are paid well to represent them. The fact that they do not usually take part in criminal planning or other aspects of criminal activity means that they cannot be prosecuted. New laws in the United States attempt to discourage this by prohibiting illegal funds to be used to hire a lawyer. However, this has not been very successful because it is difficult to prove where the money comes from, especially in those groups that also run "legitimate" businesses.

Sphere of Influence

Most active enterprise crime groups could not survive without corrupt government officials. Corruption practices range from minor bribery of police officers to "look the other way" to paying off judges and high-ranking officials. The investigative team must have some idea of the dimensions of this type of activity.

It also should be noted that not all cooperative efforts are the result of bribery. In Colombia, for example, drug cartels employ threats and other fear tactics to maintain power. Individuals who do not cooperate may find family members kidnapped or killed, or they themselves may be assaulted or even killed.

Blackmail also is used frequently as a means of keeping people in line. Usually, a person is enticed into small illegal acts, the seriousness and number of which gradually increase. When the person reaches a point at which he or she refuses to cooperate, evidence of his or her misdeeds is used to coerce further cooperation.

There are also those who will "look the other way" because the activities of the illegal group benefit their interests. It is not uncommon, for example, for the police to overlook the criminal acts of one group in order to create competition with an established group, usually in the hope that it will drive the established group out of business or at least provide information on them. The problem with this approach is that innocent people are hurt and in the end there is usually little gain for the public.

Enterprise criminals are capable of finding ways to control people even at the highest levels of government; when this occurs, prosecution becomes extremely difficult. Knowing how these activities are carried out and who is involved is important during the preliminary phase of an investigation.

Goals and Means

The means by which a group attains its goals represent its *modus operandi* or method of operation. Knowing how the group works provides the basis for building a criminal case. Enterprise criminals are likely to be very sophisticated. Generally, they would not have attained this level of criminal activity without some knowledge of how to avoid detection and prosecution. Illegal profits may be the goal, but the variety of schemes used is almost limitless.

In many cases the investigator may think he or she knows what is going on, but finds that his or her deductions are incorrect or that the criminals are creating a "smoke screen" to cover their real activities. A common problem for the investigator is the use of "go-betweens" or low-level persons to carry out the actual crimes. Drug traffickers frequently use well-paid "couriers" who are not part of the group, and are thus expendable to them.

Most white-collar crime transactions are recorded on paper or in a computer, and it is difficult to trace the illegal movement of money or goods. The point at which a transaction becomes illegal may also vary; this makes the timing of the arrest very important. This is common in fraud cases.

Proper training, research, and recruiting of specialists are extremely important in combating enterprise crime. In fact, these means are the only way law enforcement personnel can prepare for the many types and methods of criminal activity they will encounter in this kind of investigation. Police departments in the United States have begun to recruit specialists in such areas as computer crime, business fraud, and the theft of technology.

From a research standpoint, efforts are now under way to help identify those areas in which new types of crime may begin, or in which they may increase. We know, for example, that international criminal activity has increased. With this in mind, the Justice Department has established an international section.

The National Institute of Justice, which funds research in the criminal justice area, also has sponsored studies of new ways to deal with enterprise crime. Much of this research is carried out at universities—away from the day-to-day problems of an operational setting with limited resources.

A Typology of Enterprise Criminality _____

Some of the organized criminal groups operating in the United States include: the Mafia (Cosa Nostra); Colombian drug cartels; Jamaican Posses; Asian organized crime—ethnic Viet Ching (Vietnamese), Triads (Chinese), and Yakuza (Japanese); ethnic and racially related street gangs; other neighborhood street gangs; outlaw motorcycle gangs; and white-collar syndicates.

The Mafia

Although not the oldest form of organized crime in the United States, the Mafia—known also as *la Cosa Nostra* ("our thing"), the syndicate, or the mob—has managed to capture the imagination of the American people in a way that is nothing short of phenomenal. For many years the FBI refused to recognize the existence of the Mafia. It was not until a raid on a meeting of Mafia bosses in upstate New York in November of 1957 that people began to recognize the threat.

The Mafia has its roots in Sicily, a small Italian island that, to this day, spawns one of the most pernicious set of criminal enterprises in the world. Although there continues to be some relationship between the Sicilian Mafia, which in fact consists of several gangs who are frequently in conflict with one another, the American Mafia has its own unique and separate structure operating across the United States.

Although there has been some success in fighting the Mafia over the past two decades, the organization continues to be a powerful criminal cartel that operates almost with impunity in some parts of the United States. There are Mafia "families" in many cities in the United States, each with its own well-defined territory and loose agreements relative to the types of crime in which each is involved.

Despite the perceived "romantic" images of brotherhood, a code of honor, and so-called family ties, the Mafia is a vicious, violent organization that preys largely on the failures of human nature. The Mafia is successful largely because of its ability to corrupt public officials and police, its emphasis on preying upon the weak, and its development of an organizational structure difficult for law enforcement to penetrate.

Some recent accounts in the media describe the Mafia as an aged organization that has lost most of its influence. Law enforcement officials who work in this area, however, contend that the Mafia is not only thriving but has become much more sophisticated as a purveyor of a variety of criminal activities—including drug trafficking, murder, loan-sharking, prostitution, penetration of legitimate businesses, and a broad range of other illegal activities.

Colombian Drug-Trafficking Organizations

America's fascination with drugs has spawned a series of international criminal organizations that span the world. Among the most notorious are the Colombian drug cartels, which according to INTERPOL's 2003 report control approximately 80 percent of the cocaine distributed in the world.[1]

According to the Drug Enforcement Administration (DEA), the Colombian drug cartels consist of groups of independent organizations that work together on various levels—supply, distribution, and trafficking—for purposes of efficiency. The groups, which had remarkably stable leadership until the Colombian government "cracked down" on them with some success in the late 1980s, operate under a complex organizational infrastructure involving thousands of employees. Many of these relationships involve family members, but there are indications that this has changed in recent years as a result of investigative successes.

The cartels are characterized by extreme violence, corruption of officials, and even the destabilization of governments. Thousands of people in Colombia, Peru, and other countries have been murdered in the drug wars there, and the rising homicide rate in the United States is attributed in large measure to drug trafficking.

It is estimated that drug networks now exist in every major American city. The DEA defines a Class I drug trafficker as a group with five or more members that smuggles at least four kilograms of cocaine or its equivalent into the United States in a one-month period. As an example of the size and scope of such operations consider that in 1988 the DEA identified some 174 such Class I networks operating in Chicago alone. The FBI during the same year identified more than 200 such groups operating in Florida.[2]

The extensive cartel network provides high-priced lawyers, modern equipment (e.g., radios, cellular phones, airplanes, helicopters), funds for bribing officials, and a broad range of weaponry. The cartel is noted for killing informants or "turnarounds" and will go to almost any length to protect the leadership.

A major concern with regard to the cartel organization is its set of methods for money "laundering" and moving funds back to Colombia. The sums, which are measured in billions of dollars, stagger the imagination. The introduction of new banking laws and other legislation designed to stop such illegal transactions has had relatively little impact; the cartel's sophisticated accountants have devised new ways to avoid detection.

Jamaican Posses

Jamaican Posses are estimated to have as many as 10,000 members operating in at least 40 gangs or Posses in the United States, Canada, Great Britain, and the Caribbean. They are thought to have committed more than 2,000 murders since 1985. Involved primarily in drug dealing and firearms trafficking, the Posses are active in a wide variety of criminal activity, including burglaries, robberies, fraud, and auto theft. These violent gangs are considered to be one of the fastest-growing criminal enterprise groups in the United States. According to one estimate, they control 40 percent of the "crack" cocaine distributed in the country.[3]

The Posses originated in Kingston, Jamaica, and while they cooperate with one another at times, there is also some degree of rivalry and little loyalty among members. They operate throughout the United States and are frequently confused with the Rastafarians, a Jamaican group whose members smoke marijuana as part of their religious practice. Although some Rastafarians are Posse members, there is not thought to be a strong linkage between the Rastafarians and the Posses. The two groups, however, use similar methods to smuggle marijuana. As the Posses have become more sophisticated, their organizational structure has developed along a more traditional triangular model (see Figure 21.1).

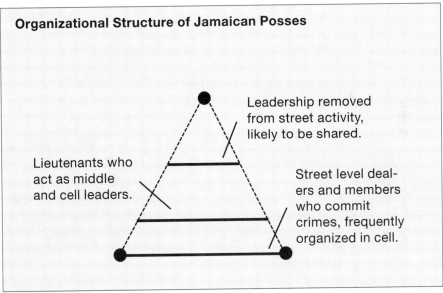

Organizational Structure of Jamaican Posses

Leadership removed from street activity, likely to be shared.

Lieutenants who act as middle and cell leaders.

Street level dealers and members who commit crimes, frequently organized in cell.

Figure 21.1
The triangular model representing the organizational structure of Jamaican Posses. *(Courtesy, U.S. General Accounting Office.)*

The Posses' leadership is not as stable as that of the Colombian cartels and several other groups, perhaps due more to law enforcement pressure and unstable organization than to other factors. Leaders tend to be Jamaican nationals who have legal status in the United States. About 70 percent of the street-level members are illegal aliens. The Immigration and Naturalization Service (INS) reports that there is no shortage of potential recruits in Jamaica who wish to join one of the groups.

The extensive network of the Posses makes it possible for them to secure forged documents and other certification to obtain passports and establish false identities. They move large quantities of illegal drugs, usually marijuana and crack cocaine, in rented trucks and trailers, storing the drugs in rented "safe" houses in various cities.

Posse members are usually heavily armed, with access to automatic weapons. They will frequently establish their operations in neighborhoods controlled by black gangs. Federal investigators believe that most of the money collected remains in the United States, and there is some suspicion that in recent years some of the groups have begun to buy property or small businesses.

Asian Criminal Groups

The development of a number of independent criminal organizations representing various Asian groups has become a source of concern to law enforcement officials in the United States and abroad. Among these organizations are the Yakuza (a Japanese-based group), Chinese Triads and Tongs, and some Vietnamese-controlled groups. Among the more difficult aspects of investigating such groups are their international connections, the use of languages other than English, and a tightly knit structure that stresses individual discipline. Most of these gangs, according to Howard Abadinsky, a Chicago-based expert on organized crime, prey on victims from their own country, many of whom are fearful of cooperating with the police.[4]

Chinese Criminal Organizations

The expansion of American-based Chinese gangs, many with international connections, has resulted in efforts by law enforcement to learn more about their operations. Of particular concern has been the influence of Tongs, many of which are listed as social organizations and are frequently involved in legitimate as well as illegal operations. Tongs involved in illegal activity will usually be affiliated with a gang, which is likely to consist of younger members. One estimate indicates that there are more than 30 Tongs operating in the United States, each with its own membership rules and independent structures.[5] Figure 21.2 illustrates the primary Tongs and their affiliated gangs that are operating in the United States. In recent years many of the gangs have begun to recruit Vietnamese immigrants, many of whom are in the country illegally.

Viet Ching and Vietnamese Gangs

During the 1980s, following the end of the Vietnam war, many Vietnamese immigrants migrated to the United States. Many of them were of Chinese ancestry, known as Viet Ching. A small number began to prey upon the Asian communities. From an investigative standpoint, very little is known about these groups.

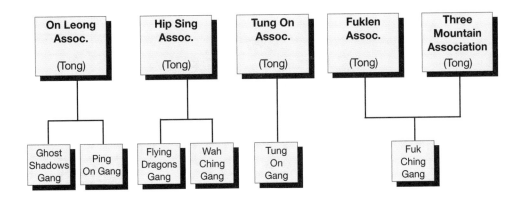

Figure 21.2
Primary Tongs and affiliated gangs in organized criminal activity. *(Courtesy, U.S. General Accounting Office.)*

Vietnamese gangs, which consist almost solely of immigrants from Vietnam and their offspring, are thought to be made up largely of former members of the Vietnamese armed forces and criminals from Vietnam. Adult gangs have a high propensity for violence, particularly within their own community, and are involved in extortion, murder, arson, and in a few cases, fraud. Vietnamese youth gangs, made up of junior and high school students, have begun to emerge in several cities, operating very much like traditional street gangs. They commit robberies, burglaries, and other street crimes, and are likely to be armed with handguns and automatic weapons. Because the crimes are generally well-planned and executed, investigators believe that many of these gangs are led by an older member. (See Figure 21.3.)

Triads

Triad societies have a long history in China, dating back more than 100 years. With the rise to power of the Chinese communists, many of the triads migrated to Taiwan and Hong Kong. Triads engage in a sophisticated set of rituals; the number three (3) represents an important symbol and source of identification and rituals. For example, each member is assigned a number, divisible by three. The term *triad* refers to the relationship between heaven, earth, and humankind.

Although there is apparently little Triad activity in the United States, their involvement in drug trafficking and forms of international crime leads some experts to believe that there is a growing relationship between Tongs and Triads.

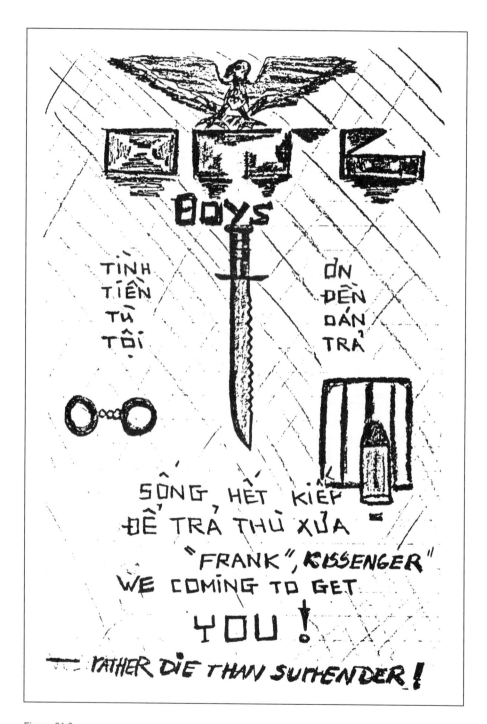

Figure 21.3
Hand-drawn flyer threatening two Orange County, California, police officers. Found in the possession of Vietnamese gang member in 1988. *(From Nontraditional Organized Crime, courtesy, United States General Accounting Office and Westminster Police Department, Westminster, California.)*

Street Gangs

One of the more disturbing trends in recent years has been the emergence of a variety of street gangs whose numbers can be extremely large and whose involvement in various forms of criminal activity is extensive. Many of them are involved in sophisticated drug trafficking activities, their operations characterized by a high degree of violence. It has been estimated that the number of individuals involved in street gangs throughout the United States may surpass 200,000. Many of these gangs are racially or ethnically structured. In Los Angeles, the Crips and the Bloods, both black gangs, are viewed as two of the most violent gangs in American history. Their operations extend across much of the United States. In Chicago, the activities of the El Rukins, a black street gang, have become legend. Their activities ranged from extortion to terrorism until the efforts of a joint FBI/local police task force virtually eliminated the leadership with a series of indictments and trials that left many of the gang's leaders in jail. Investigations of gang-related activities require special techniques and expertise. (See Figures 21.4 and 21.5.)

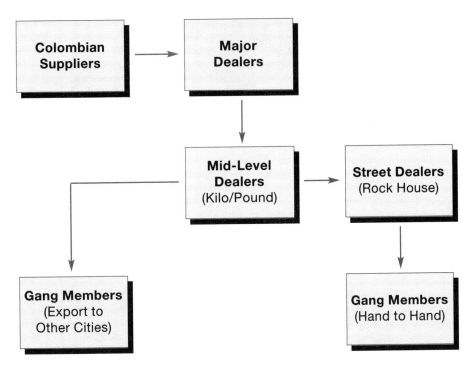

Figure 21.4
Organization of black street gang narcotics operations. *(Courtesy, U.S. General Accounting Office.)*

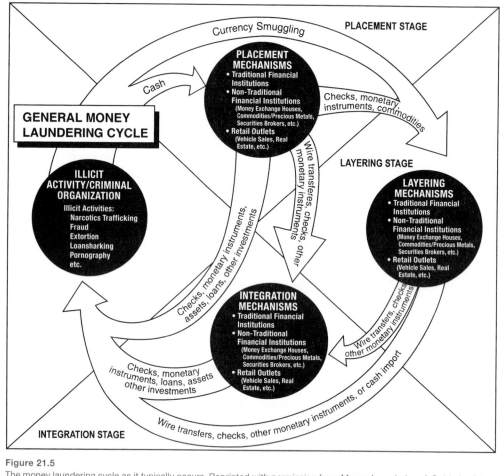

Figure 21.5

The money laundering cycle as it typically occurs. Reprinted with permission from *Money Laundering: A Guide for Criminal Investigation*, by John Madinger and Sydney A. Zalopany. Boca Raton, FL: CRC Press, 1999.

NEW DEVELOPMENTS IN CRIME

Some of the new and developing areas in which enterprise criminals operate include:

- Illegal drugs and drug trafficking—new forms

- Computer-related crime

- Theft of technology; industrial espionage

- Arms dealing

- Art and cultural object theft

- Dealing in body parts, such as kidneys and hearts

- "Kidnapping, slavery, and prostitution"—old crimes in new forms.

- Mail fraud

These represent a few of the areas in which organized crime operates; they reflect the range of activity that, from an investigative standpoint, is creating an even greater need within the law enforcement community for specialization and subspecialization. In some police departments and federal agencies, individuals have developed a particular expertise over a long period of time; when they retire, the organization is likely to be faced with a "knowledge gap" of sizable proportion. Progressive organizations have begun to build into their organization an ability to pass on such knowledge through in-service training, partnering younger investigators with those experienced in specific areas, and using retired investigators as consultants. Ultimately, as the world becomes smaller and more complex, the need for greater subspecialization will continue to increase.

The Investigation of Illegal Drugs and Drug Trafficking

Although drugs and drug trafficking have been around for several decades, the last part of the twentieth century saw some significant changes and trends. For the most part, drug-related cases have become a specialized form of investigation in the majority of departments and agencies.

Drugs are brought into the United States through many channels and by a variety of means. A key investigative activity is the development of information and intelligence relative to sources and methods of supply and the distribution networks within a city. Another important aspect of drug investigation involves tracking money. Most transactions occur in cash, but the large volume of currency, frequently in relatively small bills, makes concealing and "laundering" it extremely difficult. Drug dealers have adopted advanced methods of accounting, frequently using legitimate businesses and banks to help move funds through complicated transactions.

Most sophisticated drug dealers attempt to blend into the community. Their large expenditures, however, coupled with no visible means of support, may aid in detection. They are likely to use false credentials—drivers licenses or other forged documents—to maintain cover. Leads can be generated by developing informants among suppliers of such documents.

Generally, drug-related investigations involve four specific areas:

1. traditional investigations

2. surveillance

3. undercover and informant operations

4. cooperative inter-agency investigations

5. international investigations involving two or more countries

Traditional Investigations

Traditional investigations usually occur where there is a complainant, victim, or witness who provides information concerning a drug operation. Two aspects of such cases are somewhat different from those involving other forms of crime: (1) the need to secure evidence (illegal drugs usually are not sold to strangers), which establishes the *corpus delicti*; and (2) the frequent need to protect witnesses from the drug dealers.

In some cases the witness may also be a drug user, which can further complicate matters. Often there is also an ulterior motive for providing information, usually part of an effort to eliminate competition. In conducting such investigations it is important to make an effort to identify the drug network and the individuals within it. In today's society, it is relatively easy to arrest street-level pushers or locate "crack houses," but much more difficult to conduct successful investigations into the hierarchy of the criminal network. To do so requires patience, a willingness to explore and investigate a large number of possible clues, and usually a great deal of cooperation with other law enforcement personnel and agencies.

Surveillance

Surveillance, which makes up much of the work of drug investigators, represents the most effective means of collecting information in this area. Both electronic and visual surveillance have proved to be valuable tools. However, one of the pitfalls in such investigations is the inability, at least at the moment, to put together pieces of information in a way that makes sense. Many criminals have taken to using "code" words in conversations, which are designed to hinder eavesdropping efforts, while others move to other jurisdictions to conduct meetings. For this reason it is particularly important to record as many details as possible when working a surveillance. What may appear to be casual meetings with passersby, as well as the use of specific words—or even gestures—when communicating may prove valuable as the investigation unfolds.

Undercover and Informant Operations

Undercover and informant operations represent an important means by which intelligence and information is collected; these techniques should be viewed in most cases as a feasible way to reach as high into the criminal enterprise as possible. Although some investigators in drug investigations concentrate on that which is before them, usually the point-of-sale, the identification of the seller's contacts and source of supply is of far greater importance. The user leads to the seller, who leads to a wholesaler, who leads to an organizational structure, which leads ultimately to the means by which drugs enter the country or are produced, i.e., the source of supply.

Surveillance and undercover investigations involve a degree of specialization and training beyond the scope of this text. However, it is important to recognize that these investigations are perhaps the most dangerous in police work today. See Chapter 9 for more information on general surveillance techniques.

The use of informants in drug investigations also necessitates a high degree of care, both to protect the informant and to ensure that the information being provided is accurate and truthful. In drug-related cases, informants working for money have something to gain by providing information, even if it is false. Even those who have other reasons for informing are not likely to have humanitarian motives: they may provide information to keep the police off their backs, to eliminate the competition, or to settle an old score. Thus, it is important to ascertain an informant's motive for giving information.

Care should be taken when meeting informants, or when passing information, even over the telephone. If the information is used to make an arrest or conduct an investigation, every effort should be made to protect the source. This is easier said than done; a person who has been arrested, particularly when not for an obvious mistake, is generally looking and listening for a clue as to how he or she was "fingered." See Chapter 8 for more information on using and cultivating informants.

Cooperative Investigations

Cooperative investigations have become very commonplace, and the establishment of task forces and teams from several departments or agencies has proved to be an important part of successful drug investigation. At the outset, clear lines of responsibility and authority must be established. It is crucial that individuals recognize the importance of working as a team in every way.

A problem commonly suffered by multijurisdictional teams is a conflict over differences in policies and procedures. This can be resolved by instituting a joint training program. Individuals must be made aware of potential problems, and guidelines must be conceived of early on in the process—involving such things as who is to be notified when a case is implemented or an arrest made, what is the policy with regard to informants, what are the unit's weapons policies, and what is the chain of command. Some jurisdictions have experienced major problems with "leaks" of information, discordant positions on how an investigation should be conducted, and conflict over who is responsible for prosecution of a case. A successful drug investigation accomplishes a set of goals that is consistent with an organization's policy, aiming to bring into custody the highest individual involved who is within the scope of the law enforcement team's ability to investigate and produce a prosecutable case.

International Investigations

Investigations involving two or more countries have become commonplace in recent years, and are usually carried out by federal agencies. The Drug Enforcement Administration (DEA), the U.S. Customs Service, the Federal Bureau of Investigation, the U.S. Postal Inspection Service, and other agencies now have agents assigned to posts overseas, frequently working in cooperation with counterparts in other nations. Additionally, the Central Intelligence Agency and the U.S. military are also involved in assisting in international investigations involving organized crime and drug trafficking.

INTERPOL and EUROPOL serve as data-collection and information-exchange points, as well as intelligence sources for law enforcement agencies throughout the world. Local police can work through National Central Bureaus, which are established in countries belonging to each of these organizations. Although they do not have investigative powers, these organizations serve as important informational centers on individuals and groups.

Often overlooked by investigators are the security operations of multinational corporations, which have operations throughout the world, and often can provide a wealth of information.

Drugs

The following discussion centers on the activities of gangs and groups involved in drug-trafficking, rather than on individual sellers ("pushers") and users. Nevertheless, it is important to be familiar with the various substances most likely to be marketed by criminal enterprises.

Cocaine is a powerful addictive stimulant that directly affects the brain. Cocaine has been labeled the drug of the 1980s and 1990s, because of its extensive popularity and use during this period. However, cocaine is not a new drug. In fact, it is one of the oldest known drugs. The pure chemical, cocaine is a natural product derived from the leaves of the coca plant. A potent central nervous system stimulant and local anesthetic, it induces euphoria, confidence, and increased energy, and is accompanied physiologically by increased heart rate, dilated pupils, fever, and sweating. The "crash" following the "high" ranges from irritability and the desire for more drugs, to anxiety, hallucinations, and paranoia.[6]

Crack cocaine, sometimes referred to as rock cocaine, or free base cocaine, is a pure form of the drug that appears as a white crystal or cream-colored powder, sometimes in wet form, and frequently in a chunk or rock-like form. It is usually packaged in foil, although in recent years various forms of packaging have appeared. It is usually inhaled through a pipe, preferably a water pipe, with the high taking effect almost immediately and lasting for 10 to 20 minutes.[7]

Heroin (diacetylmorphine) is a chemical derivative of morphine that is more potent and addictive than morphine.

Marijuana is made from the dried leaves of the hemp plant. It is usually smoked for its intoxicating effect.

PCP (phencyclidine), called "angel dust" on the street, is a very potent drug that causes hallucinations and flashbacks.

Methamphetamine, crystal meth, is an addictive stimulant drug that dramatically affects the central nervous system. It is generally made in clandestine laboratories with relatively inexpensive over-the-counter ingredients.

In addition to these commonly trafficked drugs, there is a large business in amphetamines (stimulants that affect the central nervous system), barbiturates (sedatives and hypnotics that depress the central nervous system), and a newly developing group known as "designer" drugs, which are created in illicit laboratories.

Virtually all cocaine is produced in South America, entering the United States through various ports of entry by a variety of illegal means. Southwest Asia continues to dominate the heroin market in terms of production and distribution. Most heroin seizures have taken place in Southwest Asia[8] in the last decade, but in 2001 the most seizures were in the East and Southeast Asia subregion. Approximately 50 percent of heroin consumed in the United States originates in Southwest Asia, with a large proportion of the balance originating in Southeast Asia. Because drug sources and routes have begun to change as a result of pressures applied by the United States and cooperating countries, the reader should be aware that the most accurate assessment of the current situation can be obtained from the U.S. Drug Enforcement Administration (DEA).

Specialized criminal investigations require a well-planned, coordinated, step-by-step approach, usually involving more than one jurisdiction or agency. Penetration of drug rings is difficult and dangerous, and the investigative approach will frequently be determined by the type of gang under investigation. The use of undercover operatives has proved successful over the years, but the escalating caution exercised by gangs makes this tactic increasingly difficult. In recent years informants—frequently those who have been arrested and developed as "turnarounds"—have been used as an effective method for gaining permission to conduct wiretaps or other forms of electronic surveillance. This approach helps identify couriers and routes, as well as distribution points. Physical surveillance should be elaborately planned, and officers operating in teams offer the best probability of success.

When a gang has been identified, and the principals located, it is possible to monitor their activities and determine the means through which money is laundered or banked. A key aspect of the investigation is record keeping; every detail should be carefully documented for use in court. Frequently, a successful investigation will depend on the prosecution's ability to explain in minute detail (through an investigator's or informant's testimony) the means by which drugs are moved, who moved them, and who was responsible for the operation. Investigators should bear in mind that the actual handling of the drugs is usually left to relatively low-level members of the organization. The means by which these suspects pass information and money on to their leaders frequently forms the basis for a larger case. In this regard, even minute details are important, because acknowledgments are usually made in code, or through *cutouts* (individuals who know nothing other than the message being passed), and other forms of communication. The use of beepers, walkie-talkies, and cellular phones has become commonplace.

In one case, law enforcement officials reviewed the records of a paging company from which beepers had been rented, and were able to identify hundreds of contacts made between individuals. The code used was easily broken by the team conducting the investigation. For example, a specific number was used to indicate the quantity of drugs to be delivered, whether delivery was successful, and who was to carry the drugs. Although this appeared on the pager as something like "201054," the large volume of calls made it quite simple for investigators to decode meanings. Of course, the frequently called telephone numbers also proved of value, as a means of identifying both fixed locations and automobiles, through the use of a reverse directory.* Where walkie-talkies are used, it may be possible to use a scanner to identify the frequencies being used by suspects. Tapping cellular phones is somewhat more difficult, but not impossible.

---

* A reverse directory, supplied by the telephone company, provides the location where a telephone is connected.

The investigator should constantly be aware of the importance of reaching higher up into the organization as the investigation progresses. The arrest of low-level dealers or suppliers has only minimal impact on a group's operations.

RICO AND ASSET FORFEITURE
IN THE INVESTIGATIVE PROCESS

One of the more effective tools used by law enforcement over the past decade has been what is known as *asset forfeiture*. It falls under the provisions of a federal law known as RICO (Racketeer Influenced Corrupt Organization), wherein civil remedies can be used against organized criminal activity. The RICO laws apply to a broad range of organized criminal activity. Specifically, in the case of illegal drugs, the government can seize property that has been used in violation of the law or bought with illicit money. In addition, property seized by a local law enforcement officer can be turned over to a federal agent, as if the seizure had been made by federal authorities.[9] The forfeiture does not require that an individual be convicted of a crime, but only that the person's property was used for or during the commission of a crime. Through asset forfeiture provisions the government has confiscated money, houses, cars, boats, airplanes, electronic equipment, and weapons. This has not only impacted on the specific criminals targeted, but in many jurisdictions has been used as a means for law enforcement to expand their own efforts.

Federal racketeering statutes were first enacted in 1934, but a major breakthrough in the law came in 1970 with the enactment of the Racketeer Influenced and Corrupt Organizations Act (RICO), which amended existing statutes. The act prohibits four specific activities:

- Investing the proceeds of a pattern of racketeering activity in an enterprise that engages in interstate or foreign commerce;

- Acquiring or maintaining an interest in such an enterprise by means of a pattern of racketeering activity;

- Using a pattern of such activity in conducting the affairs of such an enterprise;

- Conspiracy to do any of the above.[10]

RICO also provides a provision that makes it possible for lawyers and private citizens to sue if their property was part of a criminal act covered by the statute.

In order to strengthen drug laws, the Continuing Criminal Enterprise (CCE) statute was enacted to make it a crime if six or more persons acting in concert commit a continuing series of felonies under the 1970 Drug Abuse Prevention and Control Act. The courts have ruled that a "series" involves at least three related violations. This law provides for a mandatory 20-year sentence, a fine of not more than $2 million, and the forfeiture of profits and/or interests in the enterprise.

These laws provide the backbone of the government's efforts to combat organized and enterprise crime in the United States, and have been used against foreign nationals who are involved in illegal activities in the country.

REFERENCES

1   INTERPOL, Information Sheet on Cocaine Production, 2003. *<http://www.interpol.int/Public/Drugs/ cocaine/default.asp>*

2   *Nontraditional Organized Crime: Law Enforcement Officials' Perspectives on Five Criminal Groups* (Washington, DC: U.S. General Accounting Office, September 1989), 13.

3   Ibid., 22.

4   Howard Abadinsky, *Organized Crime*, 3rd ed. (Chicago: Nelson-Hall, 1990), 255.

5   *Nontraditional Organized Crime, op. cit.*, 36-37.

6   Karen Bellinir, ed., *Drug Abuse Sourcebook: Basic Consumer Health Information about Illicit Substances of Abuse and the Diversion of Prescription Medications* (Detroit, MI: Omnigraphics, 2000).

7   "What is Crack," pamphlet published by Northeastern Metropolitan Enforcement group.

8   United Nations Office on Drugs and Crime, *Global Illicit Drug Trends 2003* (Vienna: UNODC, 2003).

9   Robert M. Lombardo, "Asset Forfeiture: Civil Remedies Against Organized Crime," in *An International Perspective on Organized Crime*, Jane Rae Buckwalter, ed. (Chicago: Office of International Criminal Justice, 1990).

10   Kenneth Carlson and Peter Finn, "Prosecuting Criminal Enterprises," *Bureau of Justice Statistics: Special Report*, November 1993, 2.

SUPPLEMENTAL READINGS

Abadinsky, Howard. *Organized Crime*. 6th ed. Belmont, CA: Wadsworth, 1999.

Albanese, Jay S. *Organized Crime in Our Times*. 4th ed. Cincinnati: Anderson, 2004.

Benson, Michael L., and Francis T. Cullen. *Combating Corporate Crime: Local Prosecutors at Work*. Boston: Northeastern University Press, 1998.

Booth, Martin. *The Dragon Syndicates: The Global Phenomenon of the Triads*. New York: Doubleday, 1999.

Einstein, Stanley, and Menachim Amir (eds.). *Organized Crime: Uncertainties and Dilemmas*. Chicago: Office of International Criminal Justice, 1999.

Finckenauer, James O., and Elin J. Waring. *The Russian Mafia in America: Immigration, Culture, and Crime*. Boston: Northeastern University Press, 1998.

Huston, Peter. *Tongs, Gangs, and Triads: Chinese Crime Groups in North America*. Boulder, CO: Paladin Press, 1995.

Kelly, Robert J. *The Upperworld and the Underworld: Case Studies of Racketeering and Business Infiltrations in the United States*. New York: Kluwer Academic/Plenum, 1999.

Kenney, Dennis J., and James O. Finckenauer. *Organized Crime in America*. Belmont, CA: Wadsworth, 1995.

Lofquist, William S., Mark A. Cohen, and Gary A. Rabe, eds. *Debating Corporate Crime*. Cincinnati: Anderson, 1997.

Lyman, Michael D. and Gary W. Potter. *Drugs in Society: Causes, Concepts and Control*. 4th ed. Cincinnati: Anderson, 2003.

Madinger, John, and Sydney A. Zalopany. *Money Laundering: A Guide for Criminal Investigators*. Boca Raton, FL: CRC Press, 1999.

Mahan, Sue, with Katherine O'Neil. *Beyond the Mafia: Organized Crime in the Americas*. Thousand Oaks, CA: Sage, 1998.

Schatzberg, Rufus, and Robert J. Kelly. *African-American Organized Crime: A Social History*. New Brunswick, NJ: Rutgers University Press, 1997.

Williams, Phil (ed.). *Russian Organized Crime: The New Threat?* Portland, OR: Frank Cass, 1997.

CHAPTER 22

The Automobile and Crime

In today's world, the automobile is sometimes used to commit a crime. If it is stolen, it becomes the object of a crime; if carjacked, its driver becomes the victim of a crime. This chapter will cover various aspects of automobile larceny, and how it and carjacking are investigated.

LARCENY DEFINED

The term *larceny* is generally misunderstood; many people think it simply means stealing or theft. In addition to motor vehicle and bicycle theft, larceny may involve shoplifting, purse snatching, picking pockets, and breaking into coin-operated machines. How then is it to be characterized?

Under the law, the crime of larceny comprises these elements:

1. the taking and removing
2. of another's personal property
3. with intent, permanently, to deprive the owner of its use.

Sometimes confused with larceny, *fraud* can be defined as a deception deliberately employed to achieve an unlawful gain. The following example excerpted from the Uniform Crime Reporting System best illustrates the distinction between the two:

> An individual drives into a gasoline station and requests gasoline be pumped into his motor vehicle. He then leaves the station without paying. What type of crime is this?

By asking for the gasoline, the individual enters into an implied contract. . . . His departure without paying constitutes the offense of Fraud. An individual who takes gasoline from a self-service station without paying commits a Larceny-theft (no implied contract). . . . Gasoline taken from a parked vehicle would be Larceny-theft.[1]

STATISTICS

From 2000 to 2001, there was an average of approximately 7,023,880 larceny-theft offenses per year; motor vehicle theft averaged approximately 1,193,230 during these years. The average value of motor vehicles reported stolen in 2001 was $6,646. The projected total value was $8.2 billion and nearly 62 percent of that value was reclaimed.[2] Most of those arrested for this crime were under 25.

WHY MOTOR VEHICLES ARE STOLEN

Joyriding

A significant number of motor vehicle thefts can be attributed to youthful offenders looking for driving or racing thrills—some acting on a dare and others acting as part of gang initiation. Increasingly, though, youths are stealing cars for profit through the sale of accessories (e.g., compact disc players) or are suppliers for professional vehicle thieves.

Transportation

Committing Another Felony

Having a mode of transportation available for a getaway following the commission of a crime can be accomplished by stealing a car. The crime could be armed robbery, kidnapping, a gang-related drive-by shooting, or a homicide. The vehicle is generally abandoned for another vehicle with a different description. If several perpetrators are involved, they may utilize two cars to frustrate apprehension at road blocks or otherwise. Sometimes the stolen vehicle is pushed into a pond, buried in underbrush, burned, or discarded in a large parking lot, shopping mall, or airport. If not discarded immediately, the possibility of its identification can be reduced by: (1) altering license plates (covering with mud, repainting or taping over numbers, or partially bending the plate) or (2) switching to plates stolen from another vehicle. Today, because information on stolen plates is computerized, thieves often steal the car on the day of the crime, before its loss is discovered and entered into the computer base.

Transitory Needs

Runaways, hitchhikers, and other transients sometimes steal cars to help them get to their destination. They frequently abandon the vehicle when the gas runs out and steal another that will also be abandoned. Gang-related drive-by shootings account for another short-term need for a stolen vehicle.

Profit Motive

Two kinds of individuals are concerned with turning a profit through the disappearance of a motor vehicle: those who steal cars (or have them stolen) for resale in domestic and foreign markets and those who dismantle them for their parts and accessories. Frequently, such crimes are the work of organized theft rings. In one 1999 case, vehicles were stolen from the United States and Canada by a group of suspects from Lebanon; it is believed that the proceeds, amounting to millions, were used to support terrorism.[3]

Organized Theft Rings

Organized theft rings usually employ youths to steal cars; frequently, they even "order" a specific type of vehicle. The youths start by stripping parked vehicles for parts (e.g., radios, tape decks and compact disc players, wheels and tires, hub caps, chrome trim, batteries, and alternators). Made bold by success, they may even remove bucket seats or even transmissions and motors. The larger parts are dismantled in *chop shops* (see below) and are then sold to illegitimate body shops. At drag strips, parts may be exchanged with unscrupulous auto enthusiasts looking for bargains. It can take less than one hour to strip a car of its accessories. Thereupon, it may be driven to a rented private garage, an illegitimate commercial one, or a salvage yard; once there, it will be dismantled for major body components (e.g., doors, fenders,

Figure 22.1
Police officers inspect bodies and a getaway car in a taped-off crime scene area after a botched holdup in September 1999. Generally, when a stolen car is used as a getaway car it is later abandoned for another vehicle that fits a different description. *(AP Photo/Gabriel Piko, La Nacion.)*

hoods, transmission, etc.). The engine's identification number must be altered before it (or the car) can be sold without being traced. On top of the dashboard at the driver's side is the most important part to be stripped from a stolen "totaled" (insurance-wise) vehicle: the vehicle identification number (VIN) metal plate.

The term *chop shop* refers to a garage or salvage yard where stolen vehicles are broken up with wrenches and other tools or cut apart with acetyline torches. Untraceable parts are sold to apparently legitimate repair shops, salvage yards, and body shops operating in collusion with chop shops. In general, chop shops are found in large cities like New York, Los Angeles, and Chicago. Few vehicles subjected to this treatment are ever recovered.

Resale

Fraudulent Title or Legal Restriction
In some resale operations, the entire vehicle, is sold, usually after repainting. It is then provided with a fraudulent title, with which a proper registration certificate can be obtained. Luxury-class cars are handled in this manner and sold (often to foreign buyers); less expensive cars may be transported to another state and sold to used-car dealers or private individuals. It is not unheard of for a vehicle to be stolen to meet the specific needs of a prospective customer. A fictitious bill of sale can be made out to obtain a registration certificate in a nontitle state, after which it can be utilized to obtain title in a title state.

Title Switching
When a vehicle is so damaged that repair costs exceed its market price, its undamaged parts are sold for salvage. The greatest value accrues from its certificate of title and VIN plate. Often thieves will steal a vehicle that matches the junked one and switch VIN plates. Together with the certificate of title, the altered vehicle can be easily sold below market price to an innocent purchaser.

Insurance Fraud

The monetary loss to insurance companies and motor vehicle owners through increased insurance rates significantly contributes to making motor vehicle larceny one of the most costly property crimes. Several illicit means are employed to extort money from insurance companies: for instance, false claims, phantom car claims, and insuring wrecks.

False Claims
One kind of false claim involves the unprincipled individual who owns and insures a car that he or she strips of the parts that can be sold or bartered. He or she then may burn or push it into a deep lake, report it stolen to the police, and file a claim with the insurance company. Often in such cases, the insurance is taken out with the express intent to defraud. In other cases, the intent may develop as the need to avoid accountability arises: the car may have been involved in a hit-and-run accident, for example, with a policy that covers minimal bodily injury. Other reasons that may prompt an insured owner to make a false stolen vehicle report arise, for instance, when there is a bitterly contested divorce and title must be turned over to a spouse or when the car is about to be repossessed by a loan company.

Phantom Car Claims

In a phantom car claim, a forged title to a nonexistent ("phantom") vehicle is utilized to obtain insurance coverage. Care must be taken that the VIN employed is not already registered. The car is then reported stolen and an insurance claim submitted.

Insuring a Wreck

Insuring a wreck is a variation of the phantom car claim fraud. In this scheme, the offender buys title to a total wreck. Observing caution with regard to the VIN (mentioned above), the wreck is insured and later reported stolen. Then a claim for its replacement cost is submitted to the insurance company.

INVESTIGATING MOTOR VEHICLE THEFT

Both the high number of motor vehicle thefts and the low clearance rate suggest that such cases are difficult to solve. The reasons are many:

1. The crime is easy to commit: most stolen cars are unlocked or keys are left in the ignition.

2. It is hard to trace stripped parts to stolen vehicles.

3. Many offenders (joyriders and those looking for temporary transportation) are quick to abandon the vehicle.

4. Car theft rings consist of organized, sophisticated professionals.

5. The sheer volume of caseload and the fact that motor vehicle thefts are crimes against property rather than persons diminish the resources the police usually can assign to these investigations.

The disparate motives involved in motor vehicle theft (joyriding, temporary transportation, profit) and the condition in which the property is ultimately found will determine the investigative path to be taken. The report of a disappearance starts the process. At this point, the detective assigned to the case will focus on known circumstances:

- Where was the vehicle parked?

- Was it locked?

- Was the key in the ignition?

- Who was the last person to use it?

- At time of theft, where was the person from whom the vehicle was stolen?

- Who else possesses keys?

- When was it last seen?

- What is the name of the title holder?

- If financed, are payments up-to-date?

- What is the name of the insurance company?

- Were there any witnesses to the theft? What are their names?

Additional information is sought concerning the vehicle: year, make, model, body style, color, VIN, license plate (number and state), plus any distinctive accessories such as bumper stickers or window decals that can help identify the vehicle. The detective should interview the person who parked the vehicle and conduct a neighborhood canvass. Computers provide a new investigative aid: they can perform correlation analysis. If a thief drove a blue Chevrolet "getaway car," for example, a computer search for that model and color may yield information about where it was stolen, as well as other circumstances concerning the theft.

Recovered Cars

Experience teaches that motive greatly influences whether a stolen car will be recovered: thieves such a joyriders and those looking for short-term transportation tend to abandon it fairly quickly. When a vehicle is stolen in order to commit another crime—bank robbery or kidnapping—investigating the major crime is of paramount importance because it is more likely to identify the perpetrator(s). Nevertheless, an effort must be made to determine who owns the vehicle and to learn what information he or she has on its disappearance and on those responsible. Cars stolen for profit are far less likely to be recovered. In each case, a neighborhood canvass might uncover information on the person(s) who discarded the dismantled remains of the car.

Figure 22.2
A VIN plate from a new car. The VIN is the most certain means of identifying a vehicle's true owner. *(Courtesy, E.S. Boyne.)*

Identifying the Vehicle

For cars that are recovered quickly, unless the plates were stolen, the license plate and the contents of the glove compartment may be sufficient to identify the owner. If not tampered with, the VIN is the most certain means of identifying the owner. VIN information can be obtained from the National Auto Theft Bureau (NATB).

Searching the Vehicle

When a vehicle is recovered, it should first be examined for fingerprints and palm prints (especially the rear view mirror). Coffee containers, soft drink bottles, paper bags, newspapers, and other debris possibly left by those who used the stolen vehicle should be collected and examined as potential evidence; cigarette butts in particular should be collected because DNA from saliva can be compared to that of any suspect. In a sexual abuse or kidnapping case, cars used to transport the victim might contain a facial tissue, handkerchief, or piece of towel that was used as a wipe or gag. If the object bears semen or saliva, it can serve as a DNA source. If the car was stripped, a criminalist should search for and photograph any tool mark or pattern evidence that outlines (in the paint) the place from which the part was removed. Such evidence is of value when there is a matching part found in the possession of a "hot parts" dealer, salvage yard, body shop, chop shop, or barter exchange.

Follow-Up Activities

Pursuant to the report of a stolen vehicle, there is follow-up—first by the patrol force and then (especially after the abandoned car is recovered) by detectives. For each follow-up investigation, the respective activity is distinctly different in procedure and purpose.

Patrol Force

The patrol force (radio car officers, in particular) should be on the lookout for vehicles bearing license plates that have been reported stolen. Other indicators can alert an observant officer to a vehicle theft—for instance, the behavior or appearance of the driver or the condition of the vehicle. Most large municipal departments now equip their patrol cars with computers, thereby allowing for a quick check for stolen license plates.

Driver Behavior or Appearance

Reckless or aggressive driver behavior such as speeding, running a red light, weaving in and out of traffic, not signaling lane changes, and/or illegal passing or tailgating should draw police attention. Also suspicious would be a driver who, on sighting a patrol car, becomes nervous and makes a sudden turn, apparently to elude the patrol car, or slows down to allow it to pass. Conversely, by holding to a speed well below the legal limit to avoid being noticed, a very cautious driver may defeat his or her purpose: experienced officers are aware of this subterfuge. If, once stopped, the driver, when asked, is unable to perform specific operations without fumbling (for instance, turn on the bright lights intermittently then permanently, or adjust the window washer to fast, delayed, slow), this should be viewed with suspicion. Personal appearance also can be a factor—for instance, a driver wearing gloves in warm weather, or a poorly dressed youth at the wheel of an expensive new car might be suspicious. Appropriate responses would include computer checking of the vehicle itself and of pertinent documents after a traffic stop.

When stopping a minority driver on suspicion, officers should be particularly sensitive; police must be able to articulate why such official action is reasonable. Racial profiling, or the appearance of such, should be avoided. In addition, if an officer orders a car to pull over and its driver attempts to get away, the departmental policy dictates whether a high-speed chase is permissible. More progressive departments generally frown on high-speed pursuit. This perilous practice, which endangers both officers and citizenry, is no longer standard operating procedure.

Condition of Vehicle

A moving vehicle offers few observable indicators that it has been stolen, but the watchful patrol officer will notice a partially covered license plate, a broken window, or a car being driven with a window open in cold or inclement weather. When ordering the driver of a suspect vehicle to pull over, the officer must not be careless; he or she should strictly adhere to the precautions taught for checking out a vehicle and its driver.

The officer looks for the following:

1. Damage signifying forced entry:

    a.   Broken window glass;

    b.   Punched out door or trunk lock;

    c.   Broken door handle; glove compartment, door, or trunk that has been pried open.

2. With regard to the car's tags:

    a.   Are front and back plates the same?

    b.   Is one plate loosely attached, covering another?

    c.   Are new bolts used to attach old plates?

    d.   Are new plates on an old vehicle?

    e.   Are impacted insects on the rear plate?

    The (NCIC) National Crime Information Center (and, increasingly, state motor vehicle departments or bureaus) can provide information on whether the vehicle has been stolen or involved in the commission of a felony. Following a license tag check, determine whether the names of owner and driver match. If not, can the driver name the registered owner?

3. With regard to the VIN plate:

    Is it damaged or altered?

4. With regard to the ignition lock:

    a.   Is it damaged or missing?

    b.   Is there other evidence of tampering?

    c.   Does the ignition key start the engine?

    d.   Does the ignition key open the driver's door?

Record Checking

State motor vehicle departments or bureaus and the National Crime Information Center (NCIC) are invaluable repositories of vehicle information.[4] They can verify that a driver's license number is issued to a particular person and specify the person's reported name, gender, address, age, social security number, height, and weight. The NCIC can also provide information concerning stolen vehicles, license plates, stolen parts, and whether a vehicle was used in the commission of a felony. Depending on the outcome of such inquiries, patrol car officers can confirm or put their suspicions to rest and act accordingly.[5]

Detectives

Recovered Vehicles

When a suspected stolen vehicle is found abandoned, the investigative path taken by a detective depends on why it was stolen in the first place. To some extent, this may be determined by its condition. The reason for the theft may also be indicated by the distance between where it was stolen and where it was abandoned. A detective is responsible for the follow-up investigation of reported stolen vehicles even when they are recovered stripped down almost totally or when they are never recovered.

Vehicle Intact or with Minor Damage

A vehicle found intact or with minor damage was probably "borrowed" by a joyrider or stolen for transportation. If abandoned a relatively short distance from the scene of the theft, it may have been taken for joyriding or to escape from a crime scene. If it is found a considerable distance from the scene of the theft, it is more likely that it was taken by transients in need of transportation. If the intent is to commit another crime, a second stolen car is often parked away from the scene and is then driven to another point and frequently left relatively close to where the perpetrator(s) live.

Joyriders

Information regarding possible joyrider suspects may be obtained from juvenile aid officers. Such officers may also know where auto parts are bartered or "fenced." In such situations, informants or undercover officers may be helpful.

Transportation Needs

Two kinds of offenders steal for transportation purposes. One type includes those looking for escape after committing a felony (robbery, kidnapping, etc.). In such a situation, investigating the felony that required the escape car is primary; if that investigation is successful, it will usually solve the vehicle theft as well. Soon after the commission of the felony, such criminals will often switch to another car, and the one they abandon is generally found not too far from the crime scene.

Figure 22.3
A Philadelphia police officer carries "chopped" parts of stolen cars in the city's East Frankford section. A high-tech locating device on a stolen car at the site led to the arrest of five people in the operation. *(AP Photo/George Widman.)*

The second type of individual who steals to meet transportation needs is generally a runaway, a hitchhiker, or something along those lines. Usually these perpetrators abandon the stolen car at some distance from where it was taken. Unless there were alert eyewitnesses or some traceable item is left behind, apprehension of the perpetrators is unlikely.

Vehicle Stripped Down

Stripped-down vehicles are sometimes dumped not too far from where they were dismantled (e.g., in a private garage, the location of which is changed with some regularity). A neighborhood inquiry may disclose an individual who is suspicious about the use to which a garage is being put. Mechanical equipment or noise not usually associated with a private parking garage may be noted and reported to police. The make and owner of a dismantled car may be disclosed through a discrete attempt to buy parts and accessories from street and shop dealers, uncovering thereby the outlet used to dispose of them. Then, through the person(s) and shop involved, a case might be built against those responsible for the vehicle theft.

Vehicle Not Recovered

A principal reason why a vehicle would not be recovered is because it was shipped out of the country, out of the state, or sold as scrap. The precinct detective is seldom able to solve such a theft. The work of sophisticated gangs must be met with resources adequate to the task—for example, insurance company investigators, the federal government, the NATB, and INTERPOL.

RETROSPECTIVE REVIEW

Throughout this text we emphasize the three major sources of information—people, physical evidence, and records. It is appropriate at this point to review vehicle larceny from this triadic perspective.

People

A somewhat diverse set of persons can be helpful to the detective, provided information is willingly given or obtained through skillful interviewing and interrogation. Commencing with the complainant, potential sources comprise neighbors, juveniles (including gang members), body shop and salvage yard workers, auto parts dealers, customs officials, NATB personnel, insurance investigators, suspects, and suspects' relatives and friends.

Physical Evidence

In general, the examination of physical evidence suspected of having been part of a vehicle is a task for the criminalist. Tools employed in dismantling a car may leave marks on the metal; such impressions may be converted into associative evidence when (and if) a suspected tool is recovered. By using an etching solution, it is possible to restore an engine number removed by sanding or by using a metal punch and hammer. When this process fails, heat from a torch may be attempted with some success.

Records

The records of state motor vehicle departments are of obvious value to the detective in that they provide the name and address of the owner of the car and identify its likely driver. When discovered on a vehicle part, VIN information can help trace ownership up to the present. To expose fraudulent claims, insurance company records are often invaluable. Even though different insurance companies are involved, arson suspects can be unearthed if suspicious car fires are computerized on a national level. INTERPOL records and commerce and shipping information often prove useful when cars are shipped to foreign countries.

Computers have the capability of storing data and later, of searching that data for the many variables related to both the car and its owner (or driver). For example:

Car	Driver
Make	Name of owner
Model	Physical description
Year	Gender and age
Color	Photograph
State	Social Security Number
License Number	

Motor vehicle theft is likely to decrease when resources commensurate with annual financial loss are made available to local and national levels of law enforcement.

CARJACKING

Carjacking differs from motor vehicle larceny in that the offender uses or threatens to use force on the victim who, unlike the victim of a motor vehicle larceny, is present when the crime is committed. A special report by Patsy Klaus and others in the Bureau of Justice Statistics offers considerable information regarding carjacking in the United States.[6]

Carjacking is defined as "the attempted or completed robbery of the victim's motor vehicle by a stranger to the victim." According to the report,

Seventy percent of all completed carjackings involved the use of firearms; in about 20 percent of attempted carjackings, the use of a knife or other unknown weapon was more likely. In 83 percent of *all* carjackings, a weapon of some kind was involved. Although injury to the victim did not result in most carjackings, it was twice as likely in those that were completed. Surprisingly, only somewhat more than one-half of attempted cases were reported to the police, but all completed carjackings were reported. Of the victims who were hurt, injuries (bruises, chipped teeth, etc.) were minor (about 13 percent), compared to the approximately 4 percent of the seriously injured who lost consciousness or were shot or knifed.[7]

Victim Characteristics

In general, the categories of people most vulnerable to nonfatal carjacking are the same as those observed to be the most vulnerable to violent crime overall. Men were more frequently victimized than women; blacks more than whites, and Hispanics more than non-Hispanics. Moreover, it was found that divorced, separated, or never-married persons were victimized more often than married or widowed persons. Urban residents were more likely to experience carjacking than suburban or rural residents, and persons under the age of 50 were more likely to be victims than those over that age. Finally, there were no clear patterns by household income.[8]

Incident/Offender Characteristics

The report also offered the following information on the carjacking phenomenon:

Carjacking incidents were about evenly divided between those committed by a lone offender and those committed by more than one offender. . . .

Males committed ninety-seven percent of carjacking incidents, and groups with both males and females committed three percent.

Fifty-eight percent of carjacking incidents were committed by offenders whom the victim perceived to be black; nineteen percent by offenders perceived to be white. In five percent of carjacking incidents, the victim(s) reported that multiple offenders of more than one race committed the crime.

Of the daytime carjacking incidents, almost 2 in 3 were completed; of the nighttime incidents less than half.

Most carjacking incidents occurred away from the victim's home. Forty percent occurred in an open area, such as on the street (other than adjacent to the victim's home or the home of a friend or neighbor), near a bus, subway or train station, or near an airport. Twenty percent occurred in parking lots of near commercial places like stores, restaurants, gas stations, and office buildings. Although carjackings often occurred away from the victim's home, they usually did not occur very far away. About sixty-five percent occurred within 5 miles of the victim's home; about five percent, more than 50 miles.

Carjacking victims received at least partial recovery of their property in 7 of 10 completed incidents. Fifteen percent of completed carjackings involved recovery of all property. Incidents with partial recovery most likely involved the recovery of vehicles either damaged or missing stolen articles.[9]

Carjacking Murders and Abductions

In some carjacking cases, infants have been abducted. Eight infants between the ages of two to 14 months were kidnapped The report stated that most of these incidents occurred during the day. About half were at a service station, supermarket, or shopping center; the other half, on the street or in a parking lot. Most offenders began the carjacking unaware of the infant's presence and within a short time left the infant and/or abandoned the car.[10]

In addition, the report divulges that

> . . . carjacking involving murder is a rare event. If all murder/auto thefts committed by strangers between 1992 and 1996 were carjackings, there would have been annual average of 27 homicides committed with a carjacking.[11]

Investigating Carjackings

People

In a carjacking case, the victim is an eyewitness. Other potential eyewitnesses may be forthcoming if a canvass is conducted in the open areas in which most carjacking incidents occur—near a transportation station, parking lot, or commercial place such as a restaurant or a gas station. Occasionally, the police stop the stolen car only to be told by the driver that it was loaned by a friend. Follow-up investigation should lead to the original offender, who then can be identified by the victim.

Records

Records should be accessed just as in the "Larceny" section of this chapter. The auxiliary assistance offered by insurance companies is likely to be less available, though, because only 35 percent of all completed carjacking incidents are reported to insurance companies.[12]

Physical Evidence

If a gun is used and discharged, some physical evidence may be found at the crime scene (e.g., cartridge casings). In addition, fingerprints and palm prints may be developed on the automobile if it is recovered. Finally, it is possible that DNA in the form of saliva on cigarette butts or facial tissue may have been left in the car when it was abandoned.

REFERENCES

[1] Uniform Crime Reporting (UCR), "Summary System: Frequently Asked Questions," 25-26, 79. (undated).

[2] U.S. Department of Justice, Federal Bureau of Investigation, *Uniform Crime Reports 1975-2001* (Washington, DC: U.S. Department of Justice).

[3] "RCMP: Car Theft Ring Finances Terrorism." United Press, International 03-02-1999.

[4] U.S. Department of Justice, National Crime Information Center, *The Investigative Tool* (Washington, DC: U.S. Government Printing Office), March 1982.

[5] Ibid., 22-25.

[6] Klaus, Patsy. "Carjacking in the United States, 1992-1996," Washington, DC: U.S. Dept. of Justice, Bureau of Justice Statistics, March 1999, NCJ 171145.

[7] Ibid., 1.

[8] Ibid., 2.

[9] Ibid., 3.

[10] Ibid., 4.

[11] *Loc. cit.*

[12] *Loc. cit.*

SUPPLEMENTAL READINGS

Cook, Claude W. *The Automobile Theft Investigator: A Learning and Reference Text for the Automobile Theft Investigator, the Police Supervisor, and the Student.* Springfield, IL: Charles C Thomas, 1987.

Evans, Dean. *Grand Theft Auto 2: Prima's Official Strategy Guide.* Rocklin, CA: Prima, 1999.

Williams, John J. *Auto Theft Countermeasures.* Albuquerque: Consumertronics, 1997.

SECTION IV

SPECIALIZED TOPICS

Section IV presents a "potpourri" from which instructors may choose topics according to their interests, or those of their students. A few chapters from the first edition have been relocated here. In addition, the reader will find some new material reflecting current law enforcement concerns.

Although the subject of Chapter 23 ("What is Crime?") is treated extensively in other criminal justice courses, the authors of this text have slanted the treatment of the subject to conform to the needs of those entering the field as detectives. The chapter makes the reader aware of the sources and importance of the case law governing their jurisdictions. Likewise, this text takes a different perspective on constitutional law than do political science and more general criminal justice courses. Concern here is with the front-line detective or police officer whose actions give rise to the questions the court is asked to settle.

Chapter 24 discusses traditional and more recent ideas bearing on the management of criminal investigations. It provides information useful to supervisors for *internal control* over investigative practice, and suggests ways to increase personnel productivity. *External control,* exercised through constitutional law as a protection from overzealous law enforcement, is considered in Chapter 25. Together, Chapters 24 and 25 cover the means by which a democratic society attempts to regulate and improve criminal investigation and, at the same time, empower its police to carry out delegated responsibilities.

The main concern of Chapter 26 is evidence. What is it? What are its rules? What is effective testimony in court? What is the relationship between cross-examination and evidence? For the investigator who hopes to aid the prosecution with effective testimony, a familiarity with the rules of evidence is indispensable.

The landmark cases revolving around Dr. Martin Luther King (Chapter 27) and Charles Lindbergh (Chapter 28) illustrate the many turns an investigation can take as it wends its way to a solution. The remaining chapters (Chapter 29 on Satanism, Cults and Ritual Crime and Chapter 30 on Raids) address some current concerns within the law enforcement community. Finally, Chapter 31 discusses the general problem of miscarriages of justice.

CHAPTER 23

What is Crime?

Any serious study looking into the understanding and control of crime gains insight from a wide variety of disciplines. A list might include history, criminal justice, political science, sociology, psychiatry, and even biology. Because the concern of this text must be narrow, it is limited to how crimes are solved—using legal means. With this in mind it would be advantageous at the outset to define some elementary terms in the field of criminal investigation: crime, criminal law, case law, and the Model Penal Code.

CRIME

The search for the meaning of this word begins with *The American Heritage Dictionary*. It defines "crime" as:

> An act committed or omitted in violation of law forbidding or commanding
> it, and for which punishment is imposed upon conviction.[1]

The dictionary does not specify what is forbidden or commanded, spell out what is required to prove guilt and obtain a conviction, or provide any guidelines for the conduct of the investigation and the presentation of evidence at trial. These details must be sought in the criminal law of each jurisdiction.

The legislature defines crime by enacting penal statutes that govern behavior for which punishment can be meted out. Behavior can be viewed as (1) inherently bad (*malum in se*, e.g., the deliberate killing of another human being), or (2) against public policy (*malum prohibitum*, e.g., committing arson in order to defraud). Public perception of crime varies over time and across cultures. For example, on the abortion issue it has shifted from *malum in se* (which anti-abortion activists still claim it to be) to a woman's legal right (as declared by the 1973 Supreme Court decision *Roe v. Wade*). Anti-abortion activists have attempted to attack *Roe* by urging state legislatures to pass restrictive abortion laws that, upon appeal, would afford the Court an opportunity to reverse itself. The scrutiny the Senate gave to the judicial nominees of Presidents Reagan and Bush reflects the fundamental disagreement in our culture in regard to abortion—and whether it is to be considered a crime.

Public perception has also changed regarding the way wealth is acquired. Many families that are today's pillars of society acquired their "old money" through now-outlawed *malum prohibitum* business practices, whereas some "new money" involves behavior that may yet be outlawed (e.g., "white-collar crime" in general, which presently is a sociological rather than a legal term).

An insight into a culture's influence on the law was expressed concisely (and with some exaggeration) by Newton N. Minow upon completing a comprehensive study of four European legal systems:

> In Germany, under the law, everything is prohibited except that which is permitted.

> In France, under the law, everything is permitted, except that which is prohibited.

> In the Soviet Union, under the law, everything is prohibited, *including* that which is permitted.

> And in Italy, under the law, everything is permitted, *especially* that which is prohibited.[2]

CRIMINAL LAW

American definitions of crimes are rooted in English common law, which in turn is based on custom and usage in England. Despite their common origin, state criminal laws can vary not only on punishment but, surprisingly, on the definition of the constituent elements of each crime. Moreover, every state's penal code has separate sections dealing respectively with *substantive* and *procedural* criminal law.

Substantive criminal law describes the forbidden acts and the punishment to be inflicted when the law is broken. *Procedural* criminal law deals with how the state may go about arresting and convicting a suspected offender.

Substantive Criminal Law

Crimes are divided into two classes: *felonies* are crimes of a more serious nature; *misdemeanors* are less serious, perhaps even trivial. A more significant distinction is made on the basis of punishment provided by statute: felonies are punishable by death or imprisonment for over one year in a state prison; misdemeanors by imprisonment for less than one year or by a fine, or both. A further distinction is inherent in the sanctions imposed: a convicted felon is prohibited from holding public office or engaging in a licensed occupation; a misdemeanant is not similarly disadvantaged.

The Elements of a Crime

The penal laws enacted by a state legislature to cover wrongful behavior spell out what constitutes a crime. The phrase *elements of the crime* describes the specific acts that, taken together, compose the crime. For example, loosely stated, the elements of burglary are: (a) breaking, (b) entering, and (c) with intent to commit a crime; the elements of robbery are: (a) the taking of property, (b) from another person, and (c) by force. If each and every element of a crime is not proved, a defendant cannot be convicted for that crime.

Corpus Delicti

The *corpus delicti* of a crime has two components: one, that each element of the crime is satisfied; two, that someone is responsible for inflicting the injury or loss that was sustained. When the state has proved the *corpus delicti* beyond a reasonable doubt, the prosecutor has met the burden of proof required for a jury (or judge) to convict.

Procedural Criminal Law

Procedural criminal law flows from the constitutions of the United States and the respective states. In its decisions, the Supreme Court interprets the United States Constitution or exercises its supervisory power over the federal system of criminal justice. Of greatest importance to procedural criminal law is the Bill of Rights—especially the Fourth through the Ninth Amendments, in which the actions permitted or forbidden the government in criminal matters are spelled out. By specifying the course of action required or prohibited in each phase of the legal process, the Bill of Rights protects the accused from unjust treatment by the state. Precisely because a violation will render illegally obtained evidence inadmissible at a subsequent trial, procedural limitations placed on investigative behavior are raised throughout this text.

CASE LAW

The language of the penal law is necessarily general, leaving it up to the trial judge to decide whether a particular set of details surrounding an alleged crime fits or does not fit its requirements. The cumulative wisdom of such judicial decisions is referred to as case law; it interprets the meaning of the law. In the language of the statute on burglary, for instance, "break" is an element of the crime. But suppose an offender is able to reach through an open window to unlock a door. Does that constitute a break? Is it a break if the door was ajar and the offender merely had to walk in? The *case law* of each state supplies the answer for that state. Should a novel issue be raised when relevant case law does not exist, the decisions of other jurisdictions are then searched to learn how the point in question was settled. Sources for the annotated statutes (state law codes) that embody the case law of each state are treated at the end of the chapter.

THE MODEL PENAL CODE

In an effort to make criminal laws more uniform, a Model Penal Code was proposed in 1962 by the American Law Institute (ALI), a nationwide body with membership drawn from the bench, the bar, and law schools. The code was intended to bring a unified approach to criminal law through an examination of its philosophical foundations, the elements that defined specific crimes, and the provisions for sentencing and correction. Its main thrust and purpose was an attempt to be organized and more civilized in using the power of the state against the individual. Professor Herbert Wechsler, a principal architect of the Model Penal Code, stated:

> . . . penal law governs the strongest force that we permit official agencies to bring to bear on individuals. Its promise as an instrument of safety is matched only by its power to destroy. If penal law is weak or ineffective, basic human interests are in jeopardy. If it is harsh or arbitrary in its impact, it works a gross injustice on those caught within its toils. The law that carries such responsibilities should surely be as rational and just as law can be.[3]

The ALI Model Penal Code has not yet been widely accepted, though some aspects have found their way into the criminal law of some states. Even if it were to be universally adopted, it is important to realize that the development of case law would continue, while the differences now found between states would most likely be diminished.

SOURCES OF STATE LAW

The best place to research cases concerning a particular type of crime in a certain state, dependency, or territory is a law school library where current law codes for all of the United States and its possessions are to be found. The codes (annotated statutes) are shelved and indexed alphabetically by state; usually there is commentary following each section of the code, and relevant cases may be cited therein. Additional research involves *Shepard's Citations*, available from LexisNexis™, which publishes a comprehensive "How To Use" booklet in conjunction with its volumes. *Shepard's* will direct the investigator to the appropriate sources where case texts and analyses are located. Online services such as LexisNexis™ and Westlaw® can be searched, as can various web sites on the Internet. Other possible sources might be a large public library or a superior court center.

REFERENCES

[1]   *The American Heritage Dictionary of the English Language*, 2nd College Edition, s.v. "crime."

[2]   Newton N. Minow, "Notable and Quotable," *The Wall Street Journal*, 4 February 1985, 22.

[3]   H. Wechsler, "The Challenge of a Model Penal Code," *Harvard Law Review*, 65 (1952),1097-1098.

SUPPLEMENTAL READINGS

Carlson, Ronald L. *Criminal Justice Procedure*. 6th ed. Cincinnati: Anderson, 1999.

Goldstein, Joseph, Alan Dershowitz, and R.D. Schwartz. *Criminal Law: Theory and Process*. 2nd ed. New York: The Free Press, 1974. Chapters 7, 9, 12.

Johnson, Herbert A., and Nancy Travis Wolfe. *History of Criminal Justice*. 3rd ed. Cincinnati: Anderson, 2003.

Klotter, John C. *Criminal Law*. 7th ed. Cincinnati: Anderson, 2004.

The Law Dictionary. 7th ed. Cincinnati: Anderson, 1997.

Travis, Lawrence F., III. *Introduction to Criminal Justice*. 4th ed. Cincinnati: Anderson, 2001.

CHAPTER 24

Managing Criminal Investigations

HISTORICAL ANTECEDENTS

When drafting the Constitution, the Founding Fathers delegated law enforcement to the states. The primary reason was historic—rooted in the age-old abuses of police power by monarchs. Charles Dickens details in *A Tale of Two Cities* the abuses of a bad king: how Louis XVI's arbitrary, spiteful use of the *lettre de cachet* and many another corrupt practice contributed to the French Revolution. The language of the Declaration of Independence summarizes George III's own "long train of continued abuses" that ultimately led American colonists to revolution before winning the right to frame a written constitution.

Another reason the founders delegated law enforcement to the states, rather than nationalizing it, was pragmatic. Crime was local in nature, few colonists had the transportation, time, or opportunity to move from settlement to settlement. When adopting the Constitution, therefore, they drafted the Tenth Amendment to reserve law enforcement for the individual states. Each state in turn enacted penal laws and gave over the enforcement and prosecution of them to its counties and subdivisions.

CONVENTIONAL INVESTIGATIVE ARRANGEMENTS

The biblical story of Cain's murder of Abel suggests that criminal behavior has been evident for centuries. Yet, it was not until the nineteenth century that police departments were formally organized in this country, appearing first in the major cities. Before long, the need for an investigative arm was recognized and, slowly, detective bureaus were established. Personnel selection was based partly on political considerations, or friendship—often that of the police chief. This practice has continued; even today in too many jurisdictions "clout" is a prerequisite to appointment as detective.

Bad practice, however, can evoke unintended consequences. This policy divided the force into separate camps—uniformed and detective. Excluded from what was perceived to be the most interesting aspect of "the job"—solving crime—the contribution of the uniformed officer was lost to what should have been a cooperative effort. In addition, the somewhat relaxed, sometimes nonexistent supervision that became the detective's lot caused a welling of animosity and envy. In New York City it was not uncommon for a uniformed officer, assigned to safeguard a crime scene until detectives arrived, to comment: "Well, here come the brains." Over time, detective bureaus tended to become insulated from the department, building their own power bases among judges, prosecutors, and politicians. This state of affairs is described by a former head of the New York City Police, Patrick V. Murphy, in *Commissioner*. In the book Murphy relates how carefully he had to tread when attempting to effect change in the detective bureau.

Detective bureaus have customarily been organized as follows: As specialists, detectives handle particular crimes (for example, homicide, automobile theft, burglary); as generalists, they handle any kind of case as reported. Specialization also can be based on a categorization of offenses into crimes against the person and crimes against property. Detectives may be assigned to central headquarters (likely in small departments), to local precincts or districts, or to the two in combination. Specialized squads are generally at central headquarters. Detectives handling run-of-the-mill cases usually work out of the precincts and call on specialists for cases judged to be important. If the victim is a prominent person or the crime promises to attract media attention, it is termed "heavy." Whether or not a detective "caught a heavy one," they still "caught all squeals" (New York jargon for cases reported during their tour of duty). Although this results in an uneven distribution of work, it is often tolerated in the belief that things average out in the long run. From a management view, however, it is an unsatisfactory division of labor, and should not be countenanced.

Crime on the streets was a major campaign issue in the 1967 Johnson-Goldwater presidential race. The upshot of the election was a flood of federal money to improve law enforcement. Funds were used in various ways. Most promising from the perspective of this chapter was the education at the college level of numerous (current and future) leaders of police departments. These professionals learned the value of and the need for empirical research; they were taught to have an open mind when attempting to translate the results into practice. A significant outcome of federally funded research into improving the criminal investigative function is described in the next section.

MANAGING CRIMINAL INVESTIGATIONS (MCI)

In the literature of the field, a collection of empirically tested suggestions for improving the criminal investigative process is called *Managing Criminal Investigations* or MCI.[1-4] Underlying MCI's conception are four considerations that govern any assessment of the investigative function:

1. Number of arrests

2. Number of cases cleared (one arrest may clear many crimes; several arrests may clear but a single crime)

3. Number of convictions

4. Number of cases accepted for prosecution

The first two considerations are fundamental to the control of criminal investigation by today's police administrators; they are the responsibility of the detective and police supervisors. The third involves the jury, judge, and especially the prosecutor. The fourth depends on the standards set by the prosecutor and the ability of the detective to meet them. To some degree, the performance of a detective can affect the outcome of all four.

The Elements of MCI

Five elements are viewed as significant in the management of criminal investigations:

1. The initial investigation

2. Case screening

3. Management of the ongoing investigation

4. Police-prosecutor relations

5. Continuous monitoring of the investigative process

The Initial Investigation

There is a major difference between traditional investigation efforts and MCI. The latter hands responsibility for the initial investigation over to the patrol officer responding to the radio call. The aim is to have the uniformed officer obtain all the information available at the crime scene, so that this task need not be repeated should a detective be assigned to continue it. There are, however, implications of this procedural change that are overlooked in the MCI literature. For instance, the patrol force needs in-depth training in the *recognition* and *preservation* of physical evidence at the crime scene—more than is customarily provided. If moved, trampled, or touched, the investigative and probative value of such evidence can be greatly diminished or even destroyed in certain situations.

Case Screening

Another important difference is the way MCI utilizes the initial information when screening a case to determine whether to close it out as unsolvable or to recommend further investigation. Experience clearly demonstrates that every case is not solvable, but from cases that were successfully investigated, empirical research has identified "solvability" factors. The presence of these factors suggests that a solution is possible if the case is pursued further. Those deemed significant are:

- Is there a witness to the crime?

- Is a suspect named?

- Can a suspect be described?

- Can a suspect be located?

- Can a suspect vehicle be identified?

- Is stolen property traceable?

- Is physical evidence present?

- Is there a distinguishable *modus operandi* (MO)?

A negative answer to all or most of these questions constitutes grounds for closing a case. If these factors are present, their quality and number must be evaluated. For this purpose, a weighing system has been developed for some crimes.[5]

Should the sum of the weighted factors in a particular case equal or exceed a specified value, additional investigation is advised. In many departments an experienced supervisor will review the initial recommendation. If the closing of a serious case is recommended, the case is reevaluated by another supervisor. Called *case screening*, this process removes cases from the workload, thus making resources available for those holding greater promise of solution. MCI also creates more time for detectives to prepare for their court testimony in cases accepted for prosecution.

Another noteworthy aspect of MCI is the significance it attaches to advising a complainant of the decision to suspend an investigation. The patrol officer, upon completion of the initial inquiry, can explain that the evidence does not justify further efforts; or, after the recommendation to suspend has been reviewed by a supervisor, an official letter can be mailed. In either event, the complainant should be instructed to report to the police any additional information that may subsequently be discovered from neighbors, later recollection, or other sources. Depending on the information's importance, a case may be reopened.

Management of the Continuing Investigation

Under traditional arrangements, a detective "caught" cases by chance. This means that the individual on duty was responsible for all cases that came in and for deciding which to pursue and which to "can," that is, keep in a personal file, off the official record as warranting no further effort. This practice has many shortcomings. One is that caseloads are uneven because they are dependent on the day of the week that the tour of duty happens to fall (weekends are the heaviest). Another shortcoming is the inefficient use of special talent. This becomes obvious when a good burglary investigator catches a sex crime, and a good sex crime investigator is assigned to a burglary. An added shortcoming is the lack of continuity resulting when a detective keeps all moves secret, is unavailable for an unexpected development, and informs no one else about the "squeal" (case). Another flaw is the fact that a detective determines the size and nature of the workload, has little accountability, and operates in an atmosphere of low visibility.

MCI's goal is to eliminate these shortcomings by establishing administrative controls and organizing investigative resources more effectively. The former may be accomplished through perceptive supervision, case review, and reporting; the latter by turning to the specialist/centralized model (while preserving its advantages and minimizing its disadvantages). The expansion of the patrol officer's role is pivotal, as is the expectation of better communication between officers and detectives.

To organize resources more effectively in selected categories of cases, MCI delegates the responsibility for a continuing investigation to the patrol force. For instance, a case having a high potential for solution may be assigned to the patrol force, thereby reducing the workload for detectives and releasing their special skills to be deployed elsewhere. Meanwhile a pool of talent can be identified in the patrol force that will be available when career advancement opportunities arise.

Police-Prosecutor Relations

The traditional practice in the criminal justice system has been for each segment to act independently with little concern for other component parts. For instance, the police seldom talk to—much less exchange ideas and opinions with—corrections officials, judges, or prosecutors. Many uniformed officers and detectives hold the not uncommon view that they have an adversarial relationship with the prosecutor's office. MCI, however, emphasizes mutual cooperation and understanding. Thus, under MCI, the prosecutor evaluates and marshals police evidence before initiating criminal proceedings to determine if the office standards for charging, indicting, and convicting an offender have been met. If they have not, the prosecutor should explain what must be done to meet those standards.

With the goals of cooperation and understanding in mind, MCI outlines five essential steps:

1. Increased consultation between executives of the agencies;

2. Increased cooperation among supervisory personnel of the agencies;

3. The use of liaison officers to communicate to police personnel the investigatory techniques and evidence standards that the prosecutor requires to file a case;

4. Improved case preparation procedures, including the use of forms and checklists;

5. Developing a system of formal and informal feedback to the police on case dispositions (dismissal, continuance, or other outcome of court action).

Improved relations depend not only on a firm commitment by both police and prosecutors, but also on common sense, a willingness to learn through trial and error, and training.

Investigative Monitoring System

A case monitoring system is set up to give administrators continuous feedback on the investigative process and the quality of personnel performance. The monitoring might focus on the percentage of cases assigned for continuing investigation, and whether the interval between assignment and case closure has changed (a reduction being desirable). If sufficiently detailed, the system will identify problems and facilitate the development of remedies. With respect to personnel performance, monitoring can be put to use in building a profile of each detective's abilities, assessing productivity, and identifying any need for retraining.

Monitoring, whether of the investigatory process or its individual members, presents difficulties not readily perceived. A basic one evolves because the systematic assessment of quantitative data requires intellectual skills that differ from those acquired through traditional investigative experience. A problem that might be encountered in a first attempt at monitoring is a methodical sabotage of MCI's intent by the investigative force, or less destructively, a grudging cooperation aimed at slowing down its implementation.

POTENTIAL BENEFITS OF AN MCI PROGRAM

Over time, successful implementation of an MCI system may allow such improvements as:

1. An increase in productivity through the better use of available resources or through tangible rewards for superior performance.

2. Reallocation of the resources made available through case screening to other endeavors, such as:

   a. Proactive investigations—aiming investigative efforts at those notorious criminals whose activities contribute disproportionately to the totality of crime in the community.
   b. Formation of Task Force Units to address specific, transitory crime problems.
   c. Better preparation of cases submitted to the prosecutor.

3. Rejection of favoritism as the basis for the selection of detectives. Utilizing the pool of talent recognized in the patrol force through monitoring, i.e., patrol officers adept in handling initial investigations. By selecting those who have demonstrated competence, it is likely that more cases will be handled and solved in a professional manner.

REFERENCES

[1] Peter W. Greenwood and Joan Petersilia, *The Criminal Investigation Process*, vol. I, *Summary and Policy Implications*, vol. III: *Observations and Analysis* (Santa Monica, CA: RAND, 1976).

[2] Ilene Greenberg and Robert Wasserman, *Managing Criminal Investigations* (Washington, DC: U.S. Government Printing Office: U.S. Department of Justice, 1979).

[3] John E. Eck, *Solving Crimes: The Investigation of Burglary and Robbery* (Washington, DC: Police Executive Research Forum, 1983).

[4] Peter B. Bloch and Donald R. Weidman, *Managing Criminal Investigations* (Washington, DC: U.S. Government Printing Office, U.S. Department of Justice, 1975).

[5] Eck, *loc. cit.*

SUPPLEMENTAL READINGS

Eck, John E. "Criminal Investigation," in *What Works in Policing? Operations and Administration Examined*, edited by Gary W. Cordner and Donna C. Hale. Cincinnati: Anderson, 1992.

Ericson, R.V. *Making Crime: A Study of Detective Work*. Toronto: Butterworth, 1981.

Fosdick, Raymond B. *American Police Systems*. New York: The Century Co., 1920.

Greenwood, P.W., J. Chaiken, and J. Petersilia. *The Criminal Investigation Process*. Lexington, MA: Heath, 1977.

Morgan, J. Brian. *The Police Function and the Investigation of Crime*. Brookfield, VT: Gower, 1990.

Murphy, Patrick V., and Thomas Plate. *Commissioner: A View from the Top of American Law Enforcement*. New York: Simon & Schuster, 1977.

Sanders, William B. *Detective Work: A Study of Criminal Investigations*. New York: The Free Press, 1979.

CHAPTER 25

Control Over Investigations Through Constitutional Law

HISTORICAL PERSPECTIVES

The quest for justice was one of the primary incentives for the colonists to come to America. Both Pennsylvania and Georgia were established in part as idealistic experiments in government: the former by Quakers seeking freedom of religion; the latter by James Oglethorpe and his settlers (some of whom, as debtors, were imprisoned in England). Other unfortunates also fled Europe for the new world and the opportunity to improve the condition of their lives.

Although subjects of the Crown, the settlers did not typically think or act as their compatriots in England. Indeed, their Dutch, Swedish, German, Scottish, and English ancestries partly accounted for this, as did the new manners and ideas that evolved from their struggle to tame a wilderness. The culture of the native American Indians also exerted an influence for change. During the next century and a half, therefore, British rule increasingly led to dissatisfaction. It culminated in "The Unanimous Declaration of the Thirteen United States of America in Congress."[1] It is revealing to note the importance the settlers attached to their colonies as sovereign states. Nowhere in the document, now known as the *Declaration of Independence*, does the word "nation" appear.

The government that would conduct the greater part of the war against the mother country was set up in 1777 under the Articles of Confederation. It took years of wrangling, however, before the articles were ratified. Reluctant to give up their sovereign rights, the states proposed a new kind of central government—one that was purposefully kept weak. Except for defense and foreign affairs, it was given little power: it could not impose taxes, control commerce, or stop quarrels among the states (in the language of the Articles, "maintain domestic tranquility"). Indeed, it could not raise money without first asking the states for approval. The tradition of a limited national government with major powers retained by its states has had immense influence over the development of law enforcement in America. The results of that tradition remain with us today.

A short time after the Revolution it was clear that the Articles of Confederation needed to be revised. To deal with the numerous problems that were manifest, the nation would need effective government. Finally, in 1787 a constitutional convention met in Independence Hall in Philadelphia, and from those historic deliberations, two particularly important governing principles emerged. The first concerned the distribution of power between the central government and the sovereign states. The powers finally given up by the 13 original states were carefully defined. One they would retain was control over the criminal law. Exemplifying the significance of this is the fact that, as late as 1963, no federal law was violated when President Kennedy was assassinated; only the penal code of Texas was applicable.

Another important principle adopted by the Founding Fathers was embedded in the writings of the French philosopher Montesquieu, in which the polar issues of oppression and freedom were examined. When authority is in the hands of one person or a power elite, he wrote, tyranny was the result. But if the executive, legislative, and judicial functions are separated, and each allowed to check and balance the other, the likelihood of tyranny would be lessened, and that of human freedom enhanced.[2] Nixon's Watergate episode reaffirmed this principle. An imperial presidency is clearly outside the Montesquieuian vision underlying the Convention's work.

The adoption of the new Constitution was delayed by the insistence of the original 13 states that a Bill of Rights (the first 10 amendments) be made an integral part of the document. These amendments placed limits only on the powers of the federal government; they were not intended to affect the authority of the states within their own domain. They had direct consequences on the Supreme Court's ability to rule on matters involving the criminal law, for defendants dissatisfied with state court decisions could not appeal to federal courts. It took 77 years and the passage of the Fourteenth Amendment to give the Court a constitutional basis to intervene in a state criminal matter. It was not until the Warren Court (1953-1969) that any extensive set of overruling decisions cloaked criminal defendants in state courts with the mantle of protection afforded by the Bill of Rights.

THE CONSTITUTION AND CRIMINAL JUSTICE _____

THE PREAMBLE

> *We the People of the United States, in Order to form a more perfect Union, establish Justice, insure domestic Tranquility, provide for the common defence, promote the general Welfare, and secure the Blessings of Liberty to ourselves and our Posterity, do ordain and establish this Constitution for the United States of America.*

As the Preamble to the Constitution asserts, the first reason for forming "a more perfect Union" is to establish justice. The basic human drives are for food, shelter, and procreation. Once these needs are provided for, the next instinct to be found universally across cultures is the quest for justice. Philosophers, writers, and political scientists endlessly speculate on the meaning of justice. Hence, those engaged in law enforcement, and especially in criminal investigation, are entrusted with an awesome task. If they carry it out improperly or insensitively, they not only dishonor themselves and their agencies, but also the aspirations of humankind.

THE ARTICLES AND AMENDMENTS

With the exception of treason, no crime is defined in the Constitution; indeed, only a few matters affecting criminal justice can be found throughout its seven Articles:

Article I (Re: The Legislative Branch)
. . . in Cases of Impeachment . . . the Party convicted shall nevertheless be liable and subject to Indictment, Trial, Judgment and Punishment, according to Law. (Section 3, par. 7).
. . . the Writ of Habeas Corpus shall not be suspended. . . . (Section 9, par. 2).
. . . no Bill of Attainder or ex post facto Law shall be passed. (Section 9, par. 3).

Article II (Re: The Executive Branch)
. . . the President . . . shall have Power to grant Reprieves and Pardons for Offenses against the United States. . . . (Section 2, par. 1).
. . . he . . . shall appoint . . . Judges of the Supreme Court. . . . (Section 2, par. 2).

Article III (Re: The Judicial Branch)
The judicial Power of the United States, shall be vested in one supreme Court. . . . (Section 1, par. 1).
. . . the supreme Court shall have appellate Jurisdiction, both as to Law and Fact, with such Exceptions, and under such Regulations as the Congress shall make. (Section 2, par. 2).
The Trial of all Crimes . . . shall be by Jury . . . (Section 2, par. 3).
Treason against the United States, shall consist only in levying War against them, or in adhering to their Enemies, giving them Aid and Comfort. No Person shall be convicted of Treason unless on the Testimony of two Witnesses to the same overt Act, or on Confession in open Court. (Section 3).

Article IV (Re: The States and its Citizens)
A Person charged in any State with Treason, Felony, or other Crime, who shall flee from Justice, and be found in another State, shall on Demand of the executive Authority of the State from which he fled, be delivered up, to be removed to the State having Jurisdiction of the Crime. (Section 2, par. 2).

Article VI (Re: The Supreme Law)
This Constitution . . . shall be the supreme Law of the Land; and the Judges in every State shall be bound thereby, any Thing in the Constitution or Laws of any State to the Contrary notwithstanding. (par. 2).

The Bill of Rights

The first 10 amendments were adopted in 1791. Several of them affect the administration of criminal justice. Past Supreme Court decisions having the greatest influence on investigative practice are based on the Fourth, Fifth, Sixth, and Eighth Amendments.

Fourth Amendment

> The right of the people to be secure in their persons, houses, papers, and effects, against unreasonable searches and seizures, shall not be violated, and no Warrants shall issue, but upon probable cause, supported by Oath or affirmation, and particularly describing the place to be searched, and the persons or things to be seized.

Fifth Amendment

> No person shall be held to answer for a capital, or otherwise infamous crime, unless on a presentment or indictment of a Grand Jury, except in cases arising in the land or naval forces, or in the Militia, when in actual service in time of War or public danger; nor shall any person be subject for the same offence to be twice put in jeopardy of life or limb; nor shall be compelled in any criminal case to be a witness against himself, nor be deprived of life, liberty, or property, without due process of law; nor shall private property be taken for public use, without just compensation.

Sixth Amendment

> In all criminal prosecutions, the accused shall enjoy the right to a speedy and public trial, by an impartial jury of the State and district wherein the crime shall have been committed, which district shall have been previously ascertained by law, and to be informed of the nature and cause of the accusation; to be confronted with the witnesses against him; to have compulsory process for obtaining Witnesses in his favor, and to have the Assistance of Counsel for his defence.

Eighth Amendment

> Excessive bail shall not be required, nor excessive fines imposed, nor cruel and unusual punishments inflicted.

Although judicial and correctional practice is affected, the Eighth Amendment has little influence over criminal investigative behavior.

Ninth Amendment

> The enumeration in the Constitution, of certain rights, shall not be construed to deny or disparage others retained by the people.

The Ninth Amendment was intended to cover any right not expressly mentioned in the first eight amendments. One text attempting to explain the Constitution writes of the Ninth: "In practice it has been of no importance."[3] Another text, well aware that "Courts virtually ignored the Ninth Amendment for 175 years after its adoption," believes its mere presence was sufficient to keep the federal government from attempting to restrict any fundamental right of a citizen, even though that right was not expressly stated in the Constitution.[4]

Tenth Amendment

> The powers not delegated to the United States by the Constitution, nor prohibited by it to the States, are reserved to the States respectively, or to the people.

The Tenth Amendment reserves for the states the area of criminal justice. Federal law enforcement agencies derive their enforcement and investigative powers from four constitutional clauses in Article 1, Section 8:

> The Congress shall have Power To lay and collect Taxes, Duties, Imposts, and Excises . . . (Clause 1);

> To regulate Commerce . . . among the several States . . . (Clause 3);

> To provide for the Punishment of counterfeiting the Securities and current Coin of the United States (Clause 6);

> To establish Post Offices and post Roads (Clause 7).

Thus, it is through Clause 3 that the FBI derives its authority to prosecute kidnapping, auto theft, Mann Act infractions (interstate prostitution), and so on. Many Treasury Department agencies are authorized through Clause 1 on taxing (which is used to regulate the sales of firearms and narcotics) or Clause 6 on counterfeiting (the Secret Service was one of the first federal policing agencies; its presidential protection duties were later acquired for reasons of convenience), whereas the postal inspector's authority has remained narrow.

Fourteenth Amendment

> Section 1. All persons born or naturalized in the United States, and subject to the jurisdiction thereof, are citizens of the United States and of the State wherein they reside. No State shall make or enforce any law which shall abridge the privileges or immunities of citizens of the United States; nor shall any State deprive any person of life, liberty, or property, without due process of law; nor deny to any person within its jurisdiction the equal protection of the laws.

THE SUPREME COURT AND CRIMINAL JUSTICE

Our federal court system rests on a very simple statement in Article 3, Section 1, of the Constitution:

> The judicial Power of the United States, shall be vested in one supreme Court, and in such inferior Courts as the Congress may from time to time ordain and establish . . .

In Section 2, Clause 2, of this Article the appellate jurisdiction of the Supreme Court is described:

. . . In all the other Cases before mentioned, the supreme Court shall have appellate Jurisdiction, both as to Law and Fact, with such Exceptions, and under such Regulations as the Congress shall make.

Thus, Congress is given the power to define what the appellate jurisdiction of the court will be. The legislative branch may increase or decrease this function of the Court as it sees fit; however, it has been reluctant to do so. If the issue is one of interpretation: whether a law or procedure—either state or federal—is in accord with the Constitution, then the power of the Court is beyond the reach of the Congress. The historic decision *Marbury v. Madison* settled this matter by ruling that the Judiciary Act of 1789 was unconstitutional in giving the Court the power to issue a writ of *mandamus*.[5]

The Judiciary Act of 1789 provided necessary congressional authorization for the Court to re-examine, reverse, or affirm the final judgments of the highest courts of the states.

. . . The Supreme Court shall also have appellate jurisdiction from the . . . courts of the several states, in the cases herein after provided for . . .[6]

The constitutionality of this act was first challenged in 1816 by a private citizen (*Martin v. Hunter's Lessee*)[7], then again in 1821 by a sovereign state (*Cohens v. Virginia*).[8] The Court affirmed its appellate review power in both cases. In addition, the Eleventh Amendment (relating to limitations on the "judicial power of the United States") was expressly held not to preclude the exercise of the Court's appellate review power even in a criminal prosecution in which the state itself is a party.[9]

From time to time, especially before the Civil War, several proposals have been introduced to abolish or limit the Court's power to review state court cases.[10] The outcome was invariably the same: rejection by the Congress. Thus, the hue and cry from law enforcement circles in the 1960s against the Warren Court decisions were nothing new. Thus far, such attempts to curb its review power have been similarly doomed.

Incorporating the Bill of Rights through the Fourteenth Amendment

The *Martin* and *Cohens* cases typify the pre-Civil War decisions of the Court that were largely concerned with working out the relationship between federal and state governments, and with solving property problems. (The *Dred Scott* decision, a leading cause of the Civil War, is an example of a property decision, as slaves were regarded as property.) In the post-Civil War era, as the nation industrialized and expanded westward, the cases brought before the Court dealt with economic concerns. In this period, the relationship between the state and federal governments was argued in strict constructionist terms, i.e., not expanded in meaning through a liberal interpretation by the Justices of the Court.

As the issues spawned by emergent federalism (the relationship of the national government to the states) were tested in the Court, it was inevitable that the intention of the 13 sovereign states to have the Bill of Rights apply only to the federal government would require interpellation; and it was upheld by the Court in 1833 (*Barron v. Balti-*

more).[11] It took another 40 years and the adoption of the Fourteenth Amendment before the argument to apply the provisions of the Bill of Rights to the states was again brought before the Court. At this time (1873) an economic issue evoked the decision in *The Slaughter-House Cases*.[12] Since then the Court has persistently declined any pleading for wholesale incorporation; that is, to apply all of the Bill of Rights to the states in one fell swoop. Even the Warren Court did it piecemeal, leaving some yet to be incorporated.

The myriad problems of the twentieth century—resulting from the closing of the frontier, the onset of industrialization, the emergence of the United States as a world power, a burgeoning population, and urban growth—have exerted their influence for change in the distribution of power between the states and the federal government. Many people argued that such change should be effected by fresh interpretations of the Constitution. In the New Deal era of the late 1930s, the Court began to adopt this idea.

Other influences also caused a re-examination of state law enforcement practice. The reports in 1931 of the National Commission on Law Observance and Enforcement (the Wickersham Commission), the rise of totalitarianism in Europe and elsewhere, and the appointment of judges whose philosophical outlook reflected New Deal liberalism all helped focus the Court's attention on individual liberties. Criminal cases that might previously have been rejected were selected for scrutiny and commentary. As a result, the highest courts of the states were on the road to being stripped of the authority to act as the final arbiters of law enforcement activities. This has profoundly affected the investigative process.

Of course, not all Supreme Court justices adopted this view at once; rather, as succeeding presidents from Franklin Roosevelt on made appointments to the Court, it was taken up in varying degrees by each justice as his or her judicial philosophy was constructed. It is worth stressing that the process of change in the Court's outlook is a general one; it is not confined to law enforcement practice alone. Throughout its history, the Court has overruled itself less than 200 times; it took 143 years to overrule 133 cases. In the 16 years of the Warren Court, however, an additional 44 cases were overruled, principally in the area of criminal law.

At the risk of oversimplification, and disregarding the nuances involved, the following explanation of the broad points of view that separate the Court into two schools (where law enforcement is concerned) should help to understand the trend. One is a legalistic or traditionalist philosophy; the other, a justice-oriented philosophy. The legalistic school favors a close adherence to and a relatively strict interpretation of the Constitution. Rather than extending supervisory power over law enforcement practice to include state agencies, it confines it to federal agencies and procedure. The term "judicial restraint" describes this outlook; "original intent" and "strict construction" also indicate that the Constitution is to be interpreted narrowly or literally. Presidents Nixon, Reagan, and Bush, as vacancies occurred on the bench, nominated those who shared their strict constructionist views of the Court's role in interpreting the Constitution.

Since the early 1940s, however, the justice-oriented school acquired support among Court members, and state criminal law enforcement practice began to be affected. The so-called judicial activist school believes that justice is the yardstick to be applied in a case, as opposed to merely using the law. In reaching decisions, this school considers the findings and fruits of scholarship in other disciplines (like sociology or psychology) when interpreting the Constitution. The more we apply civilized standards in weighing investigative behavior, the less is the likelihood that any action that shocks the conscience of the community will be tolerated. In their view, the rights of the individual are paramount, and the whole power of the state cannot be pitted against the individual without assistance of counsel.

By the last quarter of the twentieth century, through a process of selective incorporation, almost all the safeguards of the Bill of Rights had been extended to cover state law enforcement practice. To understand how this occurred, the language of the Fourteenth Amendment must be reexamined:

> All persons born or naturalized in the United States, and subject to the jurisdiction thereof, are citizens of the United States and of the State wherein they reside. No State shall make or enforce any law which shall abridge the privileges or immunities of citizens of the United States; nor shall any State deprive any person of life, liberty, or property, without due process of law; nor deny to any person within its jurisdiction the equal protection of the laws.

Through the *due process* and *equal protection* clauses of this amendment, the Court has elected to incorporate the provisions of the Bill of Rights and apply them to the states in a piecemeal fashion. Of the first eight amendments, only the Second, Third, Seventh, and the grand jury clause of the Fifth remain unincorporated. A case also can be made for the bail clause of the Eighth Amendment. In the decision extending the Sixth Amendment right to a jury trial, Justice White spoke for the Court:

> . . . many of the rights guaranteed by the first eight Amendments to the Constitution have been held to be protected against state action by the Due Process Clause of the Fourteenth Amendment. That clause now protects the right to compensation for property taken by the State;[a] the rights of speech, press, and religion covered by the First Amendment;[b] the Fourth Amendment rights to be free from unreasonable searches and seizures and to have excluded from criminal trials any evidence illegally seized;[c] the right guaranteed by the Fifth Amendment to be free of compelled self-incrimination;[d] and the Sixth Amendment right to counsel,[e] to a speedy[f] and public[g] trial, to confrontation of opposing witnesses,[h] and to compulsory process for obtaining witnesses.[i] [13]

A perusal of the footnotes will show that these cases fall largely in the decade of the 1960s; it is not coincidental that this is the last part of Chief Justice Earl Warren's term (1953-1969).

---

[a]   Chicago, *B. & Q. R. Co. v. Chicago*, 166 U.S. 226 (1897).
[b]   See, e.g., *Fiske v. Kansas*, 274 U.S. 380 (1927).
[c]   See *Mapp v. Ohio*, 367 U.S. 643 (1961).
[d]   *Malloy v. Hogan*, 378 U.S. 1 (1964).
[e]   *Gideon v. Wainwright*, 372 U.S. 335 (1963).
[f]   *Klopfer v. North Carolina*, 386 U.S. 213 (1967).
[g]   *In re Oliver*, 333 U.S. 257 (1948).
[h]   *Pointer v. Texas*, 380 U.S. 400 (1965).
[i]   *Washington v. Texas*, 388 U.S. 14 (1967)

Milestone Decisions Affecting Investigative Practice _____

Law is but one of many institutions devised by society to control social behavior. Not static, it slowly evolves with the culture of the civilization it serves. In some areas of the world, law exerts little influence on the process of criminal investigation, but in the United States its effect is far-reaching. For countries of Anglo-Saxon heritage, the primary sources are threefold: common law and doctrinal writings; the legislature; and case law through judicial interpretations. The Supreme Court exerts its greatest influence in the area of case law.

The Constitution grants original jurisdiction to the highest tribunal in a very limited number of special cases that are seldom tried before the Court. Instead, it decides cases that originate in lower federal courts or the highest appellate courts of the states. The criminal law issues it is asked to decide are of two kinds: those unwittingly created by police behavior and those involving apparently new interpretations of law or custom as urged by defendants through their attorneys. *Rochin v. California* concerned a police-created issue. In this case, overzealous enforcement exceeded the bounds of civilized practice.[14] In *Gideon v. Wainwright* defense counsel argued for a more liberal interpretation of the "right to counsel" clause.[15] Against the latter, police have little influence, but against the former they can exercise considerable control. Such control should be automatic when police investigative behavior is governed not only by the letter of the law, but also by its spirit. For better or worse (depending on one's viewpoint), criminal investigative practice has been altered by the Court. The next section traces the evolution of the Court's decisions with regard to the meaning of *probable cause*, the legal concept limiting the power of arrest and the seizure of evidence by law enforcement officers.

Probable Cause: Its Evolution and Significance _____

Statutory authority for police officers to make felony arrests without warrant is generally restricted to crimes committed in their presence, or to cases in which they have reasonable grounds for believing a person has committed (or is committing) a felony. Similarly, the "reasonable" standard applies when seeking a search warrant; there, the applicant must be a reasonably cautious person who believes that *seizable property* will be found; namely, contraband, the fruits of crime, the instruments of crime (e.g., a weapon), or other relevant evidence. Where it is to be discovered—on a particular person, or in his or her home, garage, automobile, or other particular place—must also be specified. It is in the Fourth Amendment that the term *probable cause* appears. The constitutional requirement of "reasonableness" is rooted here. In *Ker v. California*,[16] through the *due process clause* of the Fourteenth Amendment, state law enforcement agencies have had the federal interpretation of Fourth Amendment probable cause imposed on them. Crucial to law enforcement officers, this constitutional imperative governs arrests or searches with or without warrants. For this reason, a more extensive examination of probable cause (including its historical meaning) is necessary for a full understanding of this judicial view.

One of the earliest comments on the meaning of probable cause is found in *Locke v. United States* (1813).[17] Chief Justice John Marshall spoke for the court in this decision:

> The term "probable cause" according to its usual acceptation, means less than evidence which would justify condemnation; and, in all cases of seizure, has a fixed and well known meaning. It imports a seizure made under circumstances which warrant suspicion.[18]

Sixty-five years later, the concept of probable cause was modified in *Stacey v. Emery* (1878):

> . . . if the facts and circumstance before the officer are such as to warrant a man of prudence and caution in believing that the offense has been committed, it is sufficient.[19]

Thus, probable cause shifted from the bare suspicion test of Marshall to the idea of the prudent, cautious person. In *Carroll v. United States*,[20] and subsequently in *Brinegar v. United States*,[21] the term "reasonable" is added to the judicial discussion. In *Carroll*, the Court stated:

> Probable cause exists where "the facts and circumstances within their [the arresting officers'] knowledge, and of which they had reasonably trustworthy information, [are] sufficient in themselves to warrant a man of reasonable caution in the belief that" an offense has been or is being committed.[22]

Brinegar throws further light on the question:

> In dealing with probable cause, however, as the very name implies, we deal with probabilities. These are not technical; they are the factual and practical considerations of everyday life on which reasonable and prudent men, not legal technicians, act.[23]

The language of the Court seems clear. Nevertheless, the real problem of determining exactly what constitutes probable cause becomes apparent from the specific facts in a particular case. A good example is a case in which the police believed they had probable cause. Before considering it, though, the reader should be aware of another view taken from research in psychology. Toch and Shulte,[24] in a major, yet largely unpublicized paper, have shown that:

> Students who are exposed to several years of police training appear not only to have acquired information, but also to have sustained other effects. Given a task in which others predominantly perceive non-violent content, subjects with police schooling have become relatively aware of violent content.[25]

Further along in their paper the authors state:

> In the same fashion, law enforcement training can produce a revision of unconscious expectations of violence and crime. This does not mean that the law enforcer necessarily comes to exaggerate the prevalence of violence. It means that the law enforcer may come to accept crime *as a familiar personal experience*, one which he himself is not surprised to encounter. The acceptance of crime as a familiar experience in turn increases the *ability or readiness to perceive violence where clues to it are potentially available*.
>
> An "increased readiness to perceive" is highly functional. It permits the person to cope with otherwise improbable situations. The law enforcer thus learns to differentiate within violent scenes—to "detect" or "investigate" crimes; the mechanic becomes able to react with dispatch to unusual engine noises; the sonar operator can efficiently respond to infrequent underwater sounds.[26]

Finally, they make the point that:

> To the extent to which vocational training affects perception, it helps to accomplish its purpose. It increases the trainee's readiness to act in the sort of world he is likely to face.[27]

Although this study was directed to the perception of violence, it is reasonable to extrapolate from the research to other potential crime situations. In other words, it is plausible to argue that (owing to experience) the police recognize criminal behavior that the reasonable and prudent person (owing to unfamiliarity) would be unaware of and might, therefore, ignore. Hence, the law places police in the stultifying position of having information based on experience, observation, and interpretation, without the ability to employ it in decisionmaking. Is this not comparable to forbidding the physician to act on clinical observations of a patient because the "reasonable and prudent" person is unable to recognize them? To many people, this position seems indefensible, but with regard to probable cause, it is the legal view governing the conduct of police officers.

In light of Toch's and Schulte's contribution, it is opportune to examine a typical case in which police acted on the belief that they had probable cause, but in which the Supreme Court subsequently held to the contrary. In *Rios v. United States* (1960) it states:

> As in most cases involving a claimed unconstitutional search and seizure, resolution of the question requires a particular evaluation of the conduct of the officers involved. . . . At about ten o'clock on the night of February 18, 1957, two Los Angeles police officers, dressed in plain clothes and riding in an unmarked car, observed a taxicab standing in a parking lot next to an apartment house at the corner of First and Flower Streets in Los Angeles. The neighborhood has a reputation for "narcotics activity." The officers saw the petitioner look up and down the street, walk across the lot, and get into the cab. Neither officer had ever before seen the petitioner, and neither of them had any idea of his identity. Except for the reputation of the neigh-

borhood, neither officer had received information of any kind to suggest that someone might be engaged in criminal activity at that time and place. They were in possession of no arrest or search warrants.

The taxicab drove away, and the officers followed it in their car for a distance of about two miles through the city. At the intersection of First and State Streets, the cab stopped for a traffic light. The two officers alighted from their car and approached on foot to opposite sides of the cab. One of the officers identified himself as a policeman. In the next minute there occurred a rapid succession of events. The cab door was opened; the petitioner dropped a recognizable package of narcotics to the floor of the vehicle; one of the officers grabbed the petitioner as he alighted from the cab; the other officer retrieved the package; and the first officer drew his revolver.[28]

Further along in the opinion the Court comments:

> . . . upon no possible view of the circumstances revealed in the testimony of the Los Angeles officers could it be said that there existed probable cause for an arrest at the time the officers decided to alight from their car and approach the taxi in which the petitioner was riding.[29]

That the officers had insight based on their police training and experience is not considered to be proved by the fact that contraband evidence was indeed in the defendant's possession. Against this logical, defensible argument sits the dictum of *Johnson v. United States* (1948)—that an arrest is not justified by what the subsequent search discloses.[30] Some respond that this is not an exercise in logic, that because individual liberty is at stake, society cannot afford the luxury of placating police officers.

The police argument may be cogent to many in the law enforcement profession; it is rooted, however, in a *crime suppression model* of criminal justice, whereas the Court's reasoning is rooted in a *due process model*. In a democracy the latter model finds greater acceptance from lawyers (and presumably the people); the former model is more popular with the police. The judiciary attempted to explain this value conflict—a source of law enforcement dissatisfaction with many Supreme Court decisions—in *Johnson*:

> The point of the Fourth Amendment, which often is not grasped by zealous officers, is not that it denies law enforcement the support of the usual inferences which reasonable men draw from evidence. Its protection consists in requiring that those inferences be drawn by a neutral and detached magistrate instead of being judged by the officer engaged in the often competitive enterprise of ferreting out crime. Any assumption that evidence sufficient to support a magistrate's disinterested determination to issue a search warrant will justify the officers in making a search without a warrant would reduce the amendment to a nullity and leave the people's homes secure only in the discretion of police officers.[31]

The Court does not address the issue of a difference in perception resulting from the vocational training and experience of a police officer. Rather, even though reasonable persons might draw the same inference from the evidence, a neutral, "disinterested" magistrate must be called upon to make the judgment. The frustration of police (among other things, it takes time to obtain a warrant) and the increased crime suffered by society are among the costs against which the promise to "secure the blessings of liberty" must be weighed. One who is a citizen first and a police officer second is likely to support the Court's view. But the beliefs of one who is a police officer first and then a citizen would be shaped by the crime suppression model. It might profit those so persuaded to examine how confident they are that some of their law enforcement colleagues would not unwittingly, and in their minds for the best of reasons, whittle away their fundamental liberties. Present-day Americans have achieved with relatively little struggle what others paid for with great suffering. We need reminding that it is a price many people are still paying throughout the world.

CONTROL OVER INVESTIGATIVE PRACTICE

Not all Supreme Court decisions affecting law enforcement regulate or limit police conduct. Throughout the text (in Chapters 8 and 9 on informants and surveillance, for example), cases are cited that essentially support investigative practice. The landmark cases that in some way restrict or regulate investigative practice are described in Table 25.1. This furnishes a bird's eye view of the issues while providing enough information to permit further pursuit of the matter by anyone interested.

Table 25.1
Milestone Decisions Affecting Investigative Practice Under the 4th, 5th, and 6th Amendments of the United States Constitution

Fourth Amendment	Aspect of Law Enforcement Affected	Significant Cases*
Clause 1. "The right of the people to be secure in their persons, houses, papers, and effects, against unreasonable searches and seizures shall not be violated; . . ." (Concept involved: personal security and right to property.)	A. Search and seizure (Inadmissibility of evidence seized in an illegal fashion.)	**Federal Cases** *Weeks v. United States* 232 U.S. 383 (1914) **State Cases**** *Mapp v. Ohio* 367 U.S. 643 (1961)
Clause 2. ". . . and no warrant shall issue, but upon probable cause . . ." (Concept involved: arrest powers.)	B. Arrest (The meaning of probable cause—right to stop and question; right to take a person into custody; standard for obtaining a search warrant.)	**Federal Cases** *Brinegar v. United States* 338 U.S. 183 (1948) *Rios v. United States* 364 U.S. 253 (1960) *United States v. Ventresca* 380 U.S. 102 (1965) *Spinelli v. United States* 393 U.S. 410 (1969) **State Cases**** *Aguilar v. Texas* 378 U.S. 108 (1954)

Table 25.1
Milestone Decisions Affecting Investigative Practice Under the 4th, 5th, and
6th Amendments of the United States Constitution (cont.)

Fifth Amendment	Aspect of Law Enforcement Affected	Significant Cases*
Clause 3. "; nor (shall any person) be compelled in any criminal case, to be a witness against himself;" (Concept involved: compulsory self-incrimination.)	A. Confessions (Incompetent under the self-incrimination clause if not free and voluntary, no threats or violence used, no promises made, direct or indirect, or any other improper influence exerted or mild pressure employed.) B. Compulsory testimony (Evidence obtained through a legal grant of immunity on the state level cannot then be used against the person on the federal level, or vice-versa.)	**Federal Cases** *Bram v. United States* 168 U.S. 532 (1897) *Hardy v. United States* 186 U.S. 224 (1902) *Wan v. United States* 266 U.S. 1 (1924) *Smith v. United States* 348 U.S. 147 (1954) **State Cases**** *Haynes v. Washington* 373 U.S. 503 (1963) *Malloy v. Hogan* 378 U.S. 1 (1964) *Miranda v. Arizona* 384 U.S. 346 (1966) **Federal Cases** *United States v. The Saline Bank of Virginia* 1 Pet 100 (1828) *Ballman v. Fagin* 200 U.S. 186 (1906) **State Cases**** *Murphy v. The Waterfront Commission of New York Harbor* 378 U.S. 52 (1964)
Clause 3. "; nor (shall any person) be deprived of life, liberty, or property without due process of law. (Concept involved: due process)	C. Interrogation during detention (Confessions.) D. Admissibility of evidence	**Federal Cases** *McNabb v. United States* 18 U.S. 332 (1943) *Upshaw v. United States* 335 U.S. 410 (1948) *Mallory v. U.S.* 354 U.S. 449 (1957) **State Cases*** *Brown v. Mississippi* 297 U.S. 278 (1936) *Rochin v. California* 342 U.S. 165 (1952) *Miranda v. Arizona* 384 U.S. 436 (1966)
Sixth Amendment	**Aspect of Law Enforcement Affected**	**Significant Cases***
Clause 2. ". . . to be confronted with the witnesses against him;" (Concepts involved: Access to evidence, Right of cross-examination. Fundamental fairness implicit in the concept of ordered liberty.)	A. The investigator's and prosecutor's ability to persuade the individual to appear as a witness in court.	**State Cases**** *Pointer v. Texas* 380 U.S. 400 (1965)

Table 25.1
Milestone Decisions Affecting Investigative Practice Under the 4th, 5th, and
6th Amendments of the United States Constitution (cont.)

Sixth Amendment (continued)	Aspect of Law Enforcement Affected	Significant Cases*
Clause 3. ". . . and to have the assistance of counsel for his defense." (Concept involved: right to counsel, essentials of a fair trial.)	A. Adversary system of justice emphasized. B. Pretrial disclosure of investigative reports to defense counsel. (This affects the report writing efforts of investigators.)	**State Cases**** *Gideon v. Wainwright* 372 U.S. 335 (1963) *Escobedo v. Illinois* 378 U.S. 478 (1964) *Miranda v. Arizona* 384 U.S. 436 (1966) **Federal Cases** *Jencks v. United States* 353 U.S. 657 (1957) **State Cases**** *Brady v. Maryland* 373 U.S. 83 (1963)

*The terms "federal" and "state" indicate where the case originated. In a sense they are all federal cases, as the definitive decision was made by the U.S. Supreme Court.

**As a result of these decisions, federal practice and rules of criminal procedure are applied to state and local law enforcement through the "due process" clause of the 14th Amendment.

REFERENCES

1   Daniel T. Borstin, "America: Our By-product Nation," *Time*, 23 June 1975, 70.

2   Montesquieu, Charles-Louis de Secondat, *The Spirit of Laws*, 1748.

3   Bruce Findlay and Esther Findlay, *Your Rugged Constitution* (Stanford, CA: Stanford University Press, 1950), 213.

4   Paul Brest, *Processes of Constitutional Decision Making* (Boston: Little, Brown, 1975), 708.

5   *Marbury v. Madison*, 5 U.S. (1 Cranch) 137 (1803).

6   U.S. Judiciary Act 1789. Sec. 25. 1 Stat. 85.

7   *Martin v. Hunter's Lessee*, 14 U.S. (1 Wheat.) 304 (1816).

8   *Cohens v. Virginia*, 19 U.S. (6 Wheat.) 264 (1821).

9   Ibid.

10   M.S. Culp, "A Survey of the Proposals to Limit or Deny the Power of Judicial Review by the Supreme Court of the United States," *Indiana Law Journal* 4, 386 (1928).

11   *Barron v. Baltimore*, 32 U.S. (7 Pet.) 243 (1833).

12   *The Slaughter-House Cases*, 83 U.S. (16 Wall.) 36 (1873).

13   *Duncan v. Louisiana*, 391 U.S. 145 (1968).

14   *Rochin v. California*, 342 U.S. 165 (1952).

15   *Gideon v. Wainwright*, 372 U.S. 335 (1963).

16   *Ker v. California*, 374 U.S. 23, 33 (1963).

17   *Locke v. United States*, 11 U.S. (7 Cranch) 339 (1813).

18   Ibid., 348.

19   *Stacey v. Emery*, 97 U.S. 642, 645 (1878).

20   *Carroll v. United States*, 267 U.S. 132 (1925).

21   *Brinegar v. United States*, 338 U.S. 160 (1948).

22   *Carroll, supra* note 20, 162.

23   *Brinegar, supra* note 21, 175.

24   H.H. Toch and R. Schulte, "Readiness To Perceive Violence As a Result of Police Training," *British Journal of Psychology*, 52(4) (1961), 389-393.

25   Ibid., 391.

26   Ibid., 392.

27   Ibid., 393.

28   *Rios v. United States*, 364 U.S. 253, 255 (1960).

29   Ibid., 261.

30   *Johnson v. United States*, 333 U.S. 10, 16 (1948).

31   Ibid., 13-14.

SUPPLEMENTAL READINGS

del Carmen, Rolando V., and Jeffery T. Walker. *Briefs of Leading Cases in Law Enforcement.* 5th ed. Cincinnati: Anderson, 2004.

Felkenes, George T. *Constitutional Law for Criminal Justice.* 2nd ed. Englewood Cliffs, NJ: Prentice Hall, 1988.

Hogue, Arthur R. *Origins of the Common Law.* Indianapolis: Liberty Press, 1986.

Klotter, John C., Jacqueline R. Kanovitz, and Michael I. Kanovitz. *Constitutional Law.* 9th ed. Cincinnati: Anderson, 2002.

National Commission on Law Enforcement. *Report on Lawlessness in Law Enforcement.* Washington, DC: U.S. Government Printing Office, 1931. [This is Report No. 11 of the Wickersham Commission appointed by President Herbert Hoover in 1929.]

Schwartz, Bernard. *A History of the Supreme Court.* New York: Oxford University Press, 1993.

Segal, Jeffrey A., and Harold J. Spaeth. *The Supreme Court and the Attitudinal Model.* New York: Cambridge University Press, 1993.

Singer, S., and M.J. Hartman. *Constitutional Criminal Procedure Handbook.* New York: Wiley & Sons, 1986.

CHAPTER 26

Evidence and Effective Testimony

INTRODUCTION

The culmination of a criminal investigation is a courtroom trial in which the guilt of a defendant must be proved beyond a reasonable doubt and during which legally obtained evidence (thus admissible in court) is presented to a jury (or judge, if trial by jury is waived). After hearing all the evidence, the jury or judge evaluates it, determines the facts, and based upon those facts makes a judgment of "guilty" or "not guilty."

Initially and throughout this process the investigator is largely responsible for (1) establishing that a crime was committed, and (2) developing evidence to prove beyond a reasonable doubt that a particular individual is guilty of that crime. For future reference, one should carefully note the date and time when each bit of evidence became known or was developed by the investigator.

At the trial stage, it is the prosecutor's responsibility to present the evidence in court. Here, a few cautionary words about teamwork are in order: if a prosecutor and investigator do not work together, the presentation in court will be adversely affected—and so will the case against the defendant. Criminal prosecutions have been lost not only because a state's attorney had not prepared (through pretrial conferences) civilian witnesses to testify, but also because the police had not induced them to be available and in court at the proper time.

WHAT IS EVIDENCE?

Evidence is anything a judge permits to be offered in court to prove the truth or falsity of the question(s) at issue. It is classified as: testimonial, real, or demonstrative. *Testimonial evidence* is given orally by a witness. *Real evidence* is any tangible object or exhibit offered as proof. *Demonstrative evidence* can be a chart, drawing, model, illustration, or experiment. Some evidence may be classified as all three; for example, the results of forensic examinations presented in court can be testimonial, real, and/or demonstrative.

Evidence can also be classified as either direct or circumstantial. *Direct evidence* is evidence that, in itself, proves or refutes the fact at issue; for instance, a confession. Most often, direct evidence is testimonial—based on what a witness saw or heard—but it sometimes involves the other senses. *Circumstantial evidence* is indirect proof from which the fact at issue may be inferred. Most forensic testimonial evidence is circumstantial.

Direct, circumstantial, testimonial, real, and demonstrative evidence are not mutually exclusive. Testimonial evidence can be either direct or circumstantial; real evidence is also demonstrative evidence; and both real and demonstrative evidence are tangible evidence in contrast to verbal or testimonial evidence. The following scenario may clarify this:

> A bank robbery was interrupted by an off-duty police officer just entering a bank. Shots were exchanged and the officer was killed, the fleeing robber pausing long enough to pick up the fallen officer's revolver. Based on a reliable informant's tip, a search warrant was obtained and the suspect's garage searched. Evidence being found, the suspect was arrested. Later, the friend to whom he gave the gun for safekeeping voluntarily turned it over to the police.

At trial subsequently, a detective described the finding of "bait" money (handed over to the robber by the teller) buried in the dirt floor of the robber's garage. The marked money itself is real evidence. Discovering its hiding place to be the defendant's garage is an example of circumstantial evidence. The detective's witness-stand account of the discovery is testimonial evidence. The friend's witness-stand statements concerning her receipt of the police officer's revolver are examples of two kinds of evidence: testimonial and real. The photographs and a sketch showing the location of the buried loot before and after its retrieval are examples of demonstrative evidence.

A popular misconception about circumstantial evidence is that it ought not be believed; another, that it is a weak kind of evidence at best. The court, however, can insist on proper safeguards to ensure that a conviction resting solely on circumstantial evidence is sound—logical, convincing, and related to the contested issue. Circumstantial evidence can be, and often is, a most persuasive type of proof.

HISTORICAL BACKGROUND OF THE RULES OF EVIDENCE

A means for settling both civil and criminal disputes is—after food, shelter, and pro-creation—high on the list of human needs. Just as various rules have evolved to secure justice therefor, so have procedures to implement them. Historically, 16 systems have been recognized as constituting a well-defined, organized, continuous body of legal ideas and methods.[1] Two systems remain dominant in modern times.[2] One, the Romanesque, was developed in the 1200s. Known as an inquisitorial system of criminal justice, it is still operative in Continental Europe and Latin America. In this judge-directed and judge-dominated system, guilt or innocence is decided by a judge. There are few rules controlling the amount or type of evidence that must be considered. Underlying the need for few and less strict rules is the belief that a judge is better able to evaluate evidence than a jury of laypersons.

The second legal system, the Anglican, was inherited from England and is operative in the United States. Comprising an elaborate set of rules to govern the evidence that may be heard by a judge and a lay jury, it is an adversarial system in which the defendant in a criminal case is presumed innocent until proved guilty. This must be done to the satisfaction of a jury, and not solely that of a judge, as in the inquisitorial system.

Developments in the United States

During the past two centuries, a system of rules for the presentation of evidence has been established in the United States. In some instances the rules are the result of centuries of deep thought and experience. In other instances the rules have been established in a haphazard manner without much thought. Although the United States adopted the English system, rules concerning the admissibility of evidence have taken separate developmental paths and are not the same in the two countries. Due to legislation and court decisions, some of which interpret constitutional provisions, the rules for obtaining and weighing evidence are now more restrictive in the United States than in England. . . .

The rules of evidence are changed not only by court decisions, but also by congressional or legislative enactments. . . . Congress has enacted specific legislation relating to the admissibility of confessions, wiretap evidence, and eyewitness testimony. . . .

In an effort to obtain more uniformity in court procedures, the United States Supreme Court in 1972 adopted the *Rules of Evidence for United States Courts and Magistrates*. . . . However, in accordance with federal laws, the proposed rules were required to be transmitted to Congress for approval. The House Judiciary Committee wrestled with the provisions for nearly a year, and finally approved a modified version in early 1974 by a vote of 377 to 130. Before approving the Supreme Court draft of the rules of evidence, the House Judiciary Committee changed provisions concerning privileged communications.

[T]he evidence rules followed in the federal and state courts of the United States today are products of a combination of legislative acts . . . and court decisions. . . . [3]

The rules of evidence approved in 1975 are not carved in stone. It should be expected that, from time to time, they will be added to and revised.

THE RULES OF EVIDENCE

For practical purposes the rules of evidence are rules of exclusion. Emphasis is placed throughout this text, therefore, on legal investigative behavior. This means: securing a search warrant to obtain evidence, arresting only on probable cause, administering *Miranda* warnings before interrogating a suspect, and respecting the right to counsel and the need for due process. An investigator sensitive to these concerns is unlikely to have evidence that was obtained in the course of the investigation excluded at trial.

Relevancy, materiality, and competency are other grounds on which an attorney relies to exclude evidence.

> *Relevancy* is concerned with whether there is a connection between the evidence and the issue to be proved. Relevant evidence tends to prove or disprove a fact.

> *Materiality* is concerned with whether the evidence is sufficiently important to influence the outcome of the issue being contested. Does it throw enough new light on the issue to warrant taking the time for its presentation and consideration?

> *Competency* is concerned with the quality and kind of evidence being offered (or the person offering it). Competent evidence is that which is admissible under the rules of evidence for the purpose of proving a relevant fact.

As a general rule, evidence will not be excluded if neither prosecution nor defense makes an objection to its admission. Though not likely, a judge may also make a motion to exclude evidence.

Relevant Evidence

Relevant evidence—its admission and exclusion—is succinctly described in the Federal Rules of Evidence, Rules 401, 402, and 403.

> Rule 401.   *Definition of "Relevant Evidence"*
>
> "Relevant evidence" means evidence having any tendency to make the existence of any fact that is of consequence to the determination of the action more probable or less probable than it would be without the evidence.[4]

> Rule 402.   *Relevant Evidence Generally Admissible;*
>   *Irrelevant Evidence Inadmissible*
>
> All relevant evidence is admissible, except as otherwise provided by the Constitution of the United States, by Act of Congress, by these rules, or by other rules prescribed by the Supreme Court pursuant to statutory authority. Evidence which is not relevant is not admissible.[5]

Rule 403.   *Exclusion of Relevant Evidence on Grounds of Prejudice, Confusion, or Waste of Time*

Although relevant, evidence may be excluded if its probative value is substantially outweighed by the danger of unfair prejudice, confusion of the issues, or misleading the jury, or by considerations of undue delay, waste of time, or needless presentation of cumulative evidence.[6]

In summary, it would appear that logic and common sense are to be utilized when deciding whether a piece of evidence is relevant. Relevancy by itself is not sufficient, however; the evidence must also be material and competent.

Material Evidence

Lawyers and judges often treat the terms *relevant* and *material*—and particularly their opposites—*irrelevant* and *immaterial*—as interchangeable.[7] They are not, of course. In distinguishing between the two, one court wrote:

> As used with respect to evidence, "material" has a wholly different meaning from "relevant." To be relevant means to relate to the issue. To be material means to have probative weight, that is, reasonably likely to influence the tribunal in making the determination required to be made.[8]

Another view with regard to the same issue is that all material evidence is necessarily relevant, but all relevant evidence is not necessarily material. Evidence is not material if its effect on the outcome is likely to be trivial. Furthermore, evidence, though material, may be inadmissible because it is not competent.

Competent Evidence

The third prong in the test for admissibility (the most important from an investigative viewpoint) is competency. Competency involves either the nature of the evidence itself or the person through whom it is offered in court. It is interesting and informative to note that even after having consulted several law dictionaries, an intelligible definition of competent evidence remains elusive. In one dictionary, it is "to be legally qualified or legally fit";[9] in another, "the quality of evidence offered which makes it proper to be received";[10] in still another, "evidence relevant to the issues being litigated."[11]

Such definitions being of limited value, the concept involved is best understood by turning to examples of incompetent evidence. There, the most common grounds for exclusion are invoked when the evidence was obtained in violation of the United States Constitution, state and federal statutes, or rules established by courts. Increasingly, evidence obtained in violation of state constitutional provisions, as interpreted by state courts of last resort, is being held incompetent.

Constitutional Grounds

> Evidence that has been obtained in violation of the Constitution . . . is inadmissible not because it is irrelevant or immaterial but because it is incompetent *as determined by the courts* (emphasis added).[12]

Statutory Incompetence

> . . . [S]ome evidence is not admissible because a state or federal statute prohibits the admission of the evidence. For example, § 2515 of the Omnibus Crime Control and Safe Streets Act of 1968, as amended, provides that evidence obtained by wiretapping or eavesdropping, when conducted in violation of the statute, is inadmissible in any court or other offical proceeding. . . . Evidence produced in contravention of . . . similar statutes will be excluded from court use not because it is irrelevant or immaterial, but because the statutes specifically provide that the evidence is not admissible or usable in court.[13]

Similarly, evidence based on a privileged communication is not admissible by statute; any such proposed testimony is ruled out as incompetent. A privileged communication is any statement made by one person to another with whom a special relationship of trust and confidentiality exists. The most common examples include husband/wife, clergy/church member, attorney/client, and physician/patient; some jurisdictions also include accountant/client and reporter/source. A few examples of evidence deemed incompetent by court rules:

- The evidence is unreliable (hearsay evidence).

- The evidence is so prejudicial (e.g., gruesome homicide scene photographs) that it could inflame the jury and its detrimental effect outweigh by far its probative value.

- The evidence might lead to undue sympathy or hostility on the part of the jury.

- The evidence would be disruptive of trial procedure (e.g., a surprise alibi raised at the last moment while at trial).

- The evidence would waste the court's time (e.g., repetitive, cumulative evidence being unnecessary).

WHAT IS EFFECTIVE TESTIMONY?

The investigative effort reaches its final, decisive stage when the results are presented at trial to court and jury. Unless accomplished effectively, the outcome could be a disappointment: a defendant might be found guilty of a lesser count in the indictment or even found not guilty. An investigator may well ask, "What, exactly does 'accomplished effectively' mean?" Testimony that is both understandable and believable would partially fill the bill. These two qualities, together with preparation regarding substantive matters and deportment, sum up "accomplished effectively."

Understandable Testimony

It is important that investigators be able to articulate the investigative activities leading to the indictment of the defendant. The method employed (for almost all court testimony) follows a Question and Answer (Q and A) format. The investigator responds to questions from both prosecutor and defense counsel. In so doing, the investigator must speak plainly and avoid police jargon that may not be comprehensible to a lay jury. Some jurors will recognize police shorthand, but few will know what "a DD 13" is. Hence, "I forwarded a DD 13 to see if the DOA owned the car" is not informative—thus, an ineffective statement. On the other hand, "I asked the records bureau for the name of the registered owner of the vehicle bearing license plate ABC-123" is informative enough to be effective. Answers should be couched in simple, everyday language and should be responsive to the questions. The ability to do this rests in part on a mastery of the details of the investigation. Hazy answers reflect a lack of command over every detail; this can be avoided by a careful pretrial review of crime scene notes, sketches, photographs, and case reports.

Anyone called to testify for the first time is naturally apprehensive; some people, including investigators, never quite conquer this feeling. Hence, witnesses mumble and give inaudible answers even though it is axiomatic that what a juror does not understand is evidence lost. Another critical consequence of a timid presentation is that the witness's credibility is diminished. In summary, understandable and believable testimony are inseparable: what cannot be understood will not be believed.

Believable Testimony

A criminal trial has two sides. The prosecution has the burden of proof beyond a reasonable doubt, and the defense must convince the court of the state's failure to do so. The defense need prove nothing; in most cases it will deny the charge and enter testimony in support of its contention of innocence. The jury's task is to decide which facts among all those presented are to be believed.

What then makes one witness more believable than another? And how can investigators enhance their credibility? Obviously, the witness with firsthand knowledge of the details of the case, who does not have to refer to notes, and whose facts square with common sense, creates a favorable impression. The good impression is heightened further if no prejudice, direct or indirect, is expressed against the defendant. A deputy sheriff's witness-stand response to a defense question in a murder trial surely diminished his credibility the moment he declared, "I'm here to see him burn!"

Even the *appearance* of overzealousness is to be avoided. For instance, an investigator unwilling to agree to anything that might assist the defendant is likely to reply to the defense question "Isn't it possible the gun went off accidentally?" with a flat-out denial: "No, that was not possible." Ruling out *all* possibilities is something a jury would find hard to swallow. A proper response might be, "Yes, that is a possibility;" or to add "Yes, but I do not believe the facts support the likelihood of that having happened" (assuming that the facts reasonably support the added contention).

It is also appropriate when testifying to display a concern for the plight of both victim and accused, as well as an obvious sincerity when presenting the facts that led to the indictment. In summary, an investigator should avoid leaving the overall impression with a jury that he or she is an automaton reeling off names, dates, and jaded answers. Rather, the investigator should be perceived as a human being very much aware of the gravity of the situation.

Behavior and Appearance

From the moment an investigator is called to the witness stand and walks into the courtroom, he or she is under scrutiny by the jury. The witness's carriage when proceeding to the stand—and demeanor while on it—can enhance or diminish the impact of the testimony. Just as conduct is important, so too is general appearance. The investigator/witness should be groomed as for a job interview.

CROSS-EXAMINATION

The Purpose

Immediately following the investigator's direct testimony, defense counsel will begin the cross-examination; its purposes are:

1. To satisfy the obligation to a client to test any evidence being offered, if there is doubt about it.

2. To develop facts favorable to the defense.

3. To discredit the witness.

4. To destroy the character of the witness, his or her story, or both.

Facts Favorable to the Defense

It is possible to develop facts that are advantageous to the defense (1) by eliciting a response from the investigator that suggests or acknowledges illegal behavior, or (2) by showing that there were others who had a motive, were considered suspects, and have not been ruled out. Defense counsel may try to establish that prevailing conditions (e.g., weather, light, etc.) contributed to a misjudgment of the victim's behavior and provoked the reaction from the defendant.

A competent attorney will seize upon any opportunity warranted by the testimony to build the case for the defense. In a narcotics arrest, for example, no mention was made on direct examination of a fingerprint having been found on any of the glassine envelopes containing the heroin. On cross-examination, the investigator might be asked casually whether any fingerprints were found on the evidence. If, as is most likely, the answer is "no," counsel may appear to ignore the response and go on to other matters. If such an issue raised by the Q and A is ignored by the prosecutor on redirect examination, defense counsel may argue in closing that the absence of the client's fingerprint on the envelopes proves that the defendant did not handle them. Most jurors, believing that fingerprints are invariably left when touching an object, may be persuaded. Had an expert in the development of fingerprints been summoned to testify, however, the record could have been set straight—fingerprints are not necessarily found on narcotics glassine envelopes. It is the prosecutor's job to be alert to such possibilities, but an investigator who senses potential problems should bring them up with the prosecutor as soon as possible after leaving the witness stand.

Discrediting the Witness

Several approaches can be taken to discredit a witness:

1. Bringing out any latent evidence of bias or prejudice.

2. Testing the memory of the witness, the aim being to elicit statements inconsistent with or contradictory to the direct testimony.

3. Revealing, through adroit questioning, the direct testimony to be unreasonable and, therefore, of questionable credibility.

4. Showing that the direct testimony was inaccurate, mistaken, or the result of an oversight.

Destroying the Witness's Testimony

One ultimate result of the adversary system, that pits defense against prosecution, is the demolition of a case through cross-examination. This need not happen if the investigator is alert, prepared, and truthful. If a witness is untruthful (especially if it involves a crucial piece of evidence) and this is admitted to on the witness stand, the witness's testimony is destroyed in the eyes of a jury.

Strategy and Tactics

A *leading question* is one that in its very asking supplies an answer. Often, it merely requires a "yes" or "no." This is permitted on cross-examination but not on direct examination. As a strategy, leading questions allow the defense to testify (albeit indirectly). Even attorneys with fearful reputations as cross-examiners will treat a witness "with kid gloves" when leading questions help the defense. Off the stand, one investigator remarked on completing his testimony, "Well, that wasn't too bad. How come he's considered so tough?" Having elicited admissions somewhat inconsistent with direct testimony, defense counsel had let the investigator off lightly. The questioning would have been much more severe (or, as cops would put it, the "wraps would have been taken off") had his admissions not been favorable to the defense or had there been a chance to destroy rather than merely discredit him.

Some tactics intended to fulfill the ends of cross-examination include: bewildering a witness with rapid-fire questions, harassing or humiliating the witness through verbal browbeating, or intimidating or embarrassing the witness by physically approaching him or her in a confrontational way or by invading his or her personal space. Judges are supposed to protect witnesses against unfair cross-examination, but many are lenient and allow great latitude in this regard. Under these conditions, the proper response is to answer respectfully while maintaining an unruffled demeanor and exhibiting no signs of resentment. Though it may be hard to accept at the time, nothing personal is meant: counsel is merely doing a job. The investigator must bear in mind that lawyers, convinced that cross-examination is the acid test, take advantage of latitude granted by the judge. If the witness remains in command of the facts and behaves in a civil manner, there is little to fear from cross-examination.

Miscellaneous Comments

Early in an investigator's career it would be profitable to attend a few criminal trials, especially to observe a criminal lawyer renowned for cross-examination prowess. It is fair to say that there are few such matchless defense attorneys practicing in courts. Though it might be less instructive, observing a run-of-the-mill cross-examination would be less intimidating and perhaps comforting.

Objections as to Form and Substance

Investigators are often astonished and feel quite let down when on the witness stand they are prevented from testifying about what they believe a jury ought to hear. Because unfamiliarity with the rules of evidence can be responsible for this, an understanding of some rules may assuage this disappointment. An objection to a question is based either on the way it was phrased or on its substance. Attorneys use "objection as to form" when a question is unclear or confusing, improperly phrased, or argumentative. If sustained, the judge may then suggest that the question be rephrased. A question to which there is no definite answer is considered misleading and thus inadmissible "as to form." Leading questions and questions having two parts are objectionable for the same reason. Objections "as to substance" are based on the relevancy, materiality, or competency of the question; such qualities were discussed earlier in the chapter.

Alleged Prior Statements

During cross-examination, some attorneys will pick up a document and read from it. What was read then is attributed to the witness who will be asked whether he or she made the statement. Rather than offer a denial or express agreement, the witness should ask for an opportunity to read the document. Sometimes the statement will indeed be that of the witness but taken out of context. Seeing it in its entirety may enable the witness to set the record straight.

Use of Notes

It has been pointed out that it is best for an investigator to prepare for trial by being thoroughly conversant with the facts. Usually this is feasible; the exception is a complicated investigation extending over several months. In that event, it may be necessary to refer to notes and reports while testifying. Before doing so, the judge's permission is required. A witness is not permitted to read from them directly, but a review of them is allowed before answering. Scrambling through notes to locate the information is not the way to impress a jury. Credibility is enhanced when properly kept notes allow the witness to find the information promptly. The attorney may ask to see the notes, and the judge almost certainly will grant the request. Unbusinesslike, disorderly notes can be used to discredit an investigator. In addition, the fact that some are not available because they were destroyed (or not brought to court) may also create an unfavorable impression with the jury—especially if it believes the normal procedure would be to preserve them and bring them to court.

"Yes or No" Answers

If it suits the purposes of an attorney, a "yes or no" answer may be demanded of the investigator on the stand. Rather than be intimidated and accede to the demand, it is appropriate for the witness to appeal to the judge on the grounds that the answer requires qualification or explanation and that a straight "yes" or "no" would be misleading. Unless this is perceived as evasive, the judge will not hold the witness to a "yes" or "no." In appealing to the judge, the investigator also sends a message to the prosecutor to bring the matter up again on redirect examination.

Timing the Response

An investigator on the witness stand may be surprised and uncertain as to why counsel raised an objection to a particular question. Therefore, it is advisable that a question not be answered too quickly; first, to be certain that it is understood and to allow sufficient time to formulate a reply; second, to permit the prosecutor to state an objection and have the judge rule on it.

CONCLUSION

A familiarity with the rules of evidence coupled with the realization that defense counsel is merely living up to the legal duty he or she owes to the client can make a cross-examination less of an ordeal. The investigator who is thoroughly prepared and understands what constitutes effective testimony should find that the initial apprehension (felt by most investigators early in their career) will diminish and finally disappear when more experience is gained in testifying.

REFERENCES

1   John H. Wigmore, *A Panorama of the World's Legal Systems* (St. Paul, MN: West, 1928).

2   John H. Wigmore, *Wigmore on Evidence*, 4th ed., 13 vols. (Boston: Little, Brown, 1970-89).

3   John C. Klotter and Jefferson L. Ingram, *Criminal Evidence*, 8th ed. (Cincinnati: Anderson, 2004), 13-15.

4   FED. R. EVID., 401.

5   FED. R. EVID., 401.

6   FED. R. EVID., 403.

7   Klotter and Ingram, *op. cit.*, 170.

8   *Weinstock v. United States*, 231 F.2d 699 (D.C. Cir. 1956).

9   Michael M. D'Auria, G.D. Helfand, and H.F. Ryan, *Legal Terms and Concepts in Criminal Justice* (Wayne, NJ: Avery, 1983), 25.

10 *The Law Dictionary*, 7th ed. (Cincinnati: Anderson, 1997), 92.

11 Steven H. Gifis, *Law Dictionary* (Woodbury, NY: Barron's Educational Series, 1975), 38.

12 Klotter and Ingram, *op. cit.*, 206.

13 Ibid., 207.

SUPPLEMENTAL READINGS

Brown, Peter M. *The Art of Questioning: Thirty Maxims of Cross-Examination*. New York: Macmillan, 1987.

Cleary, Edward W. (gen. ed.). *McCormick on Evidence*. 3rd ed. St. Paul, MN: West, 1984.

Ehrlich, J.W. *Lost Art of Cross-Examination*. New York: Dorset Press, 1988.

Kestler, Jeffrey L. *Questioning Techniques and Tactics*. 2nd ed. Colorado Springs, CO: Shepard's/McGraw-Hill, Inc., 1992.

Klein, Irving J. *Law of Evidence for Police*. 2nd ed. St. Paul, MN: West, 1978.

Klotter, John C., and Jefferson L. Ingram. *Criminal Evidence*. 8th ed. Cincinnati: Anderson, 2004.

Moldovsky, Joel, and Rose Dewolf. *The Best Defense*. New York: Macmillan, 1975.

Reynolds, D.W. *The Truth, The Whole Truth, And Nothing But: A Police Officer's Guide to Testifying in Court*. Springfield, IL: Charles C Thomas, 1990.

Wellman, Francis L. *The Art of Cross-Examination*. New York: Gordon Press, 1976.

Whitaker, Michael W. *The Police Witness: Effectiveness in the Courtroom*. Springfield, IL: Charles C Thomas, 1985.

Wigmore, John H. *Evidence in Trials at Common Law*. Boston: Little, Brown, 1983 (12 vols. and supp.).

CHAPTER 27

Putting It All Together

The Assassination of Dr. Martin Luther King, Jr.

Strategy and *tactics* are military terms that may be fruitfully employed in considering criminal investigation. In its original and literal sense, *strategy* meant "the art of the commander-in-chief," but today it has come to mean the overall planning of operations. The term *tactics* formerly referred to the art or science of deploying the military; today it usually means the securing of any designated objective.

For every criminal investigation, the central objective is usually the same—identify the offender and gather proof of that fact. The procedures for seeking and obtaining that information are described in Parts A through C; they represent the gamut of tactics an investigator can use lawfully to reach the central objective.

A description of the investigation of the Dr. Martin Luther King, Jr. assassination is used to illustrate how a perpetrator can be identified if the resources needed to do the job are made available. Then, organized in tables and lists are: a more generalized analysis of information sources and a rundown of the various investigative results that may ensue. Presented next, to demonstrate the interaction between sources of information, is a chart that depicts a network of some investigative paths that can be followed. Finally, attention is directed toward a newer strategy: *targeted investigations*.

THE INVESTIGATION OF THE ASSASSINATION _____

This section provides an excerpt from the report of the U.S. Department of Justice Task Force appointed to review the FBI investigation of the King assassination; an analysis in tabular form of the information sources, strategies, and tactics employed in following through on investigative leads in the case; and a commentary on the investigative efforts.[1] For those interested in the apprehension of James Earl Ray after he fled Memphis, the report offers a chronology of his activities following the assassination and leading to his capture in England.[2]

Task Force Report

B. *The FBI Investigation of the Assassination*

1. *The Department of Justice Response and FBI Performance*

   a. *The Murder.* At approximately 6:00 P.M. on April 4, 1968, Dr. Martin Luther King, Jr. was standing on the balcony outside of his room at the Lorraine Motel in Memphis, Tennessee. Moments later, Dr. King was shot by a high power rifle and then rushed to St. Joseph's Hospital. At 7:05 P.M. he was pronounced dead. The cause of death was a bullet wound which tore the major neck blood vessels and severed the spinal cord at the root of the neck.

   b. *Top Priority Investigation Ordered.* The Memphis Police Department was immediately aware of the King assault and promptly notified the FBI Memphis Field Office headed by SAC Robert G. Jensen. SAC Jensen telephonically relayed the information to Washington where Director Hoover and Attorney General Clark were informed. The Memphis Field Office was directed on the evening of April 4, 1968, to immediately conduct a full investigation of the matter as a possible violation of 18 U.S.C. 241, the civil rights conspiracy statute.

   This directive soon became national in scope with SACs in all FBI Field Offices being ordered by Teletype on April 7, 1968, to participate and conduct a top priority investigation under their personal supervision. This meant all leads were to be afforded immediate, thorough and imaginative attention and all possibilities from such leads exhausted. Also, 24 hours was set as the period after receipt of a lead within which the investigation and reporting must be completed. All SACs were to bear personal responsibility for any failure to handle the investigation.

   c. *Progress of the Investigation.* The breadth of this top priority investigation is repeatedly evidenced in the Murkin files. All informant sources—racial, security and criminal—were immediately alerted and contacted for information. The KKK and other hate groups as well as individuals known to have violent proclivities were checked. The files were checked for prior threats against Martin Luther King, Jr. Name checks were continuously being made on Selective Service records, city and telephone directories, drivers license bureaus, motor vehicle divisions, financial institutions, credit records, criminal and civil records, marriage licenses, public utility rolls, unions, common carrier passenger lists and more.

      (1) *Bessie Brewer's Rooming House.* Key information was developed early at Bessie Brewer's Rooming House whence the shot was fired. Bessie Brewer, Charles A. Stephens and William C. Anchutz were interviewed and a physical description of a suspect was obtained.

Bessie Brewer, resident manager of the rooming house, explained that a "John Willard" registered with her April 4, between 3:00 P.M. and 3:30 P.M. He was first directed to Room 8, but rejected it because it had a stove and refrigerator. Instead, he asked for a sleeping room only and accepted Room 5-B in the rear of the hostelry. This room provided a window with a view of Dr. King's room at the Lorraine Motel. Mrs. Brewer described the new tenant as a white male approximately 35 years of age, 5'11" to 6' tall, weighing 180 pounds with a medium build and presenting a neat clean appearance.

Stephens, who was in his room on the afternoon of April 4, remembers hearing footsteps between Room 5-B and the bathroom. He also remembers the bathroom being occupied for considerable periods of time—20 to 30 minutes—without water running or the toilet being flushed except for the last visit. This last visit ended when he heard what he is certain was a gun shot. Interrupted by the shot, Stephens opened his door to the hallway to see a man running down the hallway carrying a large wrapped bundle. As this man ran down the hall in the direction of Anchutz, Stephens recalls believing that he had seen this person earlier that afternoon with Mrs. Brewer. Stephens described him as a white male of average build, in his 30s, 5'10" to 11" tall, weighing 165 pounds, wearing a dark suit, and presenting a neat clean appearance.

Like Stephens, Anchutz was a resident of the rooming house and in his room at the time of the shooting. Also like Stephens, Anchutz occupied a room adjacent to "John Willard." He recalls watching television in his room that afternoon when he heard a gun shot. Immediately, he went to the door and as he opened it saw a man running toward him. This man covered his face as he ran and carried a blanket wrapped bundle. Anchutz address the man, saying: "I thought I heard a shot." The man responded: "Yeah, it was a shot." Anchutz described the man as 6' tall with a slim build, in his 30s.

(2) *Canipe Amusement Company.* The Canipe Amusement Company is located at 424 South Main Street and is just a short distance from Bessie Brewer's Rooming House at 422 1/2 South Main Street. In the recessed entrance to Canipe Company a blanket wrapped bundle (presumably the bundle Stephens and Anchutz saw) containing valuable pieces of physical evidence was recovered shortly after the shooting.

The store owner, Guy W. Canipe, and two customers, Bernell Finley and Julius L. Graham, were in the store at the time of the assassination. Each was interviewed by the FBI and described hearing a "thud" which drew their attention, and as they looked to see what had happened, they observed the blanket wrapped bundle in the entrance. At the same time, they saw a man dressed in a dark suit walking rapidly south on the sidewalk away from the bundle. A few moments later, they said, a white compact automobile—possibly a Mustang—proceeded north on South Main Street at a high rate of speed. The male was described as white, approximately 30 years of age with a medium build, 5'10" to 6' tall and weighing 160 to 180 pounds.

The bundle, after being discovered at Canipe's doorway by a member of a Memphis Police Department Tactical Squad, first came into the custody of Inspector Zachary of the Memphis Police Department's Homicide Bureau. Later in the evening of April 4, 1968, between 9:00 P.M. and 10:00 P.M., Inspector Zachary delivered the bundle to SAC Jensen who immediately had it flown by agent courier to Washington for laboratory examination (Memphis 44-1987-610). The bundle contained a Model 760 Remington Gamemaster rifle, 30-06 Springfield caliber, and a blue zipper bag. The bag contained various toilet articles along, with a pair of men's underwear with laundry tags, a pair of binoculars, two cans of beer, and a paper bag bearing an advertisement for York Arms Company, Memphis, Tennessee, with a York Arms Company cash sales receipt dated April 4, 1968.

(3) *Information and Physical Evidence Tracked.* The investigation continued with emphasis on tracing all physical evidence and information received. To this end a search of all Memphis area hotels and motels was initiated for the source of the blanket and bar of soap found in the blue zipper bag. Also, registrations at area inns were examined for the unknown suspect who fled the rooming house and who might be driving a white compact automobile. At the same time, the rifle, scope, binocular, cans of beer, laundry tags and other items were tracked.

The rifle and scope were quickly traced to the Aero Marine Supply Company in Birmingham, Alabama. The rifle was sold to a "Harvey Lowmyer" March 30, 1968. The scope, along with a second rifle, was purchased March 29, 1968, but "Lowmyer" exchanged this rifle the following day for the one recovered at the Canipe Amusement Company. According to the Aero Marine salesman, "Lowmyer" explained that he talked with his brother and was advised a more powerful rifle was necessary for deer hunting in Wisconsin. However, a laboratory examination of this returned rifle revealed that it was clogged with Cosmoline (a heavy grease firearm preservative) and could not be loaded and readied to fire. The salesman also provided a physical description of "Lowmyer" which matched those previously obtained.

The paper bag and the sales receipt from York Arms Company led agents to the Memphis store where the binoculars were purchased. The York Arms salesman explained that he sold the pair of binoculars at approximately 4:00 P.M. April 4, 1968, to a white male matching the descriptions previously obtained (Memphis 44-1987

Sub A sec. 1). By checking the manufacturer's can codes and distribution records, the two beer cans were traced to Southhaven Minnow Shop, Southhaven, Mississippi.

The center of the investigation shifted from Memphis to Birmingham on April 9, when the search of Memphis inns focused on the Rebel Motel and the April 3 registration record of an Eric Starvo Galt. It was already known that the rifle and scope were purchased in Birmingham and the Galt registration also pointed to Birmingham. The registration record aroused interest because Galt registered for the night of April 3 only, listed a Birmingham address and drove a Mustang with Alabama license plates.

The possibility of a link between Eric Starvo Galt and the unknown subject was pursued in Alabama by the Birmingham and Mobile offices. In their pursuit they learned that on August 29, 1967, Galt purchased a 1966 white Mustang automobile. The Bureau agents also learned that the State of Alabama issued a motor vehicle operator's license in October 1967 to Eric Starvo Galt, 2608 Highland Avenue, Birmingham, Alabama. The physical description obtained from this license matched those previously received: white male, born July 20, 1931, 5'11" tall, 175 pounds with blue eyes and brown hair.

When the investigation moved to Galt's Birmingham address it was learned that Galt lived there in late August until early October 1967. Because of the length of this contact, emphasis was placed on developing information on Galt's background. Significantly, it learned that during his Birmingham sojourn Galt expressed an enthusiastic interest in dancing and attended dancing school there.

(4) *Los Angeles.* Soon after the Birmingham connection was uncovered Los Angeles became a focal point in the investigation. The significance of Los Angeles became apparent April 11, with the knowledge of four facts.

One, when on April 11, 1968, the Bureau located Galt's abandoned Mustang in Atlanta a search of it indicated that Galt had had it serviced twice in the Los Angeles area.

Two, also incident to the search of the Mustang, a fragment of cardboard torn from a Kleenex box was found. On it were the names and Los Angeles addresses of Anita Katzwinkel and Ginger Nance.

Three, laundry markings from the recovered underwear were tracked to Home Service Laundry and Dry Cleaning, Hollywood, California. The following day agents learned that the name Eric Starvo Galt appeared in the laundry's records.

Lastly, a pair of pliers recovered from the blue zipper bag were traced to the Romage Hardware Store which is within five blocks of Home Service Laundry and Dry Cleaning.

Since it was known that while in Birmingham Galt pursued an interest in dancing, all dance schools in the Los Angeles area were checked. Galt's name appeared in the records of the National Dance Studio, Los Angeles.

Eventually, the dance studio contact proved to be most important because it was through an interview with the dance studio owner that a photograph of Eric Starvo Galt was finally obtained. The owner keyed the agents to an interest Galt had expressed in attending a bartending school. Checking the area, the International School of Bartending was located and it provided Galt's graduation photograph. For the first time, agents were able to see and distribute a photo of their subject. To be sure of maximum dissemination, the photo was circulated among the news media.

While in Los Angeles Galt first lived at the Serrano Apartments and later at the St. Francis Hotel. Persons contacted at these locations called him a "loner" and described him as a person who kept to himself. A departure from this characterization, however, was reported by Charles Stein who, at no expense to himself, rode with Galt in the Mustang from Los Angeles to New Orleans and return.

Stein explained that he and his sister Rita Stein met Galt through their cousin Marie Martin who was working as a bar maid at the Sultan Bar located in the St. Francis Hotel. Galt had mentioned to Martin that he was planning to drive to New Orleans and she asked if he would be willing to give her cousin a ride there in order to pick up her children. He agreed, but it was Charles and not Rita who went along with Galt.

Notwithstanding the information Stein provided, the investigation moved no closer to locating Galt. New Orleans was scoured for clues and although Galt's hotel and room were located the effort was fruitless. Stein also stated Galt made several telephone calls from pay telephones along the way but an exhaustive search of countless telephone records, numbers and subscribers produced nothing. Lastly, Stein explained that Galt conditioned the ride to New Orleans on Charles Stein, Rita Stein and Marie Martin joining George Wallace's American Independent Party. Each joined but again the ensuing investigation of this lead learned nothing.

(5) *Atlanta.* On April 11, 1968, a citizen call came through to the Atlanta Police Department reporting the missing white Mustang. According to this caller and another person, both interviewed by the FBI, the abandoned Mustang was parked shortly before 9:00 A.M. April 5, 1968, by a lone man matching Galt's description. The discovery of Galt's Mustang immediately caused agents to seek out any additional contacts by Galt in Atlanta.

Because Galt was believed to use low cost rooming houses all such establishments were contacted for any sign of him. Success was found at Jimmie Dalton Gardner's Rooming House where Galt registered March 24, 1968. Although Galt was nowhere to be found, he had left evidence behind. Found in his room were a booklet, "Your Opportunities in Locksmithing" and a collection of maps. One of these maps was of the city of Atlanta with the residence of Martin Luther King, Jr., and the headquarters of SCLC [Southern Christian Leadership Conference] circled.

Other evidence of Galt's presence in Atlanta was received from the Piedmont Laundry where records showed he picked up laundry April 5, 1968.

(6) *Galt Identified as James Earl Ray.* Knowing that Galt returned to Atlanta after the assassination, all conceivable modes of transportation in, around and out of Atlanta were checked. However, Galt's trail was cold; there was no evidence as to where he fled from Atlanta.

The Bureau became worried because with each passing hour Galt's chances of avoiding capture became better and better. Therefore, the investigative emphasis shifted from following Galt's trail to identifying Galt. In an effort to accomplish this the Bureau initiated a comparative search of three identical latent fingerprints believed to be Galt's (one fingerprint was recovered from the rifle; a second from the binoculars; and a third from the map of Atlanta found in Galt's room) against fingerprints of white male fugitives. To be sure, the limitation to fugitives was purely speculative. However, the speculation paid off when on April 19, 1968, James Earl Ray's fingerprint card compared identically.

With the discovery that Eric Starvo Galt was James Earl Ray, the investigation was redirected to a search of Ray's whereabouts since the time of his April 23, 1967, escape from Missouri State Prison. Through the months of April and May the Ray-Galt steps were traced. Eventually, the Bureau was able to account for Ray's whereabouts almost continuously since his escape. Nevertheless, his trail remained cold beyond Atlanta on April 5, 1968.

In connection with their search, Ray's family was identified, located, physically surveilled and periodically interviewed for information. Also, prison inmates and associates were queried as well as his military record perused. But, no clues developed. Ray's family said they knew nothing; they had not heard from nor been in contact with James and did not know of his whereabouts. Prison inmates and associates told tales of bounties offered for the death of Dr. King but exhaustive investigations could not substantiate their claims.

Frustrated, the Director prepared a memorandum for the Attorney General dated May 13, 1968, in which he explains that extensive investigation has not resulted in any new developments beyond Atlanta, April 5. Therefore, the Director requested authorization for telephone and microphone surveillance on Ray family members. The request, however, was never acted upon.

(7) *Passport Search*. From an interview with a former cellmate of Ray's at Missouri State Prison it was learned that Ray appreciated the ease with which a person living in Canada could obtain a false passport. Though it is not clear that the cellmate's comments precipitated a search of Canadian passports issued since Ray's April 23, 1967, escape, it is known that on the request of the FBI Legat in Canada such a search was conducted by the Royal Canadian Mounted Police. A passport search was also conducted in Mexico and the United States.

Though the search went through a staggering number of applications and was based on the comparison of Ray's photograph to those submitted with the application, it proved to be the necessary break in picking up Ray's trail. At 9:30 P.M. June 1, 1968, the Legat attache, Ottawa, Canada, called the Bureau to advise that after reviewing some 175,000 applications the RCMP located a passport issued April 24, 1968, under the name Ramon George Sneyd which contained a photograph very definitely similar to Ray.

The passport was filed by the Kennedy Travel Agency in Toronto, Canada. Incident to their investigation, the Royal Canadian Mounted Police contacted the travel agency and obtained a hand printed note from Sneyd concerning his application. The note together with the passport photo and a latent palm print were forwarded to the Bureau for laboratory examination which concluded that Ray and Sneyd were the same person.

(8) *Ray Apprehended*. The Kennedy Travel Agency also provided information that Sneyd purchased a round trip air ticket from Toronto to London departing May 6 and returning May 21, 1968. But New Scotland Yard determined that Sneyd turned in the return portion of the fare and received a May 7, 1968, ticket to Lisbon, Portugal, plus a $14.60 voucher.

Immigration authorities in Lisbon were immediately contacted. It was learned that Ray had entered Lisbon May 7 but had exited for London May 17, 1968.

Stops were issued by New Scotland Yard for Sneyd. At 11:15 A.M., June 8, 1968, Ray was apprehended by officers of New Scotland Yard while he was passing through British immigration offices in the London Airport. At the time he was planning a flight to Brussels, Belgium.[3]

Investigative Summary

Although the crime occurred in Memphis, the investigation soon spread to four other cities: Birmingham, Atlanta, Los Angeles, and Washington. The interplay between physical evidence, people, governmental files, and records is made plain in Table 27.1, along with the results obtained and the strategies and tactics employed in each investigative step. The numerous blind alleys, however, have not been mentioned. For example, two unopened Schlitz beer cans abandoned in Canipe's doorway were traced to a store in Southhaven, Mississippi. From there it was a dead end, with no further clues of use to the investigation.

ANALYSIS OF INVESTIGATIVE EFFORTS

The Identification of a Latent Fingerprint

Owing to the size of the FBI national fingerprint file (around 100 million persons), there are about one billion individual fingerprints. To search for a single print was virtually impossible at the time of the King homicide investigation; accordingly, a decision was made to compare the latent impression with those of white male fugitives of which there were about 53,000. By selecting only fugitives similar in physical description to those previously obtained for "Galt," the number was reduced to approximately 2,000. This meant about 20,000 individual prints had to be compared. After some 7,000 had been scrutinized, a known fingerprint matching that of the latent was discovered: card number 405-942G bore the name James Earl Ray. An accurate physical description, many photographs from previous arrests, and known handwriting samples (in signatures on fingerprint record cards) immediately became available to further the investigation.

When the national fingerprint file is completely computerized, it will be possible to scan for a single latent print. Until then, a "cold" search involving a systematic culling of the entire file is not feasible unless the case is of national significance. At the time of the King investigation, latent impressions were useful only when a set of inked, known fingerprints was available—either from the file or, if the suspect had no fingerprint record, expressly taken for this purpose.

The Number of Unproductive and False Leads

In any criminal case involving a well-known figure, the flood of tips coming into the police department swells beyond normal bounds. When daily media coverage is coupled with a substantial reward ($155,000 in the King homicide), the information grows geometrically. Separating the significant from the insignificant tips is virtually impossible. Resources inevitably are diverted and the investigation lengthened; for departments with modest resources this could be fatal. Therefore, many have an arrangement for mutual aid, so that when one department is struck by a major case, there is staff available from others to run down all leads.

Table 27.1
Investigative Leads

SOURCES OF INFORMATION	STRATEGY/TACTICS USED
EYEWITNESSES	
I. Description of the possible assailant obtained from two sources:	Interviews.
A) The manager of the rooming house from which the shot was fired and the occupants of the room adjacent to "John Willard" the name used by the person from whose room the fatal shot was fired.	
B) The store owner and two customers of the Canipe Amusement Co. in the doorway entrance of which a blanket-wrapped bundle was dropped by a person who then walked rapidly away.	
II. Description of the escape vehicle:	Interviews.
Provided by Guy W. Canipe and the two customers in his store who heard the bundle drop. They then observed a white compact automobile proceeding north a few moments later at a high rate of speed.	
FINGERPRINTS (LATENT)	
Searching the items found in the abandoned bundle resulted in the development of two latent impressions (of the same finger) on:	Processing of evidence abandoned near the crime scene for fingerprints.
A) The binoculars (Bushnell "Banner").	
B) The rifle (Remington Model 760).	
MEMPHIS AND OTHER LOCALITIES	
Follow-up activities in Memphis and four other cities revealed useful, important information. The clue(s) that led to each city and their investigative value are indicated below:	
MEMPHIS, TENNESSEE	
The binoculars (7x35 Bushnell "Banner") were traced to the store in Memphis that sold them. The salesman provided a description of the buyer matching the descriptions of other eyewitnesses.	Use of the Memphis telephone directory to locate the New York Arms Co. Questioning of salesman who sold the binoculars. Canvass of motels, inns, hotels, and rooming houses listed in the telephone directory.
A registration record (for the night of April 3 only) is discovered in the Rebel Motel of Memphis. The guest stated on the registration that he was driving a Mustang automobile with Alabama plates. A home address in Birmingham is listed by the guest using the name Eric Starvo Galt.	

Table 27.1
Investigative Leads (cont.)

SOURCES OF INFORMATION	STRATEGY/TACTICS USED
BIRMINGHAM, ALABAMA	
The Remington rifle (Model 760) is traced to the store that sold it to a "Harvey Lowmyer" on March 30, 1968. The salesman's description of Lowmyer matches those previously obtained.	Interviewing of the salesman who sold the rifle to Lowmyer.
Records of the State of Alabama, Motor Vehicle Bureau disclose that an Eric Starvo Galt was issued an operator's license in October 1967. A street address in Birmingham was also available from this source. Further inquiry led to the information that Galt purchased a 1966 white Mustang automobile in late August 1967. The physical description of Galt matched that previously obtained from all others.	Examination of records and files maintained by the State of Alabama.
Information developed on Galt's background while in Birmingham revealed his interest in dancing and that while in that city he attended a dancing school.	Neighborhood canvass.
ATLANTA, GEORGIA	
A telephone call from a citizen to the Atlanta Police on April 11 provided the information that a white Mustang automobile had been parked and apparently abandoned by a lone man on April 5 (the day following the shooting) shortly before 9:00 A.M. The caller and another person provided descriptions that matched those already on file in the case.	Publicity through the mass media seeking information. A concerned, alert citizen cooperating with the police can help, especially if the police make it easy for the public to report their observations and suspicions.
A careful search of the abandoned Mustang revealed that it had been serviced twice in Los Angeles. A fragment torn from a Kleenex box bearing the names of two women with Los Angeles addresses was also found in the car.	Examination of the crime scene and/or the instruments of crime for clue material and trace evidence.
Processing for fingerprints of items found in a room rented by Galt in late March 1988 resulted in the development of a latent fingerprint on a map of the City of Atlanta. The residence of Dr. Martin Luther King, Jr. and the headquarters of SCLC were circled on this map. The print was the same as found on the rifle and binoculars.	Canvass of rooming houses, inns, and the like. Examination of the records and questioning of the manager and others in the rooming house.
A laundry was located where records showed Galt picked up his clean clothing on April 5, 1968.	Canvass of laundries and an examination of their records. Questioning of laundry personnel.

Table 27.1
Investigative Leads (cont.)

SOURCES OF INFORMATION	STRATEGY/TACTICS USED
LOS ANGELES, CALIFORNIA **TRACING ITEMS ABANDONED FLEEING FROM SCENE** Among the objects found in the bundle dropped in Canipe's doorway were:	Various follow-up efforts.
A) A pair of flatnose duckbill pliers with the name "Romage Hardware" stamped on the handle.	Use of reference library to track down Romage Hardware through a trade association. It was found in Los Angeles.
B) Underwear bearing the mark 02B-6.	Inquiry among law enforcement agencies (maintaining a laundry and dry cleaner mark file) as to whether they can identify the mark. Canvass of laundries in the cities connected to Galt through other evidence. A laundry five blocks from Romage Hardware store was found. The name Eric Starvo Galt appeared in its records, 02B-6 having been assigned to Galt.
The city of Los Angeles also cropped up when the Mustang automobile was located and examined.	Described above under Atlanta.
GALT'S EXPRESSED INTEREST IN DANCING Following up on Galt's attendance at a dancing studio in Birmingham, all dance schools in the Los Angeles area were contacted. Eventually, one was located in which Galt's name appeared in its records.	Canvass of all dancing schools in the Los Angeles area. Interviews of all persons having contact with Galt at the school.
The owner of the dance studio offered the information that Galt had expressed an interest in attending a bartending school. A check of bartending schools led to one that Galt had attended. A graduation photograph was provided by the school.	Canvass of all bartending schools in the area. Interviews of all persons having contact with Galt during his schooling. For the first time investigators were able to view and distribute a picture of Galt.
WASHINGTON, D.C. **LATENT FINGERPRINTS** The two latent fingerprints developed on the binoculars and rifle (abandoned upon fleeing the scene) and the latent print developed on the map of Atlanta were sent to the national fingerprint file located in FBI Headquarters. All three latents were of the same finger and were identical, thereby establishing that the person at the crime scene and the occupant of the room in Atlanta were one and the same.	Search and comparison of the latent fingerprints against known prints either in the crime file or taken for the purpose of comparison. See comments on the identification of a latent fingerprint.

In the survey of the King homicide, only productive developments were treated. Many leads requiring massive investigative effort proved unfruitful. For instance, in addition to the cities previously mentioned, other places such as New Orleans and Mexico needed canvassing—a resource allocation of considerable expense. It was very productive in the King case, but for most police departments it would have been impossible, given the far-flung locations involved. And it must also be remembered that although the Bureau has the wherewithal to investigate throughout the states, generally it does not have jurisdiction in homicides. Authorization for its investigation in King's assassination came from civil rights legislation.

The Investigative Process in General

Tables 27.2 and 27.3 indicate the major sources of information and the outcomes that could result from their diligent exploration and clever exploitation. Also covered are some possible interactions or paths that an investigator might follow in attempting to arrive at a solution to a case. Figure 27.1 summarizes the investigative activity that led to the

Table 27.2
Information Sources and Investigative Results That May Be Obtained

Crime Scene	People	Records and Files
AE. Examine: In important cases seek out forensically qualified personnel **Possible Results** R 1. Determine *what* happened. R 2. Note *modus operandi*, if any. R 3. Reconstruct the event (*how* was the crime committed). R 4. Record scene photographically with the aim of building a psychological profile of the offender. RE: **EVIDENCE LEFT AT CRIME SCENE** R 6. Search for, collect, and preserve. R 7. Record by photomacrography the details needed to establish an identity or otherwise help to link the crime scene and/or victim to the perpetrator. R 8. Tentatively establish the cause and manner of death. Confirm or disprove by autopsy. RE: **EVIDENCE TAKEN FROM THE CRIME SCENE** R 9. Search vicinity of crime scene for discarded weapon. R 10. Review pawnbroker reports. Canvass secondhand stores for stolen property. R 11. Engage the public through publicity in a widespread search for an item taken from the crime scene which may subsequently be abandoned.	BI. Interviews: BC. Complainant (victim, if any). BW. Witnesses, if any. BN. Neighbors. BO. Others (family and relatives, friends, employees, or other business associates of the victim). **Possible Results** R 12. Provide a description (and a photograph) of the suspect, the vehicle used, and/or the stolen property. R 13. Provide details to establish that the crime was committed. R 14. Provide other (often incomplete) information about the perpetrator or other possible witnesses who were near the scene about the time the crime was committed. R 15. Provide partial information that requires follow-up. R 16. Suggest a motive and/or names of possible suspect(s). R 17. Provide information that indicates that the suspect(s) had the opportunity and would be unafraid to commit the crime. R 18. Provide information (and later testimony) that the suspect (defendant) committed the crime.	CR. Consult: CL. Law enforcement files (Municipal, County, State, Federal) CO. Other governmental files CB. Business records CM. Miscellaneous sources (quasi *ad hoc* agencies, reference library, trade associations) **Possible Results** R 19. Obtain the name of a suspect. R 20. Obtain a name (and/or address) or other information that requires follow-up action (people, other records and possible physical evidence). R 21. Obtain the name (or purchaser) of a motor vehicle, weapon, or other recorded matter, i.e., name of a student or of the person assigned a specific laundry/dry cleaner mark. R 22. Obtain information about an object. What was it manufactured for, i.e., intended use? Where and how widely was it distributed? R 23. Based on crime pattern analysis, devise a strategy for surveillance of a future potential victim. R 24. Obtain information as to the habits, interests, likes, and dislikes of a suspect; places of previous employment and other activities; current and former love interests; location and names of in-laws and other relatives.

Table 27.3
Follow-up Activities

BEFORE a suspect is suggested or identified.

FU-A. Submit physical evidence to crime laboratory; latent fingerprints to Identification Bureau (if not compared in laboratory).

FU-B. Interview those whose names have resulted from the questioning of others or were acquired from a record or file suggesting possible knowledge of the crime, the circumstances surrounding it, the victim, or the perpetrator.

FU-C. Canvass neighborhood (crime scene, residences, employers) or something more specific such as motels, used car lots, opticians, schools (art, photography, dancing, beauty culture, automotive repair), supermarkets, hardware stores, laundries, and so on.

FU-D. Examine appropriate files and records.

FU-E. Contact informants.

FU-F. Establish a hot line (an exclusive telephone line) that is serviced 24 hours a day.

FU-G. Seek media coverage to locate possible witnesses, fleeing person(s), or an abandoned vehicle or weapon.

AFTER a suspect has been described, suggested, or identified.

FU-H. Have an artist's sketch prepared and distributed widely through newspaper, handbills, television and radio. If a photograph is available, distribute it.

FU-I. Contact informants re: suspect's possible involvement or whereabouts.

FU-J. Initiate a surveillance of suspect's family and relatives or others that may lead to or help locate a suspect.

FU-K. If necessary, obtain a search warrant to acquire physical evidence (exemplars) for comparison. Submit exemplars to the forensic laboratory.

FU-L. Submit to the forensic laboratory specimens of physical evidence found on or in the possession of the suspect, his/her home, automobile, or garage for analysis and comparison with any similar evidence discovered at the crime scene or on the victim, or given to the offender (e.g., marked money).

FU-M. Conduct a lineup.

POSSIBLE RESULTS

R 25. A possible suspect is suggested.

R 26. A particular individual is specifically named as the suspect, and his or her interests and activities are learned.

R 27. An individual is identified through a fingerprint or other physical evidence (firearms, shoeprint, etc.)

R 28. Hold a lineup (as a follow through to R 25 - R 27) or after questioning a suspect, if there is an eyewitness.

R 29. Establish the cause and manner of death through an autopsy.

R 30. Establish what a substance is or what it contains (e.g., poison, narcotic, ethyl alcohol) through chemical analysis.

R 31. Additional follow-up activity involving more records, people, even physical evidence, i.e., recording serial numbers of the ransom money (kidnapping); or use detective dyes to label an article that may be passed to an offender (as bait money in a bank holdup.)

POSSIBLE RESULTS

R 32. Recover stolen/abandoned (escape) vehicle.

R 33. Additional follow-up activity including identifying an object left at the crime scene or obtained from the victim when it (or its purpose) is not apparent.

R 34. A particular individual emerges as a possible suspect.

R 35. The suspect(s) is (are) cleared.

R 36. A suspect is linked to the crime scene through physical evidence (fingerprint, bullet, cartridge case, blood, glass, hair, and fibers).

---

identification of the perpetrator of the King homicide. Figure 27.2 presents a more general view of some possible investigative paths. It demonstrates how follow-up activities from the input of each of the three major sources of information—people, physical evidence and records—intertwine.

Following a perusal of the charts, it should be apparent that the permutations of response (in reaction to new, often partial, information) are manifold. One investigative supervisor's (or investigator's) follow-through steps will not necessarily be the same as another's. Availability of staff, concerns over perceived costs and benefits, the abilities and personalities of the investigator(s)—all will account for the separate paths that may be taken. Because human beings respond differently to inherently complicated situations, variations are to be expected. It would not be an exaggeration to

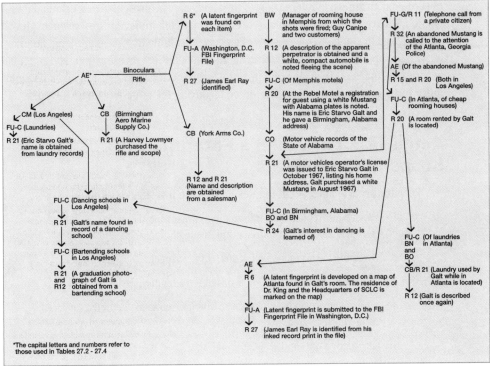

Figure 27.1
Network of Investigative Paths that Led to the Identification of James Earl Ray as the Perpetrator in the Homicide of Dr. Martin Luther King, Jr.

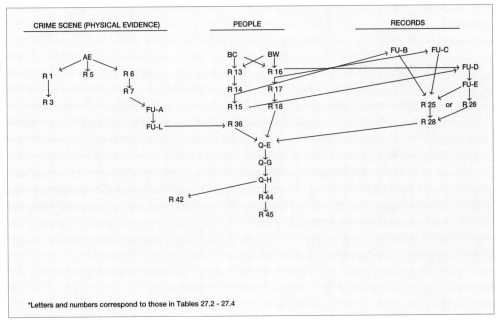

Figure 27.2
Network of Some Possible Investigative Paths Demonstrating the Interaction Between Sources of Information.

observe that an almost infinite variety of problems may be presented by a criminal investigation. Clearly, a solution is not likely to be completely reduced to a "science"; it will probably retain some characteristics of an "art." Training in logical thinking, familiarity with the application of the scientific method to criminal investigation, and practical experience (made more meaningful by retrospective, critical review) will all help to minimize variations in response to developments during the course of an investigation.

Activities: If or When a Potential Suspect Materializes

Preparatory and antecedent to questioning, the investigator should:

1. Review all reports and information concerning the crime, including forensic laboratory reports, crime scene photographs, and sketches.

2. Examine the arrest record, if any, of the suspect.

3. Interview officers who have arrested the offender previously.

4. Contact any custodial officers who may have gotten to know the suspect while incarcerated.

5. Proceed to question suspect. (See Table 27.4)

PROACTIVE MEASURES

The previous discussion largely concerns the reactive behavior of detectives—investigating a crime *after* it has been committed. *Proactive* behavior, on the other hand, involves anticipatory measures; for example, banks often provide tellers with bills whose serial numbers are recorded. Passed to a robber when such a crime is attempted, they are easy to identify.

Another proactive step is crime pattern analysis (discussed in Chapter 7), which is employed to solve a series of crimes through measures taken in the expectation of having law enforcement ready for the next attempt. A related, but relatively new, proactive approach to solving crime is termed *targeted investigation.* The difference between the two is the starting point. Pattern studies begin with the analysis of reported crimes, but targeted investigations, at least as first conceived, focus on the small group of career criminals responsible for an unduly large amount of crime. They need not be limited to career criminals, however; any serious crime problem can warrant a targeted investigation. The selection of the target must be based on a careful analysis determining the nature of the problem and possible solutions. Then, before the investigation is undertaken, a suitable strategy is developed.

Table 27.4
Questioning a (Possible) Suspect

By INTERVIEWING

Q-A. Keep *Miranda* warnings in mind—administer when necessary.

Q-B. Ascertain what he or she knows or will admit about the crime.

Q-C. Ascertain alibi, if any; check it out.

Q-D. Ask suspect to furnish or allow a search of their person, clothing, home, garage, or automobile for comparison physical evidence. If this request is denied, and if probable cause is believed to exist, seek a search warrant.

POSSIBLE RESULTS

R 37. Suspect is cleared.

R 38. Use physical evidence to reconstruct the crime and to check out the details provided as to what happened.

R 39. If not eliminated as a suspect, interview or place under surveillance persons whose identities emerge from interviewing the suspect. Records may have to be gone over again or new ones reviewed.

R 40. Crime laboratory links suspect to victim or crime scene through associative evidence.

R 41. Follow-up by interrogation.

By INTERROGATING

Q-E. Administer *Miranda* warnings.

Q-F. If there is more than one suspect, separate them and question individually. On the basis of the entire investigation reconstruct what happened and how, pointing out any discrepancies noted in the alibis and asking for an explanation or clarification. Continue to pursue such differences while conveying the impression that, because the story (or stories) don't jibe with the facts, evidence is mounting against them.

Q-G. Use evidence provided by witnesses (or conflicting accounts or alibis), records or physical evidence that points to his or her involvement in the crime

Q-H. Make any admission or confession easy.

POSSIBLE RESULTS

R 42. Suspect is cleared.

R 43. Probable cause for an arrest is not established. Review the investigation in its totality. If warranted, continue by searching for additional evidence as to the perpetrator.

R 44. Obtain an admission or confession.

R 45. Document the admission or confession.

R 46. Reconstruct how the crime was committed, based on (and to confirm details of) the confession.

R 47. After the confession urge the perpetrator to reenact the crime, noting any spontaneous comments made by him or her.

References

[1]   U.S. Department of Justice, *Report of the Department of Justice Task Force to Review the FBI Martin Luther King, Jr. Security and Assassination Investigations.* (Washington, DC: Department of Justice, 11 January 1977).

[2]   Ibid., 65-106.

[3]   Ibid., 47-62.

Supplemental Readings

Douglas, John, and Mark Olshaker. *The Anatomy of Motive*. New York: Scribner, 1999.

U.S. Department of Justice. *Report of the Department of Justice Task Force to Review the FBI Martin Luther King, Jr. Security and Assassination Investigations*. Washington, DC: Department of Justice, 11 January 1977.

Morgan, J. Brian. *The Police Function and the Investigation of Crime*. Aldershot, England: Avebury/Gower, 1990.

CHAPTER 28

Landmark Case
in Criminal Investigation
The Lindbergh Kidnapping

In order to see continuous improvement in surgical practice, most surgeons periodically review their operating procedures and the results achieved. By recognizing any drift from the norm—for better or worse—they have found that advances and mistakes can be identified. They publicize any medical advances in professional journals; meanwhile in their hospitals, corrective measures are taken to prevent the recurrence of mistakes.

This, unfortunately, does not describe the prevailing state of affairs in the field of criminal investigation: detectives seldom see past cases with a severely critical, corrective eye. While a backward look can well be an affirmative one—calling to mind more than a few successful investigations that identified, tried, and convicted the perpetrators—such negligence is not the exception but the rule. The investigator must realize that even a 60-year-old case is worth reevaluation, so long as it was well-documented from the start and the evidence preserved. These provisos apply to the Lindbergh kidnapping case. The New Jersey State Police has catalogued and kept under lock and key all the physical evidence admitted at trial; the researcher has been given access to the files.

THE LINDBERGH KIDNAPPING

In 1927 Charles A. Lindbergh became the first aviator to fly solo across the Atlantic, and the feat brought a degree of fame and acclaim unmatched by any celebrity before. With crowds of the curious dogging his every move, the shy Lindbergh took refuge in sparsely settled Hopewell, New Jersey; in 1932 he was building a house for his wife Ann Lindbergh, and 20-month-old Charles Lindbergh, Jr. On the evening of March 20 the family was settled in the partially completed residence when, shortly after the nurse put her charge down for the night, the initial report came in to the New Jersey State Police that an intruder had snatched the baby from his crib.

The handwritten ransom note left in the nursery demanded $50,000. On the paper, two blue overlapping circles were drawn; the intersecting lines formed an oval-shaped area that was colored in red. Three square holes were punched: one in each circle and one in the oval area. In subsequent communications, the perpetrator(s) would employ this "singnature" [sic] as authentication—to remove any doubt that Lindbergh was dealing with the kidnapper(s) (see Figure 28.1).

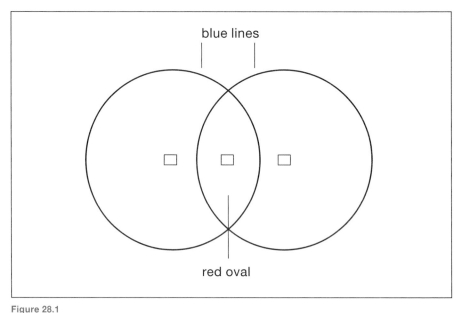

blue lines

red oval

Figure 28.1
The "singnature" [sic] on the first ransom note—to be used by the kidnapper(s) to authenticate that future notes were from them.

On the ground outside the house and just below the second-floor nursery window, investigators found two impressions; as it turned out, they had been made by the vertical uprights of a ladder. Nearby they found shoe impressions, a 3/4" wood chisel, and (a very short distance away) a ladder, which was the means of entry.

INITIAL CONTROL OF THE INVESTIGATION

After instructing the butler to notify the Hopewell Police, Lindbergh's first act was to call Colonel Henry Breckenridge, his Wall Street lawyer (after which he notified the New Jersey State Police). From that time forward, the pair would set the tone of the investigation: Employing a "take-charge" style, they demanded that the police do nothing to jeopardize the baby's return or the payment of ransom; then, by asking the New York underworld for help, they "set a thief to catch a thief." At the very least, their unprofessional, clumsy efforts bore the marks of the amateur; at most, they would seriously hinder normal investigative tactics.

Extensive press coverage meanwhile brought forth an eccentric 72-year-old retired teacher, Dr. John F. Condon. Patriotic to an extreme, and outraged that his hero needed the underworld to accomplish the return of "The Lone Eaglet" (Condon's nickname for the child), he fired off a letter to the local paper, *The Bronx Home News*, offering to be an intermediary. The kidnapper(s) accepted, also by letter to Condon, knowing what Lindbergh and Breckenridge did not—that "gangland" was not involved in the crime and had no clue as to how to get in touch with them. Seeing the "singnature"—the overlapping circles—Lindbergh agreed to the first contact. The place specified was the Woodlawn Cemetery in the Bronx; there, intermediary Condon would meet "John," who promised to return the sleeping garment. This would furnish convincing evidence that the people being dealt with were indeed holding the child.

When it arrived at Condon's house a second contact was set up, the ransom money not having been ready for the first. Lindbergh accompanied Condon this time; the ransom was paid, and though the note given to Condon told of the child's supposed whereabouts, the extensive search led nowhere. Then, 72 days after the kidnapping, a truck driver discovered the body in a wooded area five miles from the Hopewell residence.

THE POLICE INVESTIGATION

All three sources of information available to investigators were utilized in this case. Typically, police follow-through was *reactive:* people were interviewed and interrogated; physical evidence (ladder, ransom note, chisel) was examined, as were records (in particular, long-distance calls from Hopewell and from the Englewood home of Anne Lindbergh's wealthy parents.) Police follow-through also had a *proactive* side in this case, i.e., recording the serial numbers on the ransom bills. Consistent with his "take-charge" style and concerned about endangering the child, Lindbergh strongly opposed this action at first, but when the head of Treasury Department's Law Enforcement Agencies threatened to withdraw from the investigation, he submitted.

People

People, as a potential source of information, seemed to hold the most promise at the beginning of the investigation. The family's sudden decision to stay in Hopewell because of the baby's cold made Ann's family and the servants the only people privy to that change of plan. Thus, investigators consumed considerable time and effort interviewing the 29-member staff on the Morrow estate and their relatives and acquaintances, but to no avail. Nurse Betty Gow was an immediate suspect; when summoned to Hopewell to tend the baby, she had canceled a date and in so doing, had divulged the Hopewell number and the family's intentions to an outsider. What seemed a promising lead was checked out: investigators located her date, a sailor in Hartford, Connecticut. They found a milk bottle in the back seat of his car and learned that he was in the country illegally, but (except for the sailor's deportation) nothing came of this lead. Another lead involved a Morrow housemaid, Violet Sharpe. Not only had she taken the call summoning Nurse Gow to Hopewell, she aroused suspicion when she lied about her movements on the night of the kidnapping: first claiming she had gone to a movie, and when pressed, admitting to having been "picked up" at a local roadhouse. During further interviews her replies became either evasive ("I don't remember") or hostile ("that's my business"). Finally, when told she was to face more questioning (this time at the police station house), the suspect went to her room and committed suicide. Diligent follow-up again failed to establish any connection between Violet Sharpe and the crime; given the circumstances, some investigators could only ponder why an innocent person would take cyanide.

Physical Evidence

The police held three items of physical evidence: the ladder, ransom notes, and chisel. The chisel had no investigative value until years later when Hauptmann was apprehended, and his carpenter's tools were checked out; from an otherwise full set, the size missing would be the 3/4" wood chisel, identical with that found in the dirt below the nursery window. At first, little was made of the handmade ladder; then, almost a year later investigators consulted the U.S. Forestry Service. The ransom notes and other correspondence from the kidnapper were being held for comparison purposes. The method of the day was to ask a suspect to write from dictation a statement formulated by a handwriting expert from words or phrases used in the ransom note.

The Ladder

Crime laboratories were virtually nonexistent in the United States until the 1930s. The FBI laboratory began operations in 1933; New York City's laboratory, once a part of their Police Academy, was finally put in the detective bureau in 1942. With this background, it should not be surprising that New Jersey's State Police did not have the capacity to turn the kidnap ladder into an investigative lead initially—and only subsequently, into probative evidence. Ultimately, they had to seek outside expertise from Chief Wood Technologist Arthur Koehler, at the U.S. Department of Agriculture Forest Service Laboratory at Madison, Wisconsin. Koehler spent several days examining the ladder: he took it apart, then numbered each of its 11 rungs and six side rails, measured and described the kinds of wood, and noted any marks or holes. To suggest how or where the lumber was used, he looked for evidence of weathering. In retrospect, the significance of Koehler's examination relates to Piece 16 (a side rail on the top section of the three-piece ladder): thereon, he found a cluster of four nail holes. Those holes were photographed; later, they would prove to be of great probative value.

Investigative Value

Koehler observed a series of almost imperceptible marks on rails 12 and 13 (which would probably be ignored and not understood by a criminal investigator even today) and recognized that they had been made by a defective lumber mill planer. Upon closer examination and measurements, the wood specialist could say that the planer had eight knives on its face cutters and six on its edge cutters, and further, that the lumber (southern pine one-by-fours) had been fed at a speed of 230 feet per minute. A canvass of the 1,598 planing mills on the east coast disclosed that 25 had such a planer; and only one left marks with exactly the same spacing as those on rails 12 and 13. An arduous, lengthy, search of mill records enabled Koehler ultimately to locate a lumber yard in the Bronx. Its stock bore planer marks identical with those on the rails of the kidnap ladder.

Although this remarkable feat of forensic detective work was equivalent to finding the proverbial needle in the haystack, it was unproductive because Depression-day operations were on a cash-and-carry basis. The failure to keep sales records meant that purchasers' names were unavailable to investigators. Only later would a disheartened Koehler realize how close he had come to finding the kidnapper; however, his other wood clue—the four nail holes in rail 16—would provide (certainly to a criminalist) the most convincing evidence of Hauptmann's involvement.

Probative Value

The four nail holes in side rail 16 were bunched together at one end of the board, with no obvious pattern in their spacial distribution. They were made by rectangular (not round) nails, known in the trade as "cut nails." The absence of rust suggested indoor usage, protected from the elements. The nails had not been driven straight down: all four holes slanted, one at a sharp angle; hence, if the object to which this board had been nailed could be located, and the hole distribution and slope were to match rail 16's distribution and slope, this would prove they had been attached to each other. For investigators and for the criminalist such a match would depend on finding that counterpart. Unhappily for the suspect, investigators located in Hauptmann's own attic (access to which was so limited it could only be gained from a small hatchway in the ceiling of a crowded linen closet) a joist board that duplicated the cut nail holes in rail 16. This led to the inescapable conclusion that attic joist was at some time connected to rail 16.

The Ransom Money

As has already been stated, six months after Charles, Jr. was taken from his crib, the most promising of investigative leads—people—still had not led to an arrest. Because physical evidence was underemployed at the time (as it is even today), several months passed before investigators would recognize the evidentiary potential of the ladder. Meanwhile, the New York City Police Department was expending considerable investigative effort on tracing the ransom bills that were being passed (usually in the boroughs of Manhattan and the Bronx). Within a week of the ransom payment, the first bill located was deposited in a Manhattan bank. Many more were identified by fits and starts over the next two years. Then, in the middle of the third year, a man used a ten-dollar gold note to pay for fuel at a gas station in upper Manhattan. Suspecting its legality—the country was off the gold standard and Treasury had called in gold notes—the station attendant took the precaution to record the car's license plate number on the bill. This would lead to Hauptmann's arrest some 30 months after the crime.

The Ransom Notes

In all, authorities held 15 written documents from the kidnapper(s). During the course of the investigation every suspect was asked for handwriting samples. The exemplar writing, based on material prepared by a handwriting examiner, and using key words or phrases in the ransom notes, was dictated to the suspect. At trial, eight handwriting experts identified Hauptmann as the author of all the ransom notes; one defense expert declared he was not. The preponderance of testimony linking Hauptmann to the ransom demand weighed heavily on the jury to convict.

As important as the ransom notes were in convicting Hauptmann, this case could have been solved much sooner had their investigative potential been recognized. A clarification of this statement is in order.

Early in the investigation, a trio of individuals (a Department of Treasury law enforcement official, a newspaper reporter, and a forensic psychiatrist) suggested separately that use be made of the near certainty that the kidnapper(s) were based in the Bronx. They pointed out:

1. The kidnapper(s) read the *Bronx Home News;* used it to communicate with intermediary Condon.

2. Ransom bills were being passed (almost exclusively) in the Bronx or nearby upper Manhattan.

3. Bronx cemeteries were selected for the meetings with Condon.

4. A Bronx cab was hailed to deliver a sealed envelope to Condon's home. It contained instructions for a meeting between Condon and the kidnapper.

Investigators were also dealing with the likelihood that the writer of the ransom note was German. Their reasoning included:

1. The spelling of some words: "aus" for out; "ouer" for our; "gut" for good; "boad" for boat; "dank" for thank.

2. The use of a hyphen in "New-York."

3. The placement of the dollar sign after the number: 25,000$.

4. The use of the German form of salutation: "Mr Doctor John F. Condon."

A linkage of these examples suggested that a record search, limited to names in Bronx County records (i.e., applications for driving licenses and license plates), might lead to an identification. It would take considerable investigative time, with no guarantee of success. The consulting document examiner discredited the idea, offering the following rationalizations:

1. Motor vehicle registration cards are often printed; they do not provide sufficient handwriting samples to serve as a known standard.

2. The signature on the card would not necessarily match that of the ransom writings; moreover, signatures alone are not enough for comparison purposes.

From a document examiner's perspective, such reasoning may be perfectly correct; in retrospect, it was shortsighted. At this point in the investigation, the purpose of the search is to find a *lead* to a possible identification of the perpetrator; the purpose is not to look for proof that anyone so identified was indeed the kidnapper.

As a consequence, neither the New York police nor the New Jersey police followed through on the records search idea. Some years later, however, it would be tested in another kidnapping (the LaMarca-Weinberger case in 1955). In that case, more than one million records were examined; as a result, the writer of the ransom note (La Marca) was identified and convicted. The requisite handwriting sample was found in the monthly report he had filed for the United States Probation System.

THE TRIAL AND ITS AFTERMATH

Flemington, a New Jersey town of only 3,000 in the 1930s, was ill-prepared for the hordes of people wishing to take in the trial of Bruno Richard Hauptmann. There were operators for about a 100 newsreel cameras as well as several hundred more newspaper journalists and columnists (including some from England and France). In addition, numerous stage, film, and sports celebrities came, attracting 60,000 curiosity seekers.

The prevailing carnival atmosphere put the justice system to shame. The sidewalks were thronged with street hawkers selling model replicas of the kidnap ladder and "certified" locks of the baby's hair. Mindful of the infringement on the legitimacy of an otherwise competent criminal investigation were some critics who raised concerns about the distorted atmosphere that prevailed. Other critics faulted the state's evidence used to convict; the most notable among them, New Jersey's then newly elected governor, Harold Hoffman.

Through the prison warden Hauptmann sent a message to the governor asking to see him. Believing that Hauptmann wanted to confess, Hoffman agreed. However, in their face-to-face meeting, Hauptmann remained steadfast in his protestation of innocence, and pleaded for a lie detector test. He asked: Would a carpenter build a ladder that would break under his weight; or use an attic floorboard when there was a supply of lumber in the garage? And why were none of his fingerprints found on the ladder or in the nursery?

The lack of fingerprints at a crime scene is readily explained, but answers to Hauptmann's first two questions (and to others of similar thrust) would be speculative at best.

LATTER-DAY CRITICS

With the advent of World War II and Lindbergh's fall from grace (owing to an apparent bedazzlement with Nazi Germany's military might and his isolationist views), the case no longer commanded attention. But in 1976 and 1985 two books: *Scapegoat,* by Antony Scaduto, and *The Airman and the Carpenter,* by Ludovic Kennedy, created some curiosity about Bruno Richard Hauptmann's fate. A public television documentary in 1989 added fuel to the notion that Hauptmann had been the victim of unscrupulous prosecutors and police officials.

Scaduto's book maintains that evidence proving Hauptmann's innocence was suppressed; also, that the state's evidence was fabricated, distorted, or perjured. The accused, in effect, had been railroaded. Kennedy makes similar assertions. Both authors rely on self-proclaimed evidence—inadmissible in court—much of which had been the subject of sworn testimony at trial. In turn, Hauptmann's spouse sued the State of New Jersey for executing her husband "wrongfully, corruptly, and unjustly"; the civil suit was dismissed; a federal court of appeals upheld that decision.

In 1987, Professor James Fisher made a thorough examination of primary source materials in this case. A former FBI agent, then a faculty member in the department of criminal justice at Edinboro University in Pennsylvania, Fisher wrote *The Lindbergh Case* after a four-year study. He came to the following conclusions:

1. The New Jersey State Police conducted a thorough investigation under the most difficult circumstances, an investigation few modern law enforcement agencies could match if the crime were committed today. As in all investigations of celebrated crimes, the police in the Lindbergh case made mistakes and forgot to do certain things, but these errors were not major and turned out to be relatively harmless.

2. The Lindbergh case investigators and prosecutors did not fabricate any evidence of Hauptmann's guilt or suppress evidence of his innocence.

3. Hauptmann received as fair a trial as could be expected under the circumstances. The trial judge was unbiased, experienced, and competent; the jury comprised intelligent, rational people with a lot of common sense. Moreover, Hauptmann took advantage of a wide range of appeals under the guidance of a competent and dedicated attorney.

4. There is no hard evidence to support the notion that Hauptmann had the aid of accomplices.

5. The evidence clearly shows that the baby was in fact killed, and that the corpse found near the Lindbergh home 10 weeks after the crime was his.

Two more books on the Lindbergh case were published in 1993 and 1994. *Crime of the Century* censures an investigation that failed to consider Lindbergh himself a suspect. The authors assert that he was responsible for the child's death, that it resulted from a practical joke played on his wife, in which he pretended the baby had been kidnapped. Aside from the wild speculation involved in such a charge, it is hard to reconcile Lindbergh's probity evidenced by his willingness to lose face with the public when he quarreled with President Roosevelt over the rightness of declaring war on Germany with lending his consent to the electrocution of an innocent man.

In his 1994 book, *Lindbergh: The Crime*, Noel Behn speculates that Anne Lindbergh's sister Elizabeth was responsible for the baby's death and that the kidnap claim was a cover-up devised by Lindbergh and attorney Breckenridge. In both books, attention is drawn to the fact that the pair took charge of the investigation with the purpose of misleading.

Considering the importance of the kidnap ladder as evidence, it is surprising that Behn gives Arthur Koehler's work only little attention. In Ahlgren and Monier's text, the wood specialist is discredited and the means by which he traced some of the wood in the ladder to the lumber yard near Hauptmann's home is ridiculed. Investigators now realize that had sales records been kept, the case would have been solved at that time; Hauptmann's existence became known later, only because he passed a marked ransom bill. The fact that scientific expertise was involved when Koehler placed rail 16 in Hauptmann's attic is dismissed, and evidence such as the four cut nail holes in rail 16 is largely ignored.

CONCLUDING REMARKS

The Lindbergh kidnapping case provides the investigator with awareness and insight; for example:

1. The police—*not* the complainant—must take charge of the investigation. While this is ordinarily not a problem, it can become so when a complainant enjoys celebrity status sufficient to wrest control from the agency responsible. This rule was also violated in the case of President Kennedy's assassination.

2. The Lindbergh kidnapping investigation started with the premise that the crime was an inside job; by deduction, it moved to the servants in the Morrow household. Although deductive logic always leads to a correct conclusion *if* the original premise is correct, here the original premise was incorrect. Although checking out the servants was doomed to fail, inductive logic was utilized successfully when Koehler traced some of the wood in the ladder to the lumber yard nearest the Hauptmann home. However unwittingly, investigators were using the scientific method to solve this crime.

3. The value of proactive investigative measures was demonstrated when Treasury agents insisted on recording the serial numbers of the gold certificates in the ransom payment.

4. The prejudicial nature of undue publicity surrounding an investigation was raised to the conscious level for many in the field of law enforcement, but it was not until 1954 that the Supreme Court addressed the issue: because of the sensational nature of the press coverage, a new trial was ordered for Dr. Samuel Sheppard.

5. Care must be exercised in abiding by the recommendation of experts, when the advice involves an activity apparently related to—but not precisely within—their area of expertise. Follow-through in the LaMarca case demonstrated empirically that the handwriting expert's recommendation not to search Bronx County Courthouse records caused a long delay in solving the kidnapping of Charles, Jr.

SUPPLEMENTAL READINGS

Ahlgren, Gregory, and Stephen Monier. *Crime of the Century: The Lindbergh Kidnapping Hoax.* Boston: Branden, 1993.

Behn, Noel. *Lindbergh: The Crime.* New York: Atlantic Monthly Press, 1994.

Fisher, Jim. *The Lindbergh Case.* New Brunswick, NJ: Rutgers University Press, 1987.

Geis, Gilbert, and Leigh B. Bienen. *Crimes of the Century: From Leopold and Loeb to O.J. Simpson.* Boston: Northeastern University Press, 1998.

Kennedy, Ludovic. *The Airman and the Carpenter.* New York: Viking Penguin, 1985.

Scaduto, Anthony. *Scapegoat.* New York: Putnam, 1976.

Waller, George. *Kidnap.* New York: The Dial Press, 1961.

Whipple, Sidney B., ed. *The Trial of Richard Bruno Hauptmann.* Spec. ed., Birmingham, AL: The Notable Trials Library, 1989. (Selected transcriptions of the actual trial Q. & A.)

CHAPTER 29

Satanism, Cults, and Ritual Crime

DEFINITIONS

To clarify the terms used in this chapter, we will state their precise meanings and significance:

Black Mass—A rite initially fashioned by embittered "fallen-away" priests to express religious hatred; it caricatured the Roman Catholic mass. Later, the black mass would become devil worship; therein, God is ridiculed and Satan idolized, celebrants chant prayers backward, quaff blood from a chalice, or light black candles rather than white candles (sometimes made of human fat, preferably from an unbaptized infant).

Book of Shadows—a private journal record of the ritualistic or occult activities of an individual or group: what rites were performed and by whom to invoke the powers of the Evil One; what prayers and chants were said.

Cult—an organized group dedicated to the same ideal, person, or thing. Some cults merely comprise, for instance, Ford Mustang (automobile) owners, or Chicago Cub (baseball) fans; their purposes are benign, legitimate, and non-destructive. A cult is destructive when it abandons basic ethical or theological belief and moves into unlawful conduct, such as ritual abuse or terrorism. Prospective members are enticed by a charismatic leader who, looking for power, self-gratification or money, employs ritual to draw them into unethical or illegal conduct. Having lost their free will, and the ability to think for themselves as well, members become the cult's victims.

Destructive Cult—see Cult.

Devil—the supreme spirit of evil: Satan, the Prince of Evil.

Evil One—the Devil.

Ideology—the body of principles, articles of faith or accepted belief that govern a social movement, institution, large group, or individual.

Magick—Spelled with a "k" in the world of the occult, this word implies that people or natural events and forces can be influenced if not controlled through ritual, esoteric knowledge or supernatural means.

Occult—any practice that asserts secret or supernatural powers, disclosed only to the initiated. It does not necessarily signify evil, wrongdoing, crime, or satanism.

Occult crime—any statutory crime committed in the belief that some special reward or power—financial or emotional—will rebound to the benefit of the perpetrator(s). (*Per se*, there is no such thing as occult crime.)

Religion—a set of beliefs and practices that asserts the existence of an omnipotent power as the creator and governor of the universe.

Rite—the prescribed or customary manner of conducting a religious service or other solemn ceremony.

Ritual—a prescribed procedure for a ceremony or other rite that is impelled by cultural, spiritual, psychological, or sexual needs or factors, whether for good or evil.

Ritual abuse—repeated mental, physical, emotional, or spiritual assault, combined with a methodical use of symbol and ceremony to attain unhealthy or destructive consequences.

Ritual crime—any practice involving repetitive, ceremonial acts that systematically mistreat an individual physically, emotionally, or sexually. The purpose is identical with that of ritual abuse: the attainment of unhealthy or destructive consequences.

Satan—a figure of ungovernable evil: the Devil, the leader of the fallen angels, Beelzebub.

Satanism—the worship of Satan.

Satanic crime—penal law (or statutory) crime committed in the name of Satan; the motive: to fulfill a satanic ritual. (*Per se*, there is no such thing as satanic crime.)

Satanic cult—in organization and composition similar to a destructive cult, but in a satanic cult, membership and participation are generally, but not necessarily voluntary; for example, an intergenerational Satanist may want to leave the cult, others are recruited by blackmail, others are deterred by the threat of death—to individuals and possibly their families.

Commentary

To capture reader attention, it is the habit of the media to describe crime-related events with catchy words and phrases. The term "Saturday-Night Special" came to the fore in 1965; "satanic crime" and "ritual crime" are of fairly recent coinage. To the extent that these terms catch the eye, the device certainly works. Yet it also manages to distort the problem, because a careful search of the criminal law for a definition of satanic or ritual crime would be unavailing in many states.

More than a few incidents reported as satanic or occult crime might actually have been no more than juvenile pranks; meanwhile, at least some activities of real satanists go unreported—secrecy and concealment being inherent in their practice. In either event, if a complainant reports an apparently gruesome crime (and perhaps insists it is satanic), investigators should not dismiss it as unlikely and warranting of no further action. Unfortunately, this was the disastrous judgment call that responding officers made in the Jeffrey Dahmer case.[1]

The Dahmer serial murder case started when someone dialed 911. It brought three police officers to assess a complaint involving a nude and bleeding male youth, calling for help while running down an alley trying to escape Dahmer. Repairing to Dahmer's house, they allowed themselves to be convinced that, as Dahmer insisted, nothing more was amiss than a lover's quarrel. Not only that: investigating officers failed to recognize the distinctive odor of something dead, a stench so pervasive in the neighborhood that it had been the source of complaints for some time. Instead, the clue was missed and the youth left with Dahmer, only to be found murdered two months later.

When he was arrested, three human heads were discovered in Dahmer's refrigerator; elsewhere in the apartment, there were the body parts from 11 men and boys. Ultimately, Dahmer would confess to mutilating and slaying 15 males.[2] Though not an avowed satanist, in conformity with satanic practice, Dahmer admitted to having eaten the hearts of some victims. This chapter will examine satanism and some of its symbols and practices; and then will scrutinize cults and alleged satanic or cult crimes.

Before proceeding, an elementary fact needs stressing; that is: not only do skeptics abound in law enforcement, but also in the general population regarding media assertions of occult and satanic crime. This skepticism often takes the form of a challenge: "Is all this based on solid fact or pure fancy?" An example of the need to question and demand proof can be found in a recent article by journalist Debbie Nathan. She calls attention to the pervasiveness of commonplace phrases like: "ritual-crime-seminar dogma," "cult-obsessed cops regularly overlook," "cult cop teachers, most of whom have no academic training in comparative religion or other discipline," and "ritual crime seminars add to xenophobia." Nathan's own attitude is illustrated when she concludes: "At worst, cult cops will harass and even falsely accuse innocent people. At best, they have already used taxpayers' resources to chase obsessions."[3]

Kenneth Lanning, FBI Supervisory Special Agent, Behavioral Science Unit at Quantico, studied the rising concern with cults and satanism by attending numerous seminars and conferences taught by law enforcement officials, usually police officers, and by looking for hard evidence of the alleged criminal activity engaged in by satanists or cult members.

Lanning summarized what he found:

- There are individuals who believe in and are involved in satanism and the occult.

- Some of these individuals commit crime.

- There are groups of individuals who share this belief and involvement in satanism and the occult.

- Some of these groups commit crime together.

According to Lanning, some remaining unanswered questions are:

- What is the connection between the belief system and the crimes committed?

- Is there some organized conspiracy of satanic and occult believers responsible for interrelated serious crimes (i.e., molestation, murder)?

Lanning concluded:

> Law enforcement officers need to know something about satanism and the occult in order to properly evaluate their possible connections to criminal activity. The focus, however, must be on the objective investigation of violations of criminal statutes. . . . As a general rule of thumb, the law enforcement perspective can best be maintained by investigators repeatedly asking themselves what they would do if the acts in question were part of Protestant, Catholic, or Jewish activity.[4]

Equally credible investigators do not minimize the criminal importance of satanic and cult movements; to wit, journalist Larry Kahaner, and professor of religious studies, Carl Raschke. In his introduction to *Cults That Kill: Probing the Underworld of Occult Crime*, Kahaner asserts that these crimes are rarely solved; they are a new phenomenon as were narcotics in the 1960s, computer crime in the 1970s, and terrorism in the 1980s.

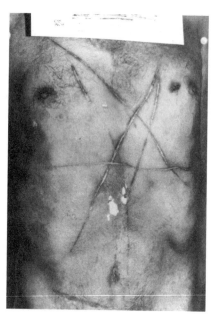

Figure 29.1
Pentagram carved on chest of an unidentified, homeless person who was kidnapped and sacrificed. *(Courtesy, Robert J. Simandl.)*

Based on interviews with the police as well as with clergy, doctors, private investigators, and victims, his text uses exact words, which were recorded and, whenever possible, corroborated. It details black-robed cultists at wooded sites ritually sacrificing or mutilating animals on altars; corpses drained of blood; satanic symbols carved on their chests (see Figure 29.1); grave robbings; occult groups connected to national drug and pornographic rings; and human sacrifices involving children.[5]

Raschke describes more than 40 incidents in the United States as being linked to satanism or the occult underworld.[6] One, the 1989 slaying and "sacrifice" of 15 victims of cult kidnappings, occurred near the Mexican city of Matamoros, across the river from Brownsville, Texas.[7] Many bodies were dismembered. Satanic ritual paraphernalia found at the scene included: a bloody altar, human body parts and the heads of chickens and goats, and an iron kettle containing a mixture of blood and flesh (brains, hearts, lungs, testicles).[8] A chapter of the book deals with the 1987 satanic murder of Steve Newberry in Joplin, Missouri, by three members of a cult of 30 called

"The Crowd."[9] One of the trio, Pete Rowland, confessed to his role in the killing. A satanic murder had been proved for the first time in an American court of law.[10]

The FBI's principal authority in this area of satanic crime continues to see things differently, according to *The Philadelphia Inquirer*:

> . . . After more than a decade spent chasing down rumors of ritual child abuse, Lanning came to the conclusion that there is little or no corroborative evidence to support the claims he wrote in a report last year. While some Satanists are practicing in the United States, he wrote, there's no reason to believe that such activities are widespread. "The public should not be frightened into believing babies are being bred and eaten, that 50,000 missing children are being murdered in human sacrifices, or that Satanists are taking over America's day care centers or institutions. . . .
>
> Lanning wrote that he himself tended to believe some of the rumors when he began investigating them. But in the report, he contended that the national hysteria over Satan was but distracting the country from the real crisis; namely, child abuse perpetrated by parents and stepparents, boyfriends.[11]

In the same article, however, widely opposing views are expressed, raising the question of what is to be believed. Consider the following:

- Larry Jones, a police lieutenant in Boise, Idaho, and founder of the Cult Impact Network, says Satanists slaughter 50,000 children each year.

- John Frattarola, author of "America's Best Kept Secret," in *Passport Magazine* says the number is 5,000.

- Michael Warnke, a controversial Christian evangelist who claims to have been a Satanic "high priest" when in college, puts the number at 2 million children "kidnapped and murdered" each year in the United States.[12]

As long as estimates of satanic practices are belittled by some and overstated by others, the careful analysis of Jeffrey S. Victor, a prominent critic of the satanic legend helps to strike some balance:

> There are people involved in criminal activities who justify their crimes with some kind of make-shift ideology of Devil worship. There are a few psychopathic murderers who call themselves Satanists. There are also some people who sexually abuse children, using rituals and perhaps, references to the Devil to manipulate the children. There are many teenagers involved in the various forms of juvenile delinquency who are also involved in "pseudo-Satanic" practices, which they may use to justify their crimes. However, these disparate forms of deviant behavior are not part of the same package.[13]

Victor's book lists 62 satanic cult episodes in the United States and Canada over a 10-year period, on which he has "reliable sources of information . . . these sources are not necessarily inclusive of all such events."[14] In the descriptions of these episodes, the following phrases are reiterated again and again:

- Kidnapping (or ritual sacrifice), (on Halloween), of a blond, blue-eyed (child or virgin)

- Animal sacrifices (or mutilations of cattle)

- Kidnapping (or attempted kidnapping) of children (or newborns)

- Human sacrifice

- Satanic or cult activity (abusing children, cult animal sacrifice, or cult murders)

- Devil worshipping cult

Perhaps the most balanced comparison can be made by juxtaposing the opinions of cult apologists with those who perceive satanism and the occult as a revival of the Salem witch hunt:

(1) Accusations of occult/satanic crime are hysterical "urban legends," invariably spread by Christian fanatics, deranged mental patients, or small children incapable of separating truth from fantasy.

FACT: While anyone can launch malicious rumors (as described above), only police, district attorneys, or duly authorized grand juries can file the sorts of criminal charges that have landed cult criminals in various prisons across the nation and in several foreign countries.

(2) Malicious cops, psychologists, and prosecutors frequently exaggerate the "witchy angle" in sensational cases to promote their own careers or personal religious beliefs.

FACT: In case after case, authorities have deliberately ignored or suppressed cult-related evidence to avoid spooking judges and jurors. Crimes with clear occult involvement are too often advertised as "only" drug-related, "simple" child molestation, and so on.

(3) When criminal charges are filed, they invariably result in dismissal or acquittal of the accused. As FBI "cult expert" Ken Lanning declares, "There is not a shred of evidence; there are no bodies and not one conviction."

FACT: Cult-related killers stand convicted of murder in 23 states and at least nine foreign countries. Numerous other occultists are now serving time for practicing their "faith" through acts of arson, rape, assault, cruelty to animals, and similar crimes. Courts in seven American states and in Canada have sustained charges of ritual child abuse in the years since 1984.

(4) When occult practitioners *are* convicted of criminal acts, they always prove to be psychotic loners, generally addicted to drugs.

> FACT: Cases involving multiple defendants—"cults," by definition—have been successfully prosecuted in at least 11 states, with similar convictions recorded in Latin America, Asia, and Africa. Charges range from vandalism and prostitution to first-degree murder; drug abuse is clearly no defense, because many occult religions consider narcotics a "sacrament."

(5) Convictions are irrelevant in any case, since the accused are not "real satanists." Satanism is an established religion, duly recognized by the U.S. Military and Internal Revenue Service. True satanists, despite their professed devotion to evil, are therefore law-abiding citizens by definition.

> FACT: As demonstrated by Jim Bakker, Jimmy Swaggart, and others, official recognition of a church is no proof against criminal acts by its leaders or membership. More to the point, "magick" religions are famous for their flexibility, defeating any effort to identify "authentic" worshipers. Author Carl Lyons, known for his friendly attitude toward organized satanism, defines a genuine satanist as "anyone who sincerely describes himself as a worshiper of the Christian Devil." The same litmus test, excluding Lucifer, might logically apply to followers of voodoo, santeria, wicca, and similar cults.

(6) If recognized occultists *do* commit criminal acts, the police, press, and public should ignore their defendant's religious beliefs, as they would if a Catholic or Presbyterian were charged with robbery. As criminologist Robert Hicks demands, "Law-enforcement investigators must remove the 'cult' from cult crime and do their jobs accordingly."

> FACT: Motives are always critical to the investigation of unsolved cases, prosecution of defendants, and prevention of future crimes. A felon's personal beliefs may be irrelevant, depending on the case; not so if his or her religion dictates or encourages commission of the crime. Where vandalism, sexual abuse, and homicide become integral parts of cult ritual, those rituals are clearly part of the problem. Police can no more divorce the "cult" from cult-related crimes than they can drop the "sex" from sexual assault or overlook the "race" in acts of racial violence.

(7) Finally, if there were really any kind of cult conspiracy, it would have been exposed by now. Somebody always talks.

> FACT: As the appended cases demonstrate, somebody *has* been talking since medieval times, and for at least a quarter century in the United States. There is no shortage of informants, witnesses, and testimony—much of it collected under oath in criminal proceedings. Even so, a brief review of history discloses how a secret order, pledged to violent crime, may flourish in the proper atmosphere.[15]

Despite these differing accounts, police departments will probably receive complaints asserting satanic or occult crime that must be investigated. What, then, is satanism? What are destructive cults? How are they investigated?

SATANISM

Most world religions believe in a hereafter, in another world to come in which some form of spiritual or physical punishment awaits the sinner. For Christians the hereafter is hell; in words from the New Testament, it is "unquenchable fire." There is also a biblical account of the proud, rebellious angel Lucifer whom God casts out of heaven. Similar legends come down from ancient Greek, Egyptian, and Hindu sources and on a cave wall in France, there is the 1,000-year old image of a horned sorcerer painted by a primitive artist-hunter that also may derive from similar devil mythology.

Clearly, primitive humankind conceived of a Devil, a Prince of Darkness, a Satan who coexisted with a God. From the beginning of time the image of Satan has been variously shaped: a serpent, dragon, goat, wolf, lion, or three-headed dog. Later, it took human form (after animal imagery was abandoned) to serve as transcendental tempter of humankind (e.g., a beautiful woman, an angel). The fact of centuries-old devil worship should not be surprising. "Satan became a figure of ungovernable evil . . . the Black Mass a horrifying but perversely satisfying ceremony that worshipped the Devil instead of a God who seemed too harsh and frightening to deal with."[16]

In the *Inferno*, the fourteenth-century poet Dante contributed to the popular visualization of Hell. His graphic imagery depicted tormented sinners in different kinds and degrees of suffering. The seventeenth-century poet John Milton (in *Paradise Lost*), however, made his devil a hero: "Satan has many of the qualities of the new men of Europe: he defies authority, pits himself against the unknown, and in his intrepid journeys from Hell, through Chaos, to newly-created earth, becomes the first explorer."[17] This view of Satan as a mirror for humankind is unusual, though. Satan is commonly perceived as a force for evil, and satanic worship is viewed as a threat to society.

An *Encyclopedia Britannica* article on satanism observes:

> Satanic cults have been documented in Europe and America as far back as the 17th century, but their earlier roots are difficult to trace, just as the number of real satanists in any period is frequently overestimated . . . Satanic worship has traditionally centered around the "Black Mass," a perverted and obscene rendition of the Christian Eucharist, and ritual magic evocations of Satan. Some recent satanist groups have supplanted those practices with rites of self-expression reminiscent of psychodrama and hyperventilation. Modern satanism is divided between underground, if not criminal, individuals and sects that view Satan as truly evil but strong and able to reward his devotees, and who serve him through pathologically repugnant and sadistic sects; and those who contend that Satan is actually maligned, representing only normal human appetites of flesh and ego unnaturally repressed by the idea of a spiritual God, and to be worshipped by rites which help one gratify those desires without harming others.[18]

The modern satanic movement took root around the turn of the century in England. There, Aleister Crowley assumed leadership over Ordo Templi Orientalis (OTO). This secret society provided Crowley, an organizing genius, the platform from which to advocate hedonistic self-fulfillment. Proclaiming himself Beast 666 (from the *Book of Revelation, 13:18*), and abetted by his belief in personal exemption from human or divine law, his behavior became depraved (i.e., characterized by deviant sexual acts, animal and human sacrifice, and other iniquities). According to Raschke, "When Crowley died in 1947, he had become the first true occult hero with a public persona in the modern epoch."[19]

Meanwhile, in the United States, Anton Szandor LaVey founded the Church of Satan in San Francisco in 1966. In 1969 he published *The Satanic Bible*; in 1972, *The Satanic Rituals: Companion to the Satanic Bible*. LaVey's approbation of every kind of vice or forbidden pleasure is summarized in nine statements:

1. Satan represents indulgence instead of abstinence!

2. Satan represents vital existence, instead of spiritual pipe dreams!

3. Satan represents undefiled wisdom, instead of hypocritical self-deceit!

4. Satan represents kindness to those who deserve it, instead of love wasted on ingrates!

5. Satan represents vengeance instead of turning the other cheek!

6. Satan represents responsibility to the responsible, instead of concern for psychic vampires!

7. Satan represents man as just another animal, sometimes better, sometimes worse than those that walk on all fours, who, because of his "divine spiritual and intellectual development," has become the most vicious animal of all!

8. Satan represents all of the so-called sins, as they all lead to physical, mental, or emotional gratification!

9. Satan has been the best friend the church has ever had, as he has kept it in business all these years![20]

Michael Aquino, a doctor of political science and Lieutenant Colonel in the U.S. Army, joined the Church of Satan a few years after it was established by LaVey. Rising rapidly in its hierarchy, Aquino became the only satanist (with the exception of LaVey) to achieve a level-IV degree.[21] Later, a disenchanted Aquino broke with LaVey and the Church of Satan to establish his own church, *Temple of Set*.

TYPES OF INVOLVEMENT[22]

Religious Satanists

Followers of Satan who operate as an organized religious body (as do the churches established by LaVey and Aquino) may be termed *orthodox* or *religious* satanists. From their theological base, they devise a mode of worship suited to their needs; this can be altered to suit any particular group. Each may perceive and refer to Satan differently (e.g., to *Temple of Set* adherents, the Devil is *Set*). Some rituals are open and public; others remain secret and impenetrable (the latter are more likely to engage in practices involving criminal violations, such as infanticide). Membership of some sodalities is inter-generational, with belief passed down from one generation to the next; in this respect, they resemble the more traditional religious institutions.

Experimental Satanists

The term *dabbler* describes persons (usually adolescents) who experiment with satanic beliefs. Disorganized for the most part, their activities mask attempts to overcome anxiety, a sense of alienation or meaninglessness in their lives, or to justify antisocial behavior. The less troubled among them may do nothing more than fill their time with role-playing fantasy games like "Dungeons and Dragons" or become obsessed with "heavy metal" music. People who do these things, it should be stressed, are not necessarily involved in satanism; nevertheless, these activities can be an initiation into the occult.

Self-Styled Satanists

The term "self-styled satanist" describes an individual encumbered with grave prob-lems, one who encourages or engages in seriously deviant behavior. A psychological pro-file will variously describe the self-styled satanist as: the loner, the underachiever, and the user of narcotics, alcohol, or pornographic material. A preoccupation with death would be a characteristic, as would a tendency to read or possess books on magick (specifically by Aleister Crowley). In addition, to enable them to handle their guilt feel-ings or justify criminal behavior, self-styled satanists often use religion. Their mode of dress may include an amulet; they may own robes, chalices, and other expensive arti-cles of the occult (secreted in a location over which they exert control and can keep private). Charles Manson, David Berkowitz ("The Son of Sam"), and serial killer Richard Ramirez ("The Night Stalker") fall into the self-styled satanist category.[23]

SATANIC CULTS

Although satanic and destructive cults share many similarities, the practices of the former are generally more depraved. (A comparison of similarities and differences is provided later in this chapter.) Satanic cults attract individuals searching for money, power, control, and/or political influence. They tend to have a ready answer to the perennial question: 'Why is there so much evil in the world if God is all-powerful?' They will assert what is for them an absolute truth; to wit: Satan is in charge on earth, and God is in charge in heaven. Further, they will explain that so long as Satan also reigns in hell, they can legitimately satisfy their desires while here on earth (and, after death, continue to do so in hell). In sum, satanists perceive themselves as petitioners who importune supernatural forces through ritual and who can, thereby, fashion events and individuals to their own liking. Their overall orientation is elitist.

At one time or another in the historical past, satanic rituals have involved the sacrifice of animals or babies (this included the drinking of their blood, which contains the life force), the eating of human flesh, and the mutilation of bodies for parts (for example, the heart, a finger of the left hand, or, as in Figure 29.2, a *right* testicle). A pentagram may be painted on the satanist's body, or carved on a victim's body (see Figure 29.1); the bodies may be ornamented with the number 666, or a drawing of the Baphomet (a goat's head located inside an inverted pentagram within the smaller of two concentric circles—see symbols on pages 760 and 761). Satanic cults employ utmost secrecy; their rituals might include child molestation, and child abuse involving incest or pornography. Such practices may be recorded in their private journal, *The Book of Shadows*.

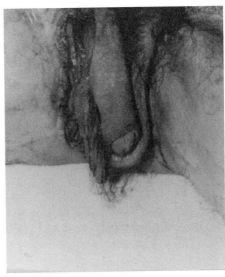

Figure 29.2
Genital mutilation. Right testicle removed in ceremonial act as part of a sacrifice or sadistic murder. Satanists believe the right testicle is a source of power. Such knowledge has significance in that such mutilation indicates motive and intent. *(Courtesy, Robert J. Simandl.)*

A description of human behavior so agonizing to read that it tests credibility was furnished by a former high priestess of a well-organized Satanic cult called "The Brotherhood." When investigators are confronted with sordid events that are completely outside their experience, they must suspend any qualms about the existence of such evil, and realize that police work can mean being apprised of the deviant activities of a John Gacy or a Jeffrey Dahmer.

NEW RELIGIOUS MOVEMENTS

Media usage of "cult" is pejorative; when describing a group's theology, terminology such as "sect" or "new religious movement" is more appropriate. When characterizing behavior that is hurtful to its membership, the use of "destructive cult" may be suitable. But the question remains: what behavioral characteristics mark the dark, potentially evil side of a cult? The following brief compilation of sundry readings sets forth some of the components that seem common to sinister (i.e., destructive) cults:

- The leader, claiming revelation from God, hands out a body of truths, not to be questioned.

- The leader is charismatic and exerts absolute control, relieving group members of the need to make decisions.

- Recruitment techniques are employed, especially with young people seeking new meanings in life; the aim, to make them feel "special," and to mitigate their sense of emptiness or restlessness. Once they accept asylum, they are forced to relinquish their identity and general well-being—all of which rebounds to the benefit of the cult leader.

- Living is communal and isolated, with absolute conformity mandated. This alleviates initial anxiety and distress owing to a lack of the normal sources of social support.

- A siege mentality prevails; there is an expectation of imminent cataclysm or holocaust.

Perhaps the best known of these cults, owing to its apocalyptic ending in Waco, Texas, is the Branch Davidians. This cult, together with its leader, David Koresh, epitomized these characteristics.

Estimates on the number of cults in the United States range from 700 to 5,000.[24] They made their appearance in the early 1970s and their numbers have mushroomed in the years that followed.[25]

DESTRUCTIVE CULT GROUPS AND SATANIC CULT GROUPS[26]

Similarities

1. There is the use of deceit in initial recruiting practices.

2. Initiates are told about more bizarre practices when it is perceived that they are "ready" to hear this information.

3. An appeal is made to a victim's need for control.

4. Victims are offered magical ways of gaining control over their destinies.

5. There is an appeal to the person's childlike need to be nurtured by a powerful figure: real (cult leader) or imaginary (Satan).

6. Answers supplied to unanswerable questions, whether the answer be valid or provable.

7. Instant gratification plus esoteric knowledge are offered, with no requirement to work for it.

8. Techniques of mind control and undue influence are employed.

9. Rituals are used. (By definition, a ritual is anything that is always done the same way. Satanic groups appear to engage in more bizarre rituals, but utilization of ritual does not distinguish them from other cults.)

10. Involvement in illegal and unethical practices.

11. Leaders are looking for self-gratification, power, and money.

12. Leaders are above-average in intelligence, often charismatic.

Differences

In reviewing differences, gradations among the various groups should be taken into consideration.

Destructive Cult Groups

1. Attract individuals who are *temporarily* disaffected, e.g., alienated youth, the divorced and widowed, and the clinically depressed.

2. Base appeal on idealistic grounds.

3. Member is often rebelling against his or her parents and usually does so under the guise of accepting parents' values.

4. Most groups do *not* use drugs.

5. Many categories* of groups exist; to simplify the structure we will identify the five basic categories:
    a. religious
    b. therapy or pseudotherapy
    c. political
    d. commercial
    e. new age

Satanic Cult Groups

1. Attract more disaffected, deviant individuals, e.g., those not within the norm in terms of mental health or who are drawn to criminal behavior.

2. Base appeal on aggressive, destructive grounds; narcissism. Financial benefits and belonging to a powerful underground society can attract acolytes.

3. Member is seeking power and rebelling; in some cases making a complete break with parents and society, and may feel excessive rage. (This profile does *not* include intergenerational members.)

---

*All groups looking for financial gain and power

4. Heavy use of drugs and so-called potions.

5. There are two basic categories of groups.

   a. nongenerational
   b. intergenerational
   Multiple types exist within each category.

6. Provides a permissive environment through which members can play out fantasies and aggressive, sadistic, and/or masochistic impulses.

7. Control of members may be accomplished by extortion.

ILLEGAL ACTS

The illegal acts of destructive cult groups vary in type and degree, not only between groups but between components within each group. Many groups lean on First Amendment guarantees; under the guise of religious fervor, many commit crimes. The following criminal acts are identified as having been committed for the groups specified. (Not all groups have involvement with all criminal acts listed.)

Destructive Cult Groups
- Child abuse, neglect, death
- Illegal and fraudulent behavior
- Drug trafficking
- Illegal weapons
- Smuggling money, cars, gems
- Fraud and deceit in recruiting, business, financial areas, tax records, fund-raising
- Illegal wiretapping
- Theft
- Harassment of families and former followers with threats, lawsuits, and foul play
- Beatings
- Sexual abuse, prostitution, and incest
- Kidnapping
- Psychological and emotional damage
- Attempted murder
- Murder
- Suicide
- Trespassing
- Illegal movement of funds
- Arson
- White-collar crimes

Satanic Cult Groups
- Child abuse
- Child prostitution
- Child pornography
- Illegal drugs
- Illegal weapons
- Fraud
- Theft
- Kidnapping
- Vandalism
- Arson
- Animal abuse/sacrifice
- Corpse abuse
- Attempted murder
- Murder
- Ritualistic abuse, ritualistic murder
- Suicide
- Harassment of former followers and victims
- Sexual abuse and incest

Lanning compiled a list of "law enforcement problems" most often linked to satanic or occult activity:

1. Vandalism
2. Desecration of churches and cemeteries
3. Thefts from churches and cemeteries
4. Teenage gangs
5. Animal mutilations
6. Teenage suicide
7. Child abuse
8. Kidnapping
9. Murder and human sacrifice[27]

The view of the Cult Awareness Network regarding illegal acts committed by destructive cults differs considerably from Lanning's much shorter list of "law enforcement problems." Just the same, when the police receive a complaint concerning behavior that appears to meet the statutory elements of a penal law crime, the responsibility to conduct an investigation is clear. When a child becomes involved in a ceremony, rite, or similar observance, some states have had the good sense to delineate which specific acts constitute the crime of *ritual abuse of a child*. Under these laws a child is any person under the age of 18 (17 in some states). The specifics of the prohibited behavior are chilling to read, and for most people they are beyond belief. One such law reads as follows:

> A person is guilty of ritual abuse of a child when he or she commits any of the following acts with, upon or in the presence of a child as part of a ceremony, rite or any similar observance:
>
> (1) actually or in simulation, tortures, mutilates, or sacrifices any warm-blooded animal or human being:
>
> (2) forces ingestion, injection or other application of any narcotic, drug, hallucinogen or anesthetic for the purpose of dulling sensitivity, cognition, recollection of or resistance to any criminal activity;
>
> (3) forces ingestion or external application, of human or animal, urine, feces, flesh, blood, bones, body secretions, non-prescribed drugs or chemical compounds;
>
> (4) involves the child in a mock, unauthorized or unlawful marriage ceremony with another person or representation of any force or deity, followed by sexual contact with the child;
>
> (5) places a living child into a coffin or open grave containing a human corpse or remains;
>
> (6) threatens death or serious harm to a child, his or her parents, family, pets, or friends that instills a well-founded fear in the child that the threat will be carried out; or
>
> (7) unlawfully dissects, mutilates, or incinerates a human corpse.[28]

The term "ritual abuse" first appeared in the 1980s as a descriptor for extremely severe multimodal child abuse.[29] Not long thereafter, allegations of perverse practices in nurseries and child day care centers appeared, of which the McMartin (Manhattan Beach, CA) preschool sexual abuse attracted national attention. The publication of *Michele Remembers* is viewed as the origin of numerous ritual cult abuse survivor stories that continue to receive attention in the mid-1990s.[30]

Ritual Mutilation[31]

A person commits the offense of ritual mutilation, when he or she mutilates, dismembers, or tortures another person as part of a ceremony, rite, initiation, observance, performance, or practice, and the victim did not consent or under such circumstances that the defendant knew or should have known that the victim was unable to render effective consent.

INVESTIGATIVE EFFORTS

The "freedom of religion" clause of the First Amendment can pose a problem in the investigation of any group that claims it as a shield. The amendment, however, defends freedom of belief, not freedom of behavior. Since its protection is not absolute, the conjuring of a spiritual connection does not necessarily legitimize every venture carried out "in the name of the Lord." If the penal law did not apply to one and all—president and clergy, rich and poor—rather than the rule of law, the result would be a reign of terror. Accordingly, the investigation of cultic activity must be based on the alleged crime; then, facts to support or disprove the complaint can be gathered from people, records, and physical evidence.

People

Individuals immediately affected by cult activities (such as members' parents, spouses, relatives, and friends) are the most likely sources of information. Although any insights they provide on their loved one may well be conjectural, they are often specific about their concerns. The aberrant behavior they observe may precipitate their lodging a complaint with the police (see Figure 29.3).

Cult survivors—people who voluntarily withdraw from a cult—are another potential source of information. They will know about its leader, its membership, and any criminal activities. Nevertheless, such informants should be regarded with a healthy skepticism; for example, Johnston, reports on a newsletter which

> . . . carries cautionary tales about Satanists purposely misleading police with strings of bizarre, conflicting stories until nothing can be believed about an incident. The newsletter also warns about storytellers out to ruin the credibility of local authorities who decide to take occult crime seriously.[32]

Law enforcement is concerned . . . with an overreaction to false reports, to exaggerated generalizations about the prevalence of the Satanic crime problem, to their own uneasiness about dealing with such sticky cases. But they're doing something about that concern.[33]

Corrective measures, therefore, take a multifaceted approach:

- Maintenance of special records on satanic-type crimes

- cooperative intelligence-gathering apparatus

- county or state task forces to coordinate investigations of satanic-related crime

Changes in Behavior:
 Adoption of a secretive demeanor
 Sudden shift to nontraditional style of clothing
 Recurring frightening nightmares
 Withdrawing from family and friends
 Attempting suicide
 Violent conduct
 Use of narcotics

Reporting Experiences:
 Episodes of insomnia
 Feelings of depression
 Involuntary muscle spasms (not drug-connected), described as a sensation of being
  in a vibrating bed or a mild earthquake
 Loss of memory or gaps in time
 Apparitions
 Poltergeist activity
 Hearing voices

Harboring Thoughts:
 Suicidal or homicidal ideas
 Hatred of the Bible

Secretly Possessing:
 Fantasy role-playing games; Tarot cards
 Crucifix displayed upside-down; occult literature
 Occult paraphernalia
  Ceremonial knife (an Athame)
  Decapitated head, or skull
  Amulet or other talisman
  Bells or gongs (to open the ceremony)
  Chalice, goblet or other ceremonial cup
  Right-handed black velvet glove

Figure 29.3
Abberant behavior exhibited by possible cult members.

- state and federal computer utilization for satanic-related crime

- standardized report forms for satanic-related crime

- development of reliable sources of information and possible informants

- allocation of adequate departmental resources

- in-depth training for specialized investigators[34]

Reformed Satanists have provided useful inside information that the law enforcement officer must keep in mind:

> . . . ceremonies are guarded by two and sometimes three rings of sentries. The outer guard will warn people out of the area; the inner ring is usually armed and will stop you . . . it will kill to keep the group from being apprehended.

> If a suicidal practitioner thinks you are a threat to their desire to die and reincarnate or resurrect, he or she might kill or hurt you (the police officer) in "defense" of this sacrifice. Remember that covens and individual solitary practitioners are equipped with knives as ceremonial tools. Therefore, consider each group or individual as armed and potentially dangerous.

> You might encounter an occultist who seems to possess "superhuman" strength. Be on guard.

> Drug-induced Satanism poses a double threat: the unpredictable effects of the drug mixed with the deviations of the practices.[35]

Investigative follow-up (if warranted by the evidence supporting the accusation) might include placing cult members under surveillance or infiltrating the cult. When human sacrifice is alleged, technical surveillance (such as a court-approved video camera) may be called for; before it can be installed, its exact location must be determined. In an outdoor scene, camera installation is a formidable if not an impossible problem. Surveillance and undercover work, because they are expensive, are justified only for more serious breaches of the law.

Pawnbrokers and "fences" can provide information if a cult engages in burglary or larceny to obtain funds. Animal control officers, child abuse investigators, school officials, and parole and probation officers can be helpful should a suspect (or cult activity) come within the scope of their duties.

Physical Evidence

Potential sources of physical evidence (in which any illegal practice is suspected) are the site(s) of the ritual(s); another would be the cult disciple's inner sanctum. Locating a ritual site can be difficult, secrecy being a paramount concern. Should the cult believe it has been discovered, it will probably be eradicated and moved. One means of avoiding detection is the use of a member's land. Game wardens, park rangers, and foresters are often responsible for exposing clandestine sites. Cemetery groundkeepers may report as vandalism what are actually attempts to steal human body parts. Such attempts may involve the larceny of decorative urns or bronze tablets and plates on mausoleums and caskets. Teenagers held for shoplifting or other minor crimes (especially when a first brush with the law) may divulge the location of rites carried out by friends or acquaintances. This could lead to evidence of criminality.

Discovery of occult paraphernalia or literature in an offspring's possessions does not necessarily mean criminal behavior. The detective who is informed on this subject can help to allay their fears. If parents believe criminal activity is involved, they may be willing to assist the investigation in the hope of deterring more destructive behavior by the offender, not to mention earning lenient treatment should a conviction result.

Recognition of Ritual Scenes or Paraphernalia

The scene of ritual ceremony will usually be bounded by a circle nine feet in diameter to protect against outside evil and keep in the power of Satan (see Figure 29.4). It may comprise an altar (marble slab, stone or wooden bench), ritual books, black candles (whole or melted), chalice or goblet, bell or drums, incense, sword or knives, and a cauldron (to hold blood, bones, even flesh). A cat-o-nine tail, a small velvet pillow, a right-handed glove, an animal mask, small cages (either holding an animal or empty), finger bones, an inverted cross; even a skull or a coffin may be present (see Figures 29.5 - 29.8). A fire pit dug in the earth is not uncommon for an outdoor scene.

It would be unusual for an investigator to come upon a live ceremony; it takes the initiated to recognize cult symbols or warning signs displayed at entrance path(s). If a ritual site is not in use, only some of the paraphernalia listed above will be present—perhaps a crude altar, melted wax, fire pit. The inner sanctum of a cultist is more likely to hold stock-in-trade articles such as: occult jewelry (i.e., a medallion with satanic symbols), crystal ball, tarot cards, Ouija board, horror-type mask(s), and mythological figurines.

Occult Symbols

A path leading to the scene of an occult ritual may be marked with warning signs and path markers; other symbols indicate what kind of ceremony is intended. Table 29.1 provides the more common examples. It is important to acquire familiarity with them, and learn how to interpret their significance.

Scene Search

The search of a suspected satanic ritual crime scene can expose the investigator to certain hazards that must be anticipated. Because secrecy and freedom from exposure are a major concern, satanists take strong protective measures. Some devices (and ritual paraphernalia) found at ritual scenes, which are employed to discourage intruders, are shown in Figure 29.9.

Figure 29.4
Ceremonial site used by teenaged experimenters. The circle measured 9 feet in diameter. *(Courtesy, Robert J. Simandl.)*

Figure 29.5
Upside down crosses constructed to mark ceremonial site shown in Figure 29.4. *(Courtesy, Robert J. Simandl.)*

Figure 29.6
Sacrificial sheep (head is to the right) found near ceremonial scene. *(Courtesy, Robert J. Simandl.)*

Figure 29.7
Head and skin of animal removed for ceremonial purposes. *(Courtesy, Robert J. Simandl.)*

Figure 29.8
Casket removed from mausoleum, opened and used in ceremony. White coloration on skull forehead is wax from drippings of the candle used in the ceremony. *(Courtesy, Robert J. Simandl.)*

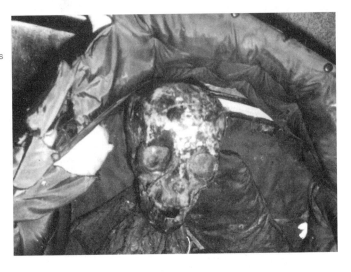

Table 29.1
Occult Symbols

Trail Markers		Directional trail markers come in many forms; some apply only to one group. A pentagram also has been used on a roadway, trail, or even a building to provide a bearing that leads to the site of the occult activity.
		The small circle in the marker sketched to the left indicates the starting place, while the path flows and ebbs as the terrain leading to the site changes.
Recognition Sign "Horned Hand"		The "horned hand" is a sign of recognition employed by those involved in occult matters.
Pentagram		Perhaps the oldest (and one of the most important) positive occult symbols. The spirit is represented at the top point. The other four points signify fire, water, earth, and air. Is also viewed as the consummate man—head at the top, feet at the bottom and arms akimbo.
Inverted Pentagram		To satanists, the inverted pentagram negates the positive nature of the pentagram. It is viewed as the degradation of the spirit into matter. It is also seen as the repudiation of the Holy Trinity. This is sometimes called the "Baphomet," which generally is depicted in a more elaborate fashion—a goat head within circles.
Triangle		This symbol is usually drawn or inscribed on the ground as part of a ritual to indicate where Satan or another demon is expected to appear as a result of conjuring. It may vary in size in contrast to that of a circle.
Circle		This symbol may be painted or inscribed to serve as a means of protection from outside evil and to keep the power or force within its boundaries. In occult ritual practice, a diameter of exactly nine feet is prescribed.

Table 29.1
Occult Symbols (cont.)

The Mark of the Beast	666 FFF	There are several symbols for Satan based on the variations of 666—the "mark of the beast." Note that "F" is the sixth letter in the alphabet. *(Revelations 13: 16-18)*
Black Mass Indicators		These symbols indicate a black mass.
Blood Ritual Symbol		This symbol is indicative of animal and human sacrifices.
Sex Ritual Symbol		This symbol may be painted on or carved in stone to show the area being used for sexual rituals.
Baphomet		A goat head inside an inverted pentagram, contained within two concentric circles, is the usual sign of the Baphomet. (See the symbol above for the inverted pentagram)

If an investigator is asked to examine a site suspected of destructive cult practices or criminal activity, he or she must adhere to the standards for a regular, traditional crime scene search. The purpose is to find any evidence of lawbreaking. Requests can come from park rangers, game wardens, and parents, or relatives and friends of someone thought to be involved with or to be the victim of a destructive cult.

For an outdoor scene the ashes remaining in a fire pit must be sifted down to a level about three feet below the surface. Bones and teeth may be uncovered; and, if discovered (and photographed), stakes used to spread-eagle captives may corroborate a tale or rumor of torture. For an indoor scene it is important to search the refrigerator for vials or bottles that appear to contain blood, and for the attendant syringes and hypodermic needles. Tucked away out of sight may be occult literature (for example, the *Book of Shadows*), student composition books, handmade drawings, poems, and essays. Such evidence can be obtained more easily from teenage "dabblers," whereas cults run by adults are usually too well organized and sophisticated to leave evidence so readily available.

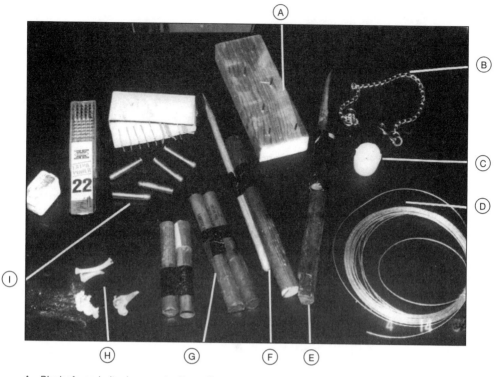

A. *Block of wood—its sharp, protruding nails were covered with leaves.*
B. *Chain used to restrain animals awaiting sacrifice.*
C. *White candle used in ceremony.*
D. *Piano wire to be strung between trees at ankle and chest height.*
E. *Filet knife attached to tree branch, used to skin animals.*
F. *Sharp pointed stake—its tip dipped into a poisonous substance.*
G. *Flares to start fire and destroy ceremonial scene.*
H. *Chicken bones.*
I. *Ammunition.*

Figure 29.9
Devices and ritual paraphernalia found at ceremonial scenes. *(Courtesy, Robert J. Simandl.)*

Occult Holidays

People celebrate special days and periods of time during the year; for example, New Year's Day, the Fourth of July, birthdays. Throughout history humankind has noted the change in seasons, marking the time to plant and harvest crops in order to feed themselves and their domesticated animals. Accordingly, occult members mark off special days for celebrations that are centered around pagan holidays and festivals.

There are several other meaningful dates—Shrovetide (three days before Ash Wednesday), St. Bartholomew's Day (August 24), and Walpurgis Night (April 30). The believer's own birthday has some significance as well. That date is the occasion to summon the power of the occult.

Occult holidays are of investigative interest because they may provide motive (i.e., what crime was committed, and why). Although it need not be proved, it may be possible to infer intent from motive, and intent is often an element of a crime. For example,

Table 29.2
Occult Holidays or Festivals

February 22	Candlemas Day honors the presentation of Jesus in the temple, and the purification of the Virgin.
March 21	Spring (Vernal) Equinox (planting time).
April 30	Beltane, also known as May Day Eve (night preceding day in the Celts way of reckoning). Named for the Celtic god, Bel, this holiday involved human sacrifice; their priests, the Druids, cut mistletoe; a ceremonial plant, it was given as a good-luck charm. Marked by great bonfires and fertility rites, Beltane was a major Celtic festival.
June 22	Summer Solstice
July 31	Lammas, the day that bread made from the first corn harvest was blessed (in England). Roman Catholics celebrate Peter's deliverance from prison (the Feast of St. Peter's Chains).
September 21	Fall (Autumnal) Equinox (harvest time).
October 31	Halloween, the beginning of the Celtic year; on this night the dead were thought to return to earth. Also known as the eve of All Saints Day or All Hallow's Eve.
December 22	Winter Solstice

a cemetery may be vandalized or desecrated, the latter charge carrying a greater penalty; thus, the charge of random overturning of tombstones might be raised from vandalism to desecration. If the crime was carried out on the eve or day of an occult holiday, this fact would suggest motive, and consequently, intent. Breaking off an angel's wings on a cemetery statue (rather than merely toppling it) is another example of intent to desecrate.

Records

In addition to information that may be recorded in any written material found, there are other potential record sources: purchase receipts for handguns, assault rifles, chemicals; records of long distance telephone calls; credit card statements; and the like.

REFERENCES

1   *New York Times*, July 29, 1991, A, 1:1.

2   *New York Times*, July 24, 1991, A, 14:1; Ju 28, 1991, IV, 7:4; Aug 2, 1991, A, 10:1; Feb 18, 1992, A, 14:1.

3   Debbie Nathan, "The Devil Makes Them Do it: While Nation's Cops Chase Demons, Taxpayers Get Burned," *In These Times*, Jul. 24 - Aug. 6, 1991, 12-13. Chicago: Institute for Public Affairs.

4   Kenneth L. Lanning, "Satanic, Occult, Ritualistic Crime: A Law Enforcement Perspective," Quantico, VA. Behavioral Science Instruction and Research Unit, FBI Academy. Undated. (also see: *The Police Chief*, Oct. 1989, 62-83).

5   Larry Kahaner, *Cults That Kill*. (New York: Warner Books, 1988), vii.

6   Carl A. Raschke, *Painted Black: From Drug Killings to Heavy Metal—The Alarming Story of How Satanism is Terrifying Our Communities* (San Francisco: Harper & Row, 1990). Chapter 3.

7   Ibid., Chapter 2.

8   Ibid., 11.

9   Ibid., 30.

10   Ibid., 56.

11   *Philadelphia Inquirer*, July 18, 1993, G-1.

12   *Loc. cit.*

13   Jeffrey S. Victor, *Satanic Panic: The Creation of a Contemporary Legend* (Chicago: Open Court, 1993), 216-217.

14   Ibid., 330.

15   Michael Newton, *Raising Hell: An Encyclopedia of Devil Worship and Satanic Crime*. (New York: Avon Books, 1993), 3-5.

16   Karen Armstrong, *A History of God*. (New York: Ballantine Books, 1993), 275.

17   Ibid., 330.

18   Philip W. Goetz, ed., *The New Encyclopoedia Brittanica*, 15th ed. (Chicago: Encyclopedia Brittanica Inc., 1985) Vol.10, 465.

19   Raschke, *op.cit.*, 95.

20   Kahaner, *op. cit.*, 71.

21   Ibid., 73.

22   Ibid., 63ff.

23   George A. Mather and Larry A. Nichols, *Dictionary of Cults, Sects, Religions and the Occult*. (Grand Rapids, MI: Zondervan, 1993), 243-245.

24   *Congressional Quarterly Researcher*, *3*(7), 387 (1993).

25   Ibid., 391.

26   Committee on Ritual Abuse, "Guidelines for Satanic Ritual Abuse" (Chicago: Cult Awareness Network, October 16, 1989).

27   Lanning, *op. cit.*

28   720 Illinois Compiled Statutes, 5/12-33 (1993 Supplement).

29   Jean Goodwin, *Rediscovering Childhood Trauma: Historical Casebook and Clinical Applications* (Washington, DC: American Psychiatric Press, 1993), 101.

30   David Lotto, "On Witches and Witch Hunts: Ritual and Satanic Cult Abuse," *J. Psychohistory*, *21*(4) 373-396 (Spring 1994), 375.

31   720 Illinois Compiled Statutes, 5/12-31 (1992).

32   Jerry Johnston, *The Edge of Evil: The Rise of Satanism in North America* (Dallas: Word Publishing, 1989), 238.

33   *Loc. cit.*

34   Ibid., 239.

35   Ibid., 240.

SUPPLEMENTAL READINGS

Boyd, A. *Blasphemous Rumours: Is Satanic Ritual Abuse Fact or Fantasy? An Investigation.* London: Fount, 1991.

Johnston, Jerry. *The Edge of Evil: The Rise of Satanism.* Dallas: Word Publishing, 1989.

Kahaner, Larry. *Cults That Kill.* New York: Warner Books, 1988.

Langone, G., and L.O. Blood. *Satanism and Occult Related Violence. What You Should Know.* Weston, MA: American Family Foundation, 1990.

Lyons, Arthur. *Satan Wants You: The Cult of Devil Worship in America.* New York: Mysterious Press, 1988.

Newton, Michael. *Raising Hell: An Encyclopedia of Devil Worship and Satanic Crime.* New York: Avon Books, 1993.

Raschke, Carl. *Painted Black.* San Francisco, CA: Harper & Row, 1990.

Richardson, J.T., J. Best, and D.G. Bromley. *The Satanist Scare.* Hawthorne, NY: Aldine de Gruyter, 1991.

Sakheim, David K., and Susan E. Divine. *Out of Darkness: Exploring Satanism and Ritual Abuse.* New York: Macmillan, 1992.

Sinason, Valerie (ed.). *Treating Survivors of Satanist Abuse.* New York: Routledge, 1994.

Smith, Michelle, and Lawrence Pazder. *Michelle Remembers.* New York: Congdon & Lattes, 1980.

Spencer, Judith. *Satan's High Priest.* New York: Pocket Books, 1997.

Tate, T. *Children for the Devil: Ritual Abuse and Satanic Crime.* London: Methuen, 1991.

Victor, Jeffrey S. *Satanic Panic.* Chicago: Open Court, 1993.

Zilliox, Larry, Jr., and Larry Kahaner. *How To Investigate Destructive Cults and Underground Groups.* Alexandria, VA: Kane Associates International, 1992.

CHAPTER 30

Raids

Reflections on
their Management

INTRODUCTION

The planning and staging of a raid requires not only considerable resources: personnel, communication systems, appropriate weaponry, and backup equipment (e.g., ambulances, fire engines), but coordination as well. A raid (whether by uniformed police, local or state detectives, or federal investigators) that is poorly conceived or ineptly conducted can provoke unwelcome publicity and harsh criticism. It is understandable that those who enforce the law perceive consequent censure with dismay (particularly when the process is rendered unfair by the 20/20 hindsight of the critics). Officers conducting a raid must assess and react to life-threatening situations within a matter of seconds; yet later, often from a distant vantage point, outsiders evaluate their performance. Because of this, it is imperative that raids be planned and staged with particular care.

Three examples will illustrate this imperative. One raid involves federal agencies, the other two involve local law enforcement. The concerns expressed below are those of opinion-makers; hence, they influence media response to newsworthy events. This factor cannot be ignored if public help and support are to be forthcoming. Law enforcement cannot afford to take a head-in-the-sand stance, writing off criticism as misguided or emanating from elements traditionally hostile to the police. Because the number of cults and political extremists who use guns to challenge government agents is on the increase, it is not unrealistic to formulate advance plans to deal with situations likely to call for a raid. There is no dearth of informed persons able to throw light on dissident groups and the way they think; law enforcement should seek them out. When a crisis does arise, and the conduct of a raid involves consultation with knowledgeable individuals, the action, if perceived as having been guided by the best available advice, can avoid criticism.

Guidance can be found in the case examples that follow. It is important to recognize, however, that law enforcement officials must ultimately bear the responsibility to save lives and property, and to see that a raid is carried out in a professional manner. Appropriate consultation provides the basis for a response to any potential fault-finding that might follow after a raid.

WACO: THE BRANCH DAVIDIANS

The first case is the ATF (Bureau of Alcohol, Tobacco, Firearms, and Explosives) raid in Waco, Texas. Executing search and arrest warrants for illegal weapons and explosives may be routine for the ATF, but the warrant under discussion here involved a religious cult. Its leader (Vernon Howell, known as David Koresh) was proclaiming himself "the Christ" who would appear and open up the Seven Seals of the *Book of Revelation*. According to a report by the U.S. Department of Treasury,

> The ensuing standoff lasted 51 days . . . when the Compound erupted in fire set by cult members after the Federal Bureau of Investigation (FBI) used tear gas to force its occupants to leave. The fire destroyed the Compound, and more than 70 residents died, many from gunshot wounds apparently inflicted by cult members.
>
> In the wake of these tragic events . . . the Executive Branch, Congress, the media, and the general public raised serious questions about ATF and FBI action at the Compound.[1]

Even harsher criticism has been forthcoming. Koresh's biblical allusion—its apocalyptic vision, specifically—should have served as a warning that far more was involved than a hostage situation and a weapons violation. Dean M. Kelley, Counsellor on Religious Liberty for the National Council of Churches, and other apocalyptic religion specialists are inclined to judge the handling of the Waco incident rather severely:

> . . . The FBI established a containment perimeter around the Mt. Carmel buildings, cut off all telephone or other communications except with its own negotiators, and settled down to a patient process of trying to talk the Davidians out of their home (termed a "compound" or even a "fortress" in federalese). This consisted of hours of listening to David Koresh expound his doctrines to sleepy negotiators struggling to follow his shifting scriptural references in their Gideon bibles. His exposition relied heavily on an Adventist and millennialist vocabulary of obscure biblical allusions, each followed by a verbal nudge—"Right?" or "Correct?"—that only deepened the agents' bewilderment. . . .
>
> After a week or so of this exercise in what federal participants began to refer to as "Bible babble," the FBI leadership on the scene grew impatient and began to use pressure tactics that tended to undercut the negotiators' efforts . . .[2]

Ironically, just as the federal government was abandoning hope of a peaceful solution, there opened up the possibility of such an outcome. Early in the siege, Koresh had promised to come out if his message could be aired on national media; he prepared an hour-long audiotape that was broadcast locally but not (he claimed) nationally. Two scholars of apocalyptic religion, Phil Arnold of the Reunion Institute in Houston and James Tabor of the University of North Carolina, studied the broadcast and believed Koresh could be reasoned with if approached within his own frame of reference. After several futile efforts to persuade the FBI to let them try, they arranged with Ron Engleman, host of a radio talk show on KGBS (to which the Davidians regularly listened), for a half hour's uninterrupted plea to David Koresh to rethink his understanding of the Fifth Seal (*Revelation* 6: 9-ll), which he believed to be unfolding at Mt. Carmel.[3]

The opinions of psychiatrist Robert Cancro are key to a fuller understanding of a group like the Branch Davidians:

> . . . they have a shared, very strongly held belief, . . . (that is) simply a rejection of the norms and ideas accepted by the rest of society.

> . . . The Branch Davidians had an apocalyptic world-view in which they expected attack from the outside world. The reason for arming themselves was . . . protection from an expected attack. They had been training . . . for a long time to defend . . . against such an effort.[4]

A subsequent publication casts blame in many directions: holding that Koresch and the Branch Davidians were not without sin, but they were also sinned against. Its criticism of the two federal bureaus involved (ATF and FBI) is unsparing.[5] In yet another book, the part played by alienated former Branch Davidians and professional "cultbusters" in molding the course of events is treated. The concern seems to be not to try to understand Koresch, but rather to demonize him.[6] As these publications make clear, relying on self-proclaimed experts can be hazardous unless their alleged expertise is carefully evaluated.

PHILADELPHIA: MOVE

An earlier incident involved MOVE, a black separatist group that seemed determined to stir up violent confrontation, not only with its neighbors but with Philadelphia's municipal government as well. The police were ultimately provoked into dropping a bomb on a row of houses occupied by MOVE. The bomb drop was deliberate; its purpose, to open a hole in the roof for the injection of tear gas. But the catastrophic fire that followed took 11 lives (men, women, and children) and destroyed an entire neighborhood of some 61 well-kept homes.

> Channel l0 news camerman Pete Kane was watching the rising flames with disbelief. Unknown to the cops on the street below, he'd been hiding in the house for more than twenty-four hours, filming the confrontation. The night before, he'd captured images of the police quietly moving into rooftop positions. Later, he'd filmed the confrontation at dawn—the thick screen of smoke that obscured the street, the first rounds of gunfire, the return burst of automatic gunfire from the police positions—and all through the long, still afternoon, when the only sound was the steady hum of compressors from the fire engines, he'd filmed the scene intermittently.[7]

The city of Philadelphia eventually rebuilt the burned homes (at a cost of more than $8 million), but despite the appointment of the Philadelphia Special Investigation Commission (the MOVE Commission), several issues went unresolved:

How does a society respond to an organization such as MOVE? How can it protect itself from those who share none of its values and beliefs and would destroy them to the roots? How can civilization withstand the awesome combination of an idea and an automatic rifle?[8]

Religious Studies Professor Nancy T. Ammerman provides some insight:

New or dissident religious groups are often "millennialist" or "apocalyptic"—they foresee . . . the emergence of a new world with themselves in leadership roles. . . .

Such new groups almost always provoke their neighbors . . . they think old ways of doing things are obsolete or evil. The resistance of outsiders to the new revelation often causes the new group to see itself as beleaguered by a hostile outside world. It may develop rituals and rhetoric of self-defense that sound and look quite aggressive, but are aimed more at reinforcing their own sense of solidarity and righteousness than at posing any real threat to outsiders.[9]

Reverberations from Philadelphia and Waco have continued to occupy press attention: *The Wall Street Journal,* hardly a severe critic of law enforcement, editorialized:

The central issue here is the credibility of the institutions invested with the power to enforce the laws. This is the bedrock beneath a stable society, even one as open as ours; for it to endure, institutions must be competent and laws rational. Are they? A look back at Waco to Philadelphia is reason to wonder.[10]

Civil damages awarded to the MOVE members (amounting to more than $1.6 million) may be the final echo of the fiery bombing in Philadelphia.

CHICAGO: THE BLACK PANTHERS

Another raid that captured worldwide attention occurred when 14 officers assigned to the Cook County (Illinois) State's Attorney's Office executed a search warrant for illegal weapons on the Black Panther Party. In the ensuing gunfire on the apartment occupied by the members, two Panthers were killed and four wounded; two officers sustaining minor injuries. The media gave full coverage to the fact that the county prosecutor's account contradicted the Panther's account of the raid. A subsequent federal grand jury report threw some light on issues engendered by the raid, and on the difficulties the grand jury experienced in ascertaining the facts:

The one group of witnesses that, perhaps, could have shed some light on what happened are the occupants of the apartment; however, without exception they declined to testify.

Thus, while there is a serious lack of corroboration of the officers' account no one has appeared before the Grand Jury with a specific allegation of wrongdoing by them. Unquestionably, the raid was not professionally planned or properly executed and the result of the raid was two deaths, four injuries and seven improper criminal charges. The grave issues of law enforcement raised by these facts are discussed elsewhere. The question here is whether the facts establish probable cause to believe that the officers involved intentionally committed acts which deprived the occupants of federally protected rights, contrary to law. The Grand Jury is unable to reach that conclusion. The physical evidence and the discrepancies in the officers' accounts are insufficient to establish probable cause to charge the officers with a willful violation of the occupants civil rights . . .[11]

In judging the facts of this case, the Grand Jury believes that the reader should keep the proper perspective. If officers of the law were on a legitimate and proper mission to search for weapons that could endanger countless persons, they should not be met with gunfire. In this case, the State's Attorney's Police did, in fact, seize and remove from public circulation nineteen weapons and a large quantity of ammunition. The fact that the raid was poorly planned and executed and evidence was mishandled, does not mean that there should have been no raid.[12]

One might speculate on the last sentence in the report. Could it be viewed as mitigating the Waco raid, making the hard facts of that action more acceptable?

As a result of considerable dissatisfaction with what the grand jury achieved, an apparently self-appointed Commission of Inquiry was created. Led by Roy Wilkins, representing the National Association for the Advancement of Colored People (NAACP), and former Supreme Court Justice Arthur Goldberg, it undertook to ascertain the facts about the raid and the killings, and determine whether prosecutable civil rights violations had occurred:

The job of the grand jury was to determine whether violations of law had occurred and to vote indictments if it found sufficient cause. Its *Report,* critical of everybody but most particularly the Panthers, has had the effect—very possibly a politically intended effect—of leaving the impression that the only crimes committed were by the Panthers, and that, even if the police were overzealous, the Panthers deserved it. It is appalling enough that although people had been killed—or perhaps more accurately murdered—the grand jury was merely investigating denials of civil rights. For that grand jury then to conclude that the victims deserved their fate, and not indict any of the perpetrators, does little except to give credit to the Panthers' foresight in being unwilling to participate in the grand jury's investigation.[13]

In its conclusion the *Report* raises profoundly important issues:

The question, "Who polices the police?" is itself difficult. When it appears that law enforcement officials are working in unison, not for justice but solely to protect some of their own, questions become that much more difficult. Who will judge the police? Who will judge the judges? And how can society expect the oppressed, or those who believe they are oppressed, to act when society's official avenues of recourse are closed to them?[14]

SUMMARY

All three raids involved search and seizure of illegal weapons and, therefore, point to the perils inherent in this law enforcement activity. The Treasury report is replete with recommendations on tactical raid operations (i.e., preparation for, execution of, and post-incident action).[15] For the untrained or unseasoned (and this includes most law enforcement personnel), a careful perusal of Treasury's analysis is vital if malfeasance is to be avoided in the future.

Should future raids be called for and if unprovidential incidents like those in Waco, Philadelphia, and Chicago are not to recur, then anticipation, planning, and preparation are key. The reader in search of provocative and informative material on the subject of apocalyptic thinking will profit from two relatively brief, lucidly written texts by scholars of religion, Robert Fuller and Elaine Pagels.[16, 17]

REFERENCES

[1] U.S. Department of the Treasury, *Report on the Bureau of Alcohol, Tobacco and Firearms Investigation of Vernon Wayne Howell, also known as David Koresh* (Washington, DC: Department of the Treasury, September 30, 1993), 1.

[2] Dean M. Kelley, "Waco, A Massacre and Its Aftermath," *First Things*, No. 53, 22-37 (May 1995).

[3] Ibid., 25-26.

[4] Kelley, *op.cit.*, 29-30.

[5] Dick J. Reavis, *The Ashes of Waco: An Investigation* (New York: Simon & Shuster, 1995).

[6] James D. Tabor and Eugene V. Gallagher, *Cults and the Battle for Religious Freedom in America* (Berkeley, CA: University of California Press, 1995).

[7] Michael Boyette (with Randi Boyette), *Let It Burn: The Philadelphia Tragedy* (Chicago: Contemporary Books, 1989), 19.

[8] Ibid., 263.

[9] Kelley, *loc cit*.

[10] *The Wall Street Journal*, 2 May 1995, A 12.

[11] United States District Court, Northern District of Illinois, Eastern Division, *Report of the January 1970 Grand Jury.* [Corrected Ed., June 1, 1970] (Washington, DC: U.S. Government Printing Office, 1970, 113.

[12] Ibid., 125.

[13] Roy Wilkins and Ramsey Clark, *A Report by the Commission of Inquiry Into the Black Panthers and the Police* (New York: Metropolitan Applied Research Center, 1973), 226.

[14] Ibid., 248.

[15] U.S. Treasury Report, *op.cit.*, B-3 through B-121.

[16] Robert Fuller, *Naming the Anti-Christ: The History of an American Obsession* (New York: Random House, 1995).

[17] Elaine Pagels, *The Origins of Satan* (New York: Random House, 1995).

SUPPLEMENTAL READINGS

Fuller, Robert. *Naming the Anti-Christ: The History of an American Obsession*. New York: Random House, 1995.

Pagels, Elaine. *The Origins of Satan*. New York: Random House, 1995.

Tabor, James D., and Eugene V. Gallagher. *Cults and the Battle for Religious Freedom in America*. Berkeley, CA: University of California Press, 1995.

U.S. Department of the Treasury. *Report on the Bureau of Alcohol, Tobacco and Firearms Investigation of Vernon Wayne Howell, also known as David Koresh*. Washington, DC: Department of the Treasury, 30 September 1993.

CHAPTER 31

Miscarriages of Justice

INTRODUCTION

William Blackstone, the preeminent English jurist, declared: "It is better that ten guilty persons escape than one innocent suffer."[1] The reality of the end of the twentieth century (at which time in Illinois and Florida more death row inmates were exonerated than executed)[2] betokens improvement in the latter but does not measure up to Blackstone's maxim. In the minds of some people, the police are at the root of justice miscarried. A careful examination of this matter, however, reveals that all of the actors in the criminal justice system play a role. Indeed, the legal profession may be more culpable and may have more to answer for than the police when one considers the behavior of prosecutors, defense attorneys, and judges.

It is the intent of this chapter to indicate how, based on newspaper accounts gathered over the last 50 years, each section of the criminal justice system has contributed to the problem. According to many, the term "miscarriage of justice" relates to those whose conviction carried the death penalty with it but who subsequently were found to be not guilty. There is less interest in cases involving wrongful convictions for lesser crimes (i.e., noncapital crimes). We now propose to extend the concept to include cases in which there was no conviction (upon trial) or the case remains unsolved. The Nicole Brown Simpson/Ronald Goldman case exemplifies the former, while the Jon Benet Ramsey case illustrates the latter. Both kinds of cases are viewed by many as a miscarriage of justice owing to the considerable attention devoted by the media to high-profile cases. In such cases, the public—without hearing the trial evidence and knowing only what is reported in newspaper or on television—makes up its collective mind. Even so, this filtered evidence is so convincing that they believe someone got away with murder or is getting away with it.

POLICE MISCONDUCT

Illicit police behavior transpires in many ways, but wrongful confessions are the most troublesome. Police depend too much upon confessions to seal the fate of the defendant and to advance their own careers. Unfortunately, some detectives, perhaps aided by a complicitous prosecutor, use illegitimate confessions to ensure a guilty finding by a jury. In an 11-year period in one county (of the more than 3,000 counties in the United States), there were 248 murder cases in which the police obtained incriminating statements that failed to secure a conviction or were thrown out by the court as tainted.[3] False confessions are regularly obtained from those who are young, who have low IQs or poor language skills, or who have been abused or coerced, and who ultimately have become submissive and compliant in the hands of their inquisitor. One critical, in-depth analysis of police interrogative behavior is a *Denver Law Review* article, "The Decision to Confess Falsely."[4] A partial list of police misdeeds that sow the seeds for miscarriages of justice include the following:

1. A search or arrest is made without a warrant or probable cause.

2. Credible leads are not pursued.

3. Serious police misconduct is covered up.

4. Interrogation is substituted for investigation.

5. Eyewitness identification is uncritically accepted.

6. Eyewitness evidence that is not supportive of the investigator's hypothesis is not reported.

7. A reluctant witness is coerced to testify to a false statement.

8. Physical evidence is fabricated or planted.

9. Exculpatory evidence is not turned over to the prosecute or defense.

10. Perjury is committed when testifying. (This is sometimes referred to as "testilying.")

11. Parents, a specialized police officer that works with juveniles, or other concerned adult are not present when a juvenile is interviewed or interrogated.

12. A nonexistent lineup is concocted to discredit a witness intent on recanting his or her identification of the defendant.

PROSECUTOR MISCONDUCT

The district attorney or the state's attorney is an elected official who heads the prosecutor's office, but it is an assistant prosecutor who tries most cases. The prosecutorial staff is responsible to the public for vigorously trying cases, especially high-profile ones. It is under these circumstances that an overzealous prosecutor is likely to overstep the bounds of legally accepted behavior. Ethically, their task is to seek justice, not just to win convictions. What action by a prosecutor rises to illegal practice? Some of the lawless steps that have been used in the past include:

1. Using an unconstitutionally tainted jury selection process.

2. Leaking brand jury evidence to sway public opinion.

3. Withholding evidence favorable to the defense or that would exonerate the defendant.

4. Using a witness who is lying in his or her testimony.

5. Holding off to the last trial day to turn over exculpatory evidence.

6. Engaging in a pattern of conduct designed to inflame and arouse the prejudice of the jury.

7. Using improper legal arguments to the jury.

8. Using a known liar and jailhouse informant to testify that the defendant confessed to him or her.

9. Denying defense the police minutes of a lineup in which a witness at first fails to identify the defendant but, in later attempts, did so.

10. Creating a false question-and-answer statement purported to be that of a witness.

11. Directing a witness to testify under a false name owing to fear of retribution.

12. Misleading judge and jury deliberately.

13. Distorting evidence to the grand jury or trial jury.

14. Not inquiring about a defendant's alleged statement that was not documented by the police but about which they testified before the grand jury.

15. Introducing tapes as evidence, alleged to contain incriminating comments cited in the indictment but not contained in the tapes.

16. Paying state money to a key witness for testimony against a known drug dealer and contract killer.

17. Failing to meet the filing date for an appeal.

Defense Counsel Misconduct

The defense attorney fills a role antithetical to that of the prosecutor, In trial work, defense counsel ranges from the "dream team" of O.J. Simpson, to the new, inexperienced law school graduate, to the older, run-down, besotted counselor. In jurisdictions not having a public defender office or law firms that do *pro bono* work, a judge can appoint a lawyer of his or her own choosing or select any lawyer present in the court room at the time to represent the defendant. In another variation (resulting from *Gideon v. Wainright*, a 1963 Supreme Court decision that proclaimed that poor defendants were entitled to a lawyer), some states devised a way of controlling costs by starting a "contract attorneys" system whereby the right to represent all of a county's defendants is awarded to the lowest bidder.[5] Under such an appointed "contract" lawyer, a poor defendant runs the risk of less-than-adequate representation. In *Strickland v. Washington*,[6] the U.S. Supreme Court cited a First Circuit decision:

> The Constitution does not guarantee a defendant a perfect defense; rather the performance standard is that of reasonably effective assistance under the circumstances then obtaining.

Under what circumstances have such actions been sufficiently ineffective to result in the challenging or overturning of a jury decision of guilty?

1. The defendant was never consulted (in private).

2. The time to prepare for the defense was too short and this matter was never raised with the judge.

3. A possible plea bargain was never discussed with the defendant.

4. A recommendation to the accused to plead guilty was made but no effort was made to negotiate a deal for leniency.

5. The possibility of severing a case in which two defendants were tried together was not discussed.

6. The scene of the alleged crime was not visited.

7. The facts testified to by a witness were not effectively checked out.

8. An adequate investigation was not conducted.

9. Suppression of the defendant's confession was not sought.

10. Defendant was not properly prepared by counsel to testify.

11. An expert witness was not cross-examined.

12. The jury was told by defense counsel that the defendant would testify in his or her own defense but he or she was never called to do so.

13. The right to closing argument was waived.

14. Defense counsel slept during a significant portion of the trial.

15. Potential legal issues were not raised, nor were objections made for the record.

16. Defense counsel had a conflict of interest and did not notify the judge.

17. Defense counsel failed to file notice of appeal within the permissible time limit.

18. Defense counsel did not display the reasonable skill and judgment expected of a competent attorney.

JUDICIAL MISCONDUCT

A trial judge is the last of the line of professionals who can alter the outcome of a trial by deviating from the detached deportment requisite for a judge. The following list embodies some of the issues raised by either the prosecution or defense concerning trial judge behavior that may have affected a case's outcome.

1. The judge knew but failed to inquire about the defense attorney's conflict of interest or allowed him or her to continue over the objections of the prosecution.

2. The judge failed to exclude (potential) jurors who had heard about the defendant's previous crime(s).

3. The judge permitted substitute defense counsel to proceed to trial without inquiring how long previous counsel would be incapacitated.

4. The judge attempted to create a racially and religiously balanced jury by granting the defendant a juror of the same religion even though the juror expressed grave doubts about his or her ability to be objective.

5. The judge ruled against defense's request to have alleged physical evidence (about which the jury was informed by the prosecution) introduced to the jury.

6. The judge allowed irrelevant evidence to be admitted.

7. The judge habitually harassed defense counsel.

8. The judge failed to read jurors an important special instruction before they deliberated.

9. The judge erred in instructing the jury.

SUPREME COURT DECISIONMAKING

The Supreme Court is the final arbiter of diametrically opposed appellate court decisions. In this role, the high court has made some regrettable decisions, especially in the light of demonstrable miscarriages of justice. Such rulings include:

1. Refusing to review state cases because of minor procedural barriers that they termed "harmless error."

2. Acquiescing in a guilty decision when the defendant was inadequately represented by counsel.

3. Expressing the belief that finality in decision is of greater importance than relief for the individual. (The Supreme Court has not been alone in touting this position. In England, Lord Denning, a senior judge, was quoted: "It is better that some innocent men remain in jail than the integrity of the English judicial system be impugned.")

PHYSICAL EVIDENCE AND THE CRIME LABORATORY

Most often a crime laboratory is located in a police department or other law enforcement agency. One of its principle functions is to examine crime scene evidence and link it (if possible) to similar evidence found in the possession of the suspect or his or her home or car. If a criminalist is able to accomplish this often and to testify effectively, members of the department will esteem him or her. Unfortunately, some criminalists have taken to falsifying their testimony. Questionable science (e.g., examination of hair before the development of DNA testing) can result in wrongful convictions. Conflicting results are not reported. Inconclusive results are reported as conclusive. In other cases, fingerprints are forged, evidence is altered or "lost," testimony is overstated or inaccurately attested to, or nonexistent qualifications are claimed in testifying before a jury.

Medical examiners, odontologists (dentists), criminalists, and other experts all can be sometimes guilty of unethical conduct. One compelling reason to distort evidence lies in the fact that criminalists generally work only for the prosecution; consequently, gaining convictions is (wrongly) regarded as their job. A more extensive treatment of malpractice in forensic laboratories is found in the book *Tainted Evidence*.[7] Similarly, the considerable impact of DNA testing on evidence in alleged wrongful conviction cases is chronicled in the book *Actual Innocence*.[8]

SUGGESTIONS FOR PROTECTING THE INNOCENT AND IMPROVING THE SYSTEM

Until the advent of DNA, it was usually difficult to prove a contention of innocence. Because DNA tests are costly, it is still difficult to challenge a conviction successfully. Even if innocence is proved in a state court, it does not mean the defendant will necessarily be freed. Appealing to the Supreme Court is not likely to be helpful either: The federal position espoused by Justice Rehnquist is that "[a] claim of actual innocence is not itself a constitutional claim."[9] Apparently, the only remedy is to seek clemency or pardon from the state governor.

Given the fact that the American criminal justice system is not foolproof, what remedies can be suggested to improve it? Dwyer, Neufeld, and Scheck have proposed a list of reforms.[10] A reformulated and supplemented list might include the following actions:

1. Videotape (or at least audio tape) all interrogations and confessions from the start.

2. Videotape lineups.

3. Improve eyewitness identification by:

   a. Verifying that the eyewitness account describes accurately what it was possible to observe under physical conditions that prevailed at the time (e.g., illumination, weather, and vantage point).

   b. Asking the eyewitness to rate how certain he or she us about the identification using a scale of 1 (low) to 10 (high).

4. Evaluate jailhouse informants and their testimony by:

    a. Determining their reputation among their peers.

    b. Finding out how often have they provided exculpatory information about a fellow convict in unrelated cases.

    c. Making sure informants' testimony is screened at the pretrial stage by a judge.

    d. Putting in writing and making available to the defense any deals made with police or prosecutor.

    e. Testing their testimony to discern whether it contains information other than that found in the press or seen on television.

    f. Seeing if their testimony leads to further evidence known only to the perpetrator and possibly the police.

    g. Ensuring that their testimony can be confirmed by extraneous evidence other than that of another inmate.

5. Assess the forensics area by:

    a. Making available to the defense all laboratory test data, including any with possible exculpatory implications.

    b. Making sure crime laboratories are free of administrative or budgetary control by the police or prosecutor. Crime lab services should be available to the defense, or a separate laboratory should be established and supported for this purpose.

6. Post-conviction DNA testing should be provided for by legislative action, similar to laws already in existence in New York, Illinois, and other states.

7. A mechanism should be created by the legislature that would:

    a. Investigate alleged wrongly convicted individuals.

    b. Monitor the caseload of appointed defense counsel, including that of public defenders.

    c. Censure and discipline misconduct by the police, defense, prosecution, or judges.

    d. Establish a "capital litigation trial bar" (CLTB) requiring minimum specific training and experience standards for counsel representing capital defendants.

    e. Allow, after conviction, a claim of innocence to be heard if new evidence is forthcoming.

8. Encourage universities to create and fund:

    a. Graduate programs in forensic science—specifically criminalistics and forensic medicine.

    b. An "innocence project" similar to the one established at the Benjamin Cardozo School of Law. Innocence projects provide representation and/or investigative assistance to prison inmates who claim to be innocent of the crimes for which they were convicted.

MISCARRIAGES OF JUSTICE IN ENGLAND

It may be of some interest to learn whether the law enforcement system in England has problems comparable to those suffered by the United States regarding justice miscarried. Several prominent cases come to mind. For example, the "Birmingham Six" walked free from jail after their convictions for the murder of 21 people in two pubs were quashed by the Court of Appeal; the "Guilford Four" were eventually released after being charged and convicted with murder for bombing a pub; and the "Maguire Seven," who were imprisoned in London for possessing explosives, had their convictions overturned in 1991. Another infamous case took place in 1953 and involved two youths accused of killing a police officer while attempting a robbery. One of the youths, Derek Bentley, was hanged for his alleged part in the killing. More than 30 years later, defense counsel in the case wrote a gripping story detailing the inappropriate behavior of the police, prosecution, and jurists. (The 1991 motion picture *Let Him Have It* was based on this story.)[11]

This brief analysis indicates that miscarriages of justice are not necessarily the exclusive domain of the United States criminal justice system. The potential problems are evident in other systems as well. All justice systems would do well to minimize the likelihood of such miscarriages continuing into the future.

REFERENCES

[1] William Blackstone, *Commentaries on the Law of England* (1765), Book 4, Ch. 27.

[2] *St. Petersburg Times* (Feb 6, 2000), 2D.

[3] Ibid.

[4] R.J. Ofshe and R. Leo, "The Decision to Confess Falsely: Rational Choice and Irrational Action." *Denver Law Review* 74:4 (1997), 979-1122.

[5] Amy Bach, "Justice on the Cheap." *The Nation* 272:20 (May 21, 2001), 25.

[6] *Strickland v. Washington*, 66 US. 668 (1984).

[7] John F. Kelly and Phillip K. Wearne, *Tainting Evidence* (New York: Free Press, 1998).

[8] Jim Dwyer, Peter Neufeld, and Barry Scheck, *Actual Innocence: Five Days to Execution and Other Dispatches from the Wrongly Convicted* (New York: Doubleday, 2000).

[9] Ibid., 71.

[10] Ibid., 255

[11] Gavin de Becker, *The Gift of Fear: Survival Signals that Protect Us from Violence* (Boston: Little, Brown, 1997).

SUPPLEMENTAL READINGS

Bedau, Hugo and Michael Radelet. *In Spite of Innocence*. Boston: Northeastern University press, 1992.

Borchard, Edwin. *Convicting the Innocent*. Cambridge, MA: DaCapo Press, 1970.

Cole, David. *No Equal Justice: Race and Class in the American Criminal Justice System*. New York: New Press, 1999.

Dwyer, Jim, Peter Neufeld, and Barry Scheck, *Actual Innocence: Five Days to Execution and Other Dispatches from the Wrongly Convicted*. New York: Doubleday, 2000.

Gianelli, Paul. "The Abuse of Scientific Evidence in Criminal Cases." *Virginia Journal of Social Policy and Law* 4, 439 (1997).

Gianelli, Paul C., and Edward J. Imwinkelried. *Scientific Evidence*. 2nd ed. Charlottesville, VA: Michie Co./LEXIS, 1993.

Loftus, Elizabeth F., and James M. Doyle. *Eyewitness Testimony: Civil and Criminal*. 3rd ed. Charlottesville, VA: Lexis Law, 1997.

O'Hara, Charles, and James Osterburg. *An Introduction to Criminalistics*. Bloomington, IN: Indiana University Press, 1972 (Chapter 47).

Parris, John. *Scapegoat*. London: Duckworth, 1991.

Protess, David, and Rob Warden. *A Promise of Justice*. New York: Hyperion, 1998.

APPENDIX 1

FBI Suggestions for Packaging Physical Evidence

FBI Suggestions for Packaging Physical Evidence

Evidence Submission

Requesting Evidence Examinations

For the most up-to-date FBI suggestions for packaging physical evidence, see the *Handbook of Forensic Services* at *http://www.fbi.gov/hq/lab/handbook/intro.htm*

All requests for evidence examinations should be in writing, addressed to the FBI Laboratory Evidence Control Center, and contain the following information:

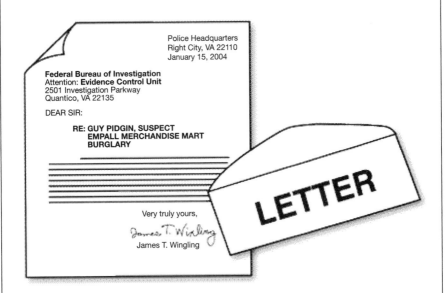

- The submitting contact person's name, agency, address, and telephone number;

- Previous case identification numbers, evidence submissions, and communications relating to the case;

- Description of the nature and the basic facts concerning the case as they pertain to the Laboratory examinations;

- The name or names of and descriptive data about the individual or individuals involved (subject, suspect, victim, or a combination of those categories) and the agency-assigned case identification number; and

- A list of the evidence being submitted herewith (enclosed) or under separate cover.

  ○ *Herewith* is limited to small items of evidence that are not endangered by transmitting in an envelope. Write on the envelope before placing evidence inside to avoid damaging or altering the evidence. The written communication should state: *Submitted herewith are the following items of evidence.*

  ○ *Separate cover* is used to ship numerous or bulky items of evidence or both. Include a copy of the communication requesting the examinations. The written communication should state: *Submitted under separate cover by (list the method of shipment) are the following items of evidence.*

- State what types of examinations are requested.

- State where the evidence should be returned and where the Laboratory report should be sent.

- Attach a statement if the evidence was examined by another expert in the same field, if there is local controversy, or if other law enforcement agencies have an interest in the case.

- State the need and reason or reasons for an expeditious examination. Do not request an expeditious examination routinely.

- Submit a separate communication for multiple cases.

Packaging and Shipping Evidence

- Prior to packaging and shipping evidence, call the pertinent unit of the Laboratory for specific instructions.

- Take precautions to preserve the evidence.

- When requesting latent print examinations, place nonporous evidence in individual protective coverings such as thick transparent envelopes or suspend in a container so that there is minimal surface contact. Place porous evidence in individual protective coverings such as paper envelopes. Stabilize the evidence to avoid movement or friction during shipment.

- Wrap and seal each item of evidence separately to avoid contamination.

- Place the evidence in a clean, dry, and previously unused inner container.

- Seal the inner container with tamper-evident or filament tape.

  - Affix **EVIDENCE** and appropriate **BIOHAZARD** or **HAZARDOUS MATERIALS** labels to the inner container. To view other hazardous materials labels, <u>click here</u>.

- If any of the evidence needs to be examined for latent prints, affix a **LATENT** label on the inner container.

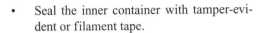

  - Affix the evidence examination request and all case information between the inner and outer containers.

- Place the sealed inner container in a clean, dry, and previously unused outer container with clean packing materials. Do not use loose Styrofoam.

- Completely seal the outer container so that opening of the container would be evident.

- Label the outer container with appropriate **BIOHAZARD** or **HAZARDOUS MATERIALS** labels.

- Address the outer container as follows:

FEDERAL BUREAU OF INVESTIGATION
ATTENTION: EVIDENCE CONTROL UNIT
2501 INVESTIGATION PARKWAY
QUANTICO, VA 22135

- Ship evidence via U.S. Postal Service Registered Mail, United Parcel Service, or Federal Express. Record the method of shipment and the tracking number or numbers on the chain-of-custody form.

- Rendered-safe explosive devices must be shipped via United Parcel Service.

- Live ammunition must be shipped via Federal Express. The following guidelines must be followed to comply with U.S. Department of Transportation regulations:

  — Pack ammunition in a cardboard container.

  — Label invoices **FEDERAL EXPRESS**.

  — The shipper's certification for restricted articles must be included.

  — The outside of the container must be labeled **ORM-D AIR, CARTRIDGES SMALL ARMS**.

  — The shipping papers must also include the weight in grams.

- The Interstate Shipment of Etiologic Agents (42 CFR Part 72) provides packaging and labeling requirements for etiologic agents (viable microorganisms or toxins that cause or may cause human disease) shipped in interstate traffic. For additional information, contact the Centers for Disease Control and Prevention at *http://www.cdc.gov/od/ohs/biosfty/shipregs.htm* or (404) 639-3235 in Atlanta, Georgia.

Package and label etiologic agents in volumes of less than 50 ml as shown in the drawings below. Place dry ice outside the secondary container.

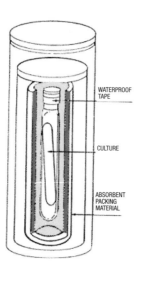

Specific guidelines are available for different types of evidence materials. See *http://www.fbi.gov/hq/lab/handbook/intro3.htm*

- Abrasives
- Adhesives
- Anthropology
- Arson
- Audio
- Bank Security Dyes
- Building Materials
- Bullet Jacket Alloys
- Bullet Leads
- Caulks
- Chemical Unknowns
- Computers
- Controlled Substances
- Cords
- Crime Scene Surveys, Documentation, and Reconstruction
- Cryptanalysis
- Disaster Squad
- DNA
- Electronic Devices
- Explosives
- Explosives Residue
- Facial Imaging
- Feathers
- Fibers
- Firearms
- Glass
- Gunshot Residue

- Hairs
- Image Analysis
- Inks
- Latent Prints
- Lubricants
- Metallurgy
- Missing Persons
- Paints
- Pepper Sprays or Foams
- Pharmaceuticals
- Photographic Images
- Polymers
- Product Tampering
- Questioned Documents
- Racketeering Records
- Ropes
- Safe Insulations
- Sealants
- Serial Numbers
- Shoeprints
- Soils
- Tapes
- Tire Treads
- Toolmarks
- Toxicology
- Videos
- Weapons of Mass Destruction
- Woods

(Courtesy, U.S. Department of Justice, Federal Bureau of Investigation, Handbook of Forensic Sciences.)

APPENDIX 2

Photographing the Crime Scene

Photographing the Crime Scene*

The hackneyed statement that "a picture is worth one thousand words" may or may not be true. However, it is certain that photography, properly performed, can be one of the most valuable aids to the police investigation. Good crime scene photography can be properly done without great expertise. This section presents a summary of the techniques and considerations bearing on comprehensive crime scene photographic coverage. The techniques involved in operating cameras and associated equipment is, however, outside the scope of this handbook.

Investigative Photographs

These are simply any photographs made to record an object or event, or to clarify a point that is relative to a matter under investigation. Many investigative photographs are made in the photographic laboratory. However, this chapter is concerned with those taken on the crime scene.

Admissibility of Photographs as Evidence

Photographs are admissible in court if the investigator can testify that they accurately depict the area he observed. The accuracy of the photograph always relates to the degree it represents the appearance of the subject matter as to form, tone, color (if applicable), and scale. Thus, the use of a lens that will record with accuracy all objects and areas in focus may not portray correct distances between objects, nor reproduce them with the proper perspective, when they are out of focal range. In such situations, the crime scene sketch and the investigator's notes play strong supporting roles.

Usually a photographic negative is considered sufficient proof to refute any allegation that a photograph has been altered. However, if enlarged photographs are made for presentation in court, a contact print without borders should also be made.

Because of the importance of scale, distances, and perspective in interpreting the photographs taken at crime scenes, it is good procedure to include a ruler or other scale measurement in the photograph, when this is practicable. However, because some courts have not allowed even this minor modification to the scene, an identical photograph without the scale indicator should also be taken.

If the photograph is to have the highest quality as evidence, it must depict the scene, persons, or objects precisely as they were found. Photography must therefore be an <u>exclusive</u> function of the crime scene search—that is, no people should be working within the scene at the time it is photographed nor should extraneous objects, such as police equipment, be included in the pictures.

Identification of Photographs

The photograph must be precisely identified, and the identifying data must be noted as each shot is taken.

The information relative to the technical history of a photograph will be recorded in the investigator's notes, which become part of the permanent record of the case.

Custody of Photographs

Custody of investigative photographs should be carefully maintained. When the film is sent by mail to a commercial processor, registered mail with return receipt should be used.

General Considerations in Field Photography

Time is an essential factor. Photography frequently will preempt other aspects of the investigation. Objects cannot be moved or examined with thoroughness until they have been photographed from all necessary angles. Because there are situations in which the object of interest undergoes significant change with the passage of time, it is very important that photographic equipment be in a constant state of readiness.

All camera positions should be recorded on the crime scene sketch. This can be done by measuring the distance from immovable objects to a vertical line extending downward from the camera lens. Photographs of interior scenes, intended to depict the area as a whole, should be taken as overlapping segments in one direction around the room or area. In making such photographs, it is best to keep the camera at about eye level, unless a tripod is used.

The most important element in police photography is maintaining perspective. Proper photographic perspective produces the same impression of relative position and size of visible objects as the actual objects do when viewed from a particular point. Any significant distortion in the perspective will reduce, or destroy altogether, its evidentiary value.

As a second rule, natural perspective can best be maintained by shooting pictures with the camera aimed so that a 90° angle is formed with opposite walls, or if outdoors, with fixed objects such as trees or the landscape.

Critical Photographic Requirements

- Approaches to the scene.

- Surrounding areas (the yard of a house in which the homicide occurred, the general area surrounding an outdoor crime scene, and so forth).

- Close-up photographs should be taken of the entrance and exit to the scene, or those most likely to have been used if these are not obvious.

- A general scenario shot showing the location of the body and its position in relation to the room or area in which it was found.

- At least two photographs of the body at 90° angles to each other. Camera should be placed as high as possible pointing downward toward the body.

- As many close-ups of the body should be taken as needed to show wounds or injuries, weapons lying near the body, and the immediate surroundings.

- After the body is moved, and after the removal of each item of evidence, the area underneath them should be photographed if there is any mark, stain, or other apparent change.

- All fingerprints which do not need further development or cannot be lifted should be photographed. Areas in which fingerprints were discovered are photographed to show the location if this area was not included in other photographs.

- Bloodstains, including locations. Color film is desirable, although not absolutely necessary. Black and white pictures must also be taken.

Photographing the Arson Scene

When photographing the arson scene, complete coverage of the damage is important. But perhaps of even greater importance are objects or areas that are suspected to have been the point or points of initiation of the fire. Close-up photographs should be made of all such objects or areas. In addition, there are several other critical points or items of interest in an arson scene that should be photographed:

- Exterior views of all structures involved in the fire.

- Interior views that give a complete representation of the damaged areas and any undamaged areas immediately adjacent.

Photographing the Burglary Scene

The photographic requirements already cited for the homicide scene apply to the burglary situation. In addition, particular attention should be paid to:

- The interior and exterior of the building.

- Damaged areas, particularly those around the points of entry and exit used by the criminal.

- Close-ups of damaged containers that were the target of the burglar—safes, jewel boxes, strong boxes, etc.

- Tool marks both close up and from a perspective that will allow the position of the mark with respect to the general scene to be noted.

- Fingerprints. Although fingerprints are of major interest to all types of investigations, they are of particular value in a burglary investigation. Fingerprints are photographed only when they are visible without development and when they cannot be lifted after they have been developed.

Photographing the Vehicle Accident

The accident scene should be photographed as soon as possible after the incident. Normally, except when photographing vehicles, the lenses should be of a normal focal length. If any lenses of an unusual length are used, considerable distortion will occur in the relative width of roads, distances between points, and so forth. Therefore, if special lenses were used, the record of the search should note the fact, and their description.

The following are the more critical aspects of interest to be photographed:

- The overall scene of the accident—from both approaches to the point of impact.

- The exact positions of the vehicles, injured persons, and objects directly connected to the accident.

- All points of impact, marks of impact, and damage to real property.

- All pavement obstructions and defects in the roadways.

- Close-ups of damage to vehicles. One photograph should show the front and one side, and another should show the rear and other side of the vehicle.

- Skid marks. If possible, photographs should be taken before the vehicle has been removed and again after it has been moved.

- Tire tracks, glass, and other associated debris.

Photographing Deceased Persons

The evidentiary value of a photograph of a deceased person is often considerably reduced by the inclusion of views that can be later alleged to be deliberately inflammatory. The unnecessary exposure of the sexual organs is a frequent case in point.

When photographing a body that is lying in a horizontal position, the camera should be placed directly over the victim's head at a height of no less than 5 feet.

Close-up photographs taken of injured parts of the body are most effective if in color, but black and white pictures must also be taken.

If the presence of wounds, blood, or other discoloration on the corpse may affect identification, the use of a lens filter may create more lifelike tones and thus aid in identification.

Photographing Live Victims and Suspects

Photographs that show areas of the body which usually are not visible when the person is clothed should be taken only under the direct supervision of the examining physician whose testimony the photographs are intended to illustrate. Thus, it is unusual that this type of photograph will be taken on the crime scene.

Before photographing any part of the female body normally covered by clothing, written consent of the subject must be obtained. If the subject is a minor, the written consent of the parent is needed and the photography must be done with witnesses present.

Photographing Fingerprints

To this point, the general requirement for close-up photographs of latent prints has been considered; however, it is important to consider also the uses that can be made of photography in the preparation and presentation of fingerprint evidence.

Fingerprints found at crime scenes may frequently be photographed and an enlargement produced that can be very useful in studying the print and comparing it with others. Fingerprints that can be seen without the aid of dusting powder should be photographed prior to dusting. There is always danger of damaging the print during the dusting process.

*   Reprinted from Richard H. Fox and Carl L. Cunningham. *Crime Scene Search and Physical Evidence Handbook.* Washington, DC: Superintendent of Documents, 1973.

APPENDIX 3

ViCAP Crime Analysis Report

ViCAP SUBMISSION CRITERIA

The ViCAP Crime Analysis Report Form has been designed to collect information regarding the following types of crimes whether or not the offender has been arrested or identified:

➤ **Solved or Unsolved Homicides/Attempted Homicides**
especially those that involve an abduction; are apparently random, motiveless, or sexually oriented; or are known or suspected to be part of a series.

➤ **Missing Persons/Kidnappings**
where the circumstances indicate a strong possibility of foul play and the victim is still missing.

➤ **Unidentified Dead Bodies**
where the manner of death is known or suspected to be homicide.

Cases where the offender has been arrested or identified should be submitted so unsolved cases in the ViCAP system can be compared to known offenders.

Public Reporting Burden for the collection of information is estimated to average one hour per response, including the time for reviewing instructions, searching existing data sources, gathering and maintaining the data needed, and completing and reviewing the collection of information. Send comments regarding this burden estimate or any other aspect of this collection of information, including suggestions for reducing this burden, to: ViCAP, FBI Academy, Quantico, VA 22135; and to the Office of Management and Budget, Paperwork Reduction Project; OMB #1110-0011, Washington, D.C., 20503.

INSTRUCTIONS

Unless otherwise stated, check as many boxes as apply for each item.

If in doubt about how to respond to a given item, be guided by your experience and good judgment. Proof beyond a reasonable doubt is not required, but do not guess either.

If there are details of the case that you believe are important but which are not covered by the questions provided in the ViCAP Crime Analysis Report, please describe them in the Narrative (Item 94).

If you wish to supplement or correct information previously reported to ViCAP, please submit a new ViCAP Report but complete only items 1-8, 12a, and the items you wish to supplement or correct. You do not need to resubmit unchanged items.

If you have questions regarding this report or its completion, call ViCAP at (800) 634-4097 or at (540) 720-4900.

If you are interested in obtaining an **offender profile** or **behavioral assessment** on this violent crime, please contact the Profiling Coordinator in the FBI Field Office nearest you. This individual will assist you with your request for a profile or behavioral assessment. Please do **NOT** submit your profiling request or materials directly to ViCAP.

Multiple Victims and/or Multiple Offenders

If your incident has **MULTIPLE VICTIMS,** you must complete a separate ViCAP Report for each victim. Offender information need not be duplicated.

If your incident has **MULTIPLE OFFENDERS,** submit only one complete ViCAP Report per victim; photocopy and attach additional Offender/Suspect pages (Items 33 - 53) as needed.

Before submitting the ViCAP Report, please make a copy for your records and for any regional or state systems to which you will be sending a copy of this report.

Mail all ViCAP Reports to: **ViCAP**
National Center For the Analysis of Violent Crime
FBI Academy
Quantico, VA 22135

Enclosing copies of Crime Scene Photographs with the ViCAP Report will assist the ViCAP staff in the analysis of your case.

A ViCAP Case Number will be assigned to your case when it is processed and will be provided to you as soon as possible. The ViCAP Case Number should be referenced in any subsequent correspondence or telephone communications with ViCAP regarding your case.

ADMINISTRATION

Date form completed

_____/_____/_____
mo   day   year

1. State System Case Number (if applicable) _____

2a. Investigating Agency _____

    2b. Address _____

      City _____ County _____

      State/ _____ ZIP _____ Country _____
      Province

3. Investigating Agency's ORI Number _____

4. Investigating Agency's Case Number _____

5. Investigator(s)'s Name, Title/Rank and Phone Number

    _____ _____-_____-_____

    _____ _____-_____-_____

6a. Name and Title/Rank of person completing this form (**if not the investigator**)

    _____

    6b. Agency _____

      Address _____

      City _____ County _____

      State/ _____ ZIP _____ Country _____
      Province

      Phone Number _____-_____-_____

7. ViCAP Report Type (**check one**):

    ❏ Original Submission of This Case
    ❏ Supplement to or Correction of Previously Submitted Information

8. Investigating Agency's Case Status (**check one**):

OPEN

    ❏ Active Investigation
    ❏ Suspended/Inactive

CLOSED

    ❏ By Arrest
    ❏ By Exceptional Means

VICTIM INFORMATION

NOTE: If there are **multiple** victims, a **separate** ViCAP form must be completed for **each** victim. Offender information need **not** be duplicated.

9. This Is Victim _____ of _____ Victim(s) in this incident.
       \#   total

10. Case Type (**check one**):

    ❑ **Murder** - Victim Deceased and Identified
    ❑ **Attempted Murder** - Victim Alive and Identified
    ❑ **Unidentified Dead Body** - Where Manner of Death Is Known or Suspected to Be Homicide
    ❑ **Missing Person** - With Evidence of Foul Play
    ❑ Other (**explain**) _____
        ❑ Victim Deceased
        ❑ Victim Alive

11. Based on your experience and the results of this investigation to date, indicate the probable Crime Type(s) and/or Motive(s) (**check all that apply**):

    ❑ Argument/Conflict   ❑ Financial Gain
    ❑ Arson   ❑ Gang-Related
    ❑ Bias/Hate   ❑ Kidnapping (18 years or older)
    ❑ Burglary   ❑ Organized Crime
    ❑ Child Abduction (under 18 years) ❑ Revenge
    ❑ Child Abuse   ❑ Robbery
    ❑ Contract Killing   ❑ Sexual Motivation
    ❑ Crime Concealment   ❑ Witness Elimination
    ❑ Domestic Homicide   ❑ Other (**describe**) _____
    ❑ Drive-by Shooting   ❑ Undetermined
    ❑ Drug-Related

12a. Name _____, _____ _____ _____
                    Last   First   Middle   Suffix -
                                                                            i.e, Jr., III

12b. Aliases including maiden name and prior married name(s)

    _____, _____ _____ _____

    _____, _____ _____ _____

    _____, _____ _____ _____

    _____, _____ _____ _____
                    Last   First   Middle   Suffix -
                                                                            i.e, Jr., III

12c. Nickname(s)/Street Name(s)

    _____ _____ _____ _____

13. Street Address _____ City _____

    County _____ State/_____ ZIP _____ Country _____
                              Province

14. Social Security Number _____

15. FBI Number _____

16. Gender (**check one**):

    ❑ Male
    ❑ Female
    ❑ Unknown

17. Race (**check all that apply**):

    ❑ Black
    ❑ White
    ❑ Hispanic
    ❑ Asian/Oriental
    ❑ American Indian/Alaskan Native
    ❑ Other (**specify**) _____
    ❑ Unknown

18. Date of Birth _____/_____/_____
                 mo   day   year

19a. Age (or best estimate) at time of incident _____ (to_____)

   19b. Apparent Physical Age _____ (**if different from item 19a**)

20. Height (or best estimate) _____ feet _____ inches (to _____ feet _____ inches)

21. Weight (or best estimate) _____ pounds (to _____ pounds)

22a. Hair Color (**check all that apply**):

    ❑ Black
    ❑ Blond
    ❑ Brown
    ❑ Gray/Silver
    ❑ Red/Auburn
    ❑ White
    ❑ Other (**describe**) _____
    ❑ Unknown

   22b. Hair Length (**check all that apply**):

    ❑ Bald or Shaved
    ❑ Balding/Receding
    ❑ Shorter than Collar Length
    ❑ Collar Length
    ❑ Shoulder Length
    ❑ Longer than Shoulder Length
    ❑ Other (**describe**) _____
    ❑ Unknown

23. Victim's Current Legal / Illegal Occupation(s)

_____   _____

_____   _____

24. Was victim affiliated with any group or organization that you think may be relevant to this crime?

   ❑ Yes (**describe**) _____
   ❑ No
   ❑ Unknown

25a. Victim's General Lifestyle(s)/Characteristic(s) (**check all that apply**):

   ❑ Heterosexual   ❑ Street Person
   ❑ Bisexual   ❑ Mentally Ill
   ❑ Homosexual   ❑ Runaway
   ❑ Transvestite   ❑ Drug User/Seller
   ❑ Prostitute   ❑ Criminal Activity
   ❑ Hitchhiker   (**describe**) _____
   ❑ Recluse   ❑ Other (**describe**) _____
   ❑ Transient   ❑ Unknown

   25b. Was the victim's lifestyle(s)/characteristic(s) a contributing factor in this crime?

   ❑ Yes
   ❑ No
   ❑ Unknown

26. Did the victim have any outstanding feature(s) not reported above (physical deformity, mental impairment, pins in bones, skeletal defects, etc.)?

   ❑ Yes (**describe**) _____
   ❑ No
   ❑ Unknown

MISSING AND UNIDENTIFIED VICTIMS

IF YOUR VICTIM IS EITHER A MISSING PERSON OR AN UNIDENTIFIED DEAD BODY, RESPOND TO ITEMS 27 THROUGH 32. OTHERWISE, GO TO ITEM 33.

27. NCIC Number _____

28. Eye Color (**check all that apply**):

   ❑ Black   ❑ Green
   ❑ Blue   ❑ Hazel
   ❑ Brown   ❑ Other (**describe**) _____
   ❑ Gray   ❑ Unknown

29. Facial Hair (**check all that apply**):

   ❑ None
   ❑ Mustache
   ❑ Beard

   ❑ Unshaven/Stubble
   ❑ Other (**describe**) _____
   ❑ Unknown

30. Characteristics of Teeth (**check all that apply**):

   ❑ No Dental Work
   ❑ Braces
   ❑ Broken/Chipped
   ❑ Crooked
   ❑ Decayed
   ❑ Dentures/Partial Plate

   ❑ Gold/Silver
   ❑ Noticeable Gaps
   ❑ Some or All Missing
   ❑ Stained
   ❑ Restorations/Fillings
   ❑ Other (**describe**) _____
   ❑ Unknown

31a. Did victim have any noticeable scars, marks or tattoos?

   ❑ Yes   ❑ No   ❑ Unknown

   31b. If yes, fill in the table below, indicating location on body, checking whether it is a scar/mark
   or a tattoo, and providing a description of the scar/mark or tattoo.

LOCATION ON BODY	SCAR OR MARK	TATTOO	DESCRIPTION
	❑	❑	
	❑	❑	
	❑	❑	
	❑	❑	
	❑	❑	
	❑	❑	

32. Give a detailed description of clothing, jewelry, glasses, and other items worn by or in possession
   of victim (when missing person last seen or when unidentified body found)

   _____

   _____

   _____

OFFENDER/SUSPECT INFORMATION

NOTE: If there are **multiple** offenders/suspects, attach additional offender pages (Items 33 through 53) for each offender/suspect.

33. The following information pertains to the (**check one**):

    ❑ Offender
    ❑ Suspect

    NOTE: From this point forward, this individual will be referred to as OFFENDER regardless of whether he/she is an offender or suspect.

34. This Is Offender _____ of _____ Offender(s) in this incident.
    _{#   total}

35. Status of this offender (**check one**):

    ❑ Unknown - Not Seen (**go to item 54**)
    ❑ Unknown - Seen
    ❑ Identified, Not in Custody
    ❑ In Custody - For This Offense - Date of Arrest _____/_____/_____
                                               mo   day   year
    ❑ In Custody - For Another Offense (**specify**) _____

                     Date of Arrest _____/_____/_____
                                               mo   day   year

    ❑ Deceased - Date of Death _____/_____/_____
                                   mo   day   year

36a. Name _____, _____ _____ _____
                 Last   First   Middle   Suffix - i.e, Jr., III

36b. Aliases including maiden name and prior married name(s)

    _____, _____ _____ _____

    _____, _____ _____ _____

    _____, _____ _____ _____

    _____, _____ _____ _____

    _____, _____ _____ _____
                 Last   First   Middle   Suffix - i.e, Jr., III

36c. Nickname(s)/Street Name(s)

    _____ _____ _____ _____

37. Street Address _____ City _____

    County _____ State/_____ ZIP _____ Country _____
                                         Province

38. Social Security Number _____

    Other SSNs Used _____ _____ _____

39. FBI Number _____

40. Gender (**check one**):

    ❏ Male
    ❏ Female
    ❏ Unknown

41. Race (**check all that apply**):

    ❏ Black
    ❏ White
    ❏ Hispanic
    ❏ Asian/Oriental
    ❏ American Indian/Alaskan Native
    ❏ Other (**describe**) _____
    ❏ Unknown

42. Date of Birth _____/_____/_____
                   mo   day   year

    Other DOBs Used _____/_____/_____ _____/_____/_____ _____/_____/_____
                          mo   day   year   mo   day   year   mo   day   year

43a. Age (or best estimate) at time of incident _____ (to _____)

    43b. Apparent Physical Age _____ (**if different from item 43a**)

44. Height (or best estimate) _____ feet _____ inches (to _____ feet _____ inches)

45. Weight (or best estimate) _____ pounds (to _____ pounds)

46a. Hair Color (**check all that apply**):

    ❏ Black
    ❏ Blond
    ❏ Brown
    ❏ Gray/Silver
    ❏ Red/Auburn
    ❏ White
    ❏ Other (**describe**) _____
    ❏ Unknown

46b. Hair Length (**check all that apply**):

- ❏ Bald or Shaved
- ❏ Balding/Receding
- ❏ Shorter Than Collar Length
- ❏ Collar Length
- ❏ Shoulder Length
- ❏ Longer than Shoulder Length
- ❏ Other (**describe**) _____
- ❏ Unknown

47a. Does the offender have any noticeable scars, marks or tattoos?

❏ Yes   ❏ No   ❏ Unknown

47b. If yes, fill in the table below, indicating location on body, checking whether it is a scar/mark or a tattoo, and providing a description of the scar/mark or tattoo.

LOCATION ON BODY	SCAR OR MARK	TATTOO	DESCRIPTION
	❏	❏	
	❏	❏	
	❏	❏	
	❏	❏	
	❏	❏	
	❏	❏	

48. Did the offender wear a disguise or mask?

- ❏ Yes (**describe**) _____
- ❏ No
- ❏ Unknown

49. Does the offender have any outstanding feature(s) not reported above (glasses, physical deformity, speech impediment, accent, odors, etc.)?

- ❏ Yes (**describe**) _____
- ❏ No
- ❏ Unknown

IDENTIFIED OFFENDER INFORMATION

If you have an offender in custody or identified, please complete items 50-53 (if known); otherwise, go to item 54. This information is requested in order to possibly associate/eliminate the offender in connection with other crimes.

50. Indicate in the table below the addresses, cities, counties, states (provinces), and countries in which offender has been employed, resided, visited, been in custody, or served in the military (indicate branch). Indicate dates if known. Attach additional sheets if necessary.

DATES From To	LOCATIONS Address / City/County	State/Province	Country	Employed	Resided	Visited	In Custody	In Military
				☐	☐	☐	☐	☐
				☐	☐	☐	☐	☐
				☐	☐	☐	☐	☐
				☐	☐	☐	☐	☐
				☐	☐	☐	☐	☐
				☐	☐	☐	☐	☐
				☐	☐	☐	☐	☐
				☐	☐	☐	☐	☐
				☐	☐	☐	☐	☐
				☐	☐	☐	☐	☐
				☐	☐	☐	☐	☐
				☐	☐	☐	☐	☐

Branch

51. Offender's Legal / Illegal Occupation(s). Include dates if known.

_____   _____   _____

_____   _____   _____

52. Offender's General Lifestyle(s)/Characteristic(s) (**check all that apply**):

❏ Heterosexual   ❏ Mentally Ill
❏ Bisexual   ❏ Street Person
❏ Homosexual   ❏ Drug User/Seller
❏ Hitchhiker   ❏ Other (**describe**) _____
❏ Transient   ❏ Unknown
❏ Prostitute

53. What was the offender's relationship to the victim? (**check all that apply**):

❏ Stranger   ❏ Parent
❏ Spouse   ❏ Friend
❏ Ex-Spouse   ❏ Acquaintance
❏ Girlfriend/Boyfriend   ❏ Relative (**describe**) _____
❏ Ex-Girlfriend/Ex-Boyfriend   ❏ Customer/Client
❏ Employee   ❏ Co-Worker
❏ Employer   ❏ Neighbor
❏ Care Provider   ❏ Other (**describe**) _____
❏ Child   ❏ Unknown

OFFENDER'S MODUS OPERANDI (M.O.)
OFFENDER'S APPROACH TO VICTIM

54. The offender's initial approach to the victim was (**check all that apply**):

    ❑ **Unknown Approach**
    ❑ By **Deception or Con**:

        ❑ Posed as Authority Figure/Police Officer
        ❑ Posed as Business Person/Customer
        ❑ Asked Victim to Model/Pose for Photos
        ❑ Offered Job, Money, Treats or Toys
        ❑ Implied Family Emergency or Illness
        ❑ Wanted to Show Something
        ❑ Asked For/Offered Assistance
        ❑ Caused/Staged Traffic Accident
        ❑ Solicited for Sex
        ❑ Offered Ride/Transportation
        ❑ Placed or Responded to Advertising
        ❑ Third Person Used to Lure Victim
        ❑ Other Deception/Con (**describe**) _____

    ❑ By **Surprise**:

        ❑ Lay in Wait - Out of Doors
        ❑ Lay in Wait - In Building
        ❑ Lay in Wait - In Vehicle
        ❑ Victim Sleeping
        ❑ Other Surprise (**describe**) _____

    ❑ By **Blitz** - Direct and immediate physical assault:

        ❑ Physically Overpowered Victim (picked up, carried away, etc.)
        ❑ Hit Victim with Hand, Fist or Clubbing Weapon
        ❑ Choked Victim
        ❑ Stabbed Victim
        ❑ Shot Victim
        ❑ Other Blitz/Assault (**describe**) _____

    ❑ **Other** Approach (**describe**) _____

55. **If relevant to the crime** describe victim's activity at the time of the initial contact between the offender and the victim, or when the victim was last seen alive prior to incident (**check all that apply**):

    ❑ Going to/from residence
    ❑ Going to/from school
    ❑ Going to/from work
    ❑ Jogging/Bicycling/Walking
    ❑ Hitchhiking
    ❑ On a date
    ❑ Prostituting
    ❑ Hunting/Camping/Fishing
    ❑ Other (**describe**) _____
    ❑ Unknown

56. Prior to, or at the time of the **initial contact** between the offender and the victim, was there an event or activity in the area that may be relevant to this crime (carnival, concert, convention, etc.)?

   ☐ Yes (**describe**) _____
   ☐ No
   ☐ Unknown

DATES AND EXACT GEOGRAPHIC LOCATIONS

57. Indicate in the table below the dates, times, and exact geographic locations of where the victim was last seen alive (prior to this incident), where the victim first came into contact with the offender, the actual murder/assault site, and the body recovery site.

	VICTIM LAST SEEN ALIVE	INITIAL CONTACT	MURDER/ ASSAULT	VICTIM/BODY RECOVERED
DATE (or date range)				
TIME (military) (or time range)				
ADDRESS (if applicable)				
CITY				
COUNTY				
STATE/ PROVINCE				
ZIP CODE				
COUNTRY				
LATITUDE				
LONGITUDE				

SPECIFIC LOCATIONS FOR EVENT SITES

Listed below are specific locations which may relate to four event sites - the victim's last known location prior to the assault/homicide, the initial contact site between the victim and the offender, the actual murder/assault site, and the victim/body recovery site. Indicate the specific locations which best describe each of the four event sites by writing in the corresponding numbers of the specific locations. The four event sites may be identical, or each of the four sites may be different. (If necessary, use more than one number for each site to describe it). If it is necessary to choose "Other", please describe the location.

58. Victim's Last Known Location _____ _____ _____ _____ (If **Other**, Describe _____)

59. Initial Contact Location _____ _____ _____ _____ (If **Other**, Describe _____)

60. Murder/Assault Location _____ _____ _____ _____ (If **Other**, Describe _____)

61. Body Recovery Location _____ _____ _____ _____ (If **Other**, Describe _____)

UNKNOWN
   0. Unknown

LIVING QUARTERS
   1. Victim's Residence
   2. Offender's Residence
   3. Dormitory
   4. Multi-Family Dwelling (apt., etc.)
   5. Rest/Nursing Home
   6. Single-Family Dwelling
   7. Transient/Temporary Quarters
   8. **Other** Living Quarters

BUSINESS
   9. Victim's Workplace
   10. Offender's Workplace
   11. Convenience Store
   12. Fast Food Restaurant
   13. Gas Station
   14. Grocery Store/Market
   15. Motel/Hotel
   16. Restaurant
   17. Shopping Mall/Center
   18. **Other** Business

TRANSPORTATION
   19. Victim's Vehicle
   20. Offender's Vehicle
   21. Bus Stop/Station
   22. Public Transportation
   23. Railroad Property
   24. Truck Stop
   25. **Other** Transportation

ENTERTAINMENT
   26. Bar/Tavern/Nightclub
   27. Circus/Fair/Carnival
   28. Party
   29. Vice Area
   30. **Other** Entertainment

PUBLIC/OTHER BUILDINGS
   31. College Campus
   32. Military Installation
   33. Office Building
   34. Public Restroom
   35. School
   36. Shed/Outbuilding/Barn
   37. Vacant Building
   38. **Other** Building

OUTDOOR LOCATIONS
   39. Alley
   40. Bridge
   41. Camping Area
   42. Cave/Mine/Quarry
   43. Cemetery
   44. Desert
   45. Dump/Landfill
   46. Field/Orchard/Farm
   47. Mountains/Hills
   48. Parking Lot/Garage
   49. Playground/Park
   50. Rest Stop/Area
   51. Road - Highway/Interstate
   52. Road - Paved/Public
   53. Road - Gravel/Dirt
   54. Trail/Jogging Path
   55. Vacant Lot
   56. Wooded Area/Forest
   57. **Other** Outdoor Location

WATER LOCATIONS
   58. Beach/Shoreline/Riverbank
   59. Canal/Inland Waterway
   60. Ditch
   61. Lake/Pond
   62. Marsh/Swamp
   63. Ocean/Bay
   64. River
   65. Stream/Creek
   66. Storm Drain/Sewer System
   67. **Other** Water Location

62. If the body recovery site involved a water location, indicate the condition of the location at the time the offender disposed of the body (**check one**):

❑ Water-filled
❑ Dry
❑ Unknown

63. If the crime scene was inside a building, indicate how the offender gained entry (**check all that apply**):

❑ Public Access
❑ Forced Entry
❑ Let in by Victim
❑ Through Unsecured Door/Window
❑ Other (**describe**) _____
❑ Unknown

EVENTS AT CRIME SCENE(S)

64a. Was the crime scene altered by the offender in any way?

❑ Yes   ❑ No   ❑ Unknown

64b. If yes, indicate how the crime scene was altered and **include details in narrative** (Item 94) (**check all that apply**):

❑ Burned Scene
❑ Cleaned Scene/Self
❑ Destroyed/Removed Evidence from Scene
❑ Disabled Phone/Security Device/Utilities at Scene
❑ Planted Evidence at Scene
❑ Ransacked Scene
❑ Staged Scene
❑ Vandalized Scene
❑ Other (**describe**) _____

65a. Was there writing or drawing **at the crime scene**? (**NOT** on the victim's body)

   ❑ Yes   ❑ No   ❑ Unknown

   65b. If yes, indicate the location(s) at the crime scene, the description(s) of the writing or drawing, and the instrument(s)/tool(s) used to write or draw at crime scene.

LOCATION AT SCENE	DESCRIPTION OF WRITING OR DRAWING	WRITING TOOL

66a. Was there writing or drawing **on the victim's body**?

   ❑ Yes   ❑ No   ❑ Unknown

   66b. If yes, indicate the location(s) on the body, the description(s) of the writing or drawing, and the instrument(s)/tool(s) used to write or draw on the body.

LOCATION ON BODY	DESCRIPTION OF WRITING OR DRAWING	WRITING TOOL

67. Was there evidence to suggest that a deliberate, unusual or symbolic act or thing had been performed on, with or near the victim (such as defecation, unique objects placed at scene, foreign substance on body, body hair shaved, etc.)?

   ❑ Yes (**describe**) _____

   _____

   ❑ No
   ❑ Unknown

CONDITION OF VICTIM WHEN FOUND

BODY DISPOSITION

68. Evidence suggests the offender disposed of the body in the following manner (**check one**):

☐ Openly Displayed or Placed to Ensure Discovery
☐ Concealed, Hidden or Placed to Prevent Discovery
☐ With an Apparent Lack of Concern as to Whether or Not the Body Was Discovered
☐ Unknown

69. Does it appear that the victim's body was intentionally placed in an unnatural or unusual position (e.g., staged or posed)?

☐ Yes (**describe**) _____
☐ No
☐ Unknown

70. Is there evidence to suggest that the offender returned to the body recovery site after disposing of the body?

☐ Yes (**describe**) _____
☐ No
☐ Unknown

71. The victim was discovered (**check all that apply**):

☐ Buried
☐ In a Vehicle
☐ In a Building
☐ In a Bathtub
☐ In a Box/Container/Dumpster
☐ Found as Skeletal Remains
☐ In Water
  ☐ Weighted Down (**describe**) _____
  ☐ Not Weighted Down
☐ Covered (**describe**) _____

☐ Face Only Covered (**describe**) _____

☐ Wrapped (**describe**) _____
☐ None of the Above

RESTRAINTS USED ON VICTIM

72a. At any time was the victim bound?

❑ Yes   ❑ No   ❑ Unknown

72b. If yes, indicate the articles used, parts of body bound, whether binding(s) were brought to scene or found at scene by offender, and whether bindings were left at scene or taken from scene by offender.

ARTICLE USED TO BIND	PARTS OF THE BODY BOUND						BINDINGS SELECTION			BINDINGS RECOVERY		
	Hands, Wrists, or Arms	Feet, Ankles, or Legs	Hands Bound to Feet	Arms Bound to Torso	Other (describe in Item 94)	Unknown	Brought to Scene by Offender	Found at Scene by Offender	Unknown if Brought or Found	Left on Victim's Body	Left at Scene (NOT on Victim)	Taken From Scene
Chain	■	■	■	■	■	■	■	■	■	■	■	■
Clothing (describe)	■	■	■	■	■	■	■	■	■	■	■	■
Flexcuffs/ Plastic Ties	■	■	■	■	■	■	■	■	■	■	■	■
Handcuffs	■	■	■	■	■	■	■	■	■	■	■	■
Rope/Cordage (describe)	■	■	■	■	■	■	■	■	■	■	■	■
Tape (describe)	■	■	■	■	■	■	■	■	■	■	■	■
Linens (describe)	■	■	■	■	■	■	■	■	■	■	■	■
Telephone/ Electrical Cord	■	■	■	■	■	■	■	■	■	■	■	■
Wire (Non-electrical)	■	■	■	■	■	■	■	■	■	■	■	■
Other (describe)	■	■	■	■	■	■	■	■	■	■	■	■
Unknown	■	■	■	■	■	■	■	■	■	■	■	■

73. At any time was the victim tied to another object?

❑ Yes (describe) _____
❑ No
❑ Unknown

74. At any time was a gag placed in or on the victim's mouth or throat?

❑ Yes (describe) _____
❑ No
❑ Unknown

75. At any time was a blindfold placed on or over the victim's eyes?

❑ Yes (describe) _____
❑ No
❑ Unknown

CLOTHING AND PROPERTY OF VICTIM

76. Clothing on victim when found (**check all that apply**):

❑ Fully Dressed
❑ Partially Dressed
   ❑ Nude from Waist Up OR Breasts/Chest Exposed
   ❑ Nude from Waist Down OR Genital Area Exposed
   ❑ Nude With Sock(s) and/or Shoe(s)
   ❑ Other (**describe**) _____
❑ Completely Nude
❑ Unknown

77. Is there evidence to suggest that the victim was redressed?

❑ Yes
❑ No
❑ Unknown

78. Is there evidence to suggest that any of the victim's clothing had been **intentionally** Ripped/ Torn or Cut by the offender?

❑ No
❑ Ripped/Torn (**describe**) _____

❑ Cut (**describe**) _____
❑ Unknown

79a. Is there evidence to suggest the offender took items from the victim and/or crime scene (these items may or may not be valuable, e.g., clothing, vehicle, driver's license, etc.)?

❑ Yes   ❑ No   ❑ Unknown

79b. If yes, indicate what items were taken (**check all that apply**):

❑ Clothing (**describe**) _____

❑ Jewelry (**describe**) _____
❑ Purse/Wallet
❑ Driver's License/Identification
❑ Credit Cards
❑ Checkbook
❑ Money
❑ Keys
❑ Vehicle
❑ Other (**describe**) _____

CAUSE(S) OF DEATH AND/OR TRAUMA

80. Indicate the Medical Examiner's/Coroner's officially listed Cause(s) of Death and any additional trauma(s) inflicted upon victim. Check all that apply. Where appropriate, indicate number of wounds.

CAUSE OF DEATH/TRAUMA	OFFICIAL CAUSE OF DEATH	ADDITIONAL TRAUMA	NUMBER OF WOUNDS
Airway Occlusion	☐	☐	
Asphyxiation	☐	☐	
Blunt Force Injury(s)	☐	☐	___
Burns (fire)	☐	☐	
Crushing Injury	☐	☐	
Cutting or Incised Wound(s)	☐	☐	___
Drowning	☐	☐	
Drug Injection/Overdose	☐	☐	
Explosive Trauma	☐	☐	
Exposure	☐	☐	
Gunshot Wound(s)	☐	☐	___
Hanging	☐	☐	
Malnutrition/Dehydration	☐	☐	
Poisoning	☐	☐	
Smoke Inhalation	☐	☐	
Smothering/Suffocation	☐	☐	
Stab Wound(s)	☐	☐	___
Strangulation (ligature)	☐	☐	
Strangulation (manual)	☐	☐	
Strangulation (undetermined)	☐	☐	
Torso Compression	☐	☐	
Undetermined	☐	☐	
Other (describe)	☐	☐	___
_____			
Unknown	☐	☐	

81. Major Trauma Location(s) (check all that apply):

☐ None
☐ Abdomen
☐ Anus
☐ Arm(s)
☐ Back
☐ Breast(s)
☐ Buttock(s)
☐ Chest
☐ Face
☐ Foot/Feet
☐ Genitalia

☐ Groin
☐ Hand(s)
☐ Head
☐ Leg(s)
☐ Lip(s)
☐ Neck
☐ Shoulder(s)
☐ Thigh(s)
☐ Other (describe) _____
☐ Unknown

82. Range of Gunfire (**check all that apply**):

❑ Distant (no stippling/tattooing)
❑ Intermediate (stippling/tattooing)
❑ Close (powder residue/tattooing)
❑ Contact
❑ Unknown

83. Extent of **Blunt Force Injury** only (this does **not** include trauma from gunshot, stabbing, etc.) (**check one**):

❑ None
❑ Minimal (minor bruising only, possibly caused by offender's slapping to control the victim)
❑ Moderate (injury inflicted which in itself could not have caused death)
❑ Severe (injury which in itself could have caused death, whether it was the cause of death or not)
❑ Extreme (injury inflicted beyond that necessary for death; overkill)
❑ Unknown

84a. Were **human** bite marks identified on victim's body?

❑ Yes   ❑ No   ❑ Unknown

84b. If yes, indicate location of bite marks on body:

_____ _____ _____ _____

85. Elements of unusual or additional assault/trauma/torture to victim (**check all that apply**):

❑ None
❑ Body Cavities or Wounds Explored/Probed
❑ Body Cavities or Genitalia Mutilated
❑ Body Set on Fire
❑ Burns (cigarette, iron, etc.)
❑ Carving on Victim (**describe**) _____
❑ Electrical Shock
❑ Evidence of Cannibalism
❑ Evidence of Vampirism
❑ Evisceration
❑ Hair Cut/Shaved:
   ❑ Head
   ❑ Pubic Area
   ❑ Other (**describe**) _____
❑ Hanged
❑ Patterned Injuries (**describe**) _____
❑ Pushed, Shoved or Thrown From Vehicle
❑ Run Over by Vehicle
❑ Skinned
❑ Stomped
❑ Whipped/Paddled
❑ Other (**describe**) _____
❑ Unknown

86a. Were body parts removed **by the offender**?

❑ Yes   ❑ No   ❑ Unknown

86b. If yes, indicate in the table below which body parts were removed, then check whether they were not recovered or recovered at scene. If recovered elsewhere, indicate location found.

BODY PART REMOVED	NOT RECOVERED	RECOVERED AT SCENE	RECOVERED ELSEWHERE (describe)
	❑	❑	
	❑	❑	
	❑	❑	
	❑	❑	
	❑	❑	
	❑	❑	

86c. Dismemberment Method (**check all that apply**):

❑ Bitten
❑ Ripped/Torn
❑ Cut - Skilled
❑ Cut - Unskilled
❑ Sawed
❑ Hacked/Chopped
❑ Other (**describe**) _____
❑ Unknown

SEXUAL ACTIVITY

87a. Is there evidence of sexual activity or attempted sexual activity with the victim?

❑ Yes   ❑ No (**go to item 89**)   ❑ Unknown

87b. Type of sexual activity or attempt (**check all that apply**):

❑ Vaginal
❑ Anal
❑ Victim Performed Oral Sex on Offender
❑ Offender Performed Oral Sex on Victim
❑ Foreign Object Insertion (**see item 87c**)
❑ Digital Penetration (**see item 87c**)
❑ Hand/Fist Insertion (**see item 87c**)
❑ Fondling
❑ Masturbation
❑ Post Mortem Sexual Activity
❑ Other (**describe**) _____
❑ Unknown

87c. If there was evidence of foreign object insertion, indicate the body location, the foreign object, and whether or not object was still in victim's body when found.

BODY LOCATION	FOREIGN OBJECT(S)	NOT IN BODY WHEN FOUND	IN BODY WHEN FOUND
Anus		❑	❑
Mouth		❑	❑
Vagina		❑	❑
Other (**specify**)		❑	❑

88. Semen Identification (**check all that apply**):

❑ None
❑ In Victim's Vagina
❑ In Victim's Anus
❑ In Victim's Mouth
❑ On Victim's Body (**describe location**) _____

❑ On Victim's Clothing (**describe location**) _____

❑ Elsewhere at Scene (**describe location**) _____

❑ Other (**describe**) _____
❑ Unknown

WEAPON INFORMATION

89a. Did offender use, display, or threaten a weapon during the commission of this crime?

☐ Yes   ☐ No (**go to item 91**)   ☐ Unknown

89b. If yes, indicate the type of weapon, whether it was a weapon of opportunity or of choice, and the weapon recovery location (**check all that apply**).

WEAPON TYPE	WEAPON SELECTION			WEAPON RECOVERY		
	Weapon of Opportunity	Weapon of Choice	Unknown	Recovered at Scene	Not Recovered	Recovered Elsewhere (**describe**)
Bludgeon/Club (**describe**)	☐	☐	☐	☐	☐	☐
Drug (**describe**)	☐	☐	☐	☐	☐	☐
Explosive Device	☐	☐	☐	☐	☐	☐
Fire/Accelerant	☐	☐	☐	☐	☐	☐
Firearm	☐	☐	☐	☐	☐	☐
Hands or Feet	☐	☐	☐	☐	☐	☐
Ligature (**describe**)	☐	☐	☐	☐	☐	☐
Poison (**describe**)	☐	☐	☐	☐	☐	☐
Stabbing/Cutting Weapon (**describe**)	☐	☐	☐	☐	☐	☐
Other (**describe**)	☐	☐	☐	☐	☐	☐

90. Firearm Characteristics:

FIREARM TYPE (handgun, rifle, shotgun, etc.)	FIREARM MAKE	CARTRIDGE CALIBER or GAUGE	# LANDS/GROOVES & DIRECTION of TWIST or PELLET SIZE

VEHICLE INFORMATION

91a. Was a vehicle known or suspected to have been used in this incident by the offender?

❏ Yes   ❏ No   ❏ Unknown

91b. What is status of ownership of vehicle? (**check all that apply**):

❏ Unknown
❏ Owned/Under Control of Victim
❏ Owned/Under Control of Offender
❏ Rented/Loaned
❏ Stolen; Not Recovered
❏ Stolen; Recovered (**specify recovery site and date**)

Street Address _____

City _____ County _____

State/_____ ZIP _____ Country _____
Province

Recovery Date _____/_____/_____
                      mo   day   year

91c. License Number _____ 91d. License State/_____ 91e. License Country _____
                                                              Province

91f. Vehicle Year _____ (or approximate range _____ to _____)

91g. Vehicle Make _____ 91h. Vehicle Model _____

91i. Body Style (**check one**):

❏ Passenger Car
❏ Van
❏ Pick-up Truck
❏ Sport/Utility
❏ Tractor-Trailer
❏ Motorcycle
❏ Station Wagon
❏ RV/Motor Home
❏ Other (**describe**) _____

91j. Color _____ (top) _____ (bottom)

91k. Distinctive features of vehicle, if any (**describe**)

_____

NOTE: If the offender owns or has access to other vehicles which may have been used in similar crimes, attach additional vehicle pages (item 91) for each vehicle.

ADDITIONAL CASE INFORMATION

92. Indicate all forensic/physical evidence items pertaining to this case that may be suitable for comparison.

    DNA from offender
    ❑ Available
    ❑ Submitted to CODIS

    Latent Prints
    ❑ Available
    ❑ Submitted to AFIS

    Projectiles/Casings
    ❑ Available
    ❑ Submitted to DRUGFIRE/IBIS

    Other Evidence _____

    _____

    _____

93. Are you aware of any other similar cases, or cases in which this offender may have been involved?

    ❑ Yes (**provide details below**) Attach additional sheets if necessary.
    ❑ No

CASE INFORMATION	CASE 1	CASE 2	CASE 3
Agency Name			
State/Province			
Case Number			
Investigator			
Telephone Number			
Victim Name			
Offense Type			
ViCAP Number			

94. Give a brief but comprehensive **NARRATIVE SUMMARY** of this case so the reader will have a clear understanding of the facts, unusual circumstances and events based upon your investigation. Include any details you believe are important for case comparison purposes - especially any that pertain to M.O. or signature aspects of the crime. Also, indicate if the offender has been suspected of, implicated in, or has admitted to other similar crimes of violence, and provide details. Also include any **unique key words or phrases** which were used by the offender during the crime.

_____

_____

_____

_____

_____

_____

_____

_____

_____

_____

_____

_____

_____

_____

_____

_____

_____

_____

_____

_____

_____

_____

_____

_____

_____

_____

_____

_____

_____

_____

_____

_____

95. List **Hold Back** Information that you **DO NOT** want discussed or disseminated outside ViCAP but which will assist in the analysis of your case.

_____

_____

_____

APPENDIX 4

Missing Person Investigation Checklists

Initial Response Investigative Checklist

The purpose of this Investigative Checklist is to provide law enforcement officers and agencies with a generic guide for the investigation of missing child cases. Law enforcement administrators should ensure that their agencies have established effective policies and procedures for the handling of missing/abducted child investigations. Compliance with an agency's standard operating procedures, by officers conducting missing child investigations, can result in efficient operations and successful resolution of the incident.

This checklist is not intended to be followed step-by-step by officers during each missing child investigation. It is meant to provide them with a framework of actions, considerations, and activities that can assist them in performing competent, productive, and successful missing/abducted children investigations. Please consult the text of this chapter for details on the items listed.

Administrative

☐ Intake report from parent/caller.

☐ Obtain basic facts, details, and a brief description of missing child and abductor.

☐ Dispatch officer to scene to conduct a preliminary investigation.

☐ Search juvenile/incident records for previous incidents related to missing child and prior police activity in area including prowlers, indecent exposure, attempted abductions, etc. Inform responding officer of any pertinent information.

☐ Broadcast known details, **on all police communications channels,** to other patrol units, other local law enforcement agencies, and surrounding law enforcement agencies and, if necessary, use NLETS telecommunication network to directly alert agencies in multi-state areas.

☐ Activate established **fugitive search plans** (prearranged plans among participating police agencies designed to apprehend fleeing fugitives) if necessary.

☐ Maintain records/recordings of telephone communications/messages.

☐ Activate established protocols for working with the media.

First Responder

☐ Interview parent(s)/person who made initial report.

☐ Verify that the child is in fact missing.

☐ Verify child's custody status.

☐ Identify the circumstances of the disappearance.

☐ Determine when, where, and by whom missing child was last seen.

☐ Interview the individuals who last had contact with the child.

☐ Identify the child's zone of safety for his or her age and developmental stage.

☐ Based on the available information, make an **initial** determination of the type of incident whether nonfamily abduction; family abduction; endangered runaway; or lost, injured, or otherwise missing.

☐ Obtain a **detailed** description of missing child/abductor/vehicles/etc.

☐ Relay detailed descriptive information to communications unit for broadcast updates.

☐ Request additional personnel if circumstances require.

☐ Request investigative assistance if necessary.

☐ Request supervisory assistance if necessary.

☐ Brief and bring up to date all additional responding personnel including supervisors and investigative staff.

☐ Ensure that everyone at the scene is identified and interviewed separately. Make sure that their interview and identifying information is properly recorded. To aid in this process, take pictures or record video images of everyone present.

   ☐ Note name, address, home/business telephone numbers of each person.
   ☐ Determine each person's relationship to missing child.
   ☐ Note information that each person may have about the child's disappearance.
   ☐ Determine when/where each person last saw the child.
   ☐ Ask each one, "What do you think happened to the child?"
   ☐ Obtain names/addresses/telephone numbers of child's friends/associates and other relatives and friends of the family.

☐ Continue to keep communications unit apprised of all appropriate developing information for broadcast updates.

☐ Obtain and note permission to search home or building where incident took place.

☐ Conduct search to include all surrounding areas including vehicles and other places of concealment.

☐ Treat the area as a crime scene.

☐ Seal/protect scene and area of child's home (including child's personal articles such as hairbrush, diary, photographs, and items with the child's fingerprints/footprints/teeth impressions) so that evidence is not destroyed during or after the initial search and to ensure that items which could help in the search for and/or identify the child are preserved. Determine if any of the child's personal items are missing. If possible, photograph/videotape those areas.

☐ Evaluate contents and appearance of child's room/residence.

☐ Obtain photographs/videotapes of missing child/abductor.

☐ Prepare reports/make all required notifications.

☐ Ensure that information regarding missing child is entered into the NCIC Missing Person File and that any information on a suspected abductor is entered into the NCIC Wanted Person File.

☐ Interview other family members, friends/associates of the child, and friends of the family to determine.

  ☐ When each last saw child.
  ☐ What they think happened to the child.

☐ Ensure that details of the case have been reported to NCMEC.

☐ Prepare and update bulletins for local law enforcement agencies, state missing children's clearinghouse, FBI, and other appropriate agencies.

☐ Prepare a flier/bulletin with the child/abductor's photograph and descriptive information. Distribute in appropriate geographic regions.

☐ Secure the child's latest medical and dental records.

☐ Establish a telephone hotline for receipt of tips and leads.

☐ Establish a leads management system to prioritize leads and ensure that each one is reviewed and followed up on.

Investigative Officer

☐ Obtain briefing from first responding officer and other on-scene personnel.

☐ Verify the accuracy of all descriptive information and other details developed during the preliminary investigation.

☐ Obtain a brief, recent history of family dynamics.

☐ Correct and investigate the reasons for any conflicting information obtained by witnesses and other individuals submitting information.

☐ Review and evaluate all available information and evidence collected.

☐ Develop an investigational plan for follow-up.

☐ Determine what additional resources and specialized services are required.

☐ Execute investigative follow-up plan.

Supervisory Responsibility

☐ Obtain briefing and written reports from first responding officer, investigators, and other agency personnel at the scene.

☐ Determine if additional personnel are needed to assist in the investigation.

☐ Determine if outside help is necessary from

  ☐ State Police.
  ☐ State Missing Children's Clearinghouse.
  ☐ FBI.
  ☐ Specialized Units.
  ☐ Victim Witness Services.
  ☐ NCMEC's Project ALERT.

☐ Ensure that all required resources, equipment, and assistance necessary to conduct an efficient investigation have been requested and expedite their availability.

☐ Establish a command post away from child's residence.

☐ Ensure coordination/cooperation among all police personnel involved in the investigation and search effort.

☐ Ensure that all required notifications are made.

☐ Ensure that all agency policies and procedures are in compliance.

☐ Conduct a criminal history check on all principal suspects and participants in the investigation.

☐ Be available to make any decisions or determinations as they develop.

☐ Utilize media (including radio, television, and newspapers) to assist in the search for missing child and maintain media relations, per established protocols, throughout the duration of the case.

Note: Periodic updates will be made in this checklist. To obtain those updates and request technical assistance on specific cases, please call NCMEC at **1-800-THE-LOST (1-800-843-5678).**

Runaway Investigative Checklist

Review all steps outlined in the "Initial Response Investigative Checklist." In addition, in cases of runaway children, consider the below listed steps.

The Initial Investigation

☐ Check agency records for recent contact with child (arrests, other activity).

☐ Review school record and interview teachers, other school personnel, classmates.

☐ Check contents of school locker.

☐ Contact community, youth-serving organizations for information.

☐ Investigate child protective agency records for abuse reports.

☐ Utilize screening procedures to develop an accurate assessment of the child.

☐ Contact the National Runaway Switchboard at **1-800-621-4000** where parents can leave a message for their child and check to see if their child has left a message for them.

The Prolonged Investigation

☐ Update initial NCIC entry by fully loading NCIC Missing Person File with all available information including medical and dental records.

☐ Consider upgrading the investigation to "Endangered" if facts warrant.

☐ Reinterview friends, classmates, and other information sources.

☐ Assist family members in the preparation of missing child posters.

☐ Provide support for family through nonprofit missing children's organization.

☐ Consider search of NCIC's Unidentified Person File, utilization of NCIC's Off-Line Search capabilities, and notification of state medical examiners by providing descriptive information and photographs of missing child.

Recovery/Case Closure

☐ Conduct a thorough interview of the child, document the results of the interview, and involve all appropriate agencies.

    ☐ Why did the child leave?
    ☐ Where did the child go?

☐ How did the child survive?
☐ Who helped the child during absence?
☐ Will the child leave again?

☐ Consider a comprehensive physical examination for the child.

☐ Make child/family aware of community services to deal with any unresolved issues.

☐ Complete an agency report of the episode that can be promptly accessed and reviewed if the child leaves again.

☐ Cancel alarms and remove the case from NCIC and other information systems.

Note: Periodic updates will be made in this checklist. To obtain those updates and request technical assistance on specific cases, please call NCMEC at **1-800-THE-LOST (1-800-843-5678).**

Family Abduction Investigative Checklist

Review all steps outlined in the "Initial Response Investigative Checklist." In addition, in cases of family abduction, consider the below listed steps.

The Initial Investigation

☐ Examine court records.

☐ Conduct background investigation of both parents.

☐ Provide tasks for left-behind parent.

☐ Interview family and friends of suspect-parent.

☐ Enter information about the child and suspect-parent into NCIC Missing Person File (Involuntary Category).

☐ Obtain and evaluate all information that may indicate location of suspect-parent.

☐ Coordinate the issuance of an arrest warrant against suspect-parent with prosecutor.

☐ Assure entry of warrant information into NCIC Missing Person File (child) and Wanted Person File (suspect-parent).

☐ Confirm entry of warrant information into NCIC Missing Person File (child) and Wanted Person File (suspect-parent).

☐ Consider use of civil procedures such as writ of habeas corpus and writ of assistance.

☐ Provide support for family through nonprofit missing children's organization.

The Prolonged Investigation

☐ Secure federal UFAP warrant, if facts support issuance.

☐ Identify and "flag" all pertinent sources of information about both child (school, medical, birth, etc.) and suspect-parent (employment, education, professional, etc.).

☐ Utilize information sources such as credit bureaus, database systems, motor vehicle bureaus, and the Federal Parent Locator Service (FPLS) to search for suspect-parent through identifiers such as social security number, name, date of birth, etc.

☐   Request U.S. Postal Service authorities to provide change of address information and assistance in setting up a mail cover on selected family members or friends of the suspect-parent.

☐   Identify and evaluate other information about suspect-parent that may provide whereabouts information such as employment records, occupational licenses, organization memberships, social interests, hobbies, and other lifestyle indicators.

☐   Assist left-behind parent in missing child poster preparation and distribution.

International Abductions

☐   Become familiar with laws of suspect-parent's country concerning custody matters.

☐   Contact U.S. Department of State for assistance in civil aspects of the abduction and potential for return of child through legal and diplomatic channels.

☐   Seek information from INTERPOL concerning criminal proceedings against the suspect-parent.

Recovery Case/Closure

☐   Arrest suspect-parent away from child, if possible.

☐   Notify child protective service workers about possible need for temporary shelter care until left-behind parent or investigator arrives.

☐   Conduct thorough interview of the child and abductor, documents the results of the interviews, and involve all appropriate agencies.

☐   Provide effective reunification techniques.

☐   Cancel alarms and remove case from NCIC and other information systems.

Note: Periodic updates will be made in this checklist. To obtain those updates and request technical assistance on specific cases, please call NCMEC   at **1-800-THE-LOST (1-800-843-5678).**

Nonfamily Abduction Checklist

Review all steps outlined in the "Initial Response Investigative Checklist." In addition, in cases of nonfamily abduction, consider the below listed steps.

The Initial Investigation

☐ Assign officer to victim's residence with the ability to record and "trap and trace" all incoming calls. Consider setting up a separate telephone line or cellular telephone for agency use.

☐ Conduct neighborhood/vehicle canvass.

☐ Compile list of known sex offenders in the region.

☐ Develop profile on possible abductor.

☐ Consider use of polygraph for parents and other key individuals.

☐ In cases of infant abduction, investigate claims of home births made in that area.

☐ Fully load NCIC Missing Person File (involuntary category) with complete descriptive, medical, and dental information.

☐ Utilize NLETS and other information systems to alert local, state, regional, and federal law enforcement agencies.

☐ Provide support for family through nonprofit missing children's organization.

The Prolonged Investigation

☐ Reread all reports and transcripts of interviews.

☐ Revisit the crime scene.

☐ Review all potential witness/suspect information obtained in the initial investigation and consider background checks on anyone identified in the investigation.

☐ Review all photographs and videotapes.

☐ Reexamine all physical evidence collected.

☐ Review child protective agency records for reports of abuse on child.

☐ Develop time lines and other visual exhibits.

☐ Reinterview key individuals.

☐ Interview delivery personnel; employees of gas, water, electric, and cable companies; taxi drivers; post office personnel; garbage handlers, etc.

☐ Critique results of the on-going investigation with appropriate investigative resources.

☐ Arrange for periodic media coverage.

☐ Utilize rewards and crimestopper programs.

☐ Contact NCMEC for photo dissemination, age-progression, and other case assistance.

☐ Update NCIC Missing Person File information as necessary.

Recovery/Case Closure

☐ Arrange for a comprehensive physical examination of the victim.

☐ Conduct a careful interview of the child, document the results of the interview, and involve all appropriate agencies.

☐ Provide effective reunification techniques.

☐ Cancel alarms and remove case from NCIC and other information systems.

☐ Perform constructive post-case critique.

Note: Periodic updates will be made in this checklist. To obtain those updates and request technical assistance on specific cases, please call NCMEC at **1-800-THE-LOST (1-800-843-5678).**

APPENDIX 5

Glossary

A

a posteriori: reasoning from empirical facts or particulars (acquired through experience or experiment) to general principles; or, from effects to causes; see *induction*

a priori: from a known or assumed cause to a necessarily related effect; from a general law to a particular instance; valid independently of observation; see *deduction*

accelerant: a volatile organic liquid used to start a fire and help it spread more rapidly

ad hoc agency: a one-purpose agency established to deal with a particularly vexatious problem (e.g., in connection with sports such as horse-racing or boxing to control "fixing" the outcome of an event, or to deal with crime on the waterfront)

admission: an express or implied statement tending to support a suspect's involvement in a crime but insufficient by itself to prove guilt

AFIS: Automated Fingerprint Identification System

agent provocateur: an individual hired to spy on the internal affairs of an organization or group, or one who is perceived as a betrayer

amplification technique: see *Polymerase Chain Reaction*

analysis: a process that starts with the whole (whether a material substance, thought, or impression) and then involves an effort to separate the whole into its constituent parts for individual study

antemortem statement: see *dying declaration*

arches: a *class characteristic* or general pattern (together with loops and whorls) used in classifying fingerprints

armed robbery: robbery involving the use of a weapon (also called *holdup, stickup, heist, hijacking*)

asphyxiation: unconsciousness or death resulting from interference with the supply of oxygen to the lungs

asset forfeiture: an act allowed by recent law by which police may seize assets which are being used in criminal enterprises

associative evidence: physical evidence that links a suspect to a crime scene or victim; a nonlegal term

B

BAI: Behavior Analysis Interview

beacon: see *beeper*

beeper: a battery-operated device that emits radio signals which permit it to be tracked by a directional finder-receiver as it moves about (also called *beacon, transponder, electronic tracking device*)

blunt force wound: a wound which is the product of neither a penetrating nor a cutting instrument

BIOS: Basic Input/Output System

boot: start up a computer, i.e., load into memory a small program that enables it to load larger programs

break: the point in an interrogation when the investigator recognizes that the subject is about to confess

bugging: eavesdropping by electronic means, such as a hidden microphone or radio transmitter; **bug**, a device used for such eavesdropping

burn the surveillance: when a surveillant's behavior causes the subject to surmise or know s/he is under surveillance

burned: when a subject's behavior signals suspicion

C

canvass: to ascertain information by systematically interviewing all people in a certain vicinity or area (in Britain called *intensive inquiry*)

career criminals: the select group of criminals responsible for an unduly large amount of crime in a particular area

case law: law created as a by-product of court decisions made in resolving unique disputes, as distinguished from statutory and constitutional law

case screening: the process by which investigative cases are removed (based on solvability factors) from the work load, making resources available for those holding greater promise of solution

certiorari: an original writ or action whereby a case is taken from an inferior to a superior court for review

chop shop: a location, often an automobile repair shop or salvage yard, where a stolen car is stripped of its parts (radio, doors, trunk lid, engine, etc.); the remains are cut up and sold for scrap metal

class characteristics: the general patterns of a type of evidence (e.g., a Cat's Paw vs. an O'Sullivan heel impression, a loop vs. an arch in a fingerprint, a .22 caliber vs. a .38 caliber weapon, etc.)

classification: the systematic arrangement of objects into categories (groups or classes) based on shared traits or characteristics; see *identification*

close surveillance: the subject is kept under constant surveillance, the aim of which is not to lose the subject even at the risk of being discovered (also called *tight surveillance*)

closed fracture: see *simple fracture*

compound fracture: a fracture with the skin broken; an open wound—perhaps with the bone exposed (also called *open fracture*)

conditioned reflex: a response discovered by Pavlov stating that an artificial stimulus or signal could, by repeated association, be substituted for a natural stimulus to cause a physiological response

confession: an oral or written statement acknowledging guilt

contact wound: a wound that results when a small weapon is fired in contact with the skin (or up to a distance of approximately two or three inches from the body)

contusion: an injury to subsurface tissue caused by a blow from a blunt instrument that does not break the skin; a hemorrhage beneath the skin; a bruise

convoy: a countermeasure to detect a surveillance; a convoy, usually a person, is employed to determine whether or not a subject is under surveillance

corpus delicti: the proof that a crime has been committed—consisting of two components: (1) that each element of the crime be satisfied, and (2) that someone is responsible for inflicting the injury or loss sustained

cracker: a person who enters a computer system illegally to commit a crime such as sabotage or theft of information

crime suppression model: a model of the criminal justice system in which the role of the criminal justice process is, first and foremost, to suppress or control crime

criminal homicide: the unlawful taking of a human life

criminalistics: the branch of forensic science concerned with the scientific examination and interpretation of the minute details of physical evidence for the purpose of aiding the criminal investigator or a judge and jury during trial

cutouts: individuals used by criminal enterprise organizations who know nothing about the operation other than the message being passed

cybercrime: crime committed using computers and the internet

D

deduction: a process of reasoning that commences with a generalization or a premise and by means of careful, systematic thinking moves to a particular fact or consequence

denature: the breaking apart of double-stranded DNA fragments by heat or chemical means, resulting in single-stranded fragments (these single strands can be combined, i.e., hybridized, with complementary single strands—called probes—to yield a DNA profile)

dermal nitrate test: an unreliable and discredited test formerly used to detect nitrates from gunpowder residue on the hand (also called *paraffin test*)

discreet surveillance: see *loose surveillance*

distant discharge wound: a wound which results when a weapon is fired from a distance of at least 24 inches for handguns, or 36 inches for rifles

DNA fingerprinting: the information obtained through multilocus probe testing of DNA

due process model: a model of the criminal justice system in which the role of the criminal justice process is, first and foremost, to preserve liberty

dying declaration: a statement made just prior to death with the knowledge of impending death; though hearsay, dying declarations are allowed into evidence in homicide cases in certain jurisdictions (also called *antemortem statement*)

E

ecotage: ecological terrorism; illegal (often violent) efforts by groups to protect the environment.

electronic tracking device: see *beeper*

elements of a crime: the specific acts that, taken together, compose a crime

elimination prints: prints of known individuals who customarily inhabit the crime scene area; used to determine whether a latent crime scene print is that of a stranger or of someone who is customarily present

enterprise crime: the broad range of crime characterized by criminal networks and illegal relationships, including but not limited to organized drug trafficking, white-collar crime, corruption, economic crime, etc.

entomology: the branch of zoology dealing with insects

entrapment: an act by a governmental agent that lures an individual into committing a crime not otherwise contemplated, for the purpose of prosecuting him or her

excusable homicide: a killing in which one person kills another by accident (without gross negligence) and without intent to injure

exemplars: specimens of physical evidence of known origin (used for comparison with similar crime scene evidence)

ex parte order: an order issued by a judge (and submitted to the appropriate federal or state judge for approval) authorizing the interception of a wire or oral communication

F

fence: a person in the business of buying stolen goods, usually for resale; to buy or sell stolen goods

fingerprint: the impression of the friction ridges on the skin surface of the last joint of the fingers and thumb

file-based credit reporting bureau: a business that collects information from creditors on how bills are paid

finished sketch: a precise rendering of a crime scene with clean, straight lines and typeset or typewritten lettering; usually prepared after leaving the crime scene with information obtained from the original rough sketch, notes, and photographs taken at the crime scene

fixed surveillance: surveillance conducted from a stationary position, such as a parked van, or room facing the subject's residence or workplace, or by posing as a street vendor or utility worker; the aim is to allow the surveillant to remain inconspicuously in one locale (also called *stakeout, plant*)

flagrante delicto: in the very act of committing a misdeed

fluoresce: to absorb ultraviolet radiation and immediately re-emit it in the visible region of the spectrum where it can be seen by the naked eye

forensic: pertaining to, connected with, or used in courts of law or public discussion and debate

forensic medicine: the use of medicine to determine the cause or time of death, or for other legal purposes (also called *legal medicine, medical jurisprudence*)

forensic odontology: the study of teeth, dentures, and bite marks for the purpose of obtaining criminal evidence, or identifying physical remains or the source of bite wounds

forensic pathology: pathology that goes beyond the normal concern for disease to the study of the causes of death—whether from natural, accidental, or criminal agency (see *pathology*)

forensic psychiatry: the study of a criminal's mental state and probable intent

forensic serology: the study of blood for the purpose of obtaining criminal evidence or for other legal purposes

forensics: a fairly new, all-encompassing term, it characterizes the scientific examination of evidence. Owing to television and motion picture shows, the term is now generic and part of the vocabulary of the average person (and, therefore, jurors)

fracture: a break or crack of a bone, cartilage, or glass

fraud: an intentional misrepresentation or deception employed to deprive another of property or a legal right or to otherwise do him or her harm.

G

Galton details: see *points of identification*

galvanic skin response (GSR): the electrical conductance of the skin, one of the physiological responses measured by the polygraph or lie detector to ascertain whether or not a subject is telling the truth

gel electrophoresis: a step in the DNA analysis process in which DNA fragments are broken apart by means of denaturing them

gene amplification: see *Polymerase Chain Reaction*

grounder: police jargon used to describe cases which are easily solved (also called *platter* or *meatball*)

H

hacker: a person who enters a computer system illegally or without permission

hearsay: statement(s) made out of court and offered in court to support the truth of the facts asserted in the statement

heavy: a case likely to attract media attention

heist: see *armed robbery*

hematoma: a localized wound in which swelling is caused by the rupture of blood vessels

hesitation marks: slight, often superficial marks (usually cuts) that typify suicide and suicide attempts

hijacking: see *armed robbery*

holdup: see *armed robbery*

homicide: the killing of one human being by another

hybridization: the process of recombining single DNA strands to form a double strand

hypnosis: a sleep-like mental state induced by a person whose suggestions are readily accepted by the subject; because it sometimes releases memories of traumatic events that are otherwise inaccessible, it is sometimes used to discover answers to significant questions, e.g., what was seen or heard during a criminal event

hypothesis: a conjecture that provisionally accounts for a set of facts; can be used as the basis for additional investigation and a guide in gathering further information

I

identification: an analytical and classification process by which an entity is placed in a predefined, limited, or restricted class (see *classification*)

identification parade: see *lineup*

identity: the result of continuing the process of classification (beyond identification) to the point where an entity is in a class by itself

in-between: a case which appears to have a solution but will require some effort

incision: a relatively clean (not ragged) cut that results when a sharp instrument is applied to a small, limited area of skin tissue

individual characteristics: the details (noted by a criminalist) in physical evidence that make possible an inference concerning the common origin of some crime scene evidence and an exemplar (or comparison specimen of known origin)

individualized: put in a class of one, thereby establishing an identity (see *identity, individual characteristics, classification, identification*)

induction: a process of reasoning based on a set of experiences or observations (particulars) from which a conclusion or generalization based on those specifics is drawn; it moves from the specific to the general

informant: an individual who discloses information to an investigator

injury: a wound, especially one in which the skin is pierced, cut, torn, or otherwise broken

inner tracing: a subclassification of a whorl fingerprint pattern, delineated by tracing a ridge line from the left delta to the right delta of a whorl pattern (also called *inner whorl*)

inorganic substance: a substance that does not contain carbon (see *organic substance*)

in situ: in its original location

INTERPOL: International **Pol**ice Organization

intensive inquiry: the British term for seeking information by canvass (see *canvass*)

interrogation: the questioning process used for a suspect, or a suspect's family, friends, or associates—people who are likely to withhold information or be deceptive

interview: the questioning process used for a victim or eyewitness—people who reasonably can be expected to disclose what they know

investigative credit reporting bureau: a business that gathers information on an individual's lifestyle and reputation

J

Jeffreys probe: a multilocus probe (see *multilocus probe test*)

judicial restraint: the application of a narrow interpretation of the constitution to issues raised in the enforcement of criminal law (also called *strict construction*)

justifiable homicide: the intentional but lawful killing of another human being (e.g., the execution of a convicted murderer)

K

kinesics: the study of the use of body movement and posture to convey meaning

L

laceration: a tearing of skin tissue, generally with ragged edges

LAN: Local **A**rea **N**etwork; a network connecting several computers that are located close to one another, allowing them to share files and devices

larceny: the crime of taking another person's property without consent and with the intent of depriving the owner of the property

latent print: a fingerprint (left when a person touches an object or surface) which is not visible unless treated (developed) in some way; *latent* is derived from the Latin word for "hidden"

LEADS: **L**aw **E**nforcement **A**gencies **D**ata **S**ystem

leakage: signals emitted in nonverbal communication

legal medicine: see *forensic medicine*

lettre de cachet: a letter bearing the seal of the sovereign, usually authorizing the imprisonment without trial of a named person

lie detector: see *polygraph*

ligature: anything that serves to bind or tie up (e.g., lamp or telephone cords, neckties, nylon hose, towels, or t-shirts are some of various ligatures used to commit homicide).

lineup: the practice of placing a suspect within a group of people lined up for the purpose of being viewed (and possibly identified as the perpetrator) by eyewitnesses (also called *identification parade*)

linkage: the production of a list of suspects based on *modus operandi* or through crime analysis patterns

loops: a *class characteristic* or general pattern (together with whorls and arches) used in classifying fingerprints

loose surveillance: a cautious surveillance wherein the loss of the subject is preferred to possible exposure (also called *discreet surveillance*)

luminesce: to absorb illumination and re-emit it at a wavelength different from the incident light; akin to fluorescence, luminescence is useful to criminal investigation in that latent fingerprints become visible because organic solids in perspiration can be detected by lasers due to their luminescence

M

macro: with regard to computers, an instruction that stands for a sequence of simpler instructions

made: to be *made* is to be detected or suspected of being a surveillant by the subject

mail cover: the printing and writing on the outside of a piece of mail, copied by postal authorities

malice aforethought: premeditation

malum in se: an act which is wrong in itself whether or not prohibited by law, e.g., the deliberate killing of another human being

malum prohibitum: an act which is prohibited by law, but is not necessarily wrong in itself, e.g., a farmer's act in burning down his barn is not unlawful in itself, but becomes so if done to defraud an insurance company

manslaughter: the unlawful killing of another without intent—express or implied—to effect death; may be voluntary or involuntary

MAPADS: **M**icrocomputer-**A**ssisted **P**olice **A**nalysis and **D**eployment **S**ystem

meatball: see *grounder*

medical jurisprudence: see *forensic medicine*

meet tracing: a subclassification of a whorl fingerprint pattern, delineated by tracing a ridge line from the left delta to the right delta of a whorl pattern (also called *meeting whorl*)

memory: the storage and retention of sensory stimuli that has been observed and encoded

mind-set: a way of thinking employing skepticism and doubt to provide foresight, and possible insight, to the creative investigator

minutiae: see *points of identification*

modus operandi (MO): an offender's pattern of operation (method of preparing for and committing a crime)

Molotov cocktail: a homemade firebomb made with an empty bottle, flammable liquid, and a wick

morphology: the general structure and shape (or form) of an entity, constituting, in criminalistics, the details used in the study and comparison of physical evidence

motherboard: the main circuit board of a computer

moving surveillance: surveillance in which the surveillant moves about in order to follow the subject

mug shot file: see *Rogues Gallery*

mugging: see *strong-arm robbery*

multilocus probe (MLP) test: a test in which one probe simultaneously binds many DNA fragments from different chromosomes

murder: the unlawful killing of another human being with malice aforethought (premeditation); killing a person during the commission of a felony also constitutes murder—even when the killing is unintentional

muscle job: see *strong-arm robbery*

mustard plaster: a form of open surveillance in which the subject is followed so closely that surveillant and subject are almost in lock step; tantamount to protective custody

mystery: a case (usually a homicide) in which no apparent solution is readily perceived, and therefore, much time and effort are in order (also called *who-done-it*)

N

narco-terrorism: drug-related terrorism with the intent to achieve a political aim

near discharge wound: a wound that is the result of firing at a distance of approximately six to 24 inches for handguns, and six to 36 inches for rifles

neutron activation analysis (NAA): a test used to detect the level of metal residue (barium and antimony) left on the skin from the primer of a gun cartridge

nol-prossing: convincing the prosecutor to agree not to proceed any further with an action; derived from *nolle prosequi (nol. pros.)*, an entry made on the court record by which the prosecutor declares that s/he will proceed no further

nonverbal communication: messages unwittingly sent through changes in facial expressions, voice quality, body movements, and the distancing of one's self from the other speaker (see *kinesics, paralinguistics, proxemics*)

O

omerta: the Mafia code of silence; secrecy sworn to by oath

open fracture: see *compound fracture*

open surveillance: surveillance in which there is little or no attempt at concealment; the subject may be and most likely is aware of the surveillance, but must not be lost (also called *rough surveillance*)

organic substance: a substance that contains carbon; all other substances are inorganic

outer tracing: a subclassification of a whorl fingerprint, delineated by tracing a ridge line from the left delta to the right delta of a whorl pattern (also called *outer whorl*)

P

paraffin test: see *dermal nitrate test*

paralinguistics: the study of the variations in the quality of the voice (pitch, intonation, loudness, softness) and their effect on the meaning conveyed

pathology: the branch of medicine that studies diseases and trauma (their causes and consequences)

pen register: a device that records all numbers dialed in a telephone, generally installed at the telephone company's central office

per se: by itself, alone; an automatic rule of exclusion

perception: the interpretation, classification, and conversion of sensory stimuli into a more durable configuration for memory

petechiae: pinhead-sized (red) dots which are minute hemorrhages found inside the eyelids and the facial skin; considered by pathologists to be a sign of strangulation

photomacrograph: a photographic image that is larger than actual size

photomicrograph: a photographic image of an object as seen through the eyepiece of a microscope

plant: *in arson investigation,* an ignition device that ignites the first fuel, or assists the initial flame to build in intensity; it may include a timing mechanism; *in surveillance,* a technique in which the surveillant remains essentially in one position or locale (also called *stakeout, fixed surveillance)*

plastic print: a three-dimensional fingerprint impression

platter: see *grounder*

points of identification: the individual characteristics found by a criminalist in physical evidence that provide the basis for establishing an identity; in a fingerprint they are called *Galton details, Galton minutiae, ridge characteristics, minutiae*; in firearms they are called *striations.*

polygraph: see *lie detector*

polymerase: a DNA enzyme used to accomplish a chain reaction that amplifies certain DNA sequences in a specimen

Polymerase Chain Reaction (PCR): a procedure that uses a DNA enzyme (polymerase) to set in motion a chain reaction that increases the quantity of certain DNA sequences in a specimen so that it can be analyzed

portrait parlé: a verbal description of a perpetrator's physical characteristics and clothing provided by an eyewitness; loosely translated as "verbal picture"

postmortem lividity: the bluish-purple color that develops after death in the undermost parts of the body—those which have been facing downward

precipitin test: a test for distinguishing human blood from animal blood

presumptive test: a sensitive, simple field test using a chemical reagent that permits detection of the slightest residues of blood; such tests are not specific for blood, are only preliminary, and are of little value in court

prima facie: at first view; sufficient in itself to prevail

proactive investigation: an investigation taken in anticipation of the commission of a crime in order to prevent it or to apprehend the offender

probable cause: a reasonable ground for suspicion, supported by circumstances sufficiently strong to justify the issuance of a search warrant or to make an arrest

probative value: the quality of evidence which serves to substantiate or help prove that a particular action took place

probe: a laboratory-tagged single-strand DNA molecule used to detect any complementary single strands of DNA obtained by denaturing the crime scene sample

profiling: the psychological assessment of a crime, in which the personality type of the perpetrator is surmised through the recognition and interpretation of visible or spoken evidence at the crime scene

procedural law: law dealing with how the state may proceed in the trial of an alleged offender

protective custody: the confinement or guardianship of an individual by law enforcement with the objective of preventing an assault or other crime against him or her

proxemics: the study of the physical distance individuals put between themselves and others, noting any shift from between an open posture and a protective one (as in folding the arms across the chest)

psychological autopsy: a technique whereby a consensus is developed by a team of experts as to the mental attitude or outlook of a deceased individual; usually used to determine whether or not a death is a suicide

psychological profile: see *profiling.*

pyromania: an irresistible impulse or compulsion to start a fire or set something on fire

pyrolysis: chemical decomposition brought about by the action of heat

Q

qualified expert: an individual about whom it is demonstrated to the court that s/he possesses specialized, relevant knowledge ordinarily not expected of the average layperson

quid pro quo: something for something, as in making a deal, e.g., plea bargaining

R

radial loop: a fingerprint pattern in which the open end leads out to the thumb

reactive investigation: investigation of a crime after it has been committed (see *proactive investigation*)

recall: to bring a previous event back from memory, usually as a verbal description of the previous event (a crime)

recognition: the act of remembering an event after some cue is provided that assists in its recollection, as when a mug shot is picked from a Rogues Gallery file or an individual from a lineup

record fingerprints: a set of an individual's fingerprints recorded in proper order on a fingerprint card using printer's ink

reliability: the extent to which an experiment, test, or measuring procedure yields consistent and reproducible results (also called *precision*)

res gestae: all of the things done or words spoken in the course of a transaction or event; a record of what was said or done in the first moments of an investigation

resolution: the capability of an optical device to separate into two or more objects (or points) what to the unaided eye appears to be one object (or point), thus yielding details not otherwise perceptible

Restriction Fragment Length Polymorphism (RFLP) analysis: DNA analysis that involves either single locus probes or multilocus probes

restriction site: a sequence of certain nucleotide combinations repeating themselves at random intervals throughout the length of the DNA chain; the term comes from the naturally occurring restriction enzymes obtained from certain bacteria

ridge characteristics: see *points of identification*

rigor mortis: the stiffening of the body after death resulting from chemical changes within muscle tissue

Rogues Gallery: a file of photographs of arrested individuals; usually includes full-face and pro-file photographs (mug shots) along with detailed physical description, age and place of birth, social security number, fingerprint classification, nicknames and aliases, *modus operandi*, etc. (also called *mug shot file*)

root directory: the main directory of a computer disk, containing files and/or subdirectories

ROM: **R**ead-**O**nly **M**emory; memory in a computer that can be read by the computer, but cannot be used for storing data

roping: placing an undercover agent on a surveillance job (see *undercover*)

rough sketch: a relatively crude, freehand representation of all essential information (including measurements) at a crime scene; it is made while at the scene

rough surveillance: see *open surveillance*

RPG: **R**ocket-**P**ropelled **G**renade

S

safe house: a rendezvous thought to be free of surveillance that is used for illegal activities such as bomb-making by terrorists

scale drawing: a drawing by a skilled draftsperson in which all distances in the finished sketch are precise and proportional

search warrant: a written order of consent, issued by a court, that specifies the place where a search is to be made and the seizable property that is to be looked for, and directs that, when such property is found, it should be brought before the court (also see *seizable property*)

sebum: the semifluid, fatty substance secreted by the sebaceous glands at the base of the hair follicles

seizable property: contraband, or the fruits or instruments of crime (e.g., a weapon, or other relevant evidence); its nature, as well as where it is to be discovered must be specified in a search warrant (see *search warrant*)

shadow: to follow secretly; to place a person under surveillance

show-up: a one-on-one confrontation wherein a suspect and eyewitness are brought together for identification purposes

single locus probe (SLP) test: a test that identifies a fragment of DNA whose sequence appears only once in a chromosome; several single locus tests can be performed using different probes

simple fracture: a fracture in which there is no break in the skin (also called *closed fracture*)

sniffer: *in arson investigation*, a catalytic combustion device employed to detect flammable vapors

speaker kill switch: a switch on a personal computer that enables and disables the speaker

stakeout: a surveillance technique in which the surveillant remains essentially in one position or locale; the term is derived from the practice of tethering animals to a stake, allowing them a short radius in which to move (also called *plant, fixed surveillance*)

stickup: see *armed robbery*

stipulation: an agreement between opposing litigants that certain facts are true

strategy: the overall planning of operations; in original military sense, "the art of the commander-in-chief"

straw ownership: a situation in which the individual or business entity on record as the owner is a front for the real owner; straw ownership is lawful if not set up for illegal purposes, but generally implies shady or questionable business practices

streamer: see *trailer*

striations: a series of roughly parallel lines of varying width, depth, and separation; scratch marks caused by irregularities or a lack of microfine smoothness of the surface of a gun barrel or on the working edge of a jimmy

strict construction: see *judicial restraint*

strings: *with regard to computers*, groups of characters entered for computer searches

strong-arm robbery: robbery involving the use of physical force (also called *mugging, muscle job*)

sublimation: a phenomenon in which a crystalline substance has the capability of changing directly to a vapor from a solid state

substantive law: law specifying which acts are forbidden and the punishment to be inflicted when the law is broken

suicide: the taking of one's own life; not a crime, but considered a grave public wrong, in many cultures

superglue procedure: a procedure for developing latent fingerprints with cyanoacrylate fuming; named for the commercial product, Super Glue

surveillance: the observation of a person, place, or thing—generally, but not necessarily, in an unobtrusive manner

surveillant: the person conducting a surveillance (see *surveillance*)

synthesis: the combining of separate parts or elements to provide a single entity

T

tactics: the means employed to secure an objective; in original military sense, the art or science of deploying in the military

tail: to follow and keep a person or vehicle under surveillance; a surveillance

tailgating: a form of open surveillance in which the subject's vehicle is closely followed

targeted investigation: an anticipatory (proactive) approach to solving crime, focusing on the small group of career criminals responsible for a large amount of crime in an area

taxonomy: the science of classification

technical surveillance: surveillance conducted by means of scientific devices which enhance hearing or seeing the subject's activities—may involve electronic eavesdropping devices (wiretaps, pen registers); electronic tracking devices (beepers), or assorted visual and infrared optical devices

terrorism: the use of force or the fear of force to achieve a political end

theory: a somewhat verified hypothesis; a scheme of thought with assumptions chosen to fit empirical knowledge or observations

tight surveillance: see *close surveillance*

toxicology: the study of poisons: their origins and properties, their identification by chemical analysis, their action upon humans and animals, and the treatment of the conditions they produce

trace evidence: physical evidence so small (in size or forensic detail) that an examination requires a stereomicroscope, a polarized light microscope, or both

transponder: see *beeper*

trailer: a device or substance used to spread a fire from one part of a structure to another (also called *streamer*)

trauma: an injury that is the result of any force—blunt, sharp, or penetrating

U

ulnar loop: a fingerprint pattern in which the open end of the loop leads out to the little finger

unconscious transference: an individual's mistaken recollection of an incident; in criminal investigation, a witness may have a mistaken recollection about a crime that implicates an individual who was not involved

undercover: in secret; an undercover agent often gets to know or work alongside the subject under investigation; an undercover agent is said to be *planted*; a form of surveillance (see *roping*)

V

validity: the extent to which an experiment, test, or procedure accurately measures that which it is purported to measure (also called *accuracy*)

Vehicle Identification Number: See *VIN*

VICAP: Violent Crime Apprehension Program

VIN: Vehicle Identification Number. The serial number that car manufacturers stamp on several motor vehicle parts (many of which are inaccessible) for the purpose of tracing and identifying car ownership.

virus: a software program that is attached illegally to a larger program and replicates itself by attaching to other programs and files, usually for the purpose of destroying or altering the primary program

voice polygraph: see *voice stress analysis*

voice stress analysis: the detection and analysis of voice changes caused by stress; alleged to be useful in determining whether or not someone is lying

W

White probe: a single locus probe

wiretap: an eavesdropping device usually attached to telephone wires to listen to private conversations

who-done-it: see *mystery*

whorls: a class characteristic or general pattern (together with loops and arches) used in classifying fingerprints

wound: an injury resulting from a blunt force or sharp instrument

X

xylotomist: an expert in the study of wood

References

Carlson, Ronald L. *Criminal Justice Procedure*. 6th ed. Cincinnati: Anderson, 1999.

Downing, Douglas and Michael Covington. *Dictionary of Computer Terms*. 2nd ed. New York: Barron's Educational Series, 1989.

The Law Dictionary. 7th ed. Cincinnati: Anderson, 1997.

Nash, Jay Robert. *Encyclopedia of World Crime Dictionary*. Wilmette, IL: CrimeBooks, 1989.

Travis, Lawrence F., III. *Introduction to Criminal Justice*. 4th ed. Cincinnati: Anderson, 2001.

Merriam-Webster's Collegiate Dictionary, 10th ed. Springfield, MA: Merriam-Webster, 1993.

INDEX

About the Authors

James W. Osterburg has long been involved in the criminal investigation process, actively engaged in the functions of teaching, research, and public service. For 20 years, Osterburg served as a sworn member of the New York City Police Department (NYPD), where he assisted in the investigation of thousands of serious crimes. He has testified in municipal, state, and federal courts on numerous occasions, and taught at the NYPD Police Academy.

His academic affiliations include professorships at the University of Illinois at Chicago, Indiana University, the University of California—Berkeley, the Baruch School of Public Administration at the City College of New York, and Sam Houston State University (as Beto Professor of Criminal Justice). A frequent participant in educational symposia, he has discussed criminal investigation, criminalistics, fingerprint characteristics, and scientific evidence.

The author of two books on criminalistics and scientific investigations, Osterburg is a regular contributor of chapters, sections, articles, and book reviews. His articles have been published in a variety of scholarly journals, including the *Journal of Criminal Law, Criminology, and Police Science;* the *Journal of the Forensic Sciences;* the *Journal of the American Statistical Association;* and the *Journal of Police Science and Administration.*

A fellow and past president of the American Academy of Forensic Sciences, Osterburg served on the *ad hoc* committee appointed by the President of the Academy to review the homicide of Robert F. Kennedy and to help resolve the controversy that arose subsequent to the conviction of Sirhan B. Sirhan regarding some of the firearms evidence. Osterburg has been a consultant to the State Department, the Department of Justice, and the Stanford Research Institute.

Richard H. Ward is Dean and Director of the Criminal Justice Center, Sam Houston State University. Prior to this appointment, Ward was Vice Chancellor for Administration and on the faculty of the University of Illinois at Chicago. Previously he served as Vice President of John Jay College of Criminal Justice at the City University of New York. He began his criminal justice career following four years in the U.S. Marine Corps and served as a detective with the New York City Police Department. Ward is the author of many books and articles—primarily on the subjects of terrorism, police corruption, and criminal investigation. He was a founder of *Law Enforcement News* and *Crime and Justice International.*

Ward has lectured at the FBI Academy and has been a visiting lecturer on crime and the media in Columbia University's School of Journalism and at Baylor University. He has been a consultant to numerous police departments in the United States and to numerous international law enforcement and criminal justice organizations. In addition to his expertise in transnational crime and international and domestic terrorism, he has directed major research projects for the federal government on police administration, counter-terrorism, and police corruption.

For many years, Ward served as Executive Director of the Office of International Criminal Justice, an internationally recognized center that promotes humane and democratic service on the part of justice-related agencies throughout the world.